COLLEGE ACCOUNTING Accounting Cycle Quick Reference

The Accounting Equation

Assets = Liabilities + Owner's Equity

Financial Statements

INCOME STATEMENT — *Reports net income or loss*

Revenues – Expenses = Net Income or Loss

STATEMENT OF OWNER'S EQUITY — *Shows changes in the owner's capital account*

Beginning Capital + Investments + Net Income – Withdrawals = Ending Capital

BALANCE SHEET — *Verifies balance of accounting equation*

Assets = Liabilities + Owner's Equity

T Account

Title	
Debit = Left	Credit = Right

Expanded Accounting Equation Showing Rules of Debit and Credit

Assets		=	Liabilities		+	Owner's Equity	
Dr.	Cr.		Dr.	Cr.		Dr.	Cr.
+	–		–	+		–	+

		Drawing		Expenses		Revenue	
		Dr.	Cr.	Dr.	Cr.	Dr.	Cr.
		+	–	+	–	–	+

College Accounting

14TH EDITION

CHAPTERS 1-15

JAMES A. HEINTZ, DBA, CPA
Professor of Accounting
University of Connecticut
Storrs, Connecticut

ROBERT W. PARRY, JR., PhD
Ernst and Young Faculty Fellow and
  Associate Professor of Accounting
Indiana University
Bloomington, Indiana

ARTHUR E. CARLSON, PhD
Professor Emeritus of Accounting
John M. Olin School of Business
Washington University in St. Louis

CONSULTING EDITOR:
Michael D. Lawence, MBA, CMA
Portland Community College
Portland, Oregon

CONSULTING EDITOR:
Joan S. Ryan, MS, MBA
Lane Community College
Eugene, Oregon

COLLEGE DIVISION South-Western Publishing Co.

Cincinnati Ohio

AV80NAA2

Copyright © 1993
by South-Western Publishing Co.
Cincinnati, Ohio

ISBN: 0-538-84601-1

3 4 5 6 7 Ki 8 7 6 5 4

Printed in the United States of America

Publisher:	Mark Hubble
Developmental Editor:	Ellen Camm
Production Editor:	Nancy Ahr
Associate Editor:	Robin Schuster
Cover and Internal Design:	Lesiak/Crampton Design
Cover and Internal Illustration:	Jud Guitteau
Internal Art:	Rick Moore
Marketing Manager:	James Sheibley Enders

Library of Congress Cataloging-in-Publication Data

The complete version of the text is cataloged as follows:

Heintz, James A.
    College accounting / James A. Heintz, Robert W. Parry, Jr., Arthur
E. Carlson. -- 14th ed., chapters 1-28
        p.   cm
    Includes index.
    ISBN 0-538-84599-6
    1. Accounting.   I. Parry, Robert W.   II. Carlson, Arthur E.
III. Title.
HF5635.C227   1992
657.044--dc20
                                                        92-14486
                                                          CIP

*P*reface

This textbook is designed for students of accounting, business administration, office technology, computer science, and other disciplines. Anyone who desires a successful career in business and nonprofit organizations must understand accounting. This book provides a thorough and efficient introduction to fundamental accounting concepts and principles. Student understanding is emphasized throughout the text.

IMPORTANT FEATURES OF THE FOURTEENTH EDITION

The basic foundation that has made this text so successful for many years has been retained in the fourteenth edition. In response to user feedback and independent reviews by accounting educators, numerous improvements have been made. The text material has been reorganized both as a whole and within specific chapters, and new materials have been added.

NEW **Learning Objectives**

Each chapter begins with learning objectives. These objectives are referenced to text material throughout each chapter by the use of marginal captions. The learning objectives are also keyed to the chapter summaries, end-of-chapter exercises and problems, test bank, and study guide.

The following illustration shows Learning Objective 5 from Chapter 3 as it appears in the margin, in the Key Points summary, and in an exercise.

5

Prepare a trial balance.

THE TRIAL BALANCE

5 A trial balance shows that the debit and credit totals are equal. A trial balance can also be used in preparing the financial statements.

EXERCISE 3A8

Trial Balance

5 The following accounts have normal balances. Prepare a trial balance for Mary's Delivery Service as of September 30, 19--.

NEW **Learning Keys**

Debits are always on the left, and credits are always on the right for *all* accounts.

Throughout the text, learning keys are placed in the margin to emphasize important new points. These keys direct student attention to such things as the application of new accounting concepts, how to journalize and post a transaction, relationships among accounts, and how to make an important calculation. A learning key from page 46 is shown in the margin.

NEW **Key Steps**

Key steps are incorporated to show students how to accomplish specific objectives. The steps are used for many purposes, including how to prepare a bank reconciliation or a work sheet, how to post subsidiary and general ledger accounts, and how to find the cause of errors in a bank reconciliation or trial balance.

NEW **Illustrations**

Accounting documents and records, diagrams, and flow charts are used throughout the text to help students visualize important concepts. There is a major increase in the use of illustrations in the fourteenth edition, particularly when any new accounting principles or procedures are introduced. Important examples are as follows:

- Use of the accounting equation. In analyzing business transactions, students must understand the impact of an event on specific accounts in the accounting equation. Throughout Chapters 2 and 3, we repeat the accounting equation as a header for each entry made for specific transactions. This enables the student to see where each account fits in the equation, how the account is increased or decreased, and the effect each entry has on the balance of the equation.
- Owner's equity umbrella. In Chapter 3, the owner's equity umbrella illustrates how revenue, expense, and drawing affect owner's equity.
- Accounting equation and financial statements. In Chapter 2, we illustrate the direct linkages between the balances in the accounting equation and the financial statements.
- Trial balance and financial statements. In Chapter 3, we show how a trial balance is used to develop a set of financial statements.
- Work sheet and financial statements. In Chapter 6, we show the linkages (a) between the Income Statement columns of the work sheet and the income statement, and (b) between the Balance Sheet columns of the work sheet and the statement of owner's equity and balance sheet.
- Work sheet and cost of goods sold. In Chapter 14, we illustrate the linkages between the information extended to the Income State-

ment columns of the work sheet and the cost of goods sold section of the income statement.

— Work sheet and closing entries. In Chapter 15, we illustrate the linkages between the Income Statement and Balance Sheet columns of the work sheet and the closing entries.

NEW   Key Points Chapter Summaries

Each chapter ends with a summary of key points. This provides an efficient way for students to review important chapter material.

NEW   Key Terms

At the end of each chapter, a list is provided of all important new terms introduced in the chapter. Each term is followed by the page number on which the term is first used in the chapter, and a definition.

Building Your Accounting Knowledge

Building Your Accounting Knowledge review questions are provided at the end of each chapter.

Demonstration Problem and Solution

A complete demonstration problem and solution are provided at the end of each chapter. The problem is a comprehensive application of key concepts and principles introduced in the chapter.

Exercises and Problems

Three complete sets of exercises and problems have been prepared to facilitate instructor usage and student learning. At the end of each chapter, there are two sets (Series A and B) of exercises and problems. A third set is available through adoption of the study guide. Each exercise reinforces one concept developed in the chapter. Each problem links related concepts. Each exercise and problem is keyed to the chapter learning objectives.

Mastery Problem

A comprehensive mastery problem follows the exercises and problems at the end of each chapter. This problem is usually similar to the demonstration problem in content and purpose, except that no solution is provided. This problem can be used either to test or to further strengthen the students' overall grasp of the chapter materials.

NEW   Comprehensive Problems

A comprehensive problem is provided at the end of Chapter 6 and Chapter 15. Each problem permits the student to review the entire accounting cycle. The Chapter 6 problem deals with a service business; a merchandising business is the focus of the Chapter 15 problem.

EMPHASIS ON SOUND PEDAGOGY

Our concern throughout the text is to facilitate student learning. Several dimensions of this sound pedagogy are worth emphasizing.

- **Worksheet acetates.** This multi-layer presentation (Chapter 5) of the worksheet provides the most effective demonstration of worksheet preparation found anywhere.
- **Accounts receivable—Notes receivable.** Notes receivable might come first on the balance sheet, but they do not come first in student understanding. Therefore, we cover the simpler, easier to understand subject of accounts receivable first (Chapter 16). Students are then better able to follow the notes receivable presentation (Chapter 17).
- **Payroll.** This sometimes difficult subject is taught in two chapters, taking advantage of the natural break between employee and employer taxes and related issues.
- **Voucher system.** This important topic is integrated into the sequence on accounting for a merchandise business (Chapters 11–15). By presenting this subject immediately following purchases and cash payments (Chapter 12), the student is shown the voucher system as a natural expansion of accounting for purchases.
- **Sales and cash receipts—Purchases and cash payments.** For sound learning and efficiency of presentation, each of these pairs of topics belongs together. The natural sequence of sales and cash receipts is reflected in Chapter 11. Similarly, Chapter 12 addresses the related activities of purchases and cash payments.
- **Statement of cash flows.** The FASB is encouraging firms to use the direct method of reporting cash flows from operating activities. But most companies currently use the indirect method. We illustrate both methods: the direct method in Chapter 24 and the indirect method in an appendix.
- **Accounting forms.** All journals, ledgers, and statements are presented on rulings. This emphasizes structure and helps students learn how to prepare these documents more quickly.
- **Color.** All journals are on blue rulings to differentiate these chronological records from ledgers and other processing documents, which are shown in yellow. Financial statements are white. Source documents vary in color, in the same manner that real-life documents do.
- **Accounting relationships.** Color is used to show accounting relationships. This helps the student see the important relationships more easily. Pages 28 and 67 are two examples of this frequently used pedagogical aid.

- **Arrow pointers and text pointers.** Arrow pointers and text pointers emphasize the derivations of numbers. For example, figure 6-3 shows number pointers that point from the source number to the resulting number, and text pointers contain additional information.
- **Accounting and Computers.** Since students must know how to use computers in today's business world, opening balances for many problems are available for general ledger and spreadsheet software. Step-by-step instructions for solving several demonstration problems are provided. These instructions allow students who have never used a computer to learn how to use a general ledger program. This general ledger program also reinforces the accounting concepts and helps students master the accounting processes more quickly and easily. Accounting and Computers instructions are provided after Chapters 4, 6, 8, 11, 12, and 15. The Accounting and Computers appendix thoroughly explains how to work the computer applications. The EPS icons in the margin beside the end-of-chapter problems identify those problems with opening balances on the general ledger disk. The 123 icons in the margin beside the end-of-chapter problems identify those problems with opening balances on the spreadsheet template disk.

MAJOR CHANGES IN ORGANIZATION

In response to customer suggestions regarding the pace and degree of difficulty of some material presented early in the previous edition, the organization has been changed.

- Old Chapters 1–5 and 8 are now Chapters 1–10. The new Chapters 1–10 focus solely on a service business because most new jobs are in service businesses. The combination journal, which was integrated in the text beginning with old Chapter 3, is presented separately in a new Chapter 7. This new chapter compares the combination journal with the general journal used in earlier chapters. Students are shown how to design a journal to achieve greater efficiency in entering transactions.
- Old Chapters 6–7, 9–10, and 16 are now Chapters 11–15. The new chapters cover accounting for purchases and sales of merchandise, use of special journals and the voucher system, and preparation of the work sheet and financial statements for a merchandise business. This focuses student attention on accounting for a merchandise business after they have learned how to use the accounting model on the simpler service business. This organization also positions the important voucher system and internal accounting control concepts earlier in the text.
- Old Chapter 15 on accounting concepts and practices has been integrated throughout the text rather than being treated as a separate topic.

- Old Chapters 11–14 covering various balance sheet accounts are now Chapters 16–19.
- Old Chapter 17 on partnerships is now Chapter 20. After learning how to account for both service and merchandise businesses, it is timely to introduce the more complicated partnership accounting at this point.
- The three chapters on bonds, statement of cash flows, and financial statement analysis are now part of a new sequence (Chapters 21–25) that emphasizes accounting for corporations.
- Old Chapters 27–29 are now Chapters 27–28. Chapter 27 discusses job order costing, which applies to both manufacturing and service businesses. Chapter 28 demonstrates the use of work sheets for a manufacturing business.

FOR THE INSTRUCTOR

- **Solutions Manual.** Solutions for all end-of-chapter materials. Separate manuals for Chapters 1 through 15 and Chapters 16 through 28.
- **Solutions Transparencies.** Solutions for all end-of-chapter materials. Separate packages for Chapters 1 through 15 and Chapters 16 through 28.
- **Instructor's Resource Guide.** Each chapter of this very helpful, comprehensive guide contains an overview, a chapter outline, teaching transparencies, an assignment table, teaching suggestions, and discussion material including a real-life problem. Information about the software and the videos is also included.
- **Test Bank.** Contains true and false questions, multiple choice questions, and problems with solutions. A microcomputer version (MicroSWAT III) of this printed material is also available.
- **Achievement Tests.** Two sets (A and B) of preprinted tests are available for each chapter. In addition, two preprinted placement test are available.
- **Teaching Transparencies.** Four-color teaching transparencies to reinforce important concepts in each chapter.
- **Videos.** Two types of videos—lecture replacement videos and videos explaining the demonstration problems for Chapters 1 through 15.

FOR THE STUDENT

- **Check Figures.** Check figures for end-of-chapter materials.
- **Electronic Problem Solver.** General ledger software with opening balances for many problems. The software also allows students to solve other problems.
- **LOTUS 1-2-3 Template Software.** Spreadsheet template software with opening balances for many problems.

- **Practice Sets**

    Lee Chang, Computer Consultant. Service business organized as a sole proprietorship using a combination journal and includes source documents. Can be used after Chapter 8.

    Northern Micro. Merchandising business organized as a sole proprietorship. Can be used after Chapter 15.

    Ryan and Lawrence Sporting Goods. Merchandising business organized as a partnership. Can be used after Chapter 20.

    Highpoint Solar Inc. Job-order manufacturing business organized as a corporation. Can be used after Chapter 28.

    Precision Fitness: Integrated Accounting—IBM. Merchandising business organized as a sole proprietorship. *Computerized.* Can be used after Chapter 15.

    QLM Cellular Phones: Integrated Accounting—IBM. Merchandising business organized as a sole proprietorship. Includes payroll. *Computerized.* Can be used after Chapter 15.

    Willett's Waterwear. Merchandising business organized as a sole proprietorship. Includes payroll and source documents. Can be used after Chapter 15.

- **Study Guide.** Includes a discussion of learning objectives, questions, exercises, problems, and practice test questions for each chapter. The study guide helps students master the materials from the chapter. Solutions are provided.

- **Working Papers.** Forms for end-of-chapter exercises, problems, and mastery problems. Separate books for Chapters 1–10, Chapters 1–15, Chapters 1–20, and Chapters 16–28.

- **Integrated Accounting.** Available for IBM and Macintosh computers. Accounting applications for proprietorships, partnerships, and corporations; service and merchandising businesses; departmentalized and nondepartmentalized businesses; and voucher systems are included.

ACKNOWLEDGMENTS

We gratefully acknowledge the many helpful suggestions from students and faculty. We would like to thank the following faculty whose suggestions have become part of this edition:

John T. Anderson
Savannah Area Technical Institute

Thomas R. Barkley
North Central Michigan College

Barbara L. Benesch
Aims Community College

Niki L. Bourke
Missoula Vo-Tech Center

Thomas S. Brooks
Southern Ohio College

James N. Carriger
Ventura College

Lois Chapin
Western Business College

Clinton Chase
Santa Barbara Business College

Mario Di Martino
Lake Washington Technical College

Ted Duzenski
Augusta Technical Institute

Jay D. Fluckiger
Ricks College

Dale Fowler
Davenport College

Scott L. Freeman
Davenport College

Michael Fritz
Portland Community College

Paul Gardiner
LDS Business College

Sherry L. Gordon
Palomar College

Stephen S. Hamilton
Lane Community College

Larry E. Hass
Glen Oaks Community College

Jeff Henderson
Kalamazoo Valley Community
College

D.F. "Duke" Hillesheim
Arizona Institute of Business and
Technology

John M. Jessup
Dickinson Warren Business College

Fred R. Jex
Macomb Community College

Linda Jones
Kaskaskia College

Sandi Jones
Hutchinson Community College

Shirly A. Kleiner
Johnson County Community College

Michael D. Lawrence
Portland Community College

Jerre Lewis
Kirtland Community College

Norbert F. Lindskog
Harold Washington College

Virginia Lumley
Jackson Business Institute

Thomas E. Lynch
Hocking College

Ann Marinoni
Lake Superior State University

Terry T. McBarnet
Maui Community College

Charles McCord
Portland Community College

Cynthia R. Middleton
University of Arkansas at Monticello

Charles Lynn Murray
Florida Community College

Darren J. Mury
Dudley Hall Career Institute

Jon Nitschke
Great Falls Vocational Technical
Center

Scott Rhude
Chaparral Career College/Educational
Management, Inc.

Lois Z. Rippe
Hawkeye Institute of Technology

Mike Rowley
West Hills Junior College

Joan S. Ryan
Lane Community College

Gene Saatmann
Tucumcari Area Vocational School

Keith Sanfter
International Business College

Joan Shaffer
International Correspondence
Schools

Curt Sharp
Lakeshore Technical College

Darlene Shimota
Jordan College

Charles R. Stanley
Southern Illinois University at
Carbondale

Rahmat O. Tavallali
Walsh College

George Wagaman
Brevard Community College

Al Walczak
Linn-Benton Community College

Nancy Weller
Grand Rapids Junior College

Nancy Wierenga
Grand Rapids Junior College

Lynda Wonacott
Portland Community College

Contents

PART TWO   *S*pecialized Accounting Procedures for Service Businesses and Proprietorships   *207*

CHAPTER 7   A PROFESSIONAL SERVICE BUSINESS: MODIFIED CASH BASIS AND COMBINATION JOURNAL   *209*

CHAPTER 8   ACCOUNTING FOR CASH   *243*

CHAPTER 9   PAYROLL ACCOUNTING: EMPLOYEE EARNINGS AND DEDUCTIONS   *277*

CHAPTER 10

PART THREE   *A*ccounting for a Merchandising Business   *339*

CHAPTER 11

CHAPTER 15

FINANCIAL STATEMENTS AND YEAR-END ACCOUNTING FOR A MERCHANDISING BUSINESS   *505*

APPENDIX A

ACCOUNTING AND COMPUTERS   *A-1*

APPENDIX B

FICA TAXES FOR 1993 AND 1992   *B-1*

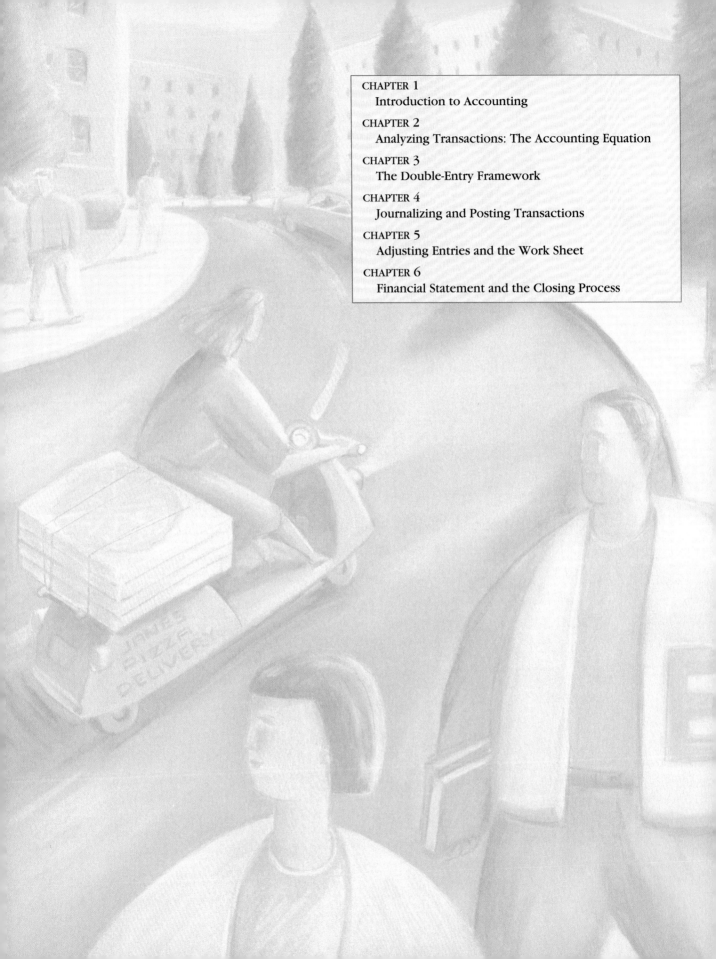

Careful study of this chapter should enable you to:

1. Describe the purpose of accounting.
2. Describe the accounting process.
3. Define three types of business ownership structures.
4. Classify different types of businesses by activities.
5. Identify career opportunities in accounting.

*I*ntroduction to Accounting

Accounting is called the language of business. It is important to understand this language in order to work effectively in the business world. Accounting clerks, bookkeepers, and accountants must understand accounting to perform their jobs. Accounting skills provide additional job opportunities for sales clerks, customer service representatives, and office workers. Small business owners need accounting knowledge to run their businesses effectively.

Knowing the language of accounting helps you understand the impact of economic events on a specific company. Whether you intend to work in accounting or in another area, it is important to have a clear understanding of this language.

THE PURPOSE OF ACCOUNTING

1

Describe the purpose of accounting.

The purpose of accounting is to provide financial information about a business to individuals and organizations. Owners, managers, creditors, and government agencies use accounting information. Other users of accounting information are customers, clients, labor unions, stock exchanges, and financial analysts. Figure 1-1 shows some of the users of accounting information and the information that they need.

THE ACCOUNTING PROCESS

2

Describe the accounting process.

Accounting is the art of gathering financial information about a business and reporting this information to users. The six major steps of the accounting process are analyzing, recording, classifying, summarizing, reporting and interpreting (figure 1-2). Computers are often used in the recording, classifying, summarizing, and reporting steps. People must analyze and interpret accounting data.

3

FIGURE 1-1 **Users of Accounting Information**

USER	INFORMATION NEEDED
Owners— Present and future	Firm's profitability and current financial condition
Managers— May or may not own business	Detailed, up-to-date information about the business to measure performance
Creditors— Present and future	Whether the firm can pay bills on time so they can decide whether or not to extend credit
Government Agencies— State, local, and national	To determine taxes that must be paid and for purposes of regulation

- **Analyzing** is looking to see what has happened and thinking about how this affects the business.
- **Recording** is entering financial information into the accounting system. Although this can be done with paper and pencil, most businesses use computers to perform routine record keeping operations.
- **Classifying** is sorting and grouping like items together rather than merely keeping a simple, diary-like record of numerous events.
- **Summarizing** is bringing the various items of information together to explain a result.
- **Reporting** is telling the results. In accounting, it is common to use tables of numbers to report results.
- **Interpreting** is deciding the importance of the various reports. This may include percentage analyses and the use of ratios to help explain how pieces of information relate to one another.

FIGURE 1-2 **The Accounting Process**

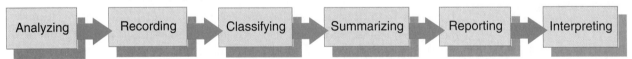

Generally accepted accounting principles (GAAP) are used during the accounting process. The Financial Accounting Standards Board develops these accounting rules, called GAAP, to provide procedures and guidelines to be followed in the accounting process.

<table>
<tr><td>3</td></tr>
<tr><td>Define three types of business ownership structures.</td></tr>
</table>

THREE TYPES OF OWNERSHIP STRUCTURES

Owners of a business need current accounting information to help determine whether the business is profitable. One or more persons may own a business, and businesses can be classified according to the number of owners. Three types of ownership structures are (1) sole proprietorship, (2) partnership, and (3) corporation (figure 1-3). Accountants provide information to owners of all three types of ownership structures.

FIGURE 1-3 **Types of Ownership Structures—Advantages and Disadvantages**

TYPES OF OWNERSHIP STRUCTURES		
Proprietorship	**Partnership**	**Corporation**
■ One owner	■ Two or more partners	■ Stockholders
■ Owner assumes all risks	■ Partners share risks	■ Stockholders have limited risk
■ Owner makes all decisions	■ Partners may disagree on how to run business	■ Stockholders may have little influence on business decisions

Sole Proprietorship

A **sole proprietorship** is owned by one person. The owner is often called a proprietor, and the proprietor is often also the manager of the business. The owner assumes all risks for the business, and personal assets can be taken to pay creditors. The advantage of a sole proprietorship is that the owner can make all of the business decisions.

Partnership

A **partnership** is owned by more than one person. One or more partners may manage the business. Like proprietors, partners assume the risks for the business, and their assets may be taken to pay creditors. An advantage of a partnership is that owners share risks and decision making. A disadvantage is that partners may disagree about the best way to run the business.

Corporation

A **corporation** is owned by stockholders (or shareholders). Corporations may have many owners, and they usually employ professional managers. The owners' risk is usually limited to their initial investment, and they usually have very little influence on the business decisions.

TYPES OF BUSINESSES

Businesses can be classified according to the type of service or product that they provide. Some businesses provide a service, while other businesses sell a product. A business that provides a service is called a **service business.** A business that purchases a product from another business to sell to customers is called a **merchandising business.** A business may make the product that it sells or it may sell a product that another business made. A business that makes a product to sell is called a **manufacturing business.** You will learn about all three types of businesses in this book. Figure 1-4 shows examples of types of businesses organized by activity.

FIGURE 1-4 **Types and Examples of Businesses Organized by Activities**

BUSINESSES THAT PROVIDE SERVICES	BUSINESSES THAT PROVIDE A PRODUCT	
Travel Agency Computer Consultant Physician Accountant Landscaping Business	Merchandising	Manufacturing
	Department Store Pharmacy Jewelry Store	Automobile Manufacturer Furniture Maker Toy Factory

CAREER OPPORTUNITIES IN ACCOUNTING

Accounting offers many career opportunities. The positions listed in the following sections require varying amounts of education and experience.

Accounting Clerk

Businesses with large quantities of accounting tasks to perform daily often employ **accounting clerks** to record, sort, and file accounting information. An accounting clerk may specialize in cash, payroll, accounts receivable, accounts payable, inventory, or purchases. As a result, they are involved with only a small portion of the total accounting responsibilities for the firm. Accounting clerks must usually have at least one year of accounting education.

Bookkeeper

Bookkeepers generally supervise the work of accounting clerks, help with daily accounting work, and summarize accounting information. In small to medium-sized businesses, the bookkeeper may also help managers and owners interpret the accounting information. Bookkeepers must usually have one to two years of accounting education and experience as an accounting clerk.

Accountant

The difference between accountants and bookkeepers is not always clear, particularly in smaller firms where bookkeepers also help analyze the accounting information. In large firms, the distinction is clearer. Bookkeepers focus on the processing of accounting data. **Accountants** design the accounting information system and focus on analyzing and interpreting information. They also look for important trends in the data and study the impact of alternative decisions.

Most accountants enter the field with a college degree in accounting. Accountants are employed in public accounting, private (managerial) accounting, and in nonprofit and governmental accounting (figure 1-5).

FIGURE 1-5 Accounting Careers

ACCOUNTING CAREERS

Private Accounting
- Accounting Information Systems
- General Accounting
- Cost Accounting
- Budgeting
- Tax Accounting
- Internal Auditing

Public Accounting
- Auditing
- Taxation
- Management Consulting

Governmental and Nonprofit Accounting

Public Accounting. Public accountants offer services in much the same way as doctors and lawyers. The public accountant can achieve professional recognition as a **Certified Public Accountant** (CPA) by meeting education and experience requirements, and passing an examination prepared by the American Institute of Certified Public Accountants.

Many CPAs work alone while others work for major accounting firms that vary in scope and size. Public accountants perform many services, which are listed in the following sections.

- **Auditing.** Auditing involves reviewing and testing to be certain that proper accounting policies and practices have been followed.

The purpose of the audit is to provide an independent opinion that the financial information about a business is fairly presented.
- **Taxation.** Tax specialists advise on tax planning, prepare tax returns, and represent clients before governmental agencies such as the Internal Revenue Service.
- **Management Consulting.** Given the financial training and business experience of public accountants, many businesses seek their advice on a wide variety of managerial issues.

CONTROLLER
$35,000-$40,000
Service company seeks financial manager to oversee all general accounting and financial reporting. PC skills important. 4+ years in corporate or public accounting will qualify.

Private Accounting (Managerial Accounting).   Many accountants are employees of private business firms. The **controller** oversees the entire accounting process and is considered the principal accounting officer of the company. Private or managerial accountants perform a wide variety of services for the business.

- **Accounting Information Systems.** Accountants in this area design and implement manual and computerized accounting systems.
- **General Accounting.** Based on the accounting data prepared by the bookkeepers and accounting clerks, the accountant prepares various reports and financial statements.
- **Cost Accounting.** The cost of producing specific products or providing services must be determined. Further analysis is also done to determine whether the products and services are produced in the most cost effective manner.
- **Budgeting.** In the budgeting process, accountants help managers develop a financial plan for the future.
- **Tax Accounting.** Instead of hiring a public accountant, a firm may have its own accountants to focus on tax planning, preparing tax returns, and dealing with the Internal Revenue Service and other governmental agencies.
- **Internal Auditing.** The main functions of an internal auditor are to review the operating and accounting control procedures adopted by management and to see that accurate and timely information is provided.

A managerial accountant can achieve professional status as a **Certified Management Accountant** (CMA) by passing a uniform examination offered by the Institute of Management Accountants. An internal auditor can achieve professional recognition as a **Certified Internal Auditor** (CIA) by passing the uniform examination offered by the Institute of Internal Auditors.

Governmental and Nonprofit Accounting.   Thousands of governmental and nonprofit organizations such as states, municipalities, educational institutions, churches, and hospitals accumulate and report information. These organizations employ a large number of accountants. While the rules are somewhat different for governmental and nonprofit organizations, many accounting procedures are similar to those found in profit-seeking organizations.

Growth in some areas will be much greater than in other areas. Notice in newspaper advertisements that accountants and accounting clerks are expected to have computer skills. Computer skills definitely increase your opportunities in your career. Almost every business needs accountants, accounting clerks, and bookkeepers. Figure 1-6 shows the expected growth for different types of businesses. Notice that growth will be greatest in the service businesses. Since you will most likely work in a service

FIGURE 1-6 **Expected Growth**

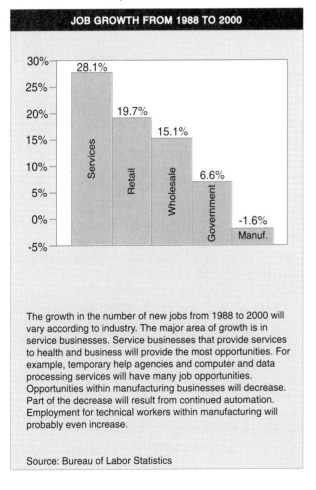

The growth in the number of new jobs from 1988 to 2000 will vary according to industry. The major area of growth is in service businesses. Service businesses that provide services to health and business will provide the most opportunities. For example, temporary help agencies and computer and data processing services will have many job opportunities. Opportunities within manufacturing businesses will decrease. Part of the decrease will result from continued automation. Employment for technical workers within manufacturing will probably even increase.

Source: Bureau of Labor Statistics

FIGURE 1-7 **Expected Demand**

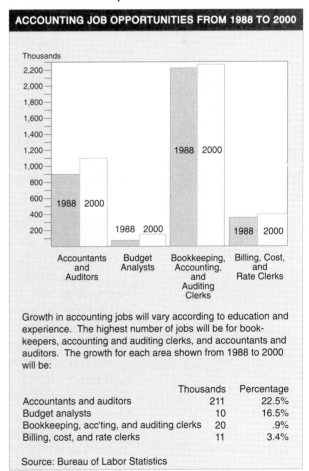

Growth in accounting jobs will vary according to education and experience. The highest number of jobs will be for bookkeepers, accounting and auditing clerks, and accountants and auditors. The growth for each area shown from 1988 to 2000 will be:

	Thousands	Percentage
Accountants and auditors	211	22.5%
Budget analysts	10	16.5%
Bookkeeping, acc'ting, and auditing clerks	20	.9%
Billing, cost, and rate clerks	11	3.4%

Source: Bureau of Labor Statistics

business, Chapters 1 through 10 of this book introduce accounting skills you will need to know to work in a service business. Chapter 11 begins the discussion about merchandising businesses. Since opportunities for accountants in manufacturing businesses will decrease, these topics are placed in the last chapters of the book. Figure 1-7 (on page 9) shows the expected demand for accounting skills.

KEY POINTS

1 The purpose of accounting is to provide financial information about a business to individuals and organizations.

2 The six major steps of the accounting process are analyzing, recording, classifying, summarizing, reporting, and interpreting.

3 Three types of business ownership structures are sole proprietorship, partnership, and corporation.

4 Different types of businesses classified by activities are a service business, a merchandising business, and a manufacturing business.

5 Career opportunities in accounting include work in private accounting, public accounting, and governmental and nonprofit accounting.

KEY TERMS

accountant 7   Designs the accounting information system and focuses on analyzing and interpreting information.

accounting 3   The art of gathering financial information about a business and reporting this information to users.

accounting clerk 6   Records, sorts, and files accounting information.

accounting information systems 8   Accountants in this area design and implement manual and computerized accounting systems.

analyzing 4   Looking to see what has happened and thinking about how this affects the business.

auditing 7   Reviewing and testing to be certain that proper accounting policies and practices have been followed.

bookkeepers 6   Generally supervise the work of accounting clerks, help with daily accounting work, and summarize accounting information.

budgeting 8   The process in which accountants help managers develop a financial plan for the future.

Certified Internal Auditor 8 An internal auditor who has achieved professional recognition by passing the uniform examination offered by the Institute of Internal Auditors.

Certified Public Accountant 7 A public accountant who has met certain education and experience requirements and has passed an examination prepared by the American Institute of Certified Public Accountants.

classifying 4 Sorting and grouping like items together rather than merely keeping a simple, diary-like record of numerous events.

controller 8 The accountant who oversees the entire accounting process in a private business firm.

corporation 5 A type of ownership structure in which stockholders own the business. The owners' risk is usually limited to their initial investment, and they usually have very little influence on the business decisions.

cost accounting 8 Determining the cost of producing specific products or providing services and analyzing for cost effectiveness.

general accounting 8 Preparing various reports and financial statements based on the accounting data prepared by the bookkeepers and accounting clerks.

generally accepted accounting principles 4 Procedures and guidelines developed by the Financial Accounting Standards Board to be followed in the accounting process.

internal auditing 8 Reviewing the operating and accounting control procedures adopted by management and seeing that accurate and timely information is provided.

interpreting 4 Deciding the importance of the various reports.

management consulting 8 Providing advice to businesses on a wide variety of managerial issues.

manufacturing business 6 A business that makes a product to sell.

merchandising business 6 A business that purchases a product from a manufacturing business to sell to customers.

partnership 5 A type of ownership structure in which more than one person owns the business.

recording 4 Entering financial information into the accounting system.

reporting 4 Telling the results of the financial information.

service business 6 A business that provides a service.

sole proprietorship 5 A type of ownership structure in which one person owns the business.

summarizing 4 Bringing the various items of information together to explain a result.

tax accounting 8 Accountants in this area focus on planning, preparing tax returns, and dealing with the Internal Revenue Service and other governmental agencies.

BUILDING YOUR ACCOUNTING KNOWLEDGE

1. What is the purpose of accounting?
2. Identify four user groups normally interested in financial information about a business.
3. Identify the six major phases of the accounting process and explain each phase.
4. Identify the three types of ownership structures and discuss the advantages and disadvantages of each.
5. Identify three types of businesses according to activities.
6. What are the main functions of an accounting clerk?
7. Name and describe three areas of specialization for a public accountant.
8. Name and describe six areas of specialization for a managerial accountant.

SERIES A

EXERCISES

APPLYING ACCOUNTING CONCEPTS

EXERCISE 1A1

Purpose of Accounting

1 Match the following users with the information needed.

1. Owners
2. Managers
3. Creditors
4. Government agencies

a. Whether the firm can pay its bills on time.
b. Detailed, up-to-date information to measure business performance (and plan for future operations)
c. To determine taxes to be paid and whether other regulations are met.
d. The firm's current financial condition.

EXERCISE 1A2

Accounting Process

2 List the six major phases of the accounting process in order (1-6) and define each.

_____ Recording
_____ Summarizing
_____ Reporting
_____ Analyzing
_____ Interpreting
_____ Classifying

SERIES B

EXERCISES

APPLYING ACCOUNTING CONCEPTS

EXERCISE 1B1

Purpose of Accounting

1 Describe the kind of information needed by the users listed.

Owners (present and future)
Managers
Creditors (present and future)
Government agencies

EXERCISE 1B2

Accounting Process

2 Match the following steps of the accounting process with their definitions.

analyzing
recording
classifying
summarizing
reporting
interpreting

a. telling the results
b. looking to see what has happened and thinking about how it affects the business
c. deciding the importance of the various reports
d. bringing together information to explain a result
e. sorting and grouping like items together
f. entering financial information into the accounting system

Careful study of this chapter should enable you to:

1. Define the accounting elements.
2. Construct the accounting equation.
3. Analyze business transactions.
4. Show the effects of business transactions on the accounting equation.
5. Prepare a simple income statement, statement of owner's equity, and balance sheet.

Analyzing Transactions: The Accounting Equation

The entire accounting process is based on one simple equation, called the accounting equation. In this chapter, you will learn how to use this equation to analyze business transactions. You also will learn how to prepare financial statements that report the effect of these transactions on a business.

THE ACCOUNTING ELEMENTS

1

Define the accounting elements.

Before the accounting process begins, the entity to be accounted for must be defined. A **business entity** is an individual, association, or organization that engages in economic activities and controls specific economic resources. This definition allows the personal and business finances of an owner to be accounted for separately. Three basic accounting elements exist for every business entity: assets, liabilities, and owner's equity.

Assets

Assets are items a business owns that will provide future benefits. Examples include money, merchandise, furniture, fixtures, machinery, buildings, and land.

Liabilities

Liabilities are items owed to another business entity. The amount owed represents a future outflow of assets resulting from a past event or transaction. Liabilities are debts that the business can pay with cash, goods, or services.

The most common liabilities are accounts payable and notes payable. An **account payable** is an unwritten promise to pay a supplier for assets purchased or for a service rendered. Formal written promises to pay suppliers or lenders specified sums of money at definite future times are known as **notes payable.**

Owner's Equity

Owner's equity is the amount by which the business assets exceed the business liabilities. Other terms for owner's equity include **proprietorship, net worth,** and **capital.** If the business has no liabilities, the owner's equity is equal to the total assets.

A business owned by one person is called a **proprietorship.** The owner, or **proprietor,** may have business assets and liabilities as well as nonbusiness assets and liabilities. For example, the proprietor probably owns a home, clothing, and a car, and perhaps owes the dentist for dental service. These are personal, nonbusiness assets and liabilities. According to the **business entity concept,** nonbusiness assets and liabilities are not included in the business entity's accounting records.

If the owner invests money or other assets in the business, the item invested is reclassified from a nonbusiness asset to a business asset. If the owner withdraws money or other assets from the business for personal use, the item withdrawn is reclassified from a business asset to a nonbusiness asset. These distinctions allow the owner to make decisions based on the financial results of the business apart from nonbusiness affairs.

The business entity's accounting records are separate from the owner's nonbusiness assets and liabilities.

2

Construct the accounting equation.

THE ACCOUNTING EQUATION

The relationship between the three basic accounting elements—assets, liabilities, and owner's equity—can be expressed in the form of a simple equation known as the **accounting equation.**

Assets = Liabilities + Owner's Equity

If you know two accounting elements, you can calculate the third element.

Total assets	$60,400
Total liabilities	−5,400
Owner's equity	$55,000

This equation shows that both outsiders and insiders have an interest in the assets of a business. *Liabilities represent the outside interests of creditors. Owner's equity represents the inside interests of owners. When two elements are known, the third can be calculated.* Assume that assets on December 31 total $60,400. On December 31, the business liabilities consist of $5,400 owed for equipment. Owner's equity is calculated by subtracting the total liabilities from the total assets, $60,400 − $5,400 = $55,000.

ASSETS = LIABILITIES + OWNER'S EQUITY

$60,400 = $5,400   + $55,000

└──────── $60,400 ────────┘

ANALYZING BUSINESS TRANSACTIONS

3

Analyze business transactions.

Three basic questions must be answered when analyzing the effects of a business transaction on the accounting equation.

1. **What happened?**
   - Make certain you understand what has happened.
2. **Which accounts are affected?**
   - Identify the accounts that are affected.
   - Classify these accounts as assets, liabilities, or owner's equity.
3. **How is the accounting equation affected?**
   - Determine which accounts increased or decreased.
   - Make certain that the accounting equation remains in balance after the transaction is entered.

EFFECT OF TRANSACTIONS ON THE ACCOUNTING EQUATION

4

Show the effects of business transactions on the accounting equation.

Each transaction affects one or more of the three basic accounting elements. A transaction increases or decreases a specific asset, liability, or owner's equity account. Assume that the following transactions occurred during June, 19--, the first month of operations for Jessica Jane's Campus Delivery Services.

Transaction (a): Investment by owner

An Increase in an Asset Offset by an Increase in Owner's Equity. Jessica Jane opened a bank account with a deposit of $2,000 for her business. The new business now has $2,000 of the asset, Cash. Since Jane contributed the asset, the owner's equity element, Jessica Jane, Capital, increases by the same amount.

	ASSETS	=	LIABILITIES	+	OWNER'S EQUITY
	Items Owned		Amounts Owed		Owner's Investment
					Jessica Jane,
	Cash	=			Capital
(a)	$2,000				$2,000

Transaction (b): Purchase of an asset for cash

An Increase in an Asset Offset by a Decrease in Another Asset. Jane decided that the best way to get around campus is on a motor scooter. Thus, she bought a motor scooter (delivery equipment) for $1,200, cash. Jane exchanged one asset, Cash, for another, Delivery Equipment. This transaction reduces Cash and creates a new asset, Delivery Equipment.

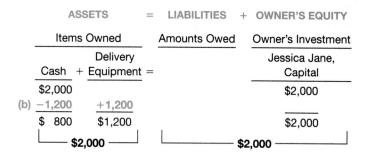

	ASSETS	=	LIABILITIES	+	OWNER'S EQUITY
	Items Owned		Amounts Owed		Owner's Investment
	Cash + Delivery Equipment =				Jessica Jane, Capital
	$2,000				$2,000
(b)	−1,200 +1,200				
	$ 800 $1,200				$2,000
	└── $2,000 ──┘		└───── $2,000 ──────┘		

Transaction (c): Purchase of an asset on account

An Increase in an Asset Offset by an Increase in a Liability. Jane hired a friend to help her, which meant that a second scooter was needed. Given Jane's limited cash, she bought the dealer's demonstration model for $900. The seller allowed Jane to spread the payments over the next three months. This transaction increased the asset, Delivery Equipment, by $900 and increased the liability, Accounts Payable, by an equal amount.

	ASSETS	=	LIABILITIES	+	OWNER'S EQUITY
	Items Owned		Amounts Owed		Owner's Investment
	Cash + Delivery Equipment =		Accounts Payable	+	Jessica Jane, Capital
	$800 $1,200				$2,000
(c)	____ + 900		+900		
	$800 $2,100		$900		$2,000
	└── $2,900 ──┘		└───── $2,900 ──────┘		

Transaction (d): Payment on a loan

A Decrease in an Asset Offset by a Decrease in a Liability. Jane paid the first installment on the scooter of $300. (See transaction (c).) This payment decreased both the asset, Cash, and the liability, Accounts Payable, by $300.

	ASSETS		=	LIABILITIES	+	OWNER'S EQUITY
	Items Owned			Amounts Owed		Owner's Investment
	Cash +	Delivery Equipment =		Accounts Payable	+	Jessica Jane, Capital
	$800	$2,100		$900		$2,000
(d)	−300			−300		
	$500	$2,100		$600		$2,000
		$2,600			$2,600	

EXPANDING THE ACCOUNTING EQUATION: REVENUES, EXPENSES, AND WITHDRAWALS

In the preceding sections, the three key accounting elements of every business entity were explained: assets, liabilities, and owner's equity. To complete the explanation, three elements must be added: revenues, expenses, and withdrawals.

Revenues

Revenues are the amount a business charges customers for products sold or services performed. Customers may pay with cash or a credit card, or they may promise to pay at a later date. Most businesses recognize revenues when earned, even if cash has not yet been received. *Revenue increases both assets and owner's equity.*

Expenses

It is important to remember that expenses do not always reduce cash.

Expenses represent the decrease in assets (or increase in liabilities) resulting from efforts to produce revenues. Common examples of expenses are rent, salaries, supplies consumed, and many taxes. As expenses are incurred, either assets are consumed (supplies), cash is paid (salaries), or a promise is made to pay cash at a future date. The promise to pay in the future represents a liability. Most businesses recognize expenses when incurred, even if cash has not yet been paid. *Expenses either decrease assets or increase liabilities; expenses always reduce owner's equity.*

If revenues exceed expenses of the period, the excess is the **net income** or net profit for the period.

Revenues Greater than Expenses = Net Income

If expenses exceed revenue of the period, the excess is a **net loss** for the period.

Expenses Greater than Revenues = Net Loss

The owner can determine the time interval used to measure net income or net loss. It may be a month, a quarter (three months), a year, or some other period of time. The concept that income determination can be made on a periodic basis is known as the **accounting period concept.** Any accounting period of twelve months is called a **fiscal year.** The fiscal year often coincides with the calendar year.

Withdrawals

Owner's Equity	
Decrease	Increase
Expenses Drawing	Revenues

Withdrawals, or **drawing,** reduce owner's equity as a result of the owner taking cash or other assets out of the business for personal use. Since earnings are expected to offset withdrawals, this reduction is viewed as temporary.

The accounting equation is expanded to include revenues, expenses, and withdrawals. Revenues increase owner's equity, while expenses and drawing reduce owner's equity.

	ASSETS	=	LIABILITIES	+		OWNER'S EQUITY			
	Items Owned		Amounts Owed		Owner's Investment	+		Earnings	
	Cash +	Del. Equip. =	Accounts Payable	+	J. Jane, Capital	−	J. Jane, Drawing +	Revenue −	Expense
Bal.	$500	$2,100	$600		$2,000				
	└── $2,600 ──┘		└────────── $2,600 ──────────┘						

EFFECT OF REVENUE, EXPENSE, AND WITHDRAWAL TRANSACTIONS ON THE ACCOUNTING EQUATION

To show the effects of revenue, expense and withdrawal transactions, the example of Jessie Jane's Campus Delivery Service will be continued. Assume that the following transactions occurred in Jane's business during June, 19--.

Transaction (e): Delivery revenues earned in cash

An Increase in an Asset Offset by an Increase in Owner's Equity Resulting from Revenue.   Jane received $500 cash from customers for delivery services. This transaction increased the asset, Cash, and increased owner's equity by $500. The increase in owner's equity is shown by increasing the revenue element called Delivery Fees by $500.

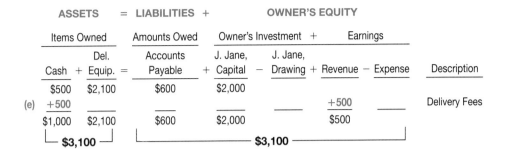

ASSETS		=	LIABILITIES	+			OWNER'S EQUITY				
Items Owned			Amounts Owed		Owner's Investment	+		Earnings			
	Del.		Accounts		J. Jane,		J. Jane,				
Cash	+ Equip. =		Payable	+	Capital	−	Drawing	+ Revenue	− Expense	Description
$500	$2,100		$600		$2,000					
(e) +500	____		____		____		____	+500	____	Delivery Fees
$1,000	$2,100		$600		$2,000			$500		
└─ **$3,100** ─┘			└──────── **$3,100** ──────────┘							

Transaction (f): Paid rent for month

A Decrease in an Asset Offset by a Decrease in Owner's Equity Resulting from an Expense.   Jane rents an office on campus. She paid $200 for office rent for June. This transaction decreased both Cash and owner's equity by $200. The decrease in owner's equity is shown by increasing an expense called Rent Expense by $200. An increase in an expense decreases owner's equity.

ASSETS		=	LIABILITIES	+			OWNER'S EQUITY				
Items Owned			Amounts Owed		Owner's Investment	+		Earnings			
	Del.		Accounts		J. Jane,		J. Jane,				
Cash	+ Equip. =		Payable	+	Capital	−	Drawing	+ Revenue	− Expense	Description
$1,000	$2,100		$600		$2,000			$500		
(f) −200	____		____		____		____	____	+200	Rent Exp.
$ 800	$2,100		$600		$2,000			$500	$200	
└─ **$2,900** ─┘			└──────── **$2,900** ──────────┘							

Transaction (g): Paid telephone bill

A Decrease in an Asset Offset by a Decrease in Owner's Equity Resulting from an Expense.   Jane paid $50 in cash for telephone service. This transaction, like the previous one, decreased both Cash and owner's equity. This decrease in owner's equity is shown by increasing an expense called Telephone Expense by $50.

ASSETS		=	LIABILITIES	+			OWNER'S EQUITY				
Items Owned			Amounts Owed		Owner's Investment	+		Earnings			
	Del.		Accounts		J. Jane,		J. Jane,				
Cash	+ Equip. =		Payable	+	Capital	−	Drawing	+ Revenue	− Expense	Description
$800	$2,100		$600		$2,000			$500	$200	
(g) −50	____		____		____		____	____	+50	Telephone Exp.
$750	$2,100		$600		$2,000			$500	$250	
└─ **$2,850** ─┘			└──────── **$2,850** ──────────┘							

Transaction (h): Delivery revenues earned on account

Revenue is recognized even though cash is not received.

An Increase in an Asset Offset by an Increase in Owner's Equity Resulting from Revenue.   Jane will extend credit to regular customers. Often delivery services are performed for which payment will be received later. This is known as offering services "on account." Since revenues are recognized when earned, an increase in owner's equity is reported by increasing a revenue account. Since cash is not received at this time, Cash cannot be increased. Instead, an increase is reported for another asset, Accounts Receivable. *The balance of Accounts Receivable reflects the amount owed to Jane by her customers.* Deliveries made on account amounted to $600. Accounts Receivable and Delivery Revenues are increased.

	ASSETS			=	LIABILITIES +		OWNER'S EQUITY				
	Items Owned				Amounts Owed	Owner's Investment +		Earnings			
	Cash +	Accts. Rec. +	Del. Equip. =		Accounts Payable	+ J. Jane, Capital	− J. Jane, Drawing	+ Revenue	− Expense	Description
	$750		$2,100		$600	$2,000		$ 500	$250	
(h)		+600						+ 600		Delivery Fees
	$750	$600	$2,100		$600	$2,000		$1,100	$250	
	$3,450				$3,450					

Transaction (i): Purchase of supplies

An Increase in an Asset Offset by a Decrease in an Asset.   Jane bought pens, paper, delivery envelopes, and other supplies for $80 cash. These supplies should last for several months. Since they will generate future benefits, the supplies should be recorded as an asset. Supplies is increased and Cash is decreased.

	ASSETS				=	LIABILITIES +		OWNER'S EQUITY				
	Items Owned					Amounts Owed	Owner's Investment +		Earnings			
	Cash +	Accts. Rec. +	Supplies +	Del. Equip. =		Accounts Payable	+ J. Jane, Capital	− J. Jane, Drawing	+ Revenue	− Expense	Description
	$750	$600		$2,100		$600	$2,000		$1,100	$250	
(i)	−80		+80								
	$670	$600	$80	$2,100		$600	$2,000		$1,100	$250	
	$3,450					$3,450					

Both supplies and insurance are recorded as assets because they will last for several months.

Transaction (j): Payment of Insurance Premium

An Increase in an Asset Offset by a Decrease in an Asset. Jane paid $200 for an eight-month liability insurance policy. Since insurance is paid in advance and will provide future benefits, it is recorded as an asset. Another asset, Prepaid Insurance, is increased and Cash is decreased.

	ASSETS					=	LIABILITIES +		OWNER'S EQUITY			
	Items Owned						Amounts Owed		Owner's Investment +		Earnings	
		Accts.		Prepaid	Del.		Accounts	J. Jane,	J. Jane,			
	Cash +	Rec. +	Supplies +	Ins. +	Equip. =		Payable	+ Capital	− Drawing	+ Revenue −	Expense	Description
	$670	$600	$80		2,100		$600	$2,000		$1,100	$250	
(j)	−200			+200								
	$470	$600	$80	$200	$2,100		$600	$2,000		$1,100	$250	
	└────────── $3,450 ──────────┘						└────────── $3,450 ──────────┘					

Transaction (k): Cash receipts from prior sales on account

An Increase in an Asset Offset by a Decrease in an Asset. Jane received $570 in cash for delivery services performed for customers earlier in the month (see transaction (h)). Receipt of this cash increases the cash account and reduces the amount due from customers reported in Accounts Receivable. *Notice that owner's equity is not affected in this transaction. Owner's equity increased in transaction (h) since revenue was recognized when it was earned rather than now when cash is received.*

	ASSETS					=	LIABILITIES +		OWNER'S EQUITY			
	Items Owned						Amounts Owed		Owner's Investment +		Earnings	
		Accts.		Prepaid	Del.		Accounts	J. Jane,	J. Jane,			
	Cash +	Rec. +	Supplies +	Ins. +	Equip. =		Payable	+ Capital	− Drawing	+ Revenue −	Expense	Description
	$ 470	$600	$80	$200	2,100		$600	$2,000		$1,100	$250	
(k)	+570	−570										
	$1,040	$ 30	$80	$200	$2,100		$600	$2,000		$1,100	$250	
	└────────── $3,450 ──────────┘						└────────── $3,450 ──────────┘					

Transaction (l): Purchase of an asset on credit making a partial payment

An Increase in an Asset Offset by a Decrease in an Asset and an Increase in a Liability. With business increasing, Jane hired a second employee and bought a third motor scooter. The scooter cost $1,500. Jane paid $300 in cash and will spread the remaining payments over the next four months. The asset Delivery Equipment increases by $1,500, Cash decreases by $300, and the liability, Accounts Payable increases by $1,200. *This transaction changed three accounts, but the accounting equation remains in balance.*

	Cash	+	Accts. Rec.	+	Supplies	+	Prepaid Ins.	+	Del. Equip.	=	Accounts Payable	+	J. Jane, Capital	−	J. Jane, Drawing	+	Revenue	−	Expense	Description
						ASSETS — Items Owned					=	LIABILITIES — Amounts Owed		OWNER'S EQUITY — Owner's Investment		+ Earnings				
	$1,040		$30		$80		$200		$2,100		$600		$2,000				$1,100		$250	
(l)	−300								+1,500		+1,200									
	$740		$30		$80		$200		$3,600		$1,800		$2,000				$1,100		$250	

Assets $4,650 — Liabilities + Owner's Equity $4,650

Transaction (m): Payment of wages

A Decrease in an Asset Offset by a Decrease in Owner's Equity Resulting From an Expense.   Jane paid her part-time employees $650 in wages. This represents a business expense. Similar to other expenses, Cash is reduced and owner's equity is reduced.

	Cash	+	Accts. Rec.	+	Supplies	+	Prepaid Ins.	+	Del. Equip.	=	Accounts Payable	+	J. Jane, Capital	−	J. Jane, Drawing	+	Revenue	−	Expense	Description
						ASSETS — Items Owned					=	LIABILITIES — Amounts Owed		OWNER'S EQUITY — Owner's Investment		+ Earnings				
	$740		$30		$80		$200		$3,600		$1,800		$2,000				$1,100		$250	
(m)	−650																		+650	Wage Exp.
	$90		$30		$80		$200		$3,600		$1,800		$2,000				$1,100		$900	

Assets $4,000 — Liabilities + Owner's Equity $4,000

Transaction (n): Deliveries made for cash and credit

An Increase in Two Assets Offset by an Increase in Owner's Equity.   Total delivery fees for the remainder of the month amounted to $900: $430 for cash and $470 on account. The revenue account increases by $900. Also, Cash increases by $430 and Accounts Receivable increases by $470. Thus, revenues increase assets and owner's equity.

	ASSETS					= LIABILITIES +		OWNER'S EQUITY				
	Items Owned					Amounts Owed	Owner's Investment +		Earnings			
		Accts.		Prepaid	Del.	Accounts	J. Jane,	J. Jane,				
	Cash +	Rec. +	Supplies +	Ins. +	Equip. =	Payable	+ Capital	− Drawing +	Revenue −	Expense	Description
	$ 90	$ 30	$80	$200	$3,600	$1,800	$2,000		$1,100	$900	
(n)	+430	+470	___	___	___	___	___	___	+900	___	Del. Fees
	$520	$500	$80	$200	$3,600	$1,800	$2,000		$2,000	$900	

ASSETS **$4,900**   LIABILITIES + OWNER'S EQUITY **$4,900**

Transaction (o): Withdrawal of cash from business

Withdrawals by the owner are reported in the drawing account. Withdrawals are the opposite of investments by the owner.

A Decrease in an Asset Offset by a Decrease in Owner's Equity Resulting from a Withdrawal by the Owner.   At the end of the month, Jane took $150 in cash from the business to buy books for her classes. Since the books are not business-related, this is a withdrawal. Withdrawals are the opposite of investments by the owner. Both owner's equity and Cash decrease.

	ASSETS					= LIABILITIES +		OWNER'S EQUITY				
	Items Owned					Amounts Owed	Owner's Investment +		Earnings			
		Accts.		Prepaid	Del.	Accounts	J. Jane,	J. Jane,				
	Cash +	Rec. +	Supplies +	Ins. +	Equip. =	Payable	+ Capital	− Drawing +	Revenue −	Expense	Description
	$520	$500	$80	$200	$3,600	$1,800	$2,000		$2,000	$900	
(o)	−150	___	___	___	___	___	___	+150	___	___	
	$370	$500	$80	$200	$3,600	$1,800	$2,000	$150	$2,000	$900	

ASSETS **$4,750**   LIABILITIES + OWNER'S EQUITY **$4,750**

Similar to the running balances in the table, the listing immediately following provides proof that the accounting equation is in balance.

Figure 2-1 shows a summary of the transactions. At the bottom of figure 2-1, the assets and their balances are compared with the liability and owner's equity accounts.

FIGURE 2-1 **Summary of Transactions Illustrated**

SUMMARY

Tran.	Cash	+ Accts. Rec.	+ Supplies	+ Prepaid Ins.	+ Del. Equip.	= Accounts Payable	+ J. Jane, Capital	− J. Jane, Drawing	+ Revenue	− Expense	Description
Bal.											
(a)	2,000						2,000				
Bal.	2,000						2,000				
(b)	(1,200)				1,200						
Bal.	800				1,200		2,000				
(c)					900	900					
Bal.	800				2,100	900	2,000				
(d)	(300)					(300)					
Bal.	500				2,100	600	2,000				
(e)	500								500		Del. Fees
Bal.	1,000				2,100	600	2,000		500		
(f)	(200)									200	Rent Exp.
Bal.	800				2,100	600	2,000		500	200	
(g)	(50)									50	Teleph. Exp.
Bal.	750				2,100	600	2,000		500	250	
(h)		600							600		Del. Fees
Bal.	750	600			2,100	600	2,000		1,100	250	
(i)	(80)		80								
Bal.	670	600	80		2,100	600	2,000		1,100	250	
(j)	(200)			200							
Bal.	470	600	80	200	2,100	600	2,000		1,100	250	
(k)	570	(570)									
Bal.	1,040	30	80	200	2,100	600	2,000		1,100	250	
(l)	(300)				1,500	1,200					
Bal.	740	30	80	200	3,600	1,800	2,000		1,100	250	
(m)	(650)									650	Wage Exp.
Bal.	90	30	80	200	3,600	1,800	2,000		1,100	900	
(n)	430	470							900		Del. Fees
Bal.	520	500	80	200	3,600	1,800	2,000		2,000	900	
(o)	(150)							150			
Bal.	370	500	80	200	3,600	1,800	2,000	150	2,000	900	

Cash....................................	$ 370	Accounts Payable.................	$1,800
Accounts Receivable.............	500	J. Jane, Capital	2,000
Supplies...............................	80	J. Jane, Drawing...................	(150)
Prepaid Insurance................	200	Delivery Fees	2,000
Delivery Equipment	3,600	Rent Expense	(200)
Total Assets	$4,750	Telephone Expense..............	(50)
		Wage Expense	(650)
		Total Liabilities and	
		Owner's Equity	$4,750

Amounts in ( ) subtracted.

FINANCIAL STATEMENTS

Prepare a simple income statement, statement of owner's equity, and balance sheet.

Three financial statements commonly prepared by a business are the income statement, statement of owner's equity, and balance sheet. The transaction information gathered and summarized in the accounting equation may be used to prepare these financial statements. Figure 2-2 shows the following:

1. A summary of the specific revenue and expense transactions and the ending balances for the asset, liability, capital, and drawing accounts from the accounting equation.
2. The financial statements and their linkages with the accounting equation and each other.

Notice that each financial statement in figure 2-2 has a heading consisting of:

1. the name of the business	Jessie Jane's Campus Delivery Service
2. the title of the statement	Income Statement, Statement of Owner's Equity, or Balance Sheet
3. the time period covered or the date of the statement.	For Month Ended June 30, 19-- or June 30, 19--

The income statement and statement of owner's equity provide information concerning transactions covering a period of time, in this case, *the month ended* June 30, 19--. The balance sheet, on the other hand, shows a picture of the business *on a specific date,* June 30, 19--.

The Income Statement

The **income statement,** sometimes called the **profit and loss statement** or **operating statement,** reports the profitability of business operations for a specific period of time. Jane's income statement shows the revenues earned for the month of June. Next, the expenses incurred as a result of the efforts made to earn these revenues are deducted. If the revenues are greater than the expenses, net income is reported. If not, a net loss is reported.

FIGURE 2-2 **Summary and Financial Statements**

Tran.	Cash	+	Accts. Rec.	+	Supplies	+	Prepaid Ins.	+	Del. Equip.	=	Accounts Payable	+	J. Jane, Capital	−	J. Jane, Drawing	+	Revenue	−	Expense	Description
(e)																	500			Del. Fees
(f)																			200	Rent Exp.
(g)																			50	Teleph. Exp.
(h)																	600			Del. Fees
(m)																	900			Del. Fees
(n)																			650	Wage Exp.
Bal.	370		500		80		200		3,600		1,800		2,000		150		2,000		900	

Column group headers:
ASSETS = LIAB. + OWNER'S EQUITY
Items Owned | Amounts Owed | Owner's Investment + | Earnings

Jessie Jane's Campus Delivery Service
Income Statement
For Month Ended June 30, 19--

Revenue		
Delivery fees		$2 000 00
Expenses		
Wage expense	$6 5 0 00	
Rent expense	2 0 0 00	
Telephone expense	5 0 00	
Total expenses		9 0 0 00
Net Income		$1 1 0 0 00

$ at top of column

Subtotal underline

Jessie Jane's Campus Delivery Service
Statement of Owner's Equity
For Month Ended June 30, 19--

Jessica Jane, capital, June 1, 19--		$2 000 00
Net income for June	$1 1 0 0 00	
Less withdrawals for June	1 5 0 00	
Increase in capital		9 5 0 00
Jessica Jane, capital, June 30, 19--		$2 950 00

$ on total

Jessie Jane's Campus Delivery Service
Balance Sheet
June 30, 19--

Assets		Liabilities	
Cash	$ 3 7 0 00	Accounts payable	$1 8 0 0 00
Accounts receivable	5 0 0 00		
Supplies	8 0 00	Owner's Equity	
Prepaid insurance	2 0 0 00	Jessica Jane, capital	2 9 5 0 00
Delivery equipment	3 6 0 0 00		
Total assets	$4 7 5 0 00	Total liab. & owner's equity	$4 7 5 0 00

Double underline

The Statement of Owner's Equity

Two types of transactions affect owner's equity:

1. Investments and withdrawals by the owner.
2. Profits and losses generated through operating activities.

The **statement of owner's equity** that reports beginning capital plus net income less withdrawals to compute ending capital, is illustrated in figure 2-2. This illustration reports these activities for June. Jane started her business with an investment of $2,000. During the month of June she earned $1,100 in net income and withdrew $150 for personal expenses. This resulted in a net increase in Jane's capital of $950. Jane's $2,000 original investment, plus the net increase of $950 results in her ending capital of $2,950.

Note that Jane's original investment and later withdrawal are taken from the accounting equation. *The net income figure could have been computed from information in the accounting equation. However, it is easier to simply transfer net income as reported on the income statement to the statement of owner's equity.* This links the income statement and statement of owner's equity.

The Balance Sheet

The **balance sheet** reports assets, liabilities, and owner's equity on a specific date. It is called a balance sheet because it confirms that the accounting equation is in balance. It is also called a **statement of financial position** or **statement of financial condition.**

As illustrated in figure 2-2, the asset and liability accounts are taken from the accounting equation and reported on the balance sheet. *Jane's June 30 capital balance could have been computed from the owner's equity accounts in the accounting equation ($2,000 − $150 + $2,000 − $900). However, it is simpler to take the June 30, 19--, capital as computed on the statement of owner's equity and transfer it to the balance sheet.* This links these two statements.

GUIDELINES FOR PREPARING FINANCIAL STATEMENTS
1. Financial statements follow a standard form with careful attention to placement, spacing, and indentions.
2. All statements have a heading with the name of the company, name of the statement, and accounting period or date.
3. Single rules (lines) indicate that the numbers above the line have been added or subtracted. Double rules (double underlines) indicate a total.

> **GUIDELINES FOR PREPARING FINANCIAL STATEMENTS, Cont'd.**
>
> **4.** Dollar signs are used at the top of columns, for totals, and beneath rulings.
> **5.** On the income statement, a common practice is to list expenses from highest to lowest dollar amount, with miscellaneous expense listed last.
> **6.** On the balance sheet, assets are listed from most liquid to least liquid. **Liquidity** measures the ease with which the asset will be converted to cash. Liabilities are listed from most current to least current.

KEY POINTS

1 The three key accounting elements are assets, liabilities, and owner's equity. Owner's equity is expanded to include revenues, expenses, and drawing.

2 The accounting equation is:

Assets = Liabilities + Owner's Equity

3 Three questions must be answered in analyzing business transactions:

1. What happened?
2. Which accounts are affected?
3. How is the accounting equation affected?

4 Each transaction affects one or more of the three basic accounting elements. The chapter transactions can be classified into five groups:

1. Increase in an asset offset by an increase in owner's equity
2. Increase in an asset offset by a decrease in another asset
3. Increase in an asset offset by an increase in a liability
4. Decrease in an asset offset by a decrease in a liability
5. Decrease in an asset offset by a decrease in owner's equity

5 The purposes of the income statement, statement of owner's equity, and balance sheet can be summarized as follows.

STATEMENT	PURPOSE
Income statement	Reports net income or loss
	Revenues – Expenses = Net Income or Loss
Statement of owner's equity	Shows changes in the owner's capital account
	Beginning Capital + Investments + Net Income – Withdrawals = Ending Capital
Balance sheet	Verifies balance of accounting equation
	Assets = Liabilities + Owner's Equity

Figure 2-3 shows the complete accounting process in terms of input, processing, and output.

▬ **Input.** Business transactions provide the necessary **input**.

FIGURE 2-3 **Input, Processing, and Output**

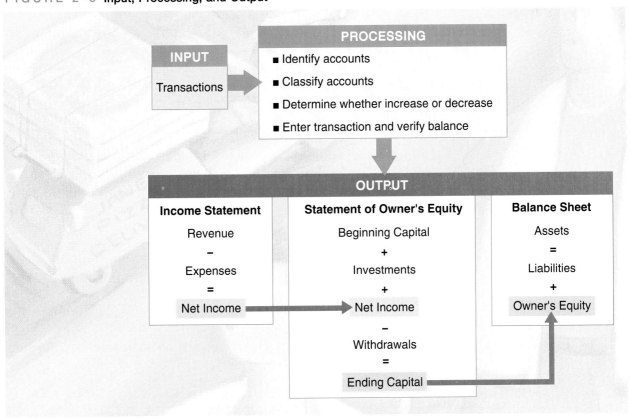

- **Processing.** Recognizing the effect of these transactions on the assets, liabilities, owner's equity, revenue, and expenses of a business is the **processing** function.
- **Output.** The financial statements are the **output**.

KEY TERMS

accounting equation 16   The accounting equation consists of the three basic accounting elements—assets = liabilities + owner's equity

accounting period concept 20   The concept that income determination can be made on a periodic basis.

account payable 16   An unwritten promise to pay a supplier for assets purchased or for a service rendered.

assets 15   Items a business owns that will provide future benefits.

balance sheet 29   Reports assets, liabilities, and owner's equity on a specific date. It is called a balance sheet because it confirms that the accounting equation is in balance.

business entity 15   An individual, association, or organization that engages in economic activities and controls specific economic resources.

business entity concept 16   The concept that states that nonbusiness assets and liabilities are not included in the business entity's accounting records.

capital 16   Another term for owner's equity, the amount by which the business assets exceed the business liabilities.

drawing 20   Withdrawals that reduce owner's equity as a result of the owner taking cash or other assets out of the business for personal use.

expenses 19   Represent the decrease in assets (or increase in liabilities) as a result of efforts to produce revenues.

fiscal year 20   Any accounting period of twelve months' duration.

income statement 27   Reports the profitability of business operations for a specific period of time (sometimes called the profit and loss statement or operating statement).

input 31   Business transactions provide the necessary input for the accounting information system.

liability 16   An item or amount of money owed to another business entity.

liquidity 30   Measures the ease with which the asset will be converted to cash.

net income 19   The excess of total revenues over total expenses for the period.

net loss 20   The excess of total expenses over total revenues for the period.

net worth 16   Another term for owner's equity, which is the amount by which the business assets exceed the business liabilities.

note payable 16   A formal written promise to pay a supplier or lender a specified sum of money at a definite future time.

operating statement 27   Another name for the income statement, which reports the profitability of business operations for a specific period of time.

output 32   The financial statements are the output of the accounting information system.

owner's equity 16   The amount by which the business assets exceed the business liabilities.

processing 32   Recognizing the effect of transactions on the assets, liabilities, owner's equity, revenue, and expense of a business.

profit and loss statement 27   Another name for the income statement, which reports the profitability of business operations for a specific period of time.

proprietor 16   The owner of a proprietorship.

proprietorship 16   A business that is owned by one person.

revenues 19   The amount a business charges customers for products sold or services performed.

statement of financial condition 29   Another name for the balance sheet, which reports assets, liabilities, and owner's equity.

statement of financial position 29   Another name for the balance sheet, which reports assets, liabilities, and owner's equity.

statement of owner's equity 29   Reports beginning capital plus net income less withdrawals to compute ending capital.

withdrawals 20   Reduce owner's equity as a result of the owner taking cash or other assets out of the business for personal use.

BUILDING YOUR ACCOUNTING KNOWLEDGE

1. Why is it necessary to distinguish between business assets and liabilities and nonbusiness assets and liabilities of a single proprietor?
2. Describe the three basic questions that must be answered when analyzing the effects of a business transaction on the accounting equation.
3. Name and define the six major elements of the accounting equation.
4. What is the function of an income statement?
5. What is the function of a statement of owner's equity?
6. What is the function of a balance sheet?

DEMONSTRATION PROBLEM

Damon Young has started his own business, Home and Away Inspections. He inspects property for buyers and sellers of real estate. Damon rents office space and has a part-time assistant to answer the phone and to help with inspections. The transactions for the month of September are as follows:

(a) Young invested cash by making a deposit in a bank account for the business, $15,000.
(b) Paid rent for September, $300.
(c) Bought a used truck for cash, $8,000.
(d) Bought tools on account from Crafty Tools, $3,000.
(e) Paid electricity bill, $50.
(f) Paid two-year premium for liability insurance on truck, $600.
(g) Received cash from clients for service performed, $2,000.
(h) Paid temporary assistant (wages) for first half of month, $200.
(i) Performed inspection services for clients on account, $1,000.
(j) Paid telephone bill, $35.
(k) Bought office supplies for cash, $100.
(l) Received cash from clients for inspections performed on account in (i), $300.
(m) Paid temporary assistant (wages) for last half of month, $250.
(n) Made partial payment on tools bought in (d), $1,000.
(o) Additional revenues earned amounted to $2,000: $1,400 for cash and $600 on account.
(p) Young withdrew cash for personal expenses, $500.

Required

1. Enter the transactions in an accounting equation similar to the following.

	ASSETS					=	LIABILITIES	+		OWNER'S EQUITY			
	Items Owned						Amounts Owed		Owner's Investment	+	Earnings		
	Accts.	Sup-	Prepaid				Accts.		D. Young,	D. Young,			
Cash +	Rec. +	plies +	Ins.	+ Tools +	Truck =		Pay.	+	Capital	− Drawing	+ Revenue	− Expense	Description

2. Compute the ending balances for all accounts.
3. Prepare an income statement for Home & Away Inspections for the month of September.
4. Prepare a statement of owner's equity for Home & Away Inspections for the month of September.

5. Prepare a balance sheet for Home & Away Inspections as of September 30 of the current year.

SOLUTION

1, 2.

	Cash	+ Accts. Rec.	+ Sup- plies	+ Prepaid Ins.	+ Tools	+ Truck	= Accts. Pay.	+ D.Young, Capital	- D.Young, Drawing	+ Revenue	- Expense	Description
ASSETS							**= LIABILITIES +**		**OWNER'S EQUITY**			
			Items Owned				Amounts Owed	Owner's Investment +		Earnings		
Bal. (a)	15,000							15,000				
Bal. (b)	15,000 (300)	0	0	0	0	0	0	15,000	0	0	0 300	Rent Exp.
Bal. (c)	14,700 (8,000)	0	0	0	0	0 8,000	0	15,000	0	0	300	
Bal. (d)	6,700	0	0	0	0 3,000	8,000	0 3,000	15,000	0	0	300	
Bal. (e)	6,700 (50)	0	0	0	3,000	8,000	3,000	15,000	0	0	300 50	Util. Exp.
Bal. (f)	6,650 (600)	0	0	0 600	3,000	8,000	3,000	15,000	0	0	350	
Bal. (g)	6,050 2,000	0	0	600	3,000	8,000	3,000	15,000	0	0 2,000	350	Inspec. Fees
Bal. (h)	8,050 (200)	0	0	600	3,000	8,000	3,000	15,000	0	2,000	350 200	Wages Exp.
Bal. (i)	7,850	0 1,000	0	600	3,000	8,000	3,000	15,000	0	2,000 1,000	550	Inspec. Fees
Bal. (j)	7,850 (35)	1,000	0	600	3,000	8,000	3,000	15,000	0	3,000	550 35	Teleph. Exp.
Bal. (k)	7,815 (100)	1,000	0 100	600	3,000	8,000	3,000	15,000	0	3,000	585	
Bal. (l)	7,715 300	1,000 (300)	100	600	3,000	8,000	3,000	15,000	0	3,000	585	
Bal. (m)	8,015 (250)	700	100	600	3,000	8,000	3,000	15,000	0	3,000	585 250	Wages Exp.
Bal. (n)	7,765 (1,000)	700	100	600	3,000	8,000	3,000 (1,000)	15,000	0	3,000	835	
Bal. (o)	6,765 1,400	700 600	100	600	3,000	8,000	2,000	15,000	0	3,000 2,000	835	Inspec. Fees
Bal. (p)	8,165 (500)	1,300	100	600	3,000	8,000	2,000	15,000	0 500	5,000	835	
Bal.	7,665	1,300	100	600	3,000	8,000	2,000	15,000	500	5,000	835	

Cash	$ 7,665	Accounts Payable	$ 2,000
Accounts Receivable ...	1,300	D.Young, Capital	15,000
Supplies	100	D.Young, Drawing	(500)
Prepaid Insurance	600	Inspection Fees	5,000
Tools	3,000	Rent Expense	(300)
Truck	8,000	Telephone Expense	(35)
Total Assets	$20,665	Wage Expense	(450)
		Utility Expense	(50)
		Total Liabilities and Owner's Equity	$20,665

3.

Home & Away Inspections
Income Statement
For Month Ended September 30, 19--

Revenue:			
Inspection fees			$5 0 0 0 00
Expenses:			
Wage expense	$4 5 0 00		
Rent expense	3 0 0 00		
Utility expense	5 0 00		
Telephone expense	3 5 00		
Total expenses			8 3 5 00
Net income			$4 1 6 5 00

4.

Home & Away Inspections
Statement of Owner's Equity
For Month Ended September 30, 19--

Damon Young, capital, September 1, 19--			$15 0 0 0 00
Net income for September	$4 1 6 5 00		
Less withdrawals for September	5 0 0 00		
Increase in capital			3 6 6 5 00
Damon Young, capital, September 30, 19--			$18 6 6 5 00

5.

Home & Away Inspections Balance Sheet September 30, 19--					
Assets			**Liabilities**		
Cash	$ 7 6 6 5 00		Accounts payable	$ 2 0 0 0 00	
Accounts receivable	1 3 0 0 00				
Supplies	1 0 0 00		**Owner's Equity**		
Prepaid insurance	6 0 0 00		D. Young, capital	18 6 6 5 00	
Tools	3 0 0 0 00				
Truck	8 0 0 0 00				
Total assets	$20 6 6 5 00		Total liab. & owner's equity	$20 6 6 5 00	

SERIES A

EXERCISES

APPLYING ACCOUNTING CONCEPTS

EXERCISE 2A1

Accounting Elements

1 Label each of the following accounts as an asset (A), a liability (L), or owner's equity (OE), using a format as follows.

Item	Account	Classification
Money in bank	Cash	
Office supplies	Supplies	
Money owed	Accounts Payable	
Office chairs	Office Furniture	
Net worth of owner	John Smith, Capital	
Money taken by owner	John Smith, Drawing	
Money owed us by customers	Accounts Receivable	

EXERCISE 2A2

The Accounting Equation

2 Using the accounting equation, compute the missing elements.

Assets	=	Liabilities	+	Owner's Equity
_____	=	$24,000	+	$10,000
$25,000	=	$18,000	+	_____
$40,000	=	_____	+	$15,000

EXERCISE 2A3

Effects of Transactions (Balance Sheet Accounts)

3 Joyce Berg has started a business. During the first month (February, 19--), the following transactions occurred. Show the effect of each transaction on the accounting equation: *Assets = Liabilities + Owner's Equity.* After each transaction, show the new account totals.

(a) Invested cash in the business, $20,000.
(b) Bought office equipment on account, $3,500.
(c) Bought office equipment for cash, $1,200.
(d) Paid cash on account to a supplier, $1,500.

<table>
<tr><td>

EXERCISE 2A4

**Effects of Transactions
(Revenue, Expense,
Withdrawals)**

</td><td>

4 Assume Joyce Berg completed the following additional transactions during February. Show the effect of each transaction on the basic elements of the expanded accounting equation: *Assets = Liabilities + Owner's Equity [Capital − Drawing + Revenue − Expenses]*. After each transaction show the new account totals.

</td></tr>
</table>

(e) Received cash from a client for professional services, $2,500.
(f) Paid cash for office rent for February, $900.
(g) Paid cash for February telephone expense, $73.
(h) Joyce Berg withdrew cash for personal use, $500.
(i) Performed services that will be paid later (on account), $1,000.
(j) Paid wages to part-time employee, $600.

<table>
<tr><td>

EXERCISE 2A5

**Financial Statement
Accounts**

</td><td>

1/5 Label each of the following accounts as an asset (A), liability (L), owner's equity (OE), revenue (R), or expense (E). Indicate the financial statement on which the account belongs: income statement (IS), statement of owner's equity (SOE), or balance sheet (B), in a format similar to the following.

</td></tr>
</table>

Account	Classification	Financial Statement
Cash		
Rent Expense		
Accounts Payable		
Service Fees		
Supplies		
Wages Expense		
John Smith, Drawing		
John Smith, Capital		
Prepaid Insurance		
Accounts Receivable		

PROBLEMS

<table>
<tr><td>

PROBLEM 2A1

The Accounting Equation

</td><td>

1 Dr. John Schleper is a chiropractor. As of December 31, he owned the following property that related to his professional practice:

</td></tr>
</table>

Cash	$ 4,750
Office Equipment	$ 6,200
X-ray Equipment	$11,680
Laboratory Equipment	$ 7,920

He also owes debts to the following business suppliers:

Chateau Gas Company $2,420
Aloe Medical Supply Company $3,740

Required

1. From the preceding information, compute the accounting elements and enter them in the accounting equation as shown below.

Assets   =   Liabilities   +   Owner's Equity

_____ = _____ + _____

2. During January, the assets increase by $7,290, and the liabilities increase by $4,210. Compute the resulting accounting equation.
3. During February, the assets decrease by $2,920, and the liabilities increase by $2,200. Compute the resulting accounting equation.

PROBLEM 2A2

Effect of Transactions on Accounting Equation

2 Albert Hirson has started a business. During the first month (April, 19--), the following transactions occurred.

(a) Invested cash in the business, $18,000.
(b) Bought office equipment on account, $4,600.
(c) Bought office equipment for cash, $1,200.
(d) Performed services and received cash, $3,300.
(e) Paid cash on account to the company that supplied the office equipment in (b) above, $2,300.
(f) Paid cash for office rent for the month, $750.
(g) Withdrew cash for personal use, $100.

Required
Show the effect of each transaction on the basic elements of the accounting equation: *Assets = Liabilities + Owner's Equity [Capital − Drawing + Revenue − Expenses]*. After each transaction, show the new account totals.

PROBLEM 2A3

Income Statement

5 Based on Problem 2A2, prepare an income statement for Albert Hirson for the month of April, 19--.

PROBLEM 2A4

Statement of Owner's Equity

5 Based on Problem 2A2, prepare a statement of owner's equity for Albert Hirson for the month of April, 19--.

PROBLEM 2A5

Balance Sheet

5 Based on Problem 2A2, prepare a balance sheet for Albert Hirson as of April 30, 19--.

SERIES B

EXERCISES

EXERCISE 2B1
Accounting Elements

1 Label each of the following accounts as an asset (A), a liability (L), or owner's equity (OE) using a format as follows.

Account	Classification
Cash	
Accounts Payable	
Supplies	
Bill Jones, Drawing	
Prepaid Insurance	
Accounts Receivable	
Bill Jones, Capital	

EXERCISE 2B2
The Accounting Equation

2 Using the accounting equation, compute the missing elements.

Assets	=	Liabilities	+	Owner's Equity
_____	=	$20,000	+	$ 5,000
$30,000	=	$15,000	+	_____
$20,000	=	_____	+	$10,000

EXERCISE 2B3
Effects of Transactions (Balance Sheet Accounts)

3 Don Coursey has started a business. During the first month (March, 19--), the following transactions occurred. Show the effect of each transaction on the accounting equation: *Assets = Liabilities + Owner's Equity.* After each transaction, show the new account totals.

(a) Invested cash in the business, $30,000.
(b) Bought office equipment on account, $4,500.
(c) Bought office equipment for cash, $1,600.
(d) Paid cash on account to a supplier, $2,000.

EXERCISE 2B4
Effects of Transactions (Revenue, Expense, Withdrawals)

4 Assume Don Coursey completed the following additional transactions during March. Show the effect of each transaction on the basic elements of the expanded accounting equation: *Assets = Liabilities + Owner's Equity [Capital − Drawing + Revenue − Expenses].* After each transaction show the new account totals.

(e) Performed services and received cash, $3,000.
(f) Paid cash for rent for March, $1,000.
(g) Paid for March telephone expense, $68.
(h) Don Coursey withdraws cash for personal use, $800.
(i) Performed services that will be paid later (on account), $900.
(j) Paid wages to part-time employee, $500.

EXERCISE 2B5

Financial Statement Accounts

1 Label each of the following accounts as an asset (A), liability (L), owner's equity (OE), revenue (R), or expense (E). Indicate the financial statement on which the account belongs: income statement (IS), statement of owner's equity (SOE), or balance sheet (B), in a format similar to the following.

Account	Classification	Financial Statement
Cash		
Rent Expense		
Accounts Payable		
Service Fees		
Supplies		
Wages Expense		
Bill Jones, Drawing		
Bill Jones, Capital		
Prepaid Insurance		
Accounts Receivable		

PROBLEMS

PROBLEM 2B1

The Accounting Equation

1 Dr. Patricia Parsons is a dentist. As of January 31, Parsons owned the following property that related to her professional practice:

Cash	$3,560
Office Equipment	$4,600
X-ray Equipment	$8,760
Laboratory Equipment	$5,940

She also owes debts to the following business suppliers:

Cupples Gas Company	$1,815
Swan Dental Lab	$2,790

Required

1. From the preceding information, compute the accounting elements and enter them in the accounting equation as shown below.

Assets	=	Liabilities	+	Owner's Equity
_____	=	_____	+	_____

2. During February, the assets increase by $4,565, and the liabilities increase by $3,910. Compute the resulting accounting equation.
3. During March, the assets decrease by $2,190, and the liabilities increase by $1,650. Compute the resulting accounting equation.

42   PART ONE   Accounting Cycle for a Service Business

PROBLEM 2B2

Effect of Transactions on Accounting Equation

2 Lee Bernstein has started a business. During the first month (October, 19--), the following transactions occurred.

(a) Invested cash in the business, $15,000.
(b) Bought office equipment on account, $3,800.
(c) Bought office equipment for cash, $1,000.
(d) Performed services and received cash, $2,700.
(e) Paid cash on account to the company that supplied the office equipment in (b) above, $1,800.
(f) Paid office rent for the month, $650.
(g) Withdrew cash for personal use, $150.

Required
Show the effect of each transaction on the basic elements of the accounting equation: *Assets = Liabilities + Owner's Equity [Capital − Drawing + Revenue − Expenses]*. After each transaction, show the new account totals.

PROBLEM 2B3

Income Statement

5 Based on Problem 2B2, prepare an income statement for Lee Bernstein for the month of October, 19--.

PROBLEM 2B4

Statement of Owner's Equity

5 Based on Problem 2B2, prepare a statement of owner's equity for Lee Bernstein for the month of October, 19--.

PROBLEM 2B5

Balance Sheet

5 Based on Problem 2B2, prepare a balance sheet for Lee Bernstein as of October 31, 19--.

MASTERY PROBLEM

Lisa Vozniak has started her own business, We Do Windows. She offers interior and exterior window cleaning for local area residents. Lisa rents a garage to store her tools and cleaning supplies and has a part-time assistant to answer the phone and handle third-story work. (Lisa is afraid of heights.) The transactions for the month of July are as follows:

(a) Vozniak invested cash by making a deposit in a bank account for the business, $8,000.
(b) Paid rent for July, $150.
(c) Bought a used van for cash, $5,000.
(d) Bought tools on account from Clean Tools, $600.
(e) Bought cleaning supplies for cash, $200.
(f) Paid temporary assistant (wages) for first half of month, $100.
(g) Paid for advertising, $75.

(h) Paid two-year premium for liability insurance on truck, $480.

(i) Received cash from clients for service performed, $800.

(j) Performed cleaning services for clients on account, $500.

(k) Paid telephone bill, $40.

(l) Received cash from clients for window cleaning performed on account in (j), $200.

(m) Paid temporary assistant (wages) for last half of month, $150.

(n) Made partial payment on tools bought in (d), $200.

(o) Additional revenues earned amounted to $800: $600 for cash and $200 on account.

(p) Vozniak withdrew cash at the end of the month for personal expenses, $100.

Required

1. Enter the above transactions in an accounting equation similar to the following.

ASSETS						=	LIABILITIES	+		OWNER'S EQUITY				
Items Owned							Amounts Owed		Owner's Investment +			Earnings		
	Accts.	Sup-	Prepaid				Accts.		Vozniak,	Vozniak,				
Cash +	Rec. +	plies +	Ins.	+ Tools +	Van =		Pay.	+	Capital	− Drawing	+ Revenue	− Expense		Description

2. Compute the ending balances for all accounts.

3. Prepare an income statement for We Do Windows for the month of July.

4. Prepare a statement of owner's equity for We Do Windows for the month of July.

5. Prepare a balance sheet for We Do Windows as of July 31, 19--.

Careful study of this chapter should enable you to:

1. Define the parts of a T account.
2. Foot and balance a T account.
3. Describe the effects of debits and credits on specific types of accounts.
4. Use T accounts to analyze transactions.
5. Prepare a trial balance.

*T*he Double-Entry Framework

The terms asset, liability, owner's equity, revenue, and expense were explained in Chapter 2. Examples showed how individual business transactions change one or more of these basic accounting elements. Each transaction had a dual effect. An increase or decrease in any asset, liability, owner's equity, revenue, or expense was *always* accompanied by an offsetting change within the basic accounting elements. The fact that each transaction has a dual effect upon the accounting elements is the basis for **double-entry accounting.**

This chapter introduces double-entry accounting. To understand double-entry accounting, you should understand how T accounts work and the role of debits and credits in accounting.

1

Define the parts of a T account.

THE T ACCOUNT

The assets of a business may consist of many items, such as cash, accounts receivable, merchandise, equipment, buildings, and land. The liabilities may consist of one or more items, such as accounts payable and notes payable. Similarly, owner's equity may consist of the owner's investments and various revenue and expense items. A separate **account** is used to record the increases and decreases in each type of asset, liability, owner's equity, revenue, and expense.

The T account gets its name from the fact that it resembles the letter T. The T account has three major parts:

1. **the title**
2. **the debit or left side**
3. **the credit or right side**

Title	
Debit = Left	Credit = Right

The debit side is always on the left and the credit side is always on the right. This is true for all types of asset, liability, owner's equity, revenue, and expense accounts.

2 · BALANCING A T ACCOUNT

Foot and balance a T account.

To determine the balance of a T account at any time, simply total the dollar amounts on the debit and credit sides. These totals are known as **footings.** The difference between the footings is called the **balance** of the account. This amount is then written on the side with the larger footing.

In Chapter 2, the accounting equation was used to analyze business transactions. This required columns to record the increases and decreases in various accounts. Let's compare this approach with the use of a T account for the transactions affecting cash. When a T account is used, increases in cash are recorded on the debit side and decreases are recorded on the credit side. Transactions for Jessie Jane's Campus Delivery are shown below.

Tran.	Cash
(a)	$ 2,000
(b)	(1,200)
(d)	(300)
(e)	500
(f)	(200)
(g)	(50)
(i)	(80)
(j)	(200)
(k)	570
(l)	(300)
(m)	(650)
(n)	430
(o)	(150)
Balance	$ 370

Cash

Debit		Credit	
(a)	2,000	(b)	1,200
(e)	500	(d)	300
(k)	570	(f)	200
(n)	430	(g)	50
footing	3,500	(i)	80
		(j)	200
		(l)	300
		(m)	650
		(o)	150
		3,130 footing	
Balance	370		

3 DEBITS AND CREDITS

Describe the effects of debits and credits on specific types of accounts.

To **debit** an account means to enter an amount on the left or debit side of the account. To **credit** an account means to enter an amount on the right or credit side of the account. *Debits may increase or decrease the balances of specific accounts. This is also true for credits. To learn to use debits and* *credits, it is best to reflect on the accounting equation. (Debit is abbreviated as Dr., and credit is abbreviated as Cr.).*

Assets	=	Liabilities	+	Owner's Equity
Dr.	Cr.	Dr.	Cr.	Dr.	Cr.
+	−	−	+	−	+

**Debits increase assets.
Debits decrease liabilities and owner's equity.
Credits increase liabilities and owner's equity.
Credits decrease assets.**

Assets

Assets are on the *left* side of the accounting equation. Therefore, *increases* are entered on the *left* (debit) side of an asset account and decreases are entered on the right (credit) side.

Liabilities and Owner's Equity

Liabilities and owner's equity are on the *right* side of the equation. Therefore, *increases* are entered on the *right* (credit) side and decreases are entered on the left (debit) side.

Normal Balances

A **normal balance** is the side of an account that is increased. Since assets are debited for increases, these accounts normally have **debit balances.** Since liability and owner's equity accounts are credited for increases, these accounts normally have **credit balances.** Figure 3-1 shows the relationship between normal balances and debits and credits.

F I G U R E 3 - 1 **Normal Balances**

ACCOUNT	ACCOUNTING EQUATION	INCREASE	DECREASE	NORMAL BALANCE
Assets	Left	Debit	Credit	Debit
Liabilities	Right	Credit	Debit	Credit
Owner's Equity	Right	Credit	Debit	Credit

Expanding the accounting equation illustrates using debits and credits for revenue, expense, and drawing. Since these accounts affect owner's equity, they are shown under the "umbrella" of owner's equity in the accounting equation in figure 3-2.

FIGURE 3-2 **The Accounting Equation and the Owner's Equity Umbrella**

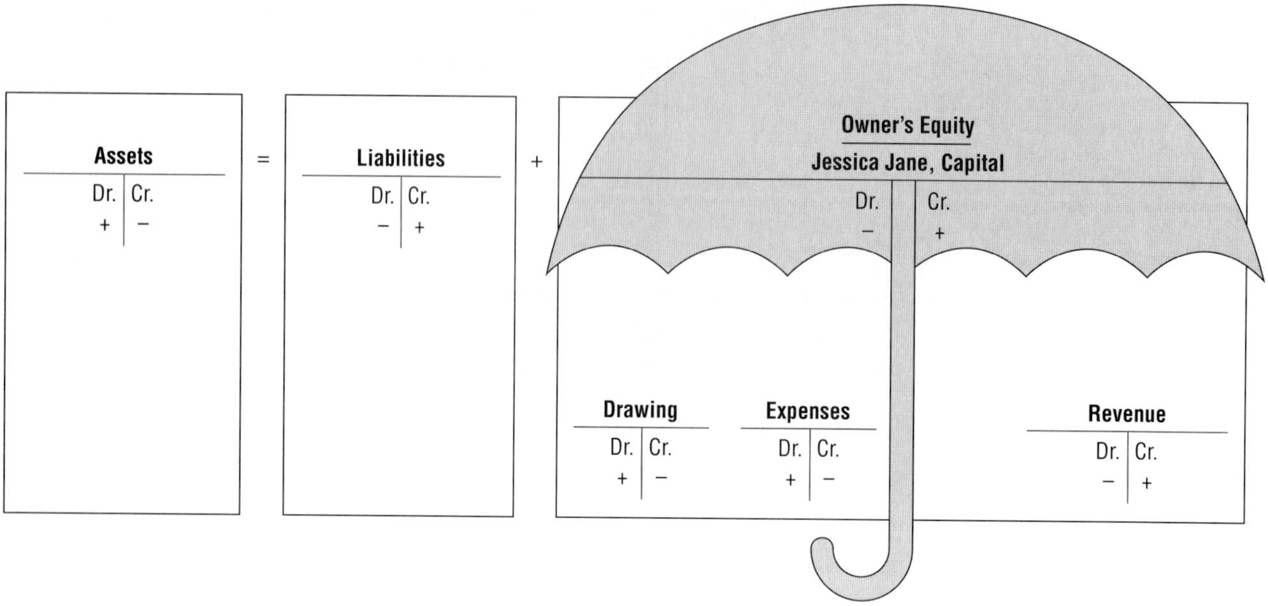

Revenues

Revenues increase owner's equity. Revenues could be recorded directly on the credit side of the owner's capital account. However, readers of financial statements are interested in the specific types of revenues earned. Therefore, specific revenue accounts like delivery fees, sales, and service fees are used. These specific accounts are credited when revenue is earned.

Expenses

Expenses decrease owner's equity. Expenses could be recorded on the debit side of the owner's capital account. However, readers of financial statements want to see the types of expenses incurred during the accounting period. Thus, specific expense accounts are maintained for items like rent, wages, advertising, and utilities. These specific accounts are debited as expenses are incurred.

You could credit the owner's capital account for revenues and debit the capital account for expenses and withdrawals. However, using specific accounts provides additional information. Remember that an increase in an expense decreases owner's equity.

Drawing

Withdrawals of cash and other assets by the owner for personal reasons decrease owner's equity. Withdrawals could be debited directly to the owner's capital account. However, readers of financial statements want to know the amount of withdrawals for the accounting period. Thus, it is easier to maintain this information in a separate account.

Normal Balances for the Owner's Equity Umbrella

Since expense and drawing accounts are debited for increases, these accounts normally have **debit balances.** Since revenue accounts are credited for increases, these accounts normally have **credit balances.** Figure 3-3 shows the normal balances for the owner's equity accounts.

FIGURE 3-3 Normal Balances for the Owner's Equity Umbrella

ACCOUNT	OWNER'S EQUITY UMBRELLA	INCREASE	DECREASE	NORMAL
Revenues	Right	Credit	Debit	Credit
Expenses	Left	Debit	Credit	Debit
Drawing	Left	Debit	Credit	Debit

 4

Use T accounts to analyze transactions.

TRANSACTION ANALYSIS

In Chapter 2, you learned how to analyze transactions by using the accounting equation. Here, we continue to use the accounting equation, but add the concept of debits and credits by using T accounts. As shown in figure 3-4, the three basic questions that must be answered when ana-

FIGURE 3-4 The Three Basic Questions Expanded

1. **What happened?**
   Make certain you understand what has happened.
2. **Which accounts are affected?**
   - Identify the accounts that are affected.
   - Classify these accounts as assets, liabilities, owner's equity, revenue, or expense.
   - *Identify the location of the accounts in the accounting equation and/or the owner's equity umbrella—left or right.*
3. **How is the accounting equation affected?**
   - Determine whether the accounts have increased or decreased.
   - *Determine whether the accounts should be debited or credited.*
   - Make certain that the accounting equation remains in balance after the transaction has been entered.
     (1) Assets = Liabilities + Owner's Equity.
     (2) Debits = Credits for every transaction.

lyzing a transaction are essentially the same but expanded for the use of T accounts. You must identify the location of the account element within the accounting equation. You must also determine whether the accounts should be debited or credited.

Debits and Credits: Asset, Liability, and Owner's Equity Accounts

Transactions (a) through (d) from Jessie Jane's Campus Delivery Service (Chapter 2) demonstrate the double-entry process for transactions affecting assets, liability, and owner's equity accounts.

As you study each transaction, answer the three questions: (1) What happened? (2) Which accounts are affected, and (3) How is the accounting equation affected? The transaction statement tells you what happened. The analysis following the illustration of each transaction tells you which accounts are affected. The illustration shows you how the accounting equation is affected.

Transaction (a): Investment by owner
Jessica Jane deposited $2,000 in a bank account for her business (figure 3-5).

FIGURE 3-5 **Transaction (a): Investment by Owner**

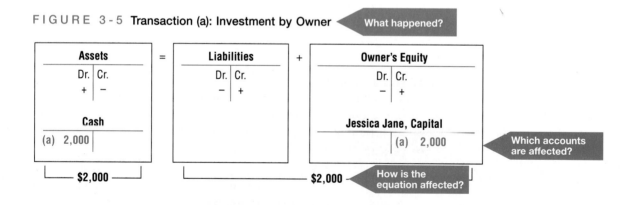

Analysis: The business acquired an asset, Cash, and gives Jessica Jane owner's equity. Remember from Chapter 2 that another name for owner's equity is capital. The owner's capital account is called Jessica Jane, Capital. The asset, Cash, is increased and Jessica Jane, Capital is increased. Debit Cash for $2,000 and credit Jessica Jane, Capital for $2,000, as shown in the table at the top of page 51.

ACCOUNT AFFECTED	CLASSIFICATION	LOCATION	INCREASE OR DECREASE	DEBIT OR CREDIT
Cash	Asset	Left	Increase	Debit
Capital	Owner's Equity	Right	Increase	Credit

Transaction (b): Purchase of an asset for cash

Jane bought a motor scooter (delivery equipment) for $1,200 cash (figure 3-6).

FIGURE 3-6 Transaction (b): Purchase of an Asset for Cash

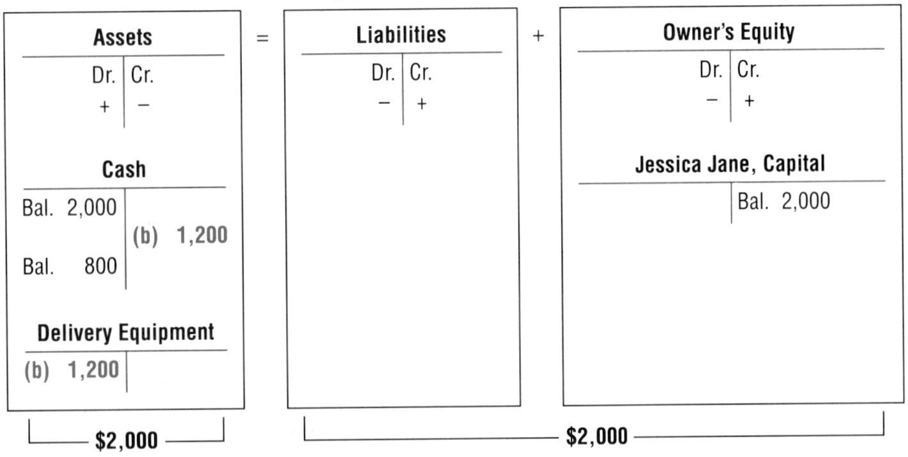

Analysis: Jane exchanged one asset, Cash, for another, Delivery Equipment. Delivery Equipment is increased and Cash is decreased. Debit Delivery Equipment and credit Cash for $1,200.

Notice that the total assets are still $2,000 as they were following transaction (a). Transaction (b) caused changes to two asset accounts, but the total assets remain the same.

ACCOUNT AFFECTED	CLASSIFICATION	LOCATION	INCREASE OR DECREASE	DEBIT OR CREDIT
Delivery Equip.	Asset	Left	Increase	Debit
Cash	Asset	Left	Decrease	Credit

Transaction (c): Purchase of an asset on account

Jane bought a second motor scooter on account for $900 (figure 3-7).

FIGURE 3-7 **Transaction (c): Purchase of an Asset on Account**

Assets		=	Liabilities		+	Owner's Equity	
Dr.	Cr.		Dr.	Cr.		Dr.	Cr.
+	–		–	+		–	+
Cash			**Accounts Payable**			**Jessica Jane, Capital**	
Bal. 800				(c) 900			Bal. 2,000
Delivery Equipment							
Bal. 1,200							
(c) 900							
Bal. 2,100							

└─── **$2,900** ───┘   └─────────── **$2,900** ───────────┘

Analysis: The asset, Delivery Equipment, increases by $900 and the liability, Accounts Payable, increases by the same amount. Debit Delivery Equipment and credit Accounts Payable for $900.

ACCOUNT AFFECTED	CLASSIFICATION	LOCATION	INCREASE OR DECREASE	DEBIT OR CREDIT
Delivery Equip.	Asset	Left	Increase	Debit
Accounts Payable	Liability	Right	Increase	Credit

Transaction (d): Payment on a loan

Jane made the first $300 payment on the scooter purchased in transaction (c) (figure 3-8).

FIGURE 3-8 **Transaction (d): Payment on a Loan**

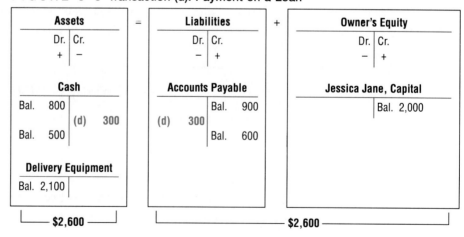

Assets		=	Liabilities		+	Owner's Equity	
Dr.	Cr.		Dr.	Cr.		Dr.	Cr.
+	–		–	+		–	+
Cash			**Accounts Payable**			**Jessica Jane, Capital**	
Bal. 800				Bal. 900			Bal. 2,000
	(d) 300		(d) 300				
Bal. 500				Bal. 600			
Delivery Equipment							
Bal. 2,100							

└─── **$2,600** ───┘   └─────────── **$2,600** ───────────┘

Analysis: This payment decreased the asset, Cash, and decreased the liability, Accounts Payable. Debit Accounts Payable and credit Cash for $300.

ACCOUNT AFFECTED	CLASSIFICATION	LOCATION	INCREASE OR DECREASE	DEBIT OR CREDIT
Accounts Payable	Liability	Right	Decrease	Debit
Cash	Asset	Left	Decrease	Credit

Notice that for each of the previous transactions (a) through (d), the debits equal credits and the accounting equation is in balance. Review transactions (a) through (d) and again identify the accounts that were affected, how they are classified (assets, liabilities, or owner's equity), and each account's location within the accounting equation.

Debits and Credits: Including Revenue, Expense, and Drawing

Revenues increase owner's equity and are on the credit side of the capital account. Expenses and drawing reduce owner's equity and are on the debit side of the capital account.

Transactions (a) through (d) involved only assets, liabilities, and the owner's capital account. The equation must be expanded to include revenues, expenses, and drawing. Remember, revenues increase owner's equity and are shown under the credit side of the capital account. Expenses and drawing decrease owner's equity and are shown under the debit side of the capital account. The expanded equation is shown in figure 3-9.

FIGURE 3-9 **The Expanded Accounting Equation**

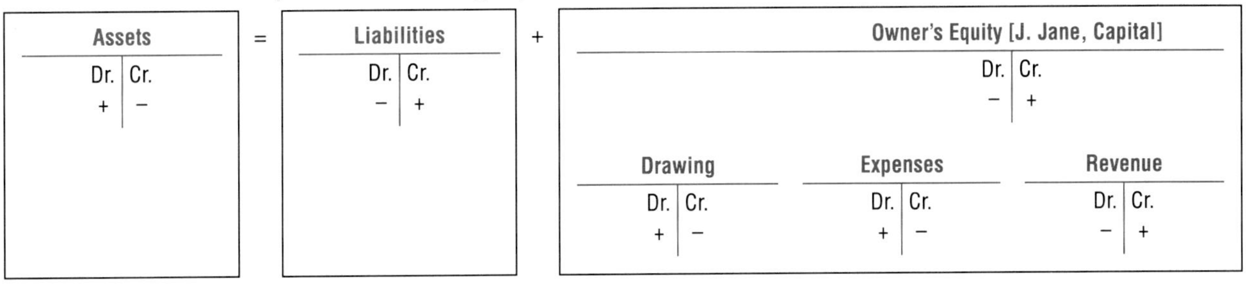

Transaction (e): Revenue earned in cash
Jane performed services and received $500 cash (figure 3-10).

FIGURE 3-10 Transaction (e): Revenue Earned in Cash

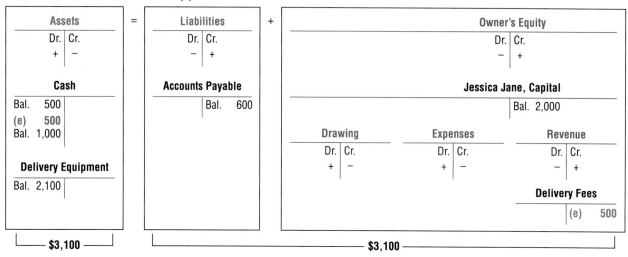

Analysis: The asset, Cash, and the revenue, Delivery Fees, increase. Debit Cash and credit Delivery Fees for $500.

ACCOUNT AFFECTED	CLASSIFICATION	LOCATION	INCREASE OR DECREASE	DEBIT OR CREDIT
Cash	Asset	Left	Increase	Debit
Delivery Fees	Revenue	Right	Increase	Credit

Transaction (f): Paid rent for month
Jane paid $200 for office rent for June (figure 3-11).

FIGURE 3-11 Transaction (f): Paid Rent for Month

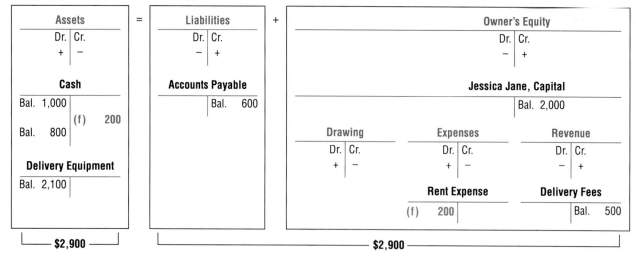

Analysis: Rent Expense increases and Cash decreases. Debit Rent Expense and credit Cash for $200.

A debit to an expense account increases that expense account and decreases owner's equity. Notice that the placement of the plus and minus signs for expenses are opposite the placement of the plus and minus signs for owner's equity. Notice that expenses are located on the left (debit) side of the owner's equity umbrella.

ACCOUNT AFFECTED	CLASSIFICATION	LOCATION	INCREASE OR DECREASE	DEBIT OR CREDIT
Rent Expense	Expense	Owner's Equity— Left Side	Expense Increases; Owner's Equity Decreases	Debit
Cash	Asset	Left	Decrease	Credit

Transaction (g): Paid telephone bill

Jane paid a bill for telephone service, $50 (figure 3-12).

FIGURE 3-12 Transaction (g): Paid Telephone Bill

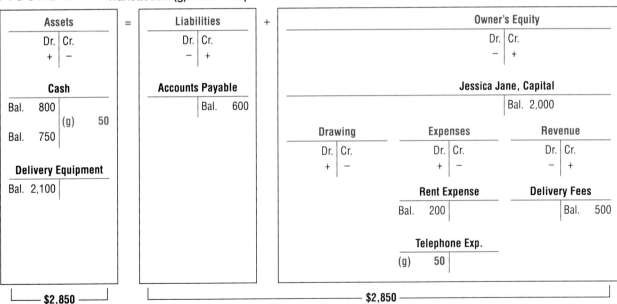

Analysis: This transaction, like the previous one, increases an expense and decreases an asset. Debit Telephone Expense and credit Cash for $50, as shown in the table at the top of page 56.

ACCOUNT AFFECTED	CLASSIFICATION	LOCATION	INCREASE OR DECREASE	DEBIT OR CREDIT
Telephone Expense	Expense	Owner's Equity— Left Side	Expense Increases; Owner's Equity Decreases	Debit
Cash	Asset	Left	Decrease	Credit

Transaction (h): Delivery revenues earned on account
Jane made deliveries on account for $600 (figure 3-13).

FIGURE 3-13 **Transaction (h): Delivery Revenues Earned on Account**

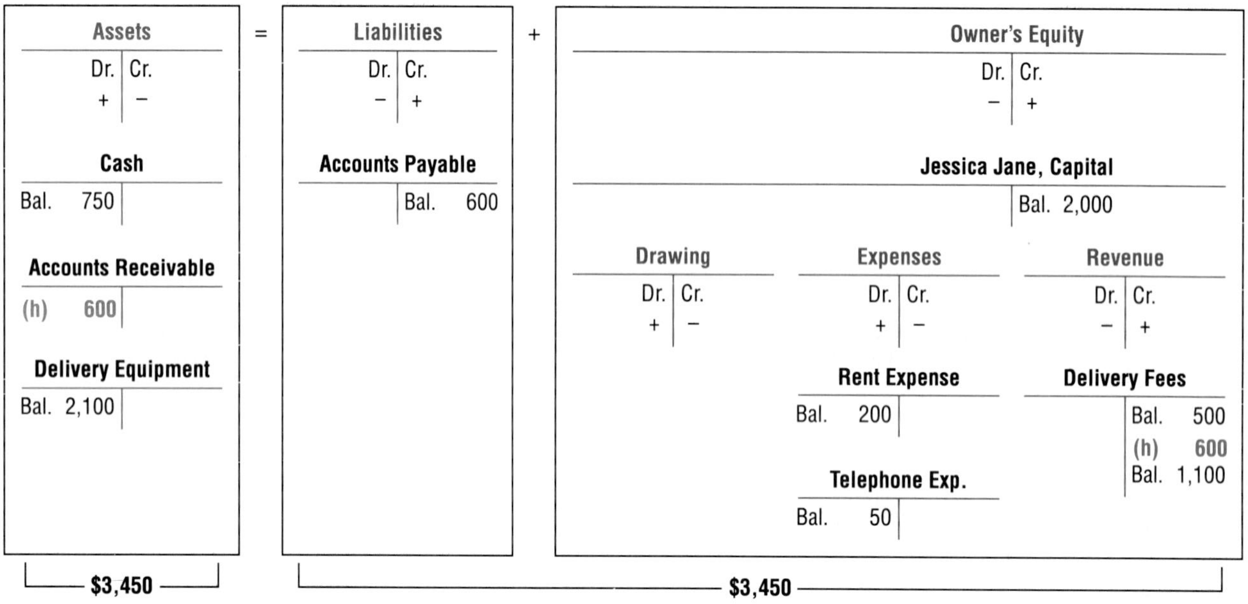

Analysis: As discussed in Chapter 2, delivery services are performed for which payment will be received later. This is called offering services "on account," or "on credit." Instead of receiving cash, Jane receives a promise that her customers will pay cash in the future. Therefore, the asset, Accounts Receivable, increases. The revenue account, Delivery Fees, also increases. Debit Accounts Receivable and credit Delivery Fees for $600.

ACCOUNT AFFECTED	CLASSIFICATION	LOCATION	INCREASE OR DECREASE	DEBIT OR CREDIT
Accounts Receivable	Asset	Left	Increase	Debit
Delivery Fees	Revenue	Right	Increase	Credit

Review transactions (e) through (h). Two of these transactions are expenses and two are revenue transactions. Each of these transactions affected the owner's equity umbrella. Three transactions affected Cash, and one transaction affected Accounts Receivable. It is important to remember that expense and revenue transactions do not always affect cash.

Notice that the debits equal credits and the accounting equation is in balance after each transaction. As you review transactions (e) through (h), identify the accounts that were affected, classify each account (assets, liabilities, owner's equity, revenue, or expense), and notice each account's location within the accounting equation and the owner's equity umbrella.

Transaction (i): Purchase of supplies

Jane bought pens, paper, delivery envelopes, and other supplies for $80 cash (figure 3-14).

F I G U R E   3 - 1 4   **Transaction (i): Purchase of Supplies**

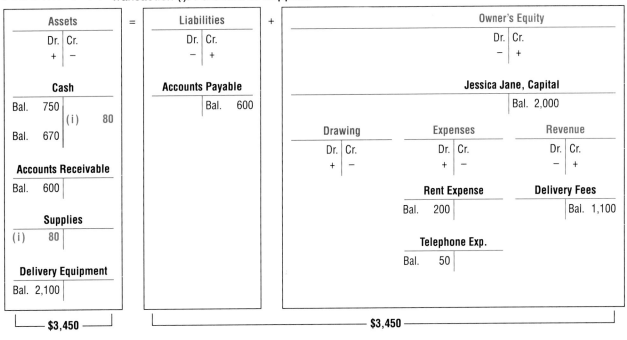

Analysis: These supplies will last for several months. Therefore, they should be recorded as an asset. An asset, Supplies, has increased, and an asset, Cash, has decreased. Debit Supplies and credit Cash for $80.

ACCOUNT AFFECTED	CLASSIFICATION	LOCATION	INCREASE OR DECREASE	DEBIT OR CREDIT
Supplies	Asset	Left	Increase	Debit
Cash	Asset	Left	Decrease	Credit

Transaction (j): Payment of insurance premium

Jane paid $200 for an eight-month liability insurance policy (figure 3-15).

F I G U R E 3 - 1 5 Transaction (j): Payment of Insurance Premium

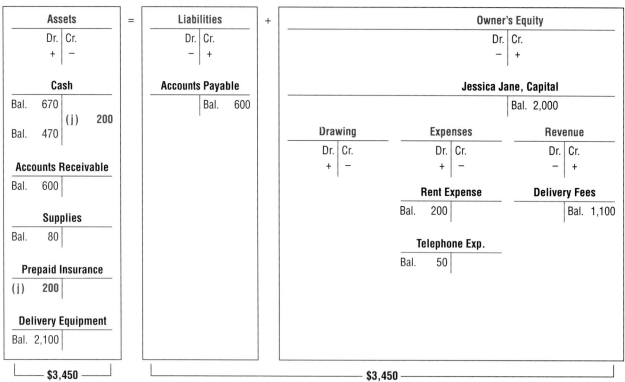

Analysis: Since insurance is paid in advance and will provide future benefits, it is treated as an asset. Therefore, one asset, Prepaid Insurance, increases, and another, Cash, decreases. Debit Prepaid Insurance and credit Cash for $200.

ACCOUNT AFFECTED	CLASSIFICATION	LOCATION	INCREASE OR DECREASE	DEBIT OR CREDIT
Prepaid Insurance	Asset	Left	Increase	Debit
Cash	Asset	Left	Decrease	Credit

Transactions (i) and (j) both involve an exchange of cash for another asset. As you analyze these two transactions and answer the three questions about these transactions, you may wonder why prepaid insurance and supplies are assets while the rent and telephone bill are expenses. Prepaid insurance and supplies are assets because they will last for more than one month. Jessica Jane pays her rent and her telephone bill each month so they are classified as expenses. If Jessica Jane paid her rent only once every three months, she would need to set up an asset account called Prepaid Rent, which she would debit when she paid the rent.

Transaction (k): Receipt of cash from prior sales on account
Jane received $570 in cash for delivery services performed for customers earlier in transaction (h) (figure 3-16).

FIGURE 3-16 Transaction (k): Receipt of Cash from Prior Sales on Account

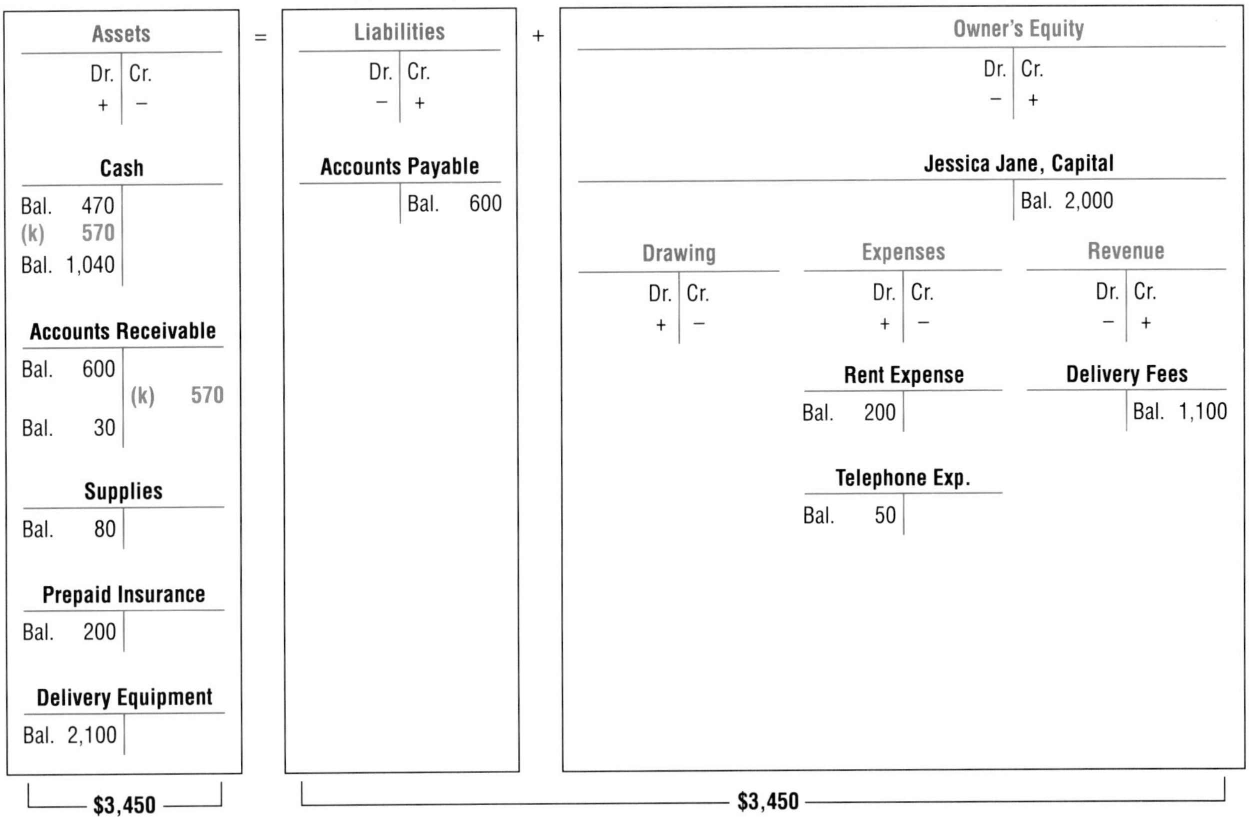

Analysis: This transaction increases Cash and reduces the amount due from customers reported in Accounts Receivable. Debit Cash and credit Accounts Receivable for $570.

As you analyze transaction (k), notice which accounts are affected and the location of these accounts in the accounting equation. Jessica Jane received cash, but this transaction did not affect revenue. The revenue was recorded in transaction (h). Transaction (k) is an exchange of one asset (Accounts Receivable) for another asset (Cash).

ACCOUNT AFFECTED	CLASSIFICATION	LOCATION	INCREASE OR DECREASE	DEBIT OR CREDIT
Cash	Asset	Left	Increase	Debit
Accounts Receivable	Asset	Left	Decrease	Credit

Transaction (I): Purchase of an asset on credit making a partial payment
Jane purchased a third motor scooter for $1,500. Jane made a down payment of $300 and spread the remaining payments over the next four months (figure 3-17).

FIGURE 3-17   Transaction (I): Purchase of an Asset on Credit Making a Partial Payment

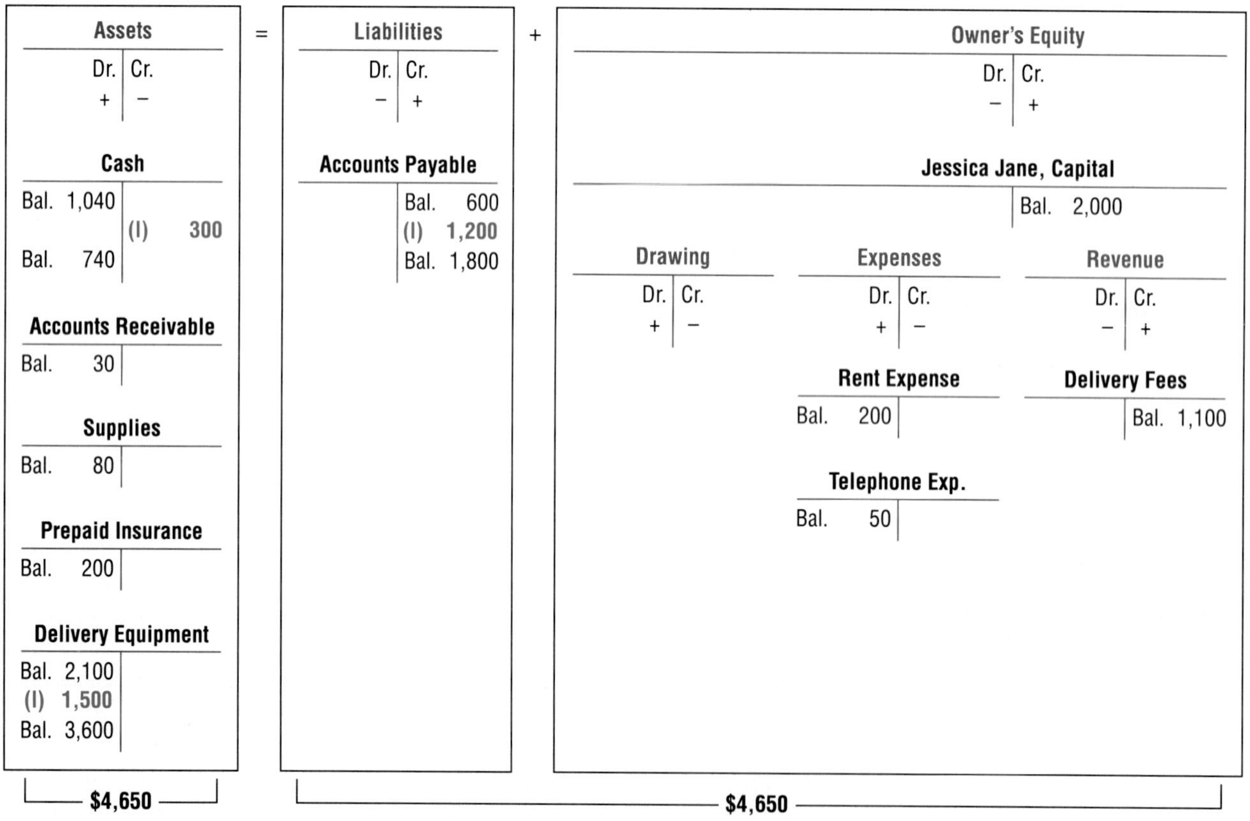

Analysis: The asset, Delivery Equipment, increases by $1,500, Cash decreases by $300 and the liability, Accounts Payable, increases by $1,200. This transaction requires one debit and two credits, but total debits ($1,500) equal total credits ($1,200 + $300), and the accounting equation remains in balance. Debit Delivery Equipment for $1,500, credit Cash for $300, and credit Accounts Payable for $1,200.

ACCOUNT AFFECTED	CLASSIFICATION	LOCATION	INCREASE OR DECREASE	DEBIT OR CREDIT
Delivery Equipment	Asset	Left	Increase	Debit
Cash	Asset	Left	Decrease	Credit
Accounts Payable	Liability	Right	Increase	Credit

Transaction (m): Payment of wages

Jane paid her part-time employees $650 in wages (figure 3-18).

FIGURE 3-18 Transaction (m): Payment of Wages

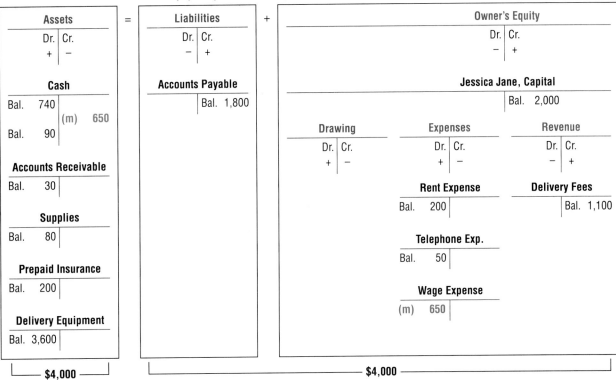

Analysis: This is an additional business expense. Expenses increase and Cash decreases. Debit Wage Expense and credit Cash for $650.

ACCOUNT AFFECTED	CLASSIFICATION	LOCATION	INCREASE OR DECREASE	DEBIT OR CREDIT
Wage Expense	Expense	Owner's Equity— Left Side	Expense Increases; Owner's Equity Decreases	Debit
Cash	Asset	Left	Decrease	Credit

Transaction (n): Deliveries made for cash and credit

Total delivery fees for the remainder of the month amounted to $900: $430 for cash and $470 on account (figure 3-19).

FIGURE 3-19 **Transaction (n): Deliveries Made for Cash and Credit**

Assets	=	Liabilities	+	Owner's Equity
Dr. + / Cr. −		Dr. − / Cr. +		Dr. − / Cr. +

Assets

Cash
Dr. (+)	Cr. (−)
Bal. 90	
(n) 430	
Bal. 520	

Accounts Receivable
Dr. (+)	Cr. (−)
Bal. 30	
(n) 470	
Bal. 500	

Supplies
| Bal. 80 | |

Prepaid Insurance
| Bal. 200 | |

Delivery Equipment
| Bal. 3,600 | |

Liabilities

Accounts Payable
Dr. (−)	Cr. (+)
	Bal. 1,800

Owner's Equity

Jessica Jane, Capital
Dr. (−)	Cr. (+)
	Bal. 2,000

Drawing
Dr. (+)	Cr. (−)

Expenses

Rent Expense
| Bal. 200 | |

Telephone Exp.
| Bal. 50 | |

Wage Expense
| Bal. 650 | |

Revenue

Delivery Fees
Dr. (−)	Cr. (+)
	Bal. 1,100
	(n) 900
	Bal. 2,000

$4,900 (Assets) $4,900 (Liabilities + Owner's Equity)

Analysis: Since the delivery fees have been earned, the revenue account increases by $900. Also, Cash increases by $430 and Accounts Receivable increases by $470. Again, one transaction impacts three accounts. Total debits ($430 + $470) equal the total credits ($900) and the equation remains in balance. Debit Cash for $430 and Accounts Receivable for $470, and credit Delivery Fees for $900.

ACCOUNT AFFECTED	CLASSIFICATION	LOCATION	INCREASE OR DECREASE	DEBIT OR CREDIT
Cash	Asset	Left	Increase	Debit
Accounts Receivable	Asset	Left	Increase	Debit
Delivery Fees	Revenue	Right	Increase	Credit

Transaction (o): Withdrawal of cash from business

At the end of the month, Jane removed $150 in cash from the business to purchase books for her classes (figure 3-20).

FIGURE 3-20 Transaction (o): Withdrawal of Cash from Business

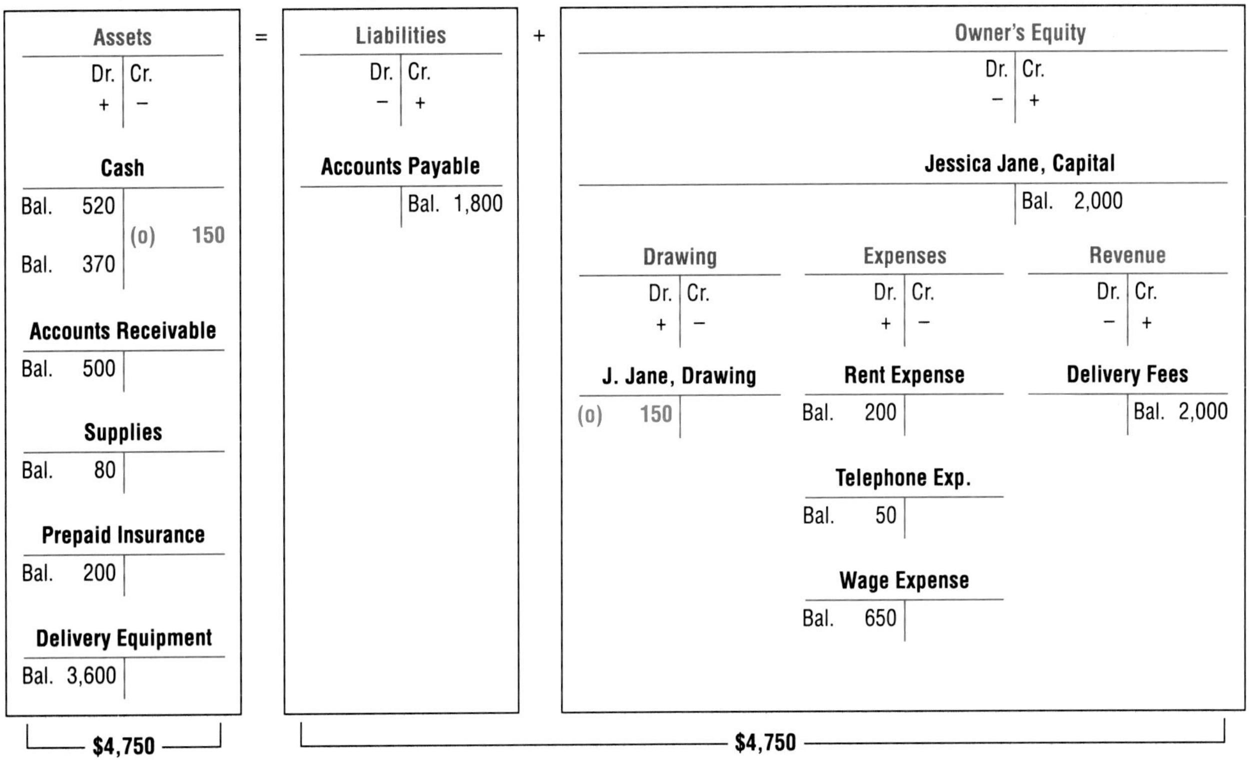

Analysis: Cash withdrawals decrease owner's equity and decrease the asset, Cash. Debit Jessica Jane, Drawing and credit Cash for $150.

Withdrawals are reported in the drawing account. Withdrawals by an owner are the opposite of an investment. You could debit the owner's capital account for withdrawals; however, using a specific account tells the user of the accounting information how much was withdrawn for the period.

ACCOUNT AFFECTED	CLASSIFICATION	LOCATION	INCREASE OR DECREASE	DEBIT OR CREDIT
Drawing	Drawing	Owner's Equity— Left Side	Drawing Increases; Owner's Equity Decreases	Debit
Cash	Asset	Left	Decrease	Credit

As you analyze transactions (l) through (o), make certain that you understand what has happened in each transaction. Identify the accounts that are affected and the locations of these accounts within the accounting equation. Notice that the accounting equation remains in balance after every transaction and debits equal credits for each transaction.

Summary of Transactions

In illustrating transactions (a) through (o), each T account for Jessie Jane's Campus Delivery Service shows a balance before and after each transaction. To focus your attention on the transaction being explained, only a single entry was shown. In practice, this is not done. Instead, each account accumulates all transactions for a period. The accounts of Jessica Jane with all transactions listed are shown in figure 3-21. Note the following:

FIGURE 3-21 Summary of Transactions (a) through (o)

1. The footings are directly under the debit (left) and credit (right) sides of the T account for those accounts with more than one debit or credit.
2. The balance is shown on the side with the larger footing.
3. The footing serves as the balance for accounts with entries on only one side of the account.
4. If an account has only a single entry, it is not necessary to enter the balance.

THE TRIAL BALANCE

5

Prepare a trial balance.

Recall the two very important rules in double-entry accounting.

1. The sum of the debits must equal the sum of the credits. This means that at least two accounts are affected by each transaction.
2. The accounting equation must remain in balance.

A trial balance provides proof that total debits equal total credits and shows that the accounting equation is in balance.

In illustrating the transactions for Jessie Jane's Campus Delivery Service, the equality of the accounting equation was verified after each transaction. Because of the large number of transactions entered each day, this is not done in practice. Instead, a trial balance is prepared periodically to determine the equality of the debits and credits. A **trial balance** is a list of all accounts showing the title and balance of each account.

A trial balance of Jessica Jane's accounts, taken on June 30, 19--, is shown in figure 3-22. The date is shown on the third line of the heading.

FIGURE 3-22 Trial Balance

Jessie Jane's Campus Delivery Service Trial Balance June 30, 19--			
ACCOUNT TITLE	ACCOUNT NO.	DEBIT BALANCE	CREDIT BALANCE
Cash		3 7 0 00	
Accounts Receivable		5 0 0 00	
Supplies		8 0 00	
Prepaid Insurance		2 0 0 00	
Delivery Equipment		3 6 0 0 00	
Accounts Payable			1 8 0 0 00
Jessica Jane, Capital			2 0 0 0 00
Jessica Jane, Drawing		1 5 0 00	
Delivery Fees			2 0 0 0 00
Rent Expense		2 0 0 00	
Telephone Expense		5 0 00	
Wage Expense		6 5 0 00	
		5 8 0 0 00	5 8 0 0 00

This trial balance provides proof that (1) in entering transactions (a) through (o) the total of the debits was equal to the total of the credits, and (2) the accounting equation has remained in balance.

A trial balance is not a formal statement or report. Normally, it is only seen by the accountant. As shown in the summary illustration on page 67, a trial balance can be used in preparing the financial statements.

KEY POINTS

1 The parts of a T account are:

	Title
Debit = Left	Credit = Right

1. **the title**
2. **the debit or left side**
3. **the credit or right side**

2 Rules for footing and balancing T accounts are:

1. The footings are directly under the debit (left) and credit (right) sides of the T account for those accounts with more than one debit or credit.
2. The balance is shown on the side with the larger footing.
3. The footing serves as the balance for accounts with entries on only one side of the account.
4. If an account has only a single entry, it is not necessary to enter the balance.

3

1. Assets are on the left side of the accounting equation. Therefore, increases are entered on the left (debit) side of an asset account and decreases are entered on the right (credit) side.
2. Liabilities and owner's equity are on the right side of the accounting equation. Therefore, increases are entered on the right (credit) side and decreases are entered on the left (debit) side.
3. Revenues are on the right side of the owner's equity umbrella. Therefore, increases are entered on the right (credit) side and decreases are entered on the left (debit) side.
4. Expenses and drawing are on the left side of the owner's equity umbrella. Therefore, increases are entered on the left (debit) side and decreases are entered on the right (credit) side.

4 Picture the accounting equation in your mind as you analyze transactions.

S U M M A R Y

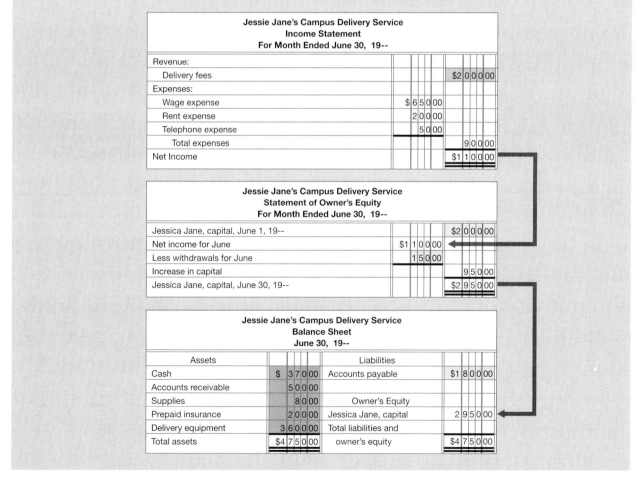

Jessie Jane's Campus Delivery Service
Trial Balance
June 30, 19--

ACCOUNT TITLE	ACCOUNT NO.	DEBIT BALANCE	CREDIT BALANCE
Cash		3 7 0 00	
Accounts Receivable		5 0 0 00	
Supplies		8 0 00	
Prepaid Insurance		2 0 0 00	
Delivery Equipment		3 6 0 0 00	
Accounts Payable			1 8 0 0 00
Jessica Jane, Capital			2 0 0 0 00
Jessica Jane, Drawing		1 5 0 00	
Delivery Fees			2 0 0 0 00
Rent Expense		2 0 0 00	
Telephone Expense		5 0 00	
Wage Expense		6 5 0 00	
		5 8 0 0 00	5 8 0 0 00

Jessie Jane's Campus Delivery Service
Income Statement
For Month Ended June 30, 19--

Revenue:		
Delivery fees		$2 0 0 0 00
Expenses:		
Wage expense	$6 5 0 00	
Rent expense	2 0 0 00	
Telephone expense	5 0 00	
Total expenses		9 0 0 00
Net Income		$1 1 0 0 00

Jessie Jane's Campus Delivery Service
Statement of Owner's Equity
For Month Ended June 30, 19--

Jessica Jane, capital, June 1, 19--		$2 0 0 0 00
Net income for June	$1 1 0 0 00	
Less withdrawals for June	1 5 0 00	
Increase in capital		9 5 0 00
Jessica Jane, capital, June 30, 19--		$2 9 5 0 00

Jessie Jane's Campus Delivery Service
Balance Sheet
June 30, 19--

Assets		Liabilities	
Cash	$ 3 7 0 00	Accounts payable	$1 8 0 0 00
Accounts receivable	5 0 0 00		
Supplies	8 0 00	Owner's Equity	
Prepaid insurance	2 0 0 00	Jessica Jane, capital	2 9 5 0 00
Delivery equipment	3 6 0 0 00	Total liabilities and	
Total assets	$4 7 5 0 00	owner's equity	$4 7 5 0 00

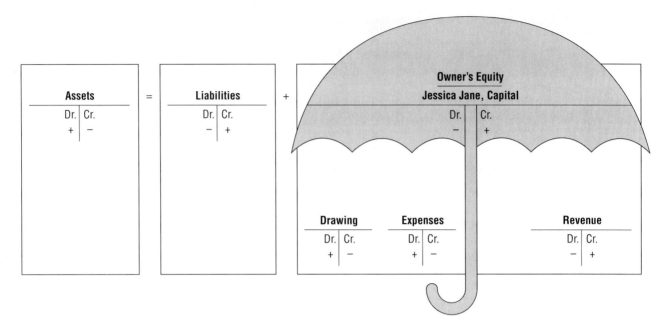

When entering transactions in T accounts:

1. The sum of the debits must equal the sum of the credits.
2. At least two accounts are affected by each transaction.
3. When finished, the accounting equation must remain in balance.

5 A trial balance shows that the debit and credit totals are equal. A trial balance can also be used in preparing the financial statements.

KEY TERMS

account 45 A separate item used to record increases and decreases in each type of asset, liability, owner's equity, revenue, and expense.

balance 46 The difference between the footings of an account.

credit 46 To enter an amount on the right side of an account.

credit balance 47 Liability, owner's equity, and revenue accounts have credit balances as their normal balances.

debit 46 To enter an amount on the left side of an account.

debit balance 47 Asset, expense, and drawing accounts have debit balances as their normal balances.

double-entry accounting 45 A system in which each transaction has a dual effect on the accounting elements.

footings 46 The total dollar amounts on the debit and credit sides of an account.

normal balance 47 The side of an account that is increased.

trial balance 65 A list of all accounts showing the title and balance of each account.

BUILDING YOUR ACCOUNTING KNOWLEDGE

1. What are the three major parts of a T account?
2. What is the left side of the T account called? the right side?
3. What is a footing?
4. What is the relationship between the revenue and expense accounts and the owner's equity account?
5. What is the function of the trial balance?

DEMONSTRATION PROBLEM

Celia Pints opened We-Buy, You-Pay Shopping Services. For a fee based on the amount of research and shopping time required, Celia and a group of associates will shop for almost anything from groceries to home furnishings. Business is particularly heavy around Christmas and in early summer when many wedding anniversaries are celebrated. The business operates from a rented store front. The associates receive a commission based on the revenues they produce and a mileage reimbursement for the use of their personal automobiles for shopping trips. The following transactions are for the month of December.

(a) Pints invested $30,000 in the business.
(b) Bought office equipment for $10,000. Pints paid $2,000 in cash and promised to pay the balance over the next four months.
(c) Paid rent for December, $500.
(d) Provided shopping services for customers on account, $5,200.
(e) Paid telephone bill, $90.
(f) Borrowed cash from the bank by signing a note payable, $5,000.
(g) Bought a computer for cash, $4,800.
(h) Collected cash from customers for services performed on account, $4,000.
(i) Paid commissions to associates for revenues generated during the first half of the month, $3,500.
(j) Paid utility bill, $600.
(k) Paid cash on account for the office equipment purchased in transaction (b), $2,000.
(l) Earned shopping fees of $13,200: $6,000 cash, $7,200 on account.
(m) Paid associates' commissions for last half of month, $7,000.
(n) Paid mileage reimbursements for the month, $1,500.
(o) Paid $1,000 on note payable to bank.
(p) Pints withdrew $2,000 for personal use.

Required
1. Enter the transactions for December in T accounts. Use the accounting equation as a guide for setting up the T accounts.

2. Foot the T accounts and determine their balances as necessary.
3. Prepare a trial balance of the accounts as of December 31 of the current year.
4. Prepare an income statement for the month ended December 31 of the current year.
5. Prepare a statement of owner's equity for the month ended December 31 of the current year.
6. Prepare a balance sheet as of December 31 of the current year.

SOLUTION

1, 2.

Assets = **Liabilities** + **Owner's Equity**

Dr. / Cr.	Dr. / Cr.	Dr. / Cr.
+ / −	− / +	− / +

Cash

(a) 30,000	(b) 2,000
(f) 5,000	(c) 500
(h) 4,000	(e) 90
(l) 6,000	(g) 4,800
45,000	(i) 3,500
	(j) 600
	(k) 2,000
	(m) 7,000
	(n) 1,500
	(o) 1,000
	(p) 2,000
	24,990
Bal. 20,010	

Accounts Receivable

(d) 5,200	(h) 4,000
(l) 7,200	
12,400	
Bal. 8,400	

Office Equipment

| (b) 10,000 | |

Computer Equipment

| (g) 4,800 | |

Accounts Payable

(k) 2,000	(b) 8,000
	Bal. 6,000

Notes Payable

(o) 1,000	(f) 5,000
	Bal. 4,000

Celia Pints, Capital

| | (a) 30,000 |

Drawing Dr. + / Cr. −

C. Pints, Drawing

| (p) 2,000 | |

Expenses Dr. + / Cr. −

Rent Expense

| (c) 500 | |

Telephone Exp.

| (e) 90 | |

Commissions Exp.

(i) 3,500	
(m) 7,000	
Bal. 10,500	

Utility Expense

| (j) 600 | |

Travel Expense

| (n) 1,500 | |

Revenue Dr. − / Cr. +

Shopping Fees

	(d) 5,200
	(l) 13,200
	Bal. 18,400

3.

We-Buy, You-Pay Shopping Services Trial Balance December 31, 19--			
ACCOUNT TITLE	ACCOUNT NO.	DEBIT BALANCE	CREDIT BALANCE
Cash		20 0 1 0 00	
Accounts Receivable		8 4 0 0 00	
Office Equipment		10 0 0 0 00	
Computer Equipment		4 8 0 0 00	
Accounts Payable			6 0 0 0 00
Notes Payable			4 0 0 0 00
Celia Pints, Capital			30 0 0 0 00
Celia Pints, Drawing		2 0 0 0 00	
Shopping Fees			18 4 0 0 00
Rent Expense		5 0 0 00	
Telephone Expense		9 0 00	
Commissions Expense		10 5 0 0 00	
Utility Expense		6 0 0 00	
Travel Expense		1 5 0 0 00	
		58 4 0 0 00	58 4 0 0 00

4.

We-Buy, You-Pay Shopping Services Income Statement For Month Ended December 31, 19--		
Revenues:		
Shopping fees		$18 4 0 0 00
Expenses:		
Commissions expense	$10 5 0 0 00	
Travel expense	1 5 0 0 00	
Utility expense	6 0 0 00	
Rent expense	5 0 0 00	
Telephone expense	9 0 00	
Total expenses		13 1 9 0 00
Net income		$ 5 2 1 0 00

5.

We-Buy, You-Pay Shopping Services Statement of Owner's Equity For Month Ended December 31, 19--			
Celia Pints, capital, December 1, 19--			$30 0 0 0 00
Net income for December	$5 2 1 0 00		
Less withdrawals for December	2 0 0 0 00		
Increase in capital			3 2 1 0 00
Celia Pints, capital, December 31, 19--			$33 2 1 0 00

6.

We-Buy, You-Pay Shopping Services Balance Sheet December 31, 19--			
Assets		**Liabilities**	
Cash	$20 0 1 0 00	Notes payable	$ 4 0 0 0 00
Accounts receivable	8 4 0 0 00	Accounts payable	6 0 0 0 00
Office equipment	10 0 0 0 00	Total liabilities	$10 0 0 0 00
Computer equipment	4 8 0 0 00		
		Owner's Equity	
		Celia Pints, capital	33 2 1 0 00
Total assets	$43 2 1 0 00	Total liab. & owner's equity	$43 2 1 0 00

SERIES A

EXERCISES

APPLYING ACCOUNTING CONCEPTS

EXERCISE 3A1

Debit and Credit Analysis

3 Complete the following questions using either "debit" or credit."

a. An increase in the asset Cash is recorded by a _____.
b. The owner's capital account is increased with a _____.
c. The account Delivery Equipment is increased with a _____.
d. The cash account is decreased with a _____.
e. An increase in the liability Accounts Payable is recorded by a _____.
f. The revenue account Delivery Fees is increased with a _____.
g. The asset Accounts Receivable is increased with a _____.
h. The account Rent Expense is increased with a _____.
i. The owner's Drawing account is increased with a _____.

EXERCISE 3A2

Analysis of T Accounts

2/3/4 Jim Arnold began a business called Arnold's Basket Corner.

1. Create T accounts for Cash; Supplies; Jim Arnold, Capital; and Utilities Expense. Identify the following transactions by letter and place on the proper side of the T accounts.
   (a) Deposited cash in the business, $5,000.
   (b) Purchased supplies for cash, $800.
   (c) Paid utility bill, $1,500.
2. Foot the T account for Cash, determine the ending balance, and enter the ending balance on the side with the larger total.

EXERCISE 3A3

Normal Balance of Account

3 Indicate whether the normal balance for each of the following accounts is a debit or a credit.

1. Cash
2. Wages Expense
3. Accounts Payable
4. Owner's Drawing
5. Supplies
6. Owner's Capital
7. Equipment

EXERCISE 3A4

Transaction Analysis

4 Sheryl Hansen started a new business on May 1, 19--. Analyze the following transactions for the first month of business using T accounts. Label each T account with the title of the account affected and then place the dollar amount on the debit or credit side.

(a) Sheryl Hansen invested cash in the business, $4,000.
(b) Bought equipment for cash, $500.
(c) Bought equipment on account, $800.
(d) Paid $300 on account from purchase in transaction (c).
(e) Owner withdrew cash for personal use, $700.

EXERCISE 3A5

Analysis of T account

2 From the transactions in Exercise 3A4, analyze the transactions affecting Cash, foot the T account, and indicate the ending balance on the side with the larger footing.

EXERCISE 3A6

Analysis of Transactions

2/4 Charlie Chadwick began a new business called Charlie's Detective Service in January, 19--. Set up T accounts for the following account titles: Cash; Accounts Receivable; Office Supplies; Computer Equipment; Office Furniture; Accounts Payable; Charles Chadwick, Capital; Charles Chadwick, Drawing; Professional Fees; Rent Expense; and Utility Expense.

The following transactions occurred during the first month of business. Record these transactions in T accounts. After all transactions are recorded, foot the accounts if necessary, and enter the total number under the last entry in small figures. If an account has entries on both sides, determine the balance and enter it on the side with the larger total.

(a) Invested cash in the business, $30,000.
(b) Bought office supplies for cash, $300.
(c) Bought office furniture for cash, $5,000.
(d) Purchased computer and printer on account, $8,000.
(e) Received cash from clients for services, $3,000.
(f) Paid cash on account for computer and printer purchased in transaction (d), $4,000.
(g) Earned professional fees on account during the month, $9,000.
(h) Paid cash for office rent for January, $1,500.
(i) Paid utility bills for the month, $800.
(j) Received cash from clients billed in transaction (g), $6,000.
(k) Withdrew cash for personal use, $3,000.

EXERCISE 3A7

Trial Balance

5 Based on the transactions recorded in Exercise 3A6, prepare a trial balance for Charlie's Detective Service as of January 31, 19--.

EXERCISE 3A8

Trial Balance

5 The following accounts have normal balances. Prepare a trial balance for Mary's Delivery Service as of September 30, 19--.

Cash	$ 5,000
Accounts Receivable	3,000
Supplies	800
Prepaid Insurance	600
Delivery Equipment	8,000
Accounts Payable	2,000
Mary Jane, Capital	10,000
Mary Jane, Drawing	1,000
Delivery Fees	9,400
Wages Expense	2,100
Rent Expense	900

EXERCISE 3A9

Income Statement

From the information in Exercise 3A8, prepare an income statement for Mary's Delivery Service for the month ended September 30, 19--.

EXERCISE 3A10

Statement of Owner's Equity

From the information in Exercise 3A8, prepare a statement of owner's equity for Mary's Delivery Service for the month ended September 30, 19--.

EXERCISE 3A11

Balance Sheet

From the information in Exercise 3A8, prepare a balance sheet for Mary's Delivery Service as of September 30, 19--.

PROBLEM 3A1

T Accounts and Trial Balance

2/4/5 Harold Long started a business in May, 19--, called Harold's Home Repair. Harold hired a part-time college student as an assistant. The following transactions occurred during May.

(a) Harold invested cash in the business, $20,000.
(b) Purchased a used van for cash, $7,000.
(c) Purchased equipment on account, $5,000.
(d) Received cash for services rendered, $6,000.
(e) Paid cash on amount owed from transaction (c), $2,000.
(f) Paid rent for the month, $900.
(g) Paid telephone bill, $200.
(h) Earned revenue on account, $4,000.
(i) Purchased office supplies for cash, $120.
(j) Paid wages to student, $600.
(k) Purchased insurance, $1,200.
(l) Received cash from services performed in transaction (h), $3,000.
(m) Paid cash for gas and oil expense on the van, $160.
(n) Purchased additional equipment for $3,000, paying $1,000 cash and spreading the remaining payments over the next 10 months.
(o) Income from services for the remainder of the month amounted to $3,200: $1,800 in cash and $1,400 on account.
(p) Owner withdrew cash at the end of the month, $2,800.

Required

1. Enter the transactions in T accounts, identifying each transaction with its corresponding letter.
2. Foot the accounts where necessary, and enter the total of each column immediately under the last entry. If an account has entries on both sides, determine the balance and enter it on the side with the larger total.
3. Prepare a trial balance as of May 31, 19--. After listing the account balances, rule a single line across the Amount columns immediately below the last item. Enter the totals on the next horizontal line and rule a double line across the Amount columns immediately under the totals.

PROBLEM 3A2

Net Income and Change in Owner's Equity

Refer to the trial balance of Harold's Home Repair in Problem 3A1 to determine the missing information. Use the following format.

1. (a) Total revenue for the month .... _____
   (b) Total expenses for the month .... _____
   (c) Net income for the month .... _____

2. (a) Harold Long's original investment in the business ...... _____

+ the net income for the month .... _____

− owner's drawing .... _____

= ending owner's equity .... _____

(b) End of month accounting equation:

ASSETS   =   LIABILITIES   + OWNER'S EQUITY

_____ = _____ + _____

PROBLEM 3A3

Financial Statements

1. Refer to the trial balance in Problem 3A1 and to the analysis of the change in owner's equity in Problem 3A2. Prepare an income statement for Harold's Home Repair for the month ended May 31, 19--.

2. Prepare a statement of owner's equity for Harold's Home Repair for the month ended May 31, 19--.

3. Prepare a balance sheet for Harold's Home Repair as of May 31, 19--.

SERIES B

EXERCISES

EXERCISE 3B1

Debit and Credit Analysis

3 Complete the following questions using either "debit" or "credit."

a. An increase in the asset Prepaid Insurance is recorded by a _____.

b. The owner's drawing account is increased with a _____.

c. The asset Accounts Receivable is decreased with a _____.

d. The liability Accounts Payable is decreased with a _____.

e. An owner's capital account is increased with a _____.

f. The revenue account Professional Fees is increased with a _____.

g. The account Repair Expense is increased with a _____.

h. The asset account Cash is decreased with a _____.

i. The asset Accounts Receivable is increased with a _____.

EXERCISE 3B2

Analysis of T Accounts

2/3/4 Bill Smith began a business called Smith's Cutlery.

1. Create T accounts for Cash; Supplies; Bill Smith, Capital; and Utilities Expense. Identify the following transactions by letter and place them on the proper side of the T accounts.

(a) Deposited cash in the business, $6,000.

(b) Purchased supplies for cash, $1,200.

(c) Paid utility bill, $900.

2. Foot the T account for Cash, determine the ending balance, and enter the ending balance on the side with the larger total.

EXERCISE 3B3
Normal Balance of Account

3 Indicate whether the normal balance for each of the following accounts is a debit or a credit.

1. Cash
2. Wages Expense
3. Accounts Payable
4. Owner's Drawing
5. Supplies
6. Owner's Capital
7. Equipment

EXERCISE 3B4
Transaction Analysis

4 George Atlas started a new business on June 1, 19--. Analyze the following transactions for the first month of business using T accounts. Label each T account with the title of the account affected and then place the dollar amount on the debit or credit side.

(a) George Atlas invested cash in the business, $7,000.
(b) Bought equipment for cash, $900.
(c) Bought equipment on account, $1,500.
(d) Paid $800 on account from purchase in transaction (c).
(e) Owner withdrew cash for personal use, $1,100.

EXERCISE 3B5
Analysis of T account

2 From the transactions in Exercise 3B4, analyze the transactions affecting Cash, foot the T account, and indicate the ending balance on the side with the larger footing.

EXERCISE 3B6
Analysis of Transactions

2/4 Nicole Lawrence began a new business called Nickie's Nylons in January, 19--. Set up T accounts for the following account titles: Cash; Accounts Receivable; Office Supplies; Computer Equipment; Office Furniture; Accounts Payable; N. Lawrence, Capital; N. Lawrence, Drawing; Professional Fees; Rent Expense; and Utility Expense.

The following transactions occurred during the first month of business. Record these transactions in T accounts. After all transactions have been recorded, foot the accounts if necessary, and enter the total number under the last entry. If an account has entries on both sides, determine the balance and enter it on the side with the larger total.

(a) Invested cash in the business, $18,000.
(b) Purchased office supplies for cash, $500.
(c) Purchased office furniture for cash, $8,000.
(d) Purchased computer and printer on account, $5,000.
(e) Received cash from clients for services, $4,000.
(f) Paid cash on account for computer and printer purchased in transaction (d), $2,000.
(g) Earned professional fees on account during the month, $7,000.
(h) Paid cash for office rent for January, $900.

(i) Paid utility bills for the month, $600.
(j) Received cash from clients that were billed previously in transaction (g), $3,000.
(k) Withdrew cash for personal use, $4,000.

EXERCISE 3B7

Trial Balance

5 Based on the transactions recorded in Exercise 3B6, prepare a trial balance for Nickie's Nylons as of January 31, 19--.

EXERCISE 3B8

Trial Balance

5 The following accounts have normal balances. Prepare a trial balance for Bill's Delivery Service as of September 30, 19--.

Cash	$ 7,000
Accounts Receivable ...	4,000
Supplies	600
Prepaid Insurance	900
Delivery Equipment	9,000
Accounts Payable	3,000
Bill Swift, Capital	12,000
Bill Swift, Drawing	2,000
Delivery Fees	12,500
Wages Expense	3,000
Rent Expense	1,000

EXERCISE 3B9

Income Statement

From the information in Exercise 3B8, prepare an income statement for Bill's Delivery Service for the month ended September 30, 19--.

EXERCISE 3B10

Statement of Owner's Equity

From the information in Exercise 3B8, prepare a statement of owner's equity for Bill's Delivery Service for the month ended September 30, 19--.

EXERCISE 3B11

Balance Sheet

From the information in Exercise 3B8, prepare a balance sheet for Bill's Delivery Service as of September 30, 19--.

P·ROBLEMS

PROBLEM 3B1

T Accounts and Trial Balance

2/4/5 Sue Jantz started a business in August, 19--, called Jantz Plumbing Service. Sue hired a part-time college student as an administrative assistant. The following transactions occurred during August.

(a) Sue invested cash in the business, $30,000.
(b) Purchased a used van for cash, $8,000.
(c) Purchased plumbing equipment on credit, $4,000.
(d) Received cash for services rendered, $3,000.
(e) Paid cash on amount owed from transaction (c), $1,000.
(f) Paid rent for the month, $700.

(g) Paid telephone bill, $100.

(h) Earned revenue on account, $4,000.

(i) Purchased office supplies for cash, $300.

(j) Paid wages to student, $500.

(k) Purchased insurance, $800.

(l) Received cash from services performed in transaction (h), $3,000.

(m) Paid cash for advertising expense, $2,000.

(n) Purchased additional plumbing equipment for $2,000, paying $500 cash and spreading the remaining payments over the next 6 months.

(o) Income from services for the remainder of the month amounted to $2,800: $1,100 in cash and $1,700 on account.

(p) Owner withdrew cash at the end of the month, $3,000.

Required

1. Enter the transactions in T accounts, identifying each transaction with its corresponding letter.

2. Foot the accounts where necessary and enter the total of each column in small figures immediately under the last entry. If an account has entries on both sides, determine the balance and enter it on the side with the larger total.

3. Prepare a trial balance as of August 31, 19--. After listing the account balances, rule a single line across the amount columns immediately below the last item. Enter the totals on the next horizontal line and rule a double line across the amount columns immediately under the totals.

PROBLEM 3B2

Net Income and Change in Owner's Equity

Refer to the trial balance of Jantz Plumbing Service in Problem 3B1 to determine the missing information. Use the following format.

1. (a) Total revenue for the month .... _____

   (b) Total expenses for the month .... _____

   (c) Net income for the month .... _____

2. (a) Sue Jantz's original investment in the business .... _____

   + the net income for the month .... _____

   − owner's drawing .... _____

   = ending owner's equity .... _____

   (b) End of month accounting equation:

   ASSETS   =   LIABILITIES   + OWNER'S EQUITY

   _____ = _____ + _____

PROBLEM 3B3

Financial Statements

1. Refer to the trial balance in Problem 3B1 and to the analysis of the change in owner's equity in Problem 3B2. Prepare an income statement for Jantz Plumbing Service for the month ended August 31, 19--.

2. Prepare a statement of owner's equity for Jantz Plumbing Service for the month ended August 31, 19--.

3. Prepare a balance sheet for Jantz Plumbing Service as of August 31, 19--.

MASTERY PROBLEM

Craig Fisher started a lawn service called Craig's Quick Cut to earn money over the summer months. The following transactions occurred during the month of June.

(a) Fisher invested $3,000 in the business.

(b) Bought mowing equipment for $1,000. Fisher paid $200 in cash and promised to pay the balance over the next four months.

(c) Paid garage rent for June, $50.

(d) Provided lawn services for customers on account, $520.

(e) Paid telephone bill, $10.

(f) Borrowed $500 from the bank by signing a note payable.

(g) Bought lawn tools, $480.

(h) Collected $400 from customers for services performed on account.

(i) Paid associates for lawn work done during the first half of the month, $350.

(j) Paid for gas and oil for the equipment, $60.

(k) Paid $200 on account for the mowing equipment purchased in transaction (b).

(l) Earned lawn fees of $1,320: $600 cash, $720 on account.

(m) Paid associates for last half of month $700.

(n) Reimbursed associates for expenses associated with using their own vehicles for transportation, $150.

(o) Paid $100 on note payable to bank.

(p) Fisher withdrew $200 for personal use.

Required

1. Enter the transactions for June in T accounts. Use the accounting equation as a guide for setting up the T accounts.
2. Foot the T accounts and determine their balances as necessary.
3. Prepare a trial balance of the accounts as of June 30 of the current year.
4. Prepare an income statement for the month ended June 30 of the current year.
5. Prepare a statement of owner's equity for the month ended June 30 of the current year.
6. Prepare a balance sheet as of June 30 of the current year.

Careful study of this chapter
should enable you to:

1. Describe the chart of
accounts as a means
of classifying
financial information.

2. Describe and explain
the purpose of source
documents.

3. Journalize
transactions.

4. Post to the general
ledger.

5. Explain how to find
and correct errors.

Journalizing and Posting Transactions

The double-entry framework of accounting was explained and illustrated in Chapter 3. Business transactions were entered directly into T accounts to demonstrate debits and credits. Now we take a more detailed look at the procedures used to account for business transactions.

This chapter traces the flow of financial data from the source documents through the accounting information system. This process includes the following steps:

1. Analyze what has happened using information from source documents and the business' chart of accounts.
2. Enter business transactions in the general journal.
3. Post entries to accounts in the general ledger.
4. Prepare a trial balance.

The flow of data from the source documents through the trial balance is shown in figure 4-1.

FIGURE 4-1 **Flow of Data from Source Documents Through Trial Balance**

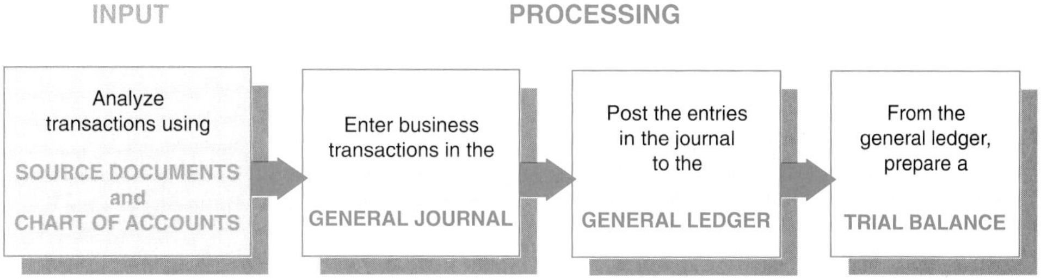

INPUT   PROCESSING

| Analyze transactions using **SOURCE DOCUMENTS** and **CHART OF ACCOUNTS** | Enter business transactions in the **GENERAL JOURNAL** | Post the entries in the journal to the **GENERAL LEDGER** | From the general ledger, prepare a **TRIAL BALANCE** |

	1

Describe the chart of accounts as a means of classifying financial information.

THE CHART OF ACCOUNTS

You learned in Chapters 2 and 3 that three basic questions must be answered when analyzing transactions:

1. What happened?
2. Which accounts are affected?
3. How is the accounting equation affected?

To determine which accounts are affected (step 2), the accountant must know which accounts the business is using. A list of all the accounts used by a business is called a **chart of accounts.**

The chart of accounts includes the account titles in numeric order for all assets, liabilities, owner's equity, revenue, and expenses. The numbering should follow a consistent pattern. In Jessie Jane's Campus Delivery Service, asset accounts begin with "1," liability accounts begin with "2," owner's equity accounts begin with "3," revenue accounts begin with "4," and expense accounts begin with "5."

A chart of accounts for Jessie Jane's Campus Delivery Service is shown in figure 4-2. Jane would not need many accounts initially because the business is new. Additional accounts can easily be added as needed.

FIGURE 4-2 Chart of Accounts

Jessie Jane's Campus Delivery Service Chart of Accounts				
Assets	**(100–199)**	**Revenues**	**(400–499)**	
111	Cash	411	Delivery Fees	Revenues begin with 4
131	Accounts Receivable			
151	Supplies	**Expenses**	**(500–599)**	Assets begin with 1
155	Prepaid Insurance	541	Rent Expense	
185	Delivery Equipment	542	Wage Expense	Expenses begin with 5
		545	Telephone Expense	
Liabilities	**(200–299)**			
218	Accounts Payable			Liabilities begin with 2
Owner's Equity	**(300–399)**			
311	Jessica Jane, Capital			Owner's Equity begins with 3
312	Jessica Jane, Drawing			

SOURCE DOCUMENTS

2

Describe and explain the purpose of source documents.

Almost any document that provides information about a business transaction can be called a **source document.** A source document triggers the analysis of what happened and its entry into the accounting system. Examples of source documents are shown in figure 4-3.

F I G U R E 4 - 3 Source Documents

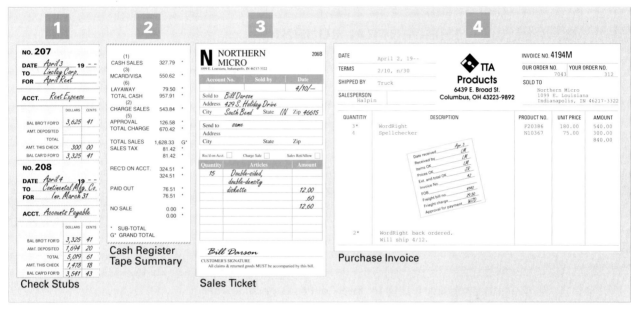

SOURCE DOCUMENTS	
EXAMPLES:	**PROVIDE INFORMATION ABOUT:**
1. Check stubs or carbon copies of checks	Cash payments
2. Receipt stubs, carbon copies of receipts, cash register tapes, or memos of cash register totals	Cash receipts
3. Copies of sales tickets or sales invoices issued to customers or clients	Sales of goods or services
4. Purchase invoices received from suppliers	Purchases of goods or services

Source documents provide objective evidence of business transactions. If anyone questions the accounting records, these documents can be used to verify the accuracy of the accounting records. For this reason, source documents are filed for possible future reference. *Having objective evidence that a transaction occurred is an important accounting concept.*

<table>
<tr><td>3</td></tr>
</table>

Journalize transactions.

A journal provides a day-by-day listing of all transactions completed by the business.

THE GENERAL JOURNAL

A day-by-day listing of the transactions of a business is called a **journal.** The purpose of a journal is to provide a record of all transactions completed by the business. The journal shows the date of each transaction, titles of the accounts to be debited or credited, and the amounts of the debits and credits.

A journal is commonly called a **book of original entry** because it is here that the first formal accounting record of a transaction is made. Although many types of journals are used in business, the simplest journal form is a two-column general journal. Any kind of business transaction may be entered into a general journal. Figure 4-4 shows a general journal. Journal pages are numbered in the upper right corner.

FIGURE 4-4 **Two-Column General Journal**

	DATE	DESCRIPTION	POST. REF.	DEBIT	CREDIT	
1	19-- ①	②	③	④	⑤	1
2						2
3						3
4						4
5						5
6						6
7						7
8						8
9						9
10						10
11						11
12						12
13						13

GENERAL JOURNAL   PAGE 1

A **two-column general journal** has only two amount columns, one for debit amounts and one for credit amounts. The column numbers in figure 4-4 correspond to the descriptions given in figure 4-5.

FIGURE 4-5   **The Columns in a Two-Column General Journal**

Column 1 Date	The year is entered in small figures at the top of the column immediately below the column heading. The year is repeated only at the top of each new page. The month is entered for the first entry on the page and for the first transaction of the month. The day of the month is recorded for every transaction, even if it is the same as the prior entry.
Column 2 Description	The account titles and a brief description of each transaction are entered in the **Description** or **Explanation** column. Each transaction affects two or more accounts. The account(s) to be debited are entered first at the extreme left of the column. The account(s) to be credited are listed on the next line, indented about one-half inch. The description should be entered immediately following the last credit entry and indented an additional one-half inch. If an entry affects more than two accounts, the entry is called a **compound entry.**
Column 3 Posting Reference	No entries are made in the **Posting Reference** column during journalizing. Entries are made in this column when the debit and credit elements are copied to the proper accounts in the ledger. This process will be explained in detail later in this chapter.
Column 4 Debit Amount	The **Debit amount column** is used to enter the amount to be debited to an account. The amount should be entered on the same line as the title of that account.
Column 5 Credit Amount	The **Credit amount column** is used to enter the amount to be credited to an account. The amount should be entered on the same line as the title of that account.

Journalizing

Entering the transactions in a journal is called **journalizing.** For every transaction, the entry should include the date, the title of each account affected, the amounts, and a brief description.

To illustrate the journalizing process, transactions for the first month of operations of Jessie Jane's Campus Delivery Service will be journalized. The transactions are listed in figure 4-6. Let's look at the steps to follow when journalizing the first transaction, Jane's initial investment of $2,000.

FIGURE 4-6 **Summary of Transactions**

Summary of Transactions
Jessie Jane's Campus Delivery Service

Transaction		
(a)	June 1	Jessica Jane invests cash in her business, $2,000.
(b)	3	Jane bought delivery equipment for cash, $1,200.
(c)	5	Jane bought delivery equipment on account from Big Red Scooters, $900.
(d)	6	Jane paid the first installment of $300 to Big Red Scooters. (See transaction (c).)
(e)	6	Jane received cash for delivery services rendered, $500.
(f)	7	Jane paid cash for June office rent, $200.
(g)	15	Jane paid a telephone bill, $50.
(h)	15	Jane made deliveries on account for a total of $600: Accounting Department ($400) and the School of Optometry ($200).
(i)	16	Jane bought supplies for cash, $80.
(j)	18	Jane paid $200 for an eight-month liability insurance policy. Coverage began on June 1.
(k)	20	Jane received $570 in cash for services performed earlier (see transaction (h)): $400 from the Accounting Department and $170 from the School of Optometry.
(l)	25	Jane bought a third scooter for $1,500 from Big Red Scooters. A down payment of $300 was made with the remaining payments expected over the next four months.
(m)	27	Jane paid part-time employees $650 in wages.
(n)	30	Total delivery fees for the remainder of the month amounted to $900: $430 for cash and $470 on account. Deliveries on account: Accounting Department, $100, and the Athletic Ticket Office, $370.
(o)	30	Jane withdrew cash from the business for personal use, $150.

Transaction (a)

June 1   Jessica Jane opened a bank account with a deposit of $2,000 for her business.

STEP 1   **Enter the date.**   Since this is the first entry on the journal page, the year is entered on the first line of the Date column (in small print at the top of the line). The month and day are entered on the same line, below the year, in the Date column.

	GENERAL JOURNAL				PAGE 1	
	DATE	DESCRIPTION	POST. REF.	DEBIT	CREDIT	
1	19-- June 1					1
2						2
3						3

STEP 2   **Enter the debit.**   Cash is entered on the first line at the extreme left of the Description column. The amount of the debit, $2,000, is entered on the same line in the Debit column.

	DATE		DESCRIPTION	POST. REF.	DEBIT	CREDIT	
			GENERAL JOURNAL			PAGE 1	
1	19-- June	1	Cash		2 0 0 0 00		1
2							2
3							3

STEP 3   **Enter the credit.**   The title of the account to be credited, Jessica Jane, Capital, is entered on the second line indented one-half inch from the left side of the Description column. The amount of the credit, $2,000, is entered on the same line in the Credit column.

	DATE		DESCRIPTION	POST. REF.	DEBIT	CREDIT	
			GENERAL JOURNAL			PAGE 1	
1	19-- June	1	Cash		2 0 0 0 00		1
2			Jessica Jane, Capital			2 0 0 0 00	2

STEP 4   **Enter the explanation.**   The explanation of the entry is entered on the next line indented an additional one-half inch. The second line of the explanation, if needed, is also indented the same distance as the first.

	DATE		DESCRIPTION	POST. REF.	DEBIT	CREDIT	
			GENERAL JOURNAL			PAGE 1	
1	19-- June	1	Cash		2 0 0 0 00		1
2			Jessica Jane, Capital			2 0 0 0 00	2
3			Owner's original investment in				3
4			delivery business.				4

To enter transaction (b), the purchase of a motor scooter for $1,200 cash, we skip a line and follow the same four steps. In practice, you probably would not skip a line to prevent inappropriate changes to entries. Note that the month and year do not need to be repeated. The day of the month must, however, be entered.

GENERAL JOURNAL · PAGE 1

	DATE		DESCRIPTION	POST. REF.	DEBIT	CREDIT	
1	19-- June	1	Cash		2 0 0 0 00		1
2			Jessica Jane, Capital			2 0 0 0 00	2
3			Owner's original investment in				3
4			delivery business.				4
5	*Skip a line*						5
6		3	Delivery Equipment		1 2 0 0 00		6
7			Cash			1 2 0 0 00	7
8			Purchase of delivery equipment				8
9			for cash.				9

The journal entries for the month of June are shown in figure 4-7.

FIGURE 4-7 **General Journal Entries**

GENERAL JOURNAL · PAGE 1

	DATE		DESCRIPTION	POST. REF.	DEBIT	CREDIT	
1	19-- June	1	Cash — *List debits first*		2 0 0 0 00		1
	Indent credits 1/2 inch		Jessica Jane, Capital			2 0 0 0 00	2
			Owner's original investment in — *Indent descript. addt'l. 1/2 inch*				3
4			delivery business.				4
5							5
6		3	Delivery Equipment		1 2 0 0 00		6
7			Cash			1 2 0 0 00	7
8			Purchase of delivery equipment				8
9			for cash.				9
							10
Space—entries easier to read		5	Delivery Equipment		9 0 0 00		11
12			Accounts Payable			9 0 0 00	12
13			Purchased delivery equipment				13
14			on acct. from Big Red Scooters.				14
15							15
16		6	Accounts Payable		3 0 0 00		16
17			Cash			3 0 0 00	17
18			Made partial payment to				18
19			Big Red Scooters.				19
20							20
21		6	Cash		5 0 0 00		21
22			Delivery Fees			5 0 0 00	22
23			Revenue from delivery services.				23

FIGURE 4-7 General Journal Entries (continued)

		DATE		DESCRIPTION	POST. REF.	DEBIT	CREDIT	
25	19-- June	7		Rent Expense		2 0 0 00		25
26				Cash			2 0 0 00	26
27				Paid office rent for June.				27
28								28
29		15		Telephone Expense		5 0 00		29
30				Cash			5 0 00	30
31				Paid telephone bill for June.				31
32								32
33		15		Accounts Receivable		6 0 0 00		33
34				Delivery Fees			6 0 0 00	34
35				Deliveries made on account for				35
36				Accounting Department ($400),				36
37				and School of Optometry ($200).				37

GENERAL JOURNAL — PAGE 1

GENERAL JOURNAL — PAGE 2

		DATE		DESCRIPTION	POST. REF.	DEBIT	CREDIT	
1	19-- June	16		Supplies		8 0 00		1
2				Cash			8 0 00	2
3				Purchased supplies for cash.				3
4								4
5		18		Prepaid Insurance		2 0 0 00		5
6				Cash			2 0 0 00	6
7				Premium for eight-month				7
8				insurance policy.				8
9								9
10		20		Cash		5 7 0 00		10
11				Accounts Receivable			5 7 0 00	11
12				On account from:				12
13				Accounting Department ($400)				13
14				School of Optometry ($170).				14
15								15
16		25		Delivery Equipment		1 5 0 0 00		16
17				Accounts Payable			1 2 0 0 00	17
18				Cash			3 0 0 00	18
19				Purch. scooter with down				19
20				pmt. of $300, and bal. on				20
21				acct. from Big Red Scooters.				21

Compound Entry

FIGURE 4-7 **General Journal Entries (concluded)**

	DATE		DESCRIPTION	POST. REF.	DEBIT	CREDIT	
23	19-- June	27	Wage Expense		6 5 0 00		23
24			Cash			6 5 0 00	24
25			Paid employees.				25
26							26
27		30	Cash		4 3 0 00		27
28			Accounts Receivable		4 7 0 00		28
29			Delivery Fees			9 0 0 00	29
30			Deliveries made for cash and on				30
31			account to: Acct. Dept. ($100)				31
32			Athletic Ticket Office ($370).				32
33							33
34		30	Jessica Jane, Drawing		1 5 0 00		34
35			Cash			1 5 0 00	35
36			Withdrawal for personal use.				36

Compound Entry →

THE GENERAL LEDGER

The journal provides a day-by-day record of business transactions. To determine the balance of specific accounts, however, the information in the journal must be copied to accounts similar to the T accounts illustrated in Chapter 3.

A complete set of all the accounts used by a business is called the **general ledger.** The general ledger provides a complete record of the transactions entered in each account. The accounts are numbered and arranged in the same order as the chart of accounts, that is, accounts are numbered and grouped by classification: assets, liabilities, owner's equity, revenue, and expense.

Four-Column Account

For purposes of illustration, the T account was introduced in Chapter 3. In actual practice, businesses are more likely to use a version of the account called the **four-column account**. A four-column account contains columns for the debit or credit transaction and columns for the debit or credit running balance. Figure 4-8 compares the cash T account from Chapter 3 for

FIGURE 4-8 **Comparison of T Account and Four-Column Account**

Cash			
(a)	2,000	(b)	1,200
(e)	500	(d)	300
(k)	570	(f)	200
(n)	430	(g)	50
	3,500	(i)	80
		(j)	200
		(l)	300
		(m)	650
		(o)	150
			3,130
Bal.	370		

GENERAL LEDGER

ACCOUNT: CASH — ACCOUNT NO. 111

DATE		ITEM	POST. REF.	DEBIT	CREDIT	BALANCE	
						DEBIT	CREDIT
19-- June	1			2 0 0 0 00		2 0 0 0 00	
	3				1 2 0 0 00	8 0 0 00	
	6				3 0 0 00	5 0 0 00	
	6			5 0 0 00		1 0 0 0 00	
	7				2 0 0 00	8 0 0 00	
	15				5 0 00	7 5 0 00	
	16				8 0 00	6 7 0 00	
	18				2 0 0 00	4 7 0 00	
	20			5 7 0 00		1 0 4 0 00	
	25				3 0 0 00	7 4 0 00	
	27				6 5 0 00	9 0 00	
	30			4 3 0 00		5 2 0 00	
	30				1 5 0 00	3 7 0 00	

Transaction Amount — Running Balance

Jessie Jane's Campus Delivery Service and a four-column cash account summarizing the same cash transactions.

As you see in figure 4-8, the primary advantage of the T account is that the debit and credit sides of the account are easier to identify. Thus, for demonstration purposes and analyzing what happened, T accounts are very helpful. However, computing the balance of a T account is cumbersome. The primary advantage of the four-column account is that it maintains a running balance.

Note that the heading for the four-column account has the account title and an account number. The account number is taken from the chart of accounts and is used in the posting process.

> The primary advantage of the four-column account over the T account is that the four-column account maintains a running balance.

Posting to the General Ledger

The process of copying the debits and credits from the journal to the ledger accounts is known as **posting.** All amounts entered in the journal must be posted to the general ledger accounts.

Posting from the journal to the ledger is done daily or at frequent intervals. There are four steps.

Steps in the Posting Process

In the ledger account:

STEP 1 Enter the date of each transaction in the Date column.

STEP 2 Enter the amount of each transaction in the Debit or Credit column and enter the new balance in the Balance columns under Debit or Credit. If the balance of the account is zero, draw a line through the Debit and Credit columns.

STEP 3 Enter the page number of the journal from which each transaction is posted in the Posting Reference column.

In the journal:

STEP 4 Enter the account number in the Posting Reference column of the journal for each transaction that is posted.

Posting references indicate that a journal entry has been posted to the general ledger.

Step 4 is the last step in the posting process since the posting references indicate which journal entries have been posted to the ledger accounts. This is very helpful, particularly if you are interrupted during the posting process. The information in the posting reference columns of the journal and ledger provides a link between the journal and ledger known as a **cross-reference.**

To illustrate the posting process, the journal entries for Jessie Jane's Campus Delivery Service will be posted. Let's post the first journal entry for the month of June. First, let's post the debit to Cash (figure 4-9).

F I G U R E 4 - 9 **Posting a Debit**

In the ledger account:

STEP 1   Enter the year, "19--," the month, "June," and the day, "1," in the Date column of the cash account.

STEP 2   Enter the amount, $2,000, in the Debit column and enter the $2,000 balance in the Balance columns under Debit.

STEP 3   Enter "J1" in the Posting Reference column since the posting came from page 1 of the journal.

In the journal:

STEP 4   Enter the cash account number 111 (see chart of accounts in figure 4-2 on page 82) in the Posting Reference column of the journal on the same line as the debit to Cash for $2,000.

Now let's post the credit portion of the first entry (figure 4-10).

FIGURE 4-10 **Posting a Credit**

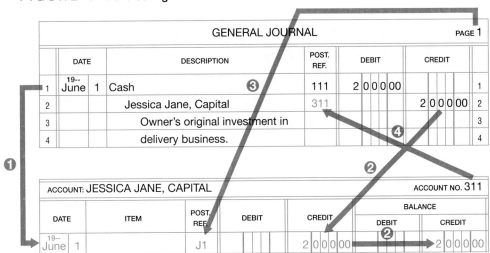

In the ledger account:

STEP 1   Enter the year, "19--," the month, "June," and the day, "1," in the Date column of the Jessica Jane, Capital account.

STEP 2   Enter the amount, $2,000, in the Credit column and enter the $2,000 balance in the Balance columns under Credit.

STEP 3   Enter "J1" in the Posting Reference column since the posting came from page 1 of the journal.

In the journal:

STEP 4   Enter the account number for Jessica Jane, Capital, 311, in the Posting Reference column.

   After posting the journal entries for Jessie Jane's Campus Delivery Service for the month of June, the general journal and general ledger would appear as in figures 4-11 and 4-12 below and on pages 95 and 96. *Note that the Posting Reference column has been filled in because the entries have been posted.*

FIGURE 4-11 **General Journal Entries After Posting**

GENERAL JOURNAL   PAGE 1

	DATE		DESCRIPTION	POST. REF.	DEBIT	CREDIT	
1	19-- June	1	Cash	111	2 0 0 0 00		1
2			Jessica Jane, Capital	311		2 0 0 0 00	2
3			Owner's original investment in				3
4			delivery business.				4
5							5
6		3	Delivery Equipment	185	1 2 0 0 00		6
7			Cash	111		1 2 0 0 00	7
8			Purchase of delivery equipment				8
9			for cash.				9
10							10
11		5	Delivery Equipment	185	9 0 0 00		11
12			Accounts Payable	218		9 0 0 00	12
13			Purchased delivery equipment				13
14			on acct. from Big Red Scooters.				14
15							15
16		6	Accounts Payable	218	3 0 0 00		16
17			Cash	111		3 0 0 00	17
18			Made partial payment to Big				18
19			Red Scooters.				19
20							20
21		6	Cash	111	5 0 0 00		21
22			Delivery Fees	411		5 0 0 00	22
23			Revenue from delivery services.				23
24							24
25		7	Rent Expense	541	2 0 0 00		25
26			Cash	111		2 0 0 00	26
27			Paid office rent for June.				27
28							28

F I G U R E 4 - 1 1 **General Journal Entries After Posting (continued)**

	DATE	DESCRIPTION	POST. REF.	DEBIT	CREDIT	
GENERAL JOURNAL					PAGE 1	
29	15	Telephone Expense	545	5 0 00		29
30		Cash	111		5 0 00	30
31		Paid telephone bill for June.				31
32						32
33	15	Accounts Receivable	131	6 0 0 00		33
34		Delivery Fees	411		6 0 0 00	34
35		Deliveries made on account for				35
36		Accounting Department ($400),				36
37		and School of Optometry ($200).				37

	DATE	DESCRIPTION	POST. REF.	DEBIT	CREDIT	
GENERAL JOURNAL					PAGE 2	
1	19-- June 16	Supplies	151	8 0 00		1
2		Cash	111		8 0 00	2
3		Purchased supplies for cash.				3
4						4
5	18	Prepaid Insurance	155	2 0 0 00		5
6		Cash	111		2 0 0 00	6
7		Premium for eight-month				7
8		insurance policy.				8
9						9
10	20	Cash	111	5 7 0 00		10
11		Accounts Receivable	131		5 7 0 00	11
12		On account from:				12
13		Accounting Department ($400)				13
14		School of Optometry ($170)				14
15						15
16	25	Delivery Equipment	185	1 5 0 0 00		16
17		Accounts Payable	218		1 2 0 0 00	17
18		Cash	111		3 0 0 00	18
19		Purch. scooter with down				19
20		pmt. of $300, and bal. on				20
21		acct. from Big Red Scooters.				21
22						22

FIGURE 4-11 **General Journal Entries After Posting (concluded)**

	DATE	DESCRIPTION	POST. REF.	DEBIT	CREDIT	
23	27	Wage Expense	542	6 5 0 00		23
24		Cash	111		6 5 0 00	24
25		Paid Employees.				25
26						26
27	30	Cash	111	4 3 0 00		27
28		Accounts Receivable	131	4 7 0 00		28
29		Delivery Fees	411		9 0 0 00	29
30		Deliveries made for cash and on				30
31		account to: Acct. Dept. ($100)				31
32		Athletic Ticket Office ($370).				32
33						33
34	30	Jessica Jane, Drawing	312	1 5 0 00		34
35		Cash	111		1 5 0 00	35
36		Withdrawal for personal use.				36

GENERAL JOURNAL — PAGE 2

FIGURE 4-12 **General Ledger After Posting**

GENERAL LEDGER

ACCOUNT: CASH — ACCOUNT NO. 111

DATE		ITEM	POST. REF.	DEBIT	CREDIT	BALANCE DEBIT	BALANCE CREDIT
19-- June	1		J1	2 0 0 0 00		2 0 0 0 00	
	3		J1		1 2 0 0 00	8 0 0 00	
	6		J1		3 0 0 00	5 0 0 00	
	6		J1	5 0 0 00		1 0 0 0 00	
	7		J1		2 0 0 00	8 0 0 00	
	15		J1		5 0 00	7 5 0 00	
	16		J2		8 0 00	6 7 0 00	
	18		J2		2 0 0 00	4 7 0 00	
	20		J2	5 7 0 00		1 0 4 0 00	
	25		J2		3 0 0 00	7 4 0 00	
	27		J2		6 5 0 00	9 0 00	
	30		J2	4 3 0 00		5 2 0 00	
	30		J2		1 5 0 00	3 7 0 00	

FIGURE 4-12 **General Ledger After Posting (continued)**

ACCOUNT: ACCOUNTS RECEIVABLE — ACCOUNT NO. 131

DATE	ITEM	POST. REF.	DEBIT	CREDIT	BALANCE DEBIT	BALANCE CREDIT
19-- June 15		J1	600 00		600 00	
20		J2		570 00	30 00	
30		J2	470 00		500 00	

ACCOUNT: SUPPLIES — ACCOUNT NO. 151

DATE	ITEM	POST. REF.	DEBIT	CREDIT	BALANCE DEBIT	BALANCE CREDIT
19-- June 16		J2	80 00		80 00	

ACCOUNT: PREPAID INSURANCE — ACCOUNT NO. 155

DATE	ITEM	POST. REF.	DEBIT	CREDIT	BALANCE DEBIT	BALANCE CREDIT
19-- June 18		J2	200 00		200 00	

ACCOUNT: DELIVERY EQUIPMENT — ACCOUNT NO. 185

DATE	ITEM	POST. REF.	DEBIT	CREDIT	BALANCE DEBIT	BALANCE CREDIT
19-- June 3		J1	1200 00		1200 00	
5		J1	900 00		2100 00	
25		J2	1500 00		3600 00	

ACCOUNT: ACCOUNTS PAYABLE — ACCOUNT NO. 218

DATE	ITEM	POST. REF.	DEBIT	CREDIT	BALANCE DEBIT	BALANCE CREDIT
19-- June 5		J1		900 00		900 00
6		J1	300 00			600 00
25		J2		1200 00		1800 00

ACCOUNT: JESSICA JANE, CAPITAL — ACCOUNT NO. 311

DATE	ITEM	POST. REF.	DEBIT	CREDIT	BALANCE DEBIT	BALANCE CREDIT
19-- June 1		J1		2000 00		2000 00

ACCOUNT: JESSICA JANE, DRAWING — ACCOUNT NO. 312

DATE	ITEM	POST. REF.	DEBIT	CREDIT	BALANCE DEBIT	BALANCE CREDIT
19-- June 30		J2	150 00		150 00	

FIGURE 4-12 **General Ledger After Posting (concluded)**

ACCOUNT: DELIVERY FEES   ACCOUNT NO. 411

DATE		ITEM	POST. REF.	DEBIT	CREDIT	BALANCE DEBIT	BALANCE CREDIT
19-- June	6		J1		5 0 0 00		5 0 0 00
	15		J1		6 0 0 00		1 1 0 0 00
	30		J2		9 0 0 00		2 0 0 0 00

ACCOUNT: RENT EXPENSE   ACCOUNT NO. 541

DATE		ITEM	POST. REF.	DEBIT	CREDIT	BALANCE DEBIT	BALANCE CREDIT
19-- June	7		J1	2 0 0 00		2 0 0 00	

ACCOUNT: WAGE EXPENSE   ACCOUNT NO. 542

DATE		ITEM	POST. REF.	DEBIT	CREDIT	BALANCE DEBIT	BALANCE CREDIT
19-- June	27		J2	6 5 0 00		6 5 0 00	

ACCOUNT: TELEPHONE EXPENSE   ACCOUNT NO. 545

DATE		ITEM	POST. REF.	DEBIT	CREDIT	BALANCE DEBIT	BALANCE CREDIT
19-- June	15		J1	5 0 00		5 0 00	

The Trial Balance

In Chapter 3, a trial balance was used to prove that the totals of the debit and credit balances in T accounts were equal. In this chapter, a **trial balance** is used to check the equality of debits and credits in the ledger accounts. A trial balance can be taken daily, weekly, monthly, or whenever desired. Before taking a trial balance, all transactions should be journalized and posted so that all transactions will be reflected in the ledger accounts.

The balances from the general ledger (figure 4-12), were used to develop the trial balance for Jessie Jane's Campus Delivery Service shown in figure 4-13.

Even though the trial balance indicates that the ledger is in balance, the ledger can still contain errors. For example, if a journal entry was made debiting or crediting the wrong accounts, or if an item was posted to the wrong account, the ledger will still be in balance. It is important, therefore, to be very careful in preparing the journal entries and in posting them to the ledger accounts.

FIGURE 4-13 Trial Balance

ACCOUNT TITLE	ACCOUNT NO.	DEBIT BALANCE	CREDIT BALANCE
Jessie Jane's Campus Delivery Service **Trial Balance** **June 30, 19--**			
Cash	111	3 7 0 00	
Accounts Receivable	131	5 0 0 00	
Supplies	151	8 0 00	
Prepaid Insurance	155	2 0 0 00	
Delivery Equipment	185	3 6 0 0 00	
Accounts Payable	218		1 8 0 0 00
Jessica Jane, Capital	311		2 0 0 0 00
Jessica Jane, Drawing	312	1 5 0 00	
Delivery Fees	411		2 0 0 0 00
Rent Expense	541	2 0 0 00	
Wage Expense	542	6 5 0 00	
Telephone Expense	545	5 0 00	
		5 8 0 0 00	5 8 0 0 00

FINDING AND CORRECTING ERRORS IN THE TRIAL BALANCE

5

Explain how to find and correct errors.

Tips are available to help if your trial balance has an error. Figure 4-14 offers hints for finding the error when your trial balance does not balance.

FIGURE 4-14 Tips for Finding Errors in the Trial Balance
Tips for Finding Errors

1. Double check your addition.
2. Find the difference between the debits and the credits.
   a. If the difference is equal to the amount of a specific transaction, perhaps you forgot to post the debit or credit portion of this transaction.

b. Divide the difference by **2.** If a debit was posted as a credit, it would mean that one transaction had two credits and no debits. The difference between the total debits and credits would be twice the amount of the debit that was posted as a credit.

c. Divide the difference by 9. If the difference is evenly divisible by 9, you may have committed a **slide** error or a **transposition** error. A slide occurs when debit or credit amounts "slide" a digit or two to the left or right when entered. For example, if $250 was entered as $25:

$$\$250 - 25 = \$225$$
$$\$225 \div 9 = 25$$

The difference is evenly divisible by 9.

A transposition occurs when two digits are reversed. For example, if $250 was entered as $520:

$$\$520 - 250 = \$270$$
$$\$270 \div 9 = 30$$

Again, the difference is evenly divisible by 9.

If the tips don't work, you must retrace your steps through the accounting process. Double check your addition for the ledger accounts and journal footings. Also trace all postings. Be patient and use this time to search for your error as an opportunity to reinforce your understanding of the flow of information through the accounting system.

Once you have found an error, there are two methods of making the correction. Although you may want to erase when correcting your homework, this is not acceptable in practice because an erasure may suggest that you are trying to hide something. Instead you should use the ruling method or make a correcting entry depending on whether the entry has been posted to the incorrect account.

Ruling Method

With the **ruling method,** draw a line through the incorrect account title or amount and write the correct information directly above the ruling. Corrections should be initialed so the source and reason for the correction can be traced. This type of correction may be made in the journal or ledger accounts as shown in figure 4-15.

FIGURE 4-15 **Ruling Method of Making a Correction**

	DATE	DESCRIPTION	POST. REF.	DEBIT	CREDIT	
1	19-- June 27	*Wage Expense* ~~Entertainment Expense~~ *HPC*		6 5 0 00		1
2		Cash			6 5 0 00	2
3		Paid employees.				3
4				*HPC*		4
5	18	Prepaid Insurance		*2 0 0 0 0* ~~2 0 00~~	*HPC*	5
6		Cash			*2 0 0 0 0* ~~2 0 00~~	6
7		Premium for eight-month				7
8		insurance policy.				8

Slide

GENERAL LEDGER

ACCOUNT: ACCOUNTS PAYABLE   ACCOUNT NO. 218

DATE	ITEM	POST. REF.	DEBIT	CREDIT	BALANCE DEBIT	BALANCE CREDIT
19-- June 5		J1		9 0 0 00		9 0 0 00
5		J1	3 0 0 00			6 0 0 00
25		J2		*HPC 1 2 0 0 0 0* ~~2 1 0 0 00~~	*HPC 1 8 0 0 0 0*	*HPC 1 8 0 0 0 0* ~~2 7 0 0 00~~

Transposition

Correcting Entry Method

If an incorrect entry has been journalized and posted to the wrong account, a **correcting entry** should be made. For example, assume that a $400 payment for Rent Expense was incorrectly debited to Repair Expense and correctly credited to Cash. This requires a correcting entry and explanation as shown in figure 4-16. Figure 4-17 shows the effects of the correcting entry on the ledger accounts.

FIGURE 4-16 **Correcting Entry Method**

	DATE	DESCRIPTION	POST. REF.	DEBIT	CREDIT	
1	19-- Sept. 25	Rent Expense	541	4 0 0 00		1
2		Repair Expense	565		4 0 0 00	2
3		To correct an error in which				3
4		a payment for rent was				4
5		debited to Repair Expense.				5

FIGURE 4-17 **Effects of Correcting Entry on Ledger Accounts**

GENERAL LEDGER

ACCOUNT: RENT EXPENSE ACCOUNT NO. 541

DATE	ITEM	POST. REF.	DEBIT	CREDIT	BALANCE DEBIT	BALANCE CREDIT
19-- Sept. 25		J6	4 0 0 00		4 0 0 00	

ACCOUNT: REPAIR EXPENSE ACCOUNT NO. 565

DATE	ITEM	POST. REF.	DEBIT	CREDIT	BALANCE DEBIT	BALANCE CREDIT
19-- Sept. 10		J5	5 0 00		5 0 00	
15		J5	4 0 0 00		4 5 0 00	
25		J6		4 0 0 00	5 0 00	

KEY POINTS

1 The chart of accounts includes the account titles in numeric order for all assets, liabilities, owner's equity, revenue, and expenses. The chart of accounts is used in classifying information about transactions.

2 Source documents trigger the analysis of what happened and its entry into the accounting system.

3 A journal provides a day-by-day listing of transactions. The journal shows the date, titles of the accounts to be debited or credited, and the amounts of the debits and credits. The steps in the journalizing process are:

1. Enter the date.
2. Enter the debit. Accounts to be debited are entered first.

3. Enter the credit. Accounts to be credited are entered after the debits and are indented one-half inch.

4. Enter the explanation. A brief explanation of the transaction should be entered in the description column on the line following the last credit. The explanation should be indented an additional one-half inch.

4 The general ledger is a complete set of all accounts used by the business. The steps in posting from the general journal to the general ledger are:

In the general ledger:

1. Enter the date of each transaction.

2. Enter the amount of each debit or credit in the Debit or Credit column and enter the new balance.

3. Enter the journal page number from which each transaction is posted in the Posting Reference column.

In the journal:

4. Enter the account number in the Posting Reference column for each debit or credit that is posted.

5 When an error is discovered, the ruling method or the correcting entry method may be used to correct the error.

KEY TERMS

book of original entry 84   The journal or the first formal accounting record of a transaction.

chart of accounts 82   A list of all the accounts used by a business.

compound entry 85   A general journal entry that affects more than two accounts.

correcting entry 101   An entry to correct an incorrect entry that has been journalized and posted to the wrong account.

Credit amount column 85   Used to enter the amount that is to be credited to an account.

cross-reference 92   The information in the Posting Reference columns of the journal and ledger that provides a link between the journal and ledger.

Date column 85   Column 1 of the general journal.

Debit amount column 85   Used to enter the amount that is to be debited to an account.

Description column 85   Used to enter the account titles of the accounts affected by each transaction and to provide a brief description of the transaction.

Explanation column 85   Used to enter the account titles and to provide a brief description of the transaction. (Also called Description column.)

four-column account 90   Contains columns for the debit or credit transaction and columns for the debit or credit running balance.

general ledger 90   A complete set of all the accounts used by a business.

journal 84   A day-by-day listing of the transactions of a business.

journalizing 85   Entering the transactions in a journal.

posting 91   Copying the debits and credits from the journal to the ledger accounts.

Posting Reference column 85   Used when the debit and credit elements are copied to the proper accounts in a ledger.

ruling method 100   A method of correcting an entry in which a line is drawn through the error and the correct information is placed above it.

slide 100   Occurs when debit or credit amounts "slide" a digit or two to the left or right.

source document 83   Almost any document that provides information about a business transaction.

transposition 100   Occurs when two digits are reversed.

trial balance 98   Proves that the totals of the debit and credit balances in the ledger accounts are equal.

two-column general journal 85   A journal with only two amount columns, one for debit amounts and one for credit amounts.

BUILDING YOUR ACCOUNTING KNOWLEDGE

1. Trace the flow of accounting information through the accounting system.
2. Explain the purpose of a chart of accounts.
3. Name the five types of financial statement classifications for which it is ordinarily desirable to keep separate accounts.
4. Name a source document that provides information about each of the following types of business transactions:
   (a) Cash payment
   (b) Cash receipt
   (c) Sale of goods or services
   (d) Purchase of goods or services
5. Where is the first formal accounting record of a business transaction usually made?
6. Describe the four steps required to journalize a business transaction in a general journal.
7. Explain the primary advantage of a four-column ledger account.
8. In what order are the accounts customarily placed in the ledger?

9. Explain the four steps required when posting the journal to the ledger.
10. What information is entered in the Posting Reference column of the journal as each amount is posted to the proper account in the ledger?
11. Explain why the ledger can still contain errors even though the trial balance is in balance. Give examples of two such types of errors.
12. What is a slide?
13. What is a transposition error?
14. What is the ruling method of correcting an error?

DEMONSTRATION PROBLEM

Maria Vietor is a financial planning consultant. She completed the following transactions during the month of December of the current year.

Dec. 1 Vietor invested cash in the business, $20,000.
3 Paid cash for December office rent, $1,000.
4 Received a check for $2,500 from Aaron Bisno, a client, for services and deposited it in the bank.
6 Paid cash to Union Electric for December heating and light, $75.
7 Received a check for $2,000 from Will Carter, a client, for services and deposited it in the bank.
12 Paid cash to Smith's Super Service for gasoline and oil purchases, $60.
14 Paid cash to Comphelp in payment for temporary secretarial services during the past two weeks, $600.
17 Bought office supplies from Cleat Office Supply on account, $280.
20 Paid cash to Cress Telephone Co. for business calls during the past month, $100.
21 Vietor withdrew cash for personal use, $1,100.
24 Paid cash to the National Multiple Sclerosis Society, $100.
27 Received cash from Ellen Thaler, a client, for services and deposited it in the bank, $2,000.
28 Paid cash to Comphelp in payment for temporary secretarial services during the past two weeks, $600.
29 Made payment on account to Cleat Office Supplies, $100.

Required
1. Record the preceding transactions in a general journal.
2. Post the entries to the general ledger.
3. Prepare a trial balance.

SOLUTION

1, 2.

					GENERAL JOURNAL							PAGE 1	
		DATE		DESCRIPTION	POST. REF.	DEBIT			CREDIT				
1	19-- Dec.	1	Cash		111	20 0 0 0 00							1
2			Maria Vietor, Capital		311				20 0 0 0 00				2
3			Owner's original investment in										3
4			consulting business.										4
5													5
6		3	Rent Expense		541	1 0 0 0 00							6
7			Cash		111				1 0 0 0 00				7
8			Paid rent for December.										8
9													9
10		4	Cash		111	2 5 0 0 00							10
11			Professional Fees		411				2 5 0 0 00				11
12			Revenue from services rendered.										12
13													13
14		6	Utilities Expense		549	7 5 00							14
15			Cash		111				7 5 00				15
16			Paid utilities.										16
17													17
18		7	Cash		111	2 0 0 0 00							18
19			Professional Fees		411				2 0 0 0 00				19
20			Revenue from services rendered.										20
21													21
22		12	Automobile Expense		546	6 0 00							22
23			Cash		111				6 0 00				23
24			Paid for gas and oil.										24
25													25
26		14	Wage Expense		542	6 0 0 00							26
27			Cash		111				6 0 0 00				27
28			Paid temporary secretaries.										28
29													29
30		17	Office Supplies		152	2 8 0 00							30
31			Accounts Payable		218				2 8 0 00				31
32			Purchased Office Supplies on										32
33			account from Cleat Office Sup.										33
34													34
35		20	Telephone Expense		545	1 0 0 00							35
36			Cash		111				1 0 0 00				36
37			Paid phone bill.										37

GENERAL JOURNAL — PAGE 2

	DATE	DESCRIPTION	POST. REF.	DEBIT	CREDIT	
1	19-- Dec. 21	Maria Vietor, Drawing	312	1 1 0 0 00		1
2		Cash	111		1 1 0 0 00	2
3		Withdrawal by Vietor.				3
4						4
5	24	Charitable Contributions Expense	557	1 0 0 00		5
6		Cash	111		1 0 0 00	6
7		Contribution to MS Society.				7
8						8
9	27	Cash	111	2 0 0 0 00		9
10		Professional Fees	411		2 0 0 0 00	10
11		Revenue from services rendered.				11
12						12
13	28	Wage Expense	542	6 0 0 00		13
14		Cash	111		6 0 0 00	14
15		Paid temporary secretaries.				15
16						16
17	29	Accounts Payable	218	1 0 0 00		17
18		Cash	111		1 0 0 00	18
19		Payment on account to Cleat				19
20		Office Supplies.				20

2.

GENERAL LEDGER

ACCOUNT: CASH   ACCOUNT NO. 111

DATE	ITEM	POST. REF.	DEBIT	CREDIT	BALANCE DEBIT	BALANCE CREDIT
19-- Dec. 1		J1	20 0 0 0 00		20 0 0 0 00	
3		J1		1 0 0 0 00	19 0 0 0 00	
4		J1	2 5 0 0 00		21 5 0 0 00	
6		J1		7 5 00	21 4 2 5 00	
7		J1	2 0 0 0 00		23 4 2 5 00	
12		J1		6 0 00	23 3 6 5 00	
14		J1		6 0 0 00	22 7 6 5 00	
20		J1		1 0 0 00	22 6 6 5 00	
21		J2		1 1 0 0 00	21 5 6 5 00	
24		J2		1 0 0 00	21 4 6 5 00	
27		J2	2 0 0 0 00		23 4 6 5 00	
28		J2		6 0 0 00	22 8 6 5 00	
29		J2		1 0 0 00	22 7 6 5 00	

ACCOUNT: OFFICE SUPPLIES   ACCOUNT NO. 152

DATE	ITEM	POST. REF.	DEBIT	CREDIT	BALANCE DEBIT	BALANCE CREDIT
19-- Dec. 17		J1	2 8 0 00		2 8 0 00	

ACCOUNT: ACCOUNTS PAYABLE   ACCOUNT NO. 218

DATE	ITEM	POST. REF.	DEBIT	CREDIT	BALANCE DEBIT	BALANCE CREDIT
19-- Dec. 17		J1		2 8 0 00		2 8 0 00
29		J2	1 0 0 00			1 8 0 00

ACCOUNT: MARIA VIETOR, CAPITAL   ACCOUNT NO. 311

DATE	ITEM	POST. REF.	DEBIT	CREDIT	BALANCE DEBIT	BALANCE CREDIT
19-- Dec. 1		J1		20 0 0 0 00		20 0 0 0 00

ACCOUNT: MARIA VIETOR, DRAWING   ACCOUNT NO. 312

DATE	ITEM	POST. REF.	DEBIT	CREDIT	BALANCE DEBIT	BALANCE CREDIT
19-- Dec. 21		J2	1 1 0 0 00		1 1 0 0 00	

ACCOUNT: PROFESSIONAL FEES   ACCOUNT NO. 411

DATE	ITEM	POST. REF.	DEBIT	CREDIT	BALANCE DEBIT	BALANCE CREDIT
19-- Dec. 4		J1		2 5 0 0 00		2 5 0 0 00
7		J1		2 0 0 0 00		4 5 0 0 00
27		J2		2 0 0 0 00		6 5 0 0 00

ACCOUNT: RENT EXPENSE   ACCOUNT NO. 541

DATE	ITEM	POST. REF.	DEBIT	CREDIT	BALANCE DEBIT	BALANCE CREDIT
19-- Dec. 3		J1	1 0 0 0 00		1 0 0 0 00	

ACCOUNT: WAGE EXPENSE   ACCOUNT NO. 542

DATE	ITEM	POST. REF.	DEBIT	CREDIT	BALANCE DEBIT	BALANCE CREDIT
19-- Dec. 14		J1	6 0 0 00		6 0 0 00	
28		J2	6 0 0 00		1 2 0 0 00	

ACCOUNT: TELEPHONE EXPENSE | ACCOUNT NO. 545

DATE	ITEM	POST. REF.	DEBIT	CREDIT	BALANCE DEBIT	BALANCE CREDIT
19-- Dec. 20		J1	1 0 0 00		1 0 0 00	

ACCOUNT: AUTOMOBILE EXPENSE | ACCOUNT NO. 546

DATE	ITEM	POST. REF.	DEBIT	CREDIT	BALANCE DEBIT	BALANCE CREDIT
19-- Dec. 12		J1	6 0 00		6 0 00	

ACCOUNT: UTILITIES EXPENSE | ACCOUNT NO. 549

DATE	ITEM	POST. REF.	DEBIT	CREDIT	BALANCE DEBIT	BALANCE CREDIT
19-- Dec. 6		J1	7 5 00		7 5 00	

ACCOUNT: CHARITABLE CONTRIBUTIONS EXPENSE | ACCOUNT NO. 557

DATE	ITEM	POST. REF.	DEBIT	CREDIT	BALANCE DEBIT	BALANCE CREDIT
19-- Dec. 24		J2	1 0 0 00		1 0 0 00	

3.

Maria Vietor, Financial Planning Consultant
Trial Balance
Dec. 31, 19--

ACCOUNT TITLE	ACCOUNT NO.	DEBIT BALANCE	CREDIT BALANCE
Cash	111	22 7 6 5 00	
Office Supplies	152	2 8 0 00	
Accounts Payable	218		1 8 0 00
Maria Vietor, Capital	311		20 0 0 0 00
Maria Vietor, Drawing	312	1 1 0 0 00	
Professional Fees	411		6 5 0 0 00
Rent Expense	541	1 0 0 0 00	
Wage Expense	542	1 2 0 0 00	
Telephone Expense	545	1 0 0 00	
Automobile Expense	546	6 0 00	
Utilities Expense	549	7 5 00	
Charitable Contrib. Exp.	557	1 0 0 00	
		26 6 8 0 00	26 6 8 0 00

EXERCISES

APPYLING ACCOUNTING CONCEPTS

EXERCISE 4A1

Source Documents

2 Source documents trigger the analysis of events requiring an accounting entry. Match the following source documents with the type of information they provide.

1. Check stubs or check register
2. Purchase invoice from suppliers (vendors)
3. Sales tickets or invoices to customers
4. Receipts or cash register tapes

a. A good or service has been sold.
b. Cash has been received by the business.
c. Cash has been paid by the business.
d. Goods or services have been purchased by the business.

EXERCISE 4A2

General Journal Entries

3 For each of the following transactions, list the account to be debited and the account to be credited in the general journal.

1. Invested cash in the business, $5,000.
2. Paid office rent, $500.
3. Bought office supplies on account, $300.
4. Received cash for services rendered (fees), $400.
5. Paid cash on account, $50.
6. Received cash for a debt owed by a customer, $100.

EXERCISE 4A3

General Ledger Accounts

3 Set up T-accounts for each of the general ledger accounts needed for Exercise 4A2 and post debits and credits to the accounts.

EXERCISE 4A4

General Journal Entries

3 Jean Jones is opening a new consulting business. Journalize the following transactions that occurred during January of the current year. Use a two-column general journal.

Jan. 1 Invested $10,000 in the business.
2 Paid office rent, $500.
3 Purchased office equipment on account, $1,500.
5 Received $750 for services rendered.
8 Paid telephone bill, $65.
10 Paid $15 for a magazine subscription (miscellaneous expense).
11 Purchased office supplies on account, $300.
15 Paid $150 on account (see Jan. 3 transaction).
18 Paid cash to part-time employee, $500.
21 Received $350 for services rendered.
25 Paid electricity bill, $85.
27 Withdrew cash for personal use, $100.
29 Paid cash to part-time employee, $500.

4 Set up four-column general ledger accounts using the following chart of accounts. Post the transactions from Exercise 4A4 to the general ledger accounts and prepare a trial balance.

Chart of Accounts

Assets		Revenue	
111	Cash	411	Consulting Fees
121	Office Supplies		
131	Office Equipment	Expenses	
		511	Rent Expense
Liabilities		521	Salary Expense
211	Accounts Payable	531	Telephone Expense
		541	Utilities Expense
Owner's Equity		551	Miscellaneous Expense
311	Jean Jones, Capital		
312	Jean Jones, Drawing		

From the information in Exercises 4A4 and 4A5, prepare an income statement, a statement of owner's equity, and a balance sheet.

From the following trial balance, prepare an income statement, a statement of owner's equity, and a balance sheet.

**TJ's Paint Service
Trial Balance
July 31, 19--**

ACCOUNT TITLE	ACCOUNT NO.	DEBIT BALANCE	CREDIT BALANCE
Cash	101	4 3 0 0 00	
Accounts Receivable	111	1 1 0 0 00	
Supplies	121	8 0 0 00	
Paint Equipment	131	9 0 0 00	
Accounts Payable	201		2 1 5 0 00
TJ Ulza, Capital	311		3 2 0 5 00
TJ Ulza, Drawing	312	5 0 0 00	
Painting Fees	411		3 6 0 0 00
Rent Expense	511	2 5 0 00	
Telephone Expense	521	5 0 00	
Electricity Expense	531	7 0 00	
Transportation Expense	541	6 0 00	
Salary Expense	551	9 0 0 00	
Miscellaneous Expense	561	2 5 00	
		8 9 5 5 00	8 9 5 5 00

5 Joe Adams bought $500 worth of office supplies on account. The following entry was recorded on May 17. Find the error(s) and correct it (them), using the ruling method.

14									14
15	19-- May	17	Office Equipment		4 0 0 00				15
16			Cash				4 0 0 00		16
17			Bought copy paper.						17
18									18

On May 25, after the transactions had been posted, Joe discovered the following entry contains an error. The cash received represents a collection on account, rather than a new sale (revenue). Correct the following error in the general journal, using the correcting entry method. Accounts Receivable is asset account no. 121.

21									21
22	19-- May	5	Cash	111	1 0 0 0 00				22
23			Service Fees	411			1 0 0 0 00		23
24			Received cash for services						24
25			previously earned.						25
26									26

3/4 Jim Andrews opened a delivery business in March. He rents a small office and has a part-time assistant. His trial balance shows accounts for the first three months of business.

Jim Andrews													
Trial Balance													
May 31, 19--													

ACCOUNT TITLE	ACCOUNT NO.	DEBIT BALANCE						CREDIT BALANCE					
Cash	101		3	8	2	6	00						
Accounts Receivable	111		1	2	1	2	00						
Office Supplies	121			6	4	8	00						
Office Equipment	131		2	1	0	0	00						
Delivery Truck	151		8	0	0	0	00						
Accounts Payable	211								6	0	0	0	00
Jim Andrews, Capital	311								4	4	7	8	00
Jim Andrews, Drawing	312		1	8	0	0	00						
Delivery Fees	411								9	8	8	0	00
Rent Expense	511			9	0	0	00						
Salary Expense	523		1	2	0	0	00						
Telephone Expense	542			1	2	6	00						
Electricity Expense	546				9	8	00						
Gas and Oil Expense	551			1	8	6	00						
Advertising Expense	562				9	0	00						
Contributions Expense	571				6	0	00						
Miscellaneous Expense	592			1	1	2	00						
		20	3	5	8		00	20	3	5	8		00

Jim's transactions for the month of June are as follows:

June 1 Paid rent, $300.

2 Performed delivery service, received $100 cash, $200 on account.

4 Paid cash for newspaper advertising, $15.

6 Bought office supplies on account, $180.

7 Received cash for delivery services rendered, $260.

9 Paid cash on account (truck payment), $200.

10 Bought a copier (office equipment)—$100 cash and $600 on account.

11 Paid cash to the Red Cross (contributions), $20.

12 Received cash for delivery services rendered, $380.

June 13 Received cash on account for services previously rendered, $100.
     15 Paid cash to a part-time worker, $200.
     16 Paid electricity bill, $36.
     18 Paid telephone bill, $46.
     19 Received cash on account for services previously rendered, $100.
     20 Jim Andrews withdrew cash for personal use, $200.
     21 Paid cash for gas and oil, $32.
     22 Paid cash on account (for office supplies), $40.
     24 Received cash for services rendered, $340.
     26 Paid cash for a magazine subscription (miscellaneous), $15.
     27 Received cash for services rendered, $180.
     27 Received cash on account, $100.
     29 Paid cash for gasoline, $24.
     30 Paid cash to a part-time worker, $200.

Required

1. Journalize the transactions for June in a two-column general journal.
2. Set up four-column general ledger accounts, entering the balances as of June 1. Post the entries from the general journal and keep running account balances.
3. Prepare a trial balance.
4. Prepare an income statement and a statement of owner's equity for the four months ended June 30.
5. Prepare a balance sheet as of June 30.

PROBLEM 4A2

Journalizing and Posting Transactions

 ◄EPS►

3/4 Annette Creighton is opening a consulting business. She will rent a small office space and pay a part-time worker to answer the telephone. Her chart of accounts is as follows:

Assets		Revenue	
101	Cash	411	Consulting Fees
111	Office Supplies		
121	Office Equipment	Expenses	
		511	Rent Expense
Liabilities		522	Salary Expense
211	Accounts Payable	524	Telephone Expense
		531	Electricity Expense
Owner's Equity		533	Transportation Expense
311	Annette Creighton, Capital	542	Advertising Expense
312	Annette Creighton, Drawing	568	Miscellaneous Expense

Annette's transactions for the first month of business are as follows:

Jan.   1 Invested $10,000 cash in the business.
     1 Paid rent, $500.
     2 Bought office supplies on account, $300.
     4 Bought office equipment on account, $1,500.
     6 Received $580 for services rendered.
     7 Paid telephone bill, $42.
     8 Paid electricity bill, $38.
   10 Received $360 for services rendered.
   12 Paid $50 on account.
   13 Paid $150 car payment (transportation expense).
   15 Paid $360 to part-time worker.
   17 Received $420 for services rendered.
   18 Withdrew $100 for personal use.
   20 Paid $26 to the newspaper for an ad.
   22 Paid $35 for gas and oil.
   24 Paid $28 for books for consulting practices (miscellaneous).
   25 Received $320 for services rendered.
   27 Paid $150 on account (for office equipment purchased).
   29 Paid $360 to part-time worker.
   30 Received $180 for services rendered.

Required
1. Journalize the transactions for January in a two-column general journal.
2. Set up four-column general ledger accounts from the chart of accounts and post the transactions from the general journal. Keep running account balances.
3. Prepare a trial balance.
4. Prepare an income statement and a statement of owner's equity for the month of January, and a balance sheet as of January 31, 19--.

PROBLEM 4A3

Financial Statements

The trial balance on page 116 represents balances in accounts at the end of a three-month period.

Required
Prepare an income statement and a statement of owner's equity for the three months ended March 31, 19--, and a balance sheet as of March 31, 19--.

ACCOUNT TITLE	ACCOUNT NO.	DEBIT BALANCE	CREDIT BALANCE
		Jones Repair Shop **Trial Balance** **March 31, 19--**	
Cash	101	3 8 2 6 00	
Accounts Receivable	111	2 1 4 6 00	
Office Supplies	121	3 8 2 00	
Repair Equipment	131	1 8 5 0 00	
Accounts Payable	211		1 3 2 6 00
B. Jones, Capital	311		4 5 0 5 00
B. Jones, Drawing	312	6 0 0 00	
Repair Fees	411		4 8 2 2 00
Rent Expense	511	7 5 0 00	
Salary Expense	523	6 6 0 00	
Electricity Expense	552	1 2 2 00	
Telephone Expense	561	8 2 00	
Advertising Expense	572	9 1 00	
Contributions Expense	588	4 0 00	
Miscellaneous Expense	593	1 0 4 00	
		10 6 5 3 00	10 6 5 3 00

SERIES B

EXERCISES

EXERCISE 4B1

Source Documents

2 What type of information is found on each of the following source documents?

1. Cash register tape
2. Sales ticket (issued to customer)
3. Purchase invoice (received from supplier or vendor)
4. Check stub

EXERCISE 4B2

General Journal Entries

3 For each of the following transactions, list the account to be debited and the account to be credited in the general journal.

1. Invested cash in the business, $1,000.
2. Performed a service on account, $200.
3. Bought office equipment on account, $500.
4. Received cash on account for services previously rendered, $200.
5. Made a payment on account, $100.

3 Set up T accounts for each general ledger account needed for Exercise 4B2 and post debits and credits to the accounts. Foot the accounts and enter the balances. Prove that total debits equal total credits.

3 Bill Jacobs opened a bicycle repair shop. Journalize the following transactions that occurred during the month of October of the current year. Use a two-column general journal.

Oct. 1 Invested cash in the business, $15,000.
      2 Paid shop rental for the month, $300.
      3 Bought bicycle parts on account, $2,000.
      5 Bought office supplies on account, $250.
      8 Paid cash for telephone bill, $38.
      9 Received cash for services, $140.
     11 Paid cash for a sports magazine subscription (miscellaneous), $15.
     12 Paid cash on account (for parts previously purchased), $100.
     14 Paid cash to part-time employee, $300.
     15 Received cash for services, $350.
     16 Paid cash for electricity bill, $48.
     19 Received cash for services, $250.
     23 Withdrew cash for personal use, $50.
     25 Paid cash on account (for office supplies previously purchased), $50.
     29 Paid cash to part-time employee, $300.

4 Set up four-column general ledger accounts using the following chart of accounts. Post the transactions from Exercise 4B4 to the general ledger accounts and prepare a trial balance.

Chart of Accounts

Assets		Revenue	
111	Cash	411	Repair Fees
121	Office Supplies		
131	Bicycle Parts	Expenses	
		511	Rent Expense
Liabilities		521	Salary Expense
211	Accounts Payable	531	Telephone Expense
		541	Utilities Expense
Owner's Equity		551	Miscellaneous Expense
311	Bill Jacobs, Capital		
312	Bill Jacobs, Drawing		

From the information in Exercises 4B4 and 4B5, prepare an income statement, a statement of owner's equity, and a balance sheet.

From the following trial balance, prepare an income statement, a statement of owner's equity, and a balance sheet.

<table>
<tr><td colspan="5" align="center">**AT's Speaker's Bureau**
Trial Balance
March 31, 19--</td></tr>
<tr><td align="center">ACCOUNT TITLE</td><td align="center">ACCOUNT NO.</td><td align="center">DEBIT BALANCE</td><td align="center">CREDIT BALANCE</td></tr>
<tr><td>Cash</td><td>101</td><td>6 6 0 0 00</td><td></td></tr>
<tr><td>Accounts Receivable</td><td>111</td><td>2 8 0 0 00</td><td></td></tr>
<tr><td>Office Supplies</td><td>121</td><td>1 0 0 0 00</td><td></td></tr>
<tr><td>Office Equipment</td><td>131</td><td>1 5 0 0 00</td><td></td></tr>
<tr><td>Accounts Payable</td><td>211</td><td></td><td>3 0 0 0 00</td></tr>
<tr><td>AT Speaker, Capital</td><td>311</td><td></td><td>6 0 9 8 00</td></tr>
<tr><td>AT Speaker, Drawing</td><td>312</td><td>8 0 0 00</td><td></td></tr>
<tr><td>Speaking Fees</td><td>411</td><td></td><td>4 8 0 0 00</td></tr>
<tr><td>Rent Expense</td><td>511</td><td>2 0 0 00</td><td></td></tr>
<tr><td>Telephone Expense</td><td>521</td><td>3 5 00</td><td></td></tr>
<tr><td>Salary Expense</td><td>531</td><td>4 0 0 00</td><td></td></tr>
<tr><td>Utilities Expense</td><td>541</td><td>8 8 00</td><td></td></tr>
<tr><td>Travel Expense</td><td>551</td><td>4 5 0 00</td><td></td></tr>
<tr><td>Miscellaneous Expense</td><td>561</td><td>2 5 00</td><td></td></tr>
<tr><td></td><td></td><td>13 8 9 8 00</td><td>13 8 9 8 00</td></tr>
</table>

EXERCISE 4B8

Finding and Correcting Errors

5 Mary Smith purchased $350 worth of office equipment on account. The following entry was recorded on April 6. Find the error(s) and correct it (them), using the ruling method.

	19--						
9	Apr.	6	Office Supplies		5 3 0 00		9
10			Cash			5 3 0 00	10
11			Purchased office equipment.				11

Later that month, after the transactions had been posted, Mary discovered the following entry contains an error. When her customer received services, Cash was debited, but no cash was received. Correct the error in the journal, using the correcting entry method. Accounts Receivable is asset account no. 121.

	19--						
28	Apr.	2	Cash	111	3 0 0 00		28
29			Service Fees	411		3 0 0 00	29
30			Fees earned.				30

PROBLEMS

3 Ann Tailor owns a suit tailoring shop. She opened business in September. She rents a small work space and has an assistant to receive job orders and process claim tickets. Her trial balance shows her account balances for the first two months of business (September and October).

Ann Tailor Trial Balance October 31, 19--			
ACCOUNT TITLE	ACCOUNT NO.	DEBIT BALANCE	CREDIT BALANCE
Cash	101	6 2 1 1 00	
Accounts Receivable	111	4 8 4 00	
Tailoring Supplies	121	1 0 0 0 00	
Tailoring Equipment	131	3 8 0 0 00	
Accounts Payable	211		4 1 2 5 00
Ann Tailor, Capital	311		6 1 3 0 00
Ann Tailor, Drawing	312	8 0 0 00	
Tailoring Fees	411		3 6 0 0 00
Rent Expense	511	6 0 0 00	
Salary Expense	522	8 0 0 00	
Telephone Expense	533	6 0 00	
Electricity Expense	555	4 4 00	
Advertising Expense	566	3 4 00	
Miscellaneous Expense	588	2 2 00	
		13 8 5 5 00	13 8 5 5 00

Ann's transactions for November are as follows:

Nov.   1 Paid rent, $300.
        2 Bought tailoring supplies on account, $150.
        3 Bought a new button hole machine on account, $300.
        5 First week's revenue: $100 cash, $300 on account.
        8 Paid $13 for newspaper advertising.
        9 Paid telephone bill, $28.
     10 Paid electric bill, $21.
     11 Received $200 on account from customers.
     12 Second week's revenue: $200 cash, $250 on account.
     15 Paid part-time worker, $400.
     16 Paid $100 on account (previously owed).
     17 Paid $12 for magazine subscription (miscellaneous).
     19 Third week's revenue: $300 cash, $150 on account.

Nov. 23 Received $300 on account from customers.
      24 Paid $13 for newspaper advertising.
      26 Paid $12 for snacks (miscellaneous).
      27 Fourth week's revenue: $200 cash, $400 on account.
      30 Received $400 on account from customers.

Required

1. Journalize the transactions for November in a two-column general journal.
2. Set up four-column general ledger accounts, entering the balances as of October 31, 19--. Post the entries from the general journal and keep running account balances.
3. Prepare a trial balance.
4. Prepare an income statement and a statement of owner's equity for the three months ended November 30, 19--.
5. Prepare a balance sheet as of November 30, 19--.

PROBLEM 4B2

Journalizing Transactions and Posting Entries

◀**EPS**▶

3/4 Don Briggs is opening an appraisal business. He will rent office space and have a part-time secretary to answer the telephone and make appraisal appointments. His chart of accounts is as follows:

Assets		Revenue	
111	Cash	411	Appraisal Fees
122	Accounts Receivable		
133	Office Supplies	Expenses	
146	Office Equipment	512	Rent Expense
		532	Advertising Expense
Liabilities		544	Telephone Expense
211	Accounts Payable	555	Electricity Expense
		562	Salary Expense
Owner's Equity		577	Transportation Expense
311	Don Briggs, Capital	592	Miscellaneous Expense
312	Don Briggs, Drawing		

Don's transactions for the first month of business are as follows:

May   1 Invested $5,000 in the business.
      2 Paid rent, $500.
      3 Bought office supplies, $100.
      4 Bought office equipment on account, $2,000.
      5 Received cash for services rendered, $280.
      8 Paid telephone bill, $38.
      9 Paid electricity bill, $42.
      10 Received cash for services rendered, $310.
      13 Paid part-time salary, $500.
      14 Paid $200 car payment.
      15 Paid $30 for advertising in the newspaper.
      18 Received $620 for services rendered.
      19 Paid $22 for gasoline.

May   21 Withdrew $50 for personal use.
        23 Paid $200 on account (for office equipment purchased earlier).
        24 Earned $500 fee, which will be paid in a week.
        26 Paid $30 for advertising in the newspaper.
        27 Paid $15 for local softball team sponsorship (Miscellaneous Expense).
        28 Paid part-time salary, $500.
        29 Received cash on account, $250.
        30 Received cash for services rendered, $280.
        31 Paid $13 for gasoline.

Required
1. Journalize the transactions for May in a two-column general journal.
2. Set up four-column general ledger accounts from the chart of accounts and post the transactions from the general journal. Keep running account balances.
3. Prepare a trial balance, income statement, statement of owner's equity, and balance sheet.

PROBLEM 4B3

Financial Statements

3 The following trial balance represents accounts at the end of a four-month period.

J. M. Jackson
Trial Balance
April 30, 19--

ACCOUNT TITLE	ACCOUNT NO.	DEBIT BALANCE	CREDIT BALANCE
Cash	101	5 8 2 0 00	
Accounts Receivable	111	2 4 1 8 00	
Office Supplies	121	3 2 4 00	
Office Equipment	131	2 1 4 4 00	
Accounts Payable	211		1 4 8 6 00
J. M. Jackson, Capital	311		6 0 0 0 00
J. M. Jackson, Drawing	312	1 2 0 0 00	
Fees	411		7 0 8 9 00
Rent Expense	511	1 0 0 0 00	
Salary Expense	523	1 0 0 0 00	
Telephone Expense	543	1 2 2 00	
Electricity Expense	554	1 4 3 00	
Advertising Expense	566	2 1 4 00	
Contributions Expense	579	9 0 00	
Miscellaneous Expense	591	1 0 0 00	
		14 5 7 5 00	14 5 7 5 00

Required

Prepare an income statement and a statement of owner's equity for the four months ended April 30, and a balance sheet as of April 30.

MASTERY PROBLEM

Barry Bird opened a summer basketball camp for children. Campers typically register for one week in June or July, arriving on Sunday and returning home the following Saturday. College players serve as cabin counselors and assist the local college and high school coaches who run the practice sessions. The registration fee includes room and board as well as basketball instruction. Barry Bird developed the following chart of accounts for his service business.

Assets			Revenue	
111	Cash		411	Registration Fees
152	Office Supplies			
154	Food Supplies		Expenses	
183	Basketball Facilities		542	Wage Expense
			545	Telephone Expense
Liabilities			549	Utility Expense
218	Accounts Payable		564	Postage Expense

Owner's Equity	
311	Barry Bird, Capital
312	Barry Bird, Drawing

The following transactions took place during the month of June.

June   1 Bird invested cash in a bank as an initial investment, $10,000.
2 Collected registration fees, $15,000.
2 Rogers Construction completed work on a new basketball court which cost $12,000. The estimated life of the facility is 5 years at which time the court will have to be resurfaced and the basketball standards, backboards and hoops will have to be replaced. Arrangements were made to pay the bill in July.
3 Bought food supplies from Acme Super Market on account, $5,000.
5 Bought office supplies on account from Gordon Office Supplies, $300.
7 Collected registration fees, $16,200.
10 Bought food supplies from Acme Super Market on account, $6,200.
10 Paid wages to camp counselors, $500.

June 14 Collected registration fees, $13,500.
     16 Bought food supplies from Acme Super Market on account, $4,000.
     17 Paid wages to camp counselors, $500.
     18 Paid postage, $85.
     21 Collected registration fees, $15,200.
     24 Bought food supplies from Acme Super Market on account for $5,500.
     24 Paid wages to camp counselors, $500.
     28 Collected registration fees, $14,000.
     30 Bought food supplies from Acme Super Market on account, $6,000.
     30 Paid wages to camp counselors, $500.
     30 Paid $26,700 to Acme Super Markets on account.
     30 Paid utility bill, $500.
     30 Paid phone bill, $120.
     30 Barry Bird withdrew cash for personal use, $2,000.

Required
1. Enter the above transactions in a general journal.
2. Post the entries to the general ledger.
3. Prepare a trial balance.

Chapter 4 Demonstration Problem

Chapter 4 contains several problems that you can work with the general ledger program called the Electronic Problem Solver. The EPS icons in the margin beside the demonstration problem and Problems 4A2 and 4B2 indicate that the opening balances for these problems have been stored on your disk.

You should have a formatted data disk to store your problems. Refer to your DOS manual for instructions on formatting a disk. You may also wish to read additional information in your DOS manual about the directories and path names on a disk.

The following instructions show you how to complete the Chapter 4 demonstration problem. Refer to Appendix A for additional information on the Electronic Problem Solver.

STEP 1 Start up your Electronic Problem Solver software using the instructions in Appendix A. (Enter ACCOUNT1 to load the software.)

STEP 2 When the first screen appears, press the Right Arrow key to move to the No option and press the Enter key to indicate that you do not want to read about the software. (Figure AC4-1)

STEP 3 If you are using 5 1/4″ disks, place Disk 2 in the disk drive.

STEP 4 Strike the Alt key to activate the pull-down menus.

STEP 5 Press Enter with the File command highlighted to pull down the File menu. (Figure AC4-2)

FIGURE AC4-1 **Opening Screen**

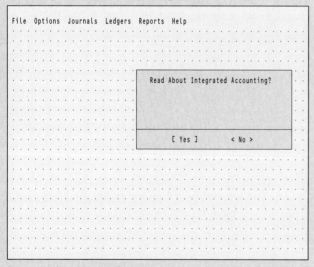

FIGURE AC4-2 **File Menu**

STEP 6   Use the Down Arrow key to highlight the Open Accounting File option and press the Enter key.

STEP 7   Make certain the Path field indicates the drive and directory of your disk. If necessary, change the Path field. For example, if your disk is in Drive A, the Path field should say **A:**. If you are using a 5 1/4" disk and Disk 2 is in Drive B, the Path field should say **B:**. If you change the Path, make certain to enter the colon (:) after the Drive name.

STEP 8   Strike the End key to activate the Directory button and press Enter to display the file directory on your disk. (Figure AC4-3)

STEP 9   Move the Down Arrow key until file name D-4 is highlighted and press Enter. Press Enter again to load the demonstration problem into memory.

STEP 10   Press the Alt key to activate the menu and press the Right Arrow key to highlight the Options menu. Press Enter to pull down the Options menu.

STEP 11   Choose the General Information option and make certain that the correct problem has been loaded. (Figure AC4-4)

FIGURE AC4-3 **Directory of Opening Balances**   FIGURE AC4-4 **General Information Screen**

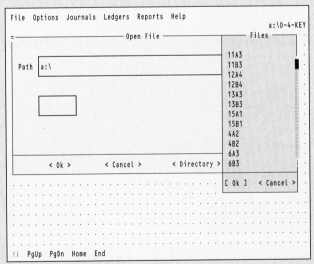

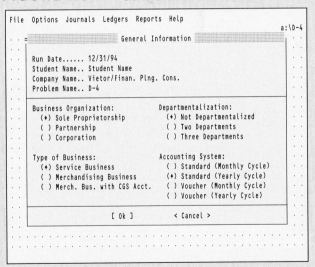

STEP 12   Enter a date of 12/31/9- (current year) in the Run Date field. (Use the Backspace key or the Left Arrow key to move the cursor.)

STEP 13   Enter your name in the Student Name field. (Notice that this problem is for a sole proprietorship and a service business. Do not change any of the buttons. Later, if you need to change the buttons, press the Space Bar beside the field that you wish to indicate. Appendix A tells you about these options.)

STEP 14   After you enter the date and your name, press the Tab key to move through the fields until you reach the Ok button. Press Enter on the Ok button to record your data.
Hint: After you enter the date and your name, you may press the Ctrl key and the Enter key simultaneously to record the data.

STEP 15   The General Journal data entry screen should automatically appear. (If it is not displayed, choose the General Journal option from the Journals menu.)

STEP 16   Enter the transaction for December 1 in the general journal. (Figure AC4-5)

      a. Enter the day and the month of the transaction in the Date field.
      b. Press the Tab key to move to the Reference field and leave the Reference field blank.
      c. Press the Tab key to move to the Acct. No. field.
      d. Enter the account number for Cash.
           Hint: Press the F1 key to display a Chart of Accounts window. Notice that Cash is Account Number 111. If you press Enter on the highlighted account number in the Chart of Accounts window, that account number will be placed in the Acct. No. field.
      e. Press the Tab key or Enter to move to the Debit field and enter the debit amount (20000.00 without the comma) in the Debit field.
      f. Enter the Capital account number and the credit amount.
      g. If you need to change the information on this screen, press the Shift key and the Tab key simultaneously to move to the previous fields and change the data.

STEP 17   Press the Ctrl key and the Enter key simultaneously to display the posting summary. (Figure AC4-6)

FIGURE AC4-5 **General Journal Data Entry**

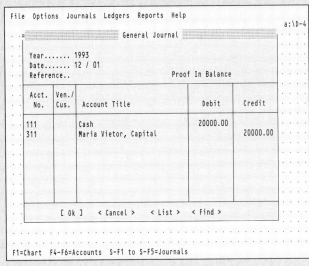

```
File  Options  Journals  Ledgers  Reports  Help
                                                        a:\D-4
 . =                       General Journal                    . . . .
 . |                                                      |    . . . .
 . | Year....... 1993                                     |    . . . .
 . | Date....... 12 / 01                                  |    . . . .
 . | Reference..                    Proof In Balance      |    . . . .
 . |                                                      |    . . . .
 . | Acct. | Ven./ |                  |          |         |    . . . .
 . | No.   | Cus.  | Account Title    | Debit    | Credit |    . . . .
 . |       |       |                  |          |         |    . . . .
 . | 111   |       | Cash             | 20000.00 |         |    . . . .
 . |       |       | Maria Vietor, Capital |     | 20000.00|   . . . .
 . |                                                      |    . . . .
 . |                                                      |    . . . .
 . |                                                      |    . . . .
 . |                                                      |    . . . .
 . |         [ Ok ]    < Cancel >    < List >   < Find >  |    . . . .
 . |                                                      |    . . . .
 . . . . . . . . . . . . . . . . . . . . . . . . . . . . . . . . . . .
F1=Chart  F4-F6=Accounts  S-F1 to S-F5=Journals
```

FIGURE AC4-6 **Posting Summary**

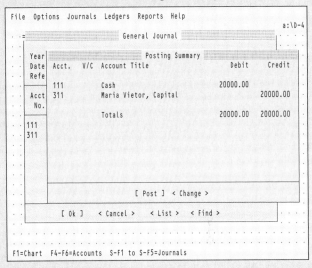

```
File  Options  Journals  Ledgers  Reports  Help
                                                        a:\D-4
 . =                       General Journal                    . . . .
 . | Year |                Posting Summary              |    . . . .
 . | Date | Acct.  V/C  Account Title    Debit   Credit |    . . . .
 . | Refe |                                             |    . . . .
 . |      | 111         Cash           20000.00         |    . . . .
 . | Acct | 311         Maria Vietor, Capital   20000.00|    . . . .
 . | No.  |                                             |    . . . .
 . |      |             Totals        20000.00 20000.00 |    . . . .
 . | 111  |                                             |    . . . .
 . | 311  |                                             |    . . . .
 . |      |                                             |    . . . .
 . |             [ Post ]   < Change >                  |    . . . .
 . |                                                     |    . . . .
 . |         [ Ok ]    < Cancel >    < List >   < Find > |    . . . .
 . . . . . . . . . . . . . . . . . . . . . . . . . . . . . . . . . . .
F1=Chart  F4-F6=Accounts  S-F1 to S-F5=Journals
```

STEP 18   Press the Enter key when the Post button is active to post the December 1 transaction. If you need to change the transaction, move the Right Arrow key to activate the Change button and press Enter.

STEP 19   Enter and post the remaining transactions for the month.

STEP 20   After you have entered all transactions, press the Alt key and pull down the Report menu either by entering the letter R or by using the arrow keys to highlight Reports and then pressing Enter.

STEP 21   Choose the Journals option.

STEP 22   Move to the field beside the General Journal option. (Figure AC4-7)

STEP 23   Press the Space Bar to place an X in the General Journal. Press Ctrl and Enter.

STEP 24   The Selection Options should display a date range of 12/01/-- to 12/31/-- to indicate the default range (all transactions). Change the date range if necessary. (Figure AC4-8)

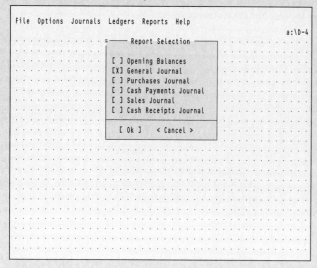

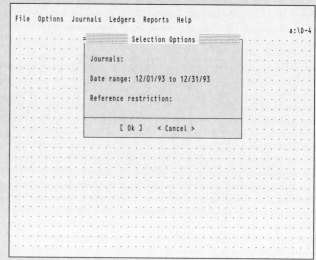

STEP 25   Press Ctrl and Enter. The general journal transactions that you entered will be displayed. (Figure AC4-9)

STEP 26   If you need to correct your transactions, refer to the section in Appendix A titled Corrections to Journal Entries.

STEP 27   Press the Alt key and the R key (or use the arrow keys) to pull down the Reports Menu. (Figure AC4-10)

FIGURE AC4-9 **General Journal Display**

FIGURE AC4-10 **Reports Menu**

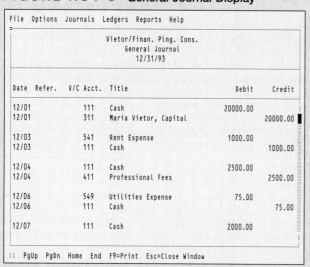

STEP 28 Move the Down Arrow key to highlight the Ledgers command.

STEP 29 Choose the Trial Balance option (press the Space Bar) and display the trial balance. (Figure AC4-11)

STEP 30 Pull down the File menu and choose the Save As command. (Figure AC4-12)

FIGURE AC4-11 **Trial Balance Display**

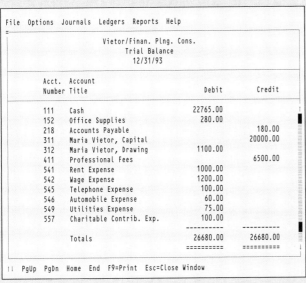

FIGURE AC4-12 **Save File Prompt**

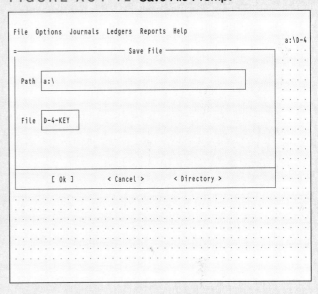

STEP 31 Save your solution on a data disk under a file name such as XXXD-4 (XXX = your initials).

STEP 32 Choose the Quit option from the File menu to end your session.

LEARNING OBJECTIVES

*A*djusting Entries and the Work Sheet

Now that you know how to journalize business transactions, post to the ledger, and prepare a trial balance, it is time to learn how to make end-of-period adjustments to the accounts listed in the trial balance. This chapter explains the need for adjustments and illustrates how they are made using a work sheet.

1

Prepare end-of-period adjustments.

Matching revenues earned with the expenses incurred during the period offers the best measure of net income.

END-OF-PERIOD ADJUSTMENTS

Throughout the accounting period, business transactions are entered in the accounting system. During the accounting period, other changes occur that affect the firm's financial condition. For example, equipment is wearing out, prepaid insurance and supplies are being used up, and employees are earning wages that have not yet been paid.

The **matching concept** in accounting requires the matching of revenues earned during an accounting period with the expenses incurred to produce the revenues. This approach offers the best measure of net income. The income statement reports earnings for a specific period of time and the balance sheet reports the assets, liabilities, and owner's equity on a specific date. Thus, before financial statements are prepared, the accounts must be brought up to date. This may require adjusting some of the accounts listed in the trial balance. Figure 5-1 lists reasons to adjust the trial balance.

FIGURE 5-1   **Reasons to Adjust the Trial Balance**

REASONS TO ADJUST THE TRIAL BALANCE
1. To report all revenues earned during the accounting period.
2. To report all expenses incurred to produce the revenues during the accounting period.
3. To accurately report the assets on the balance sheet date. Some may have been used up during the accounting period.
4. To accurately report the liabilities on the balance sheet date. Expenses may have been incurred but not yet paid.

Adjustments are made and financial statements are prepared at the end of a period called a **fiscal period.** Businesses choose different periods in which to summarize and report transactions. Some businesses prepare financial statements at the end of a 12-month period called a **fiscal year.** The fiscal year does not need to be the same as the calendar year. Some businesses schedule the fiscal year-end for a time when business is slow. In this chapter, we continue the illustration of Jessie Jane's Campus Delivery Service and will prepare adjustments at the end of the first month of operations. We will focus on the following accounts: Supplies, Prepaid Insurance, Delivery Equipment, and Wage Expense.

Supplies

During June, Jane purchased supplies consisting of paper, pens, and delivery envelopes for $80. *Since these supplies were expected to provide future benefits, Supplies, an asset, was debited at the time of the purchase.* No other entries were made to the supplies account during June. As reported on the trial balance in figure 5-2, the $80 balance remains in the supplies account at the end of the month.

FIGURE 5-2 **Trial Balance**

ACCOUNT TITLE	ACCOUNT NO.	DEBIT BALANCE	CREDIT BALANCE
Jessie Jane's Campus Delivery Service			
Trial Balance			
June 30, 19--			
Cash	111	3 7 0 00	
Accounts Receivable	131	5 0 0 00	
Supplies	151	8 0 00	
Prepaid Insurance	155	2 0 0 00	
Delivery Equipment	185	3 6 0 0 00	
Accounts Payable	218		1 8 0 0 00
Jessica Jane, Capital	311		2 0 0 0 00
Jessica Jane, Drawing	312	1 5 0 00	
Delivery Fees	411		2 0 0 0 00
Rent Expense	541	2 0 0 00	
Wage Expense	542	6 5 0 00	
Telephone Expense	545	5 0 00	
		5 8 0 0 00	5 8 0 0 00

Since it is not practical to make a journal entry for supplies expense each time an envelope is used, one adjusting entry is made at the end of the accounting period.

As supplies are used up, an expense is incurred. It is not practical, however, to make a journal entry to recognize this expense and the reduction in the supplies account every time someone uses an envelope. It is more efficient to wait until the end of the accounting period to make one adjusting entry to reflect the expense incurred for the use of supplies for the entire month.

At the end of the month, an inventory, or physical count, of the remaining supplies is taken. We learn that supplies that cost $20 were still unused at the end of June. Since Jane bought supplies costing $80, and only $20 worth remain, supplies costing $60 have been used up ($80 − $20 = $60). Thus, Supplies Expense for the month is $60. (Trial balance is abbreviated as TB in the illustrations.)

Assets		=	Liabilities		+	Owner's Equity		
Dr.	Cr.		Dr.	Cr.			Dr.	Cr.
+	−		−	+			−	+

Supplies

(TB)	80	
		(Adj.) 60
(Bal.)	20	

Drawing		Expenses		Revenue	
Dr.	Cr.	Dr.	Cr.	Dr.	Cr.
+	−	+	−	−	+

Supplies Expense

(Adj.) 60	

> **Almost all adjusting entries affect *both* the income statement and the balance sheet.**

Since $60 worth of supplies have been used up, Supplies Expense is debited and Supplies (asset) is credited for $60. Thus, supplies with a cost of $20 will be reported as an asset on the balance sheet and supplies expense of $60 will be reported on the income statement. Note that the adjusting entry affected an income statement account and a balance sheet account. This is true with almost all adjusting entries.

Balance Sheet June 30, 19--			Income Statement For Month Ended June 30, 19--		
Assets:			Expenses:		
Supplies .... $20 (unused supplies)			Supplies expense .... $60 (supplies used during June)		
	Supplies			Supplies Expense	
Before	80	Purchased during month		80	Purchased during month
Adj.	(60)	Supplies used		(20)	Supplies remaining
After	20	Supplies remaining		60	Supplies used

Prepaid Insurance

On June 18th Jane paid $200 for an eight-month liability insurance policy with coverage beginning on June 1. *Prepaid Insurance, an asset, was debited because the insurance policy is expected to provide future benefits.* The $200 balance is reported on the trial balance in figure 5-2. As the insurance policy expires with the passage of time, the asset should be reduced and an expense recognized.

> **The $200 premium covers an eight month period. The cost for June is $200 ÷ 8 = $25.**

Since the $200 premium covers an eight-month period, the cost of the expired coverage for the month of June is $25 ($200 ÷ 8 months). The adjusting entry is to debit Insurance Expense for $25 and to credit Prepaid Insurance for $25. The unexpired portion of the insurance premium will be reported on the balance sheet as Prepaid Insurance of $175 and Insurance Expense of $25 will be reported on the income statement.

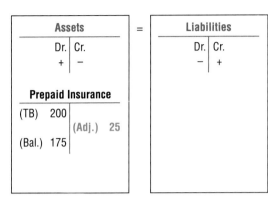

Balance Sheet June 30, 19--		Income Statement For Month Ended June 30, 19--	
Assets:		Expenses:	
Prepaid insurance $175		Insurance expense $25	
(unexpired premium)		(insurance expired during June)	
Prepaid Insurance		Insurance Expense	
Before	200 Premiums paid	200 Premiums paid	
Adj.	(25) Prepaid ins. expired	(175) Prepaid ins. remaining	
After	175 Prepaid ins. remaining	25 Prepaid ins. expired	

Wage Expense

Jane paid her part-time employees $650 on June 27th. Since then, they have earned an additional $50, but have not yet been paid. The additional wage expense must be recognized.

Since the employees have not been paid, Wages Payable, a liability, should be established. Thus, Wage Expense is debited and Wages Payable is credited for $50. Note that Wage Expense of $700 is reported on the income statement and Wages Payable of $50 is reported on the balance sheet.

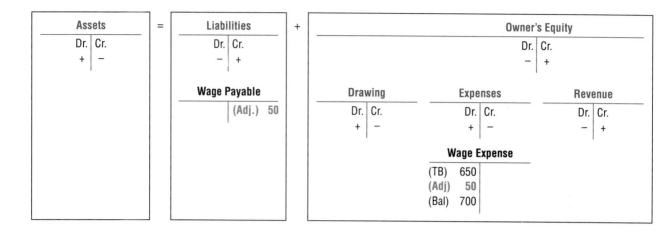

Balance Sheet June 30, 19--		Income Statement For Month Ended June 30, 19--	
Liabilities: Wages payable .... $50 (owed to employees)		Expenses: Wage expense .... $700 (incurred for June)	
	Wages Payable		Wage Expense
700	Total wage expense incurred	Before 650	Wages paid
(650)	Paid to employees	Adj. (50)	Wages owed
50	Owed to employees	After 700	Total expense

Depreciation Expense

During the month of June, Jane purchased three motor scooters. Since the scooters will provide future benefits, they were recorded as assets in the Delivery Equipment account. Under the **historical cost principle,** assets are recorded at their actual cost, in this case $3,600. This cost remains on the books until the asset is disposed of. No adjustments are made for changes in the market value of the asset.

The period of time that an asset is expected to help produce revenues is called its **useful life.** The asset's useful life expires as a result of wear and tear or because it no longer satisfies the needs of the business. As this happens, depreciation expense should be recognized and the value of the asset should be reduced. **Depreciation** provides a method of *matching* the cost of the assets against the revenues the scooters will help produce over their useful lives. There are many depreciation methods. In our example we will use the **straight-line method.**

Let's assume that Jane's motor scooters have useful lives of three years and will have no **salvage** or trade-in value at the end of that time period. Let's also assume that a full month's depreciation is recognized in the month in which an asset is purchased. The cost of the scooters that is subject to depreciation, called **depreciable cost,** is $3,600. The depreciable cost is spread over 36 months (3 years × 12 months). Thus, the straight line depreciation expense for the month of June is $100 ($3,600 ÷ 36 months).

Straight-Line Depreciation

Original Cost − Salvage Value = Depreciable Cost

$$\frac{\text{Depreciable Cost}}{\text{Estimated Useful Life}} = \frac{\$3,600}{36 \text{ months}} = \$100 \text{ per month}$$

Depreciable assets provide benefits over a longer period of time than supplies or prepaid insurance. Therefore, rather than directly crediting the asset to show that it has been used up, a *contra-asset* account is used.

When we made adjustments for supplies and prepaid insurance, the asset accounts were credited to show that they had been used up. Assets expected to provide benefits over a longer period of time, called **plant assets,** require a different approach. A record of the original cost and the amount of depreciation taken since the asset was acquired is maintained. By comparing the two amounts, the reader can estimate the relative age of the asset. Thus, instead of crediting Delivery Equipment for the amount of depreciation, a contra-asset account, Accumulated Depreciation-Delivery Equipment, is credited. A **contra-asset** has a credit balance and is deducted from the related asset account on the balance sheet.

The appropriate adjusting entry consists of a debit to Depreciation Expense—Delivery Equipment and a credit to Accumulated Depreciation—Delivery Equipment. Note the position of the Accumulated Depreciation account in the accounting equation shown below. It is shown in the asset section, directly beneath Delivery Equipment. Contra-asset accounts should always be shown along with the related asset account. Therefore, Delivery Equipment and Accumulated Depreciation—Delivery Equipment are shown together.

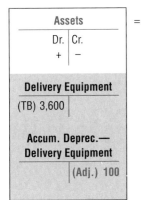
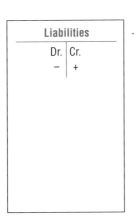

Balance Sheet June 30, 19--			Income Statement For Month Ended June 30, 19--	
Assets:			Expenses:	
Delivery equipment	$3,600		Depreciation expense	$100
Less: accum. depreciation	(100)	$3,500 (Book Value)	(Expired cost for June)	

Cost
− Accum. Dep.
_____

Book Value

The same concept is used on the balance sheet. Note that Accumulated Depreciation is reported immediately beneath the Delivery Equipment account as a deduction. The difference between these accounts is known as the **book value,** or **undepreciated cost,** of the Delivery Equipment. Book value simply means the value carried on the books or in the accounting records. It does *not* represent the market value, or selling price, of the asset.

If no delivery equipment is bought or sold during the next month, the same adjusting entry would be made at the end of July. If an income statement for the month of July and a balance sheet as of July 31 were prepared, the following would be reported for the delivery equipment.

Balance Sheet July 31, 19--			Income Statement For Month Ended July 31, 19--	
Assets:			Expenses:	
Delivery equipment	$3,600		Depreciation expense	$100
Less: accumulated depreciation	(200)	$3,400 (Book Value)	(Expired cost for July)	

Note that the cost ($3,600) remains unchanged, but that the accumulated depreciation has increased to $200. This represents *the depreciation that has accumulated* since the delivery equipment was purchased ($100 in June and $100 in July). Depreciation Expense for July is $100, the same as reported for June. Depreciation expense is reported for a specific time period.

Expanded Chart of Accounts

Several new accounts were needed to make the adjusting entries. New accounts are easily added to the chart of accounts, as shown in figure 5-3. Note the close relationship between assets and contra-assets in the numbering of the accounts. Contra-accounts carry the same number as the related asset account with a .1 suffix. For example, Delivery Equipment is account number 185 and the contra-asset account, Accumulated Depreciation: Delivery Equipment, is account number 185.1.

FIGURE 5-3 Expanded Chart of Accounts

Jessie Jane's Campus Delivery Service Chart of Accounts			
Assets	**(100–199)**	**Revenue**	**(400–499)**
111	Cash	411	Delivery Fees
131	Accounts Receivable		
151	Supplies	**Expenses**	**(500–599)**
155	Prepaid Insurance	541	Rent Expense
185	Delivery Equipment	542	Wage Expense
185.1	*Accumulated Deprec.—*	*543*	*Supplies Expense*
	Delivery Equipment	545	Telephone Expense
		547	*Depreciation Expense—*
Liabilities	**(200–299)**		*Delivery Equipment*
218	Accounts Payable	*548*	*insurance Expense*
219	*Wages Payable*		
Owner's Equity	**(300–399)**		
311	Jessica Jane, Capital		
312	Jessica Jane, Drawing		

2

Prepare a work sheet.

THE WORK SHEET

A **work sheet** pulls together all of the information needed to enter adjusting entries and prepare the financial statements. Work sheets are not financial statements and are not a formal part of the accounting system. Ordinarily, only the accountant uses a work sheet. For this reason, a work sheet is usually prepared in pencil or as a spreadsheet on a computer.

The Ten-Column Work Sheet

While a work sheet can take several forms, a common format has a column for account titles and ten amount columns grouped into five pairs. The work sheet format and the five steps in preparing the work sheet are illustrated in figure 5-4. As with financial statements, the work sheet has a heading consisting of the name of the company, name of the working paper, and the date of the accounting period just ended. The five major column headings for the work sheet are: Trial Balance, Adjustments, Adjusted Trial Balance, Income Statement, and Balance Sheet.

F I G U R E   5 - 4   **Steps in Preparing the Work Sheet**

			TRIAL BALANCE		ADJUSTMENTS		
	Name of Company **Work Sheet** **For the Month Ended June 30, 19--**						
	ACCOUNT TITLE	ACCT. NO.	DEBIT	CREDIT	DEBIT	CREDIT	
1							1
2							2
3			STEP 1:		STEP 2:		3
4			Prepare the		Prepare		4
5	(Insert Ledger		trial balance		the		5
6	Account Titles)				adjustments		6
7			Assets				7
8				Liab.			8
9				Capital			9
10			Drawing				10
11				Revenues			11
12			Expenses				12
13							13
14							14
15							15
16							16
17							17
18							18
19	(Insert additional account						19
20	titles for adjustments)						20
21							21
22							22
23							23
24							24
25							25
26							26
27							27
28							28
29							29

Preparing the Work Sheet

Let's apply the five steps required for the preparation of a work sheet to Jessie Jane's Campus Delivery Service.

STEP 1   **Prepare the trial balance.**   As shown in figure 5-5 on page 145A, the first pair of amount columns is for the trial balance. The trial balance assures

	ADJUSTED TRIAL BALANCE		INCOME STATEMENT		BALANCE SHEET		
	DEBIT	CREDIT	DEBIT	CREDIT	DEBIT	CREDIT	
1							1
2							2
3	STEP 3:			STEP 4:			3
4	Prepare the			Extend adjusted			4
5	adjusted trial balance			account balances			5
6							6
7	Assets				Assets		7
8		Liab.				Liab.	8
9		Capital				Capital	9
10	Drawing				Drawing		10
11		Revenues		Revenues			11
12	Expenses		Expenses				12
13							13
14							14
15							15
16							16
17							17
18							18
19			STEP 5:				19
20			Complete the work sheet				20
21			(1) Sum Columns				21
22			(2) Compute Net Income (Loss)				22
23							23
24							24
25							25
26			Net	Net	Net	Net	26
27			Income	Loss	Loss	Income	27
28							28
29							29

the equality of the debits and credits before the adjustment process begins. The columns should be double ruled to show that they are equal.

STEP 2   **Prepare the adjustments.**   The second pair of amount columns is used to prepare the adjusting entries. Enter the adjustments directly in these columns. When an account is debited or credited, the amount is entered on the same horizontal line as the name of the account and in the appropriate

Adjustments Debit or Credit column. Each adjusting entry made on the work sheet is identified by a small letter in parentheses.

Adjustment (a):
Supplies costing $60 were used up during June.

	Debit	Credit
Supplies Expense	60	
Supplies		60

Adjustment (b):
One month's insurance premium has expired.

	Debit	Credit
Insurance Expense	25	
Prepaid Insurance		25

Adjustment (c):
Employees earned $50 that has not yet been paid.

	Debit	Credit
Wage Expense	50	
Wages Payable		50

Adjustment (d):
Depreciation on the motor scooters is recognized.

	Debit	Credit
Depreciation Exp.—Delivery Equip.	100	
Accum. Depreciation—Delivery Equip. .		100

Supplies Expense, Insurance Expense, Wages Payable, Depreciation Expense— Delivery Equipment, and Accumulated Depreciation—Delivery Equipment must be added to the bottom of the trial balance. *Since these accounts had no balance as of June 30, they were not included in the trial balance and must be added for the adjusting entries.*

When all adjustments have been entered, each column should be totaled to assure that the debits equal the credits. Upon balancing, the columns should be double ruled.

STEP 3   **Prepare the adjusted trial balance.**   The third pair of amount columns of the work sheet is for the **adjusted trial balance.** When an account balance is not affected by entries in the Adjustments columns, the amount in the Trial Balance columns is extended directly to the Adjusted Trial Balance columns. *When an account balance is affected by an entry in the Adjustments columns, the balance to be entered in the Adjusted Trial Balance columns is increased or decreased by the amount of the adjusting entry.*

For example, in Jessie Jane's business, Supplies is listed in the Trial Balance Debit column as $80. Since the entry of $60 is in the Adjustments

Credit column, the amount extended to the Adjusted Trial Balance column is decreased to $20 ($80 − $60).

Wage Expense is listed in the Trial Balance Debit column as $650. Since $50 is in the Adjustments Debit column, the amount extended to the Adjusted Trial Balance Debit column is increased to $700 ($650 + $50).

After all extensions have been made, the Adjusted Trial Balance columns are totaled to prove the equality of the debits and the credits. Once balanced, the columns are double ruled.

STEP 4 **Extend adjusted balances to the Income Statement and Balance Sheet columns.** Each account listed in the adjusted trial balance must be extended to either the Income Statement or Balance Sheet columns. The **Income Statement columns** show the amounts that will be reported in the income statement. All revenue and expense accounts are extended to these columns.

The remaining accounts are extended to the **Balance Sheet columns.** Although called the Balance Sheet columns, these columns of the work sheet show the amounts that will be reported in the balance sheet and the statement of owner's equity. The asset and drawing accounts are extended to the Balance Sheet Debit column. The liability and owner's capital accounts are extended to the Balance Sheet Credit column.

> The Balance Sheet columns show the amounts in both the balance sheet and the statement of owner's equity.

STEP 5 **Complete the work sheet.** To complete the work sheet, first total the Income Statement columns. If the total credits (revenues) exceed the total debits (expenses), the difference represents net income. If the total debits exceed the total credits, the difference represents a net loss.

The Income Statement columns of Jane's work sheet show total credits of $2,000 and total debits of $1,135. The difference, $865, is the net income for the month of June. This amount should be added to the debit column to balance the Income Statement columns and "Net Income" should be written on the same line in the Account Title column. If the business had a net loss, the amount of the loss would be added to the Income Statement Credit column. Once balanced, the columns should be double ruled.

Finally, the Balance Sheet columns are totaled. The difference between the totals of these columns is also the amount of net income or net loss for the accounting period. If the total debits exceed the total credits, the difference is net income. If the total credits exceed the total debits, the difference is a net loss. This difference should be the same as the difference we found for the Income Statement columns.

The Balance Sheet columns of Jane's work sheet show total debits of $4,815 and total credits of $3,950. The difference of $865 represents the amount of net income for the year. This amount is added to the credit column to balance the Balance Sheet columns. If the business had a net loss, this amount would be added to the Balance Sheet Debit column. Once balanced, the columns should be double ruled.

A trick for remembering the appropriate placement of the net income and net loss is: Net Income *apart;* Net Loss *together.* Figure 5-6 illustrates this learning aid.

FIGURE 5-6 **"Net Income Apart, Net Loss Together"**

	Income Statement		Balance Sheet				Income Statement		Balance Sheet	
	Debit	Credit	Debit	Credit			Debit	Credit	Debit	Credit
	1,135	2,000	4,815	3,950			2,500	2,000	5,015	5,515
Net Income	865			865		Net Loss		500	500	
	2,000	2,000	4,815	4,815			2,500	2,500	5,515	5,515

└──── Apart ────┘   └ Together ┘

3

Describe methods for finding errors on the work sheet.

FINDING ERRORS ON THE WORK SHEET

If any of the columns on the work sheet do not balance, you must find the error before you continue. Once you are confident that the work sheet is accurate, you are ready to journalize the adjusting entries and prepare financial statements. Figure 5-7 offers tips for finding errors on the work sheet.

FIGURE 5-7 Finding Errors on the Work Sheet

TIPS FOR FINDING ERRORS ON THE WORK SHEET
1. Check the addition of all columns.
2. Check the addition and subtraction required when extending to the Adjusted Trial Balance columns.
3. Make sure the adjusted account balances have been extended to the appropriate columns.
4. See that the additional accounts needed for the adjusting entries have been extended.
5. Make sure that the net income or net loss has been added to the appropriate columns.

4

Journalize adjusting entries.

JOURNALIZING ADJUSTING ENTRIES

Remember that the work sheet simply helps the accountant organize the end-of-period work. Writing the adjustments on the work sheet has no effect on the ledger accounts. The only way to change the balance of a ledger account is to make a journal entry. Once the adjustments have been "penciled in" on the work sheet, simply copy the adjustments from the work sheet to the journal.

The adjusting entries are illustrated in figure 5-8 as they would appear in a general journal. Note that the last day of the accounting period, June 30, has been entered in the Date column and *"Adjusting Entries"* is written in the Description column prior to the first adjusting entry. No explanation is required in the Description column for individual adjusting entries.

POSTING ADJUSTING ENTRIES

5

Post adjusting entries to the general ledger.

Adjusting entries are posted to the general ledger in the same manner as all other entries, except that *"Adjusting"* is written in the Item column of the general ledger. Figure 5-8 shows the posting of the adjusting entry for supplies.

FIGURE 5-8 **Adjusting Entries and Posting the Adjusting Entry for Supplies**

GENERAL JOURNAL   PAGE 3

	DATE		DESCRIPTION	POST. REF.	DEBIT	CREDIT	
1			Adjusting Entries				1
2	19-- June	30	Supplies Expense	543	6 0 00		2
3			Supplies	151		6 0 00	3
4							4
5		30	Insurance Expense	548	2 5 00		5
6			Prepaid Insurance	155		2 5 00	6
7							7
8		30	Wage Expense	542	5 0 00		8
9			Wages Payable	219		5 0 00	9
10							10
11		30	Depreciation Exp.—Delivery Equip.	547	1 0 0 00		11
12			Accum. Depreciation—Deliv. Equip.	185.1		1 0 0 00	12

GENERAL LEDGER

ACCOUNT: SUPPLIES   ACCOUNT NO. 151

DATE		ITEM	POST. REF.	DEBIT	CREDIT	BALANCE DEBIT	BALANCE CREDIT
19-- June	16		J1	8 0 00		8 0 00	
	30	Adjusting	J3		6 0 00	2 0 00	

ACCOUNT: SUPPLIES EXPENSE   ACCOUNT NO. 543

DATE		ITEM	POST. REF.	DEBIT	CREDIT	BALANCE DEBIT	BALANCE CREDIT
19-- June	30	Adjusting	J3	6 0 00		6 0 00	

FIGURE 5 - 5   STEP 1—Prepare the Trial Balance

Jessie Jane's Campus Delivery Service
Work Sheet
For the Month Ended June 30, 19--

	ACCOUNT TITLE	TRIAL BALANCE		ADJUSTMENTS		ADJUSTED TRIAL BALANCE		INCOME STATEMENT		BALANCE SHEET		
		DEBIT	CREDIT	DEBIT	CREDIT	DEBIT	CREDIT	DEBIT	CREDIT	DEBIT	CREDIT	
1	Cash	3 7 0 00										1
2	Accounts Receivable	5 0 0 00										2
3	Supplies	8 0 00										3
4	Prepaid Insurance	2 0 0 00										4
5	Delivery Equipment	3 6 0 0 00										5
6	Accounts Payable		1 8 0 0 00									6
7	Jessica Jane, Capital		2 0 0 0 00									7
8	Jessica Jane, Drawing	1 5 0 00										8
9	Delivery Fees		2 0 0 0 00									9
10	Rent Expense	2 0 0 00										10
11	Wage Expense	6 5 0 00										11
12	Telephone Expense	5 0 00										12
13		5 8 0 0 00	5 8 0 0 00									13
14												14
15												15
16												16
17												17
18												18
19												19
20												20
21												21
22												22

STEP 1

"penciled in" on the work sheet, simply copy the adjustments from the work sheet to the journal.

The adjusting entries are illustrated in figure 5-8 as they would appear in a general journal. Note that the last day of the accounting period, June 30, has been entered in the Date column and *"Adjusting Entries"* is written in the Description column prior to the first adjusting entry. No explanation is required in the Description column for individual adjusting entries.

POSTING ADJUSTING ENTRIES

5

Post adjusting entries to the general ledger.

Adjusting entries are posted to the general ledger in the same manner as all other entries, except that *"Adjusting"* is written in the Item column of the general ledger. Figure 5-8 shows the posting of the adjusting entry for supplies.

FIGURE 5-8 **Adjusting Entries and Posting the Adjusting Entry for Supplies**

GENERAL JOURNAL PAGE 3

	DATE		DESCRIPTION	POST. REF.	DEBIT	CREDIT	
1			Adjusting Entries				1
2	19-- June	30	Supplies Expense	543	6 0 00		2
3			Supplies	151		6 0 00	3
4							4
5		30	Insurance Expense	548	2 5 00		5
6			Prepaid Insurance	155		2 5 00	6
7							7
8		30	Wage Expense	542	5 0 00		8
9			Wages Payable	219		5 0 00	9
10							10
11		30	Depreciation Exp.—Delivery Equip.	547	1 0 0 00		11
12			Accum. Depreciation—Deliv. Equip.	185.1		1 0 0 00	12

GENERAL LEDGER

ACCOUNT: SUPPLIES ACCOUNT NO. 151

DATE		ITEM	POST. REF.	DEBIT	CREDIT	BALANCE DEBIT	BALANCE CREDIT
19-- June	16		J1	8 0 00		8 0 00	
	30	Adjusting	J3		6 0 00	2 0 00	

ACCOUNT: SUPPLIES EXPENSE ACCOUNT NO. 543

DATE		ITEM	POST. REF.	DEBIT	CREDIT	BALANCE DEBIT	BALANCE CREDIT
19-- June	30	Adjusting	J3	6 0 00		6 0 00	

FIGURE 5-5 STEP 1—Prepare the Trial Balance

Jessie Jane's Campus Delivery Service
Work Sheet
For the Month Ended June 30, 19--

	ACCOUNT TITLE	TRIAL BALANCE DEBIT	TRIAL BALANCE CREDIT	ADJUSTMENTS DEBIT	ADJUSTMENTS CREDIT	ADJUSTED TRIAL BALANCE DEBIT	ADJUSTED TRIAL BALANCE CREDIT	INCOME STATEMENT DEBIT	INCOME STATEMENT CREDIT	BALANCE SHEET DEBIT	BALANCE SHEET CREDIT	
1	Cash	370 00										1
2	Accounts Receivable	500 00										2
3	Supplies	80 00										3
4	Prepaid Insurance	200 00										4
5	Delivery Equipment	3600 00										5
6	Accounts Payable		1800 00									6
7	Jessica Jane, Capital		2000 00									7
8	Jessica Jane, Drawing	150 00										8
9	Delivery Fees		2000 00									9
10	Rent Expense	200 00										10
11	Wage Expense	650 00										11
12	Telephone Expense	50 00										12
13		5800 00	5800 00									13
14												14
15												15
16												16
17												17
18												18
19												19
20												20
21												21
22												22

STEP 1

Preparing the Work Sheet

STEP 1   **Prepare the trial balance.**

- Write the heading, account titles, and the debit and credit amounts from the general ledger.
- Place a single rule across the Trial Balance columns and total the debit and credit amounts.
- Place a double rule under the columns to show that they are equal.

STEP 2   **Prepare the adjustments.**

- Record the adjustments.
- Add any accounts that did not have balances before adjusting. For this work sheet, Supplies Expense, Insurance Expense, Wages Payable, and the depreciation accounts must be added.
  - Hint: Make certain that each adjustment is on the same line as the account name and in the appropriate column.
  - Hint: Identify each adjusting entry by a letter in parentheses.
- Rule the Adjustments columns.
- Total the debit and credit columns and double rule the columns to show equality.

STEP 3   **Prepare the adjusted trial balance.**

- Extend those debits and credits that are not adjusted directly to the appropriate Adjusted Trial Balance column.
- Enter the adjusted balances in the appropriate Adjusted Trial balance column (including accounts that were added).
  - Hint: If an account has a debit and a credit, subtract the adjustment. If an account has two debits or two credits, add the adjustment.
- Single rule the Adjusted Trial Balance columns and total and double rule the Debit and Credit columns.

STEP 4   **Extend adjusted balances to the Income Statement and Balance Sheet columns.**

- Extend all revenue and expense accounts to the Income Statement columns.
- Extend the asset and drawing accounts to the Balance Sheet Debit column.
- Extend the liability and owner's capital accounts to the Balance Sheet Credit column.

STEP 5   **Complete the work sheet.**

- Rule and total the Income Statement and Balance Sheet columns.
- Calculate the difference between the Income Statement Debit and Credit columns. Calculate the difference between the Balance Sheet Debit and Credit columns.
  - Hint: If the Income Statement Credit column is larger than the Income Statement Debit column, a net income has occurred; otherwise a net loss has occurred. A net income occurs on the Balance Sheet Credit side.
  - Hint: The difference between the Balance Sheet columns and the difference between the Income Statement columns should be the same.
- Add the net income to the Income Statement Debit column or add the net loss to the Income Statement Credit column. Add the net income to the Balance Sheet Credit column or the net loss to the Balance Sheet Debit column.
- Total and rule the columns.

KEY POINTS

1 End-of-period adjustments are necessary to bring the general ledger accounts up to date prior to preparing financial statements.
Reasons to adjust the trial balance are:

1. To report all revenues earned during the accounting period.
2. To report all expenses incurred to produce the revenues.
3. To accurately report the assets on the balance sheet date. Some may have been used up during the accounting period.
4. To accurately report the liabilities on the balance sheet date. Expenses may have been incurred but not yet paid.

2 Steps in preparing the work sheet are:

1. Prepare the trial balance.
2. Prepare the adjustments.
3. Prepare the adjusted trial balance.
4. Extend the adjusted account balances to the Income Statement and Balance Sheet columns.
5. Total the Income Statement and Balance Sheet columns to compute the net income or net loss.

3 Tips for finding errors on the work sheet include:

1. Check the addition of all columns.
2. Check the addition and subtraction required when extending to the Adjusted Trial Balance columns.
3. Make sure the adjusted account balances have been extended to the appropriate columns.
4. See that the additional accounts needed for the adjusting entries have been extended.
5. Make sure that the net income or net loss has been added to the appropriate columns.

4 The adjustments are copied from the work sheet to the journal. The last day of the accounting period is entered in the Date column and "Adjusting Entries" is written in the Description column.

5 Adjusting entries are posted to the general ledger in the same manner as all other entries, except that "Adjusting" is written in the Item column of the general ledger.

KEY TERMS

adjusted trial balance 142   The third pair of amount columns of the work sheet.

Balance Sheet columns 143   The worksheet columns that show the amounts that will be reported in the balance sheet and the statement of owner's equity.

book value 138   The difference between the asset account and its related accumulated depreciation account. The value reflected by the accounting records.

contra-asset 137   Has a credit balance and is deducted from the related asset account on the balance sheet.

depreciable cost 137   The cost of an asset that is subject to depreciation.

depreciation 136   Provides a method of matching the cost of the asset against the revenues the assets produce.

fiscal period 132   Adjustments are made and financial statements are prepared at the end of this period.

fiscal year 132   A 12-month period for which financial reports are prepared.

historical cost principle 136   Under this principle, assets are recorded at their actual cost.

Income Statement columns 143   The work sheet columns that show the amounts that will be reported in the income statement.

matching concept 131   Requires the matching of revenues earned during an accounting period with the expenses incurred to produce the revenues.

plant assets 137   Assets expected to provide benefits over a long period of time.

salvage 137   Trade-in value.

straight-line method 136   The depreciable cost is divided by the estimated useful life.

undepreciated cost 138   The difference between the asset account and its related accumulated depreciation account. Also known as book value.

useful life 136   The period of time that an asset is expected to help produce revenues.

work sheet 139   Pulls together all of the information needed to enter adjusting entries and to prepare the financial statements.

BUILDING YOUR ACCOUNTING KNOWLEDGE

1. Explain the accounting concept of matching.
2. Explain the accounting concept of historical cost.

3. What is the useful life of an asset?
4. What is the purpose of depreciation?
5. What is an asset's depreciable cost?
6. Describe a plant asset.
7. What is a contra-asset?
8. What is the book value of an asset?
9. What is the market value of an asset?
10. Explain the purpose of the work sheet.
11. Identify the five major column headings on a work sheet.
12. List the five steps in preparing a work sheet.
13. Describe five techniques for finding errors on the work sheet.

DEMONSTRATION PROBLEM

Scott Rotert is a lawyer specializing in corporate tax law. Provided below is a trial balance taken on December 31, 19--.

Rotert Legal Services
Trial Balance
December 31, 19--

ACCOUNT TITLE	ACCOUNT NO.	DEBIT BALANCE	CREDIT BALANCE
Cash	111	7 000 00	
Office Supplies	152	800 00	
Prepaid Insurance	155	1 200 00	
Office Equipment	181	15 000 00	
Computer Equipment	194	6 000 00	
Notes Payable	216		5 000 00
Accounts Payable	218		500 00
Scott Rotert, Capital	311		11 400 00
Scott Rotert, Drawing	312	5 000 00	
Client Fees	411		40 000 00
Rent Expense	541	5 000 00	
Wage Expense	542	12 000 00	
Telephone Expense	545	1 000 00	
Utility Expense	549	3 900 00	
		56 900 00	56 900 00

Information for year-end adjustments:

(a) Office supplies on hand at year end amounted to $300.
(b) On January 1 of the current year, Rotert purchased office equipment which cost $15,000 with an expected life of 5 years and no salvage value.
(c) Computer equipment costing $6,000 with an expected life of three years and no salvage value was purchased on July 1 of the current year.
(d) A premium of $1,200 for a one-year insurance policy was paid on December 1.
(e) Wages earned by Rotert's part-time secretary, which have not yet been paid, amounted to $300.

Required
1. Prepare the necessary year-end adjustments on a ten-column work sheet.
2. Complete the work sheet by extending the trial balance and adjustments columns to the Adjusted Trial Balance, Income Statement, and Balance Sheet columns, and footing all columns.
3. Prepare adjusting entries in a general journal.

The solutions for the Demonstration Problem are on pages 150 and 151.

SOLUTION 1, 2.

Rotert Legal Services
Work Sheet
For the Year Ended December 31, 19--

Account Title	Trial Balance Debit	Trial Balance Credit	Adjustments Debit	Adjustments Credit	Adjusted Trial Balance Debit	Adjusted Trial Balance Credit	Income Statement Debit	Income Statement Credit	Balance Sheet Debit	Balance Sheet Credit
Cash	7 000 00				7 000 00				7 000 00	
Office Supplies	800 00			(a) 500 00	300 00				300 00	
Prepaid Insurance	1 200 00			(d) 100 00	1 100 00				1 100 00	
Office Equipment	15 000 00				15 000 00				15 000 00	
Computer Equipment	6 000 00				6 000 00				6 000 00	
Notes Payable		5 000 00				5 000 00				5 000 00
Accounts Payable		500 00				500 00				500 00
Scott Rotert, Capital		11 400 00				11 400 00				11 400 00
Scott Rotert, Drawing	5 000 00				5 000 00				5 000 00	
Client Fees		40 000 00				40 000 00		40 000 00		
Rent Expense	5 000 00				5 000 00		5 000 00			
Wage Expense	12 000 00		(e) 300 00		12 300 00		12 300 00			
Telephone Expense	1 000 00				1 000 00		1 000 00			
Utility Expense	3 900 00				3 900 00		3 900 00			
	56 900 00	56 900 00								
Office Supplies Expense			(a) 500 00		500 00		500 00			
Depr. Exp.—Off. Equip.			(b) 3 000 00		3 000 00		3 000 00			
Depr. Exp.—Comp. Equip.			(c) 1 000 00		1 000 00		1 000 00			
Accum. Dep.—Off. Equip.				(b) 3 000 00		3 000 00				3 000 00
Accum. Dep.—Comp. Equip.				(c) 1 000 00		1 000 00				1 000 00
Insurance Expense			(d) 100 00		100 00		100 00			
Wages Payable				(e) 300 00		300 00				300 00
			4 900 00	4 900 00	61 200 00	61 200 00	26 800 00	40 000 00	34 400 00	21 200 00
Net Income							13 200 00			13 200 00
							40 000 00	40 000 00	34 400 00	34 400 00

3.

	DATE		DESCRIPTION	POST. REF.	DEBIT	CREDIT	
1			Adjusting Entries				1
2	Dec.¹⁹⁻⁻	31	Office Supplies Expense		500 00		2
3			Office Supplies			500 00	3
4							4
5		31	Depreciation Expense—Office Equip.		300 00		5
6			Accum. Deprec.—Office Equip.			300 00	6
7							7
8		31	Depreciation Expense—Comp. Equip.		100 00		8
9			Accum. Deprec.—Comp. Equip.			100 00	9
10							10
11		31	Insurance Expense		10 00		11
12			Prepaid Insurance			10 00	12
13							13
14		31	Wages Expense		30 00		14
15			Wages Payable			30 00	15

GENERAL JOURNAL   PAGE 10

SERIES A

EXERCISES

APPLYING ACCOUNTING CONCEPTS

EXERCISE 5A1

Adjustment for Supplies

1 On December 31, the trial balance indicates the supplies account has a balance, prior to the adjusting entry, of $320. A physical count of the supplies inventory shows that $90 worth of supplies remains. Analyze this adjustment for supplies using T accounts, and then formally enter this adjustment in the general journal.

EXERCISE 5A2

Adjustment for Insurance

1 On December 1, a six-month liability insurance policy was purchased for $900. Analyze the required adjustment as of December 31 using T accounts, and then formally enter this adjustment in the general journal.

EXERCISE 5A3

Adjustment for Wages

1 On December 31, the trial balance shows wages expense of $600. An additional $200 of wages was earned by the employees but has not yet been paid. Analyze this adjustment for accrued wages, and then formally enter this adjustment in the general journal.

EXERCISE 5A4

Adjustment for Depreciation of Asset

1 On December 1, delivery equipment was purchased for $7,200. The delivery equipment has an estimated useful life of 4 years or 48 months and no salvage value. Analyze the necessary adjusting entry as of December 31 (one month), and then formally enter this adjustment in the general journal.

1 On June 1, 19--, a depreciable asset was acquired for $5,400. The asset has an estimated useful life of 5 years (60 months) and no salvage value. Using the straight-line depreciation method, calculate the book value as of December 31, 19--.

1 Analyze each situation and indicate the correct dollar amount for the adjusting entry. (Trial balance is abbreviated as TB.)

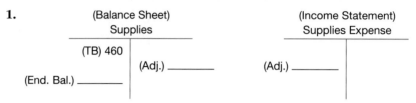

1.

(Balance Sheet) Supplies	(Income Statement) Supplies Expense
(TB) 460 (Adj.) _____	(Adj.) _____
(End. Bal.) _____	

Ending inventory of supplies is $130.

2.

(Balance Sheet) Supplies	(Income Statement) Supplies Expense
(TB) 545 (Adj.) _____	(Adj.) _____
(End. Bal.) _____	

Amount of supplies used is $320.

1 Analyze each situation and indicate the correct dollar amount for the adjusting entry.

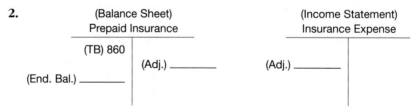

1.

(Balance Sheet) Prepaid Insurance	(Income Statement) Insurance Expense
(TB) 1,300 (Adj.) _____	(Adj.) _____
(End. Bal.) _____	

Amount of insurance expired is $900.

2.

(Balance Sheet) Prepaid Insurance	(Income Statement) Insurance Expense
(TB) 860 (Adj.) _____	(Adj.) _____
(End. Bal.) _____	

Amount of unexpired insurance is $185.

2 A partial work sheet for Jim Jacob's Furniture is shown as follows.

Jim Jacob's Furniture
Work Sheet (Partial)
For Month Ended December 31, 19--

	ACCOUNT TITLE	ACCT. NO.	TRIAL BALANCE		ADJUSTMENTS		ADJUSTED TRIAL BALANCE		
			DEBIT	CREDIT	DEBIT	CREDIT	DEBIT	CREDIT	
1	Cash		1000 00				1000 00		1
2	Supplies		850 00				200 00		2
3	Prepaid Insurance		900 00				300 00		3
4	Equipment		3600 00				3600 00		4
5	Accum. Dep.—Equip.			600 00				800 00	5
6	J. Jacobs, Capital			4000 00				4000 00	6
7	Sales Revenue			1650 00				1650 00	7
8	Wage Expense		600 00				700 00		8
9	Advertising Exp.		200 00				200 00		9
10			6250 00	6250 00					10
11	Supplies Expense						650 00		11
12	Insurance Expense						600 00		12
13	Dep. Exp.—Equip.						200 00		13
14	Wages Payable							100 00	14
15					1550 00	1550 00	6550 00	6550 00	15

The work sheet contains four adjusting entries. Indicate by letters (a) through (d) the four adjustments in the adjustment columns of the work sheet, properly matching each debit and credit.

EXERCISE 5A9

Journalizing Adjusting Entries

4 From the Adjustments columns from Exercise 5A8, journalize the four adjusting entries, on December 31, in proper general journal format.

EXERCISE 5A10

Posting Adjusting Entries

5 Two adjusting entries are in the following general journal. Post these adjusting entries to the four general ledger accounts using the four-step method of posting learned in Chapter 4. The December 15 balance in Supplies is $200 and in Wages Expense, $1,200. Use the following account numbers.

Supplies	151
Wages Payable	219
Wages Expense	542
Supplies Expense	543

	DATE		DESCRIPTION	POST. REF.	DEBIT	CREDIT	
			GENERAL JOURNAL			PAGE 9	
1			Adjusting Entries				1
2	19-- Dec.	31	Supplies Expense		8 5 00		2
3			Supplies			8 5 00	3
4							4
5		31	Wages Expense		2 2 0 00		5
6			Wages Payable			2 2 0 00	6
7							7
8							8
9							9
10							10

EXERCISE 5A11

Work Sheet Columns

2 Indicate with an (x) whether each account total should be extended to the Income Statement Debit or Credit, or to the Balance Sheet Debit or Credit columns on the work sheet.

	Income Statement		Balance Sheet	
	Debit	Credit	Debit	Credit
Cash				
Accounts Receivable				
Supplies				
Prepaid Insurance				
Delivery Equipment				
Accounts Payable				
Owners, Capital				
Owners, Drawing				
Delivery Fees				
Rent Expense				
Wage Expense				
Supplies Expense				
Insurance Expense				
Wages Payable				
Dep. Exp.—Delivery Equip.				
Accum. Deprec.—Deliv. Equip.				

EXERCISE 5A12

Analysis of Net Income or Net Loss on the Work Sheet

2 Indicate with an (x) in which columns, Income Statement Debit or Credit, or Balance Sheet Debit or Credit, a net income or a net loss would appear on a work sheet.

	Income Statement		Balance Sheet	
	Debit	Credit	Debit	Credit
Net Income	_____	_____	_____	_____
Net Loss	_____	_____	_____	_____

PROBLEMS

PROBLEM 5A1

Adjustments and Work
Sheet Showing a Net
Income

1/2 The trial balance for Jill Mason's Delivery Service as of September 30, 19--, is shown as follows:

Mason's Delivery Service
Work Sheet (Partial)
For Month Ended September 30, 19--

	ACCOUNT TITLE	ACCT. NO.	TRIAL BALANCE DEBIT	TRIAL BALANCE CREDIT	ADJUSTMENTS DEBIT	ADJUSTMENTS CREDIT	
1	Cash		1 6 0 0 00				1
2	Accounts Receivable		9 4 0 00				2
3	Supplies		6 3 5 00				3
4	Prepaid Insurance		1 2 0 0 00				4
5	Delivery Equipment		6 4 0 0 00				5
6	Accounts Payable			1 2 2 0 00			6
7	J. Mason, Capital			8 0 0 0 00			7
8	J. Mason, Drawing		1 4 0 0 00				8
9	Delivery Fees			6 2 0 0 00			9
10	Rent Expense		8 0 0 00				10
11	Wage Expense		1 5 0 0 00				11
12	Telephone Expense		1 6 5 00				12
13	Oil & Gas Expense		9 0 00				13
14	Advertising Expense		4 6 0 00				14
15	Repair Expense		2 3 0 00				15
16			15 4 2 0 00	15 4 2 0 00			16

Data to complete the adjustments are as follows:

(a) Supplies inventory as of September 30, $165.
(b) Insurance expired, $800.
(c) Depreciation on delivery equipment, $400.
(d) Wages earned by employees but not paid as of September 30, $225.

Required
1. Enter the adjustments in the adjustments columns of the work sheet.
2. Complete the work sheet.

2 Jason Armstrong started a business called Campus Escort Service. After the first month of operations, the trial balance as of November 30, 19--, is shown below.

	ACCOUNT TITLE	ACCT. NO.	TRIAL BALANCE		ADJUSTMENTS		
			DEBIT	CREDIT	DEBIT	CREDIT	
1	Cash		980 00				1
2	Accounts Receivable		590 00				2
3	Supplies		575 00				3
4	Prepaid Insurance		1300 00				4
5	Van		5800 00				5
6	Accounts Payable			960 00			6
7	J. Armstrong, Capital			10000 00			7
8	J. Armstrong, Drawing		600 00				8
9	Escort Fees			2600 00			9
10	Rent Expense		900 00				10
11	Wage Expense		1800 00				11
12	Telephone Expense		220 00				12
13	Oil & Gas Expense		100 00				13
14	Advertising Expense		380 00				14
15	Repair Expense		315 00				15
16			13560 00	13560 00			16

Campus Escort Service
Work Sheet (Partial)
For Month Ended November 30, 19--

Required

1. Analyze the following adjustments and enter them on the work sheet.
   (a) Ending inventory of supplies on November 30, $185.
   (b) Unexpired insurance as of November 30, $800.
   (c) Depreciation expense on van, $300.
   (d) Wages accrued but not paid as of November 30, $190.
2. Complete the work sheet.

PROBLEM 5A3

Journalize and Post Adjusting Entries from the Work Sheet

4/5 Refer to Problem 5A2 and the following additional information.

Account Name	Account Number	Balance in Account Before Adjusting Entry
Supplies	151	$ 575
Prepaid Insurance	155	1,300
Accum. Deprec.—Van	185.1	0
Wages Payable	219	0
Wages Expense	542	1,800
Supplies Expense	543	0
Deprec. Expense—Van	547	0
Insurance Expense	548	0

Use general journal page 5 (J5) as the posting reference for the adjusting entries in the general journal. Use page 4 (J4) for balances carried forward in the general ledger Posting Reference column for the Supplies, Prepaid Insurance, and Wages Expense accounts.

Required
1. Journalize the adjusting entries in the general journal.
2. Post the adjusting entries to the general ledger.

PROBLEM 5A4

Correcting Work Sheet with Errors

3 A beginning accounting student tried to complete a work sheet for Joyce Lee's Tax Service. The following adjusting entries were to have been analyzed and input onto the work sheet.

(a) Ending inventory of supplies as of March 31, $160.
(b) Unexpired insurance as of March 31, $520.
(c) Depreciation on office equipment, $275.
(d) Wages earned but not paid as of March 31, $110.

Required
Errors have been intentionally placed in this work sheet. Review the work sheet for addition mistakes, transpositions, and other errors and make all necessary corrections.

Errors intentionally placed in work sheet.

	ACCOUNT TITLE	ACCT. NO.	TRIAL BALANCE DEBIT	TRIAL BALANCE CREDIT	ADJUSTMENTS DEBIT	ADJUSTMENTS CREDIT	
				Lee's Tax Service **Work Sheet** **For Month Ended March 31, 19--**			
1	Cash		1 7 2 5 00				1
2	Accounts Receivable		9 6 0 00				2
3	Supplies		5 2 5 00			(a) 1 6 0 00	3
4	Prepaid Insurance		9 3 0 00			(b) 4 1 0 00	4
5	Office Equipment		5 4 5 0 00			(c) 2 7 5 00	5
6	Accounts Payable			4 8 0 00			6
7	Joyce Lee, Capital			7 5 0 0 00			7
8	Joyce Lee, Drawing		1 1 2 5 00				8
9	Professional Fees			5 7 0 0 00			9
10	Rent Expense		7 0 0 00				10
11	Wage Expense		1 4 2 0 00		(d) 1 1 0 00		11
12	Telephone Expense		1 3 0 00				12
13	Utilities Expense		1 9 0 00				13
14	Advertising Expense		3 5 0 00				14
15	Miscellaneous Expense		1 7 5 00				15
16			13 6 8 0 00	13 6 8 0 00			16
17	Supplies Expense				(a) 1 6 0 00		17
18	Insurance Expense				(b) 4 1 0 00		18
19	Depr. Exp.—Off. Equip.				(c) 2 7 5 00		19
20	Accum. Depr.—Off. Equip.						20
21	Wages Payable					(d) 1 1 0 00	21
22					9 5 5 00	9 5 5 00	22
23	Net Income						23
24							24

SERIES B

EXERCISES

EXERCISE 5B1

Adjustment for Supplies

1 On July 31, the trial balance indicates the supplies account has a balance, prior to the adjusting entry, of $430. A physical count of the supplies inventory shows that $120 of supplies remains. Analyze the adjustment for supplies using T accounts, and then formally enter this adjustment in the general journal.

EXERCISE 5B2

Adjustment for Insurance

1 On July 1, a six-month liability insurance policy was purchased for $750. Analyze the required adjustment as of July 31 using T accounts, and then formally enter this adjustment in the general journal.

	ADJUSTED TRIAL BALANCE		INCOME STATEMENT		BALANCE		
	DEBIT	CREDIT	DEBIT	CREDIT	DEBIT	CREDIT	
1	1725 00				1752 00		1
2	960 00				96 00		2
3	365 00				365 00		3
4	540 00				540 00		4
5	5175 00				5175 00		5
6		480 00				480 00	6
7		7500 00				7500 00	7
8	1125 00		1125 00				8
9		5700 00		5700 00			9
10	700 00		700 00				10
11	1420 00		1420 00			1580 00	11
12	130 00		130 00				12
13	190 00		190 00				13
14	350 00		350 00				14
15	175 00		175 00				15
16							16
17	160 00		160 00				17
18	41 00		41 00				18
19	275 00		275 00				19
20							20
21		110 00		110 00			21
22	13160 00	13790 00	4566 00	5810 00	9508 00	7980 00	22
23			1244 00			1528 00	23
24			5810 00	5810 00	9508 00	9508 00	24

EXERCISE 5B3

Adjustment for Wages

1 On July 31, the trial balance shows wages expense of $800. An additional $150 of wages was earned by the employees but has not yet been paid. Analyze the required adjustment using T accounts, and then formally enter this adjustment in the general journal.

EXERCISE 5B4

Adjustment for Depreciation of Asset

1 On July 1, delivery equipment was purchased for $4,320. The delivery equipment has an estimated useful life of 3 years or 36 months and no salvage value. Analyze the necessary adjusting entry as of July 31 (one month), and then formally enter this adjustment in the general journal.

EXERCISE 5B5

Calculation of Book Value

1 On January 1, 19--, a depreciable asset was acquired for $5,760. The asset has an estimated useful life of 4 years (48 months) and no salvage value. Use the straight-line method of depreciation to calculate the book value as of July 1, 19--.

EXERCISE 5B6

Analysis of Adjusting Entry for Supplies

1 Analyze each situation and indicate the correct dollar amount for the adjusting entry.

1.

(Balance Sheet) Supplies	(Income Statement) Supplies Expense
(TB) 540	(Adj.) _____	(Adj.) _____
(End. Bal.) _____		

Ending inventory of supplies is $95.

2.

(Balance Sheet) Supplies	(Income Statement) Supplies Expense
(TB) 330	(Adj.) _____	(Adj.) _____
(End. Bal.) _____		

Amount of supplies used is $280.

EXERCISE 5B7

Analysis of Adjusting Entry for Insurance

1 Analyze each situation and indicate the correct dollar amount for the adjusting entry.

1.

(Balance Sheet) Prepaid Insurance	(Income Statement) Insurance Expense
960	(Adj.) _____	(Adj.) _____
(End. Bal.) _____		

Amount of insurance expired is $830.

2.

(Balance Sheet) Prepaid Insurance	(Income Statement) Insurance Expense
(TB) 1,135	(Adj.) _____	(Adj.) _____
(End. Bal.) _____		

Amount of unexpired insurance is $340.

EXERCISE 5B8

Work Sheet and Adjusting Entries

2 The following shows a partial work sheet for Bill Black's Automotive.

			TRIAL BALANCE		ADJUSTMENTS		ADJUSTED TRIAL BALANCE		
	ACCOUNT TITLE	ACCT. NO.	DEBIT	CREDIT	DEBIT	CREDIT	DEBIT	CREDIT	
1	Cash		1 5 0 00				1 5 0 00		1
2	Supplies		5 2 0 00				9 0 00		2
3	Prepaid Insurance		7 5 0 00				2 0 0 00		3
4	Equipment		5 4 0 0 00				5 4 0 0 00		4
5	Accum. Dep.—Equip.			8 5 0 00				1 1 5 0 00	5
6	Bill Black, Capital			4 6 0 0 00				4 6 0 0 00	6
7	Sales Revenue			2 2 2 0 00				2 2 2 0 00	7
8	Wage Expense		7 0 0 00				9 5 0 00		8
9	Advertising Exp.		1 5 0 00				1 5 0 00		9
10			7 6 7 0 00	7 6 7 0 00					10
11	Supplies Expense						4 3 0 00		11
12	Insurance Expense						5 5 0 00		12
13	Dep. Exp.—Equip.						3 0 0 00		13
14	Wages Payable							2 5 0 00	14
15							8 2 2 0 00	8 2 2 0 00	15

Bill Black's Automotive
Work Sheet (Partial)
For Month Ended June 30, 19--

The work sheet contains four adjusting entries. Indicate by letters (a) through (d) the four adjustments in the adjustment columns of the work sheet, properly matching each debit and credit.

4 From the Adjustments columns in Exercise 5B8, journalize the four adjusting entries as of June 30, in proper general journal format.

5 Two adjusting entries are shown in the following general journal. Post these adjusting entries to the four general ledger accounts using the four-step method of posting learned in Chapter 4. Use the following account numbers.

Supplies	151
Wages Payable	219
Wages Expense	542
Supplies Expense	543

GENERAL JOURNAL						PAGE 7	
	DATE	DESCRIPTION	POST. REF.	DEBIT	CREDIT		
1		Adjusting Entries					1
2	19-- July 31	Supplies Expense		3 2 0 00			2
3		Supplies			3 2 0 00		3
4							4
5	31	Wages Expense		1 4 5 00			5
6		Wages Payable			1 4 5 00		6

<table>
<tr><td>**EXERCISE 5B11**

Completion of Work Sheet</td><td>**2** Indicate with an x whether each account total should be extended to the Income Statement Debit or Credit, or to the Balance Sheet Debit or Credit.</td></tr>
</table>

	Income Statement		Balance Sheet	
	Debit	Credit	Debit	Credit
Cash				
Accounts Receivable				
Supplies				
Prepaid Insurance				
Automobile				
Accounts Payable				
Owners, Capital				
Owners, Drawing				
Services Income				
Utilities Expense				
Wage Expense				
Supplies Expense				
Insurance Expense				
Wages Payable				
Deprec. Expense—Auto				
Accum. Deprec.—Auto				

<table>
<tr><td>**EXERCISE 5B12**

Analysis of Net Income or Net Loss on the Work Sheet</td><td>**2** Indicate with an x where the net income or net loss would appear on the work sheet.</td></tr>
</table>

	Income Statement		Balance Sheet	
	Debit	Credit	Debit	Credit
Net Income—$2,500	_____	_____	_____	_____
Net Loss—$1,900	_____	_____	_____	_____

PROBLEMS

PROBLEM 5B1

Adjustments and Work Sheet Showing a Net Income

2 Louie Long started a business called "Louie's Lawn Service". After the first month of operations the trial balance as of March 31 is shown below.

Louie's Lawn Service
Work Sheet (Partial)
For Month Ended March 31, 19--

	ACCOUNT TITLE	ACCT. NO.	TRIAL BALANCE DEBIT	TRIAL BALANCE CREDIT	ADJUSTMENTS DEBIT	ADJUSTMENTS CREDIT	
1	Cash		1 3 7 5 00				1
2	Accounts Receivable		8 8 0 00				2
3	Supplies		4 9 0 00				3
4	Prepaid Insurance		8 0 0 00				4
5	Lawn Equipment		5 7 0 0 00				5
6	Accounts Payable			7 8 0 00			6
7	L. Long, Capital			6 5 0 0 00			7
8	L. Long, Drawing		1 2 5 0 00				8
9	Services Income			6 1 0 0 00			9
10	Rent Expense		7 2 5 00				10
11	Wage Expense		1 1 4 5 00				11
12	Telephone Expense		1 6 0 00				12
13	Miscellaneous Expense		6 5 00				13
14	Advertising Expense		5 4 0 00				14
15	Repair Expense		2 5 0 00				15
16			13 3 8 0 00	13 3 8 0 00			16

Required
1. Analyze the following adjustments and enter them on a work sheet.
   (a) Ending supplies inventory as of March 31, $165.
   (b) Insurance expired, $200
   (c) Depreciation of lawn equipment, $200.
   (d) Wages earned but not paid as of March 31, $180.
2. Complete the work sheet.

PROBLEM 5B2

Adjustments and Work Sheet Showing a Net Loss

2 Cecil May started a business called "Leisure Supplies." After the first month of operations, the trial balance as of October 31, appears below.

Leisure Supplies
Work Sheet (Partial)
For Month Ended October 31, 19--

	ACCOUNT TITLE	ACCT. NO.	TRIAL BALANCE DEBIT	TRIAL BALANCE CREDIT	ADJUSTMENTS DEBIT	ADJUSTMENTS CREDIT	
1	Cash		830 00				1
2	Accounts Receivable		760 00				2
3	Supplies		625 00				3
4	Prepaid Insurance		950 00				4
5	Delivery Equipment		6 500 00				5
6	Accounts Payable			1 500 00			6
7	Cecil May, Capital			9 900 00			7
8	Cecil May, Drawing		1 100 00				8
9	Professional Fees			3 000 00			9
10	Rent Expense		1 050 00				10
11	Wage Expense		1 560 00				11
12	Telephone Expense		255 00				12
13	Oil & Gas Expense		80 00				13
14	Advertising Expense		420 00				14
15	Repair Expense		270 00				15
16			14 400 00	14 400 00			16

Required

1. Analyze the following adjustments and enter them on the work sheet.
  (a) Supplies inventory as of October 31, $210.
  (b) Unexpired insurance as of October 31, $800
  (c) Depreciation of delivery equipment, $250.
  (d) Wages earned but not paid as of October 31, $175.
2. Complete the work sheet.

Journalize and Post Adjusting Entries from the Work Sheet

4/5 Refer to Problem 5B2 and the following additional information.

Account Name	Account Number	Balance in Account Before Adjusting Entry
Supplies	151	$ 625
Prepaid Insurance	155	950
Accum. Deprec.—Van	185.1	0
Wages Payable	219	0
Wages Expense	542	1,560
Supplies Expense	543	0
Deprec. Expense—Van	547	0
Insurance Expense	548	0

Use general journal page 3 (J3) as the posting reference for the adjusting entries in the general journal. Use page 2 (J2) for balances carried forward in the General Ledger Posting Reference column for the Supplies, Prepaid Insurance, and Wages Expense accounts.

Required
1. Journalize the adjusting entries in the general journal.
2. Post the adjusting entries to the general ledger.

PROBLEM 5B4

Correcting Work Sheet with Errors

3 A beginning accounting student tried to complete a work sheet for Dick Ady's Bookkeeping Service. The following adjusting entries were to have been analyzed and entered in the work sheet.

(a) Ending inventory of supplies on July 31, $130.
(b) Unexpired insurance on July 31, $420.
(c) Depreciation of office equipment, $325.
(d) Wages earned but not paid as of July 31, $95.

Required
Review the following work sheet for addition mistakes, transpositions, and other errors and make all necessary corrections.

Errors intentionally placed in work sheet.

Ady's Bookkeeping Service
Work Sheet
For Month Ended July 31, 19--

#	ACCOUNT TITLE	TRIAL BALANCE DEBIT	TRIAL BALANCE CREDIT	ADJUSTMENTS DEBIT	ADJUSTMENTS CREDIT	ADJUSTED TRIAL BALANCE DEBIT	ADJUSTED TRIAL BALANCE CREDIT	INCOME STATEMENT DEBIT	INCOME STATEMENT CREDIT	BALANCE SHEET DEBIT	BALANCE SHEET CREDIT
1	Cash	1 365 00				1 365 00				1 356 00	
2	Accounts Receivable	845 00				845 00			845 00		
3	Supplies	620 00			(a) 490 00	130 00				130 00	
4	Prepaid Insurance	1 150 00			(b) 420 00	730 00				730 00	
5	Office Equipment	6 400 00			(c) 325 00	6 725 00				6 725 00	
6	Accounts Payable		735 00				735 00				735 00
7	Dick Ady, Capital		7 800 00				7 800 00				7 800 00
8	Dick Ady, Drawing	1 200 00				1 200 00				1 200 00	
9	Professional Fees		6 350 00				6 350 00		6 350 00		
10	Rent Expense	850 00				850 00		850 00			
11	Wage Expense	1 495 00		(d) 95 00		1 590 00		1 590 00			
12	Telephone Expense	205 00				205 00		250 00			
13	Utilities Expense	285 00				285 00		285 00			
14	Advertising Expense	380 00				380 00		380 00			
15	Miscellaneous Expense	90 00				90 00		90 00			
16		14 885 00	14 885 00								
17	Supplies Expense			(a) 490 00		490 00		490 00			
18	Insurance Expense			(b) 420 00		420 00		420 00			
19	Dep. Exp.—Off. Equip.			(c) 325 00		325 00		325 00			
20	Acc. Dep.—Off. Equip.										
21	Wages Payable				(d) 95 00		95 00				59 00
22				0	0	15 630 00	14 980 00	4 880 00	7 195 00	10 141 00	8 594 00
23	Net Income							2 315 00			1 547 00
24								7 195 00	7 195 00	10 141 00	10 141 00

MASTERY PROBLEM

Kristi Williams offers family counseling services specializing in financial and marital problems. The following trial balance was taken on December 31, 19--.

<table>
<tr><td colspan="4" align="center">**Kristi Williams Family Counseling Services**
Trial Balance
For Month Ended December 31, 19--</td></tr>
<tr><th>ACCOUNT TITLE</th><th>ACCOUNT NO.</th><th>DEBIT BALANCE</th><th>CREDIT BALANCE</th></tr>
<tr><td>Cash</td><td>111</td><td>8 7 3 0 00</td><td></td></tr>
<tr><td>Office Supplies</td><td>152</td><td>7 0 0 00</td><td></td></tr>
<tr><td>Prepaid Insurance</td><td>155</td><td>6 0 0 00</td><td></td></tr>
<tr><td>Office Equipment</td><td>181</td><td>18 0 0 0 00</td><td></td></tr>
<tr><td>Computer Equipment</td><td>194</td><td>6 0 0 0 00</td><td></td></tr>
<tr><td>Notes Payable</td><td>216</td><td></td><td>8 0 0 0 00</td></tr>
<tr><td>Accounts Payable</td><td>218</td><td></td><td>5 0 0 00</td></tr>
<tr><td>Kristi Williams, Capital</td><td>311</td><td></td><td>11 4 0 0 00</td></tr>
<tr><td>Kristi Williams, Drawing</td><td>312</td><td>3 0 0 0 00</td><td></td></tr>
<tr><td>Client Fees</td><td>411</td><td></td><td>35 8 0 0 00</td></tr>
<tr><td>Rent Expense</td><td>541</td><td>6 0 0 0 00</td><td></td></tr>
<tr><td>Salary Expense</td><td>542</td><td>9 5 0 0 00</td><td></td></tr>
<tr><td>Utility Expense</td><td>549</td><td>2 1 7 0 00</td><td></td></tr>
<tr><td>Charitable Contributions Expense</td><td>557</td><td>1 0 0 0 00</td><td></td></tr>
<tr><td></td><td></td><td>55 7 0 0 00</td><td>55 7 0 0 00</td></tr>
</table>

Information for year-end adjustments:

(a) Office supplies on hand at year end amounted to $100.
(b) On January 1 of the current year, Williams purchased office equipment that cost $18,000 with an expected life of 10 years and no salvage value.
(c) Computer equipment costing $6,000 with an expected life of three years and no salvage value was purchased on July 1 of the current year.
(d) A premium of $600 for a six-month insurance policy was paid on December 1.

Required

1. Prepare the necessary year-end adjustments on a ten-column work sheet.
2. Complete the work sheet by extending the trial balance and adjustments columns to the income statement and balance sheet columns, and footing all columns.
3. Prepare adjusting entries in a general journal.

Careful study of this chapter should enable you to:

1. Prepare financial statements with the aid of a work sheet.
2. Journalize and post closing entries.
3. Prepare a post-closing trial balance.
4. List and describe the steps in the accounting cycle.

*F*inancial Statements and the Closing Process

The work sheet, introduced in Chapter 5, is used for three major end-of-period activities:

1. Journalizing adjusting entries
2. Preparing financial statements
3. Journalizing closing entries

This chapter illustrates the use of the work sheet for preparing financial statements and closing entries. In addition, the post-closing trial balance will be explained and illustrated. All of these activities take place at the end of the fiscal year. However, to continue our illustration of Jessie Jane's Campus Delivery Service, we will demonstrate these activities at the end of the first month of operations.

1

Prepare financial statements with the aid of a work sheet.

THE FINANCIAL STATEMENTS

The work sheet prepared in Chapter 5 supplies all of the information needed to prepare an income statement, a statement of owner's equity, and a balance sheet for Jessie Jane's Campus Delivery Service. The statements for Jane's business are shown in figure 6-1 and figure 6-2.

As you refer to the statements in figure 6-1 and 6-2, notice the placement of dollar signs, single rulings, and double rulings. Dollar signs are placed at the top of each column. Single rulings indicate addition or subtraction, and double rulings are placed under totals. Notice that each statement contains three lines: (1) company name, (2) statement title, and (3) period ended or date.

FIGURE 6-1 **The Work Sheet and the Income Statement**

			INCOME STATEMENT		BALANCE SHEET		
	ACCOUNT TITLE		DEBIT	CREDIT	DEBIT	CREDIT	
1	Cash						1
2	Accounts Receivable						2
3	Supplies						3
4	Prepaid Insurance						4
5	Delivery Equipment						5
6	Accounts Payable						6
7	Jessica Jane, Capital						7
8	Jessica Jane, Drawing						8
9	Delivery Fees			2 0 0 0 00			9
10	Rent Expense		2 0 0 00				10
11	Wage Expense		7 0 0 00				11
12	Telephone Expense		5 0 00				12
13							13
14							14
15	Supplies Expense		6 0 00				15
16	Insurance Expense		2 5 00				16
17	Wages Payable						17
18	Depr. Exp.—Del. Equip.		1 0 0 00				18
19	Accum. Depr.—Del. Equip.						19
20			1 1 3 5 00	2 0 0 0 00			20
21	Net Income		8 6 5 00				21
22			2 0 0 0 00	2 0 0 0 00			22

Jessie Jane's Campus Delivery Service
Work Sheet (Partial)
For the Month Ended June 30, 19--

The Income Statement

As shown in figure 6-1, the Income Statement columns of the work sheet provide the information needed to prepare an income statement. Revenue is shown first, followed by an itemized and totaled list of expenses. Then, net income may be calculated or copied from the Income Statement columns of the work sheet. It is presented with a double ruling as the last item in the statement.

The expenses could be listed in the same order that they appear in the chart of accounts, or in descending order by dollar amount. The latter method helps the reader identify the most important expenses and is the approach illustrated in figure 6-1.

FIGURE 6-1 **The Work Sheet and the Income Statement (continued)**

Jessie Jane's Campus Delivery Service Income Statement For Month Ended June 30, 19--			
Revenue:			
Delivery fees			$2 0 0 0 00
Expenses:			
Wage expense	$7 0 0 00		
Rent expense	2 0 0 00		
Depreciation expense	1 0 0 00		
Supplies expense	6 0 00		
Telephone expense	5 0 00		
Insurance expense	2 5 00		
Total expenses		1 1 3 5 00	
Net Income		$ 8 6 5 00	

Period ended
Revenues first
Exp. large to small
Subtotal

The Statement of Owner's Equity

As shown in figure 6-2, the Balance Sheet columns of the work sheet provide the information needed to prepare a statement of owner's equity. Jane's Capital account balance and the Drawing account balance are in the Balance Sheet columns of the work sheet. The net income for the year can be found either on the work sheet at the bottom of the Balance Sheet columns, or on the income statement. With these three items of information, the statement of owner's equity can be prepared.

Be careful when using the capital account balance reported in the Balance Sheet columns of the work sheet. This account balance is the beginning balance *plus any additional investments made during the period.* Since Jane made no additional investments during June, the $2,000 balance is also the beginning balance on the statement of owner's equity.

If a business owner made additional investments during the accounting period, the owner's capital account in the general ledger must be reviewed to prepare the statement of owner's equity. Figure 6-3 illustrates this situation for another business, Dick's Shopping Service. The $5,000 balance on July 1, 19--, in Dick Balboa's general ledger capital account is the beginning balance on the statement of owner's equity. The additional investment of $3,000 made on July 5 and posted to Balboa's general ledger capital account is reported by writing "Add: Additional Investments" on the line immediately after the beginning balance. The beginning balance

If an additional investment is made during the accounting period, the owner's capital account in the general ledger must be reviewed.

FIGURE 6-2 **Using the Balance Sheet Columns of the Work Sheet to Prepare Statements**

Jessie Jane's Campus Delivery Service
Work Sheet (Partial)
For the Month Ended June 30, 19--

	ACCOUNT TITLE			BALANCE SHEET DEBIT	BALANCE SHEET CREDIT	
1	Cash			3 7 0 00		1
2	Accounts Receivable			5 0 0 00		2
3	Supplies			2 0 00		3
4	Prepaid Insurance			1 7 5 00		4
5	Delivery Equipment			3 6 0 0 00		5
6	Accounts Payable				1 8 0 0 00	6
7	Jessica Jane, Capital				2 0 0 0 00	7
8	Jessica Jane, Drawing			1 5 0 00		8
9	Delivery Fees					9
10	Rent Expense					10
11	Wage Expense					11
12	Telephone Expense					12
13						13
14						14
15	Supplies Expense					15
16	Insurance Expense					16
17	Wages Payable				5 0 00	17
18	Depr. Exp.—Del. Equip.					18
19	Accum. Depr.—Del. Equip.				1 0 0 00	19
20				4 8 1 5 00	3 9 5 0 00	20
21	Net Income				8 6 5 00	21
22				4 8 1 5 00	4 8 1 5 00	22

plus the additional investment equals the owner's total investment in the business. From this point, the preparation of the statement is the same as for businesses without additional investments.

The Balance Sheet

As shown in figure 6-2, the work sheet and the statement of owner's equity are used to prepare Jane's balance sheet. The asset and liability amounts can be found in the Balance Sheet columns of the work sheet. The ending balance in Jessica Jane, Capital, has been computed on the statement of owner's equity. This amount should be copied from the statement of owner's equity to the balance sheet.

Two important features of the balance sheet in figure 6-2 should be noted. First, it is a **report form of balance sheet,** which means that the

FIGURE 6-2 Using the Balance Sheet Columns of the Work Sheet to Prepare Statements

Jessie Jane's Campus Delivery Service Statement of Owner's Equity For Month Ended June 30, 19--			
Jessica Jane, capital, June 1, 19--			$2 0 0 0 00
Net income for June	$8 6 5 00			← Net income
Less withdrawals for June	1 5 0 00		
Increase in capital		7 1 5 00	
Jessica Jane, capital, June 30, 19--			$2 7 1 5 00

Jessie Jane's Campus Delivery Service Balance Sheet June 30, 19--			
Assets				← Date
Current assets:			
Cash	$ 3 7 0 00		
Accounts receivable	5 0 0 00		
Supplies	2 0 00		
Prepaid insurance	1 7 5 00		
Total current assets		$1 0 6 5 00	
Property, plant and equipment:			
Delivery equipment	$3 6 0 0 00		
Less accumulated depreciation	1 0 0 00	3 5 0 0 00	
Total assets		$4 5 6 5 00	
Liabilities			
Current liabilities:			
Accounts payable	$1 8 0 0 00		
Wages payable	5 0 00		
Total current liabilities		$1 8 5 0 00	
Owner's Equity			
Jessica Jane, capital		2 7 1 5 00	
Total liabilities and owner's equity		$4 5 6 5 00	

liabilities and owner's equity sections are shown below the assets section. It differs from an **account form of balance sheet** in which the assets are on the left, and the liabilities and the owner's equity sections are on the right. (See Jane's balance sheet illustrated in figure 2-2 on page 28 in Chapter 2.)

Second, it is a **classified balance sheet,** which means that similar items are grouped together on the balance sheet. Assets are classified as current assets and property, plant, and equipment. Similarly, liabilities are also

FIGURE 6-3 **Statement of Owner's Equity with Additional Investment**

GENERAL LEDGER							
ACCOUNT: DICK BALBOA, CAPITAL						ACCOUNT NO. 311	
DATE	ITEM	POST. REF.	DEBIT	CREDIT	BALANCE		
					DEBIT	CREDIT	
19-- July 1				5 0 0 0 00		5 0 0 0 00	← Amount invested July 1
5				3 0 0 0 00		8 0 0 0 00	← Amount reported on work sheet

Dick's Shopping Service
Statement of Owner's Equity
For Month Ended July 31, 19--

Dick Balboa, capital, July 1, 19--		$5 0 0 0 00
Add additional investment		3 0 0 0 00
Total investment		8 0 0 0 00
Net income for July	$2 1 0 0 00	
Less withdrawals for July	2 5 0 00	
Increase in capital		1 8 5 0 00
Dick Balboa, capital, July 31, 19--		$9 8 5 0 00

From general ledger

From work sheet

broken down into current and long-term sections. The following major balance sheet classifications are generally used.

Current assets.   **Current assets** include cash and assets that will be converted into cash or consumed within either one year or the normal operating cycle of the business, whichever is longer. An **operating cycle** is the period of time required to purchase supplies and services and convert them back into cash.

Property, Plant, and Equipment.   **Property, plant, and equipment,** also called **plant assets** or **long-term assets,** represent assets that are expected to serve the business for many years.

Current Liabilities.   **Current liabilities** are liabilities that are due within either one year or the normal operating cycle of the business, whichever is longer, and that are to be paid out of current assets. Accounts payable and wages payable are classified as current liabilities.

Long-Term Liabilities.   **Long-term liabilities,** or **long-term debt,** are obligations that are not expected to be paid within a year and do not require the use of current assets. A mortgage on an office building is an example of a long-term liability. Jane has no long-term debts. If she did, they would be listed on the balance sheet in the long-term liabilities section immediately following the current liabilities.

2

Journalize and post closing entries.

THE CLOSING PROCESS

Assets, liabilities, and the owner's capital account accumulate information across accounting periods. Their balances are brought forward for each new period. For example, the amount of cash on hand at the end of one accounting period must be the same as the amount of cash on hand at the beginning of the next. Thus, the balance reported for cash is a result of all cash transactions since the business first opened. This is true for all accounts reported on the balance sheet. For this reason, they are called **permanent accounts.**

▨ **Permanent accounts contain the results of all transactions since the business started. Temporary accounts contain information for one accounting period.**

Revenue, expense, and drawing accounts are used to accumulate information for a *specific accounting period.* At the end of the fiscal year, these accounts must be **closed,** that is, they are given zero balances so they will be prepared to accumulate new information for the next accounting period. This is known as the **closing process.** Since these accounts do not accumulate information across accounting periods they are called **temporary accounts.** The drawing account and all accounts reported on the income statement are temporary accounts and must be closed at the end of each accounting period.

The closing process is most clearly demonstrated by returning to the accounting equation and T accounts. As shown in figure 6-4, revenues, expenses, and drawing impact owner's equity and should be considered "under the umbrella" of the capital account. The effect of these accounts on owner's equity is formalized at the end of the accounting period when the balances of the temporary accounts are transferred to the owner's capital account (a permanent account) during the closing process.

F I G U R E 6 - 4 **The Closing Process**

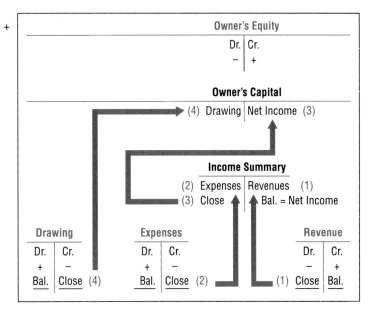

The four basic steps in the closing process are illustrated in figure 6-4. A new account, **Income Summary,** is used in the closing process. This temporary account, also called **Expense and Revenue Summary,** is used to summarize the effects of all revenue and expense accounts. This account is open during the closing process. Then it is closed to the owner's capital account. *It does not appear on any financial statement.* The four steps in the closing process are explained below.

STEP 1   **Close revenue accounts to Income Summary.**   Revenues have credit balances and increase owner's equity. Therefore, the revenue account is debited to create a zero balance. Income Summary is credited for the same amount.

STEP 2   **Close expense accounts to Income Summary.**   Expenses have debit balances and reduce owner's equity. Therefore, the expense accounts are credited to create a zero balance. Income Summary must be debited for the total of the expenses.

STEP 3   **Close Income Summary to Capital.**   The balance in Income Summary represents the net income (credit balance) or net loss (debit balance) for the period. This balance is transferred to the owner's capital account. If net income has been earned, Income Summary is debited to create a zero balance, and the owner's capital account is credited. If a net loss has been incurred, the owner's capital account is debited, and Income Summary is credited to create a zero balance. Figure 6-5 shows examples of Step 3 for net income and for net loss.

FIGURE 6-5 **STEP 3: Closing Net Income and Closing Net Loss**

EXAMPLE OF NET INCOME		EXAMPLE OF NET LOSS	
Capital		Capital	
	1,000 STEP 3 (Net Income)	STEP 3 2,000 (Net Loss)	
Income Summary		Income Summary	
(Exp.) 4,000	5,000 (Rev.)	(Exp.) 6,000	4,000 (Rev.)
STEP 3 1,000			2,000 STEP 3

STEP 4   **Close the drawing account to the owner's capital account.**   Drawing has a debit balance and reduces owner's equity. Therefore, it is credited to create a zero balance. The owner's capital account is debited.

Upon completion of these four steps, all temporary accounts have zero balances and the earnings and withdrawals for the period have been transferred to the owner's capital account. Figure 6-6 shows that the account balances are available from the work sheet.

FIGURE 6-6 Role of the Work Sheet in the Closing Process

Jessie Jane's Campus Delivery Service
Work Sheet (Partial)
For the Month Ended June 30, 19--

	ACCOUNT TITLE	INCOME STATEMENT DEBIT	INCOME STATEMENT CREDIT	BALANCE SHEET DEBIT	BALANCE SHEET CREDIT	
1	Cash			3 7 0 00		1
2	Accounts Receivable			5 0 0 00		2
3	Supplies			2 0 00		3
4	Prepaid Insurance			1 7 5 00		4
5	Delivery Equipment			3 6 0 0 00		5
6	Accounts Payable				1 8 0 0 00	6
7	Jessica Jane, Capital		STEP 1		2 0 0 0 00	7
8	Jessica Jane, Drawing	STEP 2		1 5 0 00		8
9	Delivery Fees		2 0 0 0 00			9
10	Rent Expense	2 0 0 00	STEP 4			10
11	Wage Expense	7 0 0 00				11
12	Telephone Expense	5 0 00				12
13						13
14						14
15	Supplies Expense	6 0 00				15
16	Insurance Expense	2 5 00				16
17	Wages Payable				5 0 00	17
18	Depr. Exp.—Del. Equip.	1 0 0 00				18
19	Accum. Depr.—Del. Equip.				1 0 0 00	19
20		1 1 3 5 00	2 0 0 0 00	4 8 1 5 00	3 9 5 0 00	20
21	Net Income STEP 3	8 6 5 00			8 6 5 00	21
22		2 0 0 0 00	2 0 0 0 00	4 8 1 5 00	4 8 1 5 00	22

STEP 1 Close the revenue account to Income Summary.

STEP 2 Close expense accounts to Income Summary.

STEP 3 Close Income Summary to owner's capital account.

STEP 4 Close Drawing to the owner's capital account.

Journalize Closing Entries

Of course, to actually affect the ledger accounts, the closing entries must be journalized and posted to the general ledger. As shown in figure 6-6 the balances of the accounts to be closed are readily available from the Income Statement and Balance Sheet columns of the work sheet. These balances are used to illustrate the closing entries for Jessie Jane's Campus Delivery Service in T account and general journal form in figure 6-7 and figure 6-8. Remember, closing entries are made at the end of the *fiscal year*. Closing entries at the end of June are illustrated here so you can see the completion of the accounting cycle for Jessie Jane's Campus Delivery Service.

FIGURE 6-7 Closing Entries in T Accounts

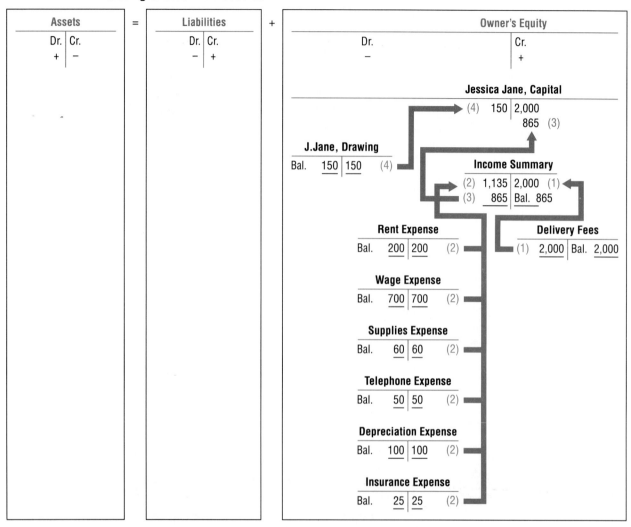

Like adjusting entries, the closing entries are made on the last day of the accounting period. "Closing Entries" is written in the Description column before the first entry and no explanations are required. Note that it is best to make one compound entry to close the expense accounts.

Post the Closing Entries

The account numbers have been entered in the Posting Reference column of the journal to show that the entries have been posted to the ledger accounts illustrated in figure 6-9. Note that "Closing" has been written in the Item column of each account to identify the closing entries. Zero account balances are recorded by drawing a line through both the debit and credit balance columns.

CHAPTER 6 Financial Statements and the Closing Process

179

FIGURE 6-8 Closing Entries in General Journal

STEP	#	DATE		DESCRIPTION	POST. REF.	DEBIT	CREDIT	#
	1			Closing Entries				1
STEP 1	2	19-- June	30	Delivery Fees	411	2 000 00		2
	3			Income Summary	331		2 000 00	3
	4							4
STEP 2	5		30	Income Summary	331	1 135 00		5
	6			Rent Expense	541		200 00	6
	7			Wage Expense	542		700 00	7
Compound entry				Supplies Expense	543		60 00	8
				Telephone Expense	545		50 00	9
	10			Depreciation Expense	547		100 00	10
	11			Insurance Expense	548		25 00	11
	12							12
STEP 3	13		30	Income Summary	331	865 00		13
	14			Jessica Jane, Capital	311		865 00	14
	15							15
STEP 4	16		30	Jessica Jane, Capital	311	150 00		16
	17			Jessica Jane, Drawing	312		150 00	17
No explanations are necessary.	18							18
	19							19
	20							20

FIGURE 6-9 Closing Entries in the General Ledger

GENERAL LEDGER

ACCOUNT: JESSICA JANE, CAPITAL — ACCOUNT NO. 311

DATE		ITEM	POST. REF.	DEBIT	CREDIT	BALANCE DEBIT	BALANCE CREDIT
19-- June	1		J1		2 000 00		2 000 00
	30	Closing	J4		865 00		2 865 00
	30	Closing	J4	150 00			2 715 00

ACCOUNT: JESSICA JANE, DRAWING — ACCOUNT NO. 131

DATE		ITEM	POST. REF.	DEBIT	CREDIT	BALANCE DEBIT	BALANCE CREDIT
19-- June	30		J2	150 00		150 00	
	30	Closing	J4		150 00	—	—

FIGURE 6-9 **Closing Entries in the General Ledger (continued)**

ACCOUNT: INCOME SUMMARY   ACCOUNT NO. 331

DATE		ITEM	POST. REF.	DEBIT	CREDIT	BALANCE DEBIT	BALANCE CREDIT
19-- June	30	Closing	J4		2 0 0 0 00		2 0 0 0 00
	30	Closing	J4	1 1 3 5 00			8 6 5 00
	30	Closing	J4	8 6 5 00			

ACCOUNT: DELIVERY FEES   ACCOUNT NO. 411

DATE		ITEM	POST. REF.	DEBIT	CREDIT	BALANCE DEBIT	BALANCE CREDIT
19-- June	6		J1		5 0 0 00		5 0 0 00
	15		J1		6 0 0 00		1 1 0 0 00
	30		J2		9 0 0 00		2 0 0 0 00
	30	Closing	J4	2 0 0 0 00			

ACCOUNT: RENT EXPENSE   ACCOUNT NO. 541

DATE		ITEM	POST. REF.	DEBIT	CREDIT	BALANCE DEBIT	BALANCE CREDIT
19-- June	7		J1	2 0 0 00		2 0 0 00	
	30	Closing	J4		2 0 0 00		

ACCOUNT: WAGE EXPENSE   ACCOUNT NO. 542

DATE		ITEM	POST. REF.	DEBIT	CREDIT	BALANCE DEBIT	BALANCE CREDIT
19-- June	27		J2	6 5 0 00		6 5 0 00	
	30	Adjusting	J3	5 0 00		7 0 0 00	
	30	Closing	J4		7 0 0 00		

ACCOUNT: SUPPLIES EXPENSE   ACCOUNT NO. 543

DATE		ITEM	POST. REF.	DEBIT	CREDIT	BALANCE DEBIT	BALANCE CREDIT
19-- June	30	Adjusting	J3	6 0 00		6 0 00	
	30	Closing	J4		6 0 00		

ACCOUNT: TELEPHONE EXPENSE   ACCOUNT NO. 545

DATE		ITEM	POST. REF.	DEBIT	CREDIT	BALANCE DEBIT	BALANCE CREDIT
19-- June	15		J1	5 0 00		5 0 00	
	30	Closing	J4		5 0 00		

FIGURE 6-9 **Closing Entries in the General Ledger (concluded)**

ACCOUNT: DEPRECIATION EXPENSE　　　　　　　　　　　ACCOUNT NO. 547

DATE	ITEM	POST. REF.	DEBIT	CREDIT	BALANCE DEBIT	BALANCE CREDIT
19-- June 30	Adjusting	J3	1 0 0 00		1 0 0 00	
30	Closing	J4		1 0 0 00		

ACCOUNT: INSURANCE EXPENSE　　　　　　　　　　　ACCOUNT NO. 548

DATE	ITEM	POST. REF.	DEBIT	CREDIT	BALANCE DEBIT	BALANCE CREDIT
19-- June 30	Adjusting	J3	2 5 00		2 5 00	
30	Closing	J4		2 5 00		

3

Prepare a post-closing
trial balance.

POST-CLOSING TRIAL BALANCE

After posting the closing entries, a **post-closing trial balance** should be prepared to prove the equality of the debit and credit balances in the general ledger accounts. The ending balance of each general ledger account that remains open at the end of the year is listed. Figure 6-10 shows the post-closing trial balance of Jane's ledger.

FIGURE 6-10 **Post-Closing Trial Balance**

Jessie Jane's Campus Delivery Service
Post-Closing Trial Balance
June 30, 19--

ACCOUNT TITLE	ACCOUNT NO.	DEBIT BALANCE	CREDIT BALANCE
Cash	111	3 7 0 00	
Accounts Receivable	131	5 0 0 00	
Supplies	151	2 0 00	
Prepaid Insurance	155	1 7 5 00	
Delivery Equipment	185	3 6 0 0 00	
Accumulated. Depr.—Delivery Equip.	185.1		1 0 0 00
Accounts Payable	218		1 8 0 0 00
Wages Payable	219		5 0 00
Jessica Jane, Capital	311		2 7 1 5 00
		4 6 6 5 00	4 6 6 5 00

4

List and describe the steps in the accounting cycle.

THE ACCOUNTING CYCLE

The steps involved in accounting for all of the business activities during an accounting period are called the **accounting cycle.** The cycle begins with the analysis of source documents and ends with a post-closing trial balance. A brief summary of the steps in the cycle follows.

Steps in the Accounting Cycle

STEP 1   Analyze source documents and journalize the transactions.

STEP 2   Post to the ledger accounts.

End of Accounting Period

STEP 3   Prepare a trial balance.

STEP 4   Determine and prepare the needed adjustments on the work sheet.

STEP 5   Complete an end-of-period work sheet.

STEP 6   Prepare an income statement, statement of owner's equity, and balance sheet.

STEP 7   Journalize the adjusting and closing entries.

STEP 8   Post the adjusting and closing entries.

STEP 9   Prepare a post-closing trial balance.

These nine steps are illustrated by number in figure 6-11.

Steps (3) through (9) are performed *as of* the last day of the accounting period. This does not mean that they are actually done on the last day. The accountant may not be able to do any of these things until the first few days (sometimes weeks) of the next period. Nevertheless, the work sheet, statements, and entries are prepared as of the closing date.

KEY POINTS

1 The work sheet is a very useful tool. It is used as an aid in preparing the:

a. adjusting entries
b. financial statements
c. closing entries

The following classifications are used for accounts reported on the balance sheet.

- **Current assets** include cash and assets that will be converted into cash or consumed within either one year or the normal operating cycle of the business, whichever is longer. An **operating cycle** is the period of

FIGURE 6-11 **Steps in the Accounting Cycle**

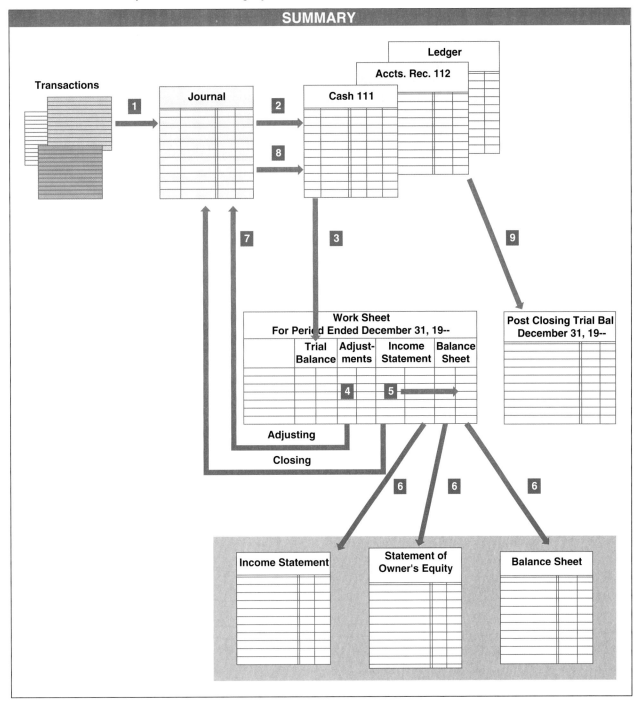

time required to purchase supplies and services and convert them back into cash.

■ **Property, plant, and equipment,** also called **plant assets** or **long-term assets,** represent assets that are expected to serve the business for many years.

■ **Current liabilities** are liabilities that are due within either one year or the normal operating cycle of the business, whichever is longer, and that are to be paid out of current assets.

■ **Long-term liabilities,** or **long-term debt,** are obligations that are not expected to be paid within a year, and do not require the use of current assets.

2 Steps in the closing process are:

1. Close revenue accounts to Income Summary.
2. Close expense accounts to Income Summary.
3. Close Income Summary to Capital.
4. Close the drawing account to the owner's capital account.

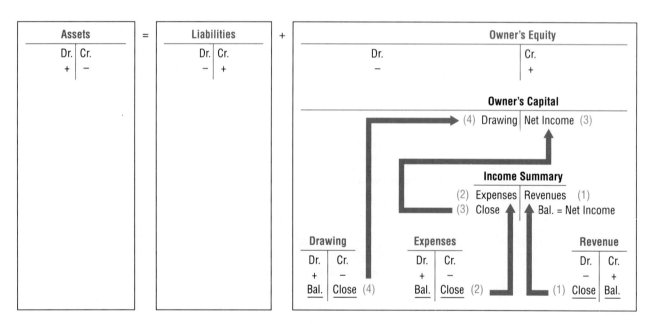

3 After posting the closing entries, a post-closing trial balance should be prepared to prove the equality of the debit and credit balances in the general ledger accounts.

Steps in the accounting cycle are:
1. Analyze source documents and journalize the transactions.
2. Post to the ledger accounts.

End of Accounting Period

3. Prepare a trial balance.
4. Determine and prepare the needed adjustments on the work sheet.
5. Complete an end-of-period work sheet.
6. Prepare an income statement, statement of owner's equity, and balance sheet.
7. Journalize the adjusting and closing entries.
8. Post the adjusting and closing entries.
9. Prepare a post-closing trial balance.

KEY TERMS

account form of balance sheet 173   The assets are on the left, and the liabilities and the owner's equity sections are on the right.

accounting cycle 182   The steps involved in accounting for all of the business activities during an accounting period.

classified balance sheet 173   Similar items are grouped together on the balance sheet.

closing process 175   The process of giving zero balances to the temporary accounts so that they can accumulate information for the next accounting period.

current assets 174   Cash and assets that will be converted into cash or consumed within either one year or the normal operating cycle of the business, whichever is longer.

current liabilities 174   Liabilities that are due within either one year or the normal operating cycle of the business, whichever is longer, and that are to be paid out of current assets.

expense and revenue summary 176   *See* Income Summary.

Income Summary 176   A temporary account used in the closing process to summarize the effects of all revenue and expense accounts.

long-term assets 174   *See* Property, plant, and equipment.

long-term debt 174   *See* Long-term liabilities.

long-term liabilities 174   Obligations that are not expected to be paid within a year and do not require the use of current assets.

operating cycle 174   The period of time required to purchase supplies and services and convert them back into cash.

permanent accounts 175   All accounts reported on the balance sheet.

plant assets 174   *See* Property, plant, and equipment.

post-closing trial balance 181   Prepared after posting the closing entries to prove the equality of the debit and credit balances in the general ledger.

property, plant, and equipment 174   Assets that are expected to serve the business for many years. Also called plant assets or long-term assets.

report form of balance sheet 172   The liabilities and the owner's equity sections are shown below the assets section.

temporary accounts 175   Accounts that do not accumulate information across accounting periods but are closed, such as the drawing account and all income statement accounts.

BUILDING YOUR ACCOUNTING KNOWLEDGE

1. Identify the source of the information needed to prepare the income statement.
2. Describe two approaches to listing the expenses in the income statement.
3. Identify the sources of the information needed to prepare the statement of owner's equity.
4. If additional investments were made during the year, what information in addition to the work sheet would be needed to prepare the statement of owner's equity?
5. Identify the sources of the information needed to prepare the balance sheet.
6. What is a permanent account? On which financial statement are permanent accounts reported?
7. Name three types of temporary accounts.
8. List the four procedures for closing the temporary accounts.
9. Describe the net effect of the four closing entries on the balance of the owner's capital account. Where else is this same amount calculated?
10. What is the purpose of the post-closing trial balance?
11. List the nine steps in the accounting cycle.

DEMONSTRATION PROBLEM

Timothy Chang owns and operates Hard Copy Printers. A work sheet for the year ended December 31, 19--, is provided below. Using this information, (1) prepare financial statements and (2) prepare closing entries.

Hard Copy Printers
Work Sheet
For the Year Ended December 31, 19--

	ACCOUNT TITLE	TRIAL BALANCE DEBIT	TRIAL BALANCE CREDIT	ADJUSTMENTS DEBIT	ADJUSTMENTS CREDIT	ADJUSTED TRIAL BALANCE DEBIT	ADJUSTED TRIAL BALANCE CREDIT	INCOME STATEMENT DEBIT	INCOME STATEMENT CREDIT	BALANCE SHEET DEBIT	BALANCE SHEET CREDIT	
1	Cash	1 180 00				1 180 00				1 180 00		1
2	Paper Supplies	3 600 00			(a) 3 550 00	50 00				50 00		2
3	Prepaid Insurance	1 000 00			(b) 505 00	495 00				495 00		3
4	Printing Equipment	5 800 00				5 800 00				5 800 00		4
5	Accounts Payable		500 00				500 00				500 00	5
6	Timothy Chang, Capital		4 530 00				4 530 00				4 530 00	6
7	Timothy Chang, Drawing	13 000 00				13 000 00				13 000 00		7
8	Printing Fees		35 100 00				35 100 00		35 100 00			8
9	Rent Expense	7 500 00				7 500 00		7 500 00				9
10	Wage Expense	6 500 00		(c) 30 00		6 530 00		6 530 00				10
11	Telephone Expense	550 00				550 00		550 00				11
12	Utilities Expense	1 000 00				1 000 00		1 000 00				12
13		40 130 00	40 130 00									13
14	Paper Supplies Expense			(a) 3 550 00		3 550 00		3 550 00				14
15	Insurance Expense			(b) 505 00		505 00		505 00				15
16	Depr. Exp.—Print Equip.			(d) 1 200 00		1 200 00		1 200 00				16
17	Acc. Depr.—Print Equip.				(d) 1 200 00		120 00				120 00	17
18	Wages Payable				(c) 30 00		30 00				30 00	18
19				5 285 00	5 285 00	41 360 00	41 360 00	20 835 00	35 100 00	20 525 00	6 260 00	19
20	Net Income							14 265 00			14 265 00	20
21								35 100 00	35 100 00	20 525 00	20 525 00	21

1.

Hard Copy Printers
Income Statement
For the Year Ended December 31, 19--

Revenue:			
Printing fees			$35 1 0 0 00
Expenses:			
Rent expense	$7 5 0 0 00		
Wage expense	6 5 3 0 00		
Paper supplies expense	3 5 5 0 00		
Depreciation expense	1 2 0 0 00		
Utilities expense	1 0 0 0 00		
Telephone expense	5 5 0 00		
Insurance expense	5 0 5 00		
Total expenses		20 8 3 5 00	
Net income		$14 2 6 5 00	

Hard Copy Printers
Statement of Owner's Equity
For the Year Ended December 31, 19--

Timothy Chang, capital, Jan. 1, 19--			$4 5 3 0 00
Net income	$14 2 6 5 00		
Less withdrawals	13 0 0 0 00		
Increase in capital		1 2 6 5 00	
Timothy Chang, capital, Dec. 31, 19--		$5 7 9 5 00	

Hard Copy Printers
Balance Sheet
December 31, 19--

Assets			
Current assets:			
Cash	$1 1 8 0 00		
Paper supplies	5 0 00		
Prepaid insurance	4 9 5 00		
Total current assets		$1 7 2 5 00	
Property, plant, and equipment:			
Printing equipment	$5 8 0 0 00		
Less accumulated depreciation	1 2 0 0 00	4 6 0 0 00	
Total assets		$6 3 2 5 00	
Liabilities			
Current liabilities:			
Accounts payable	$ 5 0 0 00		
Wages payable	3 0 00		
Total current liabilities		$ 5 3 0 00	
Owner's Equity			
Timothy Chang, capital		5 7 9 5 00	
Total liabilities and owner's equity		$6 3 2 5 00	

2.

	DATE		DESCRIPTION	POST. REF.	DEBIT	CREDIT	
1			Closing Entries				1
2	19-- Dec.	31	Printing Fees		35 1 0 0 00		2
3			Income Summary			35 1 0 0 00	3
4							4
5		31	Income Summary		20 8 3 5 00		5
6			Rent Expense			7 5 0 0 00	6
7			Wage Expense			6 5 3 0 00	7
8			Telephone Expense			5 5 0 00	8
9			Utilities Expense			1 0 0 0 00	9
10			Paper Supplies Expense			3 5 5 0 00	10
11			Insurance Expense			5 0 5 00	11
12			Depreciation Expense			1 2 0 0 00	12
13							13
14		31	Income Summary		14 2 6 5 00		14
15			Timothy Chang, Capital			14 2 6 5 00	15
16							16
17		31	Timothy Chang, Capital		13 0 0 0 00		17
18			Timothy Chang, Drawing			13 0 0 0 00	18
19							19
20							20
21							21
22							22
23							23
24							24

GENERAL JOURNAL — PAGE 4

SERIES A

EXERCISES

APPLYING ACCOUNTING CONCEPTS

EXERCISE 6A1

Income Statement

1 From the partial work sheet on page 190, prepare an income statement.

EXERCISE 6A2

Statement of Owner's Equity

1 From the partial work sheet in Exercise 6A1, prepare a statement of owner's equity, assuming no additional investment was made by the owner.

EXERCISE 6A3

Balance Sheet

1 From the partial work sheet in Exercise 6A1, prepare a balance sheet for Bill Case.

Bill Case
Work Sheet (Partial)
For Month Ended January 31, 19--

	ACCOUNT TITLE	INCOME STATEMENT DEBIT	INCOME STATEMENT CREDIT	BALANCE SHEET DEBIT	BALANCE SHEET CREDIT	
1	Cash			1 2 1 2 00		1
2	Accounts Receivable			8 9 6 00		2
3	Supplies			4 8 2 00		3
4	Prepaid Insurance			9 0 0 00		4
5	Delivery Equipment			3 0 0 0 00		5
6	Accounts Payable				1 0 0 0 00	6
7	Bill Case, Capital				4 0 0 0 00	7
8	Bill Case, Drawing			8 0 0 00		8
9	Delivery Fees		3 7 9 3 00			9
10	Rent Expense	5 0 0 00				10
11	Wage Expense	8 0 0 00				11
12	Telephone Expense	5 8 00				12
13	Electricity Expense	4 4 00				13
14	Gas and Oil Expense	3 8 00				14
15	Advertising Expense	8 0 00				15
16	Miscellaneous Expense	3 3 00				16
17	Supplies Expense	1 2 0 00				17
18	Insurance Expense	3 0 00				18
19	Wages Payable				2 0 0 00	19
20	Depr. Exp.—Del. Equip.	1 0 0 00				20
21	Accum. Depr.—Del. Equip.				1 0 0 00	21
22		1 8 0 3 00	3 7 9 3 00	7 2 9 0 00	5 3 0 0 00	22
23	Net Income	1 9 9 0 00			1 9 9 0 00	23
24		3 7 9 3 00	3 7 9 3 00	7 2 9 0 00	7 2 9 0 00	24

EXERCISE 6A4

Closing Entries (Net Income)

2 Set up the following T accounts, prepare closing entries in general journal form. Then post the closing entries to the T accounts.

Cash 111	Accounts Receivable 131	Supplies 151
1,212	896	482

Prepaid Ins. 155	Delivery Equip. 185	Accts. Payable 211
900	3,000	1,000

Bill Case, Cap. 311	Bill Case, Drawing 312	Delivery Fees 411
4,000	800	3,793

Rent Expense 541	Wage Expense 542	Telephone Exp. 545
500	800	58

Electricity Exp. 549	Gas & Oil Exp. 550	Advertising Exp. 551
44	38	80

Misc. Exp. 572	Supplies Expense 543	Insurance Exp. 548
33	120	30

Wages Payable 219	Depr. Exp.— Del. Equip. 547	Acc. Depr.— Del. Equip. 185.1
200	100	100

Income Summary 313

EXERCISE 6A5

Closing Entries (Net Loss)

2 Using the following T accounts, prepare closing entries in general journal form. Then post the closing entries to the T accounts.

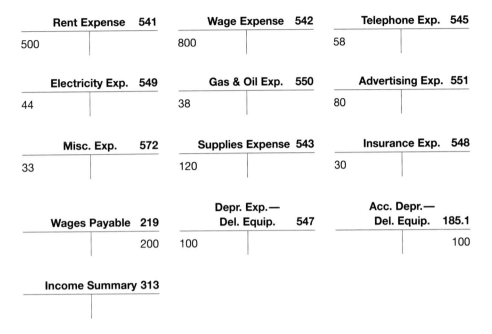

Bill Case, Cap. 311	Bill Case, Drawing 312	Delivery Fees 411
4,000	800	2,200

Rent Expense 541	Wage Expense 542	Telephone Exp. 545
500	1,800	58

Electricity Exp. 549	Gas & Oil Exp. 550	Advertising Exp. 551
44	38	80

Misc. Expense 572	Supplies Expense 543	Insurance Exp. 548
33	120	30

Wages Payable 219	Depr. Exp.— Del. Equip 547	Acc. Depr— Del. Equip. 185.1
200	100	100

Income Summary 313

PROBLEMS

1 The following shows a work sheet for Monte's Repairs.

Required
1. Prepare an income statement.
2. Prepare a statement of owner's equity.
3. Prepare a balance sheet.

Monte's Repairs
Work Sheet
For Month Ended January 31, 19--

	ACCOUNT TITLE	ACCT. NO.	TRIAL BALANCE DEBIT	TRIAL BALANCE CREDIT	ADJUSTMENTS DEBIT	ADJUSTMENTS CREDIT	
1	Cash	111	3150 00				1
2	Accounts Receivable	131	1200 00				2
3	Supplies	151	800 00			(a) 200 00	3
4	Prepaid Insurance	155	900 00			(b) 100 00	4
5	Delivery Equipment	185	3000 00				5
6	Accounts Payable	211		1100 00			6
7	Monte Eli, Capital	311		6000 00			7
8	Monte Eli, Drawing	312	1000 00				8
9	Repair Fees	411		4230 00			9
10	Rent Expense	541	420 00				10
11	Salary Expense	542	650 00		(c) 150 00		11
12	Telephone Expense	545	49 00				12
13	Gas and Oil Exp.	550	33 00				13
14	Advertising Exp.	551	100 00				14
15	Miscellaneous Exp.	572	28 00				15
16							16
17	Supplies Expense	543			(a) 200 00		17
18	Insurance Expense	548			(b) 100 00		18
19	Salary Payable	219				(c) 150 00	19
20	Depr. Exp.—Del. Eq.	547			(d) 30 00		20
21	Accum. Depr.—Del. Eq.	185.1				(d) 30 00	21
22			11330 00	11330 00	480 00	480 00	22
23	Net Income						23
24							24

	ADJUSTED TRIAL BALANCE		INCOME STATEMENT		BALANCE SHEET		
	DEBIT	CREDIT	DEBIT	CREDIT	DEBIT	CREDIT	
1	3 1 5 0 00				3 1 5 0 00		1
2	1 2 0 0 00				1 2 0 0 00		2
3	6 0 0 00				6 0 0 00		3
4	8 0 0 00				8 0 0 00		4
5	3 0 0 0 00				3 0 0 0 00		5
6		1 1 0 0 00				1 1 0 0 00	6
7		6 0 0 0 00				6 0 0 0 00	7
8	1 0 0 00				1 0 0 00		8
9		4 2 3 0 00		4 2 3 0 00			9
10	4 2 0 00		4 2 0 00				10
11	8 0 0 00		8 0 0 00				11
12	4 9 00		4 9 00				12
13	3 3 00		3 3 00				13
14	1 0 0 00		1 0 0 00				14
15	2 8 00		2 8 00				15
16							16
17	2 0 0 00		2 0 0 00				17
18	1 0 0 00		1 0 0 00				18
19		1 5 0 00				1 5 0 00	19
20	3 0 00		3 0 00				20
21		3 0 00				3 0 00	21
22	11 5 1 0 00	11 5 1 0 00	1 7 6 0 00	4 2 3 0 00	9 7 5 0 00	7 2 8 0 00	22
23			2 4 7 0 00			2 4 7 0 00	23
24			4 2 3 0 00	4 2 3 0 00	9 7 5 0 00	9 7 5 0 00	24

1 The capital account for Jessie Richards with an additional investment, and a partial work sheet are shown as follows.

Required

Prepare a statement of owner's equity.

ACCOUNT: JESSIE RICHARDS, CAPTIAL							ACCOUNT NO. 311	
DATE		ITEM	POST. REF.	DEBIT	CREDIT	BALANCE		
						DEBIT	CREDIT	
19-- Jan.	1	Bal.					4 8 0 0 00	
	18		CJ1		1 2 0 0 00		6 0 0 0 00	

Jessie Richards
Work Sheet (Partial)
For Month Ended January 31, 19--

	ACCOUNT TITLE	INCOME STATEMENT		BALANCE SHEET		
		DEBIT	CREDIT	DEBIT	CREDIT	
1	Cash			3 2 0 0 00		1
2	Accounts Receivable			1 6 0 0 00		2
3	Supplies			8 0 0 00		3
4	Prepaid Insurance			9 0 0 00		4
5	Office Equipment			2 5 0 0 00		5
6	Accounts Payable				1 9 5 0 00	6
7	Jessie Richards, Capital				6 0 0 0 00	7
8	Jessie Richards, Drawing			1 0 0 0 00		8
9	Service Fees		3 8 6 6 00			9
10	Rent Expense	6 0 0 00				10
11	Wage Expense	9 0 0 00				11
12	Telephone Expense	8 5 00				12
13	Electricity Expense	4 8 00				13
14	Gas & Oil Expense	3 2 00				14
15	Advertising Expense	2 1 00				15
16	Miscellaneous Expense	5 0 00				16
17						17
18	Supplies Expense	2 0 0 00				18
19	Insurance Expense	6 0 00				19
20	Wages Payable				1 8 0 00	20
21	Depr. Exp.—Office Equip.	5 0 00				21
22	Acc. Depr.—Office Equip.				5 0 00	22
23		2 0 4 6 00	3 8 6 6 00	10 0 0 0 00	8 1 8 0 00	23
24	Net Income	1 8 2 0 00			1 8 2 0 00	24
25		3 8 6 6 00	3 8 6 6 00	10 0 0 0 00	10 0 0 0 00	25

PROBLEM 6A3

Financial Statements, Closing Entries, Post- Closing Trial Balance

◄**EPS**►

1/2/3 Refer to the work sheet in Problem 6A1.

Required
1. Journalize the adjusting entries.
2. Journalize the closing entries.
3. Post the trial balances from the work sheet and the adjusting and closing entries to the general ledger (four-column accounts.)
4. Prepare a post-closing trial balance.
   Note: Income Summary is Account No. 313.

SERIES B

EXERCISES

EXERCISE 6B1

Income Statement

1 From the following partial work sheet, prepare an income statement.

Mary Adams
Work Sheet (Partial)
For Three Months Ended June 30, 19--

	ACCOUNT TITLE	ACCT. NO.	INCOME STATEMENT DEBIT	INCOME STATEMENT CREDIT	BALANCE SHEET DEBIT	BALANCE SHEET CREDIT	
1	Cash	111			3 2 6 2 00		1
2	Accounts Receivable	131			1 2 4 4 00		2
3	Supplies	151			8 0 0 00		3
4	Prepaid Insurance	155			6 4 0 00		4
5	Office Equipment	191			2 1 0 0 00		5
6	Accounts Payable	211				1 8 5 0 00	6
7	Mary Adams, Capital	311				6 0 0 0 00	7
8	Mary Adams, Drawing	312			2 0 0 0 00		8
9	Referral Fees	411		4 8 1 3 00			9
10	Rent Expense	541	9 0 0 00				10
11	Wage Expense	542	1 0 8 0 00				11
12	Telephone Expense	545	1 3 3 00				12
13	Utilities Expense	549	1 0 2 00				13
14	Gas and Oil Expense	550	8 8 00				14
15	Advertising Expense	551	3 4 00				15
16	Miscellaneous Expense	572	9 8 00				16
17	Supplies Expense	543	3 2 2 00				17
18	Insurance Expense	548	1 2 0 00				18
19	Wages Payable	219				2 6 0 00	19
20	Depr. Exp.—Off. Equip.	547	1 1 0 00				20
21	Acc. Depr.—Off. Equip.	191.1				1 1 0 00	21
22			2 9 8 7 00	4 8 1 3 00	10 0 4 6 00	8 2 2 0 00	22
23	Net Income		1 8 2 6 00			1 8 2 6 00	23
24			4 8 1 3 00	4 8 1 3 00	10 0 4 6 00	10 0 4 6 00	24

EXERCISE 6B2

Statement of Owner's Equity

1 From the partial work sheet in Exercise 6B1, prepare a statement of owner's equity, assuming no additional investment was made by the owner.

EXERCISE 6B3

Balance Sheet

1. From the partial work sheet in Exercise 6B1, prepare a balance sheet for Mary Adams.

EXERCISE 6B4

Closing Entries (Net Income)

2 Set up T accounts for Mary Adams (see Exercise 6B1). Prepare closing entries in general journal form, then post the closing entries to the T accounts.

EXERCISE 6B5

Closing Entries (Net Loss)

2 Set up the T accounts shown below, prepare closing entries in general journal form. Then post the closing entries to the T accounts.

Mary Adams, Cap. 311	Mary Adams, Drawing 312	Referral Fees 411
| 6,000	2,000 |	| 2,813

Rent Expense 541	Wage Expense 542	Telephone Exp. 545
900 |	1,080 |	133 |

Utilities Exp. 549	Gas & Oil Exp. 550	Advertising Exp. 551
102 |	88 |	34 |

Miscellaneous Exp. 572	Supplies Expense 543	Insurance Exp. 548
98 |	322 |	120 |

Wages Payable 219	Dep. Exp.—Off. Equip. 548	Acc. Dep.—Off. Equip. 191.1
| 260	110 |	| 110

Income Summary 313
|

PROBLEMS

PROBLEM 6B1

Financial Statements

1 A work sheet for Melissa's Consulting is shown on pages 198–199.

Required

1. Prepare an income statement.
2. Prepare a statement of owner's equity.
3. Prepare a balance sheet.

PROBLEM 6B2

Statement of Owner's Equity

1 The capital account for Jeremy Blanchard with an additional invest-ment, and a partial work sheet are shown as follows.

ACCOUNT: JEREMY BLANCHARD, CAPITAL					ACCOUNT NO. 311	
					BALANCE	
DATE	ITEM	POST. REF.	DEBIT	CREDIT	DEBIT	CREDIT
19-- Jan. 1	Bal.					3 6 0 0 00
22		CJ1		2 9 0 0 00		6 5 0 0 00

Jeremy Blanchard
Work Sheet (Partial)
For Month Ended January 31, 19--

	ACCOUNT TITLE	INCOME STATEMENT		BALANCE SHEET		
		DEBIT	CREDIT	DEBIT	CREDIT	
1	Cash			3 8 0 0 00		1
2	Accounts Receivable			2 2 0 0 00		2
3	Supplies			1 0 0 0 00		3
4	Prepaid Insurance			9 5 0 00		4
5	Repair Equipment			4 5 0 0 00		5
6	Accounts Payable				2 1 0 0 00	6
7	Jeremy Blanchard, Capital				6 5 0 0 00	7
8	Jeremy Blanchard, Drawing			1 7 0 0 00		8
9	Repair Fees		7 0 1 2 00			9
10	Rent Expense	4 5 0 00				10
11	Wage Expense	6 0 0 00				11
12	Telephone Expense	4 4 00				12
13	Electricity Expense	3 8 00				13
14	Gas and Oil Expense	6 8 00				14
15	Advertising Expense	4 9 00				15
16	Miscellaneous Expense	1 8 00				16
17						17
18	Supplies Expense	2 2 0 00				18
19	Insurance Expense	1 2 5 00				19
20	Wages Payable				1 5 0 00	20
21	Depr. Exp.—Repair Equip.	2 2 5 00				21
22	Accum. Depr.—Repair Equip.				2 2 5 00	22
23		1 8 3 7 00	7 0 1 2 00	14 1 5 0 00	8 9 7 5 00	23
24	Net Income	5 1 7 5 00			5 1 7 5 00	24
25		7 0 1 2 00	7 0 1 2 00	14 1 5 0 00	14 1 5 0 00	25

Required

Prepare a statement of owner's equity.

Work Sheet for Problem 6B1.

Melissa's Consulting
Work Sheet
For Month Ended June 30, 19--

	ACCOUNT TITLE	ACCT. NO.	TRIAL BALANCE DEBIT	TRIAL BALANCE CREDIT	ADJUSTMENTS DEBIT	ADJUSTMENTS CREDIT	
1	Cash	111	5 2 8 5 00				1
2	Accounts Receivable	131	1 0 7 5 00				2
3	Supplies	151	7 5 0 00			(a) 2 5 0 00	3
4	Prepaid Insurance	155	5 0 0 00			(b) 1 0 0 00	4
5	Office Equipment	191	2 2 0 0 00				5
6	Accounts Payable	211		1 5 0 0 00			6
7	Melissa Mebs, Cap.	311		6 0 0 0 00			7
8	Melissa Mebs, Draw.	312	8 0 0 00				8
9	Consulting Fees	411		4 2 0 4 00			9
10	Rent Expense	541	5 0 0 00				10
11	Salary Expense	542	4 0 0 00		(c) 2 0 0 00		11
12	Telephone Expense	545	4 6 00				12
13	Gas and Oil Exp.	550	2 8 00				13
14	Electricity Exp.	551	3 9 00				14
15	Advertising Exp.	552	6 0 00				15
16	Miscellaneous Exp.	572	2 1 00				16
17							17
18	Supplies Expense	543			(a) 2 5 0 00		18
19	Insurance Expense	548			(b) 1 0 0 00		19
20	Salary Payable	219				(c) 2 0 0 00	20
21	Depr. Exp.—Off. Equip.	547			(d) 1 1 0 00		21
22	Acc. Depr.—Off. Equip.	191.1				(d) 1 1 0 00	22
23			11 7 0 4 00	11 7 0 4 00	6 6 0 00	6 6 0 00	23
24	Net Income						24
25							25

	ADJUSTED TRIAL BALANCE		INCOME STATEMENT		BALANCE SHEET		
	DEBIT	CREDIT	DEBIT	CREDIT	DEBIT	CREDIT	
1	5 2 8 5 00				5 2 8 5 00		1
2	1 0 7 5 00				1 0 7 5 00		2
3	5 0 0 00				5 0 0 00		3
4	4 0 0 00				4 0 0 00		4
5	2 2 0 0 00				2 2 0 0 00		5
6		1 5 0 0 00				1 5 0 0 00	6
7		6 0 0 0 00				6 0 0 0 00	7
8	8 0 0 00				8 0 0 00		8
9		4 2 0 4 00		4 2 0 4 00			9
10	5 0 0 00		5 0 0 00				10
11	6 0 0 00		6 0 0 00				11
12	4 6 00		4 6 00				12
13	2 8 00		2 8 00				13
14	3 9 00		3 9 00				14
15	6 0 00		6 0 00				15
16	2 1 00		2 1 00				16
17							17
18	2 5 0 00		2 5 0 00				18
19	1 0 0 00		1 0 0 00				19
20		2 0 0 00				2 0 0 00	20
21	1 1 0 00		1 1 0 00				21
22		1 1 0 00				1 1 0 00	22
23	12 0 1 4 00	12 0 1 4 00	1 7 5 4 00	4 2 0 4 00	10 2 6 0 00	7 8 1 0 00	23
24			2 4 5 0 00			2 4 5 0 00	24
25			4 2 0 4 00	4 2 0 4 00	10 2 6 0 00	10 2 6 0 00	25

1/2/3 Refer to the work sheet in Problem 6B1.

Required
1. Journalize the adjusting entries.
2. Journalize the closing entries.
3. Post the trial balances from the work sheet and the adjusting and closing entries to the general ledger (four-column accounts.)
4. Prepare a post-closing trial balance.
   Note: Income Summary is Account No. 313.

MASTERY PROBLEM

Marla Woychek owns and operates Shear Brilliance Styling Salon. A year-end work sheet is provided as follows. Using this information, prepare financial statements and closing entries.

Sheer Brilliance Styling Salon
Work Sheet
For Year Ended December 31, 19--

	ACCOUNT TITLE	ACCT. NO.	TRIAL BALANCE DEBIT	TRIAL BALANCE CREDIT	ADJUSTMENTS DEBIT	ADJUSTMENTS CREDIT	
1	Cash		9 4 0 00				1
2	Styling Supplies		1 5 0 0 00			(a)1 4 5 0 00	2
3	Prepaid Insurance		8 0 0 00			(b) 6 5 0 00	3
4	Salon Equipment		4 5 0 0 00				4
5	Accounts Payable			2 2 5 00			5
6	Marla Woychek, Capital			2 7 6 5 00			6
7	Marla Woychek, Drawing		12 0 0 0 00				7
8	Styling Fees			32 0 0 0 00			8
9	Rent Expense		6 0 0 0 00				9
10	Wage Expense		8 0 0 0 00		(c) 4 0 00		10
11	Telephone Expense		4 5 0 00				11
12	Utility Expense		8 0 0 00				12
13			34 9 9 0 00	34 9 9 0 00			13
14	Styling Supplies Expense				(a)1 4 5 0 00		14
15	Insurance Expense				(b) 6 5 0 00		15
16	Depr. Exp.—Salon Equip.				(d) 9 0 0 00		16
17	Accum. Depr.—Salon Equip.					(d) 9 0 0 00	17
18	Wages Payable					(c) 4 0 00	18
19					3 0 4 0 00	3 0 4 0 00	19
20	Net Income						20
21							21

COMPREHENSIVE PROBLEM 1

THE ACCOUNTING CYCLE FOR A SERVICE BUSINESS

Bob Night opened "The General's Favorite Fishing Hole." This fishing camp is open from April through September. Guests typically register for one week arriving on Sunday afternoon and returning home the following Saturday afternoon. The registration fee includes room and board, the use of fishing boats, and professional instruction in fishing techniques. The chart of accounts for the camping operations is on page 202.

	ADJUSTED TRIAL BALANCE		INCOME STATEMENT		BALANCE SHEET		
	DEBIT	CREDIT	DEBIT	CREDIT	DEBIT	CREDIT	
1	9 4 0 00				9 4 0 00		1
2	5 0 00				5 0 00		2
3	1 5 0 00				1 5 0 00		3
4	4 5 0 0 00				4 5 0 0 00		4
5		2 2 5 00				2 2 5 00	5
6		2 7 6 5 00				2 7 6 5 00	6
7	12 0 0 0 00				12 0 0 0 00		7
8		32 0 0 0 00		32 0 0 0 00			8
9	6 0 0 0 00		6 0 0 0 00				9
10	8 0 4 0 00		8 0 4 0 00				10
11	4 5 0 00		4 5 0 00				11
12	8 0 0 00		8 0 0 00				12
13							13
14	1 4 5 0 00		1 4 5 0 00				14
15	6 5 0 00		6 5 0 00				15
16	9 0 0 00		9 0 0 00				16
17		9 0 0 00				9 0 0 00	17
18		4 0 00				4 0 00	18
19	35 9 3 0 00	35 9 3 0 00	18 2 9 0 00	32 0 0 0 00	17 6 4 0 00	3 9 3 0 00	19
20			13 7 1 0 00			13 7 1 0 00	20
21			32 0 0 0 00	32 0 0 0 00	17 6 4 0 00	17 6 4 0 00	21

The General's Favorite Fishing Hole Chart of Accounts			
Assets	**(100–199)**	**Revenues**	**(400–499)**
111	Cash	411	Registration Fees
152	Office Supplies		
154	Food Supplies	**Expenses**	**(500–599)**
155	Prepaid Insurance	541	Rent Expense
185	Fishing Boats	542	Wage Expense
185.1	Accum. Dep.—	543	Supplies Expense
	Fishing Boats	545	Telephone Expense
		547	Deprec. Exp.—
Liabilities	**(200–299)**		Fishing Boats
218	Accounts Payable	548	Insurance Expense
219	Wages Payable	549	Utility Expense
		556	Food Expense
Owner's Equity	**(300–399)**	564	Postage Expense
311	Bob Night, Capital		
312	Bob Night, Drawing		
331	Income Summary		

The following transactions took place during the month of April.

April 1 Night invested $90,000 in a bank as an initial investment.
1 Paid insurance premium for camping season, $9,000.
2 Paid rent on lodge and campgrounds for the month of April, $70,000.
2 Deposited registration fees in the bank, $35,000.
2 Purchased 10 fishing boats for $60,000. The boats have estimated lives of 10 years at which time they will be given to a local camp. Arrangements were made to pay for the boats in July.
3 Purchased food supplies from Acme Super Market on account for $7,000.
5 Purchased office supplies on account from Gordon Office Supplies, $500.
7 Deposited registration fees in the bank, $38,600.

April 10 Purchased food supplies from Acme Super Market on account for $8,200.
10 Paid wages to fishing guides, $10,000.
14 Deposited registration fees in the bank, $30,500.
16 Purchased food supplies from Acme Super Market on account for $9,000.
17 Paid wages to fishing guides, $10,000.
18 Paid postage, $150.
21 Deposited registration fees in the bank, $35,600.
24 Purchased food supplies from Acme Super Market on account for $8,500.
24 Paid wages to fishing guides, $10,000.
28 Deposited registration fees in the bank, $32,000.
30 Purchased food supplies from Acme Super Market on account for $6,000.
30 Paid wages to fishing guides, $10,000.
30 Paid $32,700 to Acme Super Markets on account.
30 Paid utility bill, $2,000.
30 Paid phone bill, $1,200.
30 Paid Bob Night $6,000 for personal use.

Required

1. Enter the above transactions in a general journal.
2. Post the entries to the general ledger.
3. Prepare a trial balance in the first two columns of a work sheet.
4. Complete the work sheet. Adjustment information for the end of April follows.
   (a) Office supplies remaining on hand, $100.
   (b) Food supplies remaining on hand, $8,000.
   (c) Insurance expired during the month of April, $1,500.
   (d) Depreciation on the fishing boats for the month of April, $1,000.
   (e) Wages accrued at the end of April, $500.
5. Prepare the income statement.
6. Prepare the statement of owner's equity.
7. Prepare the balance sheet.
8. Journalize the adjusting entries.
9. Post the adjusting entries to the general ledger.
10. Journalize the closing entries.
11. Post the closing entries to the general ledger.
12. Prepare a post-closing trial balance.

**Chapter 6
Demonstration
Problem**

The following instructions show you how to complete the Chapter 6 demonstration problem using your general ledger software (the Electronic Problem Solver). Refer to Appendix A for additional help as you complete this problem and Problems 6A3 and 6B3. Appendix A contains detailed instructions on the Electronic Problem Solver.

STEP 1   Start up your Electronic Problem Solver software. Enter ACCOUNT1 to load the software.

STEP 2   Move to No using the Right Arrow key and press Enter to move to the next screen.

STEP 3   If you are using 5¼" disks, place Disk 2 in the disk drive.

STEP 4   Strike the Alt key to activate the pull-down menus.

STEP 5   Press Enter with the File command highlighted to pull down the File menu. (Figure AC6-1)

STEP 6   Select the Open Accounting File option and press Enter.

STEP 7   Make certain the Path field indicates the drive and directory in which your disk is located. If necessary, change the Path field. Be certain to include the colon (:) after the Drive name.

STEP 8   Press the End key to activate the Directory button and press Enter to display the directory of files on your disk. (Figure AC6-2)

FIGURE AC6-1 **File Menu**

```
 File Options Journals Ledgers Reports Help
 . . . . . . . . . . . . . . . . . . . . . . .
┌──────────────────────────────┐ . . . . . . . . . . . . . . . .
│ New                          │ . . . . . . . . . . . . . . . .
│ Open Accounting File         │ . . . . . . . . . . . . . . . .
│ Save Accounting File         │ . . . . . . . . . . . . . . . .
│ Save As                      │ . . . . . . . . . . . . . . . .
│ Erase Accounting File        │ . . . . . . . . . . . . . . . .
│                              │
│ About Integrated Accounting  │ . . . . . . . . . . . . . . . .
│ Print                    F9  │ . . . . . . . . . . . . . . . .
│                              │
│ Quit                         │ . . . . . . . . . . . . . . . .
└──────────────────────────────┘
 . . . . . . . . . . . . . . . . . . . . . . .
```

FIGURE AC6-2 **Directory of Opening Balances**

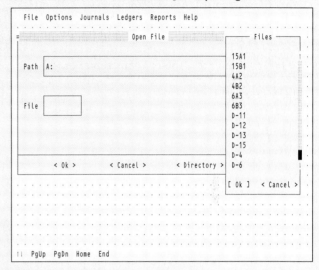

STEP 9   Select D-6 and press Enter.

STEP 10   Press Ok to load the demonstration problem into memory.

STEP 11   Press the Alt key to activate the menu bar. Move to Options and press Enter to pull down the Options menu.

STEP 12   Select General Information and Enter. Verify that the correct problem has been loaded. (Figure AC6-3)

STEP 13   Enter a date of 12/31/9-- (current year).

STEP 14   Enter your name in the Student Name field. Notice that this problem is for a sole proprietorship and a service business. Do not change any of these buttons.

STEP 15   Press the Tab key to move through the fields to the Ok button. Press Enter on Ok to record your data. (Remember that pressing the Ctrl key and the Enter key simultaneously will also record the data.)

STEP 16 Enter the adjusting entries, (a) through (d), in the general journal. Use the Tab key to move forward. The Shift and Tab keys simultaneously move backwards. (Figure AC6-4)

FIGURE AC6-3 **General Information Screen**

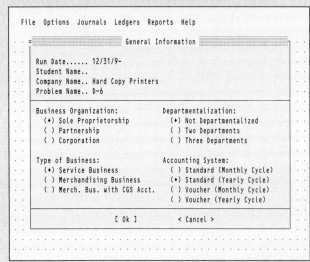

FIGURE AC6-4 **General Journal Data Entry**

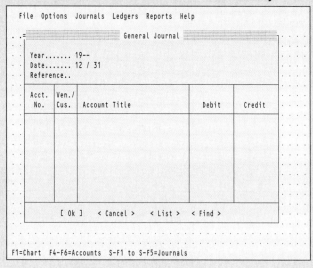

    a. Enter 12/31 in the Date field.

    b. Enter ADJ.ENT. in the Reference field.

    c. Enter the account number for Paper Supplies Expense.
Hint: Press the F1 key to display the Chart of Accounts window. Notice that Paper Supplies Expense is Account Number 543. If you press the Enter key with the account number highlighted in the Chart of Accounts window, that account number will be placed in the Acct. No. field.

    d. Press the Tab key or the Enter key to move to the Debit field and enter the debit amount (3550 without the comma).

    e. Enter the Paper Supplies account number and the credit amount.

    f. Enter the Insurance Expense account number and the debit amount.

    g. Enter the Prepaid Insurance account number and the credit amount.

    h. Enter the Wage Expense account number and the debit amount.

    i. Enter the Wages Payable account number and the credit amount.

    j. Enter the Depr. Exp.:Print. Eqpt. account number and the debit amount.

    k. Enter the Accum. Depr.:Print. Eqpt. account number and the credit amount.

l. If you need to change the infomation on this screen, press the Shift key and the Tab key simultaneously to display the previous field and enter the correct information.

STEP 17 Press the Ctrl key and the Enter key simultaneously to display the posting summary. (Figure AC6-5)

STEP 18 Press the Enter key when the Post button is active to post the adjusting entries. If you need to change the transaction, press Enter on the Change button.

STEP 19 Press the Alt key and select the Report menu.

STEP 20 Choose the Financial Statements option.

STEP 21 Press the Space bar to place an X in each box to display reports for the Income Statement, Balance Sheet, and Statement of Owner's Equity. (Figure AC6-6)

FIGURE AC6-5 **Posting Summary**

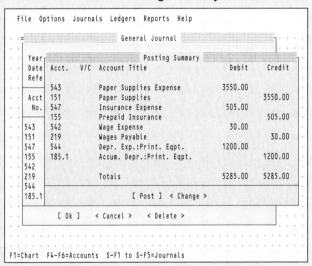

FIGURE AC6-6 **Report Selection**

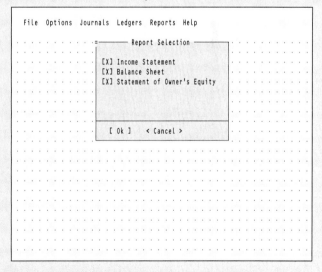

STEP 22 Press Enter on Ok to display the financial statements. Esc removes the current report from the screen and displays the next report.

STEP 23 To perform the period-end closing, press the Alt key and pull down the Options menu. (Figure AC6-7)

STEP 24   The Period-End Closing option will erase your journal entries, but the balances will be updated. Therefore, do not choose this option until you have made all necessary corrections. Select Period-End Closing from the menu and press Enter. The computer will automatically make the closing entries for the period.

STEP 25   To run a Post-Closing Trial Balance press the Alt key and select Reports. Select Ledgers. (Figure AC6-8)

FIGURE AC6-7 **Options Menu**

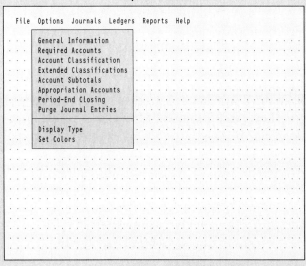

FIGURE AC6-8 **Reports Menu**

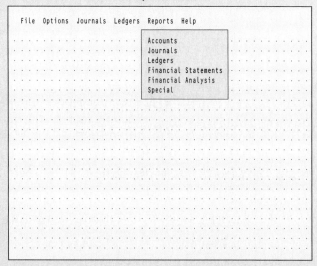

STEP 26   Press the Space Bar to place an X in the box for Trial Balance and press Enter on Ok.

STEP 27   Pull down the File menu and choose the Save As command.

STEP 28   Save your solution on a data disk under a file name such as XXXD-6 (XXX=your initials).

STEP 29   Choose the Quit option from the File menu to end your session.

PART II
*Specialized Accounting
Procedures for Service
Businesses and
Propietorships*

Careful study of this chapter should enable you to:

1. Explain the cash, modified cash, and accrual basis of accounting.

2. Describe special records for a professional service business using the modified cash basis.

3. Use the combination journal to record transactions of a professional service business.

4. Post entries from the combination journal to the general ledger.

5. Prepare a work sheet, financial statements, and adjusting and closing entries for a professional service business.

A Professional Service Business: Modified Cash Basis and Combination Journal

Throughout the first six chapters, the accrual basis of accounting for a service business was demonstrated. We also used a general journal as the book of original entry for all transactions. Not all businesses use the accrual basis of accounting, and many businesses use special journals rather than the general journal. This chapter explains the cash basis and modified cash basis of accounting. In addition, this chapter demonstrates the advantages of using a combination journal as the book of original entry.

1

Explain the cash, modified cash, and accrual basis of accounting.

ACCRUAL BASIS VERSUS CASH BASIS

Under the **accrual basis of accounting,** revenues are recorded when earned. Revenues are considered earned when a service is provided or a product sold, regardless of whether cash has been received. The accrual basis also assumes that expenses are recorded when incurred. Expenses are considered incurred when a service is received or an asset consumed, regardless of when cash is paid. The accrual basis is the best method of measuring income for most businesses.

However, the **cash basis of accounting** is used by some small businesses and by most individuals for tax purposes. Under the cash basis of accounting, revenues are recorded when cash is received and expenses are recorded when cash is paid. As shown in figure 7-1, the cash and accrual bases can result in very different measures of net income.

FIGURE 7-1 Cash Versus Accrual Accounting

	Cash Versus Accrual Accounting				
	METHOD OF ACCOUNTING				
TRANSACTION	ACCRUAL BASIS		CASH BASIS	
	EXPENSE	REVENUE	EXPENSE	REVENUE
a. Sold merchandise on account, $600.		600		
b. Paid wages, $300.	300		300	
c. Received $200 for merchandise sold on account.				200
d. Received cleaning bill for month, $250.	250			
e. Paid on account for last month's advertising, $100.			100	
	550	600	400	200
Revenue		$600		$200
Expense		550		400
Net Income (Loss)		$50		($200)
Revenues are recognized when:		earned		cash is received
Expenses are recognized when:		incurred		cash is paid

Under the modified cash basis, revenue is not recorded until cash is received. Expenses are recorded when cash is paid, except for assets with useful lives greater than one accounting period.

A third method of accounting combines aspects of the cash and accrual methods. With the **modified cash basis,** a firm uses the cash basis for recording revenues and most expenses. Exceptions are made, however, when cash is paid for assets with useful lives greater than one accounting period. For example, under a strict cash basis, if cash is paid for equipment, buildings, supplies, or insurance, the amount is immediately recorded as an expense. This recording approach would cause major distortions when measuring net income. Under the modified cash basis, cash payments like these are recorded as assets, and adjustments are made each period under the accrual basis. Thus, the modified cash basis combines the cash and accrual methods of accounting. Differences and similarities among the cash, modified cash, and accrual methods of accounting are shown in figure 7-2.

ACCOUNTING FOR A PROFESSIONAL SERVICE BUSINESS

2

Describe special records for a professional service business using the modified cash basis.

Many small professional service businesses use the modified cash basis of accounting. A few examples of professional service businesses are accounting, law, dentistry, medicine, and engineering.

FIGURE 7-2 Comparison of Cash, Modified Cash, and Accrual Methods

Entries Made Under Each Accounting Method			
EVENTS	**CASH**	**MODIFIED CASH**	**ACCRUAL**
Revenues: Perform services for cash.	Cash Sales	Cash Sales	Cash Sales
Perform services on account.	No entry.	No entry.	Accts. Rec. Sales
Expenses: Pay cash for operating expenses: wages, advertising, rent, phone, etc.	Expense Cash	Expense Cash	Expense Cash
Pay cash for prepaid items: insurance, supplies, etc.	Expense Cash	Prepaid Asset Cash	Prepaid Asset Cash
Pay cash for property, plant & equipment.	Expense Cash	P.P. & E. Asset Cash	P.P. & E. Asset Cash
End-of-period adjustments: Wages earned but not paid.	No entry.	No entry.	Wage Exp. Wages Payable
Prepaid items purchased but not used.	No entry.	Expense Prepaid Asset	Expense Prepaid Asset
Depreciation on property, plant, and equipment.	No entry.	Depreciation Exp. Accum. Depr.	Depreciation Exp. Accum. Depr.
Other events: Purchase of assets on account.	No entry.	Asset Accounts Payable	Asset Accounts Payable

Shaded area shows that sometimes modified cash basis is the same as the cash basis and sometimes it is the same as the accrual basis. For some transactions all methods are the same.

Notice that figure 7-2 shows two differences between the accrual basis and the modified cash basis. First, under the modified cash basis, no adjusting entries are made for accrued wages expenses. Second, under the modified cash basis, revenues from services performed on account are not recorded until cash is received. Thus, no accounts receivable are entered in the accounting system. This means that other records must be maintained to keep track of amounts owed by clients and patients. These records generally include an appointment record and a client or patient ledger record. These records are illustrated in figures 7-3 and 7-4.

FIGURE 7-3 **Appointment Record**

Date: 6/4/--

Time	Patient	Medical Service	Fees	Payments
8:00	Dennis Rogan	OV	40.00	40.00
15				
30	Rick Cosier	OV;EKG	120.00	
45				
9:00	George Hettenhouse	OV;MISC	50.00	
15				
30	Sam Frumer	OV;LAB	75.00	75.00
45				
10:00	Dan Dalton	OV	40.00	
15				
30	Louis Biagioni	OV;X	65.00	
45				
11:00	Mike Groomer	X	40.00	40.00
15				
30				
45				
12:00				
15				
30				
45				
1:00	Mike Tiller	OV;LAB	80.00	
15				
30	Peggy Hite	OV;PHYS	190.00	
45				
2:00				
15				
30				
45				
3:00	Vivian Winston	OV;MISC	40.00	
15				
30				
45				
4:00	Hank Davis	OV	40.00	40.00
15				
30				
45				
	Bill Sharp			150.00
	Phil Jones			80.00
	Diane Gallagher			200.00
			780.00	625.00

FIGURE 7-4 **Client or Patient Ledger Account**

Patient Name   Dennis Rogan
Address   1542 Hamilton Avenue   Cincinnati, OH   45240
Phone Number   548-1683

Date	Service Rendered	Time	Debit	Credit	Balance
19-- June 4	Office visit	8:00	40.00		
4				40.00	----

The appointment record is used to schedule appointments and to maintain a record of the services rendered, fees charged, and payments received. This information is copied to the patient ledger records, which show the amount owed by each client or patient for services performed. A copy of this record may also be used for billing purposes.

3

Use the combination journal to record transactions of a professional service business.

⬛ The totals of special journal columns are posted as one amount to the account, which saves time and reduces the possibility of posting errors.

THE COMBINATION JOURNAL

The two-column general journal illustrated in Chapter 4 can be used to enter every transaction of a business. However, in most businesses, many similar transactions involve the same account or accounts. Cash receipts and payments are good examples. Suppose a typical month has 30 transactions that result in an increase in cash and 40 transactions that cause a decrease in cash. In a two-column general journal, this would require entering the account "Cash" 70 times, using a journal line each time.

A considerable amount of time and space is saved if a journal contains **special columns** for cash debits and cash credits. At the end of the month, the special columns for cash debits and credits are totaled. The total of the Cash Debit column is posted as one amount to the debit side of the cash account, and the total of the Cash Credit column is posted as one amount to the credit side of the cash account. Thus, instead of receiving 70 postings, Cash receives only two, one debit and one credit. This method requires much less time, and the possibility of posting errors is reduced.

Special journal columns can be added for any accounts that are frequently used. Infrequently used accounts are entered in a **General Debit column** and a **General Credit column.** A journal with such special and general columns is called a **combination journal.**

Many small professional enterprises use a combination journal to record business transactions. To demonstrate the use of a combination journal, let's consider the medical practice of Dr. Ray Bonita. Dr. Bonita uses the modified cash basis of accounting. The chart of accounts for his medical practice is shown in figure 7-5.

FIGURE 7-5 **Chart of Accounts**

<table>
<tr><th colspan="4">Ray Bonita, MD
Chart of Accounts</th></tr>
<tr><th>Assets</th><th>(100–199)</th><th>Revenues</th><th>(400–499)</th></tr>
<tr><td>111</td><td>Cash</td><td>411</td><td>Medical Fees</td></tr>
<tr><td>151</td><td>Medical Supplies</td><td></td><td></td></tr>
<tr><td>152</td><td>Office Supplies</td><td>**Expenses**</td><td>**(500–599)**</td></tr>
<tr><td>155</td><td>Prepaid Insurance</td><td>541</td><td>Rent Expense</td></tr>
<tr><td>185</td><td>Medical Equipment</td><td>542</td><td>Wage Expense</td></tr>
<tr><td>185.1</td><td>Accum. Depr.—</td><td>543</td><td>Office Supplies Exp.</td></tr>
<tr><td></td><td>Medical Equip.</td><td>544</td><td>Medical Supplies Exp.</td></tr>
<tr><td>192</td><td>Office Furniture</td><td>545</td><td>Telephone Expense</td></tr>
<tr><td>192.1</td><td>Acc. Depr.—Off. Furn.</td><td>546</td><td>Laboratory Exp.</td></tr>
<tr><td></td><td></td><td>547</td><td>Depr. Exp.—Med. Eq.</td></tr>
<tr><td>**Liabilities**</td><td>**(200–299)**</td><td>548</td><td>Insurance Expense</td></tr>
<tr><td>218</td><td>Accounts Payable</td><td>559</td><td>Depr. Exp.—Off. Furn.</td></tr>
<tr><td></td><td></td><td></td><td></td></tr>
<tr><td>**Owner's Equity**</td><td>**(300–399)**</td><td></td><td></td></tr>
<tr><td>311</td><td>Ray Bonita, Capital</td><td></td><td></td></tr>
<tr><td>312</td><td>Ray Bonita, Drawing</td><td></td><td></td></tr>
<tr><td>331</td><td>Income Summary</td><td></td><td></td></tr>
</table>

The transactions for the month of June, Dr. Bonita's first month in practice, are as follows.

Summary of Transactions
Ray Bonita's Medical Practice

June 1 Ray Bonita invests $50,000 cash in his business.

2 Paid $6,000 for a one-year liability insurance policy. Coverage began on June 1.

Summary of Transactions
Ray Bonita's Medical Practice
(continued)

June   3 Bought medical equipment for cash, $22,000.
   4 Paid bill for laboratory work, $300.
   5 Bought office furniture on credit from Bittle's Furniture, $9,000.
   6 Received $5,000 cash from patients and insurance companies for medical services rendered.
   7 Paid June office rent, $2,000.
   8 Paid part-time salaries, $3,000.
   9 Bought medical supplies for cash, $250.
   15 Paid telephone bill, $150.
   15 Received $10,000 cash from patients and insurance companies for medical services rendered.
   16 Paid bill for laboratory work, $280.
   17 Paid part-time salaries, $3,000.
   19 Bought office supplies for cash, $150.
   20 Received $3,000 cash from patients and insurance companies for medical services rendered.
   22 Paid the first installment of $3,000 to Bittle's Furniture.
   23 Bought medical supplies for cash, $200.
   24 Paid bill for laboratory work, $400.
   25 Bought additional furniture from Bittle's for $3,500. A down payment of $500 was made with the remaining payments expected over the next four months.
   27 Paid part-time salaries, $2,500.
   30 Total cash received from patients and insurance companies for medical fees for the remainder of the month amounted to $7,000.
   30 Bonita withdrew cash from the business for personal use, $10,000.

Set up special columns for the most frequently used accounts.

A combination journal for Ray Bonita's medical practice is illustrated in figure 7-6. Note that special columns were set up for Cash (Debit and Credit), Medical Fees (Credit), Wage Expense (Debit), Laboratory Expense (Debit), Medical Supplies (Debit), and Office Supplies (Debit). Special columns were set up for these accounts because they are used frequently in this business. Other businesses might set up special columns for different accounts depending on the frequency of their use. Of course, we also need General Debit and Credit columns for transactions affecting other accounts.

FIGURE 7-6 **Combination Journal**

	DATE		CASH DEBIT	CASH CREDIT	DESCRIPTION	POST. REF.	
1	19-- June	1	50 000 00		Ray Bonita, Capital	311	1
2		2		6 000 00	Prepaid Insurance	155	2
3		3		22 000 00	Medical Equipment	185	3
4		4		3 00 00		—	4
5		5			Office Furniture	192	5
6					Accounts Payable—Bittle's	218	6
7		6	5 000 00			—	7
8		7		2 000 00	Rent Expense	541	8
9		8		3 000 00		—	9
10		9		2 50 00		—	10
11		15		1 50 00	Telephone Expense	545	11
12		15	10 000 00			—	12
13		16		2 80 00		—	13
14		17		3 000 00		—	14
15		19		1 50 00		—	15
16		20	3 000 00			—	16
17		22		3 000 00	Accounts Payable: Bittle's	218	17
18		23		2 00 00		—	18
19		24		4 00 00		—	19
20		25		5 00 00	Office Furniture	192	20
21					Accounts Payable—Bittle's	218	21
22		27		2 500 00		—	22
23		30	7 000 00			—	23
24		30		10 000 00	Ray Bonita, Drawing	312	24
25			75 000 00	53 730 00			25
26			(111)	(111)			26

PAGE 1

	GENERAL DEBIT	GENERAL CREDIT	MEDICAL FEES CREDIT	WAGE EXPENSE DEBIT	LAB. EXPENSE DEBIT	MEDICAL SUPPLIES DEBIT	OFFICE SUPPLIES DEBIT	
1		50 000 00						1
2	6 000 00							2
3	22 000 00							3
4					3 00 00			4
5	9 000 00							5
6		9 000 00						6
7			5 000 00					7
8	2 000 00							8
9				3 000 00				9
10						2 50 00		10
11	1 50 00							11
12			10 000 00					12
13					2 80 00			13
14				3 000 00				14
15							1 50 00	15
16			3 000 00					16
17	3 000 00							17
18						2 00 00		18
19					4 00 00			19
20	3 500 00							20
21		3 000 00						21
22				2 500 00				22
23			7 000 00					23
24	10 000 00							24
25	55 650 00	62 000 00	25 000 00	8 500 00	9 80 00	4 50 00	1 50 00	25
26	(✓)	(✓)	(411)	(542)	(546)	(151)	(152)	26

Proving the Combination Journal

Debit Columns		Credit Columns	
Cash	75,000	Cash	53,730
General	55,650	General	62,000
Wage Exp.	8,500	Medical Fees	25,000
Laboratory Exp.	980		140,730
Medical Supplies	450		
Office Supplies	150		
	140,730		

Journalizing in a Combination Journal

The following procedures were used to enter the transactions for Dr. Bonita for June.

General Columns. Enter transactions in the *general columns* in a similar manner as used for the general journal. Look at the entry for June 5 in figure 7-6.

> **a.** Enter the name of the debited account (Office Furniture) first at the extreme left of the Description column.
> **b.** Enter the amount in the General Debit column.
> **c.** Enter the name of the account credited (Accounts Payable: Bittle's) on the next line, indented about ½ inch.
> **d.** Enter the amount in the General Credit column.

General and Special Accounts. Some transactions affect both a *general account and a special account.* Look at the entry for June 1 in figure 7-6.

> **a.** Enter the name of the general account in the Description column.
> **b.** Enter the amount in the General Debit or Credit column.
> **c.** Enter the amount of the debit or credit for the special account in the appropriate special column.
> Enter all of this information on the same line.

Special Accounts. Many transactions affect only *special accounts.* Look at the entry for June 6 in figure 7-6.

> **a.** Enter the amounts in the appropriate special debit and credit columns.
> **b.** Do not enter anything in the Description column.
> **c.** Place a dash in the Posting Reference column to indicate that this amount is not posted individually. It will be posted as part of the total of the special column at the end of the month.

Description Column. In general, the **Description column** is used for the following:

> **a.** To enter the account titles for the General Debit and General Credit columns.
> **b.** To identify specific creditors when Bonita purchases assets on account (see the entry on June 5).
> *NOTE:* For firms using the accrual basis of accounting, this column also would be used to identify specific customers receiving services on account.

c. To identify amounts forwarded. When more than one page is required during an accounting period, amounts from the previous page are brought forward. In this situation, "Amounts Forwarded" is entered in the Description column on the first line.

Proving the Combination Journal

At the end of the accounting period, all columns of the combination journal should be footed. The sum of the debit columns should be compared with the sum of the credit columns to verify that they are equal. The proving of Bonita's combination journal for the month of June is shown at the bottom of figure 7-6 on page 219.

POSTING FROM THE COMBINATION JOURNAL

Post entries from the combination journal to the general ledger.

The procedures for posting a special column are different from the procedures used when posting a general column. Accounts debited or credited in the general columns are posted individually in the same manner as followed for the general journal. The procedures for posting a special column are different. Refer to the combination journal in figure 7-6, which has been posted. Figure 7-7 shows the procedures to follow in posting from a combination journal.

FIGURE 7-7 Posting from a Combination Journal

GENERAL COLUMNS   Since a combination journal is being used, enter "CJ" and the page number in each general ledger account's Posting Reference column. Once the amount has been posted to the general ledger account, the account number is entered in the **Posting Reference column** of the combination journal. The accounts in the general column should be posted daily. The check marks at the bottom of the General Debit and Credit columns indicate that these totals should not be posted.

SPECIAL COLUMNS   1. Total the special columns at the end of the accounting period.
2. Post the totals to the appropriate general ledger accounts.
3. Once posted, enter the account number beneath the column in parentheses.

The general ledger accounts for Cash, Accounts Payable, and Medical Fees are shown in figure 7-8 to illustrate the effects of this posting process.

FIGURE 7-8 **The General Ledger After Posting**

GENERAL LEDGER

ACCOUNT: CASH ACCOUNT NO. 111

DATE		ITEM	POST. REF.	DEBIT	CREDIT	BALANCE DEBIT	BALANCE CREDIT
19-- June	30		CJ1	75 000 00		75 000 00	
	30		CJ1		53 730 00	21 270 00	

ACCOUNT: ACCOUNTS PAYABLE ACCOUNT NO. 218

DATE		ITEM	POST. REF.	DEBIT	CREDIT	BALANCE DEBIT	BALANCE CREDIT
19-- June	5		CJ1		9 000 00	9 000 00	
	22		CJ1	3 000 00		6 000 00	
	25		CJ1		3 000 00	9 000 00	

ACCOUNT: MEDICAL FEES ACCOUNT NO. 411

DATE		ITEM	POST. REF.	DEBIT	CREDIT	BALANCE DEBIT	BALANCE CREDIT
19-- June	30		CJ1		25 000 00		25 000 00

FIGURE 7-9 **Determining the Cash Balance**

COMBINATION JOURNAL

		DATE		CASH DEBIT	CASH CREDIT	DESCRIPTION	POST. REF.	
1	19-- June	1	50 000 00			Ray Bonita, Capital	311	1
2		2			6 000 00	Prepaid Insurance	155	2
3		3			22 000 00	Medical Equipment	185	3
4		4			300 00		—	4
5		5				Office Furniture	192	5
6						Accounts Pay.—Bittle's	218	6
7		6	5 000 00				—	7
8		7			2 000 00	Rent Expense	541	8
9		8			300 00		—	9
10		9			250 00		—	10
11		15			150 00	Telephone Expense	545	11
12		15	10 000 00				—	12
13			65 000 00	33 700 00				13

To see the advantages of posting a combination journal as compared with the general journal, simply compare the accounts in figure 7-6 with the same accounts in Chapter 4, figure 4-11 on pages 94–96. Note the number of postings required for the general journal and combination journal.

	Number of Postings		
	General Journal	Combination Journal	
Cash	13	2	(Special columns for Cash)
Accounts Payable	3	3	(No special column)
Delivery/Medical Fees	3	1	(Special column for Medical Fees)

Using the combination journal can clearly be very efficient.

Determining the Cash Balance

Beginning cash balance
+ total cash debits
− cash credits to date

Current cash balance

The debits and credits to Cash are not posted until the end of the accounting period. Therefore, it is necessary to compute the cash balance when this information is needed. The cash balance may be computed at any time during the month by taking the beginning balance, adding total cash debits and subtracting total cash credits to date. Bonita's cash balance on June 15 would be calculated as shown in figure 7-9.

				PAGE 1							
	GENERAL		MEDICAL FEES CREDIT	WAGE EXPENSE DEBIT	LAB. EXPENSE DEBIT	MEDICAL SUPPLIES DEBIT	OFFICE SUPPLIES DEBIT			
	DEBIT	CREDIT							
1		50 000 00						1
2	6 000 00							2
3	22 000 00							3
4					30 00			4
5	9 000 00							5
6		9 000 00						6
7			5 000 00					7
8	2 000 00							8
9			3 000 00					9
10						2 50 00		10
11	1 50 00							11
12			10 000 00					12
13								13

Beginning balance	$ 0
Add cash debits	65,000
Total	65,000
Less cash credits	33,700
Cash balance, June 15	$31,300

PERFORMING END-OF-PERIOD WORK FOR A PROFESSIONAL SERVICE BUSINESS

> **5**
>
> Prepare a work sheet, financial statements, and adjusting and closing entries for a professional service business.

Once the combination journal has been posted to the general ledger, the end-of-period work sheet is prepared in the same way as described in Chapter 5. Recall that financial statements are prepared and end-of-period work is normally performed at the end of the fiscal year. For illustration purposes, we will perform these activities at the end of Bonita's first month of operations.

Preparing the Work Sheet

Bonita's work sheet is illustrated in figure 7-10. Adjustments were made for the following items:

FIGURE 7-10 Work Sheet for Ray Bonita, M.D.

	ACCOUNT TITLE	ACCT. NO.	TRIAL BALANCE DEBIT	TRIAL BALANCE CREDIT	ADJUSTMENTS DEBIT	ADJUSTMENTS CREDIT	
1	Cash	111	21 270 00				1
2	Medical Supplies	151	4 50 00			(a) 1 00 00	2
3	Office Supplies	152	1 50 00			(b) 50 00	3
4	Prepaid Insurance	155	6 000 00			(c) 50 00	4
5	Medical Equipment	185	22 000 00				5
6	Accum. Depr.—Med. Equip.	185.1				(d) 3 00 00	6
7	Office Furniture	192	12 500 00				7
8	Accum. Depr.—Off. Furn.	192.1				(e) 2 00 00	8
9	Accounts Payable	218		9 000 00			9
10	Ray Bonita, Capital	311		50 000 00			10
11	Ray Bonita, Drawing	312	10 000 00				11
12	Medical Fees	411		25 000 00			12
13	Rent Expense	541	2 000 00				13
14	Wage Expense	542	8 500 00				14
15	Office Sup. Expense	543			(b) 50 00		15
16	Medical Supplies Exp.	544			(a) 1 00 00		16
17	Telephone Expense	545	1 50 00				17
18	Laboratory Expense	546	9 80 00				18
19	Depr. Exp.—Med. Equip.	547			(d) 3 00 00		19
20	Depr. Exp.—Off. Furn.	559			(e) 2 00 00		20
21	Insurance Exp.	548			(c) 50 00		21
22			84 000 00	84 000 00	1 1 50 00	1 1 50 00	22
23	Net Income						23
24							24

Ray Bonita, M.D.
Work Sheet
For the Month Ended June 30, 19--

(a) Medical supplies remaining on June 30, $350.
(b) Office supplies remaining on June 30, $100.
(c) Prepaid insurance expired during June, $500.
(d) Depreciation on medical equipment for June, $300.
(e) Depreciation on office furniture for June, $200.

Preparing Financial Statements

No additional investment was made by Bonita during June. Thus, as we saw in Chapter 6, the financial statements can be prepared directly from the work sheet. Recall that if Bonita had made an additional investment, this amount would be identified by reviewing Bonita's capital account and would need to be reported in the statement of owner's equity. Bonita's financial statements are illustrated in figure 7-11.

	ADJUSTED TRIAL BALANCE DEBIT	ADJUSTED TRIAL BALANCE CREDIT	INCOME STATEMENT DEBIT	INCOME STATEMENT CREDIT	BALANCE SHEET DEBIT	BALANCE SHEET CREDIT	
1	21 270 00				21 270 00		1
2	350 00				350 00		2
3	100 00				100 00		3
4	5 500 00				5 500 00		4
5	22 000 00				22 000 00		5
6		300 00				300 00	6
7	12 500 00				12 500 00		7
8		200 00				200 00	8
9		9 000 00				9 000 00	9
10		5 000 00				5 000 00	10
11	1 000 00				1 000 00		11
12		25 000 00		25 000 00			12
13	2 000 00		2 000 00				13
14	8 500 00		8 500 00				14
15	50 00		50 00				15
16	100 00		100 00				16
17	150 00		150 00				17
18	980 00		980 00				18
19	300 00		300 00				19
20	200 00		200 00				20
21	500 00		500 00				21
22	84 500 00	84 500 00	12 780 00	25 000 00	71 720 00	59 500 00	22
23			12 220 00			12 220 00	23
24			25 000 00	25 000 00	71 720 00	71 720 00	24

FIGURE 7-11 Financial Statements for Ray Bonita, M.D.

Ray Bonita, M.D.
Income Statement
For Month Ended June 30, 19--

Revenue:		
Medical fees		$25 000 00
Expenses:		
Wage expense	$8 500 00	
Rent expense	2 000 00	
Laboratory expense	980 00	
Insurance expense	500 00	
Depreciation expense—medical equipment	300 00	
Depreciation expense—office furniture	200 00	
Telephone expense	150 00	
Medical supplies expense	100 00	
Office supplies expense	50 00	
Total expenses		12 780 00
Net income		$12 220 00

Ray Bonita, M.D.
Statement of Owner's Equity
For Month Ended June 30, 19--

Ray Bonita, Capital, June 1, 19--		$50 000 00
Net income for June	$12 220 00	
Less withdrawals for June	10 000 00	
Increase in capital		2 220 00
Ray Bonita, Capital, June 30, 19--		$52 220 00

Ray Bonita, M.D.
Balance Sheet
June 30, 19--

Assets			
Current assets:			
Cash	$21 270 00		
Medical supplies	350 00		
Office supplies	100 00		
Prepaid insurance	5 500 00		
Total current assets		$27 220 00	
Property, plant and equipment:			
Medical equipment	$22 000 00		
Less: Accumulated depreciation	300 00	21 700 00	
Office furniture	$12 500 00		
Less: Accumulated depreciation	200 00	12 300 00	
Total assets		$61 220 00	
Liabilities			
Current liabilities:			
Accounts payable		$ 9 000 00	
Owner's Equity			
Ray Bonita, capital		52 220 00	
Total liabilities and owner's equity		$61 220 00	

Preparing Adjusting and Closing Entries

Adjusting and closing entries are made in the combination journal in the same manner demonstrated for the general journal in Chapter 6. We simply use the Description and General Debit and Credit columns. These posted entries are illustrated in Figures 7-12 and 7-13.

FIGURE 7-12 **Adjusting Entries**

	DATE		CASH		DESCRIPTION	POST. REF.	GENERAL		
			DEBIT	CREDIT			DEBIT	CREDIT	
1					Adjusting Entries				1
2	19-- June	30			Medical Supplies Exp.	544	100 00		2
3					Medical Supplies	151		100 00	3
4		30			Office Supplies Exp.	543	50 00		4
5					Office Supplies	152		50 00	5
6		30			Insurance Expense	548	500 00		6
7					Prepaid Insurance	155		500 00	7
8		30			Depr.—Medical Equip.	547	300 00		8
9					Accum. Dep.—Med. Equip.	185.1		300 00	9
10		30			Depr. Exp.—Office Furn.	559	200 00		10
11					Accum. Dep.—Office Furn.	192.1		200 00	11

FIGURE 7-13 **Closing Entries**

	DATE		CASH		DESCRIPTION	POST. REF.	GENERAL		
			DEBIT	CREDIT			DEBIT	CREDIT	
13					Closing Entries				13
14	19-- June	30			Medical Fees	411	25 000 00		14
15					Income Summary	331		25 000 00	15
16		30			Income Summary	331	12 780 00		16
17					Rent Expense	541		2 000 00	17
18					Wage Expense	542		8 500 00	18
19					Office Supplies Exp.	543		50 00	19
20					Medical Supplies Exp.	544		100 00	20
21					Telephone Expense	545		150 00	21
22					Laboratory Expense	546		980 00	22
23					Depr. Exp.—Medical Equip.	547		300 00	23
24					Depr. Exp.—Office Furn.	559		200 00	24
25					Insurance Expense	548		500 00	25
26		30			Income Summary	331	12 220 00		26
27					Ray Bonita, Capital	311		12 220 00	27
28		30			Ray Bonita, Capital	311	10 000 00		28
29					Ray Bonita, Drawing	312		10 000 00	29

KEY POINTS

1 The three bases of accounting are cash, modified cash, and accrual. They differ on the recording of revenues and expenses as listed below.

Revenues are recorded:
    Cash: when cash is received.
    Modified Cash: when cash is received.
    Accrual: when earned.
Expenses are recorded:
    Cash: when cash is paid out.
    Modified Cash: when cash is paid out, except for property, plant and equipment and prepaid items.
    Accrual: when incurred.

2 Special records are required for a professional service business using the modified cash basis. Since accounts receivable are not entered in the accounting system, other records must be maintained to keep track of amounts owed by clients and patients. These records generally include an appointment record and a client or patient ledger record.

3 A combination journal is used by smaller businesses to improve the efficiency of recording and posting transactions. It includes general and special columns. The headings for a typical combination journal for a doctor's office are shown below.

Left side

COMBINATION JOURNAL

| DATE | CASH | | DESCRIPTION | POST. REF. |
| | DEBIT | CREDIT | | |

Right side

PAGE 1

| GENERAL | | MEDICAL FEES CREDIT | WAGE EXPENSE DEBIT | LAB. EXPENSE DEBIT | MEDICAL SUPPLIES DEBIT | OFFICE SUPPLIES DEBIT |
| DEBIT | CREDIT | | | | | |

4 Rules for posting a combination journal include:

a. Amounts entered in the general columns are posted individually to the general ledger on a daily basis.

b. The totals of the special columns are posted to the general ledger at the end of the month.

The work sheet, financial statements, adjusting entries and closing entries are prepared in the same manner as discussed in Chapters 5 and 6. Remember, however, that under the modified cash basis, adjustments are made only for prepaid items and depreciation on plant and equipment.

KEY TERMS

accrual basis of accounting 211 A method of accounting under which revenues are recorded when earned and expenses are recorded when incurred.

cash basis of accounting 211 A method of accounting under which revenues are recorded when cash is received and expenses are recorded when cash is paid.

combination journal 215 A journal with special and general columns.

Description column 220 In the combination journal, this column is used to enter the account titles for the General Debit and General Credit columns, to identify specific creditors when assets are purchased on account, and to identify amounts forwarded.

General Credit column 215 In the combination journal, this column is used to credit accounts that are infrequently used.

General Debit column 215 In the combination journal, this column is used to debit accounts that are infrequently used.

modified cash basis 212 A method of accounting that combines aspects of the cash and accrual methods. It uses the cash basis for recording revenues and most expenses, except when cash is paid for assets with useful lives greater than one accounting period.

Posting Reference column 221 In the combination journal, the account number is entered in this column after posting.

special columns 215 Columns in journals for frequently-used accounts.

BUILDING YOUR ACCOUNTING KNOWLEDGE

1. Explain when revenues are recorded under the cash basis, modified cash basis, and accrual basis of accounting.
2. Explain when expenses are recorded under the cash basis, modified cash basis, and accrual basis of accounting.
3. Explain the purpose of an appointment record.
4. Explain the purpose of a patient ledger account.
5. Explain the purpose of a special column in the combination journal.
6. Explain the purpose of the Description column in the combination journal.
7. Explain the purpose of the general columns in the combination journal.

8. How does using the combination journal save time and space in entering cash transactions?
9. What is the purpose of the proof of footings of the combination journal?
10. When an entry is posted from the combination journal to a ledger account, what information is entered in the "Post. Ref." column of the combination journal? In the "Post. Ref." column of the ledger account?

DEMONSTRATION PROBLEM

Maria Vietor is a financial planning consultant. She completed the following transactions during the month of December of the current year:

Dec. 1 Vietor invested $20,000 in the business.
      3 Paid $1,000 for December office rent.
      4 Received a check for $2,500 from Aaron Bisno, a client, for services and deposited it in the bank.
      6 Paid $75 to Union Electric for December heating and light.
      7 Received a check for $2,000 from Will Carter, a client, for services and deposited it in the bank.
      12 Paid $60 to Smith's Super Service for gasoline and oil purchases.
      14 Paid $600 to Comphelp in payment for temporary secretarial services during the past two weeks.
      17 Purchased office supplies from Cleat Office Supply on account, $280.
      20 Paid $100 to Cress Telephone Co. in payment of charges for business calls during the past month.
      21 Paid $1,100 to Vietor for personal use.
      24 Paid $100 to the National Multiple Sclerosis Society.
      27 Received a check for $2,000 from Ellen Thaler, a client, for services and deposited it in the bank.
      28 Paid $600 to Comphelp in payment for temporary secretarial services during the past two weeks.
      29 Made $100 payment on account to Cleat Office Supply.

Required

1. Enter the transactions in a combination journal. Establish special columns for Professional Fees, Wage Expense, and Automobile Expense. (Refer to the Chapter 4 Demonstration Problem to see how these transactions were recorded in a general journal. Notice that the combination journal is much more efficient.)
2. Prove the combination journal.
3. Post these transactions to a general ledger.
4. Prepare a trial balance.

SOLUTION

1,2.

COMBINATION JOURNAL   PAGE 1

DATE	DESCRIPTION	POST. REF.	CASH DEBIT	CASH CREDIT	GENERAL DEBIT	GENERAL CREDIT	PROFESSIONAL FEES CREDIT	WAGE EXPENSE DEBIT	AUTO EXPENSE DEBIT	
19-- Dec. 1	Maria Vietor, Capital	311	20 000 00			20 000 00				1
3	Rent Expense	541		1 000 00	1 000 00					2
4		—	2 500 00				2 500 00			3
6	Utilities Expense	549		7 5 00	7 5 00					4
7		—	2 000 00				2 000 00			5
12		—		6 0 00					6 0 00	6
14		—		6 0 0 00				6 0 0 00		7
17	Office Supplies	152			2 8 0 00					8
	Accounts Payable: Cleat Office Supplies	218				2 8 0 00				9
20	Telephone Expense	545		1 0 0 00	1 0 0 00					10
21	Maria Vietor, Drawing	312		1 1 0 0 00	1 1 0 0 00					11
24	Charitable Contrib. Exp.	557		1 0 0 00	1 0 0 00					12
27		—	2 000 00				2 000 00			13
28		—		6 0 0 00				6 0 0 00		14
29	Accounts Payable: Cleat Office Supplies	218		1 0 0 00	1 0 0 00					15
			26 500 00	3 735 00	2 755 00	20 280 00	6 500 00	1 200 00	6 0 00	16
			(111)	(111)	(✓)	(✓)	(411)	(542)	(546)	17

Proving the Combination Journal

Debit Columns		Credit Columns	
Cash	26,500	Cash	3,735
General	2,755	General	20,280
Wage Exp.	1,200	Professional Fees	6,500
Auto. Exp.	60		30,515
	30,515		

3.

GENERAL LEDGER

ACCOUNT: CASH   ACCOUNT NO. 111

DATE	ITEM	POST. REF.	DEBIT	CREDIT	BALANCE DEBIT	BALANCE CREDIT
19-- Dec. 31		CJ1	26 500 00		26 500 00	
31		CJ1		3 735 00	22 765 00	

ACCOUNT: OFFICE SUPPLIES   ACCOUNT NO. 152

DATE	ITEM	POST. REF.	DEBIT	CREDIT	BALANCE DEBIT	BALANCE CREDIT
19-- Dec. 17		CJ1	280 00		280 00	

ACCOUNT: ACCOUNTS PAYABLE   ACCOUNT NO. 218

DATE	ITEM	POST. REF.	DEBIT	CREDIT	BALANCE DEBIT	BALANCE CREDIT
19-- Dec. 17		CJ1		280 00		280 00
29		CJ1	100 00			180 00

ACCOUNT: MARIA VIETOR, CAPITAL   ACCOUNT NO. 311

DATE	ITEM	POST. REF.	DEBIT	CREDIT	BALANCE DEBIT	BALANCE CREDIT
19-- Dec. 1		CJ1		20 000 00		20 000 00

ACCOUNT: MARIA VIETOR, DRAWING   ACCOUNT NO. 312

DATE	ITEM	POST. REF.	DEBIT	CREDIT	BALANCE DEBIT	BALANCE CREDIT
19-- Dec. 21		CJ1	1 100 00		1 100 00	

ACCOUNT: PROFESSIONAL FEES   ACCOUNT NO. 411

DATE	ITEM	POST. REF.	DEBIT	CREDIT	BALANCE DEBIT	BALANCE CREDIT
19-- Dec. 31		CJ1		6 500 00		6 500 00

ACCOUNT: RENT EXPENSE   ACCOUNT NO. 541

DATE	ITEM	POST. REF.	DEBIT	CREDIT	BALANCE DEBIT	BALANCE CREDIT
19-- Dec. 3		CJ1	1 000 00		1 000 00	

ACCOUNT: WAGE EXPENSE   ACCOUNT NO. 542

DATE	ITEM	POST. REF.	DEBIT	CREDIT	BALANCE DEBIT	BALANCE CREDIT
19-- Dec. 31		CJ1	1 200 00		1 200 00	

ACCOUNT: TELEPHONE EXPENSE   ACCOUNT NO. 545

DATE	ITEM	POST. REF.	DEBIT	CREDIT	BALANCE DEBIT	BALANCE CREDIT
19-- Dec. 20		CJ1	100 00		100 00	

ACCOUNT: AUTOMOBILE EXPENSE ACCOUNT NO. 546

DATE	ITEM	POST. REF.	DEBIT	CREDIT	BALANCE DEBIT	BALANCE CREDIT
19-- Dec. 31		CJ1	6 0 00		6 0 00	

ACCOUNT: UTILITIES EXPENSE ACCOUNT NO. 549

DATE	ITEM	POST. REF.	DEBIT	CREDIT	BALANCE DEBIT	BALANCE CREDIT
19-- Dec. 6		CJ1	7 5 00		7 5 00	

ACCOUNT: CHARITABLE CONTRIBUTIONS EXPENSE ACCOUNT NO. 557

DATE	ITEM	POST. REF.	DEBIT	CREDIT	BALANCE DEBIT	BALANCE CREDIT
19-- Dec. 24		CJ1	1 0 0 00		1 0 0 00	

4.

Maria Vietor, Financial Planning Consultant
Trial Balance
December 31, 19--

ACCOUNT TITLE	ACCOUNT NO.	DEBIT BALANCE	CREDIT BALANCE
Cash	111	22 7 6 5 00	
Office Supplies	152	2 8 0 00	
Accounts Payable	218		1 8 0 00
Maria Vietor, Capital	311		20 0 0 0 00
Maria Vietor, Drawing	312	1 1 0 0 00	
Professional Fees	411		6 5 0 0 00
Rent Expense	541	1 0 0 0 00	
Wage Expense	542	1 2 0 0 00	
Telephone Expense	545	1 0 0 00	
Automobile Expense	546	6 0 00	
Utilities Expense	549	7 5 00	
Charitable Contributions Exp.	557	1 0 0 00	
		26 6 8 0 00	26 6 8 0 00

SERIES A

EXERCISES

APPLYING ACCOUNTING CONCEPTS

EXERCISE 7A1

Cash, Modified Cash, and Accrual Basis Accounting

1 Prepare the entry for each of the following transactions, using the (a) cash basis, (b) modified cash basis, and (c) accrual basis of accounting.

1. Purchase asset on account.
2. Make payment on asset previously purchased.
3. Purchase supplies for cash.

   4. Purchase insurance for cash.
   5. Pay cash for wages.
   6. Pay cash for telephone expense.
   7. Pay cash for new equipment.
   8. Wages earned but not paid.
   9. Prepaid item purchased but not used.
   10. Depreciation on long-term assets.

EXERCISE 7A2

Journal Entries

1 Jean Akins is opening a new consulting business. Journalize the following transactions that occurred during the month of January of the current year using the modified cash basis and a combination journal.

Jan.   1 Invested $10,000 in the business.
       2 Paid office rent, $500.
       3 Purchased office equipment on account, $1,500.
       5 Received $750 for services rendered.
       8 Paid telephone bill, $65.
      10 Paid $15 for a magazine subscription (miscellaneous expense).
      11 Purchased office supplies on account, $300.
      15 Paid $150 for one-year liability insurance policy.
      18 Paid part-time help, $500.
      21 Received $350 for services rendered.
      25 Paid electricity bill, $85.
      27 Withdrew $100 cash for personal use.
      29 Paid part-time help, $500.

EXERCISE 7A3

Journal Entries

1/3 Bill Rackes is opening a new bicycle repair shop. Journalize the following transactions that occurred during the month of October of the current year. Use the modified cash basis and a combination journal. Prove the combination journal.

Oct.   1 Invested $15,000 cash in the business.
       2 Paid shop rental for the month, $300.
       3 Purchased bicycle parts on account, $2,000.
       5 Purchased office supplies on account, $250.
       8 Paid telephone bill, $38.
       9 Received $140 for services.
      11 Paid $15 for a sports magazine subscription (miscellaneous expense).
      12 Paid $100 on account (for parts previously purchased).
      14 Paid part-time help, $300.
      15 Received $350 for services.
      16 Paid electricity bill, $48.
      19 Received $250 for services.
      23 Withdrew $50 cash for personal use.
      25 Paid $50 on account (for office supplies previously purchased).
      29 Paid part-time help, $300.

PROBLEMS

PROBLEM 7A1

Journalizing and posting transactions and preparing financial statements

3/4/5 Angela McWharton is opening an on-call nursing services business. She will rent a small office space and pay a part-time worker to answer the telephone. Her chart of accounts is as follows:

Assets		Revenue	
101	Cash	411	Nursing Care Fees
111	Office Supplies		
121	Office Equipment	Expenses	
		511	Rent Expense
Liabilities		522	Salary Expense
211	Accounts Payable	524	Telephone Expense
		531	Electricity Expense
Owner's Equity		533	Transportation Expense
311	Angela McWharton, Capital	542	Advertising Expense
312	Angela McWharton, Drawing	568	Miscellaneous Expense

Angela's transactions for the first month of business are as follows:

Jan. 1 Invested $10,000 cash in the business.
  1 Paid rent, $500.
  2 Bought office supplies on account, $300.
  4 Bought office equipment on account, $1,500.
  6 Received $580 for nursing services rendered.
  7 Paid telephone bill, $42.
  8 Paid electricity bill, $38.
  10 Received $360 for nursing services rendered.
  12 Paid $50 on account (office supplies).
  13 Paid $150 car payment (transportation expense).
  15 Paid part-time worker, $360.
  17 Received $420 for nursing services rendered.
  18 Withdrew $100 for personal use.
  20 Paid $26 to the newspaper for an ad.
  22 Paid $35 for gas and oil.
  24 Paid $28 for books on nursing care practices (miscellaneous).
  25 Received $320 for nursing services rendered.
  27 Paid $150 on account (office equipment purchased).
  29 Paid part-time worker, $360.
  30 Received $180 for nursing services rendered.

Required

1. Journalize the transactions for January using the modified cash basis and a combination journal.
2. Set up four-column general ledger accounts from the chart of accounts and post the transactions from the combination journal. Keep running account balances.

3. Determine the cash balance as of January 12 (using the combination journal).
4. Prove the combination journal.
5. Prepare a trial balance.
6. Prepare an income statement, statement of owner's equity, and balance sheet for January, 19- -.

PROBLEM 7A2

Journalizing and posting transactions and preparing financial statements

3/4/5 Sue Reyton owns a suit tailoring shop. She opened business in September. She rents a small work space and has an assistant to receive job orders and process claim tickets. Her trial balance shows her account balances for the first two months of business (September and October).

ACCOUNT TITLE	ACCOUNT NO.	DEBIT BALANCE	CREDIT BALANCE
Cash	101	6 2 1 1 50	
Office Supplies	111	4 8 4 50	
Tailoring Supplies	121	1 0 0 0 00	
Prepaid Insurance	131	1 0 0 00	
Tailoring Equipment	141	3 8 0 0 00	
Accum. Depr./Tailoring Equip.	141.1		8 0 0 00
Accounts Payable	211		4 1 2 5 00
Sue Reyton, Capital	311		5 4 3 0 00
Sue Reyton, Drawing	312	8 0 0 00	
Tailoring Fees	411		3 6 0 0 00
Rent Expense	511	6 0 0 00	
Salary Expense	522	8 0 0 00	
Telephone Expense	533	6 0 00	
Electricity Expense	555	4 4 00	
Advertising Expense	566	3 3 00	
Miscellaneous Expense	588	2 2 00	
		13 9 5 5 00	13 9 5 5 00

Sue Reyton
Trial Balance
October 31, 19--

Sue's transactions for November are as follows:

Nov. 1 Paid rent, $300.
      2 Bought tailoring supplies, on account, $150.
      3 Bought a new button hole machine on account, $3,000.

Sue's transactions, cont'd.

Nov. 5 First week's income: $400 cash.
      8 Paid $13 for newspaper advertising.
      9 Paid telephone bill, $28.
     10 Paid electric bill, $21.
     12 Second week's income: $200 cash, $300 on account.
     15 Paid part-time worker, $400.
     16 Paid $100 on account (previously owed).
     17 Paid $12 for magazine subscription (miscellaneous expense).
     19 Third week's income: $450 cash.
     21 Paid $500 for prepaid insurance for the year.
     23 Received $300 from customers (previously owed).
     24 Paid $13 for newspaper advertising.
     26 Paid $12 for snacks (miscellaneous expense).
     29 Fourth week's income: $600 cash.

Additional account numbers are:

541	Tailoring Supplies Expense
542	Office Supplies Expense
543	Insurance Expense
544	Depreciation Expense

Nov. 30 Adjustments:

(a) Tailoring supplies on hand, $450.
(b) Office supplies on hand, $284.50.
(c) Prepaid insurance expired, $150.
(d) Depreciation on tailoring equipment, $300.

Required
1. Journalize the transactions for November using the modified cash basis and a combination journal.
2. Set up four-column general ledger accounts, entering the balances as of October 31, 19--. Post the entries from the combination journal and keep running account balances.
3. Determine the cash balance as of November 13.
4. Prove the combination journal.
5. Prepare a work sheet for the three months ended November 30, 19--. Record the adjusting and closing entries in the combination journal.
6. Prepare an income statement, statement of owner's equity, and balance sheet as of November 30, 19--.

SERIES B

EXERCISES

1 Identify for each journal entry which accounting method(s) would apply.

1. Office Equipment
   Cash
      Purchased equipment for cash.

2. Office Equipment
   Accounts Payable
      Purchased equipment on account.

3. Cash
   Revenue
      Cash receipts for week.

4. Accounts Receivable
   Revenue
      Services performed on account.

5. Prepaid Insurance
   Cash
      Purchased prepaid asset.

6. Supplies
   Accounts Payable
      Purchased prepaid asset.

7. Depreciation Expense—Office Equipment
   Accum. Depr.—Office Equipment
      Depreciation for month.

8. Wages Expense
   Cash
      Paid wages for month.

9. Supplies Expense
   Supplies
      Use of prepaid expense.

10. Wages Expense
    Wages Payable
       Wages earned, not paid.

11. Telephone Expense
    Cash
       Paid telephone bill.

12. Accounts Payable
    Cash
       Payment on account.

3 Bill Miller is opening a bookkeeping services business. Journalize the following transactions that occurred during the month of March of the current year. Use the modified cash basis and a combination journal.

Mar.   1 Invested $7,500 in the business.
      3 Paid office rent, $500.
      5 Purchased office equipment on account, $800.
      6 Received $400 for services rendered.
      8 Paid telephone bill, $48.
    10 Paid $25 for a magazine subscription (miscellaneous expense).
    11 Purchased office supplies, $200.
    14 Received $520 for services rendered.
    16 Paid $200 for a one-year insurance policy.
    18 Paid part-time help, $400.
    21 Received $380 for services rendered.
    22 Paid $100 on office equipment previously purchased.
    24 Paid electricity bill, $56.
    27 Withdrew $200 for personal use.
    29 Paid part-time help, $400.
    30 Received $600 for services rendered.

EXERCISE 7B3

Journal Entries

3 Amy Anjelo opened a new delivery service. Journalize the following transactions that occurred in January of this year. Use the modified cash basis and a combination journal. Prove the combination journal.

Jan. 1 Invested $10,000 in the business.
      2 Paid shop rental for the month, $400.
      3 Purchased a delivery cart on account, $1,000.
      5 Purchased office supplies for $250.
      6 Paid the telephone bill, $51.
      8 Received $428 for delivery services.
     11 Paid the electricity bill, $37.
     12 Paid part-time employee, $480.
     13 Paid $29 for postage stamps (miscellaneous expense).
     15 Received $382 for delivery services.
     18 Paid $90 on account (for delivery cart previously purchased).
     21 Withdrew $250 for personal use.
     24 Paid $180 for a one-year liability insurance policy.
     26 Received $292 for delivery services.
     29 Paid part-time employee, $480.

PROBLEMS

PROBLEM 7B1

Journalizing and posting transactions and preparing financial statements

3/4/5 J.B. Hoyt opened a training center at the marina where he provides private waterskiing lessons. He rents a small building space at the marina, and has a part-time worker to assist him. His chart of accounts is as follows:

Assets		Revenue	
101	Cash	411	Training Fees
111	Office Supplies	Expenses	
121	Skiing Equipment	511	Rent Expense
Liabilities		522	Salary Expense
211	Accounts Payable	524	Telephone Expense
Owner's Equity		531	Repair Expense
311	J. B. Hoyt, Capital	538	Electricity Expense
312	J. B. Hoyt, Drawing	542	Transportation Expense
		568	Miscellaneous Expense

Transactions for the first month of business are as follows:

July 1 Invested $5,000 in the business.
      2 Paid rent for the month, $250.
      3 Bought office supplies, $150.
      4 Bought skiing equipment on account, $2,000.
      6 Paid telephone bill, $36.
      7 Received $200 for skiing lessons.
     10 Paid electricity bill, $28.

July 12 Paid part-time worker, $250.
      14 Received $300 for skiing lessons.
      16 Paid $60 for gas and oil (transportation expense).
      17 Received $250 for skiing lessons.
      20 Paid for repair to ski rope, $20.
      21 Paid $100 on account (for skiing equipment previously purchased).
      24 Received $310 for skiing lessons.
      26 Paid $18 for award certificates (miscellaneous expense).
      28 Paid part-time worker, $250.
      30 Received $230 for skiing lessons.
      31 Paid for repair to life jacket, $20.

Required
1. Journalize the transactions for July using the modified cash basis and a combination journal.
2. Set up four-column general ledger accounts from the chart of accounts and post the transactions from the combination journal. Keep running account balances.
3. Determine the cash balance as of July 15, 19--.
4. Prove the combination journal.
5. Prepare a trial balance.
6. Prepare an income statement, a statement of owner's equity, and a balance sheet for July, 19--.

PROBLEM 7B2

Journalizing and posting transactions and preparing financial statements

3/4/5 Molly Claussen owns a lawn care business. She opened her business in April. She rents a small shop area where she stores her equipment, and has an assistant to receive orders and process accounts. Her trial balance shows her account balances for the first two months of business (April and May).

Transactions for June are as follows:

June   1 Paid shop rent, $200.
       2 Bought office supplies, $230.
       3 Bought new landscaping equipment on account, $1,000.
       5 Paid telephone bill, $31.
       6 Received $640 for lawn care fees.
       8 Paid electricity bill, $31.
      10 Paid part-time worker, $300.
      11 Received $580 for lawn care fees.
      12 Paid $200 for a one-year insurance policy.
      14 Paid $100 on account (for landscaping equipment previously purchased).
      15 Paid $40 for gas and oil.
      19 Paid $25 for mower repairs.
      21 Received $310 for lawn care fees.
      24 Withdrew $100 for personal use.

	Molly Claussen Trial Balance May 31, 19--			
ACCOUNT TITLE	ACCOUNT NO.	DEBIT BALANCE	CREDIT BALANCE
Cash	101	4 8 4 4 00	
Office Supplies	111	2 4 3 00	
Lawn Care Supplies	121	5 8 8 00	
Prepaid Insurance	131	1 5 0 00	
Lawn Care Equipment	144	2 4 0 8 00	
Accum. Depr.—Lawn Equipment	144.1		2 4 0 00
Accounts Payable	211		1 0 8 0 00
Molly Claussen, Capital	311		5 0 0 0 00
Molly Claussen, Drawing	312	8 0 0 00	
Lawn Care Fees	411		4 0 3 3 00
Rent Expense	511	4 0 0 00	
Salary Expense	522	6 0 0 00	
Telephone Expense	533	8 8 00	
Electricity Expense	555	6 2 00	
Gas and Oil Expense	566	1 2 0 00	
Repair Expense	588	5 0 00	
		10 3 5 3 00	10 3 5 3 00

June 26 Paid $20 for edging equipment repairs.
      28 Received $480 for lawn care fees.
      29 Paid part-time worker, $300.

June 30 Adjustments:

(a) Office supplies on hand, $273. (Office Supplies Exp. 542)
(b) Lawn care supplies on hand, $300. (Lawn Care Sup. Exp. 541)
(c) Prepaid insurance expired, $100. (Insurance Exp. 543)
(d) Depreciation on lawn care equipment, $260. (Depr. Exp. 544)

Required
1. Journalize the transactions for June using the modified cash basis and a combination journal.
2. Set up four-column general ledger accounts, entering balances as of May 31, 19--. Post the entries from the combination journal and keep running account balances.
3. Determine the cash balance as of June 13.
4. Prove the combination journal.
5. Prepare a worksheet for the three months ended June 30, 19--. Record the adjusting and closing entries in the combination journal, and post to the general ledger accounts.
6. Prepare an income statement, statement of owner's equity, and balance sheet as of June 30, 19--.

MASTERY PROBLEM

Dr. James Goodbody operates a health spa. Clients typically register for one week, arriving on Sunday afternoon and returning home the following Saturday afternoon. A dietitian, physical therapist and athletic trainers are on call to assure the proper combination of diet and exercise. The following transactions took place during the month of June.

June 1 Goodbody invested $10,000.
      2 Deposited registration fees in the bank, $15,000.
      2 Rogers Construction completed work on a new tennis court which cost $12,000. The estimated life of the facility is 5 years at which time the court will have to be resurfaced. Arrangements were made to pay the bill in July.
      3 Purchased food supplies from Natural Foods on account, $5,000.
      5 Purchased office supplies on account from Gordon Office Supplies, $300.
      7 Deposited registration fees in the bank, $16,200.
     10 Purchased food supplies from Natural Foods on account, $6,200.
     10 Paid wages to staff, $500.
     14 Deposited registration fees in the bank, $13,500.
     16 Purchased food supplies from Natural Foods on account, $4,000.
     17 Paid wages to staff, $500.
     18 Paid postage, $85.
     21 Deposited registration fees in the bank, $15,200.
     24 Purchased food supplies from Natural Foods on account, $5,500.
     24 Paid wages to staff, $500.
     28 Deposited registration fees in the bank, $14,000.
     30 Purchased food supplies from Natural Foods on account, $6,000.
     30 Paid wages to staff, $500.
     30 Paid $28,700 to Natural Foods on account.
     30 Paid utility bill, $500.
     30 Paid phone bill, $120.
     30 James Goodbody withdrew $2,000 for personal use.

Required
1. Enter the transactions in a combination journal. Establish special columns for Registration Fees, Wage Expense, and Food Supplies.
2. Prove the combination journal.
3. Post these transactions to a general ledger.
4. Prepare a trial balance.

LEARNING OBJECTIVES

Careful study of this chapter should enable you to:

1. Describe how to open and use a checking account.
2. Prepare a bank reconciliation.
3. Describe how to operate a petty cash fund.
4. Use the Cash Short and Over account.

*A*ccounting for Cash

Cash is an asset that is quite familiar and important to all of us. We generally think of **cash** as the currency and coins in our pockets and the money we have in our checking accounts. To a business, cash also includes checks received from customers, money orders, and bank cashier's checks.

Because it plays such a central role in operating a business, cash must be carefully managed and controlled. A business should have a system of **internal control**—a set of procedures designed to ensure proper accounting for transactions. For good internal control of cash transactions, all cash received should be deposited daily in a bank. All disbursements, except for payments from petty cash, should be made by check.

1

Describe how to open and use a checking account.

CHECKING ACCOUNT

The key documents and forms required in opening and using a checking account are the signature card, deposit tickets, checks, and bank statements.

Opening a Checking Account

To open a checking account, each person authorized to sign checks must complete and sign a **signature card** (figure 8-1). The bank uses this card to verify the depositor's signature on any banking transactions. The depositor's social security number or business identification number is shown on the card to identify the depositor. A business identification number can be obtained from the Internal Revenue Service.

FIGURE 8-1 **Signature Card**

LAST NAME, FIRST NAME, MIDDLE INITIAL			ACCT #	
			TYPE	
			DATE	INIT.
STREET ADDRESS		TOWN	STATE	ZIP

I CERTIFY THAT THE NUMBER SHOWN ON THIS FORM IS MY CORRECT TAXPAYER IDENTIFICATION NUMBER AND THAT I AM NOT SUBJECT TO BACKUP WITHHOLDING.

SIGNATURE 1	DATE OF BIRTH / /	SOCIAL SECURITY NO.
SIGNATURE 2		
SIGNATURE 3		

Making Deposits

A **deposit ticket** (figure 8-2) is a detailed listing of items being deposited. Currency, coins, and checks are listed separately. Each check should be identified by its **ABA (American Bankers Association) Number.** This number is the small fraction printed in the upper right hand corner of each check. The number is used to sort and route checks throughout our banking system. Only the numerator of the fraction normally is used in identifying checks on the deposit ticket.

FIGURE 8-2 **Deposit Ticket**

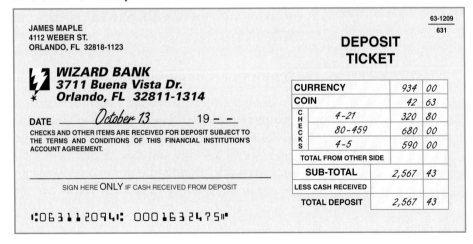

The deposit ticket and all items being deposited are delivered or mailed to the bank. A receipt for the deposit is then given or mailed to the depositor by the bank.

Endorsements.   Each check being deposited must be endorsed by the depositor. The **endorsement** consists of stamping or writing the depositor's name and sometimes other important information on the back of the check, near the left end. There are two basic types of endorsements.

1. **Blank endorsement**—the depositor simply signs the back of the check. This makes the check payable to any bearer.
2. **Restrictive endorsement**—the depositor adds words such as "For deposit," "Pay to any bank," or "Pay to Daryl Beck only," to restrict the payment of the check.

A widely used business practice when endorsing checks for deposit is to use a rubber stamp on the back of the check. The check shown in figure 8-3 has been stamped with a restrictive endorsement.

FIGURE 8-3 **Restrictive Endorsement**

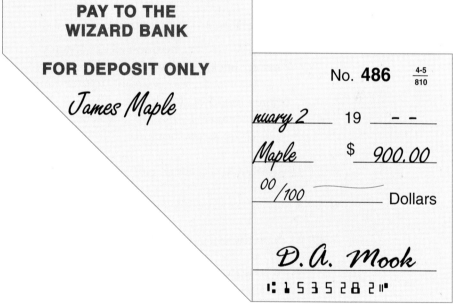

Automated Teller Machines.   Many banks now make **automated teller machines** available at all times to depositors for making deposits or withdrawals. Each depositor has a plastic card (figure 8-4) and a code number. The depositor inserts the card into the machine, keys in the "password" code number, indicates whether the transaction is a withdrawal or a deposit, and keys in the amount. The machine has a drawer or door for the withdrawal or deposit.

FIGURE 8-4 **Automated Teller Machine Card**

Writing Checks

A **check** is a document ordering a bank to pay cash from a depositor's account. There are three parties to every check:

1. **Drawer**—the depositor who orders the bank to pay the cash.
2. **Drawee**—the bank on which the check is drawn.
3. **Payee**—the person being paid the cash.

Checks used by businesses are usually bound in the form of a book. In some checkbooks, each check is attached to a **check stub** (figure 8-5) that contains space to record all relevant information about the check. Other times the checkbook is accompanied by a small register book in which the relevant information is noted.

Three steps should be followed in preparing a check.

STEP 1   Complete the check stub or register.

STEP 2   Enter the date, payee name, and amount on the check.

STEP 3   Sign the check.

It is important that the check stub is completed first so that the drawer retains a record of each check issued. If this information is not recorded, it can be difficult to determine the proper journal entry for the transaction.

The payee name is entered on the first long line on the check, followed by the amount in figures. The amount in words is then entered on the second long line. If the amount shown on the check in figures does not agree with the amount shown in words, the bank usually contacts the drawer for the correct amount or returns the check unpaid.

The most critical point in preparing a check is signing it, and this should be done last. The signature authorizes the bank to pay cash from the drawer's account. The check signer should make sure that all other aspects of the check are correct before signing it.

Figure 8-5 shows properly completed checks and stubs.

FIGURE 8-5 **Checks and Check Stubs**

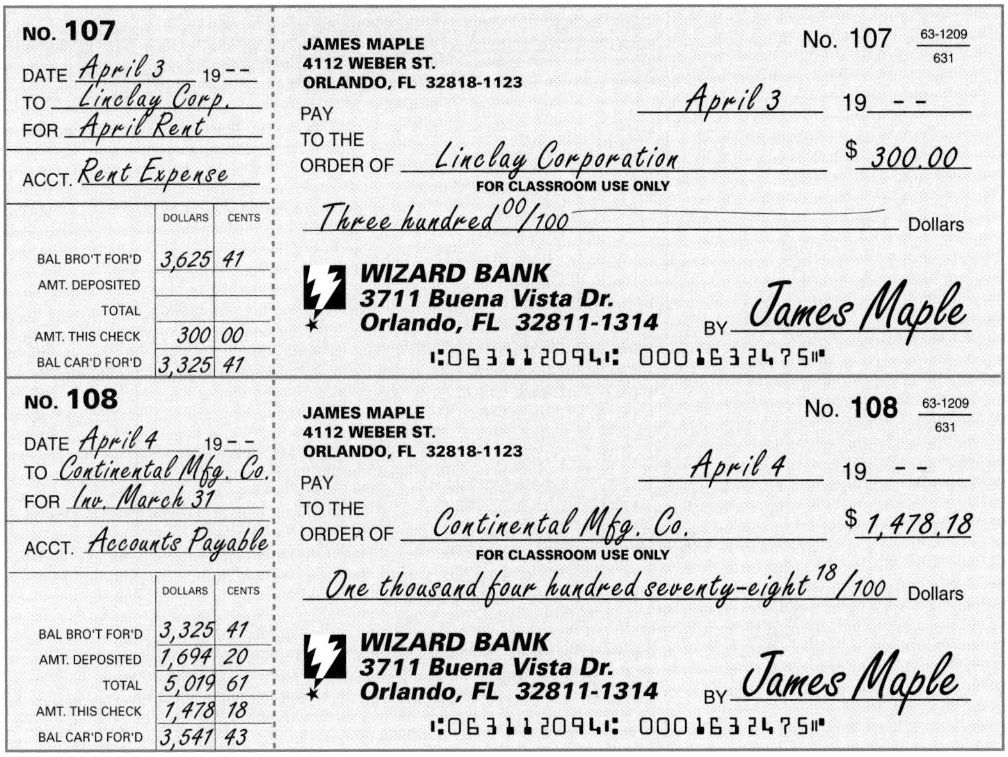
NO. 107
DATE April 3 19--
TO Linclay Corp.
FOR April Rent
ACCT. Rent Expense

	DOLLARS	CENTS
BAL BRO'T FOR'D	3,625	41
AMT. DEPOSITED		
TOTAL		
AMT. THIS CHECK	300	00
BAL CAR'D FOR'D	3,325	41

JAMES MAPLE
4112 WEBER ST.
ORLANDO, FL 32818-1123
No. 107 63-1209/631
April 3 19 --
PAY TO THE ORDER OF Linclay Corporation $ 300.00
FOR CLASSROOM USE ONLY
Three hundred 00/100 Dollars
WIZARD BANK
3711 Buena Vista Dr.
Orlando, FL 32811-1314
BY James Maple
⑆063112094⑆ 0001632475⑈

NO. 108
DATE April 4 19--
TO Continental Mfg. Co.
FOR Inv. March 31
ACCT. Accounts Payable

	DOLLARS	CENTS
BAL BRO'T FOR'D	3,325	41
AMT. DEPOSITED	1,694	20
TOTAL	5,019	61
AMT. THIS CHECK	1,478	18
BAL CAR'D FOR'D	3,541	43

JAMES MAPLE
4112 WEBER ST.
ORLANDO, FL 32818-1123
No. 108 63-1209/631
April 4 19 --
PAY TO THE ORDER OF Continental Mfg. Co. $ 1,478.18
FOR CLASSROOM USE ONLY
One thousand four hundred seventy-eight 18/100 Dollars
WIZARD BANK
3711 Buena Vista Dr.
Orlando, FL 32811-1314
BY James Maple
⑆063112094⑆ 0001632475⑈

Bank Statement

A statement of account issued by a bank to each depositor once a month is called a **bank statement.** Figure 8-6 is a bank statement for a checking account. The statement shows:

1. The balance at the beginning of the period.
2. Deposits and other amounts added during the period.
3. Checks and other amounts subtracted during the period.
4. The balance at the end of the period.

With the bank statement, the depositor receives **cancelled checks** (the depositor's checks paid by the bank during the period) and any other forms representing items added to or subtracted from the account.

FIGURE 8-6 **Bank Statement**

Statement			**WIZARD BANK**

James Maple
4112 Weber St.
Orlando, FL 32818-1123

Reference Number	16 3247 5	Page Number	
Statement Date	Nov. 21, 19--		
Statement Instructions			

Beginning Balance	No. of Deposits and Credits	We have added these deposits and credits totaling	No. of withdrawals and charges	We have subtracted these withdrawals and charges totaling	Resulting in a statement balance of
$2,721.51	2	$2,599.31	15	$3,572.73	$1,748.09

Document Count	Average Daily Balance this statement period	Minimum balance this statement period	Date	Amount

If your account does not balance, please see reverse side and report any discrepancy to our Customer Service Department.

Date	Description	Amount	Balance
10/20	Beginning Balance		2,721.51
10/27	Check No. 207	-242.00	2,479.51
10/28	Check No. 212	-68.93	2,410.58
10/28	Check No. 213	-58.00	2,352.58
10/29	Deposit	867.00	3,219.58
11/3	Deposit	1,732.31	4,951.89
11/3	Check No. 214	-18.98	4,932.91
11/3	Check No. 215	-229.01	4,703.90
11/3	Check No. 216	-452.13	4,251.77
11/3	Check No. 217	-94.60	4,157.17
11/10	Check No. 218	-1,800.00	2,357.17
11/10	NSF	-200.00	2,157.17
11/10	Check No. 220	-32.42	2,124.75
11/10	Check No. 221	-64.08	2,060.67
11/10	Check No. 222	-210.87	1,849.80
11/18	Check No. 223	-18.00	1,831.80
11/18	Check No. 225	-23.31	1,808.49
11/18	Check No. 226	-58.60	1,749.89
11/19	Service Charge	-1.80	1,748.09

EC - Error Correction
CM - Credit Memo
DM - Debit Memo
        NSF - Not Sufficient Funds   **TR - Wire Transfer**

2
Prepare a bank reconciliation.

RECONCILING THE BANK STATEMENT

On any given day, it is unlikely that the balance in the cash account on the depositor's books (the book balance) will be the same as on the bank's books (the bank balance). This can be because of errors, but it mostly is caused by timing differences.

Deposits

Suppose there are cash receipts of $600 on April 30. These cash receipts would be recorded on the books on April 30 and a deposit of $600 would be sent to the bank. The deposit would not reach the bank, however, until at least the following day, May 1. This timing difference in recording the $600 of cash receipts is illustrated in figure 8-7. Notice that on April 30, the balances in the depositor's books and in the bank's books will differ.

FIGURE 8-7 **Depositor and Bank Records—Deposits**

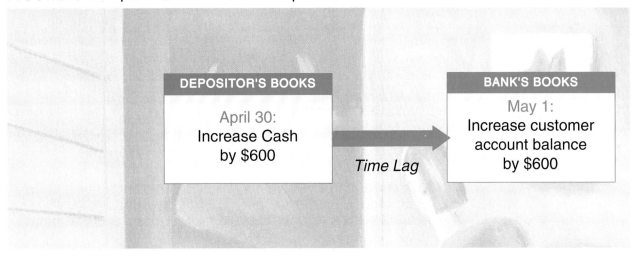

Cash Payments

Similar timing differences occur with cash payments. Suppose a check for $350 is written on April 30. This cash payment would be recorded on the books on April 30 and the check sent to the payee. The check probably would not clear the bank, however, until several days later. This timing difference in recording the $350 cash payment is illustrated in figure 8-8. Notice once again that on April 30, the balances in the depositor's books and the bank's books differ.

FIGURE 8-8 **Depositor and Bank Records—Cash Payments**

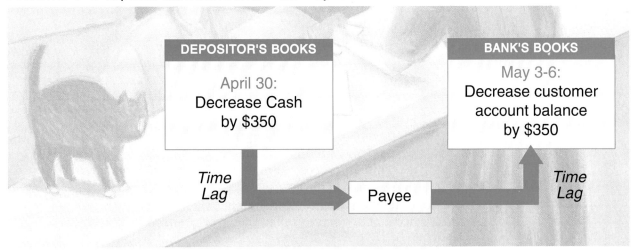

Reasons for Differences Between Bank and Book Balances

When the bank statement is received, the depositor compares the book and bank balances to identify the items that explain the difference between the two balances. This process of bringing the book and bank balances into agreement is called preparing a **bank reconciliation.**

The most common reasons for differences between the book and bank balances are the following:

1. **Outstanding checks.** Checks issued during the period that have not been presented to the bank for payment before the statement is prepared.
2. **Deposits in transit.** Deposits that have not reached or been recorded by the bank before the statement is prepared.
3. **Service charges.** Bank charges for services such as check printing and processing.
4. **Collections.** Collections of promissory notes or charge accounts made by the bank on behalf of the depositor.
5. **Not sufficient funds (NSF) checks.** Checks deposited by the depositor that are not paid because the drawer did not have sufficient funds.
6. **Errors.** Errors made by the bank or the depositor in recording cash transactions.

Steps in Preparing the Bank Reconciliation

Use the following three steps in preparing the bank reconciliation.

STEP 1   Identify deposits in transit and any related errors.

STEP 2   Identify outstanding checks and any related errors.

STEP 3   Identify additional reconciling items.

Deposits in Transit and Related Errors.   Follow these steps:

1. Compare deposits listed on the bank statement with deposits in transit on last month's bank reconciliation. All of last month's deposits in transit should appear on the current month's bank statement.
2. Compare the remaining deposits on the bank statement with deposits listed in the accounting records. Any deposits listed in the accounting records but not on the bank statement are deposits in transit on the current bank reconciliation.
3. If the individual deposit amounts on the bank statement and in the accounting records differ, the error needs to be corrected.

Outstanding Checks and Related Errors.   Follow these steps:

1. Compare cancelled checks with the bank statement and the accounting records. If the amounts differ, the error needs to be corrected.
2. As each cancelled check is compared with the accounting records, place a check mark on the check stub or other accounting record to indicate that the check has cleared.
3. Any checks written that have not been checked off represent outstanding checks on the bank reconciliation.

Additional Reconciling Items.   Compare any additions and deductions on the bank statement that are not deposits or checks with the accounting records. Items that the bank adds to the account are called **credit memos.** Items that the bank deducts from the account are called **debit memos.** Any of these items not appearing in the accounting records represent additional items on the bank reconciliation.

Illustration of a Bank Reconciliation

A general format for the bank reconciliation is shown in figure 8-9. Not all of the reconciling items shown in this illustration would be in every bank reconciliation, but this format is helpful in determining where to put items.

FIGURE 8-9 **Bank Reconciliation Format**

Bank statement balance		$_____
Add: Deposits in transit	$_____	
Bank errors	_____	
Subtotal		$_____
Deduct: Outstanding checks	$_____	
Bank errors	_____	
Adjusted bank balance		$_____
Book balance		$_____
Add: Bank credit memos	$_____	
Book errors	_____	
Subtotal		$_____
Deduct: Bank debit memos	$_____	
Book errors	_____	
Adjusted book balance		$_____

To illustrate the preparation of a bank reconciliation, we will use the James Maple bank statement shown in figure 8-6. That statement shows a balance of $1,748.09 as of November 21. The balance in Maple's check stubs and general ledger cash account is $2,293.23. The three steps described on page 250 were used to identify the following items, and the reconciliation in figure 8-10 was prepared.

1. A deposit of $637.02 on November 21 on the books had not been received by the bank. The deposit in transit is added to the balance on the bank statement. Maple has received the funds but the amount has not yet been counted by the bank.
2. Check numbers 219, 224, and 227 are outstanding. The amount of these outstanding checks is subtracted from the balance on the bank statement. The funds have been disbursed by Maple but have not yet been paid out by the bank.
3. Check number 214 was written for $18.98, but was entered on the check stub and on the books as $19.88. This $.90 error is added to the balance on the books because an extra $.90 has been deducted from the book balance.
4. The bank returned an NSF check of $200. This amount is deducted from the balance on the books. The bank has reduced Maple's balance by this amount but Maple has not yet recorded it.
5. The bank service charge was $1.80. This amount is deducted from the balance on the books. The bank has reduced Maple's balance by this amount but Maple has not yet recorded it.

FIGURE 8-10 Bank Reconciliation

James Maple Bank Reconciliation November 21, 19--		
Bank statement balance, November 21		$1 748 09
Add deposit in transit		637 02
		$2 385 11
Deduct outstanding checks:		
No. 219	$200 00	
No. 224	25 00	
No. 227	67 78	292 78
Adjusted bank balance		$2 092 33
Book balance, November 21		$2 293 23
Requires jrnl. entry ▶ Add error on stub for check no. 214		90
		$2 294 13
Requires jrnl. entry ▶ Deduct: NSF check	$200 00	
Bank service charge	1 80	201 80
Adjusted book balance		$2 092 33

Journal Entries

Only two kinds of items appearing on a bank reconciliation require journal entries:

1. Errors in the books.
2. Bank additions and deductions that do not already appear in the accounting records.

Note the three items in the lower portion of the bank reconciliation in figure 8-10. These are items the bank knew about, but the company did not. A journal entry is required for each item.

The $.90 item is an error in the accounting records that occurred when the check amount was incorrectly entered. Assuming the $18.98 was in payment of an account payable, the entry to correct this error is:

4		Cash			90			4
5		Accounts Payable				90		5
6								6

The $200 NSF check is a bank charge for a check deposited by Maple that proved to be worthless. This amount must be deducted from the book balance. Assuming the $200 was received from a customer on account, the following journal entry is required.

7		Accounts Receivable		200 00			7
8		Cash			200 00		8
9							9

The $1.80 bank service charge is a fee for bank services received by Maple. The bank has deducted this amount from Maple's account. Bank service charges are usually small and are charged to Miscellaneous Expense.

10		Miscellaneous Expense		1 80			10
11		Cash			1 80		11
12							12

Electronic Funds Transfer

Electronic funds transfer (EFT) uses a computer rather than money or checks to complete transactions with the bank. This technique is being used increasingly today. Applications include payrolls, social security payments, and retail purchases.

Errors in the books and bank additions and deductions that are not in the accounting records require journal entries.

Heavy use of EFT can present a challenge in preparing bank reconciliations. Many of the documents handled in a purely manual environment disappear when EFT is used. Bank accounts are just one of many areas where computers require accountants to think in new ways.

3				

THE PETTY CASH FUND

Describe how to operate a petty cash fund.

For good control over cash, payments generally should be made by check. Unfortunately, payment of very small amounts by check can be both inconvenient and inefficient. For example, the time and cost required to write a check for $.70 to pay for mailing a letter might be greater than the cost of the postage. Therefore, businesses customarily establish a **petty cash fund** to pay for small items with cash. "Petty" means small, and both the amount of the fund and the maximum amount of any bill that can be paid from the fund are small.

Establishing a Petty Cash Fund

To establish a petty cash fund, a check is written to the petty cash custodian for the amount that is to be set aside in the fund. The amount may be $50, $100, $200, or any amount considered necessary. The journal entry to establish a petty cash fund of $100 would be as follows.

3			Petty Cash			1 0 0 00			3
4			Cash				1 0 0 00		4

Petty cash is an asset that is listed immediately below Cash on the balance sheet.

The custodian cashes the check and places the money in a petty cash box. For good control, the custodian should be the only person authorized to make payments from the fund. The custodian should be able to account for the full amount of the fund at any time.

Making Payments from a Petty Cash Fund

A receipt called a **petty cash voucher** (figure 8-11) should be prepared for every payment from the fund. The voucher shows the name of the payee, the purpose of the payment, and the account to be charged for the payment. Each voucher should be signed by the custodian and by the person receiving the cash. The vouchers should be numbered consecutively and should be accounted for.

FIGURE 8-11 **Petty Cash Voucher**

PETTY CASH VOUCHER		
No. _2_		
Date _December 8, 19--_		
Paid to _James Maple_	$	¢
For _Client Luncheon_	15	75
Charge to _Travel & Entertainment Expense_		
Remittance received _James Maple_	Approved by _John E. Berra_	

Petty Cash Payments Record

When a petty cash fund is maintained, a formal record is often kept of all payments from the fund. The **petty cash payments record** (figure 8-12) is a special multi-column record that supplements the regular accounting records. The headings of the Distribution of Payments columns may vary, depending upon the types of expenditures.

The petty cash payments record of James Maple, a business consultant, is shown in figure 8-12 on pages 256–257. A narrative of the petty cash transactions shown in figure 8-12 follows.

Dec. 1   Maple issued a check for $200 payable to Tina Blank, Petty Cash Custodian. Blank cashed the check and placed the money in a secure cash box.

A notation of the amount received is made in the Description column of the petty cash payments record. In addition, this transaction is entered in the journal as follows:

	19--						
8	Dec.	1	Petty Cash		2 0 0 00		8
9			Cash			2 0 0 00	9
10			To establish petty cash fund.				10

FIGURE 8-12 **James Maple's Petty Cash Payments Record**

	DAY	DESCRIPTION		VOU. NO.	TOTAL AMOUNT	AUTO EXP.	
1		Amounts Forwarded					1
2	1	Received in fund	200.00				2
3	5	Automobile repairs		1	32 80	32 80	3
4	8	Client luncheon		2	15 75		4
5	9	James Maple, personal use		3	30 00		5
6	15	Typewriter repairs		4	28 25		6
7	17	Traveling expense		5	14 50		7
8	19	Washing automobile		6	8 00	8 00	8
9	22	Postage expense		7	9 50		9
10	29	Postage stamps		8	30 00		10
11					168 80	40 80	11
12	31	Balance	31.20				12
13	31	Replenished fund	168.80				13
14		Total	200.00				14

During the month of December, the following payments were made from the petty cash fund:

Dec. 5   Paid $32.80 to Jerry's Auto for servicing the company automobile. Voucher no. 1.

     8   Reimbursed Maple $15.75 for the amount spent in entertaining a client at lunch. Voucher no. 2.

     9   Gave Maple $30 for personal use. Voucher no. 3.

         There is no special Distribution column for entering amounts withdrawn by the owner for personal use. Therefore, this $30 payment is entered in the Amount column at the extreme right of the petty cash payments record.

   15   Paid $28.25 for typewriter repairs. Voucher no. 4.

   17   Reimbursed Maple $14.50 for travel expenses. Voucher no. 5.

   19   Paid $8.00 to Big Red Car Care for washing the company automobile. Voucher no. 6.

   22   Paid $9.50 for mailing a package. Voucher no. 7.

   29   Paid $30 for postage stamps. Voucher no. 8.

Replenishing the Petty Cash Fund

The petty cash fund should be replenished whenever the fund runs low, and at the end of each accounting period so that the accounts are brought

F I G U R E   8 - 1 2 **James Maple's Petty Cash Payments Record**

FOR THE MONTH OF December 19--					PAGE 1
			DISTRIBUTION OF PAYMENTS		
	POST. EXP.	TRAVEL/ ENTERT. EXP.	MISC. EXP.	ACCOUNT	AMOUNT
1					
2					
3					
4		15 75			
5				James Maple, Drawing	30 00
6			28 25		
7		14 50			
8					
9	9 50				
10	30 00				
11	39 50	30 25	28 25		30 00
12					
13					
14					

up to date. The petty cash payments record is proved by footing all of the amount columns. The sum of the footings of the Distribution columns should equal the footing of the Total Amount column. After proving the footings, the totals are entered and the record is ruled as shown in figure 8-12.

The information in the petty cash payments record is then used to replenish the petty cash fund. On December 31, a check for $168.80 is issued to the petty cash custodian. The journal entry to record the replenishment of the fund is as follows:

	19--					
18	Dec.	31	Automobile Expense	40 80		18
19			Postage Expense	39 50		19
20			Travel & Entertainment Expense	30 25		20
21			Miscellaneous Expense	28 25		21
22			James Maple, Drawing	30 00		22
23			Cash		168 80	23
24			Repl. of petty cash fund.			24
25						25
26						26
27						27
28						28
29						29

Note two important aspects of the functioning of a petty cash fund.

Once the petty cash fund is established, no further entries are made to Petty Cash unless the amount of the fund is being changed. No posting is done from the petty cash payments record.

1. Once the fund is established by debiting Petty Cash and crediting Cash, no further entries are made to Petty Cash. Notice in the journal entry to replenish the fund that the debits are to appropriate expense accounts and the credit is to Cash. Only if the amount of the fund itself is being changed would there be a debit or credit to Petty Cash.

2. The petty cash payments record is strictly a supplement to the regular accounting records. No posting is done from this record.

4

Use the cash short and over account.

CASH SHORT AND OVER

Businesses generally must be able to make change when customers pay for goods or services received. An unavoidable part of this change-making process is that errors can occur. It is important to know whether such errors have occurred and how to account for them.

Businesses commonly use cash registers with tapes that accumulate a record of the day's receipts. The amount of cash according to the tapes can be compared with the amount of cash in the register to determine the existence and amount of any error. For example, assume a cash shortage is identified for June 19.

Receipts per register tapes	$963
Cash count	961
Cash shortage	$ 2

Similarly, assume a cash overage is identified for June 20.

Receipts per register tapes	$814
Cash count	815
Cash overage	$ 1

We account for such errors by using an account called Cash Short and Over. The register tapes on June 19 showed receipts of $963, but only $961 in cash was counted. The journal entry on June 19 to record the revenues and cash shortage would be:

23	19-- June	19	Cash		961 00			23
24			Cash Short and Over		2 00			24
25			Service Fees			963 00		25

The entry on June 20 to record the revenues and cash overage would be:

23		20	Cash		815 00			23
24			Service Fees			814 00		24
25			Cash Short and Over			1 00		25

The Cash Short and Over account is used to accumulate cash shortages and overages throughout the accounting period. At the end of the period, a debit balance in the account (a net shortage) is treated as Miscellaneous Expense. A credit balance in the account (a net overage) is treated as Miscellaneous Revenue.

KEY POINTS

1 Three steps to follow in preparing a check are:

1. Complete the check stub or register.
2. Enter the date, payee name, and amount on the check.
3. Sign the check.

2 The most common reasons for differences between the book and bank cash balances are:

1. Outstanding checks
2. Deposits in transit
3. Bank service charges
4. Bank collections for the depositor
5. NSF checks
6. Errors by the bank or the depositor

Three steps to follow in preparing a bank reconciliation are:

1. Identify deposits in transit and any related errors.
2. Identify outstanding checks and any related errors.
3. Identify additional reconciling items.

Only two kinds of items on a bank reconciliation require journal entries:

1. Errors on the depositor's books.
2. Bank additions and deductions that do not already appear in the accounting records.

3 Two important aspects of the functioning of a petty cash fund are:

1. Once the fund is established, subsequent entries do not affect the petty cash account balance, unless the amount of the fund itself is being changed.
2. The petty cash payments record is supplemental to the regular accounting records. No posting is done from this record.

4 Cash shortages and overages are accounted for using the Cash Short and Over account. A debit balance in this account represents expense; a credit balance represents revenue.

KEY TERMS

ABA (American Bankers Association) Number 244 The small fraction printed in the upper right hand corner of each check.

automated teller machines 245 Banks have these machines so that depositors can make withdrawals or deposits at any time.

bank reconciliation 250 Bringing the book and bank balances into agreement.

bank statement 247 A statement of account issued by a bank to each depositor once a month.

blank endorsement 245 The depositor signs on the back of the check, making the check payable to any bearer.

cancelled checks 247 The depositor's checks paid by the bank during the period.

cash 243 To a business, cash includes checks received from customers, money orders, and bank cashier's checks, in addition to currency and coins.

check 246 A document ordering a bank to pay cash from a depositor's account.

check stub 246 In some checkbooks, each check is attached to a check stub that contains space for relevant information.

credit memos 251 Items that the bank adds to the account.

debit memos 251 Items that the bank deducts from the account.

deposit ticket 244 A detailed listing of items being deposited.

deposits in transit 250 Deposits that have not reached or been recorded by the bank before the statement is prepared.

drawee 246 The bank on which the check is drawn.

drawer 246 The depositor who orders the bank to pay the cash.

electronic funds transfer (EFT) 253 Using a computer rather than money or checks to complete transactions with the bank.

endorsement 245   Stamping or writing the depositor's name and sometimes other important information on the back of the check.

internal control 243   A set of procedures designed to ensure proper accounting for transactions.

not sufficient funds (NSF) checks 250   Checks deposited by the depositor that are not paid because the drawer did not have sufficient funds.

outstanding checks 250   Checks issued during the period that have not been presented to the bank for payment before the statement is prepared.

payee 246   The person being paid the cash.

petty cash fund 254   A fund established to pay for small items.

petty cash payments record 255   A special multi-column record that supplements the regular accounting records.

petty cash voucher 254   A receipt that is prepared for every payment from the petty cash fund.

restrictive endorsement 245   The depositor adds words such as "For deposit" to restrict the payment of the check.

service charges 250   Bank charges for services such as check printing and processing.

signature card 243   A card that is completed and signed by each person authorized to sign checks.

BUILDING YOUR ACCOUNTING KNOWLEDGE

1. Why must a signature card be filled out and signed to open a checking account?
2. Explain the difference between a blank endorsement and a restrictive endorsement.
3. Who are the three parties to every check?
4. What are the three steps to follow in preparing a check?
5. What are the most common reasons for differences between the book and bank cash balances?
6. What are the three steps to follow in preparing a bank reconciliation?
7. What two kinds of items on a bank reconciliation require journal entries?
8. Name three applications of electronic funds transfer in current use.
9. What is the purpose of a petty cash fund?
10. What should be prepared every time a petty cash payment is made?
11. At what two times should the petty cash fund be replenished?
12. From what source is the information obtained for issuing a check to replenish the petty cash fund?
13. What does a debit balance in the cash short and over account represent? What does a credit balance in this account represent?

DEMONSTRATION PROBLEM

Jason Kuhn's check stubs indicated a balance of $4,573.12 on March 31. This included a record of a deposit of $926.10 mailed to the bank on March 30, but not credited to Kuhn's account until April 1. In addition, the following checks were outstanding on March 31.

> No. 462, $524.26
> No. 465, $213.41
> No. 473, $543.58
> No. 476, $351.38
> No. 477, $197.45

The bank statement showed a balance of $5,419.00 as of March 31. The bank included a service charge on its March 31 statement with the date of 3/29 in the amount of $4.10. In matching the cancelled checks and record of deposits with the stubs, it was discovered that check no. 456, to Office Suppliers, Inc., for $93 was erroneously recorded on the stub for $39, causing the bank balance on that stub and those following to be $54 too large.

Kuhn maintains a $200.00 petty cash fund. His petty cash payments record showed the following totals at the end of March of the current year.

Automobile Expense	32.40
Postage Expense	27.50
Charitable Contributions Expense	35.00
Telephone Expense	6.20
Travel & Entertainment Expense	38.60
Miscellaneous Expense	17.75
Jason Kuhn, Drawing	40.00
Total	$197.45

This left a balance of $2.55 in the petty cash fund.

Required
1. Prepare a bank reconciliation for Jason Kuhn as of March 31, 19--.
2. Journalize the entries that should be made by Kuhn on his books as of March 31, 19--: (a) as a result of the bank reconciliation and (b) to replenish the petty cash fund.
3. Show proof that, after these entries, the total of the cash and petty cash account balances equals $4,715.02.

SOLUTION

1.

<table>
<tr><td colspan="3" align="center">**Jason Kuhn**
Bank Reconciliation
March 31, 19--</td></tr>
<tr><td>Balance per bank statement, March 31</td><td></td><td>$5 4 1 9 00</td></tr>
<tr><td>Add deposit in transit, March 30</td><td></td><td>9 2 6 10</td></tr>
<tr><td></td><td></td><td>$6 3 4 5 10</td></tr>
<tr><td>Deduct outstanding checks:</td><td></td><td></td></tr>
<tr><td>   No. 462</td><td>$5 2 4 26</td><td></td></tr>
<tr><td>   No. 465</td><td>2 1 3 41</td><td></td></tr>
<tr><td>   No. 473</td><td>5 4 3 58</td><td></td></tr>
<tr><td>   No. 476</td><td>3 5 1 38</td><td></td></tr>
<tr><td>   No. 477</td><td>1 9 7 45</td><td>1 8 3 0 08</td></tr>
<tr><td>Adjusted bank balance, March 31</td><td></td><td>$4 5 1 5 02</td></tr>
<tr><td></td><td></td><td></td></tr>
<tr><td>Balance per check stub March 31</td><td></td><td>$4 5 7 3 12</td></tr>
<tr><td>Deduct: Bank service charge</td><td>$ 4 10</td><td></td></tr>
<tr><td>   Error on stub for check no. 456</td><td>5 4 00</td><td>5 8 10</td></tr>
<tr><td>Adjusted check stub balance</td><td></td><td>$4 5 1 5 02</td></tr>
<tr><td></td><td></td><td></td></tr>
</table>

2. a.

	19-- Mar.	31						
9	Mar.	31	Miscellaneous Expense		4 10			9
10			Accounts Payable—Office Sup., Inc.		5 4 00			10
11			Cash			5 8 10		11
12			Bank transactions for March.					12
13								13

b.

14		31	Automobile Expense		3 2 40			14
15			Postage Expense		2 7 50			15
16			Charitable Contributions Expense		3 5 00			16
17			Telephone Expense		6 20			17
18			Travel & Entertainment Expense		3 8 60			18
19			Miscellaneous Expense		1 7 75			19
20			Jason Kuhn, Drawing		4 0 00			20
21			Cash			1 9 7 45		21
22			Replenishment of petty cash					22
23			fund—check no. 477					23

3.

Cash in bank:	
Check stub balance, March 31	$4,573.12
Less bank charges	58.10
Adjusted cash in bank	$4,515.02
Cash on hand:	
Petty cash fund	$ 2.55
Add replenishment	197.45
Adjusted cash on hand	$ 200.00
Total cash in bank and petty cash on hand	$4,715.02

SERIES A

EXERCISES

APPLYING ACCOUNTING CONCEPTS

EXERCISE 8A1

Checking Account Terms

1 Match the following words with their definitions.

1. An endorsement where the depositor simply signs on the back of the check.
2. An endorsement which contains words like "For Deposit Only" together with the signature.
3. A card filled out and signed by each person authorized to sign checks on an account.
4. The depositor who orders the bank to pay cash from the depositor's account.
5. The bank on which the check is drawn.
6. The person being paid the cash.
7. A check which has been paid by the bank and is being returned to the depositor.

a. signature card
b. cancelled check
c. blank endorsement
d. drawer
e. restricted endorsement
f. drawee
g. payee

EXERCISE 8A2

Prepare Deposit Ticket

1 Based on the following information, prepare a deposit ticket.

Date:		January 15, 19--
Currency:		$334.00
Coin:		26.00
Checks:	No. 4-11	311.00
	No. 80-322	108.00
	No. 3-9	38.00

EXERCISE 8A3

Prepare Check and Stub

1 Based on the following information, prepare a check and stub.

Date:	January 15, 19--
Check to:	J. M. Suppliers
Amount:	$150.00
For:	Office Supplies
Balance forward:	$2,841.50
Deposit:	(From Exercise 8A2)
Signature:	Sign your name

EXERCISE 8A4

Bank Reconciliation Terminology

2 In a similar format, indicate whether the action at the left will result in an addition to (+) or subtraction from (−) the ending bank balance or the ending checkbook balance.

	Ending Bank Balance	Ending Checkbook Balance
a. Deposits in transit to the bank	____	____
b. Error in checkbook, was recorded as $32 but was actually $23	____	____
c. Service fee charged by bank	____	____
d. Outstanding checks	____	____
e. NSF check deposited earlier	____	____
f. Error in checkbook, was recorded as $22 but was actually $12	____	____
g. Bank credit memo advising they collected a note for us	____	____

EXERCISE 8A5

Prepare Journal Entries for Bank Reconciliation

2 Based on the following bank reconciliation information, prepare the journal entries.

Karen Henderson
Bank Reconciliation
September 30, 19--

Balance per bank statement, Sept. 30			$5,326.40
Add deposits in transit, Sept. 29	$352.00		
	116.00		468.00
			$5,794.40
Deduct outstanding checks:			
No. 387	$324.50		
No. 393	11.80		
No. 395	36.20		372.50
Adjusted bank balance, Sept. 30			$5,421.90
Book balance, Sept. 30			$5,840.20
Deduct: Error on check 391*	$10.00		
NSF check	400.00		
Service fee	8.30		418.30
Adjusted book balance			$5,421.90

*Accounts Payable was debited in original entry.

Petty Cash Journal Entries

3 Based on the following petty cash information, prepare (a) the journal entry to establish a petty cash fund, and (b) the journal entry to replenish the petty cash fund.

On January 1, 19--, a check is written in the amount of $150 to establish a petty cash fund. During January, the following vouchers are written for cash removed from the petty cash drawer:

Voucher	Account Debited	Amount
1	Telephone Expense	$ 3.50
2	Automobile Expense	11.00
3	J. Adams, Drawing	50.00
4	Postage Expense	8.50
5	Charitable Contributions Expense	10.00
6	Miscellaneous Expense	28.00

Cash Short and Over Entries

4 Based on the following information, prepare the weekly entries for cash receipts from sales revenue and cash short and over.

Date	Cash Register Receipt Amount	Actual Cash Counted
April 2	$268.50	$266.50
9	237.75	233.50
16	309.25	311.00
23	226.50	224.00
30	318.00	322.00

PROBLEMS

Bank Reconciliation and Related Journal Entries

2 The balance in the checking account as of October 30 is $3,184.00. The bank statement shows an ending balance of $2,856.00. The following information is discovered by comparing checks deposited and written, and noting service fees, and other debit and credit memos shown on the bank statement.

Deposits in transit:	10/28	$300.00
	10/29	280.00
Outstanding checks:	No. 2826	$ 58.00
	No. 2829	122.00
	No. 2833	360.00
Bank service charge:		$ 20.00
NSF check:		278.00
Error on check no. 2818:	Checkbook shows it was for $28, but was actually written for $18. Accounts Payable was debited.	

Required

1. Prepare a bank reconciliation as of October 30, 19--.
2. Prepare the required journal entries.

PROBLEM 8A2
Petty Cash Record and Journal Entries

3 On May 1 a petty cash fund was established for $150. The following vouchers were issued during May:

Date	Voucher No.	Purpose	Amount
May 1	1	postage due	$ 3.50
3	2	supplies	11.00
5	3	auto repair (misc.)	22.00
7	4	drawing (J. Adams)	25.00
11	5	donation (Red Cross)	10.00
15	6	travel expenses	28.00
22	7	postage stamps	3.50
26	8	telephone call	5.00
30	9	donation (Boy Scouts)	30.00

Required

1. Prepare the journal entry to establish the petty cash fund.
2. Record the vouchers in the petty cash record. Total and rule the petty cash record.
3. Prepare the journal entry to replenish the petty cash fund. Make the appropriate entry in the petty cash record.

PROBLEM 8A3
Cash Short and Over Entries

4 Listed below are the weekly cash register tape amounts for sales and the related cash counts during the month of July.

	Cash Register Tape	Cash in Drawer
July 2	$289.50	$287.00
9	311.50	311.50
16	306.00	308.50
23	317.50	315.00
30	296.00	299.50

Required

1. Prepare the journal entries to record the cash sales and cash short and over for each of the five weeks.
2. Post to the Cash Short and Over account.
3. Determine the ending balance of the Cash Short and Over account. Does it represent an expense or revenue?

SERIES B

EXERCISES

EXERCISE 8B1

Checking Account Terms

1 Match the following words with their definitions.

1. Banking number used to identify checks for deposit tickets.
2. A card filled out to open a checking account.
3. A machine from which withdrawals can be taken or deposits made to accounts.
4. A place where relevant information is recorded about a check.
5. A set of procedures designed to ensure proper accounting for transactions.
6. A statement of account issued to each depositor once a month.
7. A detailed listing of items being deposited to an account.

a. bank statement
b. deposit ticket
c. signature card
d. internal control
e. check stub
f. ATM
g. ABA number

EXERCISE 8B2

Prepare Deposit Ticket

1 Based on the following information, prepare a deposit ticket.

Date:	November 15, 19--	
Currency:		$283.00
Coin:		19.00
Checks:	No. 3-22	201.00
	No. 19-366	114.00
	No. 3-2	28.00

EXERCISE 8B3

Prepare Check and Stub

1 Based on the following information, prepare a check and stub.

Date:	November 15, 19--
Check to:	R. J. Smith Co.
Amount:	$120.00
For:	Payment on account
Balance forward:	$3,181.00
Deposit:	(from Exercise 8B2)
Signature:	Sign your name

EXERCISE 8B4

Bank Reconciliation Terminology

2 In a similar format, indicate whether the action at the left will result in an addition to ($+$) or subtraction from ($-$) the ending bank balance or the ending checkbook balance.

	Ending Bank Balance	Ending Checkbook Balance
a. Service fee of $12 charged by bank	_____	_____
b. Outstanding checks	_____	_____
c. Error in checkbook—check recorded as $36 was actually for $28	_____	_____
d. NSF check deposited earlier	_____	_____

	Ending Bank Balance	Ending Checkbook Balance
e. Bank credit memo advising they collected a note for us	_____	_____
f. Deposits in transit to the bank	_____	_____
g. Error in checkbook—check recorded as $182 was actually for $218	_____	_____

EXERCISE 8B5

Prepare Journal Entries for Bank Reconciliation

2 Based on the following bank reconciliation information, prepare the journal entries.

Rebecca Reilly
Bank Reconciliation
July 31, 19--

Balance bank statement, July 31			$3 826 00
Add deposits in transit, July 31	$2 185 0		
	1 125 0		3 31 00
			$4 157 00
Deduct outstanding checks:			
No. 385	$3 085 0		
No. 403	2 11 40		
No. 410	98 10		6 18 00
Adjusted bank balance, July 31			$3 539 00
Balance per checkbook, July 31			$3 834 00
Add error on check 391*:			1 2 00
			$3 846 00
Deduct: NSF check	$2 97 00		
Service fee	10 00		3 07 00
Adjusted checkbook balance			$3 539 00

*Accounts Payable was debited in original entry.

EXERCISE 8B6

Petty Cash Journal Entries

3 Based on the following petty cash information, prepare (a) the journal entry to establish a petty cash fund, and (b) the journal entry to replenish the petty cash fund.

On October 1, 19--, a check is written in the amount of $100 to establish a petty cash fund. During October, the following vouchers are written for cash taken from the petty cash drawer:

Voucher	Account Debited	Amount
1	Postage Expense	$ 8.50
2	Miscellaneous Expense	12.00
3	B. Jones, Drawing	35.00
4	Telephone Expense	7.50
5	Charitable Contributions Expense	15.00
6	Automobile Expense	22.00

Cash Short and Over Entries

4 Based on the following information, prepare the weekly entries for cash receipts from sales revenue and cash short and over.

Date	Cash Register Receipt Amount	Actual Cash Counted
June 1	$330.00	$333.00
8	297.00	300.00
15	233.00	231.00
22	302.00	296.50
29	316.00	312.00

PROBLEMS

Bank Reconciliation and Related Journal Entries

2 The bank statement shows an ending balance of $3,628.00. The balance in the checking account as of November 30, is $4,120.00. The following information is discovered by comparing checks deposited and written, and noting service fees and other debit and credit memos shown on the bank statement.

Deposits in transit:	11/26	$250.00
	11/28	325.00
Outstanding checks:	No. 322	$128.00
	No. 324	86.00
	No. 327	224.00
Bank service charge:		$ 12.00
NSF check:		323.00
Error on check no. 321:	Checkbook shows it was for $32, but was actually written for $52. Accounts Payable was debited.	

Required
1. Prepare a bank reconciliation as of November 30, 19--.
2. Prepare the required journal entries.

Petty Cash Record and Journal Entries

3 On July 1, a petty cash fund was established by L. Bean for $100. The following vouchers were issued during July.

Date	Voucher No.	Purpose	Amount
1	1	office supplies	$ 3.00
3	2	donation (Goodwill)	15.00
5	3	travel expenses	5.00
7	4	postage due	2.00
8	5	office supplies	4.00
11	6	postage due	3.50
15	7	telephone call	5.00
21	8	travel expenses	11.00
25	9	withdrawal by owner	20.00
26	10	copier repair (misc.)	18.50

Required

1. Prepare the journal entry to establish the petty cash fund.
2. Record the vouchers in the petty cash record. Total and rule the petty cash record.
3. Prepare the journal entry to replenish the petty cash fund. Make the appropriate entry in the petty cash record.

<table>
<tr><td>PROBLEM 8B3</td></tr>
<tr><td>Cash Short and Over Entries</td></tr>
</table>

4 Listed below are the weekly cash register tape amounts for sales and the related cash counts during the month of July.

		Cash Register Tape	Cash in Drawer
Aug.	1	$292.50	$295.00
	8	305.00	301.50
	15	286.00	286.00
	22	330.25	332.75
	29	298.50	295.00

Required

1. Prepare the journal entries to record the cash sales and cash short and over for each of the five weeks.
2. Post to the Cash Short and Over account.
3. Determine the ending balance of the Cash Short and Over account. Does it represent an expense or revenue?

MASTERY PROBLEM

Turner Excavation maintains a checking account and has decided to open a petty cash fund.

Required

1. Record each of the following transactions in either a journal or a petty cash payments record:

July 2 Established a petty cash fund by issuing check no. 301 for $100.00.
   5 Issued check no. 302 to pay office rent, $650.00.
   5 Paid $25.00 from the petty cash fund for postage. Voucher no. 1.
   7 Paid $30.00 from the petty cash fund for delivery of flowers for the secretaries (Miscellaneous Expense). Voucher no. 2.
   8 Paid $20.00 from the petty cash fund to repair a tire on the company truck. Voucher no. 3.

July 12 Paid $22.00 from the petty cash fund for a newspaper advertisement. Voucher no. 4.

13 Issued check no. 303 to replenish the petty cash fund. (Foot, prove, total, and rule the petty cash payments record. Record the balance and the amount needed to replenish the fund in the Description column of the petty cash payments record.)

15 Issued check no. 304 for office equipment, $525.00.

17 Issued check no. 305 for the purchase of supplies, $133.00.

18 Issued check no. 306 to pay attorney fees, $1,000.

20 Paid $26.00 from the petty cash fund to reimburse an employee for expenses incurred to repair the company truck. Voucher no. 5.

24 Paid $12.50 from the petty cash fund for telephone calls made from a phone booth. Voucher no. 6.

28 Paid $25.00 from the petty cash fund as a contribution to the YMCA. Voucher no. 7.

30 Issued check no. 307 to newspaper for an advertisement $200.20.

31 Issued check no. 308 to replenish the petty cash fund. (Foot, prove, total, and rule the petty cash payments record. Record the balance and the amount needed to replenish the fund in the Description column of the petty cash payments record.)

2. The following bank statement was received in the mail. Deposits were made on July 6 for $3,500.00 and on July 29 for $2,350.00. The checkbook balance on July 31 is $4,331.55. Prepare a bank reconciliation and make any necessary journal entries. Notice the discrepancy in check no. 302 that cleared the bank for $655.00. This check was written on July 5 for rent expense, but was incorrectly entered on the check stub and in the journal as $650.00.

F I G U R E   8 - 1 3   **Bank Statement**

Statement						Merchant's National Bank

Turner Excavation
220 Main Street
Oakhurst, NJ 07755-1461

Reference Number 16 3247 5
Statement Date July 31, 19--
Statement Instructions

Page Number

Beginning Balance $1,250.25	No. of Deposits and Credits 1	We have added these deposits and credits totaling $3,500.00	No. of withdrawals and charges 6	We have subtracted these withdrawals and charges totaling $1,512.50	Resulting in a statement balance of $3,237.75
Document Count	Average Daily balance this statement period		Minimum balance this statement period	Date	Amount

If your account does not balance , please see reverse side and report any discrepancy to our Customer Service Department.

Date	Description	Amount	Balance
7/1	Beginning Balance		1,250.25
7/5	Check No. 301	-100.00	1,150.25
7/8	Check No. 302	-655.00	495.25
7/9	Deposit	3,500.00	3,995.25
7/15	Check No. 303	-97.00	3,898.25
7/20	Check No.304	-525.00	3,373.25
7/28	Check No.305	-133.00	3,240.25
7/31	Sevice Charge	-2.50	3,237.75

EC-Error Correction   OD-Overdrawn   RC-Return Check Charge
                          TR-Wire Transfer   D/N-Day/Night

Depositor agrees and Bank accepts business upon the terms and conditions of Bank's rules and regulations now in effect or as may be hereafter adopted.

Chapter 8 Demonstration Problem

Chapter 8 contains several problems that you can complete if you have a LOTUS 1-2-3 spreadsheet program. The 123 icon in the margin beside selected problems indicates that the opening balances for these problems have been entered on a template disk. This template disk is available from your instructor. You must have a LOTUS 1-2-3 spreadsheet program to use the template disk.

The following instructions show you how to complete the Chapter 8 demonstration problem. Refer to Appendix A for additional information on accounting spreadsheet applications.

STEP 1 Place your template disk with the opening data in the data drive.

STEP 2 Start up your spreadsheet software using the instructions in the documentation that is provided with the spreadsheet program. The template disk contains a command that causes the spreadsheet program to load an opening screen. (Figure AC8-1)

STEP 3 When the opening screen appears, press the Alt key and the letter I to read the instructions. (Figure AC8-2)

FIGURE AC8-1 **Opening Screen**

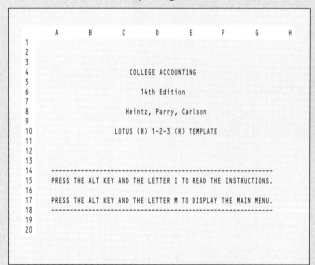

```
          A     B     C     D     E     F     G     H
 1
 2
 3
 4                   COLLEGE ACCOUNTING
 5
 6                      14th Edition
 7
 8                  Heintz, Parry, Carlson
 9
10                LOTUS (R) 1-2-3 (R) TEMPLATE
11
12
13
14     --------------------------------------------------
15     PRESS THE ALT KEY AND THE LETTER I TO READ THE INSTRUCTIONS.
16
17     PRESS THE ALT KEY AND THE LETTER M TO DISPLAY THE MAIN MENU.
18     --------------------------------------------------
19
20
```

FIGURE AC8-2 **Instructions Display**

```
          A     B     C     D     E     F     G     H
 1
 2           INSTRUCTIONS FOR USING THE LOTUS 1-2-3
 3                      TEMPLATE DISK
 4
 5     (1)  Insert your copy of the PROBLEMS disk into the drive.
 6     (2)  Load LOTUS 1-2-3 into the computer.
 7     (3)  The opening screen will appear.
 8     (4)  Press the Alt key and the letter I simultaneously to read these
 9          instructions.
10     (5)  Press the Alt key and the letter P to print these instructions.
11     (6)  After you have read these instructions, follow the instructions
12          at the bottom of this screen to load the Main Menu. The Main
13          Menu displays a list of problems.
14     (7)  From the Main Menu, press the Alt key and the specified letter
15          to load the problem you wish to work.
16     (8)  After you have loaded a problem, the following menu will be
17          displayed:
18
19                      Go Print Save Quit
20
```

STEP 4 After you have read the instructions, press the Alt key and the letter M to load the Main Menu. (Figure AC8-3)

STEP 5 From the Main Menu, press the Alt key and the letter A to load the demonstration problem for Chapter 8.

STEP 6 After you have loaded the problem, the following menu will be displayed: Go Print Save Quit.

STEP 7 Press the Enter key with the highlight bar positioned on Go. The highlight bar will then be positioned in the Student Name cell.

STEP 8 Enter your name in the Student Name cell and the Section Number in the Section Number cell.

STEP 9 Use the arrow keys to move the highlight bar. Enter the data from the demonstration problem into the appropriate cells in the spreadsheet. (Figures AC8-4, AC8-5, and AC8-6)

FIGURE AC8-3 **Problems Menu**

```
        A    B      C        D       E     F       G        H
   1
   2
   3                  C O L L E G E    A C C O U N T I N G
   4    -----------------------------------------------------------
   5
   6    ALT A   Demonstration Problem 8    ALT J   Problem 16B3
   7    ALT B   Problem 8A1                ALT K   Problem 17A3
   8    ALT C   Problem 8B1                ALT L   Problem 17B3
   9    ALT D   Demonstration Problem 9    ALT M   Problem 18A3
  10    ALT E   Problem 9A3                ALT N   Problem 18B3
  11    ALT F   Problem 9B3                ALT O   Problem 19A3
  12    ALT G   Problem 10A1               ALT P   Problem 19B3
  13    ALT H   Problem 10B1               ALT Q   Problem 26A4
  14    ALT I   Problem 16A3               ALT R   Problem 26B4
  15
  16
  17          -------------------------------------------
  18          CHOOSE THE APPROPRIATE OPTION BY PRESSING
  19          THE ALT KEY AND THE LETTER SIMULTANEOUSLY
  20          -------------------------------------------
```

FIGURE AC8-4 **Data Entered— Lines 13 through 24**

```
        A    B      C        D       E     F       G        H
   5
   6    ------------------------------------------------------------
   7    A    B      C        D       E     F       G        H
   8    ------------------------------------------------------------
   9    9 (1)                             Jason Kuhn
  10    10                             Bank Reconciliation
  11    11                               March 31, 19--
  12    12 ---------------------------------------------------------
  13    13 Balance per bank statement, March 31            $5,419.00
  14    14 Add:  Deposit in transit,  March 30                926.10
  15    15                                                 ----------
  16    16                                                 $6,345.10
  17    17 Deduct outstanding checks
  18    18                                       $524.26
  19    19                                        213.41
  20    20                                        543.58
  21    21                                        351.38
  22    22                                        197.45   1,830.08
  23    23                                       --------- ----------
  24    24 Adjusted bank balance, March 31                 $4,515.02
```

FIGURE AC8-5 **Data Entered—**
Lines 25 through 44

```
      A    B            C            D       E       F        G        H
25  25                                                              ==========
26  26 Balance, per check stub, March 31                          $4,573.12
27  27 Deduct: Bank service charge                        $4.10
28  28        Error in recording check                    54.00     58.10
29  29                                                             ----------
30  30 Adjusted check stub balance                                $4,515.02
31  31                                                              ==========
32  32
33  33
34  34
35  35 (2) Record the necessary entries.
36  36
37  37                                               Debit    Credit
38  38                                              ---------- ----------
39  39 March 31 Miscellaneous Expense                 4.10
40  40          Accts. Pay.--Office Suppliers, Inc.   54.00
41  41             Cash                                          58.10
42  42                (a) Bank transactions for March.
43  43
44  44 March 31 Automobile Expense                    32.40
```

FIGURE AC8-6 **Data Entered—**
Lines 45 through 64

```
      A    B       C            D           E      F       G        H
45  45       Postage Expense                             27.50
46  46       Charitable Contributions Expense            35.00
47  47       Telephone Expense                            6.20
48  48       Travel & Entertainment Expense              38.60
49  49       Miscellaneous Expense                       17.75
50  50       Jason Kuhn, Drawing                         40.00
51  51          Cash                                               197.45
52  52             (b) Replenishment of petty cash fund.
53  53
54  54 (3)   Cash in bank:
55  55          Check stub balance, March 31                    $4,573.12
56  56          Less bank charges                                  58.10
57  57                                                           ----------
58  58          Adjusted cash in bank                            $4,515.02
59  59
60  60       Cash on hand:
61  61          Petty cash fund                                    $2.55
62  62          Add replenishment                                 197.45
63  63                                                           ----------
64  64          Adjusted cash on hand                             $200.00
```

STEP 10   After you enter the data from the demonstration problem, press the Alt key and the letter M to return to the Menu.

STEP 11   If you wish to save your data, remove your template disk and place a formatted data disk in the data drive before you choose Save.
CAUTION: If you choose the Save option without placing a different data disk in the drive, you will save data over the opening balances.

STEP 12   Choose the Quit option to clear the spreadsheet from memory.

STEP 13   If you wish to load another problem, press /FR and retrieve the file named Menu to display the available opening balances.

STEP 14   When you wish to quit the spreadsheet program, press /QY.

LEARNING OBJECTIVES

Careful study of this chapter should enable you to:

1. Distinguish between employees and independent contractors.
2. Calculate employee earnings and deductions.
3. Prepare payroll records.
4. Account for employee earnings and deductions.
5. Describe various payroll record-keeping methods.

*P*ayroll Accounting: Employee Earnings and Deductions

The only contact most of us have had with payroll is to have received a paycheck. Very few of us have seen the large amount of record keeping needed to produce that paycheck.

Employers maintain complete payroll accounting records for two reasons. First, payroll costs are major expenditures for most companies. Payroll accounting records provide data useful in analyzing and controlling these expenditures. Second, federal, state, and local laws require employers to keep payroll records. Companies must accumulate payroll data both for the business as a whole and for each employee.

1

Distinguish between employees and independent contractors.

EMPLOYEES AND INDEPENDENT CONTRACTORS

Not every person who performs services for a business is considered an employee. An **employee** works under the control and direction of an employer. Examples include secretaries, maintenance workers, salesclerks, and plant supervisors. In contrast, an **independent contractor** performs a service for a fee and does not work under the control and direction of the company paying for the service. Examples of independent contractors include public accountants, real estate agents, and doctors.

The distinction between an employee and an independent contractor is very important for payroll purposes. Government laws and regulations regarding payroll apply only to employees. Thus, employers must deduct certain taxes, maintain payroll records, and file reports for all employees, but not for independent contractors. The payroll accounting procedures described in this chapter apply only to employer/employee relationships.

2

Calculate employee earnings and deductions.

EMPLOYEE EARNINGS AND DEDUCTIONS

Two steps are required to determine how much to pay an employee for a pay period.

1. Calculate total earnings.
2. Determine the amounts of deductions.

Salaries and Wages

Compensation for managerial or administrative services usually is called **salary.** A salary normally is expressed in biweekly, monthly, or annual terms. Compensation for skilled or unskilled labor usually is referred to as **wages.** Wages ordinarily are expressed in terms of hours, weeks, or units produced. The terms "salaries" and "wages" often are used interchangeably in practice.

The **Fair Labor Standards Act (FLSA)** requires employers to pay overtime at 1½ times the regular rate to any hourly employee who works over 40 hours in a week. Some companies pay a higher rate for hours worked on Saturday or Sunday, but this is not required by the FLSA. In addition, some salaried employees are exempt from the FLSA rules.

Computing Total Earnings

Compensation usually is based on the time worked during the payroll period. Sometimes earnings are based on sales or units of output during the period. When compensation is based on time, a record must be kept of the time worked by each employee. Time cards (figure 9-1) are helpful for this purpose. In large businesses with computer-based timekeeping systems, plastic cards or badges with special codes (figure 9-2) can be used.

To illustrate the computation of total earnings, we can use the time card of Helen Kuzmik in figure 9-1. The card shows that Kuzmik worked a total of 55 hours:

Monday—Friday: 5 × 9 hours	45
Saturday	6
Sunday	4
Total hours worked	55 hours

Kuzmik's regular rate of pay is $12 per hour. She is paid 1½ times the regular rate for hours in excess of 40 per week, and twice the regular rate for hours on Sunday. Kuzmik's total earnings for the week ended December 19, are computed as follows:

40 hours × $12	$480
11 hours × $18 (1½ × $12 = $18)	198*
4 hours (on Sunday) × $24 (2 × $12 = $24)	96
Total earnings for the week	$774

*Kuzmik worked 9 hours each day Monday through Friday and 6 hours on Saturday—a total of 51 hours. Forty hours are paid for at the regular rate and 11 hours at time and a half.

FIGURE 9-1 Time Card

Westly, Inc. Time Card - Hourly Payroll								

Period Ending — **Mo.** *Dec.* **Day** *19* **Yr.** *19--*

Name of Dept. *Sales*

NAME (Print) Last *Kuzmik* **First** *Helen*

Payroll No. *25-1* **Section** *A*

1st. wk.	M	T	W	Th	F	Sa	Su	Totals
Reg. Sched.	8	8	8	8	8			40
Over-time	1	1	1	1	1	6		11
Dbl. Time					4			4
1st. wk.	M	T	W	Th	F	Sa	Su	Totals
Reg. Sched.								
Over-time								

Remarks

I certify that to the best of my knowledge the above is a true report of the attendance of the employee named.

T.M.

Department Head

FIGURE 9-2 Bar-Code Time Card

EAST CORP.

Robin Brown

Name

004866

An employee who is paid a regular salary may also be entitled to premium pay for overtime. If this is the case, it is necessary to compute the regular hourly rate of pay before computing the overtime rate. To illustrate, assume that Linda Swaney receives a regular salary of $2,288 a month and is paid 1½ times the regular hourly rate for hours in excess of 40 per week. Swaney's overtime rate of pay is computed as follows:

$2,288 × 12 months	$27,456 annual pay
$27,456 ÷ 52 weeks	$528.00 pay per week
$528.00 ÷ 40 hours	$13.20 pay per regular hour
$13.20 × 1½	$19.80 overtime pay per hour

If Swaney worked 50 hours during the week ended December 19, her total earnings for the week would be computed as follows:

40 hours × $13.20	$528.00
10 hours × $19.80	198.00
Total earnings for the week	$726.00

Deductions from Total Earnings

An employee's total earnings are called **gross pay.** Various deductions are made from gross pay to yield take-home or **net pay.** Deductions from gross pay fall into three major categories:

1. Federal (and possibly state and city) income tax withholding
2. Employees' FICA tax withholding
3. Voluntary deductions

Employees Income Tax Withholding.   Employers are required by federal law to withhold certain amounts from the total earnings of each employee. These withholdings are applied toward the payment of the employee's federal income tax. Four factors determine the amount to be withheld from an employee's gross pay each pay period.

1. Total earnings
2. Marital status
3. Number of withholding allowances claimed
4. Length of the pay period

Withholding Allowances.   Each employee is required to furnish the employer with an Employee's Withholding Allowance Certificate, Form W-4 (figure 9-3). The marital status of the employee and the number of allowances claimed on Form W-4 determine the dollar amount of earnings subject to withholding. A **withholding allowance** exempts a specific dollar amount of an employee's gross pay from federal income tax withholding. In general, each employee is permitted one personal withholding allowance, one for a spouse who does not also claim an allowance, and one for each dependent.

An allowance certificate completed by Ken Istone is shown below. Istone is married, has a spouse who is not employed, and has four dependent children. On line 5 of the W-4 form, Istone claims 6 allowances, calculated as follows:

Personal allowance	1
Spouse allowance	1
Allowances for dependents	4
Total withholding allowances	6

FIGURE 9-3 **Withholding Allowance Certificate (Form W-4)**

Wage-Bracket Method.   Most employers use the **wage-bracket method** to determine the amount of tax to be withheld from an employee's pay. Employers trace the employee's gross pay for a specific time period into the appropriate wage-bracket table provided by the Internal Revenue Service. These tables cover various time periods, and there are separate tables for single and married taxpayers. Copies are provided in *Circular E—Employer's Tax Guide,* which may be obtained from any local Internal Revenue Service office.

A portion of a weekly income tax wage-bracket withholding table for married persons is illustrated in figure 9-4. Assume that Ken Istone (who claims 6 allowances) had gross earnings of $425 for the week ending December 19, 19--. The table is used as follows:

1. Find the row for wages of "at least $420, but less than $430."
2. Find the column headed "6 withholding allowances."
3. Where the row and column cross, $16.00 is the amount to be withheld.

1. **Find the row for wages.**
2. **Find the column for withholding allowances.**
3. **Find the amount where they cross.**

FIGURE 9-4 Federal Withholding Tax Table

| WEEKLY Payroll Period — Employee MARRIED | | | | | | | | | | | |
| And the wages are- | | And the number of withholding allowances claimed is— | | | | | | | | | | |
At least	But less than	0	1	2	3	4	5	6	7	8	9	10 or more
		The amount of income tax to be withheld shall be—										
280	290	33	26	20	14	8	2	0	0	0	0	0
290	300	34	28	22	15	9	3	0	0	0	0	0
300	310	36	29	23	17	11	5	0	0	0	0	0
310	320	37	31	25	18	12	6	0	0	0	0	0
320	330	39	32	26	20	14	8	1	0	0	0	0
330	340	40	34	28	21	15	9	3	0	0	0	0
340	350	42	35	29	23	17	11	4	0	0	0	0
350	360	43	37	31	24	18	12	6	0	0	0	0
360	370	45	38	32	26	20	14	7	1	0	0	0
370	380	46	40	34	27	21	15	9	3	0	0	0
380	390	48	41	35	29	23	17	10	4	0	0	0
390	400	49	43	37	30	24	18	12	6	0	0	0
400	410	51	44	38	32	26	20	13	7	1	0	0
410	420	52	46	40	33	27	21	15	9	2	0	0
420	430	54	47	41	35	29	23	16	10	4	0	0
430	440	55	49	43	36	30	24	18	12	5	0	0
440	450	57	50	44	38	32	26	19	13	7	1	0
450	460	58	52	46	39	33	27	21	15	8	2	0
460	470	60	53	47	41	35	29	22	16	10	4	0
470	480	61	55	49	42	36	30	24	18	11	5	0
480	490	63	56	50	44	38	32	25	19	13	7	0
490	500	64	58	52	45	39	33	27	21	14	8	2
500	510	66	59	53	47	41	35	28	22	16	10	3
510	520	67	61	55	48	42	36	30	24	17	11	5
520	530	69	62	56	50	44	38	31	25	19	13	6
530	540	70	64	58	51	45	39	33	27	20	14	8
540	550	72	65	59	53	47	41	34	28	22	16	9
550	560	73	67	61	54	48	42	36	30	23	17	11
560	570	75	68	62	56	50	44	37	31	25	19	12
570	580	76	70	64	57	51	45	39	33	26	20	14
580	590	78	71	65	59	53	47	40	34	28	22	15
590	600	79	73	67	60	54	48	42	36	29	23	17
600	610	81	74	68	62	56	50	43	37	31	25	18
610	620	82	76	70	63	57	51	45	39	32	26	20
620	630	84	77	71	65	59	53	46	40	34	28	21

❶ Find the row for wages.
❷ Find the column for withholding allowances.
❸ Find the amount where they cross.

If there are state or city income taxes, withholding generally is handled in one of two ways. (1) Forms and tables similar to the Internal Revenue Service are used. (2) An amount equal to a percentage of the federal withholding amount is withheld.

Employees' FICA Tax Withholding.   The Federal Insurance Contributions Act requires employers to withhold **FICA taxes** from employees' earnings. FICA taxes are commonly referred to as social security taxes. These taxes are intended to provide pensions, disability benefits, and health insurance for retired persons.

Congress has frequently changed the tax rates and the maximum amounts of earnings subject to FICA taxes. These changes, however, do not affect the accounting procedures for payroll. In this text, we will assume an overall rate of 7.5% applied to maximum earnings of $55,000.[1] Refer to Appendix B for a discussion of the current FICA rates and maximum amounts.

To illustrate the calculation of FICA taxes, assume the following earnings for Sarah Cadrain:

	Earnings	
Pay Period	Week	Year-to-Date
Nov. 8–14	$1,100	$48,400
......	.	.
......	.	.
......	.	.
Dec. 13–19	$1,260	$55,800

For the week of November 8-14, FICA taxes on Cadrain's earnings would be:

$$\frac{\text{Gross Pay}}{\$1,100} \times \frac{\text{Tax Rate}}{7.5\%} = \frac{\text{Tax}}{\$82.50}$$

During the week of December 13-19, Cadrain's earnings for the calendar year went over the $55,000 FICA maximum by $800 ($55,800 − 55,000). Therefore, $800 of her $1,260 earnings for the week would not be subject to the FICA tax.

Year-to-date earnings	$55,800
FICA maximum	55,000
Amount *not* subject to FICA tax	$ 800

The FICA tax on Cadrain's December 13–19 earnings would be:

Gross pay	$1,260.00
Amount *not* subject to FICA tax	800.00
Amount subject to FICA tax	$ 460.00
Tax rate	7.5%
FICA tax	$ 34.50

For the rest of the calendar year through December 31, Cadrain's earnings would not be subject to FICA taxes.

Voluntary Deductions. In addition to the mandatory deductions from employee earnings for income and FICA taxes, many other deductions are

---

[1]FICA taxes are actually split into two rates and applied to employee earnings up to different maximum amounts in each calendar year. FICA taxes include OASDI (old-age, survivors and disability insurance) and HI (hospital insurance). OASDI taxes may also be referred to as social security taxes, and HI taxes may be referred to as Medicare taxes. For 1992, the OASDI rate was 6.2% on a maximum amount of $55,500, and the HI rate was 1.45% on a maximum amount of $130,200.

possible. These deductions are usually voluntary and depend on specific agreements between the employee and employer. Examples of voluntary deductions are:

1. United States savings bond purchases
2. Health insurance premiums
3. Credit union deposits
4. Pension plan payments
5. Charitable contributions

Computing Net Pay

An employee's net pay for the period is computed by subtracting all tax withholdings and voluntary deductions from the gross pay. Ken Istone's net pay for the week ended December 19 would be calculated as follows.

Gross pay		$425.00
Deductions:		
Federal income tax withholding	$16.00	
FICA withholding	31.88	
Health insurance premiums	10.00	
Total deductions		57.88
Net pay		$367.12

3

Prepare payroll records.

PAYROLL RECORDS

Payroll records should provide the following information for each employee:

1. Name, address, social security number, marital status, number of withholding allowances.
2. Gross amount of earnings, date of payment, and period covered by each payroll.
3. Gross amount of earnings accumulated for the year.
4. Amount of any taxes or other items withheld.

Three types of payroll records are used to accumulate this information.

1. The payroll register
2. The payroll check with earnings statement attached
3. The employee's earnings record

These records can be prepared by either manual or automated methods. The illustrations in this chapter are based on a manual system. The forms and procedures illustrated are equally applicable to both manual and automated systems.

Payroll Register

A **payroll register** is a multi-column form used to assemble the data required at the end of each payroll period. Figure 9-5 illustrates Westly, Inc.'s payroll register for the payroll period ended December 19, 19--.

FIGURE 9-5 **Payroll Register**

PAYROLL

	NAME	EMPLOYEE NO.	ALLOW-ANCES	MARITAL STATUS	EARNINGS				TAXABLE EARNINGS		
					REGULAR	OVER-TIME	TOTAL	CUMULATIVE TOTAL	UNEMPLOY. COMP.	FICA	
1	Cadrain, Sarah	4	M	1 1 0 0 00	1 6 0 00	1 2 6 0 00	55 8 0 0 00		4 6 0 00	1
2	Gunther, James	1	S	8 6 0 00	4 0 00	9 0 0 00	43 4 0 0 00		9 0 0 00	2
3	Istone, Ken	6	M	4 2 5 00		4 2 5 00	22 0 2 5 00		4 2 5 00	3
4	Kuzmik, Helen	2	M	4 8 0 00	2 9 4 00	7 7 4 00	31 0 0 0 00		7 7 4 00	4
5	Raines, Russell	3	M	4 4 0 00		4 4 0 00	22 3 4 0 00		4 4 0 00	5
6	Swaney, Linda	2	S	5 2 8 00	1 9 8 00	7 2 6 00	27 5 0 0 00		7 2 6 00	6
7	Tamin, Paul	5	M	4 9 0 00		4 9 0 00	25 6 5 0 00		4 9 0 00	7
8	Wiles, Harry	1	S	3 0 0 00		3 0 0 00	6 3 0 0 00	3 0 0 00	3 0 0 00	8
9					4 6 2 3 00	6 9 2 00	5 3 1 5 00	234 0 1 5 00	3 0 0 00	4 5 1 5 00	9

Time cards, pay rates

Prior per. total + current per. earnings

Current below $7,000 cumul. total

Current below $55,000 cumul. total

FIGURE 9-5 **Payroll Register (Right half)**

REGISTER— WEEK ENDED 12/19/--

	DEDUCTIONS						NET PAY	CK. NO.	
	FEDERAL INC. TAX	FICA TAX	HEALTH INS.	UNITED WAY	OTHER	TOTAL			
1	2 0 4 00	3 4 50				2 3 8 50	1 0 2 1 50	409	1
2	1 3 8 00	6 7 50		2 0 00		2 2 5 50	6 7 4 50	410	2
3	1 6 00	3 1 88	1 0 00			5 7 88	3 6 7 12	411	3
4	9 7 00	5 8 05	1 3 00	2 0 00		1 8 8 05	5 8 5 95	412	4
5	3 8 00	3 3 00	1 3 00			8 4 00	3 5 6 00	413	5
6	1 2 2 00	5 4 45				1 7 6 45	5 4 9 55	414	6
7	3 3 00	3 6 75	1 0 00			7 9 75	4 1 0 25	415	7
8	3 6 00	2 2 50				5 8 50	2 4 1 50	416	8
9	6 8 4 00	3 3 8 63	4 6 00	4 0 00		1 1 0 8 63	4 2 0 6 37		9

Withholding Tax Table

7.5% × FICA taxable earnings

Specific employer-employee agreements

Detailed information on earnings, taxable earnings, deductions, and net pay is provided for each employee. The sources of key information in the register are indicated in figure 9-5.

Westly, Inc., has eight employees. The first $55,000 of earnings of each employee is subject to FICA tax. The Cumulative Total column, under the Earnings category, shows that Sarah Cadrain has exceeded this limit during the period. Thus only $460 of her earnings for this pay period are subject to FICA tax, as shown in the Taxable Earnings columns. The Taxable Earnings columns are needed for determining the FICA tax and the employer's payroll taxes. Employer payroll taxes are discussed in Chapter 10.

											PAYROLL REGISTER
					EARNINGS				**TAXABLE EARNINGS**		
	NAME	EMPLOYEE NO.	ALLOW- ANCES	MARITAL STATUS	REGULAR	OVER- TIME	TOTAL	CUMULATIVE TOTAL	UNEMPLOY. COMP.	FICA	
1	Cadrain, Sarah		4	M	1 1 0 0 00	1 6 0 00	1 2 6 0 00	55 8 0 0 00		4 6 0 00	1
2											2

Regular deductions are made from employee earnings for federal income tax and FICA tax. In addition, voluntary deductions are made for health insurance and United Way contributions, based on agreements with individual employees.

After the data for each employee have been entered, the amount columns in the payroll register should be footed and the footings verified as follows:

Regular earnings		$4,623.00
Overtime earnings		692.00
Gross earnings		$5,315.00
Deductions:		
Federal income tax	$684.00	
FICA tax	338.63	
Health insurance premiums	46.00	
United Way	40.00	1,108.63
Net amount of payroll		$4,206.37

In a computerized accounting system, the payroll software performs this proof. An error in the payroll register could cause the payment of an incorrect amount to an employee. It also could result in sending an incorrect amount to the government or other agencies for whom funds are withheld.

Payroll Check

Employees may be paid in cash or by check. In some cases today, the employee does not even handle the paycheck. Rather, payment is made by **direct deposit** or electronic funds transfer (EFT) by the employer to the employee's bank. The employee receives the deduction stub from the check and a printed deposit receipt. Payment by check or direct deposit provides better internal accounting control than payment by cash.

Many businesses prepare a single check for the net amount of the total payroll and deposit it in a special payroll bank account. Individual paychecks are then drawn on that account for the amount due to each employee. The following entry is made to record the deposit.

12	19-- Dec.	19	Payroll Cash		4 2 0 6 37			12
13			Cash			4 2 0 6 37		13

Data needed to prepare a paycheck for each employee are contained in the payroll register. In a computer-based system, the paychecks normally are prepared at the same time as the payroll register. The employer furnishes a statement of payroll deductions to each employee along with each paycheck. Paychecks with detachable stubs, like the one for Ken Istone illustrated in figure 9-6, are widely used for this purpose. Before the check is deposited or cashed, the employee should detach the stub and keep it.

F I G U R E   9 - 6 **Paycheck and Deduction Stub**

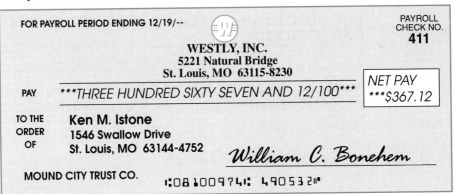

WESTLY, INC.
St. Louis, MO
STATEMENT OF EARNINGS

	Earnings			Deductions					Net Pay	Ck. No.
Date	Regular	Overtime	Total	Federal Inc. Tax	Fica Tax	Health Ins.	United Way	Total		
12/19/--	425.00		425.00	16.00	31.88	10.00		57.88	367.12	411
Year-to- Date	20,375.00	1,650.00	22,025.00	933.00	1,651.88	484.00		3,068.88	18,956.12	

Employee's Earnings Record

A separate record of each employee's earnings is called an **employee's earnings record.** An employee's earnings record for Ken M. Istone for a portion of the last quarter of the calendar year is illustrated in figure 9-7.

The information in this record is obtained from the payroll register. In a computer-based system, the employee's earnings record can be updated at the same time the payroll register is prepared.

Istone's earnings for four weeks of the last quarter of the year are shown on this form. Note that the entry for the pay period ended December 19 is the same as that in the payroll register illustrated in figure 9-5. This linkage between the payroll register and the employee's earnings record always exists. The payroll register provides a summary of the earnings of all employees for each pay period. The earnings record provides a summary of the annual earnings of an individual employee.

The earnings record illustrated in figure 9-7 is designed to accumulate both quarterly and annual totals. The employer needs this information to prepare several reports. These reports will be discussed in Chapter 10.

ACCOUNTING FOR EMPLOYEE EARNINGS AND DEDUCTIONS

4

Account for employee earnings and deductions.

The payroll register described in the previous section provides complete payroll data for each pay period. But the payroll register is not a journal. We still need to make a journal entry for payroll.

FIGURE 9-7 Employee's Earnings Record (Left half)

19-- PERIOD ENDING	EARNINGS				TAXABLE EARNINGS		DEDUCTIONS	
	REGULAR	OVERTIME	TOTAL	CUMULATIVE TOTAL	UNEMP. COMP.	FICA	FEDERAL INC. TAX	CITY TAX
11/28	425 00	75 00	500 00	20 600 00			28 00	37 50
12/5	425 00	75 00	500 00	21 100 00			28 00	37 50
12/12	425 00	75 00	500 00	21 600 00			28 00	37 50
12/19	425 00		425 00	22 025 00			16 00	31 88

SEX	DEPARTMENT	OCCUPATION	SOCIAL SECURITY NO.	MARITAL STATUS	EXEMPTIONS
M ✓ F	Maintenance	Service	393-58-8194	M	6

EMPLOYEE'S EARNINGS RECORD

Journalizing Payroll Transactions

The totals at the bottom of the columns of the payroll register in figure 9-5 show the following information.

Regular earnings		$4,623.00
Overtime earnings		692.00
Gross earnings		$5,315.00
Deductions:		
Federal income tax	$684.00	
FICA tax	338.63	
Health insurance premiums	46.00	
United Way	40.00	1,108.63
Net amount of payroll		$4,206.37

The payroll register column totals thus provide the basis for the following journal entry:

19-- Dec. 19	Wage and Salary Expense	5 3 1 5 00	
	Employees Income Tax Payable		6 8 4 00
	FICA Tax Payable		3 3 8 63
	Health Insurance Premiums Payable		4 6 00
	United Way Contributions Payable		4 0 00
	Cash		4 2 0 6 37
	Payroll for week ended Dec. 19.		

FIGURE 9-7 Employee's Earnings Record (Right half)

FOR PERIOD ENDED	19--							
		DEDUCTIONS					NET PAY	
HEALTH INS.	UNITED WAY	OTHER			TOTAL	CK. NO.	AMOUNT	
1 0 00					7 5 50	387	4 2 4 50	
1 0 00					7 5 50	395	4 2 4 50	
1 0 00					7 5 50	403	4 2 4 50	
1 0 00					5 7 88	411	3 6 7 12	

PAY RATE	DATE OF BIRTH	DATE EMPLOYED	NAME—LAST	FIRST	MIDDLE	EMP. NO.
$425/wk	8/17/64	1/3/87	Istone	Ken	M.	3

This entry is the same whether or not the business uses a special payroll bank account. The only difference is the payee for the $4,206.37 check(s). With a special payroll bank account, a single check is written to "Payroll Cash." Otherwise, individual checks totaling $4,206.37 are written to the employees.

Notice two important facts about this entry. First, Wage and Salary Expense is debited for the *gross pay* of the employees. The expense to the employer is the gross pay, not the employees' net pay after deductions. Second, a separate account is kept for each earnings deduction.

The accounts needed in entering earnings deductions depend upon the deductions involved. It helps in understanding the accounting for these deductions if we recognize what the employer is doing. In deducting amounts from employees' earnings, the employer is simply serving as an agent for the government and other groups. Amounts that are deducted from an employee's gross earnings must be paid by the employer to these groups. Therefore, a separate account should be kept for the liability for each type of deduction.

To help us understand the journal entry for payroll, let's examine the accounts involved. The six accounts affected by the payroll entry shown above are as follows.

> **Wage and Salary Expense is debited for the *gross pay*. A separate account is kept for each earnings deduction. Cash or Payroll Cash is credited for the *net pay*.**

ACCOUNT	CLASSIFICATION
Wage and Salary Expense	Expense
Employees Income Tax Payable	Liability
FICA Tax Payable	Liability
Health Insurance Premiums Payable	Liability
United Way Contributions Payable	Liability
Cash (or Payroll Cash)	Asset

Wage and Salary Expense

This account is debited for the gross pay of all employees for each pay period. Sometimes separate payroll accounts are kept for the employees of different departments. Thus separate accounts may be kept for Office Salaries Expense, Sales Salaries Expense, and Factory Wage Expense.

Wage and Salary Expense

Debit	Credit
gross pay of employees for each pay period	

Employees Income Tax Payable

This account is credited for the total federal income tax withheld from employees' earnings. The account is debited for amounts paid to the Internal Revenue Service. When all of the income taxes withheld have been paid, the account will have a zero balance. A state or city income tax payable account is used in a similar manner.

Employees Income Tax Payable

Debit	Credit
payment of income tax previously withheld	federal income tax withheld from employees' earnings

FICA Tax Payable

This account is credited for (1) the FICA tax withheld from employees' earnings and (2) the FICA tax imposed on the employer. FICA taxes imposed on the employer are discussed in Chapter 10. The account should be debited for amounts paid to the Internal Revenue Service. When all of the FICA taxes have been paid, the account will have a zero balance.

FICA Tax Payable

Debit	Credit
payment of FICA tax previously withheld or imposed	FICA taxes (1) withheld from employees' earnings and (2) imposed on the employer

Other Deductions

Health Insurance Premiums Payable is credited for health insurance contributions deducted from an employee's pay. The account is debited for the subsequent payment of these amounts to the health insurer. The United Way contributions payable account is used in a similar manner.

5

Describe various payroll record-keeping methods.

PAYROLL RECORD-KEEPING METHODS

You probably noticed that the same information appears in several places in the payroll records—in the payroll register, paycheck and stub, and employee's earnings record. If all records are prepared by hand (a **manual**

system), this could mean recording exactly the same information several times. If an employer has many employees, this can be inefficient. Various systems are available to make payroll accounting more efficient and accurate.

Mechanical Payroll System

In a **mechanical system,** all payroll data are entered into accounting machines once each pay period, as shown in figure 9-8. These machines then provide output in the form of a payroll register, paychecks, and earnings records. Some of these machines even do the math necessary in preparing the payroll.

FIGURE 9-8 **Mechanical Payroll System**

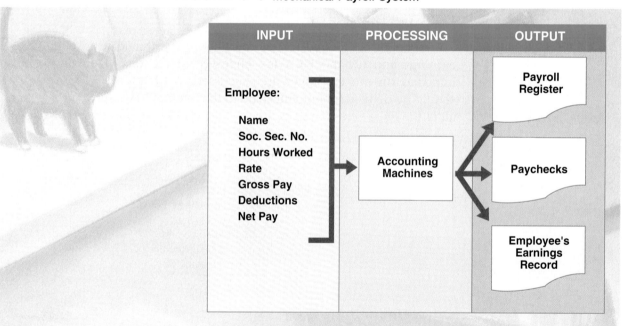

Electronic Payroll System

In an **electronic system,** only the employee number and hours worked need to be entered into a computer each pay period, as shown in figure 9-9. All other payroll data needed to prepare the payroll records can be stored in the computer. The computer uses the employee number and hours worked to determine the gross pay, deductions, and net pay. The payroll register, checks, and employee's earnings records are provided as outputs.

FIGURE 9-9 Electronic Payroll System

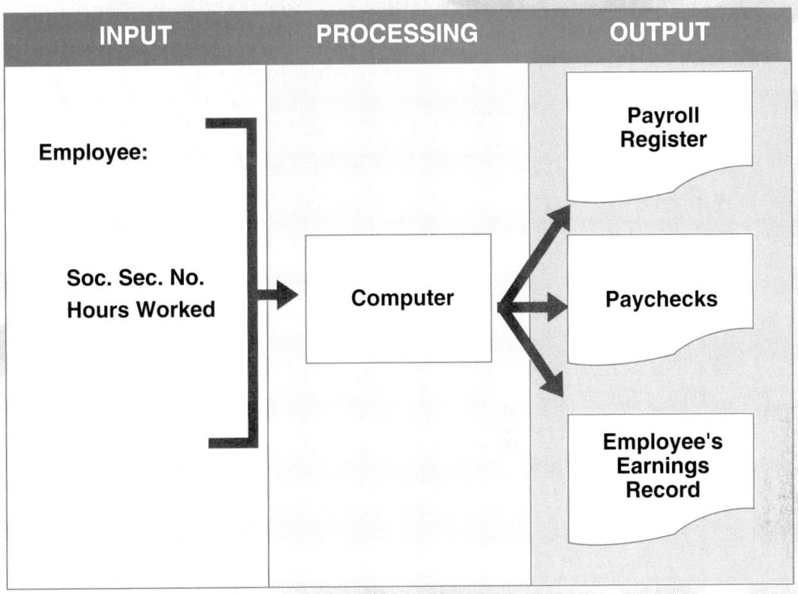

The same inputs and outputs are required in all of the different payroll record-keeping systems. Even with a computer, the data required for payroll processing have to be entered into the system. The outputs—the payroll register, paychecks, and employee earnings records—are basically the same under each system.

KEY POINTS

1 Payroll accounting procedures apply only to employees, not to independent contractors.

2 Two steps are required to determine how much to pay an employee for a pay period:

1. Calculate total earnings.
2. Determine the amounts of deductions.

Deductions from gross pay fall into three categories:

1. Employees income tax withholding.
2. Employees FICA tax withholding.
3. Voluntary deductions.

Four factors determine the amount to be withheld from an employee's gross pay each pay period:

1. Total earnings
2. Marital status
3. Number of withholding allowances claimed
4. Length of the pay period

3 The payroll register and the employee's earnings record are linked. The payroll register provides a summary of earnings of all employees for each pay period. The earnings record provides a summary of the annual earnings of an individual employee.

The totals at the bottom of the columns of the payroll register provide the basis for the journal entry for payroll.

4 Amounts withheld or deducted by the employer from employee earnings are credited to liability accounts. The employer must pay these amounts to the proper government groups and other appropriate groups.

5 In a manual payroll system, the same information may need to be recorded several times. Mechanical and electronic payroll systems are much more efficient.

KEY TERMS

direct deposit 286   The employee does not handle the paycheck; payment is made by the employer (directly) to the employee's bank.

electronic system 292   Payroll system in which only the employee number and hours worked need to be entered into a computer each pay period.

employee 277   Works under the control and direction of an employer.

employee's earnings record 288   A separate record of each employee's earnings.

Fair Labor Standards Act (FLSA) 278   Requires employers to pay overtime at $1\frac{1}{2}$ times the regular rate to any hourly employee who works over 40 hours in a week.

FICA taxes 282   Social security taxes which are intended to provide pensions, disability benefits, and health insurance for retired persons.

gross pay 280   An employee's total earnings.

independent contractor 277   Performs a service for a fee and does not work under the control and direction of the company paying for the service.

manual system 291   Payroll system in which all records are prepared by hand.

mechanical system 292   Payroll system in which all payroll data are entered into accounting machines only one time each pay period.

net pay 280   Gross pay less mandatory and voluntary deductions.

payroll register 285   A multi-column form used to assemble the data required at the end of each payroll period.

salary 278   Compensation for managerial or administrative services.

wage-bracket method 281   Employers determine the amount to withhold from an employee's gross pay for a specific time period from the appropriate wage-bracket table provided by the IRS.

wages 278   Compensation for skilled or unskilled labor.

withholding allowance 280   Exempts a specific dollar amount of an employee's gross pay from federal income tax withholding.

BUILDING YOUR ACCOUNTING KNOWLEDGE

1. Why is it important for payroll accounting purposes to distinguish between an employee and an independent contractor?
2. Name three major categories of deductions from an employee's gross pay.
3. Identify the four factors that determine the amount of federal income tax that is withheld from an employee's pay each pay period.
4. In general, an employee is entitled to withholding allowances for what purposes?
5. Identify the three payroll records usually needed by an employer.
6. Describe the information contained in the payroll register.
7. Why is it important to foot and verify the footings of the payroll register after the data for each employee have been entered?
8. Distinguish between the payroll register and the employee's earnings record.
9. Explain what an employer does with the amounts withheld from an employee's pay.
10. Explain why mechanical and electronic systems are commonly used in payroll accounting.

DEMONSTRATION PROBLEM

Carole Vohsen operates a beauty salon known as Carole's Coiffures, and has five employees. All are paid on a weekly basis. Carole's Coiffures uses a payroll register, individual employee's earnings records, a journal, and standard general ledger of accounts.

The payroll data for each employee for the week ending January 21, 19--, are given below. Employees are paid time and a half for work over 40 hours a week, and double time for work on Sunday.

Name	Employee No.	No. of Allow.	Marital Status	Total Hrs. Worked Jan 15–21	Rate	Total Earnings Jan 1–14
DeNourie, Katie	1	2	M	44	$11.50	$1,058.00
Garriott, Pete	2	1	M	40	12.00	1,032.00
Martinez, Sheila	3	3	M	39	12.50	987.50
Parker, Nancy	4	4	M	42	11.00	957.00
Shapiro, John	5	2	M	40	11.50	931.50

Sheila Martinez is the assistant manager of Carol's Coiffures. Her social security number is 500-88-4189, and she was born April 12, 1959. Sheila was employed September 1 of last year.

Carole's Coiffures uses a federal income tax withholding table. A portion of this weekly table is provided on page 282. FICA tax is withheld at the rate of 7.5%, and city earnings tax at the rate of 1%, both applied to gross pay. Garriott and Parker each have $10 withheld for group life insurance. All employees, except Shapiro, have $4 withheld for health insurance. DeNourie, Martinez, and Shapiro each have $15 withheld to be invested in the beauticians' credit union. Garriott and Shapiro each have $18.75 withheld under a savings bond purchase plan.

Carol's Coiffures' payroll is met by drawing checks on its regular bank account. This week, the checks were issued in sequence, beginning with no. 811.

Required
1. Prepare a payroll register for Carol's Coiffures for the week ending January 21, 19--. (In the Taxable Earnings/Unemployment Compensation column, enter the same amounts as in the FICA column.) Foot the amount columns, prove the footings, enter the totals, and rule with single and double lines.
2. Prepare an employee's earnings record for Sheila Martinez for the week ending January 21, 19--.
3. Assuming that the wages for the week ending January 21 were paid on January 23, prepare the journal entry for the payment of this payroll.
4. Post the entry in no. 3 to the affected accounts in the ledger of Carole's Coiffures.

SOLUTION

1.

PAYROLL REGISTER

	EMPLOYEE NO.	NAME	ALLOW-ANCES	MARITAL STATUS	EARNINGS			CUMULATIVE TOTAL	TAXABLE EARNINGS	
					REGULAR	OVER-TIME	TOTAL		UNEMPLOY. COMP.	FICA
1	1	DeNourie, Katie	2	M	460 00	69 00	529 00	1587 00	529 00	529 00
2	2	Garriott, Pete	1	M	480 00		480 00	1512 00	480 00	480 00
3	3	Martinez, Sheila	3	M	487 50		487 50	1475 00	487 50	487 50
4	4	Parker, Nancy	4	M	440 00	33 00	473 00	1430 00	473 00	473 00
5	5	Shapiro, John	2	M	460 00		460 00	1391 50	460 00	460 00
6					2327 50	102 00	2429 50	7395 50	2429 50	2429 50
7										
8										

FOR WEEK ENDED   January 21, 19--

	DEDUCTIONS								NET PAY	CK. NO.
	FEDERAL INC. TAX	FICA TAX	CITY TAX	LIFE INS.	HEALTH INS.	CREDIT UNION	OTHER	TOTAL		
1	56 00	39 68	5 29		4 00	15 00		119 97	409 03	811
2	56 00	36 00	4 80	10 00	4 00		U.S. Savings Bond 18 75	129 55	350 45	812
3	44 00	36 56	4 88		4 00	15 00		104 44	383 06	813
4	36 00	35 48	4 73	10 00	4 00			90 21	382 79	814
5	47 00	34 50	4 60			15 00	U.S. Savings Bond 18 75	119 85	340 15	815
6	239 00	182 22	24 30	20 00	16 00	45 00	37 50	564 02	1865 48	
7										
8										

2.

EMPLOYEE'S EARNINGS RECORD

19-- PERIOD ENDING	EARNINGS				TAXABLE EARNINGS		DEDUCTIONS	
	REGULAR	OVERTIME	TOTAL	CUMULATIVE TOTAL	UNEMP. COMP.	FICA	FEDERAL INC. TAX	CITY TAX
1/7								
1/14								
1/21	4 8 7 50		4 8 7 50	1 4 7 5 00	4 8 7 50	4 8 7 50	4 88	4 4 00
1/28								

SEX		DEPARTMENT	OCCUPATION	SOCIAL SECURITY NO.	MARITAL STATUS	EXEMP- TIONS
M	F ✓	Beauty Salon	Asst. Manager	500-88-4189	M	3

FOR PERIOD ENDED January 21, 19--

DEDUCTIONS						NET PAY	
FICA TAX	LIFE INS.	HEALTH INS.	CREDIT UNION	OTHER	TOTAL	CK. NO.	AMOUNT
3 6 56		4 00	1 5 00		1 0 4 44	813	3 8 3 06

PAY RATE	DATE OF BIRTH	DATE EMPLOYED	NAME—LAST	FIRST	MIDDLE	EMP. NO.
$12.50	4/12/59	9/1/--	Martinez	Sheila		3

3.

GENERAL JOURNAL   PAGE 1

	DATE		DESCRIPTION	POST. REF.	DEBIT	CREDIT	
1	19-- Jan.	23	Wage and Salary Expense	542	2 4 2 9 50		1
2			Employees Inc. Tax Payable	214		2 3 9 00	2
3			City Earnings Tax Payable	225		2 4 30	3
4			FICA Tax Payable	211		1 8 2 22	4
5			Life Insurance Premiums Pay.	226		2 0 00	5
6			Health Insurance Premiums Pay.	227		1 6 00	6
7			Credit Union Contributions Pay.	228		4 5 00	7
8			Savings Bond Deductions Pay.	229		3 7 50	8
9			Cash	111		1 8 6 5 48	9
10			Payroll for week end. Jan. 21.				10

4.

ACCOUNT: Cash   ACCOUNT NO. 111

DATE	ITEM	POST. REF.	DEBIT	CREDIT	BALANCE DEBIT	BALANCE CREDIT
19-- Jan. 23		J1		1 86 5 48		

ACCOUNT: FICA Tax Payable   ACCOUNT NO. 211

DATE	ITEM	POST. REF.	DEBIT	CREDIT	BALANCE DEBIT	BALANCE CREDIT
19-- Jan. 23		J1		1 82 22		

ACCOUNT: Employees Income Tax Payable   ACCOUNT NO. 214

DATE	ITEM	POST. REF.	DEBIT	CREDIT	BALANCE DEBIT	BALANCE CREDIT
19-- Jan. 23		J1		2 39 00		

ACCOUNT: City Earnings Tax Payable   ACCOUNT NO. 225

DATE	ITEM	POST. REF.	DEBIT	CREDIT	BALANCE DEBIT	BALANCE CREDIT
19-- Jan. 23		J1		2 4 30		

ACCOUNT: Life Insurance Premiums Payable   ACCOUNT NO. 226

DATE	ITEM	POST. REF.	DEBIT	CREDIT	BALANCE DEBIT	BALANCE CREDIT
19-- Jan. 23		J1		2 0 00		

ACCOUNT: Health Insurance Premiums Payable   ACCOUNT NO. 227

DATE	ITEM	POST. REF.	DEBIT	CREDIT	BALANCE DEBIT	BALANCE CREDIT
19-- Jan. 23		J1		1 6 00		

ACCOUNT: Credit Union Contributions Payable   ACCOUNT NO. 228

DATE	ITEM	POST. REF.	DEBIT	CREDIT	BALANCE DEBIT	BALANCE CREDIT
19-- Jan. 23		J1		4 5 00		

ACCOUNT: Savings Bonds Deductions Payable						ACCOUNT NO. 229	
		POST. REF.	DEBIT	CREDIT	BALANCE		
DATE	ITEM				DEBIT	CREDIT	
19-- Jan. 23		J1		37 50			

ACCOUNT: Wage and Salary Expense						ACCOUNT NO. 542	
		POST. REF.	DEBIT	CREDIT	BALANCE		
DATE	ITEM				DEBIT	CREDIT	
19-- Jan. 23		J1	2 429 50				

EXERCISES

APPLYING ACCOUNTING CONCEPTS

EXERCISE 9A1

Computing Net Pay

2 Mary Sue Guild works for Davis Construction Co., which pays its employees time and a half for all hours worked in excess of 40 per week. Guild's pay rate is $10.00 per hour. Her wages are subject to federal income tax and to FICA tax deductions at the rate of 7.5%. She is married and claims 4 tax exemptions. Guild has a ½ hour lunch break during an 8½ hour day. Her time card is shown below.

Name	Mary Sue Guild					
Week Ending		March 30, 19--				
					Hours Worked	
Day	In	Out	In	Out	Regular	Overtime
M	7:57	12:05	12:35	4:33	8	
T	7:52	12:09	12:39	5:05	8	1/2
W	7:59	12:15	12:45	5:30	8	1
T	8:00	12:01	12:30	6:31	8	2
F	7:56	12:05	12:34	4:30	8	
S	8:00	10:31				2 1/2

Complete the following:

a. _____ hours straight time × $10.00 per hour .... $_____
b. _____ hours overtime × $15.00 per hour .... $_____
c. Total gross wages .... $_____
d. Federal income tax withholding
(from tax tables in figure 9-4, page 282) .... $_____
e. FICA withholding at 7.5% .... $_____
f. Total withholding .... $_____
g. Net pay .... $_____

EXERCISE 9A2
Computing Weekly Gross Pay

2 Ryan Lawrence's regular hourly rate is $15.00. He receives time and a half for any time worked over 40 hours a week, and double time for work on Sunday. During the past week, Lawrence worked 8 hours each day Monday through Thursday, 10 hours on Friday, and 5 hours on Sunday.
Compute Lawrence's gross pay for the past week.

EXERCISE 9A3
Computing Overtime Rate of Pay and Gross Weekly Pay

2 Bill Smith receives a regular salary of $2,600 a month and is paid 1½ times the regular hourly rate for hours in excess of 40 per week.

a. Calculate Smith's overtime rate of pay.
b. Calculate Smith's total gross weekly pay if he works 45 hours during the week.

EXERCISE 9A4
Computing Federal Income Tax

2 Using the table in figure 9-4 on page 282, determine the amount of federal income tax an employer should withhold weekly for married employees with the following total earnings and withholding allowances.

Total Weekly Earnings	Number of Allowances	Amount of Withholding
a. $327.90	2	_____
b. $410.00	1	_____
c. $438.16	5	_____
d. $518.25	0	_____
e. $603.98	6	_____

EXERCISE 9A5
Calculating FICA Tax

2 Assume a FICA tax rate of 7.5% is applied to maximum earnings of $55,000. Calculate the FICA tax for the following situations.

Accumulated Pay Before Current Weekly Payroll	Current Gross Pay	Year-to-Date Earnings	FICA Maximum	Amount Not Subject to FICA	Amount Subject to FICA	FICA Tax Withheld
$22,000	$1,200	____	$55,000	____	____	____
$54,000	$4,200	____	$55,000	____	____	____
$53,200	$3,925	____	$55,000	____	____	____
$56,000	$4,600	____	$55,000	____	____	____

EXERCISE 9A6
Payroll Transactions

4 On December 31, the payroll register of Hamstreet & Sons' indicated the following column totals:

Wage and Salary Expense	$8,700.00
Employees Income Tax Payable	$ 920.00
FICA taxable at 7.5%	$7,300.00
United Way Contributions Payable	$ 200.00

Determine the amount of FICA taxes to be withheld and record the journal entry for the payroll, crediting Cash for the net pay.

EXERCISE 9A7
Payroll Journal Entry

4 Journalize the following data taken from the payroll register of University Printing as of April 15, 19--.

Regular earnings	$5,418.00
Overtime earnings	824.00
Deductions:	
Federal income tax	593.00
FICA tax	468.15
Pension plan	90.00
Health insurance premiums	225.00
United Way	100.00

PROBLEMS

PROBLEM 9A1
Gross Pay, Deductions, and Net Pay

2/4 Doug Davis works for Northwest Supplies and is paid time and a half for all work in excess of 40 hours per week. His rate of pay is $8.50 per hour and during the last week of January of the current year he worked 48 hours. Davis is married and claims 4 exemptions on his W-4 form. His weekly wages are subject to the following deductions.

a. FICA tax at 7.5%.
b. Employees income tax (use figure 9-4 on page 282)
c. Health insurance premium, $85.00
d. Credit union contributions, $125.00
e. United Way contributions, $10.00

Required
1. Compute Davis' regular pay, overtime pay, gross pay, and net pay.
2. Journalize the payment of his wages for the week ending January 31, crediting Cash for the net amount.

PROBLEM 9A2
Payroll Register and Payroll Journal Entry

2/3/4 The Wray Publishing Company pays its employees time and a half for all hours in excess of 40 per week. All of its employees are married. The following information for the first week of pay for this calendar year has been gathered from the time cards of the following employees.

Name	Hours Worked	Pay Rate	No. of Allow.	Mar. Stat.	Health Ins.	Credit Union	United Way
Cox, Barbara J.	40	$8.00 per hour	1	M	20.00	80.00	
Ellis, Judy C.	44	$12.00 per hour	4	M	30.00		5.00
Gray, Bill R.	48	$400 per week	1	M	20.00		
Hall, Cecil B.	40	$500 per week	3	M	25.00	75.00	5.00
Lee, Janice R.	40	$7.50 per hour	2	M	22.00		
Pitcher, Jon S.	43	$9.00 per hour	5	M	33.00	35.00	
Tucker, Roy A.	45	$10.00 per hour	1	M	20.00		10.00
Wilson, Pam E.	40	$600 per week	5	M	33.00	95.00	5.00
Yates, Keith M.	40	$12.00 per hour	2	M	22.00	25.00	5.00

Required

1. Complete the payroll register using a FICA tax rate of 7.5%. This is the first payroll of the current year and all pay is subject to the FICA tax. Use figure 9-4 on page 282 to calculate the federal income tax. Foot the amount columns, prove the footings, enter the totals, and rule with single and double lines.

2. Prepare a journal entry to record the payment to the employees. Date the entry as of January 8, 19--. Assume the company credits the total net pay to the Cash account. Begin the payroll checks with check no. 711.

PROBLEM 9A3

Payroll Register, Employee's Earnings Record, Payroll Journal Entry

2/3/4 Don McCullum operates a travel agency known as Don's Luxury Travel, and has five employees. All are paid on a weekly basis. The travel agency uses a payroll register, individual employee's earnings records, and a general journal.

Don's Luxury Travel uses a weekly federal income tax withholding table. The payroll data for each employee for the week ended March 22, 19--, are given below. Employees are paid time and a half for working over 40 hours a week.

Name	Employee No.	No. of Allow.	Marital Status	Total Hrs. Worked March 16–22	Rate	Total Earnings Jan 1–Mar. 15
Anderson, Loren	1	4	M	45	$11.00	$5,280.00
Carson, Judy	2	1	M	40	12.00	5,760.00
Ellis, Susan	3	3	M	43	9.50	4,560.00
Knox, Wayne	4	1	M	39	11.00	5,125.50
Peters, Jim	5	2	M	40	10.50	4,720.50

FICA Tax is withheld at the rate of 7.5%, and city earnings tax at the rate of 1%, both applied to gross pay. Anderson and Knox each have $10 withheld for group life insurance. All employees, except Peters, have $5.00 withheld for health insurance. Anderson, Carson and Knox each have $20 withheld to be invested in the Travel Agencies credit union. Carson and Ellis each have $18.75 withheld under a savings bond purchase plan.

Don's Luxury Travel's payroll is met by drawing checks on its regular bank account. The checks were issued in sequence, beginning with check no. 423.

Required

1. Prepare a payroll register for Don's Luxury Travel for the week ended March 22, 19--. Foot the amount columns, prove the footings, enter the totals, and rule with single and double lines.

2. Assuming that the wages for the week ended March 22 were paid on March 24, prepare the journal entry for the payment of this payroll.

3 Refer to Problem 9A3. Don's Luxury Travel keeps employee earnings records.

Required

For the week ended March 22, complete an employee's earnings record for Judy Carson, whose social security number is 544-67-1283. Carson is employed as a manager in the ticket sales department. She was born on May 8, 1959, and was hired on June 1 of last year.

SERIES B

EXERCISES

2 Tom Hallinan works for Sylvania Construction Co., which pays its employees time and a half for all hours worked in excess of 40 per week. Hallinan's pay rate is $12.00 per hour. His wages are subject to federal income tax and to FICA tax deductions at the rate of 7.5%. He is married and claims 5 tax exemptions. Hallinan has a ½ hour lunch break during an 8½ hour day. His time card is shown below.

Name	Tom Hallinan					
Week Ending			March 30, 19--			
					Hours Worked	
Day	In	Out	In	Out	Regular	Overtime
M	7:55	12:02	12:32	5:33	8	1
T	7:59	12:04	12:34	6:05	8	1 1/2
W	7:59	12:05	12:35	4:30	8	
T	8:00	12:01	12:30	5:01	8	1/2
F	7:58	12:02	12:31	5:33	8	1
S	7:59	9:33				1 1/2

Complete the following:

a. _____ hours straight time × $12.00 per hour .... $_____
b. _____ hours overtime × $18.00 per hour .... $_____
c. Total gross wages .... $_____
d. Federal income tax withholding
     (from tax tables in figure 9-4, page 282) .... $_____
e. FICA withholding at 7.5% .... $_____
f. Total withholding .... $_____
g. Net pay .... $_____

EXERCISE 9B2

Computing Weekly Gross Pay

2 William Brown's regular hourly rate is $12.00. He receives time and a half for any time worked over 40 hours a week, and double time for work on Sunday. During the past week, Brown worked 8 hours each day Monday through Thursday, 11 hours on Friday, and 6 hours on Sunday.

Compute Brown's gross pay for the past week.

EXERCISE 9B3

Computing Overtime Rate of Pay and Gross Weekly Pay

2 Mike Fritz receives a regular salary of $2,800 a month and is paid 1½ times the regular hourly rate for hours in excess of 40 per week.

a. Calculate Fritz's overtime rate of pay.

b. Calculate Fritz's total gross weekly pay if he works 46 hours during the week.

EXERCISE 9B4

Computing Federal Income Tax

2 Using the table in figure 9-4 on page 282, determine the amount of federal income tax an employer should withhold weekly for married employees with the following total earnings and withholding allowances.

	Total Weekly Earnings	Number of Allowances	Amount of Withholding
a.	$346.32	4	_____
b.	$390.00	3	_____
c.	$461.39	2	_____
d.	$522.88	6	_____
e.	$612.00	0	_____

EXERCISE 9B5

Calculating FICA Tax

2 The FICA tax rate is 7.5% applied to a maximum earnings of $55,000. Calculate the FICA tax for the following situations.

Accumulated Pay Before Current Weekly Payroll	Current Gross Pay	Year-to-Date Earnings	FICA Maximum	Amount Not Subject to FICA	Amount Subject to FICA	FICA Tax Withheld
$31,000	$1,500	_____	$55,000	_____	_____	_____
$53,000	$2,860	_____	$55,000	_____	_____	_____
$53,800	$3,140	_____	$55,000	_____	_____	_____
$56,000	$2,920	_____	$55,000	_____	_____	_____

EXERCISE 9B6

Journalizing Payroll Transactions

4 On November 30, the payroll register of Webster & Smith indicated the following column totals:

Wage and Salary Expense	$9,400.00
Employees Income Tax Payable	$ 985.00
FICA taxable at 7.5%	$8,600.00
United Way Contributions Payable	$ 100.00

Determine the amount of FICA taxes to be withheld and record the journal entry for the payroll, crediting Cash for the net pay.

EXERCISE 9B7

Payroll Journal Entry

4 Journalize the following data taken from the payroll register of Himes Bakery as of June 12, 19--.

Regular earnings	$6,520.00
Overtime earnings	950.00
Deductions:	
Federal income tax	782.00
FICA tax	560.25
Pension plan	80.00
Health insurance premiums	190.00
United Way	150.00

PROBLEMS

PROBLEM 9B1

Gross Pay, Deductions, and Net Pay

2/4 Kathy Miller works for Columbia Industries and is paid time and a half for all work in excess of 40 hours per week. Her rate of pay is $9.00 per hour and during the last week of January of the current year she worked 46 hours. Miller is married and claims 5 exemptions on her W-4 form. Her weekly wages are subject to the following deductions.

a. FICA tax at 7.5%
b. Employees income tax (use figure 9-4 on page 282)
c. Health insurance premium, $92.00
d. Credit union contributions, $110.00
e. United Way contributions, $5.00

Required
1. Compute Miller's regular pay, overtime pay, gross pay, and net pay.
2. Journalize the payment of her wages for the week ending January 31, crediting Cash for the net amount.

PROBLEM 9B2

Payroll Register and Payroll Journal Entry

2/3/4 The Portland Fuel Company pays its employees time and a half for all hours in excess of 40 per week. All of its employees are married. The following information for the first week of pay for this calendar year has been gathered from the time cards of the following employees.

Name	Hours Worked	Pay Rate	No. of allow.	Health Ins.	Credit Union	United Way
Abbot, Ken L.	43	$9.00 per hour	2	22.00	35.00	5.00
Catt, Katie S.	44	$10.00 per hour	1	20.00	10.00	5.00
Davis, Terry A.	40	$450 per week	2	22.00		
Fox, Alice J.	46	$500 per week	5	33.00	55.00	
Gnatt, Bill M.	45	$6.75 per hour	3	25.00		
Lee, Joyce R.	40	$12.00 per hour	2	32.00		
Mason, Bob H.	40	$10.00 per hour	1	20.00		10.00
Quick, Otis, J.	40	$600 per week	4	30.00	65.00	5.00
Wilson, Susan B.	42	$12.00 per hour	3	25.00		

Required

1. Complete the payroll register using a FICA tax rate of 7.5%. This is the first payroll of the current year and all pay is subject to the FICA tax. Use figure 9-4 on page 282 to calculate the federal income tax.

2. Prepare a journal entry to record the payment to the employees. Assume the company credits the total net pay to the Cash account. Begin the payroll checks with check no. 657. Date the journal entry as of January 8, 19--.

PROBLEM 9B3

Payroll Register, Employee's Earnings Record, Payroll Journal Entry

2/3/4 Karen Jolly operates a bakery known as Karen's Cupcakes, and has five employees. All are paid on a weekly basis. Karen's Cupcakes uses a payroll register, individual employee's earnings records, and a general journal.

Karen's Cupcakes uses a weekly federal income tax withholding table. The payroll data for each employee for the week ended February 15, 19--, are given below. Employees are paid time and a half for working over 40 hours a week.

Name	Employee No.	No. of Allow.	Marital Status	Total Hrs. Worked Feb. 9–15	Rate	Total Earnings Jan. 1–Feb. 15
Brown, William	1	1	M	40	$10.00	$2,400.00
Hastings, Gene	2	4	M	45	12.00	3,360.00
Ridgeway, Ruth	3	3	M	46	8.75	2,935.00
Smith, Judy	4	4	M	42	11.00	2,745.00
Turville, Dolores	5	1	M	39	10.50	2,650.75

FICA Tax is withheld at the rate of 7.5%, and city earnings tax at the rate of 1%, both applied to gross pay. Hastings and Smith each have $20 withheld for group life insurance. All employees except Brown have $15.00 withheld for health insurance. Ridgeway, Smith, and Turville each have $25 withheld to be invested in the bakers credit union. Hastings and Smith each have $18.75 withheld under a savings bond purchase plan.

Karen's Cupcakes payroll is met by drawing checks on its regular bank account. The checks were issued in sequence, beginning with no. 365.

Required

1. Prepare a payroll register for Karen's Cupcakes for the week ended February 15, 19--. Foot the amount columns, prove the footings, enter the totals, and rule with single and double lines.

2. Assuming that the wages for the week ended February 15 were paid on February 17, prepare the journal entry for the payment of this payroll.

<table>
<tr><td>PROBLEM 9B4</td></tr>
<tr><td>Employee's Earnings
Record</td></tr>
</table>

3 Refer to Problem 9B3. Karen's Cupcakes keeps employees' earnings records.

Required

For the week ended February 15, complete an employee's earnings record for William Brown whose social security number is 342-73-4681. Brown is employed as a baker in the desserts department. He was born on August 26, 1949, and was hired on October 1 of last year.

MASTERY PROBLEM

Abigail Trenkamp owns and operates a collection agency. Listed below are the name, number of allowances claimed, information from time cards on hours worked each day, and the hourly rate of each employee. All employees are married. All hours worked in excess of 8 hours on week days are paid at the rate of time and a half. All weekend hours are paid at double time.

The employer uses a weekly federal income tax withholding table. A portion of this weekly table is provided in the chapter on page 282. (The table is also in the working papers.) FICA tax is withheld at the rate of 7.5% for the first $55,000 earned. State income tax is withheld at the rate of 2.5% of gross earnings, and a city earnings tax is withheld at the rate 1% of gross earnings. Berling, Salzman, and Thompson each have $20 withheld for group life insurance. Each employee, except Merz and Menick, has $5 withheld for health insurance. All of the employees use direct deposit to the credit union for varying amounts as listed below. Heimbrock, Townsley, and Morris each have $18.25 withheld under a savings bond purchase plan.

Trenkamp Collection Agency
Payroll Information for the Week Ending November 18, 19--

Employee Name	No.	No. of Allow.	Marital Status	Regular Hours Worked							Hourly Rate	Credit Union Deposit	Total Earnings 1/1–11/18
				S	S	M	T	W	T	F			
Berling, James	1	3	M	2	2	9	8	8	9	10	12.00	129.60	30,525.00
Merz, Linda	2	4	M	4	3	8	8	8	8	11	10.00	117.00	28,480.00
Goetz, Ken	3	5	M	0	0	6	7	8	9	10	11.00	91.30	25,500.00
Menick, Judd	4	2	M	8	8	0	0	8	8	9	11.00	126.50	22,625.00
Morris, Ruth	5	3	M	0	0	8	8	8	6	8	13.00	98.80	28,730.00
Heimbrock, Jacob	6	2	M	0	0	8	8	8	8	8	17.00	136.00	54,800.00
Townsley, Sarah	7	2	M	4	0	6	6	6	6	4	9.00	64.80	21,425.00
Salzman, Ben	8	4	M	6	2	8	8	6	6	6	11.00	110.00	6,635.00
Layton, Esther	9	4	M	0	0	8	8	8	8	8	11.00	88.00	5,635.00
Thompson, David	10	5	M	0	2	10	9	7	7	10	11.00	108.90	29,635.00
Wissman, Celia	11	2	M	8	0	4	8	8	8	9	13.00	139.10	24,115.00

The Trenkamp Collection Agency follows the practice of drawing a single check for the net amount of the payroll and depositing the check in a special payroll account at the bank. Individual checks issued were numbered consecutively beginning with no. 331.

Required

1. Prepare a payroll register for Trenkamp Collection Agency for the week ending November 18, 19--. (In the Taxable Earnings/ Unemployment Compensation column, enter $365 for Salzman and $440 for Layton. Leave this column blank for all other employees.) Foot the amount columns, prove the footings, enter the totals, and rule with single and double lines.

2. Assuming that the wages for the week ending November 18 were paid on November 21, prepare the journal entry for the payment of this payroll.

3. The current employee's earnings record for Ben Salzman is provided in the working papers. Update Salzman's earnings record to reflect the November 18 payroll. Although this information should have been entered earlier, complete the required information on the earnings record. The necessary information is provided below.

Name	Ben F. Salzman
Sex	Male
Department	Administration
Occupation	Office Manager
S.S. No.	446-46-6321
Marital Status	Married
Exemptions	4
Pay Rate	$11.00 per hour
Birth Date	3/4/59
Date Employed	7/22/--

Careful study of this chapter should enable you to:

1. Describe and calculate employer payroll taxes.
2. Account for employer payroll taxes expense.
3. Describe employer reporting and payment responsibilities.
4. Describe and account for workers' compensation insurance.

*P*ayroll Accounting: Employer Taxes and Reports

The taxes we discussed in Chapter 9 had one thing in common—they all were levied on the employee. The employer withheld them from employees' earnings and paid them to the government. They were not an expense of the employer.

In this chapter, we will examine several taxes that are imposed directly on the employer. All of these taxes represent additional payroll expenses of the employer.

1

Describe and calculate employer payroll taxes.

EMPLOYER PAYROLL TAXES

Most employers are subject to FICA taxes and FUTA (Federal Unemployment Tax Act) taxes. An employer may also be subject to state unemployment taxes.

Employer's FICA Tax

The **employer FICA tax** is levied on employers at the same rate and on the same earnings base as the employee FICA tax. As explained in Chapter 9, in this text we assume a rate of 7.5% applied to maximum earnings of $55,000. Thus, the employer is required to pay FICA tax at a rate of 7.5% on the first $55,000 of each employee's earnings.

■ *Use the payroll register to compute employer payroll taxes.*

The payroll register we saw in Chapter 9 is a key source of information for computing employer payroll taxes. That payroll register is reproduced in figure 10-1. The Taxable Earnings FICA column shows that $4,515 of

311

FIGURE 10-1 **Payroll Register**

				EARNINGS				TAXABLE EARNINGS		
	NAME	ALLOW-ANCES	MARITAL STATUS	REGULAR	OVER-TIME	TOTAL	CUMULATIVE TOTAL	UNEMPLOY. COMP.	FICA	
1	Cadrain, Sarah	4	M	1100 00	160 00	1260 00	5580 00		460 00	1
2	Gunther, James	1	S	860 00	40 00	900 00	4340 00		900 00	2
3	Isotone, Ken	6	M	425 00		425 00	22025 00		425 00	3
4	Kuzmik, Helen	2	M	480 00	294 00	774 00	31000 00		774 00	4
5	Raines, Russell	3	M	440 00		440 00	22340 00		440 00	5
6	Swaney, Linda	2	S	528 00	198 00	726 00	27500 00		726 00	6
7	Tamin, Paul	5	M	490 00		490 00	25650 00		490 00	7
8	Wiles, Harry	1	S	300 00		300 00	6300 00	300 00	300 00	8
				4623 00	692 00	5315 00	234015 00	300 00	4515 00	

employee earnings were subject to FICA tax for the pay period. The employer's FICA tax on these earnings is computed as follows:

$$\frac{\text{FICA Taxable Earnings}}{\$4,515} \times \frac{\text{Tax Rate}}{.075} = \frac{\text{Tax}}{\$338.63}$$

This amount plus the employees FICA taxes withheld must be paid by the employer to the Internal Revenue Service.

Self-Employment Tax

Individuals who own and run their own business are considered self-employed. These individuals can be viewed as both employer and employee. They do not receive salary or wages from the business, but they do have earnings in the form of the business net income. **Self-employment income** is the net income of a trade or business run by an individual. Currently, the law requires persons earning self-employment income of $400 or more to pay a **self-employment tax.** Self-employment tax is a contribution to the federal social security (FICA) program. The tax rate is about double the FICA rate, and is applied to the same income base as is used for the FICA tax.

One half of the self-employment tax is a personal expense of the owner of the business. The other half is similar to the employer FICA tax paid for each employee. This portion of the tax is considered a business expense and is debited to Self Employment Tax. If the entire self-employment tax is paid with business funds, the half that is a personal expense should be debited to the owner's drawing account.

WEEK ENDED 12/19 19--							
DEDUCTIONS						**NET PAY**	**CK. NO.**
FEDERAL INC. TAX	FICA TAX	HEALTH INS.	UNITED WAY	OTHER	TOTAL		
1	204 00	34 50				238 00	1 021 50	409
2	138 00	67 50		20 00		225 50	674 50	410
3	16 00	31 88	10 00			57 88	367 12	411
4	97 00	58 05	13 00	20 00		188 05	585 95	412
5	38 00	33 00	13 00			84 00	356 00	413
6	122 00	54 45				176 45	549 55	414
7	33 00	36 75	10 00			79 75	410 25	415
8	36 00	22 50				58 50	241 50	416
9	684 00	338 63	46 00	40 00		1 108 63	4 206 37	

Employer's FUTA Tax

The **FUTA (Federal Unemployment Tax Act) tax** is levied only on employers. It is not deducted from employees' earnings. The purpose of this tax is to raise funds to administer the federal/state unemployment compensation program. The maximum amount of earnings subject to the FUTA tax and the tax rate can be changed by Congress. We will assume a rate of 0.8% applied to maximum earnings of $7,000 for each employee.

To illustrate the computation of the FUTA tax, refer again to figure 10-1. The Taxable Earnings Unemployment Compensation column shows that only $300 of employee earnings were subject to the FUTA tax. This amount is so low because the payroll period is late in the calendar year (December 19, 19--). It is common for most employees to exceed the $7,000 earnings limit by this time. The FUTA tax is computed as shown in figure 10-2.

FIGURE 10-2 **Computation of FUTA Tax**

$$\underset{\$300.00}{\underline{\text{FUTA Taxable Earnings}}} \times \underset{.008}{\underline{\text{Tax Rate}}} = \underset{\$2.40}{\underline{\text{Tax}}}$$

Employer's State Unemployment Tax (SUTA)

The **state unemployment tax (SUTA)** is also levied only on employers. The purpose of this tax is to raise funds to pay unemployment benefits. Tax rates and unemployment benefits vary among the states. In addition, most states have a **merit-rating system** to encourage employers to provide regular employment to workers. If an employer has very few employees on unemployment compensation, the employer qualifies for a lower state unemployment tax rate. We will assume a rate of 5.4% applied to maximum earnings of $7,000 for each employee.

Refer to the payroll register in figure 10-1. As we saw with the FUTA tax, only $300 of employee earnings for this pay period are subject to the state unemployment tax. The tax is computed as shown in figure 10-3.

FIGURE 10-3 **Computation of SUTA Tax**

	UNEMPLOY. COMP.
5	
6	
7	
8	3 0 0 00
9	3 0 0 00

$$\frac{\text{State Unemployment Taxable Earnings}}{\$300.00} \times \frac{\text{Tax Rate}}{.054} = \frac{\text{Tax}}{\$16.20}$$

2

Account for employer payroll taxes expense.

ACCOUNTING FOR EMPLOYER PAYROLL TAXES

Now that we have computed the employer payroll taxes, we need to journalize them. It is common to debit all employer payroll taxes to a single account—Payroll Taxes Expense. However, we usually credit separate liability accounts for FICA, FUTA, and SUTA Payable.

Journalizing Employer Payroll Taxes

The employer payroll taxes computed in the previous section can be summarized as follows:

Employer's FICA tax	$338.63
FUTA tax	2.40
SUTA tax	16.20
Total employer payroll taxes	$357.23

These amounts provide the basis for the following journal entry:

3	19-- Dec.	19	Payroll Taxes Expense		3 5 7 23			3
4			FICA Tax Payable			3 3 8 63		4
5			FUTA Tax Payable			2 40		5
6			SUTA Tax Payable			1 6 20		6
7			Employer payroll taxes					7
8			for week ended Dec. 19.					8

It is helpful to review the steps to prepare this journal entry for employer payroll taxes.

STEP 1   Obtain the taxable earnings amounts from the Taxable Earnings columns of the payroll register. In this case, FICA taxable earnings were $4,515; Unemployment Compensation taxable earnings were $300.

STEP 2   Compute the amount of employer FICA tax by multiplying the FICA taxable earnings by 7.5%.

STEP 3   Compute the amount of FUTA tax by multiplying the Unemployment Taxable earnings by 0.8%.

STEP 4   Compute the amount of SUTA by multiplying the Unemployment Taxable earnings by 5.4%.

STEP 5   Prepare the appropriate journal entry using the amounts computed in steps 2-4.

To understand the journal entry for employer payroll taxes, the accounts involved should be examined.

Payroll Taxes Expense

The FICA, FUTA, and SUTA taxes imposed on the employer are expenses of doing business. It would be possible to use a separate expense account for each of these taxes, but a single account entitled Payroll Taxes Expense is commonly used. Each of the employer taxes is debited to this same expense account.

Payroll Taxes Expense

Debit	Credit
FICA, FUTA, and SUTA taxes imposed on the employer	

FICA Tax Payable

This is the same liability account used in Chapter 9 to record the FICA tax withheld from employees earnings. The account is credited to enter the FICA tax imposed on the employer. It is debited when the tax is paid to the Internal Revenue Service (IRS). When all of the FICA taxes have been paid, the account will have a zero balance.

FICA Tax Payable

Debit	Credit
payment of FICA tax.	FICA taxes (1) withheld from employees' earnings and (2) imposed on the employer.

FUTA Tax Payable

A separate liability account entitled FUTA Tax Payable is kept for the employer's FUTA tax. This account is credited for the tax imposed on employers under the Federal Unemployment Tax Act. The account is debited when this tax is paid. When all of the FUTA taxes have been paid, the account will have a zero balance.

FUTA Tax Payable

Debit	Credit
payment of FUTA tax.	FUTA tax imposed on the employer.

SUTA Tax Payable

A separate liability account entitled SUTA Payable is kept for the state unemployment tax. This account is credited for the tax imposed on employers under the state unemployment compensation laws. The account is debited when these taxes are paid. When all of the state taxes have been paid, the account will have a zero balance.

State Unemployment Tax Payable

Debit	Credit
state unemployment tax paid.	state unemployment tax imposed on the employer

Total Payroll Cost of an Employee

It is interesting to note what it really costs to employ a person. The employer must, of course, pay the gross wages of an employee. In addition, the employer must pay payroll taxes on employee earnings up to certain dollar limits.

To illustrate, assume that an employee earns $25,000 a year. The total cost of this employee to the employer is calculated as follows:

Gross wages	$25,000
Employer FICA tax, 7.5% of $25,000	1,875
State unemployment tax, 5.4% of $7,000	378
FUTA tax, 0.8% of $7,000	56
	$27,309

Thus, the total payroll cost of employing a person whose stated compensation is $25,000 is $27,309. Employer payroll taxes clearly are a significant cost of doing business.

REPORTING AND PAYMENT RESPONSIBILITIES

3

Describe employer reporting and payment responsibilities.

Employer payroll reporting and payment responsibilities fall into four areas:

1. Federal income tax withholding and FICA taxes
2. FUTA taxes
3. State unemployment taxes
4. Employee Wage and Tax Statement (W-2)

Federal Income Tax Withholding and FICA Taxes

Three important aspects of employer reporting and payment responsibilities for federal income tax withholding and FICA taxes are:

1. Determining when payments are due
2. Use of Form 8109, Federal Tax Deposit Coupon
3. Use of Form 941, Employer's Quarterly Federal Tax Return

When Payments are Due.   The date by which federal income tax withholding and FICA taxes must be paid depends on the amount of these taxes. Figure 10-4 summarizes the deposit rules stated in *Circular E—Employer's Tax Guide*. In general, the larger the undeposited amount is, the more frequently payments must be made. For simplicity, we will assume that deposits must be made 15 days after the end of each month.

FIGURE 10-4 **Summary of Deposit Rules**

UNDEPOSITED AMOUNT	DEPOSIT DUE
1. Less than $500 at the end of the quarter.	1. Pay with Form 941 at end of the month following end of the quarter.
2. Less than $500 at the end of the month.	2. No deposit required. Carry forward taxes to following month within quarter.
3. $500 or more but less than $3,000 at end of the month.	3. Deposit 15 days after end of the month.
4. $3,000 or more but less than $100,000 at end of any 8th-monthly period (Day 3, 7, 11, 15, 19, 22, 25, and last day of each month).	4. Deposit within 3 working days after the end of that 8th-monthly period.
5. $100,000 or more during any 8th-monthly period.	5. Deposit by the end of the next banking day.

Form 8109. Deposits are made at a Federal Reserve bank or other authorized commercial bank using Form 8109, Federal Tax Deposit Coupon (figure 10-5). The **employer identification number (EIN)** shown on this form is obtained by the employer from the IRS. This number identifies the employer and must be shown on all payroll forms and reports filed with the IRS.

FIGURE 10-5 **Federal Tax Deposit Coupon (Form 8109)**

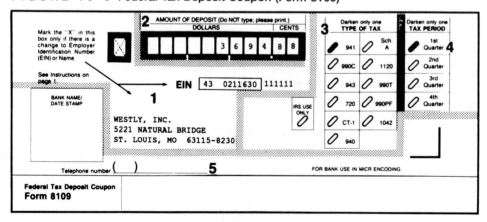

The $3,694.88 deposit shown in figure 10-5 for Westly, Inc. was for the following taxes:

Employees income tax withheld from wages		$1,654.80
FICA tax:		
Withheld from employees wages	$1,020.04	
Imposed on employer	1,020.04	2,040.08
Amount of check		$3,694.88

The journal entry for this deposit would be as follows.

2		Employees Income Tax Payable	1 6 5 4 80		2
3		FICA Tax Payable	2 0 4 0 08		3
4		Cash		3 6 9 4 88	4
5		Deposit of FICA taxes and			5
6		employee FIT.			6

Form 941.   Form 941, Employer's Quarterly Federal Tax Return must be filed with the IRS at the end of the month following each calendar quarter. This form is a report of employee federal income tax and FICA tax withholding, and employer FICA taxes for the quarter. A completed form for Westly Inc. for the first quarter of the calendar year is shown in figure 10-6. Instructions for completing the form are provided with the form and in *Circular E.*

Notice that Lines 6a and 7 in Figure 10-6 show the taxable social security and Medicare wages. As discussed in Chapter 9 on page 283, the FICA rate includes these two rates (OASDI—6.2% and HI—1.45%). Notice on Lines 6a and 7 that these two rates are 12.4% (6.2% × 2) and 2.9% (1.45% × 2). These rates include both employer and employee rates.

FUTA Taxes

Federal unemployment taxes must be calculated on a quarterly basis. If the accumulated liability exceeds $100, the total must be paid to a Federal Reserve bank or other authorized commercial bank. The total is due the last day of the first month following the close of the quarter. If the liability is $100 or less, no deposit is necessary. The amount is simply added to the amount to be deposited for the next quarter. FUTA taxes are deposited using Form 8109 (figure 10-5).

Assume that Westly, Inc.'s accumulated FUTA tax liability for the first quarter of the calendar year is $310. Westly would use Form 8109 to deposit this amount on April 30. The journal entry for this transaction would be as follows:

6	19-- Apr.	30	FUTA Tax Payable	3 1 0 00		6
7			Cash		3 1 0 00	7
8			Paid federal unemployment tax.			8

Form 940.   In addition to making quarterly deposits, employers are required to file an annual report of federal unemployment tax on Form 940. This form must be filed with the IRS by January 31 following the end of the calendar year. Figure 10-7 shows a completed Form 940 for Westly, Inc. Instructions for completing the form are provided with the form and in *Circular E.*

FIGURE 10-6 Employer's Quarterly Federal Tax Return (Form 941)

Form **941**
(Rev. January 1992)
Department of the Treasury
Internal Revenue Service

4141

Employer's Quarterly Federal Tax Return

▶ See Circular E for more information concerning employment tax returns.

Please type or print.

Your name, address, employer identification number, and calendar quarter of return. (If not correct, please change.)

If address is different from prior return, check here ▶ ☐

Name (as distinguished from trade name)

Date quarter ended
MARCH 27, 19--

Trade name, if any
WESTLEY, INC.

Employer identification number
43-0211630

Address (number and street)
5221 NATURAL BRIDGE,

City, state, and ZIP code
ST. LOUIS, MO 63115-8230

OMB No. 1545-0029
Expires 5-31-93

T
FF
FD
FP
I
T

IRS Use

1 1 1 1 1 1 1 1 1 1 1 2 3 3 3 3 3 4 4 4
5 5 5 6 7 8 8 8 8 8 9 9 9 10 10 10 10 10 10 10 10 10 10

If you do not have to file returns in the future, check here . ▶ ☐   Date final wages paid . . . ▶ _____

If you are a seasonal employer, see **Seasonal employers** on page 2 and check here . . ▶ ☐

1	Number of employees (except household) employed in the pay period that includes March 12th ▶	**1**	8
2	Total wages and tips subject to withholding, plus other compensation . . . . ▶	**2**	41,875 00
3	Total income tax withheld from wages, tips, pensions, annuities, sick pay, gambling, etc. ▶	**3**	4,095 40
4	Adjustment of withheld income tax for preceding quarters of calendar year (see instructions) . ▶	**4**	- 0 -
5	Adjusted total of income tax withheld (line 3 as adjusted by line 4—see instructions) . .	**5**	4,095 40
6a	Taxable social security wages (Complete line 7) $ 41,875 00 × 12.4% (.124) =	**6a**	5,192 50
b	Taxable social security tips $ × 12.4% (.124) =	**6b**	- 0 -
7	Taxable Medicare wages and tips $ 41,875 00 × 2.9% (.029) =	**7**	1,214 38
8	Total social security and Medicare taxes (add lines 6a, 6b, and 7)	**8**	6,406 88
9	Adjustment of social security and Medicare taxes (see instructions for required explanation) .	**9**	- 0 -
10	Adjusted total of social security and Medicare taxes (line 8 as adjusted by line 9—see instructions) . ▶	**10**	6,406 88
11	Backup withholding (see instructions)	**11**	- 0 -
12	Adjustment of backup withholding tax for preceding quarters of calendar year . . .	**12**	- 0 -
13	Adjusted total of backup withholding (line 11 as adjusted by line 12)	**13**	- 0 -
14	**Total taxes** (add lines 5, 10, and 13)	**14**	10,502 28
15	Advance earned income credit (EIC) payments made to employees, if any . . . . . ▶	**15**	
16	Net taxes (subtract line 15 from line 14). **This should equal line IV below** (plus line IV of Schedule A (Form 941) if you have treated backup withholding as a separate liability) . . .	**16**	10,502 28
17	Total deposits for quarter, including overpayment applied from a prior quarter, from your records . ▶	**17**	10,502 28
18	**Balance due** (subtract line 17 from line 16). This should be less than $500. Pay to Internal Revenue Service . ▶	**18**	

19 **Overpayment,** if line 17 is more than line 16, enter excess here ▶ $ _____ and check if to be:
☐ Applied to next return **OR** ☐ Refunded.

Record of Federal Tax Liability (You must complete if line 16 is $500 or more and Schedule B is not attached.) See instructions before checking these boxes.

If you made deposits using the 95% rule, check here ▶ ☐   If you are a first time 3-banking-day depositor, check here . . ▶ ☐

Show tax liability here, **not deposits.** The IRS gets deposit data from FTD coupons.

Date wages paid		First month of quarter		Second month of quarter		Third month of quarter
1st through 3rd	A		I		Q	
4th through 7th	B		J		R	
8th through 11th	C		K		S	
12th through 15th	D		L		T	
16th through 19th	E		M		U	
20th through 22nd	F		N		V	
23rd through 25th	G		O		W	
26th through the last	H		P		X	
Total liability for month	I	3,694.88	II	3,301.77	III	3,505.63

DO NOT Show Federal Tax Deposits Here

▶ **IV** Total for quarter (add lines **I, II,** and **III**). **This should equal line 16 above** . . . . . ▶   10,502.28

Sign Here

Under penalties of perjury, I declare that I have examined this return, including accompanying schedules and statements, and to the best of my knowledge and belief, it is true, correct, and complete.

Signature ▶ *William P. Jones*   Print Your Name and Title ▶ *Treasurer*   Date ▶ 4/30/--

For Paperwork Reduction Act Notice, see page 2.   Cat. No. 17001Z

FIGURE 10-7 Employer's Annual Federal Unemployment (FUTA) Tax Return, Form 940

Form **940**	**Employer's Annual Federal Unemployment (FUTA) Tax Return**	OMB No. 1545-0028

Department of the Treasury
Internal Revenue Service

▶ For Paperwork Reduction Act Notice, see separate instructions.

		T	
	Name (as distinguished from trade name) Calendar year	FF	
If incorrect, make any necessary change. ▶	Trade name, if any WESTLEY, INC.	FD	
		FP	
	Address and ZIP code Employer identification number	I	
	5221 NATURAL BRIDGE [43-0211630]	T	
	ST. LOUIS, MO 63115-8230		

A Did you pay all required contributions to state unemployment funds by the due date of Form 940? (If a 0% experience rate is granted, check "Yes" and see instructions.) . . . .   ☒ **Yes** ☐ **No**
 If you checked the "Yes" box, enter the amount of contributions paid to state unemployment funds . ▶ $ ....

B Are you required to pay contributions to only one state? . . . .   ☒ **Yes** ☐ **No**
 If you checked the "Yes" box: (1) Enter the name of the state where you have to pay contributions ▶ MISSOURI
 (2) Enter your state reporting number(s) as shown on state unemployment tax return. ▶ 319-855
 If you checked the "No" box, be sure to complete Part III and see the instructions.

C If any part of wages taxable for FUTA tax is exempt from state unemployment tax, check the box. (See the instructions.). . . . . ☐

If you will not have to file returns in the future, check here, complete, and sign the return . . . . ▶ ☐
If this is an Amended Return, check here . . . . ▶ ☐

Part I Computation of Taxable Wages *(to be completed by all taxpayers)*

				Amount paid			
1	Total payments (including exempt payments) during the calendar year for services of employees.		**1**			168,954	00
2	Exempt payments. (Explain each exemption shown, attach additional sheets if necessary.) ▶		**2**				
3	Payments of more than $7,000 for services. Enter only the amounts over the first $7,000 paid to each employee. Do not include payments from line 2. Do not use the state wage limitation		**3**	114,254	00		
4	Total exempt payments (add lines 2 and 3).				**4**	114,254	00
5	**Total taxable wages** (subtract line 4 from line 1). . . . . ▶				**5**	54,700	00
6	Additional tax resulting from credit reduction for unpaid advances to the state of Michigan. Enter the wages included on line 5 above for that state and multiply by the rate shown. (See the instructions.) Enter the credit reduction amount here and in Part II, line 2, or Part III, line 5: Michigan wages _____ × .008 = ... ▶				**6**		

Part II Tax Due or Refund *(Complete if you checked the "Yes" boxes in both questions A and B and did not check the box in C.)*

1	FUTA tax. Multiply the wages in Part I, line 5, by .008 and enter here.	**1**	437	60
2	Enter amount from Part I, line 6	**2**		
3	Total FUTA tax (add lines 1 and 2) . . . . ▶	**3**	437	60
4	Total FUTA tax deposited for the year, including any overpayment applied from a prior year . .	**4**	419	60
5	Balance due (subtract line 4 from line 3). This should be $100 or less. Pay to the Internal Revenue Service.	**5**	18	00
6	Overpayment (subtract line 3 from line 4). Check if it is to be: ☐ Applied to next return, or ☐ Refunded . . . . ▶	**6**		

Part IV Record of Quarterly Federal Tax Liability for Unemployment Tax *(Do not include state liability)*

Quarter	First	Second	Third	Fourth	Total for year
Liability for quarter	310.00	96.00	13.60	18.00	437.60

Under penalties of perjury, I declare that I have examined this return, including accompanying schedules and statements, and to the best of my knowledge and belief, it is true, correct, and complete, and that no part of any payment made to a state unemployment fund claimed as a credit was or is to be deducted from the payments to employees.

Signature ▶ *William P. Jones*   Title (Owner, etc.) ▶ *Treasurer*   Date ▶ 1/31/- -

SUTA Taxes

Deposit rules and forms for state unemployment taxes vary among the states. Deposits usually are required on a quarterly basis. Assume that

Westly's accumulated state unemployment liability for the first quarter of the calendar year is $1,980. The journal entry for the deposit of this amount with the state on April 30 would be as follows:

	19--					
10	Apr.	30	SUTA Tax Payable	1 9 8 0 00		10
11			Cash		1 9 8 0 00	11
12			Paid state unemployment tax.			12

Employee Wage and Tax Statement

By January 31 of each year, employers must furnish each employee with a Wage and Tax Statement, Form W-2 (figure 10-8). This form shows the total amount of wages paid to the employee and the amounts of taxes withheld during the preceding taxable year. Information needed to complete this form is contained in the employee's earnings record.

FIGURE 10-8 **Wage and Tax Statement, Form W-2**

1 Control number						
		OMB No. 1545-0008				
2 Employer's name, address, and ZIP code		**6** Statutory employee ☐ Deceased ☐ Pension plan ☐ Legal rep. ☐ 942 emp. ☐ Subtotal ☐ Deferred compensation ☐ Void ☐				
Westley, Inc.		**7** Allocated tips		**8** Advance EIC payment		
5221 Natural Bridge						
St. Louis, MO 63115-8230		**9** Federal income tax withheld *909.00*		**10** Wages, tips, other compensation *22,450.00*		
3 Employer's identification number *43 0211630*	**4** Employer's state I.D. number *21 686001*	**11** Social security tax withheld *1,683.75*		**12** Social security wages *22,450.00*		
5 Employee's social security number *393-58-8194*		**13** Social security tips		**14** Medicare wages and tips		
19 Employee's name, address, and ZIP code		**15** Medicare tax withheld		**16** Nonqualified plans		
Ken M. Istone		**17**		**18** Other		
1546 Swallow Drive						
St. Louis, MO 63144-4752						
20	**21**	**22** Dependent care benefits		**23** Benefits included in Box 10		
24 State income tax	**25** State wages, tips, etc.	**26** Name of state	**27** Local income tax *231.80*	**28** Local wages, tips, etc. *22,450.00*	**29** Name of locality *St. Louis Co.*	

Copy 1 **For State, City, or Local Tax Department**   Department of the Treasury—Internal Revenue Service

Multiple copies of Form W-2 are needed for the following purposes:

- Copy A—Employer sends to Social Security Administration.
- Copy B—Employee attaches to federal income tax return.

- Copy C—Employee attaches to state or local income tax return.
- Copy D—Employee retains for his or her own records.
- Copy E—Employer retains for business records.

Summary of Reports and Payments

Keeping track of the many payroll reports, deposits, and due dates can be a challenge for an employer. Figure 10-9 shows a calendar that highlights the due dates for the various reports and deposits. The calendar assumes the following for an employer:

1. Undeposited FIT (federal income tax) and FICA taxes of $500 to $3,000 at the end of each month.
2. Undeposited FUTA taxes of more than $100 at the end of each quarter.
3. SUTA taxes must be deposited quarterly.

FIGURE 10-9 Payroll Calendar

January

S	M	T	W	T	F	S
			1	2	3	4
5	6	7	8	9	10	11
12	13	14	15	16	17	18
19	20	21	22	23	24	25
26	27	28	29	30	31	

February

S	M	T	W	T	F	S
						1
2	3	4	5	6	7	8
9	10	11	12	13	14	15
16	17	18	19	20	21	22
23	24	25	26	27	28	29

March

S	M	T	W	T	F	S
1	2	3	4	5	6	7
8	9	10	11	12	13	14
15	16	17	18	19	20	21
22	23	24	25	26	27	28
29	30	31				

April

S	M	T	W	T	F	S
			1	2	3	4
5	6	7	8	9	10	11
12	13	14	15	16	17	18
19	20	21	22	23	24	25
26	27	28	29	30		

May

S	M	T	W	T	F	S
					1	2
3	4	5	6	7	8	9
10	11	12	13	14	15	16
17	18	19	20	21	22	23
24	25	26	27	28	29	30
31						

June

S	M	T	W	T	F	S
	1	2	3	4	5	6
7	8	9	10	11	12	13
14	15	16	17	18	19	20
21	22	23	24	25	26	27
28	29	30				

July

S	M	T	W	T	F	S
			1	2	3	4
5	6	7	8	9	10	11
12	13	14	15	16	17	18
19	20	21	22	23	24	25
26	27	28	29	30	31	

August

S	M	T	W	T	F	S
						1
2	3	4	5	6	7	8
9	10	11	12	13	14	15
16	17	18	19	20	21	22
23	24	25	26	27	28	29
30	31					

September

S	M	T	W	T	F	S
		1	2	3	4	5
6	7	8	9	10	11	12
13	14	15	16	17	18	19
20	21	22	23	24	25	26
27	28	29	30			

October

S	M	T	W	T	F	S
				1	2	3
4	5	6	7	8	9	10
11	12	13	14	15	16	17
18	19	20	21	22	23	24
25	26	27	28	29	30	31

November

S	M	T	W	T	F	S
1	2	3	4	5	6	7
8	9	10	11	12	13	14
15	16	17	18	19	20	21
22	23	24	25	26	27	28
29	30					

December

S	M	T	W	T	F	S
		1	2	3	4	5
6	7	8	9	10	11	12
13	14	15	16	17	18	19
20	21	22	23	24	25	26
27	28	29	30	31		

File Forms 940, 941, state unemployment tax report, and send W-2 to employees.

File form 941 and state unemployment tax report.

Deposit FIT and FICA taxes from previous month.

<table>
<tr><td>4</td></tr>
</table>

Describe and account for workers' compensation insurance.

WORKERS' COMPENSATION INSURANCE

Most states require employers to carry workers' compensation insurance. **Workers' compensation insurance** provides insurance for employees who suffer a job-related illness or injury.

The employer usually pays the entire cost of workers' compensation insurance. The cost of the insurance depends on the number of employees, the riskiness of the job, and the company's accident history. For example, the insurance premium for workers in a chemical plant could be higher than for office workers. Employers generally can obtain the insurance either from the state in which they operate, or from a private insurance company.

The employer usually pays the premium at the beginning of the year, based on the estimated payroll for the year. At the end of the year, after the actual amount of payroll is known, an adjustment is made. If the employer has overpaid, a credit is received from the state or insurance company. If the employer has underpaid, an additional premium is paid.

As an example of how to account for workers' compensation insurance, assume that Lockwood Co. expects its payroll for the year to be $210,000. If Lockwood's insurance premium rate is 0.2%, its payment for workers' compensation insurance at the beginning of the year would be as follows:

Estimated Payroll	Rate	Estimated Insurance Premium
$210,000	× .002 =	$420.00

The journal entry for the payment of this $420 premium would be:

1		Workers' Compensation Insurance Expense	4 2 0 00			1
2		Cash		4 2 0 00		2
3		Paid insurance premium.				3

If Lockwood's actual payroll for the year is $220,000, Lockwood would owe an additional premium at year end, computed as follows:

Payroll		Rate		Insurance Premium
$220,000	×	.002	=	$440.00
Less estimated premium paid				420.00
Additional premium due				$ 20.00

The adjusting entry at year end for this additional expense would be:

5		Workers' Compensation Insurance Expense	2 0 00			5
6		Workers' Compensation Insurance Pay.		2 0 00		6
7		Adjustment for insurance premium.				7

In T account form, the total Workers' Compensation Insurance Expense of $440.00 would look like this.

Worker's Compensation Insurance Expense

420.00	
20.00	
440.00	

If Lockwood's actual payroll for the year is only $205,000, Lockwood would be due a refund, computed as follows:

Payroll		Rate		Insurance Premium
$205,000	×	.002	=	$410.00
Less estimated premium paid				420.00
Refund due				$ (10.00)

The adjusting entry at year end for this refund due would be:

9		Insurance Refund Receivable		1 0 00		9
10		Workers' Compensation Insurance Exp.			1 0 00	10
11		Adjustment for insurance premium.				11

In T account form, the total Workers' Compensation Insurance Expense of $410 would look as follows:

Worker's Compensation Insurance Expense

420.00	10.00
410.00	

KEY POINTS

1/2 Employer payroll taxes represent additional payroll expenses of the employer. The journal entry for payroll taxes is:

8		Payroll Taxes Expense		X XX		8
9		FICA Tax Payable			X XX	9
10		FUTA Tax Payable			X XX	10
11		SUTA Tax Payable			X XX	11

The steps to be followed in preparing this journal entry are:

1. Obtain the taxable earnings amounts from the Taxable Earnings columns of the payroll register.
2. Compute the amount of employer FICA tax by multiplying the FICA taxable earnings by 7.5%.
3. Compute the amount of FUTA tax by multiplying the Unemployment Taxable earnings by 0.8%.
4. Compute the amount of SUTA tax by multiplying the Unemployment Taxable earnings by 5.4%.
5. Prepare the appropriate journal entry using the amounts computed in steps 2-4.

3 Employer payroll reporting and payment responsibilities fall into four areas:

1. Federal income tax withholding and FICA taxes
2. FUTA taxes
3. State unemployment taxes
4. Employee Wage and Tax Statement (W-2)

Key forms needed in reporting and paying employer payroll taxes are:

1. Form 8109, Federal Tax Deposit Coupon
2. Form 941, Employer's Quarterly Federal Tax Return
3. Form 940, Employer's Annual Federal Unemployment Tax Return

By January 31 of each year, employers must provide each employee with a Wage and Tax Statement, Form W-2.

4 Employers generally are required to carry and pay the entire cost of workers' compensation insurance.

KEY TERMS

employer FICA tax 311   Tax levied on employers at the same rate and on the same earnings base as the employee FICA tax.

Employer Identification Number (EIN) 318   A number that identifies the employer on all payroll forms and reports filed with the IRS.

FUTA (Federal Unemployment Tax Act) tax 313   A tax levied on employers to raise funds to administer the federal/state unemployment compensation program.

merit-rating system 314   A system to encourage employers to provide regular employment to workers.

self-employment income 312   The net income of a trade or business run by an individual.

self-employment tax 312   A contribution to the federal social security (FICA) program.

state unemployment tax (SUTA) 314   A tax levied on employers to raise funds to pay unemployment benefits.

workers' compensation insurance 324   Provides insurance for employees who suffer a job-related illness or injury.

BUILDING YOUR ACCOUNTING KNOWLEDGE

1. Why do employer payroll taxes represent an additional expense to the employer, whereas the various employee payroll taxes do not?
2. At what rate and on what earnings base is the employer's FICA tax levied?
3. What is the purpose of the FUTA tax and who must pay it?
4. What is the purpose of the state unemployment tax and who must pay it?
5. What accounts are affected when employer payroll tax expenses are properly recorded?
6. Identify all items that are debited or credited to the FICA Tax Payable account.
7. Explain why an employee whose gross salary is $20,000 costs an employer more than $20,000 to employ.
8. What is the purpose of Form 8109, the Federal Tax Deposit Coupon?
9. What is the purpose of Form 941, the Employer's Quarterly Federal Tax Return?
10. What is the purpose of Form 940, the Employer's Annual Federal Unemployment Tax Return?
11. What information appears on Form W-2, the employee's Wage and Tax Statement?
12. What is the purpose of workers' compensation insurance and who must pay for it?

DEMONSTRATION PROBLEM

The totals line from Hart Company's payroll register for the week ending December 31, 19--, is as follows:

	NAME	EMPLOYEE NO.	ALLOW-ANCES	MARITAL STATUS	EARNINGS				TAXABLE EARNINGS		
					REGULAR	OVER-TIME	TOTAL	CUMULATIVE TOTAL	UNEMPLOY. COMP.	FICA	
1	Totals				3 5 0 0 00	3 0 0 00	3 8 0 0 00	197 6 0 0 00	4 0 0 00	3 8 0 0 00	1

PAYROLL REGISTER

FOR PERIOD ENDED   December 31,19--

	DEDUCTIONS						NET PAY	CK. NO.	
	FEDERAL INC. TAX	FICA TAX	HEALTH INS.	UNITED WAY	OTHER	TOTAL			
1	3 8 0 00	2 8 5 00	5 0 00	1 0 0 00		8 1 5 00	2 9 8 5 00		1

Payroll taxes are imposed as follows: FICA tax—7.5%; FUTA tax—0.8%; SUTA tax—5.4%

Required
1. **a.** Prepare the journal entry for payment of this payroll on December 31, 19--.
   b. Prepare the journal entry for the employer's payroll taxes for the period ending December 31, 19--.
2. Hart Company had the following balances in its general ledger *after* the entries for part (A) were made:

Employees Income Tax Payable	$1,520.00
FICA Tax Payable	$2,280.00
Federal Unemployment Tax Payable	$ 27.20
State Unemployment Tax Payable	$ 183.60

   c. Prepare the journal entry for payment of the liabilities for employees' federal income taxes and FICA taxes on January 15, 19--.
   d. Prepare the journal entry for payment of the liability for federal unemployment tax on January 31, 19--.
   e. Prepare the journal entry for payment of the liability for state unemployment tax on January 31, 19--.
3. Hart Company paid a premium of $280 for workers' compensation insurance based on estimated payroll as of the beginning of the year. Based on actual payroll as of the end of the year, the premium is $298.
   f. Prepare the adjusting entry to reflect the underpayment of the insurance premium.

SOLUTION

	DATE		DESCRIPTION	POST. REF.	DEBIT	CREDIT	
	GENERAL JOURNAL					PAGE 1	
1	19-- Dec.	31	Wage and Salary Expense		3 8 0 0 00		1
2			Employees Income Tax Payable			3 8 0 00	2
3			FICA Tax Payable			2 8 5 00	3
4			Health Insurance Premiums Payable			5 0 00	4
5			United Way Payable			1 0 0 00	5
6			Cash			2 9 8 5 00	6
7							7
8	Dec.	31	Payroll Taxes Expense		3 0 9 80		8
9			FICA Tax Payable			2 8 5 00	9
10			FUTA Tax Payable			3 20	10
11			State Unemployment Tax Payable			2 1 60	11
12							12
13	Jan.	15	Employees Income Tax Payable		1 5 2 0 00		13
14			FICA Tax Payable		2 2 8 0 00		14
15			Cash			3 8 0 0 00	15
16							16
17	Jan.	31	Federal Unemployment Tax Payable		2 7 20		17
18			Cash			2 7 20	18
19							19
20	Jan.	31	State Unemployment Tax Payable		1 8 3 60		20
21			Cash			1 8 3 60	21
22							22
23	Jan.	31	Workers' Comp. Insurance Expense		1 8 00		23
24			Workers' Comp. Insurance Payable			1 8 00	24

SERIES A

EXERCISES

APPLYING ACCOUNTING CONCEPTS

EXERCISE 10A1

Journal Entry for Employer Payroll Taxes

1/2 A section of the payroll register for Barney's Bagels for the week ended July 15 is shown below. The state unemployment tax rate is 5.4%, and the federal unemployment tax rate is 0.8%, both on the first $7,000 of earnings. The FICA tax rate is 7.5% on the first $55,000 of earnings.

Barney's Bagels
Payroll Register

Taxable Earnings

	Unemploy. Comp.	FICA
Totals	10,500.00	12,200.00

1. Calculate the employer's payroll tax expense.

2. Prepare the journal entry to record the employer's payroll tax expense for the week ending July 15, of the current year.

EXERCISE 10A2

Employer Payroll Taxes

1/2 Taxable earnings for several employees for the week ended March 12, 19--, are shown as follows.

	Taxable Earnings	
Employee Name	Unemploy. Comp.	FICA
Aus, Glenn E.	200.00	700.00
Duckworth, Charles K.	350.00	350.00
Knapp, Carol S.	—	1,200.00
Mueller, Deborah F.	125.00	830.00
Yeager, Jackie R.	35.00	920.00

Calculate the employer's payroll tax expense and prepare the journal entry as of March 12, 19--, assuming that FUTA tax is 0.8%, state unemployment tax is 5.4%, and FICA tax is 7.5%.

EXERCISE 10A3

Taxable Earnings and Employer's Payroll Tax Journal Entry

1/2 Selected information from the payroll register of Raynette's Boutique for the week ended September 14, 19--, is presented as follows. FICA tax is 7.5% on the first $55,000 of earnings on each employee. Federal unemployment tax is 0.8%, and state unemployment tax is 5.4% on the first $7,000 of earnings.

	Cumulative Pay Before Current	Current Gross	Taxable Earnings	
Employee Name	Earnings	Pay	Unemploy. Comp.	FICA
Adams, John R.	$ 6,800	$1,250		
Ellis, Judy A.	6,300	1,100		
Lewis, Arlene S.	54,200	2,320		
Mason, Jason W.	53,900	2,270		
Yates, Ruby L.	27,650	1,900		
Zielke, Ronald M.	58,730	2,680		

Calculate the amount of taxable earnings for unemployment and FICA tax, and prepare the journal entry to record the employer's payroll tax as of September 14, 19--.

EXERCISE 10A4

Journal Entry for Payment of Employer's Payroll Taxes

3 Bruce Brown owns a business called Brown Construction Co. and does his banking at the Citizens National Bank in Portland, Oregon. The amounts in his general ledger for the withholding of payroll taxes and the employee's withholding of FICA and Employees Federal Income Tax Payable as of March 15th of the current year show the following:

FICA payable (includes both employer and employee) $3,750.00
FUTA payable .... $ 200.00
SUTA payable $1,350.00
Employees income tax payable $2,275.00

Journalize the payment of the Form 941 deposit (i.e. FICA and federal income tax) to the Citizens National Bank, and the payment of the state unemployment tax to the state of Oregon as of March 15, 19--.

EXERCISE 10A5
Total Cost of Employee

1 J.B. Kenton employs Sharla Knox at a salary of $32,000 a year. Kenton is subject to employer FICA taxes at a rate of 7.5% on Sharla's salary. In addition, Kenton must pay state unemployment tax at a rate of 5.4%, and federal unemployment tax at a rate of 0.8% on the first $7,000 of Knox's salary.

Compute the total cost to Kenton of employing Knox for the year.

EXERCISE 10A6
Workers' Compensation Insurance and Adjustment

4 General Manufacturing estimated that its total payroll for the coming year would be $425,000. The workers' compensation insurance premium rate is 0.2%.

1. Calculate the estimated worker's compensation insurance premium and prepare the journal entry for the payment as of January 2, 19--.
2. Assume that General Manufacturing's actual payroll for the year is $432,000. Calculate the total insurance premium owed, and prepare a journal entry as of December 31, 19--, to record the adjustment for the underpayment. The actual payment of the additional premium will take place in January of the next year.

PROBLEMS

PROBLEM 10A1
Calculating Payroll Tax Expense and Preparing Journal Entry

1/2 Selected information from the payroll register of Anderson's Dairy for the week ended May 7, 19--, is shown as follows. State unemployment tax is withheld at the rate of 5.4% and the federal unemployment tax is withheld at the rate of 0.8%, both on the first $7,000 of earnings. FICA tax on the employer is a matching 7.5% imposed on the first $55,000 of earnings.

Employee Name	Cumulative Pay Before Current Earnings	Current Weekly Earnings	Taxable Earnings Unemploy. Comp.	FICA
Barnum, Alex	$ 6,750	$ 820.00		
Duel, Richard	6,340	725.00		
Hunt, J. B.	23,460	1,235.00		
Larson, Susan	6,950	910.00		
Miller, Denise	53,480	2,520.00		
Swan, Judy	15,470	1,125.00		
Yates, Keith	28,675	1,300.00		

Required
1. Calculate the employer payroll taxes for each employee.
2. Prepare the journal entry to record the employer payroll taxes as of May 7, 19--.

2 The Cascade Company has four employees. All are paid on a monthly basis. The fiscal year of the business is July 1 to June 30. Payroll taxes are imposed as follows:

1. FICA tax to be withheld from employees' wages, 7.5% on the first $55,000 of earnings.
2. FICA tax imposed on the employer, 7.5% on the first $55,000 of earnings.
3. SUTA tax, 5.4% on the first $7,000 of earnings.
4. FUTA tax, 0.8% on the first $7,000 of earnings.

The accounts kept by the Cascade Company include the following:

Account Number	Title	Balance on July 1
111	Cash	$50,200.00
211	FICA Tax Payable	1,800.00
212	FUTA Tax Payable	164.00
213	SUTA Tax Payable	810.00
214	Employees Income Tax Payable	1,015.00
261	Savings Bond Deductions Payable	350.00
542	Wages and Salary Expense	–0–
552	Payroll Taxes Expense	–0–

The following transactions relating to payrolls and payroll taxes occurred during July and August.

July 15   Paid $2,815.00 covering the following June taxes:

FICA tax	$ 1,800.00
Employees income tax withheld	1,015.00
Total	$ 2,815.00

31   July payroll:

Total wage and salary expense		$12,000.00
Less amounts withheld:		
FICA Tax	$ 900.00	
Employees Income Tax	1,020.00	
Savings Bond Payable	350.00	2,270.00
Net amount paid		$ 9,730.00

31   Purchased savings bonds for employees, $700.00
31   Data for completing employer's payroll taxes expense for July:

FICA taxable wages	$12,000.00
Unemployment taxable wages	$ 3,000.00

Aug. 15   Paid $2,820.00 covering the following July taxes:

FICA tax	$ 1,800.00
Employees Income Tax Payable	$ 1,020.00

15   Paid state unemployment tax for the quarter, $972.00
15   Paid FUTA tax, $188.00

Required
1. Journalize the preceding transactions using a two-column journal.
2. Open T accounts for the payroll expense and liabilities, then post the beginning balances and the previous transactions.

PROBLEM 10A3

Workers' Compensation Insurance and Adjustment

4 Willamette Manufacturing estimated that its total payroll for the coming year would be $650,000. The workers' compensation insurance premium rate is 0.3%.

Required

1. Calculate the estimated workers' compensation insurance premium and prepare the journal entry for the payment as of January 2, 19--.
2. Assume that Willamette Manufacturing's actual payroll for the year is $672,000. Calculate the total insurance premium owed, and prepare a journal entry as of December 31, 19--, to record the adjustment for the underpayment. The actual payment of the additional premium will take place in January of the next year.
3. Assume instead, that Willamette Manufacturing's actual payroll for the year is $634,000. Prepare a journal entry as of December 31, 19--, for the total amount that should be refunded. The refund will not be received until the next year.

SERIES B

EXERCISES

EXERCISE 10B1

Journal Entry for Employer Payroll Taxes

1/2 A section of the payroll register for Kathy's Cupcakes for the week ended June 21, 19--, is shown below. The state unemployment tax rate is 5.4% and the federal unemployment tax rate is 0.8%, both on the first $7,000 of earnings. The FICA tax rate is 7.5% on the first $55,000 of earnings.

Kathy's Cupcakes
Payroll Register

Taxable Earnings

	Unemploy. Comp.	FICA
Totals	12,310.00	15,680.00

1. Calculate the employer's payroll tax expense.
2. Prepare the journal entry to record the employer's payroll tax expense for the week ending June 21 of the current year.

EXERCISE 10B2

Employer Payroll Taxes

1/2 Taxable earnings for several employees for the week ended April 7, 19--, are shown below.

Employee Name	Taxable Earnings Unemploy. Comp.	FICA
Boyd, Glenda, L.	300.00	850.00
Evans, Sheryl N.	225.00	970.00
Fox, Howard J.	830.00	830.00
Jacobs, Phyllis J.	—	1,825.00
Rawlins, William R.	25.00	990.00

Calculate the employer's payroll tax expense and prepare the journal entry as of April 7, 19--, assuming that FUTA tax is 0.8%, SUTA tax is 5.4%, and FICA tax is 7.5%.

EXERCISE 10B3

Taxable Earnings and Employer's Payroll Tax Journal Entry

1/2 Selected information from the payroll register of Howard's Cutlery for the week ended October 7, 19--, is presented below. FICA tax is 7.5% on the first $55,000 of earnings on each employee. Federal unemployment tax is 0.8%, and state unemployment tax is 5.4% on the first $7,000 of earnings.

Employee Name	Cumulative Pay Before Current Earnings	Current Gross Pay	Taxable Earnings Unemploy. Comp.	FICA
Carlson, David J.	$ 6,635	$ 950		
Davis, Patricia S.	6,150	1,215		
Lewis, Arlene S.	54,375	2,415		
Nixon, Robert R.	53,870	1,750		
Shippe, Lance W.	24,830	1,450		
Watts, Brandon Q.	59,200	2,120		

Calculate the amount of taxable earnings for unemployment and FICA tax, and prepare the journal entry to record the employer's payroll tax for Howard's Cutlery as of October 7, 19--.

EXERCISE 10B4

Journal Entry for Payment of Employer's Payroll Taxes

3 Francis Baker owns a business called Baker Construction Co. and does her banking at the American National Bank in Seattle, Washington. The amounts in her general ledger for the withholding of payroll taxes and the employee's withholding of FICA and employees federal income tax as of May 15th of the current year show the following:

FICA payable (includes both employer and employee) $6,375.00
FUTA payable .... $ 336.00
SUTA payable $2,268.00
Employees federal income tax payable $4,830.00

Journalize the payment of the Form 941 deposit (i.e. FICA and federal income tax) to the American National Bank, and the payment of the state unemployment tax to the state of Washington as of May 15, 19--.

EXERCISE 10B5

Total Cost of Employee

1 B. F. Goodson employs Eduardo Gonzales at a salary of $46,000 a year. Goodson is subject to employer FICA taxes at a rate of 7.5% on Eduardo's salary. In addition, Goodson must pay state unemployment tax at a rate of 5.4%, and federal unemployment tax at a rate of 0.8% on the first $7,000 of Gonzales' salary.

Compute the total cost to Goodson of employing Gonzales for the year.

4 Columbia Industries estimated that its total payroll for the coming year would be $385,000. Workers' compensation insurance premium rate is 0.2%.

1. Calculate the estimated worker's compensation insurance premium and prepare the journal entry for the payment as of January 2, 19--.
2. Assume that Columbia Industries' actual payroll for the year is $396,000. Calculate the total insurance premium owed, and prepare a journal entry as of December 31, 19--, to record the adjustment for the underpayment. The actual payment of the additional premium will take place in January of the next year.

PROBLEMS

1/2 Selected information from the payroll register of Wray's Drug Store for the week ended July 7, 19-- is shown below. State unemployment tax is withheld at the rate of 5.4% and federal unemployment tax is withheld at the rate of 0.8%, both on the first $7,000 of earnings. FICA tax on the employer is a matching 7.5% imposed on the first $55,000 of earnings.

| | | | Taxable Earnings | |
| | Cumulative Pay Before Current | Current Weekly | Unemploy. | |
Employee Name	Earnings	Earnings	Comp.	FICA
Ackers, Alice	$ 6,460	$ 645.00		
Conley, Dorothy	27,560	1,025.00		
Davis, James	6,850	565.00		
Lawrence, Kevin	52,850	2,875.00		
Rawlings, Judy	16,350	985.00		
Tester, Leonard	22,320	835.00		
Wray, Raynette	53,460	2,540.00		

Required
1. Calculate the employer payroll taxes for each employee.
2. Prepare the journal entry to record the employer payroll taxes as of July 7, 19--.

2 The Oxford Company has five employees. All are paid on a monthly basis. The fiscal year of the business is June 1 to May 31. Payroll taxes are imposed as follows:

1. FICA tax to be withheld from employees' wages, 7.5% on the first $55,000 of earnings.
2. FICA tax imposed on the employer, 7.5% on the first $55,000 of earnings.
3. State unemployment tax, 5.4% on the first $7,000 of earnings.
4. FUTA tax imposed on the employer, 0.8% on the first $7,000 of earnings.

The accounts kept by the Oxford Company include the following:

Account Number	Title	Balance on June 1
111	Cash	$48,650.00
211	FICA Tax Payable	2,250.00
212	FUTA Tax Payable	360.00
213	State Unemployment Tax Payable	920.00
214	Employees Income Tax Payable	1,345.00
261	Savings Bond Deductions Payable	525.00
542	Wages and Salary Expense	–0–
552	Payroll Taxes Expense	–0–

The following transactions relating to payrolls and payroll taxes occurred during June and July.

June 15   Paid $3,595.00 covering the following May taxes:

FICA tax	$ 2,250.00
Employees income tax withheld	1,345.00
Total	$ 3,595.00

30   June payroll:

Total wage and salary expense		$15,000.00
Less amounts withheld:		
FICA Tax	$ 1,125.00	
Employees Income Tax	1,280.00	
Savings Bonds Payable	525.00	2,930.00
Net amount paid		$12,070.00

30   Purchased savings bonds for employees, $1,050.00
30   Data for completing employer's payroll taxes expense for June:

FICA taxable wages	$15,000.00
Unemployment taxable wages	$ 4,500.00

July 15   Paid $3,530.00 covering the following May taxes:

FICA tax	$ 2,250.00
Employees Income Tax Payable	$ 1,280.00

15   Paid state unemployment tax, $1,163.00
15   Paid FUTA tax, $396.00

Required
1. Journalize the preceding transactions using a two-column general journal.
2. Open T accounts for the payroll expense and liabilities, then post the beginning balances and the previous transactions.

PROBLEM 10B3

Workers' Compensation Insurance and Adjustment

4 Multnomah Manufacturing estimated that its total payroll for the coming year would be $540,000. The workers' compensation insurance premium rate is 0.2%.

Required
1. Calculate the estimated workers' compensation insurance premium and prepare the journal entry for the payment as of January 2, 19--.
2. Assume that Multnomah Manufacturing's actual payroll for the year is $562,000. Calculate the total insurance premium owed, and prepare a journal entry as of December 31, 19--, to record the adjustment for the underpayment. The actual payment of the additional premium will take place in January of the next year.
3. Assume instead, that Multnomah Manufacturing's actual payroll for the year is $548,000. Prepare a journal entry as of December 31, 19--, for the total amount that should be refunded. The refund will not be received until the next year.

MASTERY PROBLEM

The totals line from Nix Company's payroll register for the week ending March 31, 19--, is as follows:

PAYROLL REGISTER

	NAME	EMPLOYEE NO.	ALLOW-ANCES	MARITAL STATUS	EARNINGS				TAXABLE EARNINGS		
					REGULAR	OVER-TIME	TOTAL	CUMULATIVE TOTAL	UNEMPLOY. COMP.	FICA	
1	Totals				5 4 0 0 00	1 0 0 00	5 5 0 0 00	71 5 0 0 00	5 0 0 0 00	5 5 0 0 00	1

FOR PERIOD ENDED   March 31,19--

	DEDUCTIONS						NET PAY	CK. NO.	
	FEDERAL INC. TAX	FICA TAX	HEALTH INS.	LIFE INS.	OTHER	TOTAL			
1	5 0 0 00	4 1 2 50	1 6 5 00	2 0 0 00		1 2 7 7 50	4 2 2 2 50		1

Payroll taxes are imposed as follows: FICA tax—7.5%; FUTA tax--0.8%; SUTA tax--5.4%

Required
1. **a.** Prepare the journal entry for payment of this payroll on March 31, 19--.
   b. Prepare the journal entry for the employer's payroll taxes for the period ending March 31, 19--.

2. Nix Company had the following balances in its general ledger *before* the entries for part (A) were made:

Employees Income Tax Payable	$1,500.00
FICA Tax Payable	$2,478.00
Federal Unemployment Tax Payable	$ 520.00
State Unemployment Tax Payable	$3,510.00

    c. Prepare the journal entry for payment of the liabilities for federal income taxes and FICA taxes on April 15, 19--.

    d. Prepare the journal entry for payment of the liability for federal unemployment tax on April 30, 19--.

    e. Prepare the journal entry for payment of the liability for state unemployment tax on April 30, 19--.

3. Nix Company paid a premium of $420 for workers' compensation insurance based on the estimated payroll as of the beginning of the year. Based on actual payroll as of the end of the year, the premium is only $400.

    f. Prepare the adjusting entry to reflect the overpayment of the insurance premium at the end of the year (12/31/--).

PART III
Accounting for a Merchandising Business

Careful study of this chapter should enable you to:

1. Define merchandise sales transactions.
2. Describe and use merchandise sales accounts.
3. Describe and use the sales journal and accounts receivable ledger.
4. Describe and use the cash receipts journal and accounts receivable ledger.
5. Prepare a schedule of accounts receivable.

Accounting for Sales and Cash Receipts

For the last ten chapters, we have learned how to account for a service business. We are now ready to consider accounting for a different kind of business—merchandising. A **merchandising business** purchases merchandise such as clothing, furniture, or computers, and sells that merchandise to customers.

This chapter examines how to account for the sale of merchandise using the accrual basis of accounting. We will learn how to use four new accounts, two special journals, and a subsidiary ledger.

Define merchandise sales transactions.

MERCHANDISE SALES TRANSACTIONS

A **sale** is a transfer of merchandise from one business or individual to another in exchange for cash or a promise to pay cash. Sales procedures and documents can vary greatly, depending on the nature and size of the business.

Retailer

Retail businesses generally sell to customers who enter the store, select the merchandise they want, and bring it to a salesclerk. The salesclerk enters the sale in some type of electronic cash register which generates a receipt for the customer. A copy of the receipt is retained in the register.

Most registers can print a summary of the day's sales activity, like the one in figure 11-1. This summary can be used to journalize sales in the accounting records.

FIGURE 11-1 **Cash Register Tape Summary**

```
        (1)
    CASH SALES           327.79  *
        (3)
    MCARD/VISA           550.62  *
        (6)
    LAYAWAY               79.50  *
    TOTAL CASH           957.91  *
        (2)
    CHARGE SALES         543.84  *
        (5)
    APPROVAL             126.58  *
    TOTAL CHARGE         670.42  *

    TOTAL SALES        1,628.33  G*
    SALES TAX             81.42  *
                         81.42  *

    REC'D ON ACCT.       324.51  *
                        324.51  *

    PAID OUT             76.51   *
                         76.51   *

    NO SALE               0.00   *
                          0.00   *

    *  SUB-TOTAL
    G* GRAND TOTAL
```

An additional document often created as evidence of a sale in a retail business is a **sales ticket** (figure 11-2). One copy of the sales ticket is given to the customer and the other copy is sent to accounting.

Wholesaler

We can see in figure 11-3 that the wholesaler plays a different role from the retailer in the marketing chain. Retailers usually sell to final consumers, whereas wholesalers tend to sell to retailers. This causes the wholesale sales transaction process to differ, as shown in figure 11-4.

Customers commonly send in written orders to buy merchandise from wholesalers. When the customer purchase order arrives, who the customer is and what is being ordered are determined. Since wholesalers typically make sales on account, credit approval is needed. Three copies of a **sales invoice** are then generated. One is shipped with the merchandise, one is sent to the customer as a bill for the merchandise, and one is sent to accounting to record the sale. Figure 11-5 shows the customer copy of a sales invoice for Alladin Electric Supply.

FIGURE 11-2 **Sales Ticket**

FIGURE 11-3 **Marketing Chain**

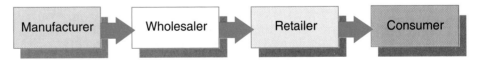

Credit Memorandum

Both retailers and wholesalers sometimes have customers return goods or seek price reductions for damaged goods. Merchandise returned by the customer for a refund is called a **sales return.** Reductions in the price of

F I G U R E   1 1 - 4   **Wholesale Sales Transaction Process**

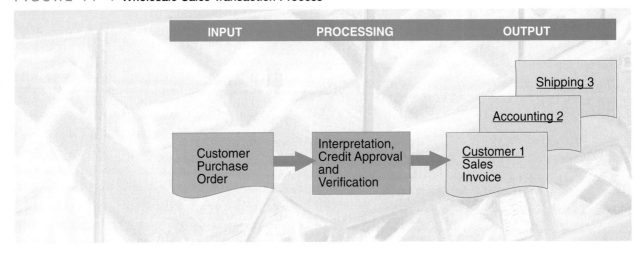

F I G U R E   1 1 - 5   **Sales Invoice**

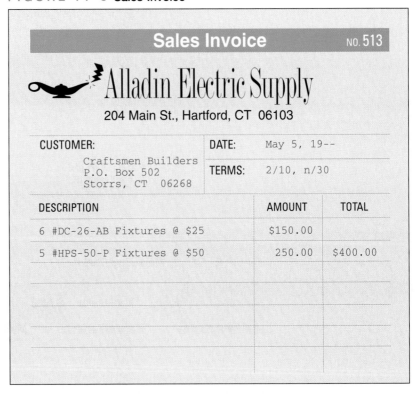

merchandise granted by the seller because of defects or other problems with the merchandise are called **sales allowances.** When credit is given for merchandise returned or for an allowance, a **credit memo** is issued for the amount involved. One copy is given to the customer and one copy is sent to accounting. Figure 11-6 shows a credit memo issued by Northern Micro for merchandise returned by a customer.

FIGURE 11-6 Credit Memo

NORTHERN MICRO 72

1099 E. Louisiana, Indianapolis, IN 46217-3322

Date April 2, 19--

Name Susan Chang

Address 337 Elm Street

City Noblesville State IN Zip 46060-3377

Sales Number			OK	
Cash Refund	Mdse. Order	Charge ✓	Gift	Amount $42.00

Quantity	Articles	Amount
2	Printer Ribbons	$40.00
	Tax	2.00
		$42.00

Forty-two 00/100 ——— Dollars

Reason Not needed

Rec'd. Stock By Laura Murphy

x Susan Chang
Customer's Signature

MERCHANDISE SALES ACCOUNTS

2 **Describe and use merchandise sales accounts.**

To account for merchandise sales transactions, we need to know how to use four new accounts.

1. Sales
2. Sales Tax Payable
3. Sales Returns and Allowances
4. Sales Discounts

Sales Account

The sales account is a temporary owner's equity account in which the revenue earned from the sale of merchandise is entered. The account is credited for the selling price of merchandise sold during the period.

Sales

	Credit to enter the selling price of merchandise sold.

If a $100 sale is made for cash, the following entry is made.

5			Cash				1 0 0 00				5
6			Sales						1 0 0 00	6

If the same sale is made on account, the entry is:

5			Accounts Receivable				1 0 0 00				5
6			Sales						1 0 0 00	6

Sales Tax Payable Account

When sales tax is imposed on merchandise sold, a separate account is kept for Sales Tax Payable. This is a liability account that is credited for the amount of tax imposed on sales. The account should be debited for the amount of the tax paid to the proper taxing authority or for the amount of the tax on merchandise returned by customers. A credit balance in the account indicates the amount owed to the taxing authority for taxes collected.

Sales Tax Payable

Debit	Credit
to enter payment of tax to taxing authority or adjustment of tax on merchandise returned by customers.	to enter tax imposed on sales

If a cash sale for $100 plus 5% sales tax (5% × $100 = $5) occurs, the following entry is made.

11			Cash				1 0 5 00				11
12			Sales						1 0 0 00	12
13			Sales Tax Payable						5 00	13

If the same sale is made on account, the following entry is made.

11		Accounts Receivable		1 0 5 00		11
12		Sales			1 0 0 00	12
13		Sales Tax Payable			5 00	13

The debit to Accounts Receivable indicates that the amount owed by customers to the firm has increased. Since the buyer has accepted the merchandise and promised to pay for it, revenue is recognized by crediting the Sales account. Sales Tax Payable is credited because the amount of sales tax owed to the taxing authority has increased.

Sales Returns and Allowances Account

Sales Returns and Allowances is a temporary owner's equity account in which sales returns and sales allowances are debited. It is a contra-sales account reported as a deduction from Sales on the income statement.

Sales Returns and Allowances

Debit
to enter returns
and allowances.

Look at the credit memo in figure 11-6 on page 345. The entry for the return of these printer ribbons by Susan Chang would be:

19		Sales Returns and Allowances		4 0 00		19
20		Sales Tax Payable		2 00		20
21		Accts. Receivable (Susan Chang)			4 2 00	21

Debit Sales Returns and Allowances for the amount of the sale excluding the sales tax.

Note carefully the parts of this entry. Sales Returns and Allowances is debited for the amount of the sale, *excluding* the sales tax. Sales Tax Payable is debited separately for the sales tax on the original sale amount. Accounts Receivable is credited for the total amount originally billed to Chang.

Sales Discounts Account

Some businesses offer **cash discounts** to encourage prompt payment by customers who buy merchandise on account. Some possible credit terms are shown in figure 11-7.

FIGURE 11-7 **Credit Terms**

TERMS	MEANING
2/10, n/30*	2% discount off sales price if paid within 10 days Total amount due within 30 days
1/10, n/30	Same as 2/10, n/30, except 1% discount instead of 2%
2/eom, n/60	2% discount if paid before end of month Total amount due within 60 days
3/10 eom	3% discount if paid within 10 days after end of month

*See Figure 11-5. A discount of $8 (2% × $400) is allowed if this invoice is paid by May 15 (invoice date of May 5 + 10 days).

To the seller, cash discounts are considered **sales discounts.** The Sales Discounts account is a temporary owner's equity account in which any cash discounts allowed are debited. Like Sales Returns and Allowances, Sales Discounts is a contra-sales account reported as a deduction from Sales on the income statement.

Sales Discounts

Debit
to enter cash
discounts.

If merchandise is sold for $100 with credit terms of 2/10, n/30, and cash is received within the discount period, the following entries are made.

At time of sale:

23		Accounts Receivable	1 0 0 00		23
24		Sales		1 0 0 00	24

At time of collection:

26		Cash	9 8 00		26
27		Sales Discounts	2 00		27
28		Accounts Receivable		1 0 0 00	28

3

Describe and use the sales journal and accounts receivable ledger.

JOURNALIZING AND POSTING SALES TRANSACTIONS

To illustrate the journalizing and posting of sales transactions, Northern Micro, a retail computer business, is used. Assume that the following sales transactions occurred during the first three weeks of April, 19--.

Apr. 4   Made sale no. 133C on account to Enrico Lorenzo, $1,520 plus $76 sales tax.

10   Made sale no. 134C on account to Brenda Myers, $440 plus $22 sales tax.

18   Made sale no. 105D on account to Edith Walton, $980 plus $49 sales tax.

21   Made sale no. 202B on account to Susan Chang, $620 plus $31 sales tax.

24   Made sale no. 162A on account to Heidi Switzer, $1,600 plus $80 sales tax.

These transactions could be entered in a general journal as shown in figure 11-8.

FIGURE 11-8 **Sales Entered in General Journal**

	19-- Apr.					
5	Apr.	4	Accounts Receivable	1 5 9 6 00		5
6			Sales		1 5 2 0 00	6
7			Sales Tax Payable		7 6 00	7
8			Sale no. 133C.			8
9						9
10		10	Accounts Receivable	4 6 2 00		10
11			Sales		4 4 0 00	11
12			Sales Tax Payable		2 2 00	12
13			Sale no. 134C.			13
14						14
15		18	Accounts Receivable	1 0 2 9 00		15
16			Sales		9 8 0 00	16
17			Sales Tax Payable		4 9 00	17
18			Sale no. 105D.			18
19						19
20		21	Accounts Receivable	6 5 1 00		20
21			Sales		6 2 0 00	21
22			Sales Tax Payable		3 1 00	22
23			Sale no. 202B.			23
24						24
25		24	Accounts Receivable	1 6 8 0 00		25
26			Sales		1 6 0 0 00	26
27			Sales Tax Payable		8 0 00	27
28			Sale no. 162A.			28
29						29

Notice that each of these entries involved the same three accounts. The same account title had to be recorded four times to make these four entries. Similarly, to post these entries to the general ledger, four separate postings would have to be made to each of the three accounts, a total of twelve postings.

This repetition is inefficient. Fortunately, there is a much more efficient way to record sales on account. This is done by using a **special journal** designed for recording only certain kinds of transactions.

Sales Journal

Use a sales journal to streamline posting and journalizing of sales on account.

A **sales journal** is a special journal used to record only sales on account. By using a sales journal, we can streamline our journalizing and posting of sales on account.

To illustrate, let's reconsider the five sales on account of Northern Micro. They are entered in the sales journal in figure 11-9. The sales journal provides separate columns for Accounts Receivable Dr., Sales Cr., and Sales Tax Payable Cr., the three accounts used repeatedly in the general journal in figure 11-8. A sale is recorded in the sales journal by entering the following information:

1. Date
2. Sale number
3. Customer
4. Dollar amounts

There is no need to enter any general ledger account titles.

FIGURE 11-9 **Northern Micro Sales Journal**

	DATE	SALE NO.	TO WHOM SOLD	POST. REF.	ACCOUNTS RECEIVABLE DR.	SALES CR.	SALES TAX PAYABLE CR.	
1	19-- Apr. 4	133C	Enrico Lorenzo		1 5 9 6 00	1 5 2 0 00	7 6 00	1
2	10	134C	Brenda Myers		4 6 2 00	4 4 0 00	2 2 00	2
3	18	105D	Edith Walton		1 0 2 9 00	9 8 0 00	4 9 00	3
4	21	202B	Susan Chang		6 5 1 00	6 2 0 00	3 1 00	4
5	24	162A	Heidi Switzer		1 6 8 0 00	1 6 0 0 00	8 0 00	5
6								6

SALES JOURNAL — PAGE 6

The sales journal in figure 11-9 is designed for a company, like Northern Micro, that charges sales tax. For a wholesaler, or any other company that does not charge sales tax, a sales journal like that in figure 11-10 would be sufficient. In this case, there is only a single amount column headed Accounts Receivable Dr./Sales Cr. With no sales tax, the Accounts Receivable Dr. and Sales Cr. amounts are identical for each sale. Thus only a single column is needed.

FIGURE 11-10 **Sales Journal Without Sales Tax**

			SALES JOURNAL			PAGE 1	
	DATE	SALE NO.	TO WHOM SOLD	POST. REF.	ACCOUNTS RECEIVABLE DR./ SALES CR.		

Posting from the Sales Journal

Posting from the sales journal is also very efficient. Each general ledger account used in the sales journal requires only one posting each period. Figure 11-11 illustrates the general ledger posting process for Northern Micro's sales journal for the month of April.

FIGURE 11-11 **Posting the Sales Journal to the General Ledger**

SALES JOURNAL   Page 6

Date	Sale No.	To Whom Sold	Post. Ref.	Accounts Receivable Dr.	Sales Cr.	Sales Tax Payable Cr.	
19--							
Apr. 4	133C	Enrico Lorenzo....		1,596.00	1,520.00	76.00	
10	134C	Brenda Myers.......		462.00	440.00	22.00	
18	105D	Edith Walton		1,029.00	980.00	49.00	
21	202B	Susan Chang		651.00	620.00	31.00	
24	162A	Heidi Schwitzer....		1,680.00	1,600.00	80.00	
				5,418.00	5,160.00	258.00	①
				(131)	(411)	(221)	④

②

GENERAL LEDGER (Partial)

ACCOUNT Accounts Receivable   ACCOUNT NO. 131

		Post.			Balance	
Date	Item	Ref.	Debit	Credit	Debit	Credit
19--						
Apr. 1	Bal.	✓			12,000.00	
③ 30		S6	5,418.00		17,418.00	

ACCOUNT Sales Tax Payable   ACCOUNT NO. 221

		Post.			Balance	
Date	Item	Ref.	Debit	Credit	Debit	Credit
19--						
③ Apr. 30		S6		258.00		258.00

ACCOUNT Sales   ACCOUNT NO. 411

		Post.			Balance	
Date	Item	Ref.	Debit	Credit	Debit	Credit
19--						
Apr. 1	Bal.	✓				27,000.00
③ 30		S6		5,160.00		32,160.00

The steps in the posting procedure from the sales journal to the general ledger at the end of each month are indicated in figure 11-11, as follows:

STEP 1   Foot the amount columns, verify that the total of the debit column equals the total of the credit columns, and rule the columns.

STEP 2   Post the column totals to the general ledger accounts indicated in the column headings.

STEP 3   Insert the date in the Date column, and the initial "S" and the sales journal page number in the Posting Reference column of each ledger account.

STEP 4   Insert the general ledger account numbers immediately below the column totals.

The sales and accounts receivable accounts in the general ledger are now completely up to date. But Northern Micro has a problem. It has no complete record of the account receivable from *individual customers*. To run the business properly, Northern Micro needs this information.

A common approach to keeping a record of each customer's account receivable is to use a **subsidiary accounts receivable ledger.** This is a separate ledger containing an individual account receivable for each customer, usually in alphabetical order. A summary accounts receivable account called a **controlling account** is still maintained in the general ledger. The accounts receivable ledger is "subsidiary" to this account.

The use of the accounts receivable subsidiary ledger is illustrated in figure 11-12. The accounts receivable ledger is posted *daily* so that current information is available for each customer at all times. The steps in posting from the sales journal to the accounts receivable ledger as shown in figure 11-12 follow.

STEP 1   Post the individual sale amount to the customer's account on the date the sale occurs.

STEP 2   Insert the date in the Date column, and the initial "S" and the sales journal page number in the Posting Reference column of each customer account.

STEP 3   Insert a check mark (√) in the Posting Reference column of the sales journal to indicate that the amount has been posted.

The total of the accounts receivable ledger balances equals the Accounts Receivable balance in the general ledger.

Note the relationship between the sales journal, accounts receivable subsidiary ledger, and general ledger. All individual entries in the sales journal are posted to the accounts receivable ledger. The totals of all entries in the sales journal are posted to the general ledger accounts. After the posting of the accounts receivable ledger and the general ledger is completed, the

FIGURE 11-12 **Posting the Sales Journal to the Accounts Receivable Ledger**

SALES JOURNAL   Page 6

Date	Sale No.	To Whom Sold	Post Ref.	Accounts Receivable Dr.	Sales Cr.	Sales Tax Payable Cr.
19-- Apr. 4	133C	Enrico Lorenzo....	✓	1,596.00	1,520.00	76.00
10	134C	Brenda Myers.......	✓	462.00	440.00	22.00
18	105D	Edith Walton	✓	1,029.00	980.00	49.00
21	202B	Susan Chang	✓	651.00	620.00	31.00
24	162A	Heidi Schwitzer....	✓	1,680.00	1,600.00	80.00
			③	5,418.00	5,160.00	258.00
				(131)	(411)	(221)

ACCOUNTS RECEIVABLE SUBSIDIARY LEDGER (Partial)

NAME Helen Avery
ADDRESS 1739 Woodsage Trace, Indianapolis, IN 46237-1199

Date	Item	Post. Ref.	Debit	Credit	Balance
19-- Apr. 1	Bal.	✓			2,302.00

NAME Susan Chang
ADDRESS 337 Elm Street, Noblesville, IN 46060-3377

Date	Item	Post. Ref.	Debit	Credit	Balance
19-- ② Apr. 21		S6	651.00		651.00

NAME Enrico Lorenzo
ADDRESS 5240 Tousley Court, Indianapolis, IN 46224-5678

Date	Item	Post. Ref.	Debit	Credit	Balance
19-- ② Apr. 4		S6	1,596.00		1,596.00

NAME Brenda Myers
ADDRESS 581 Acorn Way, Zionsville, IN 46077-2154

Date	Item	Post. Ref.	Debit	Credit	Balance
19-- ② Apr. 10		S6	462.00		462.00

NAME Heidi Schwitzer
ADDRESS 5858 Wildflower Cir., Bloomington, NY 47401-6209

Date	Item	Post. Ref.	Debit	Credit	Balance
19-- Apr. 1	Bal.	✓			1,883.00
② 24		S6	1,680.00		3,563.00

NAME Ken Ulmet
ADDRESS 5260 Eagle Creek, Indianapolis, IN 46254-8275

Date	Item	Post. Ref.	Debit	Credit	Balance
19-- Apr. 1	Bal.				3,315.00

NAME Edith Walton
ADDRESS 1113 Stones Crossing, Zionsville, IN 46077-6601

Date	Item	Post. Ref.	Debit	Credit	Balance
19-- ② Apr. 18		S6	1,029.00		1,029.00

NAME Vivian Winston
ADDRESS 124 Main St., Zionsville, IN 46077-1358

Date	Item	Post. Ref.	Debit	Credit	Balance
19-- Apr. 1	Bal.	✓			4,500.00

①

GENERAL LEDGER (Partial)

ACCOUNT Accounts Receivable   **ACCOUNT NO.** 131

Date	Item	Post. Ref.	Debit	Credit	Balance Debit	Balance Credit
19-- Apr. 1	Bal.	✓			12,000.00	
30		S6	5,418.00		17,418.00	

ACCOUNT Sales Tax Payable   **ACCOUNT NO.** 221

Date	Item	Post. Ref.	Debit	Credit	Balance Debit	Balance Credit
19-- Apr. 30		S6		258.00		258.00

ACCOUNT Sales   **ACCOUNT NO.** 411

Date	Item	Post. Ref.	Debit	Credit	Balance Debit	Balance Credit
19-- Apr. 1						27,000.00
30		S6		5,160.00		32,160.00

total of the accounts receivable ledger balances should equal the Accounts Receivable balance in the general ledger. *Remember, the accounts receivable ledger is simply a detailed listing of the same information that is summarized in Accounts Receivable in the general ledger.*

Sales Returns and Allowances

Enter sales returns and allowances in the general journal.

If a customer returns merchandise or is given an allowance for damaged merchandise, a general journal entry is required. *Remember, the sales journal can be used only to enter sales on account.* Assume that on May 5, Susan Chang returns two printer ribbons costing $40 plus $2 sales tax. These were part of the sale to her on April 21. The general journal entry, general ledger posting, and accounts receivable ledger posting for this transaction are illustrated in figure 11-13.

FIGURE 11-13 **Accounting for Sales Returns and Allowances**

GENERAL JOURNAL — Page 4

Date	Description	Post. Ref.	Debit	Credit
19--				
May 5	Sales Returns & Allowances	411.1	40.00	
	Sales Tax Payable	221	2.00	
	Accounts Receivable (S. Chang)	131 / ✓		42.00
	Returned Merch. - C.M. #75	③ ④		

ACCOUNTS RECEIVABLE SUBSIDIARY LEDGER (Partial)

NAME Susan Chang
ADDRESS 337 Elm Street, Noblesville, IN 46060-3377 ②

Date	Item	Post. Ref.	Debit	Credit	Balance
19--					
May 1	Bal.	✓			651.00
5		J4		42.00	609.00

③ Indicates general ledger account has been posted.
④ Indicates customer account has been posted.

GENERAL LEDGER (Partial)

ACCOUNT Accounts Receivable — ACCOUNT NO. 131

Date	Item	Post. Ref.	Debit	Credit	Balance Debit	Credit
19--						
May 1	Bal.	✓			14,331.00	
5		J4		42.00	14,289.00	

ACCOUNT Sales Tax Payable — ACCOUNT NO. 221

Date	Item	Post. Ref.	Debit	Credit	Balance Debit	Credit
19--						
May 1	Bal.	✓				563.00
5		J4	2.00			561.00

ACCOUNT Sales Returns & Allowances — ACCOUNT NO. 411.1

Date	Item	Post. Ref.	Debit	Credit	Balance Debit	Credit
19--						
May 1	Bal.	✓			274.00	
5		J4	40.00		314.00	

The general journal entry is made in the usual manner. The postings are made daily and require special attention. The debits to Sales Returns and Allowances and Sales Tax Payable are posted to the general ledger accounts, and posting references are inserted in the general journal and general ledger accounts. To post the Accounts Receivable credit for a sales return as shown in figure 11-13, use the following steps.

STEP 1   Post the amounts to the general ledger accounts and insert the initial "J" and the general journal page number (4) in the Posting Reference columns.

STEP 2   Post the same amount to the customer account in the accounts receivable ledger and insert the same posting reference (J4) in the Posting Reference column.

STEP 3   To indicate that the general ledger has been posted, insert the account number (131) and a slash (/) in the Posting Reference column of the general journal.

STEP 4   To indicate that the customer account has been posted, insert a check mark (√) following the slash in the Posting Reference column of the general journal.

JOURNALIZING AND POSTING CASH RECEIPTS

4

Describe and use the cash receipts journal and accounts receivable ledger.

Just as sales transactions occur frequently in most businesses, so also do cash receipt transactions. Sales on account lead to cash receipts, which could be entered in the general journal. For example, assume that Northern Micro receives cash from Enrico Lorenzo for sale no. 133C on April 14. The transaction could be recorded in the general journal as follows.

25	19-- Apr.	14	Cash		1 5 9 6 00		25
26			Accounts Rec./Enrico Lorenzo			1 5 9 6 00	26

Most businesses also regularly make cash sales. A general journal can be used to record cash sales. The following general journal shows cash sales of $500 recorded in the general journal on May 5.

2	19-- May	5	Cash		5 0 0 00		2
3			Sales			5 0 0 00	3

In addition, an increasing amount of sales today are made using bank credit cards. Bank credit card sales are similar to cash sales because the cash is available to the business as soon as the credit card slips are deposited in the bank. But not all of the cash is available. The bank charges a fee to the business for processing the credit card items. Thus, on a sale of

$100, the bank might charge a fee of $4 (4%). The following general journal shows this credit card sale recorded on May 6.

5		6	Cash			9 6 00		5
6			Bank Credit Card Expense			4 00		6
7			Sales				1 0 0 00	7

Note two important features of the three journal entries illustrated above.

1. Each involves a debit to Cash.
2. Each would occur quite frequently in a business.

If the general journal were used to record all such transactions, the journalizing and posting process would be repetitive and inefficient.

In the previous section of this chapter, it was illustrated how sales on account could be journalized and posted more efficiently by using a sales journal. Using a special journal to record cash receipts transactions also increases efficiency.

Cash Receipts Journal

A **cash receipts journal** is a special journal used to record only cash receipts transactions. To illustrate its use, we will continue with the transactions of Northern Micro. Northern Micro's cash receipts journal for the month of April is shown in figure 11-14. Five types of cash receipts transactions are shown.

1. Collections on account (three separate items)
2. Cash sales (shown in summary form for the month)
3. Bank credit card sales (shown in summary form for the month)
4. Rent revenue
5. Borrowing from the bank

FIGURE 11-14 **Northern Micro Cash Receipts Journal**

				CASH RECEIPTS JOURNAL			
	DATE		ACCOUNT CREDITED	POST. REF.	GENERAL CR.		
1	19-- Apr.	14	Enrico Lorenzo				1
2		20	Brenda Myers				2
3		28	Edith Walton				3
4		30					4
5		30					5
6		30	Rent Revenue		6 0 0 00		6
7		30	Notes Payable		3 0 0 0 00		7

The following transactions are recorded in the cash receipts journal in figure 11-14.

Apr. 14   Received cash on account from Enrico Lorenzo for sale no. 133C, $1,596.
20   Received cash on account from Brenda Myers for sale no. 134C, $462.
28   Received cash on account from Edith Walton for sale no. 105D, $1,029.
30   Cash sales for the month are $3,600 plus tax of $180.
30   Bank credit card sales for the month are $2,500 plus tax of $125. Bank credit card expenses on these sales is $100.
30   Received cash for rent revenue, $600.
30   Borrowed cash from the bank, $3,000.

Northern Micro's cash receipts journal provides separate columns for Accounts Receivable Cr., Sales Cr., Sales Tax Payable Cr., Bank Credit Card Expense Dr., and Cash Dr. These are the accounts most frequently affected by Northern Micro's cash receipts transactions. In addition, a General Cr. column is provided for credits to any other accounts affected by cash receipts transactions.

A cash receipt is recorded in the cash receipts journal by entering the following information:

1. Date
2. Account credited (if applicable)
3. Dollar amounts

The Account Credited column is used for two purposes:

1. To identify the customer name for any collection on account. This column is used whenever the Accounts Receivable Cr. column is used.
2. To enter the appropriate account name whenever the General Cr. column is used.

PAGE 7

	ACCOUNTS RECEIV. CR.	SALES CR.	SALES TAX PAY. CR.	BANK CREDIT CARD EXPENSE DR.	CASH DR.	
1	1 5 9 6 00				1 5 9 6 00	1
2	4 6 2 00				4 6 2 00	2
3	1 0 2 9 00				1 0 2 9 00	3
4		3 6 0 0 00	1 8 0 00		3 7 8 0 00	4
5		2 5 0 0 00	1 2 5 00	1 0 0 00	2 5 2 5 00	5
6					6 0 0 00	6
7					3 0 0 0 00	7

Note that this means there are times when the Account Credited column is left blank. This would be whenever the entry is for cash sales or bank credit card sales.

The cash receipts journal in figure 11-14 is designed for a company like Northern Micro, which charges sales tax, makes bank credit card sales, and offers no cash discounts. For a wholesaler who does not charge sales tax, makes no bank credit card sales, and does offer cash discounts, a cash receipts journal like the one in figure 11-15 would be used. Recall that a special journal should be designed with column headings for frequently used accounts. Thus, the cash receipts journal in figure 11-15, has no Sales Tax Payable Cr. or Bank Credit Card Expense Dr. column. Instead, a Sales Discount Dr. column is provided. In this way, the common cash receipts transactions of the wholesaler can be easily and efficiently recorded.

> Use a cash receipts journal to record cash receipts transactions only. A retail business would probably use column headings for Sales Tax Payable Cr. and Credit Card Expense Dr. A wholesale business would probably use a column heading for Sales Discount Dr. Both would have a Cash Dr. column.

FIGURE 11-15 Cash Receipts Journal without Sales Tax

	DATE	ACCOUNT CREDITED	POST. REF.	GENERAL CR.	ACCOUNTS RECEIV. CR.	SALES CR.	SALES DISCOUNT DR.	CASH DR.	

CASH RECEIPTS JOURNAL — PAGE 1

Posting the Cash Receipts Journal

The general ledger posting process for Northern Micro's cash receipts journal is illustrated in figure 11-16.

On a daily basis:

STEP 1 Post each amount in the General Cr. column to the appropriate general ledger account.

STEP 2 Insert the date in the Date column and the initials "CR" and the cash receipts journal page number in the Posting Reference column of each ledger account.

STEP 3 Insert the general ledger account numbers in the Posting Reference column of the cash receipts journal.

At the end of each month:

STEP 4 Foot the amount columns, verify that the total of the debit columns equals the total of the credit columns, and rule the columns.

STEP 5 Post each column total except the General Cr. column to the general ledger account indicated in the column headings.

FIGURE 11-16 **Posting the Cash Receipts Journal to the General Ledger**

CASH RECEIPTS JOURNAL   Page 7

Date	Account Credited	Post. Ref.	General Cr.	Accounts Receivable Cr.	Sales Cr.	Sales Tax Pay. Cr.	Bank Credit Card Exp. Dr.	Cash Dr.
19-- Apr. 4	Enrico Lorenzo			1,596.00				1,596.00
10	Brenda Myers			462.00				462.00
18	Edith Walton	⑧		1,029.00				1,029.00
30		✓			3,600.00	180.00		3,780.00
30		✓			2,500.00	125.00	100.00	2,525.00
30	Rent Revenue	451	600.00					600.00
30	Notes Payable	216	3,000.00					3,000.00
		③	3,600.00	3,087.00	6,100.00	305.00	100.00	12,992.00 ④
			(✓)	(131)	(411)	(221)	(553)	(111) ⑦
			⑧					⑤

GENERAL LEDGER (Partial)

ACCOUNT Cash   ACCOUNT NO. 111

Date	Item	Post. Ref.	Debit	Credit	Balance Debit	Balance Credit
19-- Apr. 1	Bal.	✓			20,000.00	
⑥ 30		CR7	12,992.00		32,992.00	

ACCOUNT Accounts Receivable   ACCOUNT NO. 131

Date	Item	Post. Ref.	Debit	Credit	Balance Debit	Balance Credit
19-- Apr. 1	Bal.	✓			12,000.00	
30		S6	5,418.00		17,418.00	
① ⑥ 30		CR7		3,087.00	14,331.00	⑤

ACCOUNT Notes Payable   ACCOUNT NO. 216

Date	Item	Post. Ref.	Debit	Credit	Balance Debit	Balance Credit
19-- Apr. 1	Bal.	✓				6,000.00
② 30		CR7		3,000.00		9,000.00

ACCOUNT Sales Tax Payable   ACCOUNT NO. 221

Date	Item	Post. Ref.	Debit	Credit	Balance Debit	Balance Credit
19-- Apr. 30		S6		258.00		258.00
⑥ 30		CR7		305.00		563.00

ACCOUNT Sales   ACCOUNT NO. 411

Date	Item	Post. Ref.	Debit	Credit	Balance Debit	Balance Credit
19-- Apr. 1	Bal.	✓				27,000.00
30		S6		5,160.00		32,160.00
⑥ 30		CR7		6,100.00		38,260.00

ACCOUNT Rent Revenue   ACCOUNT NO. 451

Date	Item	Post. Ref.	Debit	Credit	Balance Debit	Balance Credit
19-- Apr. 1	Bal.	✓				1,800.00
② 30		CR7		600.00		2,400.00

ACCOUNT Bank Credit Card Expense ACCOUNT NO. 553

Date	Item	Post. Ref.	Debit	Credit	Balance Debit	Balance Credit
19-- Apr. 1	Bal.	✓			430.00	
⑥ 30		CR7	100.00		530.00	

STEP 6   Insert the date in the Date column and the initials "CR" and the cash receipts journal page number in the Posting Reference column of each ledger account.

STEP 7   Insert the general ledger account numbers immediately below each column total except the General Cr. column.

STEP 8   Insert a check mark ($\sqrt{}$) in the Posting Reference column of the cash receipts journal for the cash sales and bank credit card sales, and immediately below the General Cr. column.

The general ledger accounts affected by the cash receipts transactions are now up to date. Postings to the accounts receivable ledger also must be made. These postings are made daily. Posting procedures are as follows, as shown in figure 11-17.

STEP 1   Post the individual cash receipt to the customer's account on the date the receipt occurs.

STEP 2   Insert the date in the Date column, and the initials "CR" and the cash receipts journal page number in the Posting Reference column of each customer account.

STEP 3   Insert a check mark ($\sqrt{}$) in the Posting Reference column of the cash receipts journal to indicate that the amount has been posted.

5

Prepare a schedule of accounts receivable.

SCHEDULE OF ACCOUNTS RECEIVABLE

All postings to the general ledger and accounts receivable subsidiary ledger are now complete. At this point, the Accounts Receivable balance in the general ledger should equal the sum of the customer balances in the accounts receivable ledger.

To verify that the sum of the accounts receivable ledger balances equals the Accounts Receivable balance, a **schedule of accounts receivable** is prepared. This is an alphabetical listing of customer accounts and balances, usually prepared at the end of the month. The schedule of accounts receivable for Northern Micro as of April 30 is illustrated in figure 11-18 on page 362.

This schedule is prepared from the list of customer accounts in the accounts receivable ledger. The total calculated in the schedule is compared with the balance in Accounts Receivable in the general ledger. Note that the $14,331 total listed in the schedule equals the Accounts Receivable balance shown in figure 11-17. If the schedule total and the Accounts

FIGURE 11-17 **Posting the Cash Receipts Journal to the Accounts Receivable Ledger**

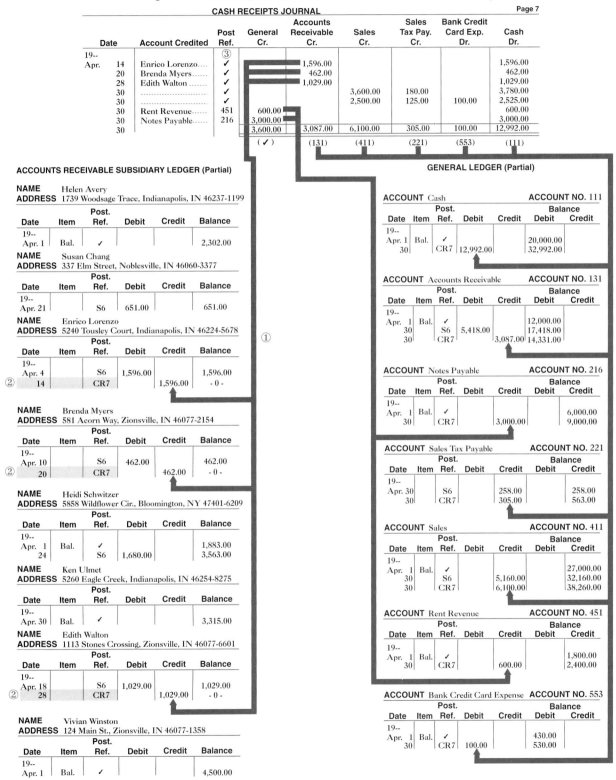

FIGURE 11-18 Schedule of Accounts Receivable

Northern Micro Schedule of Accounts Receivable April 30, 19--	
Helen Avery	2 3 0 2 00
Susan Chang	6 5 1 00
Heidi Schwitzer	3 5 6 3 00
Ken Ulmet	3 3 1 5 00
Vivian Winston	4 5 0 0 00
	14 3 3 1 00

Receivable balance do not agree, the error must be located and corrected. To find the error, use the following procedures.

STEP 1   Verify the total of the schedule.

STEP 2   Verify the postings to the accounts receivable ledger.

STEP 3   Verify the postings to Accounts Receivable in the general ledger.

KEY POINTS

1 A merchandising business buys and sells merchandise. Retailers generally make sales in the store. Important accounting documents are cash register tapes and sales tickets. Wholesalers generally ship merchandise to customers. A key accounting document is the sales invoice. When customers return merchandise or obtain price adjustments, a credit memo is issued.

2 Four accounts are used in accounting for merchandise sales transactions:

1. Sales
2. Sales Tax Payable
3. Sales Returns and Allowances
4. Sales Discounts

3 A sales journal is a special journal for recording sales on account. A sale is recorded by entering the:

1. Date
2. Sale number
3. Customer
4. Dollar amounts

To post from the sales journal to the general ledger:

1. Foot, verify the equality of, and rule the amount columns.
2. Post column totals to the general ledger accounts.
3. Insert the date and posting reference in the ledger accounts.
4. Insert the account numbers below the column totals in the sales journal.

To post from the sales journal to the accounts receivable ledger:

1. Post individual sale amounts to customer accounts.
2. Insert the date and posting reference in the customer accounts.
3. Insert a check mark ($\sqrt{}$) in the Posting Reference column of the sales journal.

Sales returns and allowances are recorded in the general journal.

4 A cash receipts journal is a special journal for recording cash receipts. A cash receipt is recorded by entering the:

1. Date
2. Account credited (if applicable)
3. Dollar amounts

To post from the cash receipts journal to the general ledger:

On a daily basis:

1. Post General Cr. column amounts to the general ledger.
2. Insert the date and posting reference in the accounts.
3. Insert the account numbers in the Posting Reference column of the cash receipts journal.

At the end of each month:

4. Foot, verify the equality of, and rule the amount columns.
5. Post specific account column totals to the general ledger.
6. Insert the date and posting reference in the accounts.
7. Insert the account numbers below the specific account column totals.
8. Insert a check mark ($\sqrt{}$) in the Posting Reference column for the cash sales and bank credit card sales, and below the General Cr. column.

To post from the cash receipts journal to the accounts receivable ledger:

1. Post individual cash receipts to customer accounts.
2. Insert the date and posting reference in the customer accounts.
3. Insert a check mark ($\sqrt{}$) in the Posting Reference column of the cash receipts journal.

5 The schedule of accounts receivable is used to verify that the sum of the accounts receivable ledger balances equals the Accounts Receivable balance.

KEY TERMS

cash discounts 347   A discount to encourage prompt payment by customers who buy merchandise on account.

cash receipts journal 356   A special journal used to record only cash receipts transactions.

controlling account 352   A summary account maintained in the general ledger with a subsidiary ledger (for example, the accounts receivable ledger).

credit memo 344   A document issued when credit is given for merchandise returned or for an allowance.

merchandising business 341   Purchases merchandise such as clothing, furniture, or computers, and sells that merchandise to its customers.

sale 341   A transfer of merchandise from one business or individual to another in exchange for cash or a promise to pay cash.

sales allowances 344   Reductions in the price of merchandise granted by the seller because of defects or other problems with the merchandise.

sales discounts 348   To the seller, cash discounts are considered sales discounts.

sales invoice 342   A document that is generated to bill the customer who made the purchase.

sales journal 350   A special journal used to record only sales on account.

sales return 343   Merchandise returned by the customer for a refund.

sales ticket 342   An additional document often created as evidence of a sale in a retail business.

schedule of accounts receivable 360   An alphabetical listing of customer accounts and balances, usually prepared at the end of the month.

special journal 350   A journal designed for recording only certain kinds of transactions.

subsidiary accounts receivable ledger 352   A separate ledger containing an individual account receivable for each customer, usually in alphabetical order.

BUILDING YOUR ACCOUNTING KNOWLEDGE

1. Identify the sales documents commonly used in retail and wholesale businesses.
2. What is the purpose of a credit memo?
3. Describe how each of the following accounts is used: (1) Sales, (2) Sales Tax Payable, (3) Sales Returns and Allowances, and (4) Sales Discounts.
4. List four items of information about each sale entered in the sales journal.

5. What steps are followed in posting from the sales journal to the general ledger?
6. What steps are followed in posting from the sales journal to the accounts receivable ledger?
7. How is the posting of Sales Returns and Allowances from the general journal to the general ledger and accounts receivable ledger different from the normal posting process?
8. List three items of information about each cash receipt entered in the cash receipts journal.
9. What steps are followed in posting from the cash receipts journal to the general ledger?
10. What steps are followed in posting from the cash receipts journal to the accounts receivable ledger?
11. If the total of the schedule of accounts receivable does not agree with the Accounts Receivable balance, what procedures should be used to search for the error?

DEMONSTRATION PROBLEM

Karen Hunt operates an audio-video store. The books of original entry include a sales journal, a cash receipts journal, and a general journal. The following transactions related to sales on account and cash receipts occurred during April:

April 3 Sold merchandise on account to Susan Haberman, $159.50 plus tax of $11.17. Sale no. 41.
      4 Sold merchandise on account to Glenn Kelly, $299.95 plus tax of $21.00. Sale no. 42.
      6 Received $69.50 from Tera Scherrer on account.
      7 Issued a credit memorandum for $42.75 which included the tax of $2.80 to Kenneth Watt for merchandise returned that had been sold on account.
     10 Received $99.95 from Kellie Cokley on account.
     11 Sold merchandise on account to Victor Cardona, $499.95 plus tax of $35.00. Sale no. 43.
     14 Received $157.00 from Kenneth Watt in full settlement of account.
     17 Sold merchandise on account to Susan Haberman, $379.95 plus tax of $26.60. Sale no. 44.
     19 Sold merchandise on account to Tera Scherrer, $59.95 plus tax of $4.20. Sale no. 45.
     21 Issued a credit memorandum to Glenn Kelly for $53.45 which included the tax of $3.50 for merchandise returned that had been sold on account.

April 24 Received $299.95 from Victor Cardona on account.
25 Sold merchandise on account to Kellie Cokley, $179.50 plus tax of $12.57. Sale no. 46.
26 Received $250.65 from Susan Haberman on account.
28 Sold merchandise on account to Kenneth Watt, $49.95 plus tax of $3.50. Sale no. 47.
30 Bank credit card sales for the month are $1,220.00 plus tax of $85.40. Bank credit card expense on these sales is $65.27.
30 Cash sales for the month are $2,000.00 plus tax of $140.00.

Hunt had the following general ledger account balances as of April 1:

Account Title	Account No.	General Ledger Balance on 4/1
Cash	111	$5,000.00
Accounts Receivable	131	1,208.63
Sales Tax Payable	221	72.52
Sales	411	8,421.49
Sales Returns & Allowances	411.1	168.43
Bank Credit Card Expense	553	215.00

Hunt also had the following accounts receivable ledger account balances as of April 1:

Customer	Accounts Receivable Balance
Victor Cardona 6300 Washington Blvd. St. Louis, MO 63130-9523	$299.95
Kellie Cokley 4220 Kingsbury Blvd. St. Louis, MO 63130-1645	$99.95
Susan Haberman 9421 Garden Ct. Kirkwood, MO 63122-1878	$79.98
Glenn Kelly 6612 Arundel Pl. Clayton, MO 63150-9266	$379.50
Tera Scherrer 315 W. Linden St. Webster Groves, MO 63119-9881	$149.50
Kenneth Watt 11742 Fawnridge Dr. St. Louis, MO 63131-1726	$199.75

Required

1. Open a T account general ledger and a T account subsidiary accounts receivable ledger for Hunt's Audio-Video Store as of April 1 of the current year. Enter the April 1 balance of each of the above accounts in the T accounts on the appropriate side, with a check mark to the left of each balance.

2. Enter each transaction either in a three-column sales journal, a six-column cash receipts journal, or a general journal.

3. Post directly from each of the three journals to the proper customers' accounts in the subsidiary accounts receivable ledger. Each subsidiary ledger account should show the initials "S," "CR," or "J," followed by the appropriate journal page number as a posting reference for each transaction.

4. Enter the totals and rule the sales journal and the cash receipts journal. Foot the general journal to prove the equality of debits and credits. Complete the summary posting of the cash receipts and sales journals and the individual posting of the general journal to the proper general ledger accounts. Each general ledger account should show the initials "S," "CR," or "J," followed by the appropriate journal page number as a posting reference for each transaction.

5. Foot and balance all general and subsidiary ledger accounts.

6. Prove the balance of the summary accounts receivable account by preparing a schedule of accounts receivable as of April 30, based on the subsidiary accounts receivable ledger.

SOLUTION

1, 3, 4, 5.

Accounts Receivable Ledger

Victor Cardona

19--				19--		
Apr.	1 Bal. √		299.95	Apr. 24	CR8	299.95
	11	S5	534.95			
			834.90			
			534.95			

Kellie Cokley

19--				19--		
Apr.	1 Bal. √		99.95	Apr. 10	CR8	99.95
	25	S5	192.07			
			292.02			
			192.07			

Susan Haberman

19--				19--		
Apr.	1 Bal. √		79.98	Apr. 26	CR8	250.65
	3	S5	170.67			
	17	S5	406.55			
			657.20			
			406.55			

Tera Scherrer

19--				19--		
Apr.	1 Bal. √		149.50	Apr. 6	CR8	69.50
	19	S5	64.15			
			213.65			
			144.15			

1, 3, 4, 5.   Accounts Receivable Ledger (Continued)

Glenn Kelly

19--				19--			
Apr. 1	Bal. ✓		379.50	Apr. 21		J7	53.45
4	S5		320.95				
			700.45				
			647.00				

Kenneth Watt

19--				19--			
Apr. 1	Bal. ✓		199.75	Apr. 7		J7	42.75
28	S5		53.45	14		CR8	157.00
			253.20				199.75
			53.45				

General Ledger

Cash   111

19--			
Apr. 1	Bal. ✓	5,000.00	
30	CR8	4,257.18	
		9,257.18	

Bank Credit Card Exp.   553

19--			
Apr. 1	Bal. ✓	215.00	
30	CR8	65.27	
		280.27	

Accounts Receivable   131

19--				19--			
Apr. 1	Bal. ✓	1,208.63		Apr. 7	J7		42.75
30	S5	1,742.79		21	J7		53.45
		2,951.42		30	CR8		877.05
		1,978.17					973.25

Sales   411

				19--			
				Apr. 1	Bal. ✓		8,421.49
				30	S5		1,628.75
				30	CR8		3,220.00
							13,270.24

Sales Tax Payable   221

19--				19--			
Apr. 7	J7		2.80	Apr. 1	Bal. ✓		72.52
21	J7		3.50	30	S5		114.04
			6.30	30	CR8		225.40
							411.96
							405.66

Sales Returns & Allow.   411.1

19--			
Apr. 1	Bal. ✓	168.43	
7	J7	39.95	
21	J7	49.95	
		258.33	

4.

		CASH RECEIPTS JOURNAL					
	DATE	ACCOUNT CREDITED	POST. REF.	GENERAL CR.			
1	19-- Apr. 6	Tera Scherrer	✓				1
2	10	Kellie Cokley	✓				2
3	14	Kenneth Watt	✓				3
4	24	Victor Cardona	✓				4
5	26	Susan Haberman	✓				5
6	30						6
7	30						7
8							8
9							9

2.

	DATE		DESCRIPTION	POST. REF.	DEBIT	CREDIT	
			GENERAL JOURNAL			PAGE 7	
1	19-- Apr.	7	Sales Returns & Allowances	411.1	3 9 95		1
2			Sales Tax Payable	221	2 80		2
3			Accounts Receivable (K. Watt)	131/✓		4 2 75	3
4							4
5		21	Sales Returns & Allowances	411.1	4 9 95		5
6			Sales Tax Payable	221	3 50		6
7			Accounts Receivable (G. Kelly)	131/✓		5 3 45	7
8					9 6 20	9 6 20	8

2, 3, 4.

	DATE		SALE NO.	TO WHOM SOLD	POST. REF.	ACCOUNTS RECEIVABLE DR.	SALES CR.	SALES TAX PAYABLE CR.	
				SALES JOURNAL				PAGE 5	
1	19-- Apr.	3	41	Susan Haberman	✓	1 7 0 67	1 5 9 50	1 1 17	1
2		4	42	Glenn Kelly	✓	3 2 0 95	2 9 9 95	2 1 00	2
3		11	43	Victor Cardona	✓	5 3 4 95	4 9 9 95	3 5 00	3
4		17	44	Susan Haberman	✓	4 0 6 55	3 7 9 95	2 6 60	4
5		19	45	Tera Scherrer	✓	6 4 15	5 9 95	4 20	5
6		25	46	Kellie Cokley	✓	1 9 2 07	1 7 9 50	1 2 57	6
7		28	47	Kenneth Watt	✓	5 3 45	4 9 95	3 50	7
8		30				1 7 4 2 79	1 6 2 8 75	1 1 4 04	8
9						(131)	(411)	(221)	9

	ACCOUNTS RECEIV. CR.	SALES CR.	SALES TAX PAY. CR.	BANK CREDIT CARD EXPENSE DR.	CASH DR.	
					PAGE 8	
1	6 9 50				6 9 50	1
2	9 9 95				9 9 95	2
3	1 5 7 00				1 5 7 00	3
4	2 9 9 95				2 9 9 95	4
5	2 5 0 65				2 5 0 65	5
6		1 2 2 0 00	8 5 40	6 5 27	1 2 4 0 13	6
7		2 0 0 0 00	1 4 0 00		2 1 4 0 00	7
8	8 7 7 05	3 2 2 0 00	2 2 5 40	6 5 27	4 2 5 7 18	8
9	(131)	(411)	(221)	(553)	(111)	9

6.

Hunt's Audio-Video Store Schedule of Accounts Receivable April 30, 19--				
Victor Cardona		5	3 4	95
Kellie Cokley		1	9 2	07
Susan Haberman		4	0 6	55
Glenn Kelly		6	4 7	00
Tera Scherrer		1	4 4	15
Kenneth Watt			5 3	45
	1	9	7 8	17

SERIES A

EXERCISES

APPLYING ACCOUNTING CONCEPTS

EXERCISE 11A1

Sales Documents

1 For each document or procedure listed below, indicate whether it would be used for a retail business, or a wholesale business.

1. sales ticket
2. sales invoice
3. credit approval
4. cash register tape summary
5. credit memorandum
6. customer purchase order

EXERCISE 11A2

Sales Transactions and Accounts

2 Using T accounts for Cash, Accounts Receivable, Sales Tax Payable, Sales, Sales Returns and Allowances, and Sales Discounts, enter the following sales transactions.

1. No sales tax.
  (a) Merchandise is sold for $300 cash.
  (b) Merchandise is sold on account for $285.
  (c) Payment is received for merchandise sold on account.
2. 5% sales tax.
  (a) Merchandise is sold for $300 cash plus sales tax.
  (b) Merchandise is sold on account for $285 plus sales tax.
  (c) Payment is received for merchandise sold on account.
3. Cash and credit sales, with returned merchandise.
  (a) Merchandise is sold for $325 cash.
  (b) $25 of merchandise sold for $325 is returned for refund.
  (c) Merchandise is sold on account for $350.
  (d) $35 of merchandise sold for $350 is returned for a credit.
  (e) Payment is received for balance owed on merchandise sold on account.
4. 5% sales tax, with returned merchandise.
  (a) Merchandise is sold on account for $400 plus sales tax.
  (b) Merchandise totaling $40 is returned.

(c) Balance on account is paid in cash.

(d) Merchandise is sold for $280 cash plus sales tax.

(e) $20 of merchandise sold for $280 cash is returned for refund.

5. Sales on account, with 2/10, n/30 cash discount.

(a) Merchandise is sold on account for $350.

(b) The balance is paid within the discount period.

EXERCISE 11A3

Computing Net Sales

2 Based on the following information, compute net sales.

Gross sales	$3,580
Sales returns and allowances	428
Sales discounts	73

EXERCISE 11A4

Journalizing Sales Transactions

3 Enter the following transactions (a) in a general journal, and (b) in a sales journal. Use a 6% sales tax rate.

May 1 Sold $2,000 merchandise on account plus sales tax (receipt no. 488—J. Adams).

4 Sold $1,800 merchandise on account plus sales tax (receipt no. 489—B. Clark).

8 Sold $1,500 merchandise on account plus sales tax (receipt no. 490—A. Duck).

11 Sold $1,950 merchandise on account plus sales tax (receipt no. 491—E. Hill).

EXERCISE 11A5

Journalizing Sales Returns and Allowances

3 Enter the following transactions in a general journal and post them to the appropriate general ledger and accounts receivable ledger accounts.

June 1 John B. Adams returned $56 of merchandise previously purchased on account (receipt no. 329).

6 Marie L. Philips returned $33 of merchandise previously purchased on account (receipt no. 321).

8 L. B. Greene returned $28 of merchandise previously purchased on account (receipt no. 299).

EXERCISE 11A6

Journalizing Cash Receipts

4 Enter the following transactions (a) in a general journal and (b) in a cash receipts journal.

July 3 James Alcott paid $300 on account.

10 Cash sales for the week, $1,280.

14 Betty Harris paid $248 on account.

15 J. L. Brett paid $189 on account.

18 Cash sales for the week, $1,322.

EXERCISE 11A7

Schedule of Accounts Receivable

5 From the accounts receivable ledger shown, prepare a schedule of accounts receivable as of August 31, 19--.

ACCOUNTS RECEIVABLE SUBSIDIARY LEDGER

NAME B & G Distributors   TERMS 2/10, n/30

ADDRESS 2628 Burlington Avenue, Chicago, IL 60604

DATE		ITEM	POST. REF.	DEBIT	CREDIT	BALANCE
19-- Aug.	3		S1		1 3 8 0 00	1 3 8 0 00
	8		J1	1 4 0 00		1 2 4 0 00

NAME P. L. Davis   TERMS 2/10, n/30

ADDRESS 1422 SW Pacific, Chicago, IL 60603

DATE		ITEM	POST. REF.	DEBIT	CREDIT	BALANCE
19-- Aug.	5		S1		2 1 3 6 00	2 1 3 6 00
	11		CR1	2 1 3 6 00		-0-

NAME B. J. Hinschliff & Co.   TERMS 2/10, n/30

ADDRESS 133 College Blvd, Des Plaines, IL 60611

DATE		ITEM	POST. REF.	DEBIT	CREDIT	BALANCE
19-- Aug.	15		S1		1 1 0 6 00	1 1 0 6 00
	21		S1		3 8 4 00	1 4 9 0 00

NAME Sally M. Pitts   TERMS 2/10, n/30

ADDRESS 213 East 29th Place, Chicago, IL 60601

DATE		ITEM	POST. REF.	DEBIT	CREDIT	BALANCE
19-- Aug.	21		S1		8 3 8 00	8 3 8 00

NAME Trendsetter, Inc.   TERMS 2/10, n/30

ADDRESS 28 Industrial Way, Chicago, IL 60600

DATE		ITEM	POST. REF.	DEBIT	CREDIT	BALANCE
19-- Aug.	28		S1		1 0 1 8 00	1 0 1 8 00

PROBLEMS

PROBLEM 11A1

| Sales Journal |

3 J. K. Bekins owns a retail business and made the following sales during the month of August, 19--. There is a 5% sales tax on all sales.

Aug. 1 Sale no. 213, $2,800 plus sales tax to Jones Manufacturing Co.
3 Sale no. 214, $3,300 plus sales tax to R. B. Smith & Co.
7 Sale no. 215, $1,210 plus sales tax to Andy Harris, Inc.
11 Sale no. 216, $2,440 plus sales tax to Ardis McKenzie.
18 Sale no. 217, $3,100 plus sales tax to R. B. Smith & Co.
22 Sale no. 218, $1,100 plus sales tax to Jones Manufacturing Co.
30 Sale no. 219, $2,810 plus sales tax to Ardis McKenzie.

Required
1. Record the transactions in the sales journal. Total and rule the journal and prove column totals.
2. Post from the sales journal to the general ledger accounts and to the accounts receivable ledger accounts.

PROBLEM 11A2

| Cash Receipts Journal |

4 Zebra Imaginarium, a retail business, had the following cash receipts during December, 19--. The sales tax is 6%.

Dec. 1 Received $1,360 on account from Michael Anderson.
2 Received $382 on account from Ansel Manufacturing.
7 Cash receipts for the week, $3,160 plus sales tax. Bank credit card charges for the week, $1,000 plus sales tax. Bank credit card fee is 3%.
8 Received $880 on account from W. J. Beemer.
11 Michael Anderson returned $60 of merchandise for a credit.
14 Cash receipts for the week, $2,800 plus sales tax. Bank credit card charges for the week, $800 plus sales tax. Bank credit card fee is 3%.
20 Received $1,110 on account from Tom Wilson.
21 Ansel Manufacturing returned $22 of merchandise for a credit.
22 Cash receipts for the week, $3,200 plus sales tax.
24 Received $2,000 on account from Rachel Carson.

Required
1. Record the transactions in the cash receipts journal. Total and rule the journal and prove the column totals. Use the general journal to record sales returns and allowances.
2. Post the journals to the general ledger and to the accounts receivable ledger accounts.

P R O B L E M   1 1 A 3

Sales Journal, Cash Receipts Journal, General Journal

3/4 Owens Distributors is a retail business. The following sales, returns, and cash receipts are for March, 19--. There is an 8% sales tax.

March 1 Sale no. 33C, $1,800 plus sales tax to Able & Co.
       3 Sale no. 33D, $2,240 plus sales tax to R. J. Kalas, Inc.
       5 Able & Co. returned $30 of merchandise for a credit (credit memorandum no. 66).
       7 Cash receipts for the week, $3,160 plus sales tax.
      10 Received payment from Able & Co.
      11 Sale no. 33E, $1,210 plus sales tax to Blevins Bakery.
      13 Received payment from R. J. Kalas for sale 33D.
      14 Cash receipts for the week, $4,200 plus sales tax.
      16 Blevins Bakery returned $44 of merchandise for a credit (credit memorandum no. 67).
      18 Sale no. 33F, $2,620 plus sales tax to R. J. Kalas, Inc.
      20 Received payment from Blevins Bakery for sale 33E.
      21 Cash receipts for the week, $2,400 plus sales tax.
      25 Sale no. 33G, $1,915 plus sales tax to Blevins Bakery.
      27 Sale no. 33H, $2,016 plus sales tax to Thompson Group.
      28 Cash receipts for the week, $3,500 plus sales tax.

Required
1. Record the transactions in the sales journal, the cash receipts journal, and the general journal. Total and rule where appropriate at the end of the month.
2. Post from the journals to the general ledger and accounts receivable ledger accounts.

P R O B L E M   1 1 A 4

Schedule of Accounts Receivable

5 Based on the information provided in Problem 11A3, prepare a schedule of accounts receivable for Owens Distributors as of March 31, 19--. Note whether the accounts receivable account balance in the general ledger agrees with the schedule of accounts receivable total.

S E R I E S   B

E X E R C I S E S

E X E R C I S E   1 1 B 1

Sales Documents

1 Indicate whether the following documents and procedures are for a retail business or for a wholesale business.

1. A cash register receipt is given to the customer.
2. Credit approval is required since sales are almost always "on account."
3. A summary of the day's sales activities is generated for business accounting purposes.
4. Three copies of the sales invoice are prepared: one for shipping, one for the customer (as a bill), and one for accounting.
5. A sales ticket is given to a customer and another copy goes to accounting.
6. The sales process begins with a customer purchase order.

7. The sales invoice itemizes what is sold, its cost, and the total amount owed.

EXERCISE 11B2

Sales Transactions and
Accounts

2 Using T accounts for Cash, Accounts Receivable, Sales Tax Payable, Sales, Sales Returns and Allowances, and Sales Discounts, enter the following sales transactions.

1. No sales tax.
  (a) Merchandise is sold for $250 cash.
  (b) Merchandise is sold on account for $225.
  (c) Payment is received for merchandise sold on account.
2. 6% sales tax.
  (a) Merchandise is sold for $250 cash plus sales tax.
  (b) Merchandise is sold on account for $225 plus sales tax.
  (c) Payment is received for merchandise sold on account.
3. Cash and credit sales, with returned merchandise.
  (a) Merchandise is sold for $481 cash.
  (b) $18 of merchandise sold for $481 is returned for a refund.
  (c) Merchandise is sold on account for $388.
  (d) $24 of merchandise sold for $388 is returned for a credit.
  (e) Payment is received for balance owed on merchandise sold on account.
4. 6% sales tax, with returned merchandise.
  (a) Merchandise is sold on account for $480 plus sales tax.
  (b) Merchandise totaling $30 is returned.
  (c) The balance on the account is paid in cash.
  (d) Merchandise is sold for $300 cash plus sales tax.
  (e) $30 of merchandise sold for $300 cash is returned for a refund.
5. Sales on account, with 2/10, n/30 cash discount.
  (a) Merchandise is sold on account for $280.
  (b) The balance is paid within the discount period.

EXERCISE 11B3

Computing Net Sales

2 Based on the following information, compute net sales.

Gross sales	$2,880
Sales returns and allowances	322
Sales discounts	56

EXERCISE 11B4

Journalizing Sales
Transactions

3 Enter the following transactions (a) in a general journal, and (b) in a sales journal. Use a 5% sales tax rate.

Sept. 1 Sold $1,800 merchandise on account plus sales tax (sale no. 228—K. Smith).

3 Sold $3,100 merchandise on account plus sales tax (sale no. 229—J. Arnes).

5 Sold $2,800 merchandise on account plus sales tax (sale no. 230—M. Denison).

7 Sold $1,900 merchandise on account plus sales tax (sale no. 231—B. Marshall).

3 Enter the following transactions in a general journal and post them to the appropriate general ledger and accounts receivable ledger accounts.

June   1 Marie L. Phillips returned $38 of merchandise previously purchased on account (receipt no. 33).
    11 John B. Adams returned $52 of merchandise previously purchased on account (receipt no. 34).
    15 L. B. Greene returned $26 of merchandise previously purchased on account (receipt no. 35).

4 Enter the following transactions (a) in the general journal and (b) in a cash receipts journal.

Nov.   1 Jean Harris paid $500 on account.
    12 Marc Anselmo paid $323 on account.
    15 Cash sales, $3,221.
    18 Will Moon paid $286 on account.
    25 Cash sales, $2,801.

5 From the accounts receivable ledger shown, prepare a schedule of accounts receivable as of November 30, 19--.

ACCOUNTS RECEIVABLE SUBSIDIARY LEDGER

NAME   James L. Adams Co.   TERMS 2/10, n/30
ADDRESS   24481 McAdams Road, Dallas, TX 77001

DATE	ITEM	POST. REF.	DEBIT	CREDIT	BALANCE
19-- Nov. 1		S11		3 1 8 0 00	3 1 8 0 00
5		J8	1 8 0 00		3 0 0 0 00
7		S11		2 0 0 00	3 2 0 0 00

NAME   Trish Berens   TERMS 2/10, n/30
ADDRESS   34 West 55th Avenue, Fort Worth, TX 76310

DATE	ITEM	POST. REF.	DEBIT	CREDIT	BALANCE
19-- Nov. 3		S11		1 3 6 0 00	1 3 6 0 00

NAME   M and T Jenkins, Inc.   TERMS 2/10, n/30
ADDRESS   100 NW Richfield, Austin, TX 78481

DATE	ITEM	POST. REF.	DEBIT	CREDIT	BALANCE
19-- Nov. 5		S11		2 6 2 8 00	2 6 2 8 00
12		CR11	2 6 2 8 00		- 0 -

NAME	R & J Travis				TERMS	2/10, n/30
ADDRESS	288 Beacon Street, Dallas, TX 79301					

DATE	ITEM	POST. REF.	DEBIT	CREDIT	BALANCE
19-- Nov. 22		S11		1 8 4 2 00	1 8 4 2 00

PROBLEMS °

PROBLEM 11B1

Sales Journal

3 T. M. Maxwell owns a retail business and made the following sales transactions during the month of July, 19--. There is a 7% sales tax on all sales.

July 1 Sale no. 101, $1,300 plus sales tax to Andy Harris, Inc.
      8 Sale no. 102, $1,090 plus sales tax to Ardis McKenzie.
    15 Sale no. 103, $3,200 plus sales tax to Jones Manufacturing.
    21 Sale no. 104, $2,400 plus sales tax to Ardis McKenzie.
    24 Sale no. 105, $1,200 plus sales tax to R. B. Smith & Co.
    29 Sale no. 106, $2,210 plus sales tax to Andy Harris, Inc.

Required
1. Record the transactions in the sales journal. Total and rule the journal and prove column totals.
2. Post the sales journal to the general ledger accounts and to the accounts receivable ledger accounts.

PROBLEM 11B2

Cash Receipts Journal

4 Color Florists, a retail business, had the following cash receipts during January, 19--. The sales tax is 5%.

Jan. 1 Received $880 on account from Michael Anderson.
     3 Received $271 on account from W. J. Beemer.
     5 Cash receipts for the week, $2,800 plus sales tax. Bank credit card charges for the week, $1,200 plus sales tax. Bank credit card fee is 3%.
     8 Received $912 on account from Rachel Carson.
    11 Michael Anderson returned $40 of merchandise for a credit.
    12 Cash receipts for the week, $3,100 plus sales tax. Bank credit card charges for the week, $1,900 plus sales tax. Bank credit card fee is 3%.
    15 Received $1,100 on account from Tom Wilson.
    18 Tom Wilson returned $31 of merchandise for a credit.
    19 Cash receipts for the week, $2,230 plus sales tax.
    25 Received $318 on account from Ansel Manufacturing.

Required
1. Record the transactions in the cash receipts journal. Total and rule the journal and prove the column totals. Use the general journal to record sales returns and allowances.

2. Post the journals to the general ledger and to the accounts receivable ledger accounts.

3/4 Paul Jackson owns a retail business. The following sales, returns, discounts, and cash receipts are for April, 19--. There is a 7% sales tax.

April   1 Sale no. 111, $2,100 plus sales tax to O. L. Meyers.
       3 Sale no. 112, $1,000 plus sales tax to Andrew Plaa.
       6 O. L. Meyers returned $50 of merchandise from sale no. 111 for a credit (credit memorandum no. 42).
       7 Cash receipts for the week, $3,240 plus sales tax.
       9 Received payment from O. L. Meyers for sale no. 111.
      12 Sale no. 113, $980 plus sales tax to Melissa Richfield.
      14 Cash receipts for the week, $2,180 plus sales tax.
      17 Melissa Richfield returned $40 of merchandise for a credit (credit memorandum no. 43).
      19 Sale no. 114, $1,020 plus sales tax to Kelsay Munkres.
      21 Cash receipts for the week, $2,600 plus sales tax.
      24 Sale no. 115, $920 plus sales tax to O. L. Meyers.
      27 Sale no. 116, $1,320 plus sales tax to Andrew Plaa.
      28 Cash receipts for the week, $2,800 plus sales tax.

Required
1. Record the transactions in the sales journal, the cash receipts journal, and the general journal. Total and rule where appropriate at the end of the month.
2. Post from the journals to the general ledger and accounts receivable ledger accounts.

5 Based on the information provided in Problem 11B3, prepare a schedule of accounts receivable for Paul Jackson as of April 30, 19—. Note whether the accounts receivable account balance in the general ledger agrees with the schedule of accounts receivable total.

MASTERY PROBLEM

If the working papers for this textbook are not used, omit the Mastery Problem.

Geoff and Sandy Harland own and operate Wayward Kennel and Pet Supply where the motto is "If your pet is not becoming to you, he should be coming to us." The Harlands maintain a sales tax payable account throughout the month to account for the 6% sales tax. They use a sales journal, a cash receipts journal, and a general journal. The following sales and cash collections took place during the month of September.

Sept. 1 Sold a fish aquarium on account to Ken Shank for $125.00 plus tax of $7.50, terms n/30. Sale no. 101.

      3 Sold dog food on account to Nancy Truelove for $68.25 plus tax of $4.10, terms n/30. Sale no. 102.

      5 Sold a bird cage on account to Jean Warkentin for $43.95 plus tax of $2.64, terms n/30. Sale no. 103.

      8 Cash sales for the week were $2,332.45 plus tax of $139.95.

    10 Cash received for boarding and grooming services, $625.00 plus tax of $37.50.

    11 Jean Warkentin stopped by the store to point out a minor defect in the bird cage recently purchased. The Harlands offered a sales allowance of $10.00 on the price of the cage which satisfied Jean Warkentin.

    12 Sold a cockatoo on account to Tully Shaw for $1,200.00 plus tax of $72.00, terms n/30. Sale no. 104.

    14 Received $256.00 cash on account from Jayne Brown.

    15 Jayne Brown returned merchandise sold for $93.28 including tax.

    16 Received $58.25 cash on account from Nancy Truelove.

    17 Cash sales for the week were $2,656.85 plus tax of $159.41.

    18 Cash received for boarding and grooming services $535.00 plus tax of $32.10.

    19 Received $63.25 cash on account from Ed Cochran.

    20 Sold pet supplies on account to Susan Hays for $83.33 plus tax of $5.00, terms n/30. Sale no. 105.

    21 Sold three Labrador Retriever puppies to All American Day Camp for $375.00 plus tax of $22.50, terms n/30. Sale no. 106.

    22 Cash sales for the week were $3,122.45 plus tax of $187.35.

    23 Cash received for boarding and grooming services $515.00 plus tax of $30.90.

    25 Received $132.50 cash on account from Ken Shank.

    26 Received $72.35 cash on account from Nancy Truelove.

    27 Received $273.25 cash on account from Joe Gloy.

    28 Borrowed $11,000.00 to be used for the purchase of a pet limousine.

    29 Cash sales for the week were $2,835.45 plus tax of $170.13.

    30 Cash received for boarding and grooming services $488.00 plus tax of $29.28.

Required

1. Enter the transactions for the month of September in the proper journals.
2. Enter the totals and rule the journals where appropriate.
3. Post the entries to the general and subsidiary ledgers.
4. Prepare a schedule of accounts receivable.
5. Compute the net sales for the month of September.

Chapter 11 Demonstration Problem

The following instructions show you how to complete the Chapter 11 demonstration problem. Refer to Appendix A for additional help as you complete this problem and Problems 11A3 and 11B3.

STEP 1   Load the Electronic Problem Solver software and the opening balance file for Demonstration Problem D-11.

STEP 2   Select the Options Menu and the General Information screen. Enter a date of 04/30/-- (current year) and your name. Do not change any buttons (these buttons indicate that this is a sole proprietorship and a merchandising business). Press Enter on Ok or press the Ctrl key and the Enter key simultaneously.

STEP 3   Enter all April transactions selecting either the Sales Journal, Cash Receipts Journal, or the General Journal command from the Journals menu. You must use a customer number when you enter the Accounts Receivable account. Press the F3 key to display a customer list showing customer numbers. The computer automatically debits the Accounts Receivable account on the sales journal (figure AC11-1). The computer automatically debits the Cash account on the cash receipts journal (figure AC11-2). Use the general journal to enter sales returns (figure AC11-3).

FIGURE AC11-1 **Sales Journal Data Entry**

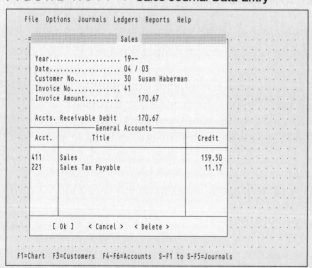

FIGURE AC11-2 **Cash Receipts Journal Data Entry**

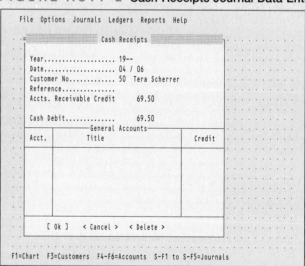

STEP 4   After you enter all transactions, select the Journals command from the Reports menu, and press the space bar to place an X in each box to display the general journal, sales journal, and cash receipts journal. Press Enter on Ok.

STEP 5 The Selection Options should display a date range of 04/01/-- to 04/30/-- to indicate the default range (all transactions). Change the date range if necessary. Press Enter on Ok.

STEP 6 Each journal will be displayed showing the April transactions. (Figure AC11-4 shows the sales journal display.)

FIGURE AC11-3 **General Journal Data Entry**   FIGURE AC11-4 **Sales Journal Display**

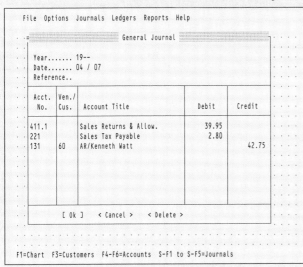

```
File Options Journals Ledgers Reports Help

===============General Journal================

Year....... 19--
Date....... 04 / 07
Reference..

Acct. |Ven./
No.   |Cus. |Account Title        |Debit |Credit

411.1 |     |Sales Returns & Allow.|39.95 |
221   |     |Sales Tax Payable     | 2.80 |
131   | 60  |AR/Kenneth Watt       |      | 42.75




      [ Ok ]    < Cancel >    < Delete >


F1=Chart  F3=Customers  F4-F6=Accounts  S-F1 to S-F5=Journals
```

```
File Options Journals Ledgers Reports Help
=
                Hunt's Audio-Video Store
                      Sales Journal
                       04/30/--

Date  Refer.  V/C Acct.  Title             Debit    Credit
04/03  41     30  131   AR/Susan Haberman  170.67
04/03  41         411   Sales                       159.50
04/03  41         221   Sales Tax Payable            11.17

04/04  42     40  131   AR/Glenn Kelly     320.95
04/04  42         411   Sales                       299.95
04/04  42         221   Sales Tax Payable            21.00

04/11  43     10  131   AR/Victor Cardona  534.95
04/11  43         411   Sales                       499.95
04/11  43         221   Sales Tax Payable            35.00



↑↓  PgUp  PgDn  Home  End  F9=Print  Esc=Close Window
```

STEP 7 If you need to correct your transactions, refer to section in Appendix A titled Corrections to Journal Entries.

STEP 8 Display ledger reports by selecting the Ledgers command from the Reports menu. Press the space bar to place an X in each box to display the general ledger, schedule of accounts receivable, and accounts receivable ledger. Press Enter on Ok.

STEP 9 Press Enter on Ok to accept the account number range (general ledger) and the customer number range (accounts receivable ledger).

STEP 10 The general ledger will show the April transactions and account activity and balances for each account. The schedule of accounts receivable will display account balances as of April 30 for each customer. The accounts receivable ledger will show the April transactions and account activity and balances for each customer.

STEP 11 Choose the Save As command from the File menu, and save your solution on a data disk under a file name such as D-11XXX (XXX=your initials). Choose the Quit option from the File menu to end your session.

381

LEARNING OBJECTIVES

Careful study of this chapter should enable you to:

1. Define merchandise purchases transactions.

2. Account for merchandise purchases.

3. Describe and use the purchases journal and accounts payable ledger.

4. Describe and use the cash payments journal and accounts payable ledger.

5. Prepare a schedule of accounts payable.

*A*ccounting for Purchases and Cash Payments

In Chapter 11 we learned how to account for sales in a merchandising business. This chapter continues the study of the merchandising business by examining how to account for merchandise purchases using the accrual basis of accounting. We will learn how to use four new accounts, two more special journals, and another subsidiary ledger.

1

Define merchandise purchases transactions.

MERCHANDISE PURCHASES TRANSACTIONS

In everyday language, purchases can refer to almost anything we have bought. For a merchandising business, however, **purchases** refers to merchandise acquired for resale. These are the goods a business buys for the sole purpose of selling them to its customers.

Purchasing procedures and documents can vary, depending on the nature and size of a business. For example, in a small business, the buying might be done by the owner or a single employee, and might require only part-time attention. In a large business, there might be a separate purchasing department with a full-time manager and staff. In addition, the procedures and documents used can be affected by whether purchases are made on account or for cash.

The flowchart in figure 12-1 shows some of the major documents used in the purchasing process of a merchandising business. In discussing the purchasing process, a business that makes purchases on account and has a purchasing department is illustrated.

FIGURE 12-1 **Purchasing Process Documents**

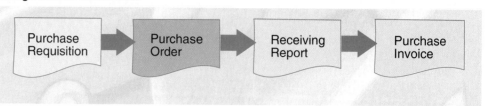

Purchase Requisition

A **purchase requisition** is a form used to request the purchasing department to purchase merchandise or other property. Any authorized person or department can prepare this form. Figure 12-2 shows a purchase requisition used by Northern Micro. One copy of this form is sent to the purchasing department and one is kept by the department that prepared the requisition.

FIGURE 12-2 **Purchase Requisition**

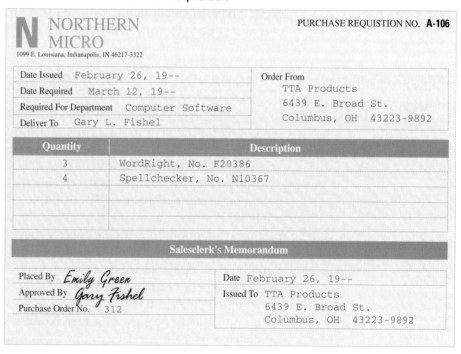

Purchase Order

The purchasing department reviews and approves the purchase requisition and prepares a purchase order. A **purchase order** is a written order to buy goods from a specific vendor (supplier). Figure 12-3 shows a purchase order prepared by Northern Micro based on the purchase requisition in figure 12-2. One copy of the purchase order is sent to the vendor to order the goods, and one copy is kept in the purchasing department. Other copies can be sent to the accounting department, the department that prepared the purchase requisition, and the receiving area.

FIGURE 12-3 **Purchase Order**

Receiving Report and Purchase Invoice

When the merchandise is received, a **receiving report** indicating what has been received is prepared. The receiving report can be a separate form, or a copy of the vendor's purchase invoice can be used for this purpose. A rubber stamp has been used to imprint a type of receiving report on the face of the vendor invoice in figure 12-4. The receiving clerk has indicated on the form the date and condition of the goods received.

FIGURE 12-4 **Purchase Invoice**

DATE	March 2, 19--			INVOICE NO. **4194H**	
TERMS	2/10, n/30		**TTA** **Products** 6439 E. Broad St. Columbus, OH 43223-9892	OUR ORDER NO. 7043	YOUR ORDER NO. 312
SHIPPED BY	Truck			SOLD TO	
SALESPERSON	Halpin			Northern Micro 1099 E. Louisiana Indianapolis, IN 46217-3322	

QUANTITY	DESCRIPTION	PRODUCT NO.	UNIT PRICE	AMOUNT
3	WordRight	F20386	180.00	540.00
4	Spellchecker	N10367	75.00	300.00
				840.00

Date received _____ March 3
Received by _____ LM
Items OK _____ LM
Prices OK _____ LM
Ext. and total OK _____ JR
Invoice no. _____ 42
FOB _____
Freight bill no. _____ 4140
Freight charge _____ 29.50
Approval for payment _____ T.J.Q.

A document prepared by the seller as a bill for the merchandise shipped is called an **invoice.** To the seller, this is a sales invoice, as explained in Chapter 11. To the buyer, this is a **purchase invoice.** Figure 12-4 shows an invoice sent by TTA Products to Northern Micro for the goods ordered with the purchase order in figure 12-3.

The accounting department compares the purchase invoice with the purchase requisition, purchase order, and receiving report. If the invoice is for the goods ordered and the correct price, the invoice is paid by the due date.

Cash and Trade Discounts

Notice that the invoice in figure 12-4 shows terms of 2/10, n/30. These are the same credit terms discussed in Chapter 11. A discount is available if the bill is paid within the discount period. The only difference is that we are now looking from the buyer's point of view rather than the seller's. We will see how to account for these discounts later in the chapter.

Another type of discount, called a **trade discount,** is often offered by manufacturers and wholesalers. This discount is a reduction from the list or catalog price offered to different classes of customers. Trade discounts are usually shown as a deduction from the total amount of the invoice. For example, the invoice in figure 12-5 includes a trade discount of 10%. The amount to be entered in the accounting records for this invoice is $756, the net amount after deducting the trade discount of $84. Trade discounts represent a reduction in the price of the merchandise and should not be entered in the accounts of either the seller or the buyer.

FIGURE 12-5 **Purchase Invoice with Trade Discount**

We need to be careful in computing the cash discount when an invoice has both cash and trade discounts. The cash discount applies to the *net amount* after deducting the trade discount. For example, the cash discount and amount to be paid on the invoice in figure 12-5 would be calculated as follows:

Gross amount	$840.00
Less 10% trade discount	84.00
Net amount	$756.00
Less 2% cash discount	15.12
Amount to be paid	$740.88

2

Account for merchandise purchases accounts.

MERCHANDISE PURCHASES ACCOUNTS

To account for merchandise purchases transactions, we need to know how to use four new accounts.

1. Purchases
2. Purchases Returns and Allowances
3. Purchases Discounts
4. Freight In

Purchases Account

The purchases account is a temporary owner's equity account in which the cost of merchandise purchased is debited.

Purchases

Debit to enter the cost of merchandise purchased.

If a $100 purchase is made for cash, the following entry is made.

3		Purchases	1 0 0 00		3
4		Cash		1 0 0 00	4

If the same purchase is made on account, the entry is:

3		Purchases	1 0 0 00		3
4		Accounts Payable		1 0 0 00	4

Purchases Returns and Allowances Account

Purchases Returns and Allowances is a temporary owner's equity account in which purchases returns and purchases allowances are credited. It is a contra-purchases account reported as a deduction from Purchases on the income statement.

Purchases returns and allowances are similar to the sales returns and allowances we discussed in Chapter 11. We are simply looking at returns and allowances from the buyer's point of view. If merchandise is returned to a supplier, or the supplier grants a price reduction because of defects or other problems with merchandise purchased, Purchases Returns and Allowances is credited.

Purchases Returns and Allowances

	Credit to enter the cost of merchandise returned and allowances received.

If merchandise that was purchased on account for $200 is defective and is returned to the supplier, the following entry is made:

9		Accounts Payable		2 0 0 00			9
10		Purchases Returns and Allowances			2 0 0 00		10

If the same merchandise is retained but the supplier grants a price reduction of $45 because of the defects, the entry would be:

12		Accounts Payable		4 5 00			12
13		Purchases Returns and Allowances			4 5 00		13

Purchases Discounts Account

Purchases Discounts is a temporary owner's equity account in which any cash discounts allowed on purchases are credited. Like Purchases Returns and Allowances, Purchases Discounts is a contra-purchases account reported as a deduction from Purchases on the income statement.

Purchases Discounts

	Credit for cash discounts taken.

If merchandise is purchased for $100 on account, with credit terms of 2/10, n/30, the following entry is made.

15		Purchases		1 0 0 00			15
16		Accounts Payable			1 0 0 00		16

If payment for the merchandise is subsequently made within the discount period, the entry is:

18		Accounts Payable		1 0 0 00			18
19		Cash			9 8 00		19
20		Purchases Discounts			2 00		20

Note the parts of this entry. Accounts Payable is debited for $100, the full amount of the invoice, because the entire debt has been paid. Cash is credited for only $98 because that is all that was required to pay the debt. The difference of $2 ($100 − $98) is credited to Purchases Discounts, which represents a reduction in the purchase price of the merchandise. That is why Purchases Discounts is deducted from Purchases on the income statement.

Freight-In Account

Freight-In is a cost of goods sold account in which transportation charges on merchandise purchases are debited. Freight-In is reported as an addition to Purchases on the income statement.

Freight-In

Debit for transportation charges on merchandise purchases.	

Transportation charges are expressed in FOB (free on board) terms, that indicate who is responsible for paying the freight costs. **FOB shipping point** means that transportation charges are paid by the buyer. **FOB destination** means that transportation charges are paid by the seller.

When the terms are FOB shipping point, either the freight charges will be listed separately on the purchase invoice, or a separate freight bill will be sent. Assume Northern Micro receives an invoice for $400 plus freight charges of $38. The entry for this purchase is:

22		Purchases		4 0 0 00		22
23		Freight-In		3 8 00		23
24		Accounts Payable			4 3 8 00	24

Assume instead that Northern Micro receives an invoice for $400 for the same merchandise, shipped FOB shipping point. Northern Micro then receives a separate bill from the transportation company for $38. These two transactions are entered as follows.

22		Purchases		4 0 0 00		22
23		Accounts Payable			4 0 0 00	23
24						24
25		Freight-In		3 8 00		25
26		Accounts Payable			3 8 00	26

When the terms are FOB destination, generally no freight charges appear on the purchase invoice. The buyer simply records the purchase at the amount of the invoice. The Freight-In account is not used in recording this purchase.

Computation of Gross Profit

Gross profit is the difference between net sales and cost of merchandise sold.

An important step in determining net income for a merchandising business is the calculation of its gross profit. **Gross profit** (also called **gross margin**) is the difference between net sales and cost of merchandise sold. Gross profit provides very important information. It tells management the amount of sales dollars available to cover expenses after covering the cost of the merchandise sold.

By using three of the four new accounts described in Chapter 11, the four new accounts described above, and the merchandise inventory balances, we can compute gross profit. To illustrate, assume that Northern Micro has the following sales, purchases, and merchandise inventory balances for the year ended December 31, 19--.

Sales	$200,500
Sales returns and allowances	1,200
Purchases	105,000
Purchases returns and allowances	800
Purchases discounts	1,000
Freight-In	300
Merchandise inventory, January 1, 19--	26,000
Merchandise inventory, December 31, 19--	18,000

Use these balances to compute net sales, net purchases, cost of merchandise sold, and gross profit, as shown in figure 12-6. The following four steps in computing gross profit are labeled in the figure.

STEP 1   Compute net sales.

STEP 2   Compute merchandise available for sale.

STEP 3   Compute cost of merchandise sold.

STEP 4   Compute gross profit.
(Net sales − cost of merchandise sold = gross profit)

FIGURE 12-6 **Computation of Gross Profit**

Sales				200 5 0 0 00	
Less: Sales returns and allowances				1 2 0 0 00	
Net sales					199 3 0 0 00
Cost of merchandise sold					
Merchandise inventory, Jan. 1				26 0 0 0 00	
Purchases			105 0 0 0 00		
Less: Purchases returns and allow.	8 0 0 00				
Purchases discounts	1 0 0 0 00		1 8 0 0 00		
Net purchases			103 2 0 0 00		
Add freight-in			3 0 0 00		
Cost of merchandise purchased				103 5 0 0 00	
Merchandise available for sale				129 5 0 0 00	
Less merchandise inventory, Dec. 31				18 0 0 0 00	
Cost of merchandise sold					111 5 0 0 00
Gross profit					87 8 0 0 00

Figure 12-6 also illustrates the computation of cost of merchandise sold. Cost of merchandise sold is the beginning inventory plus the merchandise available for sale minus the ending inventory.

> Cost of Merchandise Sold:
> Beginning Inventory + Merchandise Available for Sale − Ending Inventory

JOURNALIZING AND POSTING PURCHASES TRANSACTIONS

3

Describe and use the purchases journal and accounts payable ledger.

To illustrate the journalizing and posting of purchases transactions, we will continue with the transactions of Northern Micro. Assume the following purchases on account occurred during the month of April.

Apr. 4 Purchased merchandise from Compucraft, $3,300. Invoice no. 631, dated Apr. 2, terms n/30.

8 Purchased merchandise from Datasoft, $2,500. Invoice no. 632, dated Apr. 6, terms n/30.

Apr. 11 Purchased merchandise from EZX, $8,700. Invoice no. 633, dated Apr. 9, terms 1/15, n/30.

17 Purchased merchandise from Printpro, $800. Invoice no. 634, dated Apr. 16, terms n/30.

23 Purchased merchandise from Televax, $5,300. Invoice no. 635, dated Apr. 22, terms 1/10, n/30.

These transactions could be entered in a general journal as shown in figure 12-7.

FIGURE 12-7 **Purchases Entered in General Journal**

	DATE		DESCRIPTION	POST. REF.	DEBIT	CREDIT	
			GENERAL JOURNAL			PAGE 1	
1	19-- Apr.	4	Purchases		3 3 0 0 00		1
2			Accounts Payable			3 3 0 0 00	2
3			Purchase no. 631				3
4							4
5		8	Purchases		2 5 0 0 00		5
6			Accounts Payable			2 5 0 0 00	6
7			Purchase no. 632				7
8							8
9		11	Purchases		8 7 0 0 00		9
10			Accounts Payable			8 7 0 0 00	10
11			Purchase no. 633				11
12							12
13		17	Purchases		8 0 0 00		13
14			Accounts Payable			8 0 0 00	14
15			Purchase no. 634				15
16							16
17		23	Purchases		5 3 0 0 00		17
18			Accounts Payable			5 3 0 0 00	18
19			Purchase no. 635				19

The same problem occurs with this approach to recording purchases that occurred in Chapter 11 with sales transactions. The same account titles had to be recorded five times to make these five entries. Similarly, to post these entries to the general ledger, five separate postings would have to be made to each of the two accounts, a total of ten postings.

Fortunately, there is a more efficient way to record purchases on account. A purchases journal is used.

Purchases Journal

A **purchases journal** is a special journal used to record only purchases on account. By using a purchases journal, both journalizing and posting of purchases on account can be much more efficient.

Using a purchases journal can make both journalizing and posting much more efficient.

To illustrate, let's reconsider the five purchases on account of Northern Micro. They are entered in the purchases journal in figure 12-8. Northern Micro's purchases journal has a single column for Purchases Dr./Accounts Payable Cr., the two accounts used repeatedly in the general journal in figure 12-7. A purchase is recorded in the purchases journal by entering the following information:

1. Date
2. Invoice number
3. Supplier (from Whom Purchased)
4. Dollar amount

There is no need to enter any general ledger account titles.

FIGURE 12-8 **Northern Micro Purchases Journal**

	DATE	INVOICE NO.	FROM WHOM PURCHASED	POST. REF.	PURCHASES DR. ACCTS. PAY. CR.	
1	19-- Apr. 4	631	Compucraft		3 3 0 0 00	1
2	8	632	Datasoft		2 5 0 0 00	2
3	11	633	EZX Corp		8 7 0 0 00	3
4	17	634	Printpro Corp		8 0 0 00	4
5	23	635	Televax, Inc		5 3 0 0 00	5
6	30				20 6 0 0 00	6

(Table title: PURCHASES JOURNAL — PAGE 8)

The purchases journal in figure 12-8 is designed for a company like Northern Micro, whose suppliers generally pay freight charges. For a company that frequently pays freight charges as part of the purchase price of merchandise, a purchases journal like the one in figure 12-9 would be used. In this case, there are three columns: (1) Purchases Dr., (2) Freight-In Dr., and (3) Accounts Payable Cr. Each special journal should be designed for the particular needs of the company using it.

FIGURE 12-9 **Purchases Journal with Freight-In Column**

	DATE	INVOICE NO.	FROM WHOM PURCHASED	POST. REF.	PURCHASES DR.	FREIGHT-IN DR.	ACCTS. PAY. CR.	

(Table title: PURCHASES JOURNAL)

Posting from the Purchases Journal

Each general ledger account used in the purchases journal requires only one posting each period. Figure 12-10 illustrates the general ledger posting process for Northern Micro's purchases journal for the month of April.

FIGURE 12-10 **Posting the Purchases Journal to the General Ledger**

PURCHASES JOURNAL — Page 8

Date	Invoice No.	From Whom Purchased	Post Ref.	Purchases Dr./ Accts. Pay. Cr.
19--				
Apr. 4	631	Compucraft		3,300.00
8	632	Datasoft		2,500.00
11	633	EZX Corp.		8,700.00
17	634	Printpro Corp.		800.00
23	635	Televax, Inc.		5,300.00
30				20,600.00
				(511) (218)

GENERAL LEDGER (Partial)

ACCOUNT Accounts Payable   ACCOUNT No. 218

Date	Item	Post. Ref.	Debit	Credit	Balance Debit	Balance Credit
19--						
Apr. 1	Bal.	✓				8,800.00
30		P8		20,600.00		29,400.00

ACCOUNT Purchases   ACCOUNT No. 511

Date	Item	Post. Ref.	Debit	Credit	Balance Debit	Balance Credit
19--						
Apr. 1	Bal.	✓			16,500.00	
30		P8	20,600.00		37,100.00	

The steps in the procedure of posting from the purchases journal to the general ledger are indicated in figure 12-10, as follows:

STEP 1 Foot the amount column and post the total to the Purchases and Accounts Payable accounts in the general ledger.

STEP 2 Insert the date in the Date column, and the initial "P" and the purchases journal page number in the Posting Reference column of each ledger account.

STEP 3 Insert the Purchases and Accounts Payable account numbers immediately below the column total in the purchases journal.

The Purchases and Accounts Payable resulting from merchandise purchases on account are now up to date in the general ledger. A record can be kept of the amount owed to each supplier by using a **subsidiary accounts payable ledger.** This is a separate ledger containing an individual account payable for each supplier. A summary account payable called a controlling account is maintained in the general ledger. The accounts payable ledger is "subsidiary" to this account.

The use of the accounts payable ledger is illustrated in figure 12-11. This ledger is posted daily. Procedures for posting from the purchases journal to the accounts payable ledger are as listed on page 397 and as shown in figure 12-11.

FIGURE 12-11 Posting the Purchases Journal to the Accounts Payable Ledger

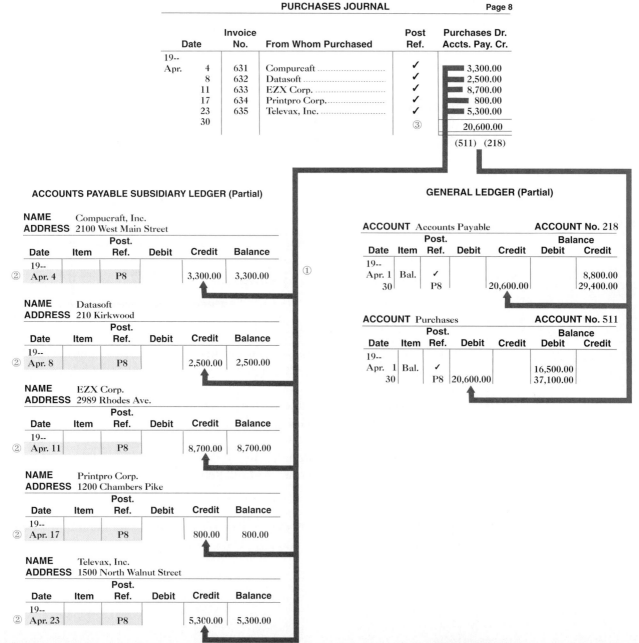

STEP 1   Post the individual purchase amounts to the supplier's account on the date the purchase occurs.

STEP 2   Insert the date in the Date column, and the initial "P" and the purchases journal page number in the Posting Reference column of each supplier account.

STEP 3   Insert a check mark (√) in the Posting Reference column of the purchases journal to indicate that the amount has been posted.

NOTE: After the posting of the accounts payable ledger and general ledger is completed, the total of the accounts payable ledger balances should equal the Accounts Payable balance in the general ledger.

Purchases Returns and Allowances

> Enter purchases returns and allowances in the general journal.

If a buyer returns merchandise or is given an allowance for damaged merchandise, a general journal entry is required. Remember, the purchases journal can only be used to enter purchases on account. Assume that on May 4, Northern Micro returns $200 of merchandise to Televax, Inc. These goods were part of the purchase made on April 23. The general journal entry, general ledger posting, and accounts payable ledger posting for this transaction are illustrated in figure 12-12.

F I G U R E   1 2 - 1 2   **Accounting for Purchases Returns and Allowances**

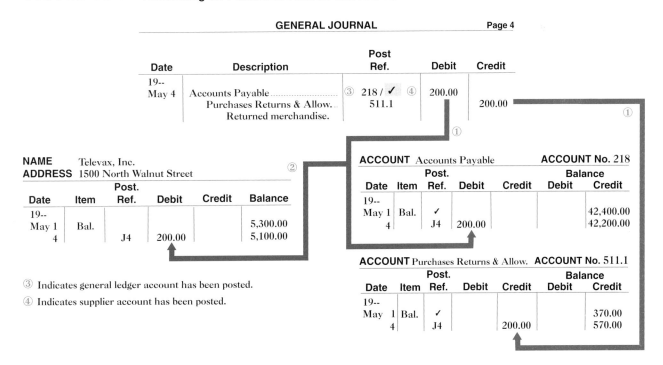

The general journal entry is made in the usual manner. The Purchases Returns and Allowances credit is posted to the general ledger account, and the posting reference is inserted in the general journal and general ledger account. To post the Accounts Payable debit for a purchases return, we use the following procedures.

STEP 1   Post the amount to the general ledger account and insert the initial "J" and the general journal page number (4) in the Posting Reference column.

STEP 2   Post the same amount to the supplier account in the accounts payable ledger and insert the same posting reference (J4) in the Posting Reference column.

STEP 3   To indicate that the general ledger has been posted, insert the account number (218) and a slash (/) in the Posting Reference column of the general journal.

STEP 4   To indicate that the supplier account has been posted, insert a check mark (√) following the slash in the Posting Reference column of the general journal.

4

Describe and use the cash payments journal and accounts payable ledger.

JOURNALIZING AND POSTING CASH PAYMENTS

We saw in Chapter 11 how a cash receipts journal could be used to efficiently record cash receipts transactions. Cash payments transactions generally occur just as frequently as cash receipts transactions, so a special journal for cash payments also can be quite useful.

Cash Payments Journal

A **cash payments journal** is a special journal used to record only cash payments transactions. To illustrate its use, we will record the cash payments transactions of Northern Micro. Northern Micro's cash payments

FIGURE 12-13 **Northern Micro Cash Payments Journal**

	DATE	CK NO.	ACCOUNT DEBITED	POST. REF.	GENERAL DR.	
				CASH PAYMENTS JOURNAL		
1	19-- Apr. 2	307	Rent Expense		2 4 0 0 00	1
2	4	308				2
3	10	309	B.B. Small			3
4	14	310	Notes Payable		2 0 0 0 00	4
5	22	311	Gary Fishel, Drawing		1 6 0 0 00	5
6	24	312	EZX Corp.			6
7	30				6 0 0 0 00	7

journal for the month of April is shown in figure 12-13. Five types of cash payments transactions are shown.

1. Payment of an expense
2. Cash purchase
3. Payment of an account payable (two separate items)
4. Payment of a note payable
5. Withdrawal by the owner

A cash payments journal is used to record only cash payments. A business may use separate columns for Accounts Payable Dr., Purchases Dr., Purchases Discounts Cr., and Cash Cr. in addition to a General Dr. column.

Northern Micro's cash payments journal provides separate columns for Accounts Payable Dr., Purchases Dr., Purchases Discounts Cr., and Cash Cr. These are the accounts most frequently affected by Northern Micro's cash payments transactions. In addition, a General Dr. column is provided for debits to any other accounts affected by cash payments transactions. For good internal control over cash payments, all payments (except out of petty cash) should be made by check. Therefore, the cash payments journal also includes a Check No. column.

A cash payment is recorded in the cash payments journal by entering the following information:

1. Date
2. Check number
3. Account debited (if applicable)
4. Dollar amounts

The Account Debited column is used for two purposes:

1. To identify the supplier name for any payment on account. This column is used whenever the Accounts Payable Dr. column is used.
2. To enter the appropriate account name whenever the General Dr. column is used.

Note that the column is left blank if the entry is for cash purchases.

PAGE 12

	ACCOUNTS PAYABLE DR.	PURCHASES DR.	PURCHASES DISCOUNTS CR.	CASH CR.	
1				2 4 0 0 00	1
2		1 4 0 0 00		1 4 0 0 00	2
3	4 8 0 0 00			4 8 0 0 00	3
4				2 0 0 0 00	4
5				1 6 0 0 00	5
6	8 7 0 0 00		8 7 00	8 6 1 3 00	6
7	13 5 0 0 00	1 4 0 0 00	8 7 00	20 8 1 3 00	7

Posting the Cash Payments Journal

The general ledger posting process for Northern Micro's cash payments journal is illustrated in figure 12-14.

The steps in the process are as follows:

On a daily basis:

STEP 1   Post each amount in the General Dr. column to the appropriate general ledger account.

STEP 2   Insert the date in the Date column and the initials "CP" and the cash payments journal page number in the Posting Reference column of each ledger account.

STEP 3   Insert the general ledger account numbers in the Posting Reference column of the cash payments journal.

At the end of each month:

STEP 4   Foot the amount columns, verify that the total of the debit columns equals the total of the credit columns, and rule the columns.

STEP 5   Post each column total except the General Dr. column to the general ledger account indicated in the column headings.

STEP 6   Insert the date in the Date column and the initials "CP" and the cash payments journal page number in the Posting Reference column of each ledger account.

STEP 7   Insert the general ledger account numbers immediately below each column total except the General Dr. column.

STEP 8   Insert a check mark (√) in the Posting Reference column of the cash payments journal for the cash purchases, and immediately below the General Dr. column.

Postings from the cash payments journal to the accounts payable subsidiary ledger also must be made. These postings are made daily. Posting procedures are as follows, as shown in figure 12-15.

STEP 1   Post the individual cash payment to the supplier's account on the date the payment occurs.

STEP 2   Insert the date in the Date column, and the initials "CP" and the cash payments journal page number in the Posting Reference column of each supplier account.

STEP 3   Insert a check mark (√) in the Posting Reference column of the cash payments journal to indicate that the amount has been posted.

FIGURE 12-14 **Posting the Cash Payments Journal to the General Ledger**

CASH PAYMENTS JOURNAL — Page 12

Date	Check No.	Account Debited	Post. Ref.	General Dr.	Accounts Payable Dr.	Purchases Dr.	Purchases Discounts Cr.	Cash Cr.
19-- Apr. 2	307	Rent Expense ③	541	2,400.00				2,400.00
4	308	⑧	✓			1,400.00		1,400.00
10	309	B.B. Small			4,800.00			4,800.00
14	310	Notes Payable ③	216	2,000.00				2,000.00
22	311	Gary Fishel, Drawing ③	312	1,600.00				1,600.00
24	312	EZX Corp.			8,700.00		87.00	8,613.00
30				6,000.00	13,500.00	1,400.00	87.00	20,813.00 ④
				(✓) ⑧	(218)	(511)	(511.2)	(111) ⑦

GENERAL LEDGER (Partial)

ACCOUNT Cash   ACCOUNT No. 111

Date	Item	Post. Ref.	Debit	Credit	Balance Debit	Balance Credit
19-- Apr. 1	Bal.	✓			20,000.00	
30		CR7	12,992.00		32,992.00	
⑥ 30		CP12		20,813.00	12,179.00	

ACCOUNT Notes Payable   ACCOUNT No. 216

Date	Item	Post. Ref.	Debit	Credit	Balance Debit	Balance Credit
19-- Apr. 1	Bal.	✓				6,000.00
② 14		CP12	2,000.00			4,000.00

ACCOUNT Accounts Payable   ACCOUNT No. 218

Date	Item	Post. Ref.	Debit	Credit	Balance Debit	Balance Credit
19-- Apr. 1	Bal.	✓				8,800.00
30		P8		20,600.00		29,400.00
⑥ 30		CP12	13,500.00			15,900.00

ACCOUNT Gary L. Fishel, Drawing   ACCOUNT No. 312

Date	Item	Post. Ref.	Debit	Credit	Balance Debit	Balance Credit
19-- Apr. 1	Bal.	✓			4,500.00	
② 22		CP12	1,600.00		6,100.00	

ACCOUNT Purchases   ACCOUNT No. 511

Date	Item	Post. Ref.	Debit	Credit	Balance Debit	Balance Credit
19-- Apr. 1	Bal.	✓			17,400.00	
30		P8	20,600.00		38,000.00	
⑥ 30		CP12	1,400.00		39,400.00	

ACCOUNT Purchase Discounts   ACCOUNT No. 511.2

Date	Item	Post. Ref.	Debit	Credit	Balance Debit	Balance Credit
19-- Apr. 1	Bal.	✓				330.00
⑥ 30		CP12		87.00		417.00

ACCOUNT Rent Expense   ACCOUNT No. 541

Date	Item	Post. Ref.	Debit	Credit	Balance Debit	Balance Credit
19-- Apr. 1	Bal.	✓			6,600.00	
② 2		CP12	2,400.00		9,000.00	

F I G U R E 1 2 - 1 5 **Posting the Cash Payments Journal to the Accounts Payable Ledger**

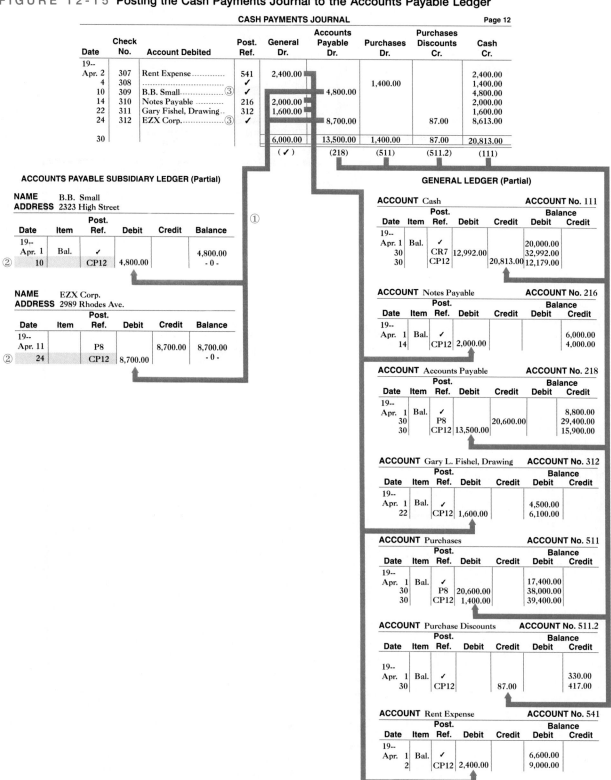

Date	Check No.	Account Debited	Post. Ref.	General Dr.	Accounts Payable Dr.	Purchases Dr.	Purchases Discounts Cr.	Cash Cr.
19--								
Apr. 2	307	Rent Expense.............	541	2,400.00				2,400.00
4	308	....	✓			1,400.00		1,400.00
10	309	B.B. Small............③	✓		4,800.00			4,800.00
14	310	Notes Payable	216	2,000.00				2,000.00
22	311	Gary Fishel, Drawing..	312	1,600.00				1,600.00
24	312	EZX Corp.............③	✓		8,700.00		87.00	8,613.00
30				6,000.00	13,500.00	1,400.00	87.00	20,813.00
				(✓)	(218)	(511)	(511.2)	(111)

CASH PAYMENTS JOURNAL — Page 12

ACCOUNTS PAYABLE SUBSIDIARY LEDGER (Partial)

NAME B.B. Small
ADDRESS 2323 High Street

Date	Item	Post. Ref.	Debit	Credit	Balance
19--					
Apr. 1	Bal.	✓			4,800.00
10		CP12	4,800.00		- 0 -

NAME EZX Corp.
ADDRESS 2989 Rhodes Ave.

Date	Item	Post. Ref.	Debit	Credit	Balance
19--					
Apr. 11		P8		8,700.00	8,700.00
24		CP12	8,700.00		- 0 -

GENERAL LEDGER (Partial)

ACCOUNT Cash   ACCOUNT No. 111

Date	Item	Post. Ref.	Debit	Credit	Balance Debit	Balance Credit
19--						
Apr. 1	Bal.	✓			20,000.00	
30		CR7	12,992.00		32,992.00	
30		CP12		20,813.00	12,179.00	

ACCOUNT Notes Payable   ACCOUNT No. 216

Date	Item	Post. Ref.	Debit	Credit	Balance Debit	Balance Credit
19--						
Apr. 1	Bal.	✓				6,000.00
14		CP12	2,000.00			4,000.00

ACCOUNT Accounts Payable   ACCOUNT No. 218

Date	Item	Post. Ref.	Debit	Credit	Balance Debit	Balance Credit
19--						
Apr. 1	Bal.	✓				8,800.00
30		P8		20,600.00		29,400.00
30		CP12	13,500.00			15,900.00

ACCOUNT Gary L. Fishel, Drawing   ACCOUNT No. 312

Date	Item	Post. Ref.	Debit	Credit	Balance Debit	Balance Credit
19--						
Apr. 1	Bal.	✓			4,500.00	
22		CP12	1,600.00		6,100.00	

ACCOUNT Purchases   ACCOUNT No. 511

Date	Item	Post. Ref.	Debit	Credit	Balance Debit	Balance Credit
19--						
Apr. 1	Bal.	✓			17,400.00	
30		P8	20,600.00		38,000.00	
30		CP12	1,400.00		39,400.00	

ACCOUNT Purchase Discounts   ACCOUNT No. 511.2

Date	Item	Post. Ref.	Debit	Credit	Balance Debit	Balance Credit
19--						
Apr. 1	Bal.	✓				330.00
30		CP12		87.00		417.00

ACCOUNT Rent Expense   ACCOUNT No. 541

Date	Item	Post. Ref.	Debit	Credit	Balance Debit	Balance Credit
19--						
Apr. 1	Bal.	✓			6,600.00	
2		CP12	2,400.00		9,000.00	

5

Prepare a schedule of accounts payable.

SCHEDULE OF ACCOUNTS PAYABLE

All postings to the general ledger and accounts payable ledger are now complete. At this point, the Accounts Payable balance in the general ledger should equal the sum of the supplier balances in the accounts payable ledger.

To verify that the sum of the accounts payable ledger balances equals the Accounts Payable balance, a **schedule of accounts payable** is prepared. This is an alphabetical listing of supplier accounts and balances, usually prepared at the end of the month. The schedule of accounts payable for Northern Micro as of April 30 is illustrated in figure 12-16.

FIGURE 12-16 Schedule of Accounts Payable

Northern Micro Schedule of Accounts Payable April 30, 19--	
Compucraft	3 3 0 0 00
Datasoft	2 5 0 0 00
Printpro	8 0 0 00
Televax	5 3 0 0 00
TTA Products, Inc.	4 0 0 0 00*
	15 9 0 0 00

*The $4,000 amount for TTA Products, Inc. is a balance from April 1.

This schedule is prepared from the list of supplier accounts in the accounts payable ledger. The total calculated in the schedule is compared with the balance in Accounts Payable in the general ledger. Note that the $15,900 total listed in the schedule equals the Accounts Payable balance shown in figure 12-15. If the schedule total and the Accounts Payable balance do not agree, the error must be located and corrected. To find the error, use the following procedures.

STEPS IN LOCATING DISAGREEMENT IN THE SCHEDULE AND ACCOUNTS PAYABLE
1. Verify the total of the schedule.
2. Verify the postings to the accounts payable ledger.
3. Verify the postings to Accounts Payable in the general ledger.

K E Y   P O I N T S

1 Major documents used in the purchasing process are the purchase requisition, purchase order, receiving report, and purchase invoice.

2 Four accounts are used in accounting for merchandise purchases transactions:

1. Purchases
2. Purchases Returns and Allowances
3. Purchases Discounts
4. Freight-In

3 A purchases journal is a special journal for recording purchases on account. A purchase is recorded by entering the:

1. Date
2. Invoice number
3. Supplier
4. Dollar amount

To post from the purchases journal to the general ledger:

1. Foot, verify the equality of, and rule the amount columns.
2. Insert the date and posting reference in the accounts.
3. Insert the Purchases and Accounts Payable account numbers below the column total.

To post from the purchases journal to the accounts payable ledger:

1. Post individual purchase amounts to supplier accounts.
2. Insert the date and posting reference in the customer accounts.
3. Insert a check mark ($\sqrt{}$) in the Posting Reference column of the purchases journal.

Purchases returns and allowances are recorded in the general journal.

4 A cash payments journal is a special journal for recording cash payments. A cash payment is recorded by entering the:

1. Date
2. Check number
3. Account debited (if applicable)
4. Dollar amounts

To post from the cash payments journal to the general ledger:

On a daily basis:

1. Post General Dr. column amounts to the general ledger.
2. Insert the date and posting reference in the accounts.
3. Insert the account numbers in the Posting Reference column of the cash payments journal.

At the end of each month:

4. Foot, verify the equality of, and rule the amount columns.
5. Post account column totals to the appropriate general ledger accounts.
6. Insert the date and posting reference in the accounts.
7. Insert the account numbers below the specific account column totals.
8. Insert a check mark (√) in the Posting Reference column for the cash purchases, and below the General Dr. column.

To post from the cash payments journal to the accounts payable ledger:

1. Post individual cash payments to supplier accounts.
2. Insert the date and posting reference in the customer accounts.
3. Insert a check mark (√) in the Posting Reference column of the cash payments journal.

5 The schedule of accounts payable is used to verify that the sum of the accounts payable ledger balances equals the Accounts Payable balance.

KEY TERMS

cash payments journal 398   A special journal used to record only cash payments transactions.

FOB destination 390   Transportation charges are paid by the seller.

FOB shipping point 390   Transportation charges are paid by the buyer.

gross margin 391   See gross profit.

gross profit 391   The difference between net sales and cost of merchandise sold.

invoice 386   A document prepared by the seller as a bill for the merchandise shipped. To the seller, this is a sales invoice. To the buyer, this is a purchase invoice.

purchase invoice 386   A document prepared by the seller as a bill for the merchandise shipped. To the buyer, this is a purchase invoice.

purchase order 385   A written order to buy goods from a specific vendor (supplier).

purchase requisition 384   A form used to request the purchasing department to purchase merchandise.

purchases 383   Merchandise acquired for resale to customers.

purchases journal 394   A special journal used to record only purchases on account.

receiving report 385   A report indicating what has been received.

schedule of accounts payable 403   An alphabetical listing of supplier accounts and balances, usually prepared at the end of the month.

subsidiary accounts payable ledger 396   A separate ledger containing an individual account payable for each supplier.

trade discount 386   A reduction from the list or catalog price offered to different classes of customers.

BUILDING YOUR ACCOUNTING KNOWLEDGE

1. Identify the major documents commonly used in the purchasing process.
2. Distinguish between a cash discount and a trade discount.
3. Describe how each of the following accounts is used: (1) Purchases, (2) Purchases Returns and Allowances, (3) Purchases Discounts, and (4) Freight In.
4. How are cost of merchandise sold and gross profit computed?
5. List four items of information about each purchase entered in the purchases journal.
6. What steps are followed in posting from the purchases journal to the general ledger?
7. What steps are followed in posting from the purchases journal to the accounts payable ledger?
8. What procedures are used to post Purchases Returns and Allowances from the general journal to the general ledger and accounts payable ledger?
9. List four items of information about each cash payment entered in the cash payments journal.
10. What steps are followed in posting from the cash payments journal to the general ledger?
11. What steps are followed in posting from the cash payments journal to the accounts payable ledger?
12. If the total of the schedule of accounts payable does not agree with the Accounts Payable balance, what procedures should be used to search for the error?

DEMONSTRATION PROBLEM

Jodi Rutman operates a retail pharmacy. The books of original entry include a purchases journal in which purchases of merchandise on account are entered, a cash payments journal in which all cash payments (except petty cash) are entered, and a general journal in which entries such as purchases returns and allowances are made. A subsidiary ledger is used for accounts payable. The following are the transactions related to purchases and cash payments for the month of June.

June   1   Purchased merchandise from Sullivan Co. on account for $234.20. Invoice no. 71 dated June 1, terms 2/10, n/30.

       2   Issued check no. 536 for $1,000.00 in payment of rent (Rent Expense) for June.

       5   Purchased merchandise from Amfac Drug Supply on account for $562.40. Invoice no. 72 dated June 2, terms 1/15, n/30.

June   7 Purchased merchandise from University Drug Co. on account for $367.35. Invoice no. 73 dated June 5, terms 3/10 eom.

9 Issued check no. 537 to Sullivan Co. in payment of invoice no. 71 less 2% discount.

12 Received a credit memorandum from Amfac Drug Supply for $46.20 for merchandise returned that was purchased on June 5.

14 Purchased merchandise from Mutual Drug Co. on account for $479.40. Invoice no. 74 dated June 14, terms 2/10, n/30.

15 Received a credit memorandum from University Drug Co. for $53.70 for merchandise returned that was purchased on June 7.

16 Issued check no. 538 to Amfac Drug Supply in payment of invoice no. 72 less the credit memorandum of June 12, and less 1% discount.

23 Issued check no. 539 to Mutual Drug Co. in payment of invoice no. 74 less 2% discount.

27 Purchased merchandise from Flites Pharmaceuticals on account for $638.47. Invoice no. 75 dated June 27, terms 2/10 eom.

30 Issued check no. 540 for $270.20 to Dolgin Candy Co. for a cash purchase of merchandise.

Required

1. Enter the transactions in a purchases journal, a five-column cash payments journal, and a general journal. Enter the totals and rule the purchases and cash payments journals.
2. Post from the journals to the general ledger accounts and the accounts payable subsidiary ledger. (In posting from these three journals, the page number preceded by the initials "J", "P", or "CP", should be placed in the Post. Ref. column of the general or subsidiary ledger account involved.) Then, update the account balances.
3. Prepare a schedule of accounts payable from the partial subsidiary ledger in the problem. Show that the total of accounts payable in the schedule equals the difference between the June 1 balance and the June 30 balance of Accounts Payable in the general ledger.

SOLUTION

1, 2.

	DATE		INVOICE NO.	FROM WHOM PURCHASED	POST. REF.	PURCHASES DR. ACCTS. PAY. CR.	
1	19-- June	1	71	Sullivan Co.	✓	234 20	1
2		5	72	Amfac Drug Supply	✓	562 40	2
3		7	73	University Drug. Co.	✓	367 35	3
4		14	74	Mutual Drug. Co.	✓	479 40	4
5		27	75	Flites Pharmaceuticals	✓	638 47	5
6						2281 82	6
7						(511) (218)	7

PURCHASES JOURNAL — PAGE 2

CASH PAYMENTS JOURNAL

	DATE		CK NO.	ACCOUNT DEBITED	POST. REF.	GENERAL DR.	
1	19-- June	2	536	Rent Expense	541	1 0 0 0 00	1
2		9	537	Sullivan Co.	✓		2
3		16	538	Amfac Drug Supply	✓		3
4		23	539	Mutual Drug Co.	✓		4
5		30	540		✓		5
6						1 0 0 0 00	6
7						(✓)	7

GENERAL JOURNAL

PAGE 4

	DATE		DESCRIPTION	POST. REF.	DEBIT	CREDIT	
1	19-- June	12	Accts. Payable (Amfac Drug Supply)	218/✓	4 6 20		1
2			Purchases Returns & Allow.	511.1		4 6 20	2
3		15	Accts. Payable (University Drug Co.)	218/✓	5 3 70		3
4			Purchases Returns & Allow.	511.1		5 3 70	4

2.

GENERAL LEDGER

ACCOUNT Cash   ACCOUNT NO. 111

DATE	ITEM	POST. REF.	DEBIT	CREDIT	BALANCE DEBIT	BALANCE CREDIT
19-- June 1	Balance	✓			9 1 8 0 00	
30		CP4		2 4 8 0 57	6 6 9 9 43	

ACCOUNT Accounts Payable   ACCOUNT NO. 218

DATE	ITEM	POST. REF.	DEBIT	CREDIT	BALANCE DEBIT	BALANCE CREDIT
19-- June 1	Balance	✓				6 2 1 7 69
12		J4	4 6 20			6 1 7 1 49
15		J4	5 3 70			6 1 1 7 79
30		P2		2 2 8 1 82		8 3 9 9 61
30		CP4	1 2 2 9 80			7 1 6 9 81

	ACCOUNTS PAYABLE DR.	PURCHASES DR.	PURCHASES DISCOUNTS CR.	CASH CR.	
1				1 000 00	1
2	234 20		4 68	229 52	2
3	516 20		5 16	511 04	3
4	479 40		9 59	469 81	4
5		270 20		270 20	5
6	1 229 80	270 20	19 43	2 480 57	6
	(218)	(511)	(511.2)	(111)	7

PAGE 4

ACCOUNT **Purchases** ACCOUNT NO. 511

DATE		ITEM	POST. REF.	DEBIT	CREDIT	BALANCE DEBIT	BALANCE CREDIT
19-- June	1	Balance	✓			13 826 25	
	30		P2	2 281 82		16 108 07	
	30		CP4	270 20		16 378 27	

ACCOUNT **Purchases Returns and Allowances** ACCOUNT NO. 511.1

DATE		ITEM	POST. REF.	DEBIT	CREDIT	BALANCE DEBIT	BALANCE CREDIT
19-- June	1	Balance	✓				312 63
	12		J4		46 20		358 83
	15		J4		53 70		412 53

ACCOUNT **Purchases Discount** ACCOUNT NO. 511.2

DATE		ITEM	POST. REF.	DEBIT	CREDIT	BALANCE DEBIT	BALANCE CREDIT
19-- June	1	Balance	✓				211 45
	30		CP4		19 43		230 88

ACCOUNT **Rent Expense** ACCOUNT NO. 541

DATE		ITEM	POST. REF.	DEBIT	CREDIT	BALANCE DEBIT	BALANCE CREDIT
19-- June	1	Balance	✓			5 000 00	
	2		CP4	1 000 00		6 000 00	

3.

ACCOUNTS PAYABLE LEDGER (Partial)

ACCOUNT   Amfac Drug Supply

DATE		ITEM	POST. REF.	DEBIT	CREDIT	BALANCE
19-- June	5		P2		562 40	562 40
	12		J4	46 20		516 20
	16		CP4	516 20		-0-

ACCOUNT   Flites Pharmaceuticals

DATE		ITEM	POST. REF.	DEBIT	CREDIT	BALANCE
19-- June	27		P2		638 47	638 47

ACCOUNT   Mutual Drug Co.

DATE		ITEM	POST. REF.	DEBIT	CREDIT	BALANCE
19-- June	14		P2		479 40	479 40
	23		CP4	479 40		- 0 -

ACCOUNT   Sullivan Co.

DATE		ITEM	POST. REF.	DEBIT	CREDIT	BALANCE
19-- June	1		P2		234 20	234 20
	9		CP4	234 20		- 0 -

ACCOUNT   University Drug Co.

DATE		ITEM	POST. REF.	DEBIT	CREDIT	BALANCE
19-- June	7		P2		367 35	367 35
	15		J4	53 70		313 65

Rutman Pharmacy
Schedule of Accounts Payable
June 30, 19--

Flites Pharmaceuticals	638 47
University Drug Co.	313 65
Total	952 12
Proof	
Balance of Accounts Payable, June 30	7 169 81
Less balance of Accounts Payable, June 1	6 217 69
Difference	952 12

EXERCISES

**Purchasing Documents
and Flow Chart Labeling**

EXERCISE 12A1

APPLYING ACCOUNTING CONCEPTS

1 A partially completed flowchart showing some of the major documents commonly used in the purchase function of a merchandise business is presented below. Identify documents 1, 3, and 4.

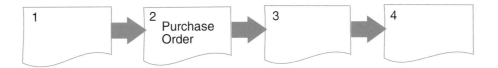

EXERCISE 12A2

**Net Amount with Trade
Discount and Cash
Discount**

1 Merchandise was purchased on account from Jacob's Distributors on May 17, 19--. The purchase price was $2,000, subject to a 10% trade discount and credit terms of 2/10, n/30.

1. Calculate the net amount to record the invoice, subject to the 10% trade discount.
2. Calulate the amount to be paid on this invoice within the discount period.
3. Journalize the purchase of the merchandise on May 17th in a two-column general journal. Journalize the payment on May 27th (within the discount period).

EXERCISE 12A3

**Purchase Transactions
and T Accounts**

2 Using T accounts for Cash, Accounts Payable, Purchases, Purchases Returns and Allowances, Purchases Discounts, and Freight-In, enter the following purchase transactions. Identify each transaction with its corresponding letter.

1. Purchase of merchandise with cash.
   (a) Merchandise is purchased for cash, $1,500.
   (b) Merchandise listed at $3,500, subject to a trade discount of 15%, is purchased for cash.
2. Purchase of merchandise on account with credit terms.
   (a) Merchandise is purchased on account, credit terms 2/10, n/30, $2,000.
   (b) Merchandise is purchased on account, credit terms 3/10, n/30, $1,200.
   (c) Payment is made on invoice (a) within the discount period.
   (d) Payment is made on invoice (b) too late to receive the cash discount.

3. Purchase of merchandise on account with return of merchandise.
   (a) Merchandise is purchased on account, credit terms 2/10, n/30, $4,000.
   (b) Merchandise is returned for credit before payment is made, $500.
   (c) Payment is made within the discount period.
4. Purchase of merchandise with freight in.
   (a) Merchandise is purchased on account $2,500, plus freight charges of $100. Terms of the sale were FOB shipping point.
   (b) Payment is made for the cost of merchandise and the freight charge.

EXERCISE 12A4

Cost of Merchandise Sold

2 The following data were taken from the accounts of Division Hardware, a small retail business. Determine the cost of merchandise sold.

Merchandise inventory, beginning of period	$25,000
Purchases during the period	85,000
Purchases returns and allowances during the period	3,000
Purchases discounts taken during the period	2,000
Freight-in on merchandise purchased during the period	1,500
Merchandise inventory, end of period.	20,000

EXERCISE 12A5

Journalizing Transactions in Purchases Journal and General Journal

3

1. Journalize the following transactions in a general journal.

May   3   Purchased merchandise from Compusales, $5,000. Invoice no. 421, dated May 1, terms n/30.

       9   Purchased merchandise from Microdata, $4,000. Invoice no. 422, dated May 8, terms 2/10, n/30.

     18   Purchased merchandise from ABC distributors, $6,500. Invoice no. 423, dated May 15, terms 1/15, n/30.

     23   Purchased merchandise from Quickfax, $8,000. Invoice no. 424, dated May 22, terms 1/10, n/30.

2. Journalize the transactions in a purchases journal with the following column headings.

PURCHASES JOURNAL					PAGE 5
DATE	INVOICE NO.	FROM WHOM PURCHASED		POST. REF.	PURCHASES DR. ACCTS. PAY. CR.

Journalize Purchase Returns and Allowances and Post to General Ledger and Accounts Payable Ledger

3 Using page 3 of a general journal and the following general ledger accounts and accounts payable accounts, journalize and post the following transactions.

July 7 Merchandise returned to Starcraft Industries, $700.
15 Merchandise returned to XYZ Inc., $450.
27 Merchandise returned to Datamagic, $900.

General Ledger

Account No.	Account	Balance
218	Accounts Payable	$10,650.00
511.1	Purchases Returns and Allowances	

Accounts Payable Subsidiary Ledger

Name	Balance
Datamagic	$2,600.00
Starcraft Industries	4,300.00
XYZ Incorporated	3,750.00

Cash Payments Journal

4 Landmark Industries uses a cash payments journal. Prepare a cash payments journal using the same format and account titles as illustrated in the chapter. Record the following payments for merchandise purchased.

Sept. 5 Issued check no. 318 to Clinton Corp. for merchandise purchased August 28, $6,000, terms 2/10, n/30. Payment is made within the discount period.
12 Issued check no. 319 to Mitchell Company for merchandise purchased September 2, $7,500, terms 1/10, n/30. Received a credit memo from Mitchell Company for merchandise returned, $500. Payment is made within the discount period after deduction for the return dated Sept 8.
19 Issued check no. 320 to Expert Systems for merchandise purchased August 19, $4,100, terms n/30.
27 Issued check no. 321 to Graphic Data for merchandise purchased September 17, $9,000, terms 2/10, n/30. Payment is made within the discount period.

Preparation of Schedule of Accounts Payable

5 Prepare a schedule of accounts payable for Ryan's Express, as of October 31, 19--. Ryan's Express, a retail business, has the following balances in the accounts payable subsidiary ledger.

Accounts Payable Subsidiary Ledger

Name	Balance
Columbia Products	$5,350.00
Favorite Fashions	4,280.00
Rustic Legends	4,740.00

PROBLEM 12A1

Purchases Journal

3 J. B. Speck, owner of Speck's Galleria, made the following purchases of merchandise on account during the month of September, 19--.

Sept.   3 Purchase invoice no. 415, $2,650, from Smith Distributors.
        8 Purchase invoice no. 416, $3,830, from Michaels Wholesaler.
       11 Purchase invoice no. 417, $3,140, from J. B. Sanders & Co.
       18 Purchase invoice no. 418, $2,250, from Bateman & Jones, Inc.
       23 Purchase invoice no. 419, $4,160, from Smith Distributors.
       27 Purchase invoice no. 420, $1,980, from Anderson Company.
       30 Purchase invoice no. 421, $2,780, from Michaels Wholesaler.

Required
1. Record the transactions in the purchases journal. Total and rule the journal and prove the totals.
2. Post from the purchases journal to the general ledger accounts and to the accounts payable ledger accounts.

PROBLEM 12A2

Purchases Journal, General Ledger, Accounts Payable Ledger

3 The purchases journal of Kevin's Kettle, a small retail business, is shown as follows.

	DATE		INVOICE NO.	FROM WHOM PURCHASED	POST. REF.	PURCHASES DR. ACCTS. PAY. CR.	
1	19-- Jan.	2	101	Nikki's Neckties		1 5 0 0 00	1
2		3	102	Billie's Boutique		1 2 4 0 00	2
3		7	103	Tower Records		2 1 8 0 00	3
4		12	104	Michael's Mementos		9 7 5 00	4
5		18	105	Henderson & Company		2 3 5 0 00	5
6		25	106	Billie's Boutique		8 8 0 00	6
7						9 1 2 5 00	7

PURCHASES JOURNAL PAGE 1

Required
1. Post the total of the purchases journal to the appropriate general ledger accounts.
2. Post the individual purchase amounts to the accounts payable subsidiary ledger.

PROBLEM 12A3

Cash Payments Journal, Accounts Payable Ledger and General Ledger

4 Sam Stephens operates a retail variety store. The books of original entry include a cash payments journal and a subsidiary ledger. All cash payments (except petty cash) are entered in the cash payments journal. The subsidiary ledger is used for accounts payable. Following are the transactions related to cash payments for the month of May:

May 1 Issued check no. 526 for $1,200 in payment of rent (Rent Expense) for May.

 3 Issued check no. 527 to Moyer's Distributors in payment of merchandise purchased on account, $1,800, less a 3% discount. Check was written for $1,746.

 7 Issued check no. 528 to Baker & Johnson, for $2,750 in payment of merchandise purchased on account. A cash discount was not allowed.

 12 Issued check no. 529 to Fantastic Toys for merchandise purchased on account, $2,600, less a 1% discount. Check was written for $2,574.

 15 Issued check no. 530 to City Power and Light for $860 (Utilities Expense).

 18 Issued check no. 531 for $2,400, to A-1 Warehouse for a cash purchase of merchandise.

 26 Issued check no. 532 to Gateway Outlet for merchandise purchased on account, $1,900, less a 2% discount. Check was written for $1,862.

 30 Issued check no. 533 for $600 to Mercury Transit Company for freight charges on merchandise purchased.

 31 Issued check no. 534 for $1,500 to Town Merchants for a cash purchase of merchandise.

Required

1. Enter the transactions in a five-column cash payments journal. Enter the totals and rule the cash payments journal.

2. Post from the cash payments journal to the general ledger and the accounts payable ledger.

PROBLEM 12A4

Purchases Journal, Cash
Payments Journal,
General Journal

3/4 Freddy Flint owns a small retail business called Flint's Fantasy. The following purchases, returns, and discounts are for July, 19--.

July 1 Paid rent for the month, $1,500.00. Issued check no. 414.

 1 Purchased merchandise on account from Tang's Toys, invoice no. 311, $2,700, terms 2/10,n/30.

 3 Purchased merchandise on account from Smith & Company, invoice no. 312, $3,100, terms 1/10,n/30.

 5 Returned $500 of merchandise purchased from Tang's Toys, receiving a credit on the amount owed.

 8 Purchased merchandise on account from Debbie's Dolls, invoice no. 313, $1,900, terms 2/10,n/30.

 11 Paid amount owed to Tang's Toys, less return of July 5 and less 2% discount. Issued check no. 415.

 13 Paid amount owed to Smith & Company, less 1% discount. Issued check no. 416.

July 15 Returned $400 of merchandise purchased from Debbie's Dolls, receiving a credit on the amount owed.

18 Paid the amount owed to Debbie's Dolls, less return of July 15 and less 2% discount. Issued check no. 417.

25 Purchased merchandise on account from Allied Business, invoice no. 314, $2,450, terms n/30.

26 Purchased merchandise on account from Tang's Toys, invoice no. 315, $1,980, terms 2/10,n/30.

29 Purchased merchandise on account from Smith & Company, invoice no. 316, $3,460, terms 1/10,n/30.

31 Freddy Flint withdrew $2,000 for personal use. Issued check no. 418.

31 Issued check no. 419, for $975.00 to Glisan Distributors for a cash purchase of merchandise.

Required

1. Enter the transactions in a purchases journal, a five-column cash payments journal, and a general journal. Assume cash and the owner's capital account has a beginning balance of $20,000.

2. Post from the journals to the general ledger and accounts payable ledger accounts.

PROBLEM 12A5

Schedule of Accounts Payable

5 Based on the information provided in Problem 12A4, prepare a schedule of accounts payable for Flint's Fantasy as of July 31, 19--. Notice whether or not the accounts payable account balance in the general ledger agrees with the schedule of accounts payable total.

SERIES B

EXERCISES

EXERCISE 12B1

Purchasing Documents and Flow Chart Labeling

1 A partially completed flowchart showing some of the major documents commonly used in the purchase function of a merchandise business is presented as follows. Identify documents 1, 2, and 4.

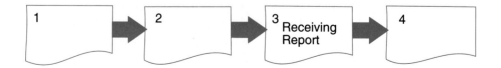

<table>
<tr><td>

EXERCISE 12B2

Net Amount with Trade Discount and Cash Discount

</td></tr>
</table>

1 Merchandise was purchased on account from Grant's Distributors on June 12, 19--. The purchase price was $5,000, subject to a 10% trade discount and credit terms of 3/10, n/30.

1. Calculate the net amount to record the invoice, subject to the 10% trade discount.
2. Calculate the amount to be paid on this invoice within the discount period.
3. Journalize the purchase of the merchandise on June 12th and the payment on June 22nd (within the discount period) in a two-column general journal.

<table>
<tr><td>

EXERCISE 12B3

Purchase Transactions and T Accounts

</td></tr>
</table>

2 Using T accounts for Cash, Accounts Payable, Purchases, Purchases Returns and Allowances, Purchases Discounts, and Freight-In, enter the following purchase transactions. Identify each transaction with its corresponding letter.

1. Purchase of merchandise with cash.
   (a) Merchandise is purchased for cash, $2,300.
   (b) Merchandise listed at $4,000, subject to a trade discount of 10%, is purchased for cash.
2. Purchase of merchandise on account with credit terms.
   (a) Merchandise is purchased on account, credit terms 2/10, n/30, $4,000.
   (b) Merchandise is purchased on account, credit terms 3/10, n/30, $2,800.
   (c) Payment is made on invoice (a) within the discount period.
   (d) Payment is made on invoice (b) too late to receive the cash discount.
3. Purchase of merchandise on account with return of merchandise.
   (a) Merchandise is purchased on account, credit terms 2/10, n/30, $5,600.
   (b) Merchandise is returned for credit before payment is made, $600.
   (c) Payment is made within the discount period.
4. Purchase of merchandise with freight in.
   (a) Merchandise is purchased on account $3,800, plus freight charges of $200. Terms of the sale were FOB shipping point.
   (b) Payment is made for the cost of merchandise and the freight charge.

<table>
<tr><td>

EXERCISE 12B4

Cost of Merchandise Sold

</td></tr>
</table>

2 The following data were taken from the accounts of Burnside Bedknobs, a retail business. Determine the cost of merchandise sold.

Merchandise inventory, beginning of period	$40,000
Purchases during the period	90,000
Purchases returns and allowances during the period	4,000
Purchases discounts taken during the period	3,500
Freight-in on merchandise purchased during the period	2,500
Merchandise inventory, end of period	42,000

Journalizing Transactions in Purchases Journal and General Journal

3

1. Journalize the following transactions in a general journal.

Jan.   3 Purchased merchandise from Execusales, $7,000. Invoice no. 516, dated Jan. 1, terms 2/10, n/30.
       12 Purchased merchandise from Microbit, $11,000. Invoice no. 517, dated Jan. 10, terms n/30.
       19 Purchased merchandise from J.B. Buck, $8,200. Invoice no. 518, dated Jan. 18, terms 1/10, n/30.
       26 Purchased merchandise from Memoryone, $5,400. Invoice no. 519, dated Jan. 25, terms 1/15, n/30.

2. Journalize the transactions in a purchases journal with the following column headings.

PURCHASES JOURNAL					PAGE 5
	DATE	INVOICE NO.	FROM WHOM PURCHASED	POST. REF.	PURCHASES DR. ACCTS. PAY. CR.

Journalize Purchase Returns and Allowances and Post to General Ledger and Accounts Payable Ledger

3 Using page 3 of a general journal and the following general ledger accounts and accounts payable accounts, journalize and post the following transactions.

Mar.   5 Merchandise returned to Tower Industries, $500.
       11 Merchandise returned to A & D Arms, $625.
       23 Merchandise returned to Mighty Mansion, $275.

General Ledger

Account No.	Account	Balance
218	Accounts Payable	$8,350.00
511.1	Purchases Returns and Allowances	

Accounts Payable Subsidiary Ledger

Name	Balance
A & D Arms	$2,300.00
Mighty Mansion	1,450.00
Tower Industries	4,600.00

Entries in a Cash Payments Journal

4 Sandcastles Northwest uses a cash payments journal. Prepare a cash payments journal using the same format and account titles as illustrated in the chapter. Record the following payments for merchandise purchased.

April   5 Issued check no. 429 to Standard Industries for merchandise purchased April 3, $8,000, terms 2/10, n/30. Payment is made within the discount period.

April 19 Issued check no. 430 to Finest Company for merchandise purchased April 10, $5,300, terms 1/10, n/30. Received a credit memo from Finest Company for merchandise returned, $300. Payment is made within the discount period after deduction for the return dated April 12.

21 Issued check no. 431 to Funny Follies for merchandise purchased March 21, $3,250, terms n/30.

29 Issued check no. 432 to Classic Data for merchandise purchased April 20, $7,000, terms 2/10, n/30. Payment is made within the discount period.

EXERCISE 12B8
Preparation of Schedule of Accounts Payable

5 Crystal's Candles, a retail business, has the following accounts payable subsidiary ledger balances on November 30. Prepare a schedule of accounts payable for Crystal's Candles, as of November 30, 19--.

Accounts Payable Subsidiary Ledger

Name	Balance
Carl's Candle Wax	$3,480.00
Handy Supplies	2,960.00
Wishy Wicks	4,125.00

PROBLEMS

PROBLEM 12B1
Purchases Journal

3 Ann Benton, owner of Benton's Galleria, made the following purchases of merchandise on account during the month of October, 19--.

Oct. 2 Purchase invoice no. 321, $1,950, from Boggs Distributors.
7 Purchase invoice no. 322, $2,915, from Wolfs Wholesaler.
10 Purchase invoice no. 323, $3,565, from Kennington & Co.
16 Purchase invoice no. 324, $2,845, from Fritz & McCord, Inc.
24 Purchase invoice no. 325, $3,370, from Boggs Distributors.
26 Purchase invoice no. 326, $2,240, from Sanderson Company.
31 Purchase invoice no. 327, $1,630, from Wolfs Wholesaler.

Required

1. Record the transactions in the purchases journal. Total and rule the journal and prove the totals.
2. Post from the purchases journal to the general ledger accounts and to the accounts payable ledger accounts.

PROBLEM 12B2

Purchases Journal,
General Ledger, Accounts
Payable Ledger

3 The purchases journal of Ryan's Rats Nest, a small retail business, is shown as follows.

	DATE		INVOICE NO.	FROM WHOM PURCHASED	POST. REF.	PURCHASES DR. ACCTS. PAY. CR.	
1	19-- Jan.	3	121	Stacy's Stash		2 2 4 5 00	1
2		5	122	Andrew & Walsh		2 9 6 0 00	2
3		9	123	Michael's Mansion		1 3 4 0 00	3
4		15	124	Smith and Johnson Co.		3 2 8 0 00	4
5		21	125	Himes Incorporated		6 5 0 00	5
6		30	126	Andrew & Walsh		9 4 5 00	6
7						11 4 2 0 00	7

PURCHASES JOURNAL   PAGE 1

Required
1. Post the total of the purchases journal to the appropriate general ledger accounts.
2. Post the individual purchase amounts to the accounts payable subsidiary ledger.

PROBLEM 12B3

Cash Payments Journal,
Accounts Payable Ledger,
and General Ledger

4 Kay Strobeck operates a retail variety store. The books of original entry include a cash payments journal and a subsidiary ledger. All cash payments (except petty cash) are entered in the cash payments journal. The subsidiary ledger is used for accounts payable. Following are the transactions related to cash payments for the month of May:

May   1 Issued check no. 426 for $1,300 in payment of rent (Rent Expense) for May.

4 Issued check no. 427 to Camm's Distributors in payment of merchandise purchased on account, $2,100, less a 3% discount. Check was written for $2,037.

7 Issued check no. 428 to Cole & Pearson for $3,100 in payment of merchandise purchased on account. A cash discount was not allowed.

11 Issued check no. 429 to Toy Corner for merchandise purchased on account, $2,300, less a 1% discount. Check was written for $2,277.

15 Issued check no. 430 to County Power and Light for $750. (Utilities Expense).

19 Issued check no. 431 for $1,750, to Builders Warehouse, for a cash purchase of merchandise.

May 25 Issued check no. 432 to Troutman Outlet for merchandise purchased on account, $2,200, less a 2% discount. Check was written for $2,156.

30 Issued check no. 433 for $400 to Rapid Transit Company for freight charges on merchandise purchased.

31 Issued check no. 434 for $1,175 to City Merchants for a cash purchase of merchandise.

Required

1. Enter the transactions in a five-column cash payments journal. Enter the totals and rule the cash payments journal.
2. Post from the cash payments journal to the general ledger and the accounts payable ledger.

PROBLEM 12B4

Purchases Journal, Cash
Payments Journal,
General Journal

 ◄**EPS**►

3/4 Debbie Mueller owns a small retail business called Debbie's Doll House. The following purchases, returns, and discounts are for July, 19--.

July 1 Paid rent for the month, $1,400.00. Issued check no. 314.

1 Purchased merchandise on account from Topper's Toys, invoice no. 211, $2,500, terms 2/10,n/30.

3 Purchased merchandise on account from Jones & Company, invoice no. 212, $2,800, terms 1/10,n/30.

5 Returned $400 of merchandise purchased from Topper's Toys receiving a credit on the amount owed.

8 Purchased merchandise on account from Downtown Merchants, invoice no. 213, $1,600, terms 2/10,n/30.

11 Paid amount owed to Topper's Toys, less return of July 5 and less 2% discount. Issued check no. 315.

13 Paid amount owed to Jones & Company, less 1% discount. Issued check no. 316.

15 Returned $600 of merchandise purchased from Downtown Merchants receiving a credit on the amount owed.

18 Paid the amount owed to Downtown Merchants, less return of July 15 and less 2% discount. Issued check no. 317.

25 Purchased merchandise on account from Columbia Products, invoice no. 214, $3,200, terms n/30.

26 Purchased merchandise on account from Topper's Toys, invoice no. 215, $1,430, terms 2/10,n/30.

29 Purchased merchandise on account from Jones & Company, invoice no. 216, $2,970, terms 1/10,n/30.

31 Debbie Mueller withdrew $2,500 for personal use. Issued check no. 318.

31 Issued check no. 319 for $1,050.00 to Burnside Warehouse for a cash purchase of merchandise.

Required

1. Enter the transactions in a purchases journal, a five-column cash payments journal, and a general journal. Assume cash and owner's capital has a beginning balance of $20,000.

2. Post from the journals to the general ledger and accounts payable ledger accounts.

PROBLEM 12B5

Schedule of Accounts Payable

5 Based on the information provided in Problem 12B4, prepare a schedule of accounts payable for Debbie's Doll House as of July 31, 19--. Notice whether or not the accounts payable account balance in the general ledger agrees with the schedule of accounts payable total.

MASTERY PROBLEM

If the working papers for the textbook are not used, omit the Mastery Problem.

Michelle French owns and operates Books and More, a retail book store. The following purchases and cash payment transactions took place during the month of June:

June 1 Purchased books on account from Irving Publishing Company for $2,100. Invoice no. 101, terms 2/10, n/30, FOB destination.

2 Made payment on account to North-Eastern Publishing Company for goods purchased on May 23, terms 2/10, n/30. Issued check no. 300 for $1,960.00, the $2,000.00 invoice amount less the 2% discount.

3 Purchased books on account from Broadway Publishing Inc. for $3,200.00. Invoice no. 102, subject to 20% and 10% trade discounts, and invoice terms of 3/10, n/30, FOB shipping point.

3 Paid shipping charges of $250.00 to Mayday Shipping for delivery from Broadway Publishing Company. Issued check no. 301.

4 Paid $625.00 rent for the month of June. Issued check no. 302.

8 Purchased books on account from North-Eastern Publishing Company for $5,825.00. Invoice no. 103, terms 2/eom, n/60, FOB destination.

10 Received a credit memorandum from Irving Publishing Company for $550.00. Books had been returned because the covers were on upside down.

13 Made payment on account to Broadway Publishing Inc. for the purchase made on June 3. Issued check no. 304.

June 28 Made the following purchases:

Inv. No.	Company	Amount	Terms
104	Broadway Pub. Inc.	$2,350.00	2/10, n/30 FOB destination
105	North-Eastern Pub. Co.	4,200.00	2/eom, n/60 FOB destination
106	Riley Publishing Co.	3,450.00	3/10, n/30 FOB destination

    30 Paid utilities for month of June to Taylor County Utility Co. Issued check no. 305 for $325.

    30 French withdrew $4,500 for personal use. Issued check no. 306.

    30 Made payment on account to Irving Publishing Company for purchase made on June 1 less returns made on June 10. Check no. 307 was issued.

    30 Made payment to North-Eastern Publishing Company for purchase made on June 8. Issued check no. 308.

    30 Purchased books at an auction. Issued check no. 309 for $1,328.

Required

1. Enter the above transactions in the appropriate journals.
2. Total and rule the purchases journal and cash payments journal.
3. Post from the journals to the general ledger accounts and the accounts payable subsidiary ledger.
4. Prepare a schedule of accounts payable.
5. If merchandise inventory was $35,523 on January 1 and $42,100.00 as of June 30, prepare the cost of merchandise sold section of the income statement for the six months ended June 30, 19--.

Chapter 12 Demonstration Problem

The following instructions show you how to complete the Chapter 12 demonstration problem. Refer to Appendix A for additional help as you complete this problem and Problems 12A4 and 12B4.

STEP 1 Load the Electronic Problem Solver software and the opening balance file for Demonstration Problem D-12.

STEP 2 Select the Options Menu and the General Information screen. Enter a date of 06/30/-- (current year) and your name. Do not change any buttons (these buttons indicate that this is a sole proprietorship and a merchandising business). Record your data.

STEP 3 Enter all June transactions selecting the Purchases Journal, Cash Payments Journal, or General Journal commands from the Journal menu. You must use a vendor number when you enter the Accounts Payable account. Press the F2 key to display a vendor list showing vendor numbers. The computer automatically credits the Accounts Payable account on the purchases journal (figure AC12-1). The computer automatically credits the Cash account on the cash payments journal (figure AC12-2). Use the general journal to enter purchases returns (figure AC12-3).

Note: On those cash payments with discounts (June 9, 16, and 23), you must enter the discount amount in the Debit column of the cash payments journal preceded by a minus (−) sign (figure 12-4).

FIGURE AC12-1 **Purchases Journal Data Entry**   FIGURE AC12-2 **Cash Payments Journal Data Entry**

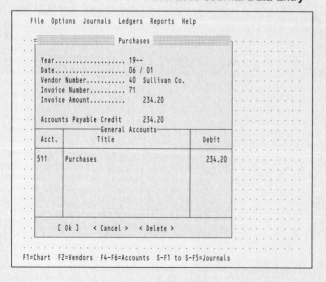

FIGURE AC12-3 **General Journal Data Entry**

FIGURE AC12-4 **Cash Payments Journal Data Entry with Purchases Discount**

```
File  Options  Journals  Ledgers  Reports  Help

═══════════════ General Journal ═══════════════

    Year....... 19--
    Date....... 06 / 12
    Reference..

  ┌──────┬──────┬─────────────────────┬────────┬────────┐
  │ Acct.│ Ven./│                     │        │        │
  │ No.  │ Cus. │  Account Title      │ Debit  │ Credit │
  ├──────┼──────┼─────────────────────┼────────┼────────┤
  │ 218  │ 10   │ AP/Amfac Drug Supply│ 46.20  │        │
  │ 511.1│      │ Purch. Returns & Allow.│     │ 46.20  │
  │      │      │                     │        │        │
  │      │      │                     │        │        │
  │      │      │                     │        │        │
  │      │      │                     │        │        │
  │      │      │                     │        │        │
  ├──────┴──────┴─────────────────────┴────────┴────────┤
  │        [ Ok ]    < Cancel >    < Delete >           │
  └─────────────────────────────────────────────────────┘

F1=Chart  F2=Vendors  F4-F6=Accounts  S-F1 to S-F5=Journals
```

```
File  Options  Journals  Ledgers  Reports  Help

═══════════════ Cash Payments ═══════════════

    Year................ 19--
    Date................ 06 / 09
    Vendor Number....... 40  Sullivan Co.
    Check Number........ 537
    Accts. Pay. Debit ...... 234.20

    Cash Credit............. 229.52
  ┌─────────────── General Accounts ───────────────┐
  │ Acct. │        Title         │    Debit        │
  ├───────┼──────────────────────┼─────────────────┤
  │ 511.2 │ Purchases Discounts  │   -4.68         │
  │       │                      │                 │
  │       │                      │                 │
  │       │                      │                 │
  │       │                      │                 │
  ├───────┴──────────────────────┴─────────────────┤
  │     [ Ok ]    < Cancel >    < Delete >         │
  └────────────────────────────────────────────────┘

F1=Chart  F2=Vendors  F4-F6=Accounts  S-F1 to S-F5=Journals
```

STEP 4 After you enter all transactions, select the Journals command from the Reports menu, and press the space bar to place an X in each box to display the general journal, purchases journal, and cash payments journal. Press Enter on Ok.

STEP 5 Verify that the date range on the Selection Options screen indicates 06/01/-- to 06/30/--. Change the dates if necessary. Press Enter on Ok to display the transactions.

STEP 6 If you need to correct your transactions, refer to the section in Appendix A titled Corrections to Journal Entries.

STEP 7 Display ledger reports by selecting Ledgers from the Reports menu. Press the space bar to place an X in each box to display the general ledger, schedule of accounts payable, and accounts payable ledger. Press Enter on Ok.

STEP 8 Press Enter on Ok to accept the account number range (general ledger) and the vendor number range (accounts payable ledger).

STEP 9 After displaying the reports, choose the Save As command from the File menu, and save your solution on a data disk under a file name such as D-12XXX (XXX=your initials).

STEP 10 Choose the Quit option to end your session.

Careful study of this chapter should enable you to:

1. Describe how a voucher system is used to control expenditures.

2. Prepare a voucher.

3. Describe and use a voucher register.

4. Describe the payment process using a voucher system.

5. Describe and use a check register.

*T*he Voucher System

Chapter 12 demonstrated how merchandise purchases on account can be efficiently recorded in a purchases journal. In this chapter, we will learn to use a special journal for recording all purchases of assets and services of any kind. Chapter 12 also demonstrated how cash payments can be efficiently recorded in a cash payments journal. In this chapter, we will learn how to use another type of journal for recording cash payments.

The two new journals introduced in this chapter provide more than an efficient way to record transactions. We will see that they are an important part of what is called a voucher system.

INTERNAL CONTROL OF EXPENDITURES

1

Describe how a voucher system is used to control expenditures.

To be successful, management must have adequate control of the operations of the business. One area of operations that is particularly important to control is the expenditure process. When we think of controlling business resources, most of us tend to emphasize control over revenues. In fact, control of expenditures is just as important.

Management needs to see that expenditures are being made only for goods and services needed by the business and at a fair price. In a small business, management does so by direct involvement with the expenditure process. But as a business grows larger, management cannot continue such direct involvement. Instead, in medium and large size businesses, management controls expenditures by using an appropriate internal control system.

Elements of Internal Control

Internal controls are the set of procedures used to ensure that all the activities of the business are properly accounted for. A full discussion of internal controls is a subject for an advanced text. Our attention will be limited to three elements of internal control that are particularly important for expenditures.

1. Segregation of duties
2. Authorization procedures and related responsibilities
3. Accounting procedures

Segregation of duties means that:

1. Different employees should be responsible for different parts of a transaction
2. Employees who account for transactions should not also have custody of the assets.

For example, one employee should order goods, and a different employee should pay for them. Similarly, one employee should record the purchase of goods, and a different employee should be responsible for storing the goods. This segregation of duties provides a built-in check of one employee by another. One employee cannot obtain goods for personal use without being caught by another employee.

Authorization procedures and related responsibilities means that every business activity should be properly authorized. In addition, it should be possible to identify who is responsible for every activity that has occurred. For example, to acquire new equipment, a signed document should authorize the purchase. After the purchase is made, this signed document shows who is responsible for the action.

Accounting procedures means that accounting documents and records should be used so that all business transactions are recorded. For example, every purchase that occurs should be supported by a document. These documents should be prenumbered, used in sequence, and subsequently accounted for. In this way, the business can be sure that it has made a record of each transaction.

Voucher System

The three elements of internal control described above can be combined to control expenditures by using a voucher system. A **voucher system** is a control technique that requires that every acquisition and subsequent payment be supported by an approved voucher. A **voucher** is a document that shows that an acquisition is proper and that payment is authorized.

The purchasing portion of a voucher system operates basically as shown in figure 13-1. The purchase requisition, purchase order, receiving report, and purchase invoice were explained and illustrated in Chapter 12. Recall that an authorized person or department prepares a purchase requisition to indicate the need for goods. The purchasing department reviews the purchase requisition and prepares a purchase order to send to the supplier. When the goods are received, a receiving report is prepared. A copy of each of these documents is sent to the vouchers payable section.

F I G U R E   1 3 - 1   **Voucher System—Purchasing Process**

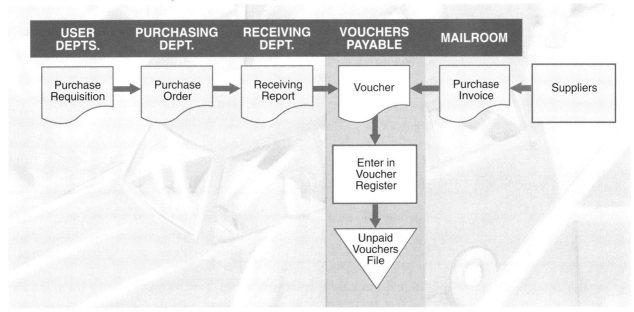

When the purchase invoice arrives, it is compared with the purchase requisition, purchase order, and receiving report. If the purchase invoice is:

- for the goods ordered (purchase requisition and purchase order),
- at the correct price (purchase order),
- and for the correct quantity (receiving report),

then a voucher (figure 13-3) is prepared. This is the first key control provided by the voucher system. If any aspect of the purchase is improper, it will be caught when the voucher is prepared.

After the voucher is prepared and approved, it is entered in a special journal called a voucher register. It then is filed by due date.

The completed voucher provides the basis for paying the supplier's invoice on the due date. This is the second key control provided by the voucher system. No payment may be made without an approved voucher. The payment process will be discussed later in this chapter.

The voucher system contains elements of internal control such as segregation of duties, authorization to order the goods and prepare the voucher, and accounting procedures that require prenumbering and accounting for the supporting documents.

Notice how the three elements of internal control can be seen in this system. (1) *Duties are segregated* because different employees order, receive, and record the purchases. (2) *Authorization* is required to order the goods, and to prepare the voucher. (3) The *accounting procedures* require prenumbering and accounting for the purchase requisitions, purchase orders, receiving reports, and vouchers. This means that every recorded purchase is supported by five documents:

1. The voucher
2. The purchase invoice
3. The receiving report
4. The purchase order
5. The purchase requisition

This provides management with strong assurance that purchases are properly controlled.

2

Prepare a voucher.

PREPARING A VOUCHER

To illustrate the preparation of a voucher and how a voucher system works, we will extend the Northern Micro transactions from Chapter 12. In this chapter, we assume that Northern Micro uses a voucher system, and several transactions are added.

When a purchase invoice (figure 13-2) is received from a supplier, the voucher section performs the following procedures.

STEP 1   Compare the invoice with the purchase requisition, purchase order, and receiving report to determine that:

   a. the quantity was requisitioned (purchase requisition), ordered (purchase order), and received (receiving report)
   b. the price and credit terms are proper (purchase order)

STEP 2   Judge whether the purchase is appropriate for the business.

STEP 3   Verify all computations on the invoice (quantity × price, and any discounts).

After performing these procedures, the voucher can be prepared. Many acceptable formats for vouchers can be used. A commonly used form is illustrated in figure 13-3. This voucher was prepared based on the purchase invoice in figure 13-2.

The front of the voucher usually shows the voucher number, date, supplier, and what was purchased. The back indicates the accounts to be debited and the payment date, check number, and amount.

FIGURE 13-2   **Purchase Invoice**

EZX ᶜᵒʳᵖ   Invoice No. 4973

2989 Rhodes Ave., Chicago, IL 60658

Sold to: **Date:**   4/9/--
Northern Micro   **Your Order No:** 319
1099 E. Louisiana   **Terms:** 1/15, n/30
Indianapolis, IN 46217

Quantity	Description	Unit Price	Total
3	P75 Computers	$1,900.00	$5,700.00
3	Q19 Laser Printers	1,000.00	3,000.00
			$8,700.00

FIGURE 13-3   **Voucher**

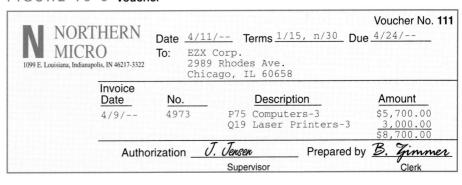

				Voucher No. **111**

N NORTHERN MICRO
1099 E. Louisiana, Indianapolis, IN 46217-3322

Date 4/11/--   Terms 1/15, n/30   Due 4/24/--
To: EZX Corp.
      2989 Rhodes Ave.
      Chicago, IL 60658

Invoice Date	No.	Description	Amount
4/9/--	4973	P75 Computers-3	$5,700.00
		Q19 Laser Printers-3	3,000.00
			$8,700.00

Authorization   *J. Jensen*   Prepared by *B. Zimmer*
                Supervisor   Clerk

Voucher No. **111**

Account Debited	Account No.	Amount	Summary	
Purchases	511	$8,700.00	Invoice	$8,700.00
			Discount	87.00
			Net	$8,613.00

Payment
Date   4/24/--   Check No.   437   Amount $8,613.00

Approved: Distribution *J.G.*   Payment *B.Z.*

The prenumbered voucher in figure 13-3 was prepared using the following steps.

STEP 1   On the front side of the voucher, insert:

    a. voucher date
    b. invoice terms
    c. due date
    d. supplier name and address
    e. invoice date
    f. description of items purchased
    g. invoice amount

STEP 2   On the back side, insert the accounts and amounts to be debited.

After these steps are completed, the voucher clerk (B. Zimmer) signs the voucher and has it approved by the voucher section supervisor (J. Jensen). The "Payment" section on the back of the voucher is not completed until the voucher is paid on the due date. The $87 purchases discount will be recorded when the voucher is paid.

3

Describe and use a voucher register.

A voucher register is used to record purchases of all types of assets and services.

VOUCHER REGISTER

After the voucher is completed and approved, it is entered in a voucher register. A **voucher register** is a special journal used to record purchases of all types of assets and services. You can think of a voucher register as an expanded purchases journal like the one we saw in Chapter 12. *In fact, if a voucher register is used, it replaces the purchases journal.*

Northern Micro's voucher register is illustrated in figure 13-4. It has four debit columns—for Purchases, Supplies, Wages Expense, and Sundry

FIGURE 13-4 **Voucher Register**

	DATE	VOUCHER NO.	ISSUED TO	PURCHASES DR.	
			VOUCHER REGISTER FOR MONTH OF April	19--	
1	4/2/--	107	Triumph Leasing		1
2	4/4/--	108	Compucraft	3 3 0 0 00	2
3	4/8/--	109	Datasoft	2 5 0 0 00	3
4	4/9/--	110	Bemon Office Supply		4
5	4/11/--	111	EZX Corporation	8 7 0 0 00	5
6	4/15/--	112	Payroll Bank Acct.		6
15	TOTALS			20 6 0 0 00	15

Accounts, and a credit column for Vouchers Payable. The Sundry Accounts Dr. column is used for transactions affecting account titles other than those with special column headings. The voucher register also has a "Payment" column which is used when the voucher is paid. As with any special journal, the exact number and types of debit and credit columns to use depends on the nature of the business.

A voucher is recorded in the voucher register by entering the following information.

1. Date
2. Voucher number
3. Person or business to whom the voucher is issued
4. Dollar amounts of debits and credits

The entry for voucher no. 111 (figure 13-3) was made on April 11.

Filing Unpaid Vouchers

After the voucher is entered in the voucher register, the voucher and supporting documents (purchase requisition, purchase order, receiving report, and purchase invoice) are stapled together. This "voucher packet" is then filed in an **unpaid vouchers file,** normally by due date. Alternatively, vouchers can be filed by supplier name. Filing by due date is preferred because this helps management plan for cash needs. It also helps ensure that vouchers are paid on the due date and cash discounts are taken.

The unpaid vouchers file is like an accounts payable subsidiary ledger grouped by due date rather than supplier.

An interesting feature of the unpaid vouchers file is that it is like an accounts payable subsidiary ledger. The main difference is that payables are grouped by due date rather than by supplier. For most businesses that use a voucher system, the unpaid vouchers file in fact serves as an accounts payable subsidiary ledger. Northern Micro uses this approach.

	SUPPLIES DR.	WAGES EXP. DR.	SUNDRY ACCOUNTS DR.			VOUCHERS PAYABLE CR.	PAYMENT		
			ACCOUNT	POST. REF.	AMOUNT		DATE	CK. NO.	
1			Rent Exp.		2 400 00	2 400 00	4/2/--	421	1
2						3 300 00			2
3						2 500 00			3
4	1 60 00					1 60 00	4/25/--	438	4
5						8 700 00	4/24/--	437	5
6		8 30 00				8 30 00	4/15/--	430	6
15	2 80 00	1 700 00			3 760 00	26 340 00			15

PAGE 4

Posting from the Voucher Register

Both individual and summary postings are required from the voucher register to the general ledger. Figure 13-5 illustrates the general ledger posting process for Northern Micro's voucher register for the month of April.

The steps in the posting procedure are indicated in figure 13-5, as follows:

On a daily basis:

STEP 1   Post each amount from the Sundry Accounts Dr. column to the appropriate general ledger account.

STEP 2   Insert the date in the Date column and the initials "VR" and the voucher register page number in the Posting Reference column of each general ledger account.

STEP 3   Insert the general ledger account numbers in the Posting Reference column of the Sundry Accounts Dr. column of the voucher register.

At the end of each month:

STEP 4   Foot the amount columns, verify that the total of the debit columns equals the total of the credit column, and rule the columns.

STEP 5   Post each column total except the Sundry Accounts Dr. column to the general ledger account indicated in the column headings.

STEP 6   Insert the date in the Date column and the initials "VR" and the voucher register page number in the Posting Reference column of each ledger account.

STEP 7   Insert the general ledger account numbers immediately below each column total except the Sundry Accounts Dr. column.

STEP 8   Insert a check mark ($\sqrt{}$) immediately below the Sundry Accounts Dr. column.

Note that the payables account in figure 13-5 can be called either Vouchers Payable or Accounts Payable. Even though the voucher system is used, many businesses still use the Accounts Payable title. On the balance sheet, the Accounts Payable title is almost always used.

No posting to an accounts payable subsidiary ledger is necessary for Northern Micro. They use the unpaid vouchers file as their accounts payable subsidiary ledger. The unpaid vouchers file was already updated when the vouchers were filed after being entered in the voucher register.

F I G U R E   1 3 - 5   **Posting Voucher Register to General Ledger**

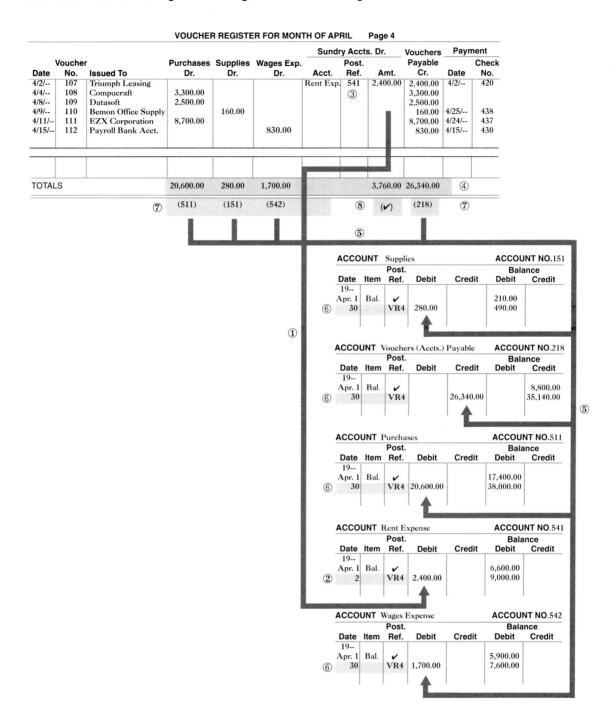

4

Describe the payment process using a voucher system.

THE PAYMENT PROCESS USING A VOUCHER SYSTEM

The payment process when a voucher system is used is illustrated in figure 13-6.

FIGURE 13-6 **Voucher System—Payment Process**

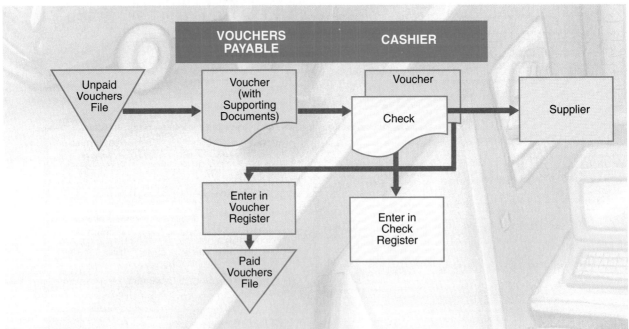

On the due date, the voucher is pulled from the unpaid vouchers file. The voucher is given to the person responsible for preparing and signing checks (for Northern Micro, the cashier). The cashier reviews each voucher and supporting documents to see that the expenditure is proper. The check is then prepared and signed, and is sent to the supplier. It is important for internal control that no check be prepared without a supporting voucher, and that the check be mailed as soon as it is signed.

Ordinary checks may be used to make payments, but under the voucher system, voucher checks often are used. A **voucher check** is a check with space for entering data about the voucher being paid. Northern Micro's voucher check to pay voucher no. 111 (figure 13-3) is shown in figure 13-7.

The voucher check has two parts:

1. The check itself, which is similar to an ordinary check
2. A statement attached which provides information regarding the invoice being paid and any deductions.

FIGURE 13-7 **Voucher Check**

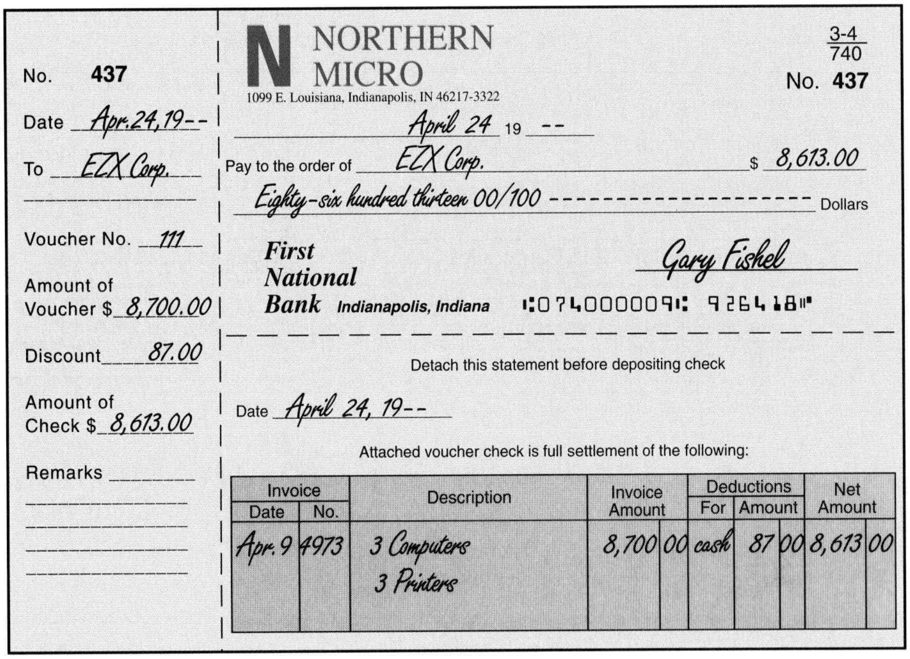

In addition, the voucher check stub identifies the voucher number being paid.

After the voucher has been paid, the cashier completes the "Payment" section on the back of the voucher. The voucher and supporting documents are then cancelled to indicate payment. This prevents a voucher from being processed again to create a duplicate payment. The cancelled voucher and supporting documents are then returned to the vouchers payable section. They are filed either numerically or by supplier in a **paid vouchers file.** In either case, the numerical sequence should be accounted for to identify possible missing or duplicate vouchers.

CHECK REGISTER

5

Describe and use a check register.

A copy of the check is used to enter the payment in a check register. A **check register** is a special journal used to record all checks written in a voucher system. Northern Micro's check register is illustrated in figure 13-8.

A check register is similar to the cash payments journal we saw in Chapter 12 (figure 12-13). A key difference is that the check register has only three amount columns—Vouchers Payable Dr., Purchases Discounts Cr., and Cash Cr. Recall that in a voucher system, every purchase of assets or services must be supported by a voucher. This means that every purchase has been recorded in a voucher register before any payment can be made.

A check register is similar to a cash payments journal except that only three amounts columns are used—Vouchers Payable Dr., Purchases Discounts Cr., and Cash Cr.

FIGURE 13-8 **Check Register**

	DATE	CHECK NO.	PAYEE	VOUCHERS PAYABLE DR. NO.	VOUCHERS PAYABLE DR. AMOUNT	PURCHASES DISCOUNTS CR.	CASH CR.	
			CHECK REGISTER FOR MONTH OF April 19--				PAGE 4	
1	4/1/--	420	Payroll Bank Acct.	106	8 7 0 00		8 7 0 00	1
2	4/2/--	421	Triumph Leasing	107	2 4 0 0 00		2 4 0 0 00	2
6	4/24/--	437	EZX Corporation	111	8 7 0 0 00	8 7 00	8 6 1 3 00	6
7	4/25/--	438	Bemon Office Supplies	110	1 6 0 00		1 6 0 00	7
8	4/29/--	443	TTA Products	100	1 5 0 0 00		1 5 0 0 00	8
9	TOTALS				24 2 0 0 00	1 7 9 00	24 0 2 1 00	9

Thus, the only possible debit in the check register is to Vouchers Payable, and the only possible credits are to Purchases Discounts and Cash. When a business uses the voucher system and a voucher register, the check register replaces the cash payments journal.

A check is recorded in the check register by entering the following information.

1. Date
2. Check number
3. Payee
4. Voucher number
5. Amounts

The entry for the voucher check in figure 13-7 can be seen on April 24. The check entering process also affects the voucher register. As shown in the diagram in figure 13-6, the canceled voucher is used to enter the payment of the vouchers in the voucher register. A portion of the voucher register in figure 13-4 is reproduced in figure 13-9, with the Payment column filled in for voucher no. 111. Both the date of payment and the check number are inserted to indicate that the voucher has been paid.

FIGURE 13-9 **Partial Voucher Register**

	DATE	VOUCHER NO.	ISSUED TO	PURCHASES DR.	
			VOUCHER REGISTER FOR MONTH OF April 19--		
5	4/11/--	111	EZX Corporation	8 7 0 0 00	5
6					6
7					7

Posting from the Check Register

Only summary postings are required from the check register. At the end of each month, the following procedures for posting from the check register to the general ledger are performed, as indicated in figure 13-10.

STEP 1   Foot the amount columns, verify that the total of the debit column equals the total of the credit columns, and rule the columns.

STEP 2   Post each column total to the general ledger account indicated in the column headings.

STEP 3   Insert the date in the Date column and the initials "CK" and the check register page number in the Posting Reference column of each ledger account.

STEP 4   Insert the general ledger account numbers immediately below each column total.

Schedule of Unpaid Vouchers

It was explained earlier that most businesses that use a voucher system do not keep an accounts payable subsidiary ledger. It is still desirable, however, to verify each month that the sum of the individual amounts owed to creditors equals the Vouchers Payable balance. For this purpose, a schedule of vouchers payable (figure 13-11) is prepared. Note that the $10,940 total listed in the schedule equals the vouchers payable balance shown in figure 13-10.

This schedule is prepared from either the voucher register or the unpaid vouchers file. Every blank in the Payment column of the voucher register represents an unpaid voucher to include in the schedule. Similarly, each voucher in the unpaid vouchers file can be included in the schedule.

		SUPPLIES DR.	WAGES EXP. DR.	SUNDRY ACCOUNTS DR.			VOUCHERS PAYABLE CR.	PAYMENT		
				ACCOUNT	POST. REF.	AMOUNT		DATE	CK. NO.	
5							8 7 0 0 00	4/24/--	437	5
6										6
7										7

PAGE 4

FIGURE 13-10 Posting Check Register to General Ledger

CHECK REGISTER FOR MONTH OF APRIL **Page 4**

Date	Check No.	Payee	Vouchers Payable Dr. No.	Vouchers Payable Dr. Amt.	Purchases Discounts Cr.	Cash Cr.	
4/1/--	420	Payroll Bank Acct.	106	870.00		870.00	
4/2/-	421	Triumph Leasing	107	2,400.00		2,400.00	
4/24/--	437	EZX Corporation	111	8,700.00	87.00	8,613.00	
4/25/--	438	Bemon Office Supplies	110	160.00		160.00	
4/29/--	443	TTA Products	100	1,500.00		1,500.00	
Totals				24,200.00	179.00	24,021.00	①
				(218)	(511.2)	(111)	④

②

ACCOUNT Cash **ACCOUNT NO.** 111

	Date	Item	Post. Ref.	Debit	Credit	Balance Debit	Balance Credit
	19--						
	Apr. 1	Bal.	✔			20,000.00	
	30		CR7	12,992.00		32,992.00	
③	30		CK4		24,021.00	8,971.00	

ACCOUNT Vouchers (Accts) Payable **ACCOUNT NO.** 218

	Date	Item	Post. Ref.	Debit	Credit	Balance Debit	Balance Credit
	19--						
	Apr. 1	Bal.	✔				8,800.00
	30		VR4		26,340.00		35,140.00
③	30		CK4	24,200.00			10,940.00

ACCOUNT Purchases Discounts **ACCOUNT NO.** 511.2

	Date	Item	Post. Ref.	Debit	Credit	Balance Debit	Balance Credit
	19--						
	Apr. 1	Bal.	✔				330.00
③	30		CK4		179.00		509.00

FIGURE 13-11 Schedule of Vouchers Payable

Northern Micro
Schedule of Vouchers Payable
April 30, 19--

TTA Products, Inc.	4 0 0 0 00
Datasoft	2 5 0 0 00
Compucraft	3 3 0 0 00
Printpro	8 0 0 00
Indy Utilities	3 4 0 00
	10 9 4 0 00

If the schedule total and the Vouchers Payable balance do not agree, the error must be located and corrected. To find the error, use the following procedures.

STEP 1   Verify the total of the schedule.

STEP 2   Review the voucher register or the unpaid vouchers file to be sure none were missed or counted twice.

STEP 3   Verify the postings to Vouchers Payable in the general ledger.

Accounting for Returns, Allowances, and Partial Payments

For a voucher system to provide good control of expenditures, vouchers must be carefully handled and recorded. This includes both the initial creation and recording of the voucher, and its subsequent payment. Because the voucher is such an important control device, special procedures are needed when the amount of the voucher needs to be changed.

Purchases Returns and Allowances.   If a complete return is made of merchandise costing $670 and a credit memo is received from the supplier, the following procedures are performed.

1. The return is noted on the voucher, the credit memo is attached, and the voucher is placed in the paid vouchers file.
2. The return is noted in the Payment column of the voucher register, as follows:

	DATE	VOUCHER NO.	ISSUED TO	PURCHASES DR.	VOUCHERS PAYABLE CR.	PAYMENT DATE	CK. NO.	
1	May 6	121	Compumax	670 00	670 00	5/9	Ret.	1

3. A general journal entry is made to record the return.

5			Vouchers Payable		670 00			5
6			Purchases Returns and Allowances			670 00		6

If a partial return of $250 is made of merchandise costing $670 and a credit memo is received, the following procedures are performed.

1. The return is noted on the voucher, the credit memo is attached, and the voucher is returned to the unpaid vouchers file.

2. The return is noted in the voucher register in the Payment column, as follows:

	DATE	VOUCHER NO.	ISSUED TO	PURCHASES DR.	VOUCHERS PAYABLE CR.	PAYMENT		
						DATE	CK. NO.	
1	May 6	121	Compumax	6 7 0 00	6 7 0 00	5/9	Ret.	1

3. A general journal entry is made to record the return.

8			Vouchers Payable		2 5 0 00			8
9			Purchases Returns and Allowances			2 5 0 00		9

4. When the voucher is paid for the original amount less the return, the payment is noted in the Payment column of the voucher register, as follows:

	DATE	VOUCHER NO.	ISSUED TO	PURCHASES DR.	VOUCHERS PAYABLE CR.	PAYMENT		
						DATE	CK. NO.	
1	May 6	121	Compumax	6 7 0 00	6 7 0 00	5/9	Ret.	1
2						5/21	451	2

Partial Payments. If partial payments (installments) are planned at the time a purchase is made, a separate voucher is prepared for each payment. Each voucher and payment is then recorded in the voucher register and check register in the normal manner.

If a partial payment is made after a voucher is created and entered, the original voucher is cancelled and new vouchers are created. Assume that merchandise is purchased for $600. Subsequently, a partial payment of only $200 is made. The following procedures are used to account for these events.

1. A general journal entry is made to cancel the original voucher.

11			Vouchers Payable		6 0 0 00			11
12			Purchases			6 0 0 00		12

2. A notation is made in the Payment column of the voucher register.

	DATE	VOUCHER NO.	ISSUED TO	PURCHASES DR.	VOUCHERS PAYABLE CR.	PAYMENT		
						DATE	CK. NO.	
1	May 3	118	PC-Time	6 0 0 00	6 0 0 00	5/7	V/122/123	1

3. Two new vouchers for $200 and $400 are prepared and entered in the voucher register. The payment of the $200 voucher is noted in the Payment column.

	DATE	VOUCHER NO.	ISSUED TO	PURCHASES DR.	VOUCHERS PAYABLE CR.	PAYMENT DATE	PAYMENT CK. NO.	
2	May 7	122	PC-Time	2 0 0 00	2 0 0 00	5/7	447	2
3	7	123	PC-Time	4 0 0 00	4 0 0 00			3

K E Y   P O I N T S

1 The three elements of internal control that are combined to control expenditures in a voucher system are:

1. Segregation of duties
2. Authorization procedures and related responsibilities
3. Accounting procedures

2 In a voucher system, every acquisition and subsequent payment must be supported by a voucher.

When a purchase invoice arrives, the voucher section verifies the quantity, price, and computations on the invoice. In addition, the appropriateness of the purchase is evaluated before preparing the voucher.

3 A voucher is recorded in a voucher register by entering the following information:

1. Date
2. Voucher number
3. Person or business to whom the voucher is issued
4. Dollar amounts of debits and credits

After entry in the voucher register, vouchers are filed in an unpaid vouchers file, normally by due date.

The voucher register is posted to the general ledger as follows:

On a daily basis:
1. Post Sundry Accounts Dr. amounts to the general ledger
2. Insert the date and posting reference in the accounts
3. Insert the account numbers in the posting reference column of the voucher register

At the end of each month:
4. Foot, verify the equality of, and rule the amount columns
5. Post specific account column totals to the general ledger
6. Insert the date and posting reference in the accounts

7. Insert the account numbers below the specific account column totals in the voucher register
8. Insert a check mark below the Sundry Accounts Dr. column

4 After a voucher is paid, the voucher and supporting documents should be canceled to prevent processing them again to create a duplicate payment.

A check is recorded in the check register by entering the following information:

1. Date
2. Check number
3. Payee
4. Voucher number
5. Amounts

5 The check register is posted to the general ledger as follows:

1. Foot, verify the equality of, and rule the amount columns
2. Post column totals to the general ledger accounts
3. Insert the date and posting reference in the accounts
4. Insert the account numbers below the column totals in the check register

To verify that the sum of the individual amounts owed to creditors equals the Vouchers Payable balance, a schedule of unpaid vouchers is prepared.

Special procedures are required when purchases returns and allowances or partial payments occur in a voucher system.

KEY TERMS

check register 437   A special journal used to record all checks written in a voucher system.

internal controls 427   Sets of procedures used to ensure that all activities of the business are properly accounted for.

paid vouchers file 437   Contains vouchers paid and cancelled and filed either numerically or by supplier.

unpaid vouchers file 433   Vouchers and supporting documents stapled together and filed either by due date (preferred) or by supplier until paid.

voucher 428   A document that shows that an acquisition is proper and that payment is authorized.

voucher check 436   A check with space for entering data about the voucher being paid.

voucher register 432 A special journal used to record purchases of all types of assets and services.

voucher system 428 A control technique that requires that every acquisition and subsequent payment be supported by an approved voucher.

BUILDING YOUR ACCOUNTING KNOWLEDGE

1. What three elements of internal control are particularly important for controlling expenditures?
2. What two key controls over expenditures are provided by the voucher system?
3. When a purchase invoice is received from a supplier, what procedures are performed by the voucher section?
4. List four items of information about each voucher entered in the voucher register.
5. Why is it desirable to file unpaid vouchers by due date?
6. What steps are followed in posting from the voucher register to the general ledger?
7. After a voucher is paid, what should be done with the voucher and supporting documents? Why?
8. List five items of information about each check entered in the check register.
9. What steps are followed in posting from the check register to the general ledger?
10. If the total of the schedule of vouchers payable does not equal the Vouchers Payable balance, what procedures should be used to search for the error?
11. If a partial return of merchandise is made, what procedures are used in a voucher system?
12. If a partial payment is made after a voucher has been created and entered for the full amount of a purchase, what procedures are used in a voucher system?

DEMONSTRATION PROBLEM

Harpo Inc. operates a retail novelty store. The following are transactions related to operations for the month of March:

March 2 Issued check no. 450 for $500 to Tremont Rental in payment of February rent. Voucher no. 313.

        3 Purchased merchandise from Gail's Gags for $550, terms 2/15, n/60. Voucher no. 314.

March 4 Purchased merchandise from Silly Sam's for $200, terms 2/10, n/60. Voucher no. 315.

10 Issued check no. 451 for $500 less $10 discount to Jerry's Jokes. Voucher no. 310.

12 Received a credit memorandum from Silly Sam's for $100 for returned merchandise that was purchased on March 4.

14 Issued check no. 452 for $250 to Resource Supplies. Voucher no. 311.

16 Purchased merchandise from Giggles for $700, terms 2/10, n/30. Voucher no. 316.

18 Issued check no. 453 to Gail's Gags for purchase made on March 3 less 2% discount. Voucher no. 314.

19 Issued check no. 454 for $750 to Donnelly's. Voucher no. 312.

21 Purchased merchandise from Creations for $870, terms 3/15, n/60. Voucher no. 317.

25 Purchased supplies from Hal's Supply for $120, terms 3/10, n/30. Voucher no. 318.

31 Issued check no. 455 to Silly Sam's for purchase made on March 4 less returns made on March 12. Voucher no. 315.

31 Issued check no. 456 for $1,250 to Payroll Bank Account in payment of wages for the month of March. Voucher no. 319.

Required

Following are selected general ledger accounts and their opening balances as well as a portion of the voucher register for February.

1. Enter the transactions in the voucher register, check register, and general journal.
2. Post the transactions to the general ledger accounts.
3. Prepare a schedule of vouchers payable and compare the March 31 balance to that in the general ledger.

GENERAL LEDGER

ACCOUNT Cash — ACCOUNT NO. 111

DATE	ITEM	POST. REF.	DEBIT	CREDIT	BALANCE DEBIT	BALANCE CREDIT
19-- Mar. 1	Balance	✓			6 0 0 0 00	

ACCOUNT Supplies — ACCOUNT NO. 151

DATE	ITEM	POST. REF.	DEBIT	CREDIT	BALANCE DEBIT	BALANCE CREDIT
19-- Mar. 1	Balance	✓			4 0 0 00	

ACCOUNT Vouchers (Accts.) Payable   ACCOUNT NO. 218

DATE	ITEM	POST. REF.	DEBIT	CREDIT	BALANCE DEBIT	BALANCE CREDIT
19-- Mar. 1	Balance	✓				1 5 0 0 00

ACCOUNT Purchases   ACCOUNT NO. 511

DATE	ITEM	POST. REF.	DEBIT	CREDIT	BALANCE DEBIT	BALANCE CREDIT
19-- Mar. 1	Balance	✓			4 2 5 0 00	

ACCOUNT Purchases Returns and Allowances   ACCOUNT NO. 511.1

DATE	ITEM	POST. REF.	DEBIT	CREDIT	BALANCE DEBIT	BALANCE CREDIT
19-- Mar. 1	Balance	✓				1 0 0 00

ACCOUNT Purchases Discounts   ACCOUNT NO. 511.2

DATE	ITEM	POST. REF.	DEBIT	CREDIT	BALANCE DEBIT	BALANCE CREDIT
19-- Mar. 1	Balance	✓				5 0 00

ACCOUNT Rent Expense   ACCOUNT NO. 541

DATE	ITEM	POST. REF.	DEBIT	CREDIT	BALANCE DEBIT	BALANCE CREDIT
19-- Mar. 1	Balance	✓			1 0 0 0 00	

ACCOUNT Wages Expense   ACCOUNT NO. 542

DATE	ITEM	POST. REF.	DEBIT	CREDIT	BALANCE DEBIT	BALANCE CREDIT
19-- Mar. 1	Balance	✓			2 5 0 0 00	

		VOUCHER REGISTER FOR MONTH OF February		19--	
	DATE	VOUCHER NO.	ISSUED TO	PURCHASES DR.	
1	2/24/--	310	Jerry's Jokes	500 00	1
2	2/26/--	311	Resource Supplies		2
3	2/26/--	312	Donnelly's	750 00	3
4					4
5					5

SOLUTION

1.

		VOUCHER REGISTER FOR MONTH OF February		19--	
	DATE	VOUCHER NO.	ISSUED TO	PURCHASES DR.	
1	2/24/--	310	Jerry's Jokes	500 00	1
2	2/26/--	311	Resource Supplies		2
3	2/26/--	312	Donnelly's	750 00	3
4					4
5					5

		VOUCHER REGISTER FOR MONTH OF March		19--	
	DATE	VOUCHER NO.	ISSUED TO	PURCHASES DR.	
1	3/2/--	313	Tremont Rental		1
2	3/3/--	314	Gail's Gags	550 00	2
3	3/4/--	315	Silly Sam's	200 00	3
4					4
5	3/16/--	316	Giggles	700 00	5
6	3/21/--	317	Creations	870 00	6
7	3/25/--	318	Hal's Supply		7
8	3/31/--	319	Payroll Bank Acct.		8
9	TOTALS			2320 00	9
10				(511)	10
11					11
12					12

PAGE 6

	SUPPLIES DR.	WAGES EXP. DR.	SUNDRY ACCOUNTS DR.			VOUCHERS PAYABLE CR.	PAYMENT		
			ACCOUNT	POST. REF.	AMOUNT		DATE	CK. NO.	
1						5 0 0 00			1
2	2 5 0 00					2 5 0 00			2
3						7 5 0 00			3
4									4
5									5

PAGE 6

	SUPPLIES DR.	WAGES EXP. DR.	SUNDRY ACCOUNTS DR.			VOUCHERS PAYABLE CR.	PAYMENT		
			ACCOUNT	POST. REF.	AMOUNT		DATE	CK. NO.	
1						5 0 0 00	3/10/--	451	1
2	2 5 0 00					2 5 0 00	3/14	452	2
3						7 5 0 00	3/19	454	3
4									4
5									5

PAGE 7

	SUPPLIES DR.	WAGES EXP. DR.	SUNDRY ACCOUNTS DR.			VOUCHERS PAYABLE CR.	PAYMENT		
			ACCOUNT	POST. REF.	AMOUNT		DATE	CK. NO.	
1			Rent Exp.	541	5 0 0 00	5 0 0 00	3/2/--	450	1
2						5 5 0 00	3/18	453	2
3						2 0 0 00	3/12	Ret.	3
4							3/31	455	4
5						7 0 0 00			5
6						8 7 0 00			6
7	1 2 0 00					1 2 0 00			7
8		1 2 5 0 00				1 2 5 0 00	3/31	456	8
9	1 2 0 00	1 2 5 0 00			5 0 0 00	4 1 9 0 00			9
10	(151)	(542)			(✓)	(218)			10
11									11
12									12

1.

	DATE	CHECK NO.	PAYEE	VOUCHERS PAYABLE DR.		PURCHASES DISCOUNTS CR.	CASH CR.	
				NO.	AMOUNT			
1	3/2/--	450	Tremont Rental	313	5 0 0 00		5 0 0 00	1
2	3/10/--	451	Jerry's Jokes	310	5 0 0 00	1 0 00	4 9 0 00	2
3	3/14/--	452	Resource Supplies	311	2 5 0 00		2 5 0 00	3
4	3/18/--	453	Gail's Gags	314	5 5 0 00	1 1 00	5 3 9 00	4
5	3/19/--	454	Donnelly's	312	7 5 0 00		7 5 0 00	5
6	3/31/--	455	Silly Sam's	315	1 0 0 00		1 0 0 00	6
7	3/31/--	456	Payroll Bank Acct.	319	1 2 5 0 00		1 2 5 0 00	7
8					3 9 0 0 00	2 1 00	3 8 7 9 00	8
9					(218)	(511.2)	(111)	9

CHECK REGISTER FOR MONTH OF March   19--   PAGE 6

2.

GENERAL LEDGER

ACCOUNT: Cash   ACCOUNT NO. 111

DATE	ITEM	POST. REF.	DEBIT	CREDIT	BALANCE DEBIT	BALANCE CREDIT
19-- Mar. 1	Balance	✓			6 0 0 0 00	
31		CK6		3 8 7 9 00	2 1 2 1 00	

ACCOUNT: Supplies   ACCOUNT NO. 151

DATE	ITEM	POST. REF.	DEBIT	CREDIT	BALANCE DEBIT	BALANCE CREDIT
19-- Mar. 1	Balance	✓			4 0 0 00	
31		VR7	1 2 0 00		5 2 0 00	

ACCOUNT: Vouchers (Accts.) Payable   ACCOUNT NO. 218

DATE	ITEM	POST. REF.	DEBIT	CREDIT	BALANCE DEBIT	BALANCE CREDIT
19-- Mar. 1	Balance	✓				1 5 0 0 00
12		J3	1 0 0 00			1 4 0 0 00
31		VR7		4 1 9 0 00		5 5 9 0 00
31		CK6	3 9 0 0 00			1 6 9 0 00

ACCOUNT: Purchases   ACCOUNT NO. 511

DATE	ITEM	POST. REF.	DEBIT	CREDIT	BALANCE DEBIT	BALANCE CREDIT
19-- Mar. 1	Balance	✓			4 2 5 0 00	
31		VR7	2 3 2 0 00		6 5 7 0 00	

ACCOUNT: Purchases Returns and Allowances					ACCOUNT NO. 511.1	
DATE	ITEM	POST. REF.	DEBIT	CREDIT	BALANCE	
					DEBIT	CREDIT
19-- Mar. 1	Balance	✓				1 0 0 00
12		J3		1 0 0 00		2 0 0 00

ACCOUNT: Purchases Discounts					ACCOUNT NO. 511.2	
DATE	ITEM	POST. REF.	DEBIT	CREDIT	BALANCE	
					DEBIT	CREDIT
19-- Mar. 1	Balance	✓				5 0 00
31		CK6		2 1 00		7 1 00

ACCOUNT: Rent Expenses					ACCOUNT NO. 541	
DATE	ITEM	POST. REF.	DEBIT	CREDIT	BALANCE	
					DEBIT	CREDIT
19-- Mar. 1	Balance	✓			1 0 0 0 00	
2		VR7	5 0 0 00		1 5 0 0 00	

ACCOUNT: Wages Expense					ACCOUNT NO. 542	
DATE	ITEM	POST. REF.	DEBIT	CREDIT	BALANCE	
					DEBIT	CREDIT
19-- Mar. 1	Balance	✓			2 5 0 0 00	
31		VR7	1 2 5 0 00		3 7 5 0 00	

1.

		GENERAL JOURNAL				PAGE 3	
	DATE	DESCRIPTION	POST. REF.	DEBIT	CREDIT		
1	19-- Mar. 12	Vouchers Payable	218	1 0 0 00			1
2		Purchases Returns & Allow.	511.1		1 0 0 00		2
3		Received credit memorandum					3
4		from Silly Sam's.					4
5							5
6							6
7							7
8							8
9							9
10							10

3.

Harpo, Inc. Schedule of Vouchers Payable March 31, 19--					
Giggles		7	0	0	00
Creations		8	7	0	00
Hal's Supply		1	2	0	00
	1	6	9	0	00
Balance in Vouchers Payable, March 31	$1	6	9	0	00

SERIES A

EXERCISES

APPLYING ACCOUNTING CONCEPTS

EXERCISE 13A1

Purchasing Process Using a Voucher System

1 In the flow chart below, identify the documents and records which illustrate the voucher process.

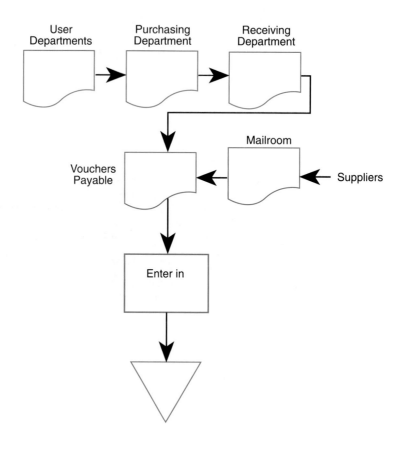

2 Prepare a voucher similar to the one shown in figure 13-3 on page 433 from the following purchase invoice.

The supplier, Sportime Corp., sent 12 Prince Spectrum rackets with a unit price of $130 and 2 DuraLink nets with a unit price of $110. Assume that the cash discount will be taken; enter your initials authorizing payment.

Sportime Corp.
6825 Kentucky Ave.
Louisville, KY 40258-4111

Invoice No. **163**

Sold to
Mitchell & Jenkins Sporting Goods
12191 E. Washington St.
Indianapolis, IN 46201-3216

Date May 6, 19--

Terms 2/10, n/30

Quantity	Description	Unit Price	Total
12	Prince Spectrum racket	$130.00	$1,560.00
2	DuraLink net	110.00	220.00
			$1,780.00

Received by *S. Miller*

Date *5/7/--*

3 Enter the following vouchers into a voucher register for the month of June, 19--, as shown in figure 13-4 on pages 432 and 433.

Voucher	Amount	Date	Issued To	Purpose
331	$ 600	6/1	Middleton Electric	Payment of rent for June
332	480	6/5	Bristow Distributors	Merchandise on account
333	700	6/9	MicroLabs, Inc.	Merchandise on account
334	122	6/11	Miller Office Supply	Prepaid office supplies
335	802	6/13	Brabham Products	Merchandise on account
336	3,000	6/15	Payroll	Bimonthly paychecks
337	850	6/21	Bristow Distributors	Merchandise on account

The following vouchers were paid:

Voucher	Date Paid	Check No.
331	6/10	498
332	6/14	499
333	6/18	501
335	6/20	502
336	6/15	500
337	6/30	503

EXERCISE 13A4

Payment Process Using a Voucher System

4 Prepare and label a flow chart illustrating the payment process using a voucher system. Use the symbols as shown in Exercise 13A1. Identify documents and records.

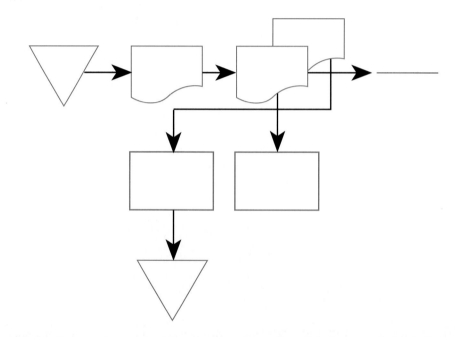

EXERCISE 13A5

Check Register

5 The following information, taken from the voucher register, is evidenced by unpaid vouchers. Enter the appropriate information into a check register for the month of August, 19--, as shown in figure 13-8 (check register) on page 438. The discount amounts shown are deducted from the voucher amounts. Total and rule the register.

Date	Voucher No.	Amount	Pay To	Ck. No.	Purpose	Discount Amount
8/5	111	$ 800	Armos Bros.	406	Merchandise on account	$ 8.00
8/7	108	500	H&L Realty	407	Rent	
8/11	113	380	Excel Products	408	Merchandise on account	$ 7.60
8/13	109	640	Bell & Mason	409	Merchandise on account	$12.80
8/15	115	2,000	Payroll	410	Bimonthly paychecks	

Date	Voucher No.	Amount	Pay To	Ck. No.	Purpose	Discount Amount
8/19	117	$ 888	B. G. Hammer	411	Merchandise on account	$17.76
8/25	119	250	Office Pro, Inc.	412	Office supplies	
8/31	120	2,000	Payroll	413	Bimonthly paychecks	

Return of Merchandise and Partial Payments

3 Enter the following merchandise returns and partial payments in a general journal and in a voucher register where appropriate:

Sept. 10 Merchandise purchased from XYZ Co. for $800, voucher no. 203, is returned. A credit memo is received, attached to the voucher, and the voucher is placed in the paid vouchers file.

20 A partial return of merchandise is made for $200, voucher no. 206. A credit memo is received, attached to the voucher, and the voucher is returned to the unpaid vouchers file.

24 A partial payment of merchandise is made for $300 on voucher no. 208, that was for $600. Plan to pay the remaining $300 in two weeks (new vouchers are issued). Check no. 682.

28 A partial return of merchandise is made for $80, voucher no. 204. A credit memo is received, attached to the voucher, and the voucher is returned to the unpaid vouchers file.

Schedule of Vouchers Payable

3 Prepare a schedule of vouchers payable for Randalls Appliances, based on information found in the voucher register on page 456.

PROBLEMS

Voucher Register, Posting to General Ledger

3 Bradshaw Electronics had the following transactions for the month of July, 19--. No subsidiary accounts payable ledger is used; instead, a schedule of vouchers payable can be prepared from information in the voucher register.

Voucher	Amount	Date	Issued To	Purpose	Payment Date	Ck. No.
206	$ 300	7/1	Parkhouse, Inc.	Payment of rent	7/1	318
207	850	7/3	G. B. Reynolds	Merchandise	7/18	320
208	120	7/5	Richardson's	Office supplies		
209	900	7/9	Seymour Supply	Merchandise	7/19	321
210	1,000	7/15	Payroll	Paychecks	7/15	319

Voucher	Amount	Date	Issued To	Purpose	Payment Date	Ck. No.
211	$ 580	7/21	Pressman's	Merchandise		
212	620	7/28	T. R. Canady Co.	Merchandise		
213	328	7/30	Excelsior Ltd.	Merchandise		
214	1,000	7/31	Payroll	Paychecks	7/31	322

VOUCHER REGISTER FOR MONTH OF January 19--

	DAY	VOUCHER NO.	ISSUED TO	PURCHASES DR.	
1	1	101	Blackmoor, Inc.	600 00	1
2	3	102	Bremer Office Supplies		2
3	6	103	Kettles and Kabrus	280 00	3
4	7	104	Moore & Johnson		4
5	11	105	Kitchen Kaboodle	300 00	5
6	13	106	Blackmoor, Inc.	375 00	6
7	16	107	Payroll		7
8	21	108	Rich & Associates	400 00	8
9	29	109	Darin Elwood Co.	219 00	9
10				2174 00	10

PAGE 1

	SUPPLIES DR.	WAGES EXP. DR.	SUNDRY ACCOUNTS DR.			VOUCHERS PAYABLE CR.	PAYMENT		
			ACCOUNT	POST. REF.	AMOUNT		DATE	CK. NO.	
1						600 00	1/11	2	1
2	118 00					118 00			2
3						280 00	1/24	4	3
4			Rent Exp.	511	500 00	500 00	1/7	1	4
5						300 00			5
6						375 00			6
7		1000 00				1000 00	1/16	3	7
8						400 00			8
9						219 00			9
10	118 00	1000 00			500 00	3792 00			10

Required

1. Enter the transactions for July, 19--, in the voucher register.
2. Post the voucher register totals to the general ledger.
3. Prepare a schedule of vouchers payable.

<table>
<tr><td>

PROBLEM 13A2

Check Register, Posting to General Ledger

</td></tr>
</table>

5 The transactions for the month of August, 19--, follow. A voucher register is used, but no subsidiary accounts payable ledger is kept. Assume terms of 2/10, n/30, and assume that all discounts are taken.

Date	Voucher No.	Amount	Pay To	Ck. No.	Purpose
8/3	108	$ 800	M. Pearson	111	August rent
8/5	109	550	K. B. Adams Co.	112	Merchandise on account
8/8	111	300	Quality Paper	113	Office supplies
8/11	113	600	Paulson Group	114	Merchandise on account
8/15	115	2,000	Payroll	115	Bimonthly payroll
8/17	116	720	Peerson, Inc.	116	Merchandise on account
8/22	118	380	K. B. Adams Co.	117	Merchandise on account
8/25	121	440	Wilson's	118	Merchandise on account
8/31	123	2,000	Payroll	119	Bimonthly payroll

Required

1. Enter the transactions for August, 19--, in the check register.
2. Post the check register totals to the general ledger.

<table>
<tr><td>

PROBLEM 13A3

Voucher Register, Check Register, Posting, and Schedule of Vouchers Payable

</td></tr>
</table>

3/4/5 Betty Classic is owner of the Classic Candle Shop. The following transactions occurred during April, 19--. The Classic Candle Shop uses a voucher register, a check register, and a general ledger, but does not keep a subsidiary accounts payable ledger. Unpaid vouchers are filed and listed at the end of the month.

Vouchers Issued:

Date	No.	Issued To	Amount	Purpose	Terms
4/1	1101	Landmark Realty	$ 500	Rent for April	
4/3	1102	Wax House	280	Merchandise	2/10, n/30
4/5	1103	Designs West	490	Merchandise	2/10, n/30
4/9	1104	Crane Stationers	180	Office supplies	
4/11	1105	Magic Solutions	600	Merchandise	2/10, n/30
4/15	1106	Payroll	1,500	Bimonthly payroll	
4/23	1107	Wax House	510	Merchandise	1/10, n/30
4/25	1108	Baskets & More	440	Merchandise	2/10, n/30
4/28	1109	Magic Solutions	450	Merchandise	2/10, n/30
4/30	1110	Payroll	1,500	Bimonthly payroll	

Checks Issued:

Date	No.	Issued To	Voucher No.	Amount	Discount	Vouchers Payable Dr.
4/1	928	Landmark Realty	1101	$ 500		
4/9	929	Crane Stationers	1104	180		
4/11	930	Wax House	1102	280		
4/15	931	Payroll	1106	1,500		

Date	No.	Issued To	Voucher No.	Amount	Discount	Vouchers Payable Dr.
4/19	932	Designs West	1103	$ 490		
4/30	933	Payroll	1110	1,500		

Required

1. Enter the transactions for April in the voucher register. Total and rule the register. Update the Payment column when vouchers are paid.
2. Enter the transactions for April in the check register. Be sure to take discounts where appropriate. Total and rule the register.
3. Post the voucher register and the check register to the general ledger.
4. Prepare a schedule of vouchers payable.

PROBLEM 13A4

Voucher Register, Check Register, General Journal (Returns and Partial Payments)

3/4/5 Richard Harris is the owner of Harris's Appliance Store. The following transactions occurred during May, 19--. Harris's Appliance Store uses a voucher register, a check register, and a general journal.

Vouchers Issued:

Date	No.	Issued To	Amount	Purpose	Terms
5/1	208	McPherson's Co.	$ 800	Rent for May	
5/3	209	Welding Supply Co.	280	Merchandise	2/10, n/30
5/7	210	Quality Office Supply	118	Prepaid supplies	
5/10	211	Piper's, Inc.	440	Merchandise	2/10, n/30
5/12	212	Manley's Wholesale	620	Merchandise	2/10, n/30
5/15	213	Payroll	1,000	Bimonthly checks	
5/19	214	Welding Supply Co.	860	Merchandise	2/10, n/30
5/22	217	Quality Office Supply	210	Prepaid supplies	
5/25	218	Regicnal Distributors	460	Merchandise	1/10, n/30
5/28	219	Pringle's & Co.	600	Merchandise	2/10, n/30
5/31	220	Payroll	1,000	Bimonthly checks	

Returns and Partial Payments:

5/5	209	Returned $40 of merchandise—credit memo received, attached to voucher and returned to unpaid vouchers file.
5/10	211	Returned $440 of merchandise—credit memo received, attached to voucher and filed in paid vouchers file.
5/21	214	Partial payment of $430 is made (see check register)—plan to pay the remaining $430 in two weeks (new vouchers 215 and 216 are issued).

Checks Issued:

Date	No.	Issued To	Voucher No.	Amount	Discount	Vouchers Payable Dr.
5/1	411	McPherson's Co.	208	$ 800		
5/7	412	Quality Office Supply	210	118		
5/11	413	Welding Supply Co.	209	240		
5/15	414	Payroll	213	1,000		
5/21	415	Welding Supply Co.	214	430		
5/23	416	Manley's Wholesale	212	620		
5/31	417	Payroll	218	1,000		

Required

1. Enter the transactions for May in the voucher register. Total and rule the register. Update the Payment column when vouchers are paid.
2. Enter the transactions for May in the check register. Be sure to take discounts where appropriate. Total and rule the register.
3. Enter the returns and partial payments in the general journal. Update the Payment column of the voucher register when appropriate.

SERIES B

EXERCISES

EXERCISE 13B1

Purchasing Process Using a Voucher System

1 In the following flow chart, identify the departments and other sources of the documents and records that illustrate the voucher process.

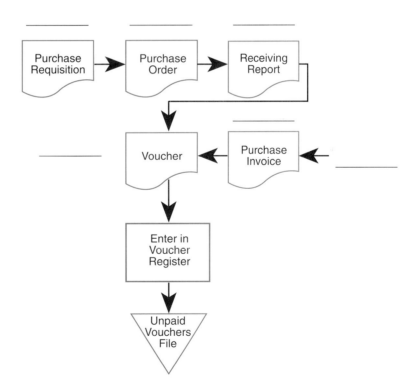

EXERCISE 13B2

Preparing a Voucher

2 Prepare a voucher similar to the one shown in figure 13-3 on page 431 from the following purchase invoice.

The supplier, Sportime Corp. sent 33 cases of Sport tennis balls at $30 a case and 14 Wilke racket covers at $25 each. Assume that the cash discount will be taken; enter your initials authorizing payment.

Sportime Corp.
6825 Kentucky Ave.
Louisville, KY 40258-4111

Invoice No. **164**

Sold to
Mitchell & Jenkins Sporting Goods
12191 E. Washington St.
Indianapolis, IN 46201-3216

Date   May 6, 19--

Terms   2/10, n/30

Quantity	Description	Unit Price	Total
33 cases	Sport tennis balls	$30.00	$ 990.00
14	Wilke racket covers	25.00	350.00
			$1340.00

Received by   *S. Miller*
Date   *5/7/--*

EXERCISE 13B3

Voucher Register

3 Enter the following vouchers into a voucher register for the month of July, 19--, as shown in figure 13-4 on pages 432 and 433.

Voucher	Amount	Date	Issued To	Purpose
431	$ 400	7/1	Basetown Management	Payment of rent for July
432	680	7/5	Repro Distributors	Merchandise on account
433	300	7/9	MirrorLabs, Inc.	Merchandise on account
434	110	7/11	Owens Office Supply	Prepaid office supplies
435	352	7/13	Richards Products	Merchandise on account
436	2,500	7/15	Payroll	Bimonthly paychecks
437	350	7/21	Repro Distributors	Merchandise on account

The following vouchers were paid:

Voucher	Date Paid	Check No.
431	7/10	598
432	7/14	599
433	7/18	601
435	7/20	602
436	7/15	600

4 In the following flow chart, supply the missing documents and records illustrating the payment process using a voucher system.

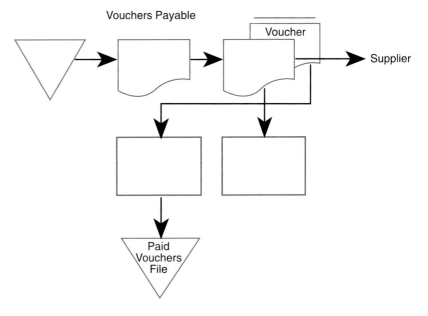

Vouchers Payable

Voucher

Supplier

Paid
Vouchers
File

5 The following information, taken from the voucher register, is evidenced by unpaid vouchers. Enter the appropriate information into a check register for the month of September, 19--, as shown in figure 13-8 (check register) on page 438. The discount amounts shown are deducted from the voucher amounts. Total and rule the register.

Date	Voucher No.	Amount	Pay To	Ck. No.	Purpose	Discount Amount
9/5	1111	$ 600	Brian Bros.	2814	Merchandise on account	$ 6.00
9/7	1108	400	B&J Realty	2815	Rent	
9/11	1113	280	Trycl Products	2816	Merchandise on account	$ 5.60
9/13	1114	540	Myro & Smith	2817	Merchandise on account	$10.80
9/15	1109	2,200	Payroll	2818	Bimonthly paychecks	
9/19	1117	488	T. M. Kingley	2819	Merchandise on account	$ 4.88
9/25	1123	150	Bly Stationers	2820	Office supplies	
9/30	1120	2,200	Payroll	2821	Bimonthly paychecks	

3 Enter the following merchandise returns and partial payments in a general journal and in a voucher register where appropriate.

Sept. 15 Merchandise purchased from Arbiters, Inc. for $700, voucher no. 204, is returned. A credit memo is received, attached to the voucher, and the voucher is placed in the paid vouchers file.

Sept. 20 A partial return of merchandise is made for $300, voucher no. 203. A credit memo is received, attached to the voucher, and the voucher is returned to the unpaid vouchers file.

25 A partial payment of merchandise is made for $150 on voucher no. 206, which was for $350. Plan to pay the remaining $200 in two weeks (new vouchers are issued). Check no. 682.

30 A partial return of merchandise is made for $20, voucher no. 208. A credit memo is received, attached to the voucher, and the voucher is returned to the unpaid vouchers file.

EXERCISE 13B7

Schedule of Vouchers Payable

3 Prepare a schedule of vouchers payable for M. B. Jacobs, based on information found in the following voucher register.

VOUCHER REGISTER FOR MONTH OF March 19--

PAGE 3

	DAY	VOUCHER NO.	ISSUED TO	PURCHASES DR.	SUPPLIES DR.	WAGES EXP. DR.	SUNDRY ACCOUNTS DR. ACCOUNT	POST. REF.	AMOUNT	VOUCHERS PAYABLE CR.	PAYMENT DATE	CK. NO.	
1	1	306	Richland Associates				Rent Exp.		300 00	300 00	3/2	806	1
2	4	307	Carlson & Son	800 00	180 00					800 00	3/11	808	2
3	6	308	Wilson Office Supplies							180 00	3/8	807	3
4	9	309	Black & Brewer	600 00						600 00			4
5	12	310	Kreklow Company	380 00						380 00	3/18	810	5
6	16	311	Payroll			1 000 00				1 000 00	3/16	809	6
7	21	312	Anderson Enterprises	260 00						260 00			7
8	24	313	Carlson & Son	410 00						410 00			8
9	28	314	Wilson Office Supplies		98 00					98 00			9
10	31	315	Payroll			1 000 00				1 000 00	3/31	811	10
11				2 450 00	278 00	2 000 00			300 00	5 028 00			11

Voucher Register, Posting to General Ledger

3 Lazertown Sounds had the following transactions for the month of July, 19--. No subsidiary accounts payable ledger is used; instead, a schedule of vouchers payable can be prepared from information in the voucher register.

Voucher	Amount	Date	Issued To	Purpose	Payment Date	Ck. No.
771	$ 500	7/1	Milltown Realty	Payment of rent	7/1	330
772	850	7/4	Deringer Electronics	Merchandise	7/11	332
773	320	7/7	Smith's	Office supplies	7/8	331
774	380	7/11	Breck Sound Supply	Merchandise	7/21	334
775	1,500	7/15	Payroll	Paychecks	7/15	333
776	680	7/21	Clear Tone Disks	Merchandise		
777	410	7/28	Deringer Electronics	Merchandise		
778	228	7/29	Smith's	Office supplies		
779	1,500	7/31	Payroll	Paychecks	7/31	335

Required
1. Enter the transactions for July, 19--, in the voucher register. Total and rule the voucher register.
2. Post the voucher register totals to the general ledger.
3. Prepare a schedule of vouchers payable.

Check Register, Posting to General Ledger

5 The following transactions are for the month of August, 19--. A voucher register is used, but no subsidiary accounts payable ledger is kept. Assume terms of 2/10, n/30, and assume that all discounts are taken.

Date	Voucher No.	Amount	Pay To	Ck. No.	Purpose
8/2	108	$600	Realty Co.	211	August rent
8/5	111	238	Tri-Cities Co.	212	Merchandise on account
8/8	112	412	Miller's	213	Merchandise on account
8/10	115	108	A&E Office Co.	214	Office supplies
8/15	114	900	Payroll	215	Bimonthly payroll
8/18	118	620	Blythe Mill	216	Merchandise on account
8/22	119	512	Tri-Cities Co.	217	Merchandise on account
8/27	122	816	Miller's	218	Merchandise on account
8/31	123	900	Payroll	219	Bimonthly payroll

Required
1. Enter the transactions for August, 19--, in the check register.
2. Post the check register totals to the general ledger.

Voucher Register, Check Register, Posting, and Schedule of Vouchers Payable

3/4/5 Jane Hledik is owner of the Hledik Lawn Supply. The following transactions occurred during April, 19--. Hledik Lawn Supply uses a voucher register, a check register, and a general ledger, but does not keep a subsidiary accounts payable ledger. Unpaid vouchers are filed and listed at the end of the month.

Vouchers Issued:

Date	No.	Issued To	Amount	Purpose	Terms
4/2	662	Brenner's	$600	Rent for April	
4/4	663	Lawn Care Wholesale	300	Merchandise	2/10, n/30
4/7	664	Southern Supply	128	Office supplies	
4/10	665	Clay's Chemicals	420	Merchandise	1/20, n/30
4/13	666	Mendel & Son	530	Merchandise	2/10, n/30
4/15	667	Payroll	950	Bimonthly payroll	
4/19	668	Lawn Care Wholesale	570	Merchandise	1/10, n/30
4/27	669	Southern Supply	99	Office supplies	
4/29	670	Lakeside Fertilizer	280	Merchandise	2/10, n/30
4/30	671	Payroll	950	Bimonthly payroll	

Checks Issued:

Date	No.	Issued To	Voucher No.	Amount	Discount	Vouchers Payable Dr.
4/2	748	Brenner's	662	$600		
4/7	749	Southern Supply	664	128		
4/11	750	Lawn Care Wholesale	663	300		
4/15	751	Payroll	667	950		
4/20	752	Mendel & Son	666	530		
4/30	753	Payroll	671	950		

Required

1. Enter the transactions for April in the voucher register. Total and rule the register. Update the Payment column when vouchers are paid.
2. Enter the transactions for April in the check register. Be sure to take discounts where appropriate. Total and rule the register.
3. Post the voucher register and the check register to the general ledger.
4. Prepare a schedule of vouchers payable.

PROBLEM 13B4

Voucher Register, Check Register, General Journal (Returns and Partial Payments)

3/4/5 Michael Blake is the owner of Blake's Appliance Store. The following transactions occurred during May, 19--. Blake's Appliance Store uses a voucher register, a check register, and a general ledger.

Vouchers Issued:

Date	No.	Issued To	Amount	Purpose	Terms
5/1	308	Johnson & Smith	$ 500	Rent for May	
5/3	309	Wilson Supply Co.	380	Merchandise	2/10, n/30
5/7	310	B & J Office Supply	138	Prepaid supplies	
5/10	311	P. T. Benkley Co.	540	Merchandise	2/10, n/30
5/12	312	Wesley's Wholesale	720	Merchandise	2/10, n/30
5/15	313	Payroll	1,000	Bimonthly checks	
5/19	314	Wilson Supply Co.	660	Merchandise	2/10, n/30
5/22	317	B & J Office Supply	120	Prepaid supplies	
5/25	318	Eastern Distributors	360	Merchandise	1/10, n/30
5/28	319	Tremble's & Co.	400	Merchandise	2/10, n/30
5/31	320	Payroll	1,000	Bimonthly checks	

Returns and Partial Payments:

5/5	309	Returned $50 of merchandise—credit memo received, attached to voucher and returned to unpaid vouchers file.
5/11	311	Returned $540 of merchandise—credit memo received, attached to voucher and filed in paid vouchers file.
5/21	314	Partial payment of $330 is made (see check register)—plan to pay the remaining $330 in two weeks (new vouchers 315 and 316 are issued).

Checks Issued:

Date	No.	Issued To	Voucher No.	Amount	Discount	Vouchers Payable Dr.
5/1	411	Johnson & Smith	308	$ 500		
5/7	412	B & J Office Supply	310	138		
5/11	413	Wilson Supply Co.	309	330		
5/15	414	Payroll	313	1,000		
5/21	415	Wilson Supply Co.	314	330		
5/23	416	Wesley's Wholesale	312	720		
5/31	417	Payroll	318	1,000		

Required

1. Enter the transactions for May in the voucher register. Total and rule the register. Update the Payment column when vouchers are paid.
2. Enter the transactions for May in the check register. Be sure to take discounts where appropriate. Total and rule the register.
3. Enter the returns and partial payments in the general journal. Update the Payment column of the voucher register when appropriate.

MASTERY PROBLEM

Sunshine Flower Shop just began operations in the month of July. Following are the transactions that occurred:

July 1 Purchased merchandise from Thorny Wholesale for $600. Voucher no. 1.

2 Issued check no. 1 for $1,000 to Strongs Rental for July rent. Voucher no. 2.

3 Purchased merchandise from Flowerbed Inc. for $470, terms 2/15, n/60, FOB shipping point. Voucher no. 3.

7 Issued check no. 2 to Thorny Wholesale for $300 partial payment for goods purchased on July 1. Voucher no. 1.

9 Paid $20 shipping charges to Charlie's Trucking for delivery from Flowerbed Inc. Issued check no. 3.

15 Issued check no. 4 for $600 to Payroll Bank Account for wages. Voucher no. 7.

July 16 Purchased merchandise from Petals Co. for $377.00, terms 2/15, n/30. Voucher no. 8.

   17 Purchased merchandise from Weeds Plus for $436, terms 3/15, n/60. Voucher no. 9.

   18 Issued check no. 5 to Flowerbed Inc. for goods purchased on July 3 less discount. Voucher no. 3.

   23 Purchased supplies from Staples Supply for $150. Voucher no. 10.

   31 Issued check no. 6 to Petals Co. for foods purchased on July 16 less discount. Voucher no. 8.

   31 Issued check no. 7 for $600 to Payroll Bank Account for wages. Voucher no. 11.

Required

The general ledger accounts are listed below. The $6,000 with which the Flower Shop began business is entered in the Cash account. Only this account has a beginning balance.

Cash	111
Supplies	151
Vouchers (Accts.) Payable	218
Purchases	511
Purchases Discounts	511.2
Freight-In	512
Rent Expense	541
Wages Expense	542

1. Enter all transactions in the voucher register, check register, and general journal.
2. Post the transactions to the general ledger.
3. Prepare a schedule of vouchers payable and compare the July 31 balance to that in the general ledger.

Adjustments and the Work Sheet for a Merchandising Business

In Chapters 11 through 13, we learned how to account for the day-by-day transactions of a merchandising business. In this chapter, we will focus on end-of-period adjustments and the preparation of the work sheet. In Chapter 15 we will complete the accounting cycle by preparing financial statements and closing entries.

A work sheet for a merchandising firm is very similar to the work sheet prepared for a service business in Chapter 5. It is used to prepare adjustments for supplies, prepaid insurance, wages earned but not paid, depreciation, and other necessary year-end adjustments. A merchandising firm must also make an adjustment to properly report the amount of merchandise inventory held at the end of the accounting period. While revisiting the work sheet, we will also introduce a new adjustment for unearned revenue.

1

Prepare an adjustment for merchandise inventory.

ADJUSTMENT FOR MERCHANDISE INVENTORY

Figure 14-1 reviews the entries made when a business buys and sells merchandise. Note that the Merchandise Inventory account is never debited or credited during the year.

FIGURE 14-1 **Review of Entries for Purchase and Sale of Merchandise.**

TRANSACTION	ENTRY		
Purchase of merchandise	Purchases	xxx	
	Accounts Payable or Cash		xxx
Sale of merchandise	Accounts Receivable or Cash	xxx	
	Sales		xxx

Since sales and purchases have taken place during the year, the beginning balance of the inventory account no longer provides an accurate picture of the inventory held at the end of the period. This means that an adjustment must be made to remove the beginning inventory and to enter the ending inventory in the Merchandise Inventory account. The quantity of inventory on hand at the end of the accounting period is determined by taking a physical count of the goods on hand. This process is referred to as a **physical inventory.** The cost of these goods is determined by reviewing the accounting records. Of course, this year's ending inventory becomes next year's beginning inventory.

To illustrate the adjustment for merchandise inventory, let's assume that Ponder's Bike Parts had a beginning merchandise inventory of $25,000. During the year the entries shown in figure 14-1 were made as merchandise was purchased and sold. At the end of the accounting period, a physical inventory of the merchandise determined that merchandise which cost $30,000 was still on hand. This indicates that the firm purchased more merchandise than it sold.

As shown in figure 14-2, the inventory adjustment is made in two steps.

STEP 1   The beginning inventory ($25,000) is removed from the Merchandise Inventory account by crediting Merchandise Inventory. Income Summary is debited because this amount is used in the calculation of Cost of Goods Sold. Cost of Goods Sold is an expense on the income statement.

STEP 2   The ending inventory ($30,000) is entered by debiting Merchandise Inventory. Income Summary is credited because this amount also is used in the calculation of Cost of Goods Sold. After making the second adjustment, the balance in the Merchandise Inventory account is $30,000 which reflects the inventory on hand at the end of the accounting period.

F I G U R E   1 4 - 2 **Two step adjustment for merchandise inventory.**

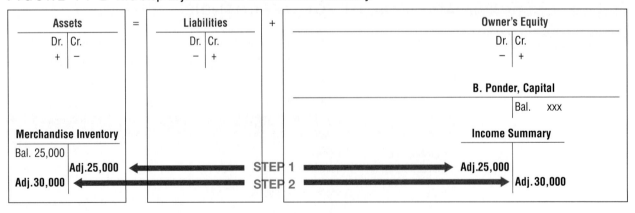

The two step adjustment process is a bit unusual. Perhaps the best way to explain the reason for this approach is by illustrating how these adjustments are made on the work sheet and how the work sheet information is used to prepare the income statement. Figure 14-3, shown on page 469, illustrates a partial work sheet for Ponder's Bike Parts and the Cost of Goods Sold section of the income statement.

The inventory adjustments are made following the two step process described above.

STEP 1	Income Summary	25,000	
	Merchandise Inventory		25,000
STEP 2	Merchandise Inventory	30,000	
	Income Summary		30,000

Note that both the debit of $25,000 and the credit of $30,000 made to the Income Summary account are extended to the Adjusted Trial Balance and Income Statement columns. *This is the only time that the individual figures, rather than the net amount, are extended on the work sheet.* It is done in this case because the individual amounts are needed for the calculation of cost of goods sold on the income statement. As shown in figure 14-3, all of the information needed for the preparation of the income statement is in the income statement columns of the work sheet. This is the result of using the two step adjustment process for inventory, and extending both the debit and credit made to the Income Summary account.

ADJUSTMENT FOR UNEARNED REVENUE

2

Prepare an adjustment for unearned revenue.

Some businesses require payment before delivering a product or performing a service. Examples include insurance companies, magazine publishers, apartment complexes, college food services, and theater companies which sell season tickets. The cash received in advance is called **unearned revenue.** Since the cash has been received in advance, the company owes the customers the product or service, or must refund their money. Thus, unearned revenue is reported as a *liability* on the balance sheet.

To illustrate, let's assume that the Brown County Playhouse sells season tickets for five plays produced throughout the year. Tickets sell for $10 each and a maximum of 1,000 seats can be sold for each play. For simplicity, let's assume that all shows sell out during the first week that

FIGURE 14-3 Calculation of Cost of Goods Sold using information in the Income Statement columns of the work sheet.

Ponder's Bike Parts
Work Sheet (Partial)
For the Year Ended December 31, 19--

ACCOUNT TITLE	TRIAL BALANCE DEBIT	TRIAL BALANCE CREDIT	ADJUSTMENTS DEBIT	ADJUSTMENTS CREDIT	ADJUSTED TRIAL BALANCE DEBIT	ADJUSTED TRIAL BALANCE CREDIT	INCOME STATEMENT DEBIT	INCOME STATEMENT CREDIT	BALANCE SHEET DEBIT	BALANCE SHEET CREDIT
Merch. Inv.	25 000 00		(2) 30 000 00	(1) 25 000 00	30 000 00		Begin. Inv. 25 000 00	End. Inv. 30 000 00	30 000 00	
Income Sum.			(1) 25 000 00	(2) 30 000 00	25 000 00	30 000 00	25 000 00	30 000 00		
Purchases	80 000 00				80 000 00		80 000 00			
Purch. Ret. & Allow.		1 000 00				1 000 00		1 000 00 Pur. R & A		
Purch. Discount		5 000 0				5 000 0		5 000 0 Pur. Discounts		
Freight-In	7 000 0				7 000 0		7 000 0 Freight-In			

Cost of Goods Sold

Cost of Goods Sold			
Merchandise inventory, January 1			25 000 00
Purchases		80 000 00	
Less purchases returns and allowances	1 000 00		
Less purchases discounts	5 000 0	1 500 00	
Net purchases		78 500 00	
Add freight-in		7 000 0	
Cost of merchandise purchased			79 200 00
Merchandise available for sale			104 200 00
Less merchandise inventory, Dec. 31			30 000 00
Cost of goods sold			74 200 00

season tickets are available for sale. As shown in figure 14-4, the sale of the tickets would be recorded as follows:

8		(1)	Cash	50 0 0 0 00		8
9			Unearned Ticket Revenue		50 0 0 0 00	9
10			($10 × 1,000 seats × 5 shows)			10
11						11

To prepare financial statements following production of the third show, an adjusting entry is made to recognize that $30,000 ($10 × 1,000 seats × 3 shows) in ticket revenue has been earned. To do this, the following adjusting entry is made.

12	(Adj.)	Unearned Ticket Revenue	30 0 0 0 00		12
13		Ticket Revenue		30 0 0 0 00	13
14					14

The remaining balance of $20,000 in Unearned Ticket Revenue is reported as a current liability on the balance sheet.

FIGURE 14-4 Entries for Unearned Revenues

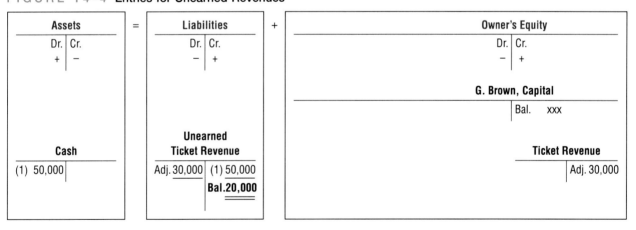

Let's take a look at where the new accounts for a merchandising firm fit into a chart of accounts. Recall that the chart of accounts follows the form of the accounting equation (Assets = Liabilities + Owner's Equity + Revenue − Expense). A chart of accounts for Northern Micro is provided in figure 14-5. Note the classification of the new accounts introduced for a merchandising firm.

FIGURE 14-5 **Chart of Accounts for Northern Micro**

Northern Micro Chart of Accounts			
Assets*		**Sales Revenue**	
Current Assets		411	Sales
111	Cash	411.1	Sales Returns and
131	Accounts Receivable		Allowances
141	Merchandise Inventory	411.2	Sales Discounts
151	Supplies	**Other Revenue**	
155	Prepaid Insurance	412	Subscriptions Revenue
Property, Plant and Equipment		431	Interest Revenue
161	Land	**Cost of Goods Sold**	
171	Building	511	Purchases
171.1	Accum. Depr—Bldg.	511.1	Purchases Returns and
181	Store Equipment		Allowances
181.1	Accum. Depr.—	511.2	Purchases Discounts
	Store Equipment	512	Freight-In
Liabilities		**Operating Expenses**	
216	Notes Payable	542	Wages Expense
218	Accounts Payable	543	Supplies Expense
219	Wages Payable	545	Telephone Expense
221	Sales Tax Payable	547	Depreciation Expense
230	Unearned Subscrp.	548	Insurance Expense
	Revenue	549	Utilities Expense
262	Mortgage Payable	551	Advertising Expense
		572	Miscellaneous Expense
Owner's Equity			
311	Gary L. Fishel, Capital	**Other Expenses**	
312	Gary L. Fishel, Drawing	581	Interest Expense
331	Income Summary		
*Words in bold type represent headings and not account titles.			

Merchandise Inventory is listed as a current asset, Unearned Subscriptions Revenue is listed as a liability, and Subscriptions Revenue is listed as an other revenue. Since Sales Returns & Allowances and Sales Discounts are deducted from Sales on the income statement, they are **contra revenue** accounts. As such, they are given the same account number as Sales (411) with a ".1" or ".2" extension.

Purchases, Purchases Returns & Allowances, Purchases Discounts and Freight-In are used to compute Cost of Goods Sold. Thus, they are listed under this heading. Since Purchases Returns & Allowances and Purchases Discounts are deducted from the Purchases account when computing cost of goods sold, they are often called **contra cost** accounts. They are given the same number as Purchases (511) with the ".1" and ".2" extensions.

Interest Expense is classified as "Other Expense" instead of being listed under "Operating Expenses" because it represents the expense of obtaining money to do business, rather than an expense directly associated with operating the business.

PREPARING A WORK SHEET FOR A MERCHANDISING FIRM

Prepare a work sheet for a merchandising firm.

The work sheet for a merchandising firm is very similar to the one you learned about in Chapter 5 for a service business. Recall the five steps taken to prepare a work sheet.

STEP 1   Prepare the trial balance.

STEP 2   Prepare the adjustments.

STEP 3   Prepare the adjusted trial balance.

STEP 4   Extend the adjusted trial balance to the Income Statement and Balance Sheet columns.

STEP 5   Total the Income Statement and Balance Sheet columns to compute the net income or net loss.

The work sheet format and the five steps taken when preparing the work sheet are illustrated in figure 14-6. Note that the new accounts introduced for a merchandising firm and the Unearned Revenue account are highlighted so you can see their proper placement and extensions. (The abbreviation BI stands for beginning inventory; EI stands for ending inventory.) Pay particular attention to the extension of the Income Summary account. Both the debit and credit amounts for this account must be extended.

FIGURE 14-6 **Overview of Work Sheet for a Merchandising Firm**

Name of Company
Work Sheet
For the Month Ended June 30, 19--

	ACCOUNT TITLE	ACCT. NO.	TRIAL BALANCE		ADJUSTMENTS		
			DEBIT	CREDIT	DEBIT	CREDIT	
1	– – – – – – – – – – –		Step 1:		Step 2:		1
2	– – – – – – – – – – –		Prepare a		Prepare		2
3	(Insert Ledger Account Titles)		Trial Balance		the		3
4					Adjustments		4
5			Assets				5
6			Mdse. Inv. (BI)		EI	BI	6
7							7
8				Liab.			8
9				Unearned			9
10				Revenues			10
11							11
12				Capital			12
13			Drawing				13
14							14
15				Revenues			15
16				Sales			16
17			Sales R&A				17
18			Sales Disc.				18
19							19
20							20
21			Expenses				21
22			Purchases				22
23				Pur. R&A			23
24				Pur. Disc.			24
25			Freight-				25
26			In				26
27	Income Summary				XXXXX	XXXXX	27
28	– – – – – – – – – – –						28
29	– – – – – – – – – – –						29
30	(Insert additional account						30
31	titles for adjustments)						31
32							32
33							33
34							34
35							35

	ADJUSTED TRIAL BALANCE		INCOME STATEMENT		BALANCE SHEET		
	DEBIT	CREDIT	DEBIT	CREDIT	DEBIT	CREDIT	
1	Step 3:		Step 4:				1
2	Prepare the		Extend Adjusted				2
3	Adjusted Trial		Account Balances				3
4	Balance						4
5	Assets				Assets		5
6	Mdse. Inv. (EI)				Mdse. Inv. (EI)		6
7							7
8		Liab.				Liab.	8
9		Unearned				Unearned	9
10		Revenues				Revenues	10
11							11
12		Capital				Capital	12
13	Drawing				Drawing		13
14							14
15		Revenue		Revenue			15
16		Sales		Sales			16
17	Sales R&A		Sales R&A				17
18	Sales Disc.		Sales Disc.				18
19							19
20							20
21	Expenses		Expenses				21
22	Purchases		Purchases				22
23		Pur. R&A		Pur. R&A			23
24		Pur. Disc.		Pur. Disc.			24
25	Freight-		Freight-				25
26	In		In				26
27	xxxxx	xxxxx	xxxxx	xxxxx			27
28							28
29			Step 5:				29
30			Complete the work sheet				30
31			1) Sum Columns				31
32			2) Compute Net Income (Loss)				32
33							33
34			Net	Net	Net	Net	34
35			Income	Loss	Loss	Income	35

Adjustments For Northern Micro

Before preparing a work sheet for Northern Micro, let's review the preparation of adjustments in T account form. Year-end adjustment information for Northern Micro is provided in figure 14-7. Adjusting entries based on this information are illustrated in figure 14-8.

FIGURE 14-7 **Year End Adjustment Data for Northern Micro**

(a–b) Based on a physical count, it was determined that merchandise inventory costing $18,000 is on hand as of December 31, 19--.

(c) Supplies remaining at the end of the year, $400.

(d) Unexpired insurance on December 31, $600.

(e) Depreciation expense on the building for 19-- was $4,000.

(f) Depreciation expense on the store equipment for 19-- was $3,000.

(g) Wages earned but not paid as of December 31, $450.

(h) Unearned subscriptions revenue as of December 31, $2,000.

Preparing A Work Sheet For Northern Micro

Let's prepare a work sheet for Northern Micro following the five steps illustrated in figure 14-6.

STEP 1 The Trial Balance columns are completed by copying the balances of all accounts from the general ledger (not shown).

STEP 2 The adjustments are entered. These entries are exactly the same as those made in T account form in figure 14-8.

STEP 3 Extensions are made to the Adjusted Trial Balance columns. Note that both the debit and credit amounts for Income Summary are extended.

STEP 4 The adjusted trial balances are extended to the Income Statement and Balance Sheet columns.

STEP 5 The work sheet (figure 14-9, on pages 478 and 479) is completed by totaling the Income Statement and Balance Sheet columns. The difference between the debits and credits for each pair of columns represents the net income or net loss.

F I G U R E   1 4 - 8   **Adjusting Entries for Northern Micro**

Assets	=	Liabilities	+	Owner's Equity

Assets

Dr. | Cr.
+ | −

Merchandise Inventory

Bal. 26,000	(a) 26,000
(b) 18,000	
Bal. 18,000	

Supplies

Bal. 1,800	(c) 1,400
Bal. 400	

Prepaid Insurance

Bal. 2,400	(d) 1,800
Bal. 600	

Accum. Deprec.—Building

	Bal. 16,000
	(e) 4,000
	Bal. 20,000

Accum. Deprec.—Store Equipment

	Bal. 15,000
	(f) 3,000
	Bal. 18,000

Liabilities

Dr. | Cr.
− | +

Wages Payable

	(g) 450

Unearned Subscript. Revenue

	Bal. 12,000
(h) 10,000	
	Bal. 2,000

Owner's Equity

Dr. | Cr.
− | +

G. Fishel, Capital

	Bal. xxx

Income Summary

(a) 26,000	(b) 18,000

Supplies Expense

(c) 1,400	

Insurance Expense

(d) 1,800	

Deprec. Exp.—Bldg.

(e) 4,000	

Deprec. Exp.—Store Equipment

(f) 3,000	

Wages Expense

(g) 450	

Subscription Rev.

	(h) 10,000

FIGURE 14-9　STEPS 1-5: Completion of the Work Sheet for Northern Micro

Northern Micro
Work Sheet
For the Year Ended December, 31, 19--

	TRIAL BALANCE		ADJUSTMENTS		ADJUSTED TRIAL BALANCE		INCOME STATEMENT		BALANCE SHEET	
ACCOUNT TITLE	DEBIT	CREDIT	DEBIT	CREDIT	DEBIT	CREDIT	DEBIT	CREDIT	DEBIT	CREDIT
1 Cash	20 000 00				20 000 00				20 000 00	
2 Accounts Receivable	15 000 00				15 000 00				15 000 00	
3 Merchandise Inv.	26 000 00		(b)18 000 00	(a) 26 000 00	18 000 00				18 000 00	
4 Supplies	1 800 00			(c) 1 400 00	400 00				400 00	
5 Prepaid Insurance	2 400 00			(d) 1 800 00	600 00				600 00	
6 Land	10 000 00				10 000 00				10 000 00	
7 Building	90 000 00				90 000 00				90 000 00	
8 Acc. Depr.—Building		16 000 00		(e) 4 000 00		20 000 00				20 000 00
9 Store Equipment	50 000 00				50 000 00				50 000 00	
10 Acc. Depr.—Store Eq.		15 000 00		(f) 3 000 00		18 000 00				18 000 00
11 Notes Payable		5 000 00				5 000 00				5 000 00
12 Accounts Payable		10 000 00				10 000 00				10 000 00
13 Sales Tax Payable		1 500 00				1 500 00				1 500 00
14 Unearned Sub. Rev.		12 000 00	(h)10 000 00			2 000 00				2 000 00
15 Mortgage Payable		30 000 00				30 000 00				30 000 00
16 Gary L. Fishel, Capital		114 400 00				114 400 00				114 400 00
17 Gary L. Fishel, Drawing	20 000 00				20 000 00				20 000 00	

Ending Inventory

Account	STEP 1 Debit	STEP 1 Credit	STEP 2 Debit	STEP 2 Credit	STEP 3 Debit	STEP 3 Credit	STEP 4 Debit	STEP 4 Credit	STEP 5 Debit	STEP 5 Credit
18 Sales		200 500 00				200 500 00		200 500 00		
19 Sales Ret. & Allow.	1 200 00				1 200 00		1 200 00			
20 Interest Revenue		900 00				900 00		900 00		
21 Purchases	105 000 00				105 000 00		105 000 00			
22 Purch. Ret. & Allow.		800 00				800 00		800 00		
23 Purchases Discounts		1 000 00				1 000 00		1 000 00		
24 Freight-In	300 00				300 00		300 00			
25 Wages Expense	42 000 00		(g) 450 00		42 450 00		42 450 00			
26 Telephone Expense	350 00				350 00		350 00			
27 Utilities Expense	12 000 00				12 000 00		12 000 00			
28 Advertising Expense	250 00				250 00		250 00			
29 Miscellaneous Expense	225 00				225 00		225 00			
30 Interest Expense	315 00				315 00		315 00			
31	407 100 00	407 100 00								
32 Income Summary			(a) 26 000 00	(b) 18 000 00	26 000 00 BI	18 000 00 EI	26 000 00 BI	18 000 00 EI		
33 Supplies Expense			(c) 1 400 00		1 400 00		1 400 00			
34 Insurance Expense			(d) 1 800 00		1 800 00		1 800 00			
35 Depr. Exp.—Building			(e) 4 000 00		4 000 00		4 000 00			
36 Depr. Exp.—Store Eq.			(f) 3 000 00		3 000 00		3 000 00			
37 Subscriptions Rev.				(h) 1 000 00		1 000 00		1 000 00		
38 Wages Payable				(g) 450 00		450 00				450 00
39			64 650 00	64 650 00	432 550 00	432 550 00	208 550 00	231 200 00	224 000 00	201 350 00
40 Net Income							22 650 00			22 650 00
41							231 200 00	231 200 00	224 000 00	224 000 00

Extended both debit & credit (Income Summary)

<table>
<tr><td>**4**</td></tr>
<tr><td>Journalize adjusting entries for a merchandising firm.</td></tr>
</table>

ADJUSTING ENTRIES

As you recall, making the adjustments on the work sheet has no effect on the actual accounts in the general ledger. To enter the adjustments into the accounting system, journal entries must be made. The adjusting entries for Northern Micro are illustrated in figure 14-10.

FIGURE 14-10 **Adjusting Entries for Northern Micro**

GENERAL JOURNAL PAGE 3

	DATE		DESCRIPTION	POST. REF.	DEBIT	CREDIT	
1			Adjusting Entries				1
2	19-- Dec.	31	Income Summary		26 000 00		2
3			Merchandise Inventory			26 000 00	3
4							4
5		31	Merchandise Inventory		18 000 00		5
6			Income Summary			18 000 00	6
7							7
8		31	Supplies Expense		1 400 00		8
9			Supplies			1 400 00	9
10							10
11		31	Insurance Expense		1 800 00		11
12			Prepaid Insurance			1 800 00	12
13							13
14		31	Depreciation Expense—Building		4 000 00		14
15			Accum. Depreciation—Building			4 000 00	15
16							16
17		31	Depreciation Expense—Store Equip.		3 000 00		17
18			Accum. Depr.—Store Equip.			3 000 00	18
19							19
20		31	Wages Expense		450 00		20
21			Wages Payable			450 00	21
22							22
23		31	Unearned Subscriptions Revenue		1 000 00		23
24			Subscriptions Revenue			1 000 00	24
25							25
26							26
27							27
28							28
29							29
30							30

K E Y   P O I N T S

1/2 Extra care is required for the end-of-period adjustment for merchandise inventory and the related extensions on the work sheet. The two step adjustment process in T account form and the work sheet treatment for Northern Micro are reviewed in this section.

3 Steps to follow when preparing a work sheet.

1. Prepare the trial balance.
2. Prepare the adjustments.
3. Prepare the adjusted trial balance.
4. Extend the adjusted trial balance to the Income Statement and Balance Sheet columns.
5. Total the Income Statement and Balance Sheet columns to compute the net income or net loss.

4 The worksheet is a useful tool when preparing end-of-period adjustments and financial statements. Remember: The work sheet is NOT a formal part of the accounting system. Adjustments made on the work sheet must be entered in a journal and posted to the ledger.

The two step adjustment for Merchandise Inventory in T account form follows.

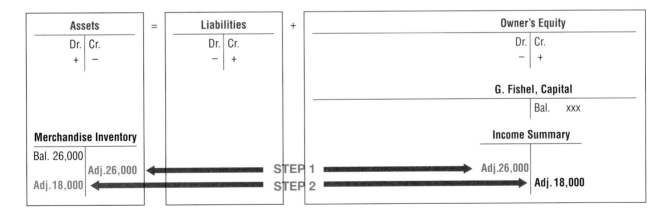

The adjustment and extension for the account Merchandise Inventory on the work sheet, and the calculation of cost of goods sold using information in the Income Statement columns of the work sheet follows.

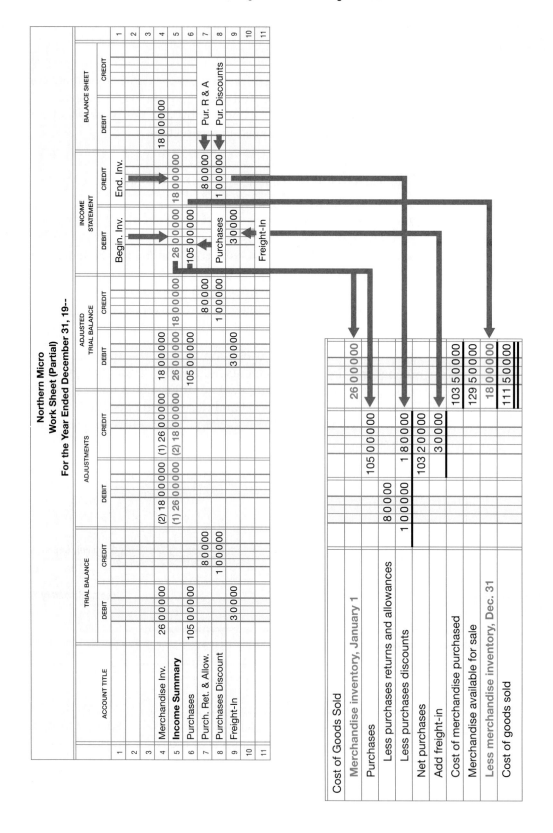

Northern Micro
Work Sheet (Partial)
For the Year Ended December 31, 19--

K E Y   T E R M S

contra cost 473 Accounts that are deducted from the Purchases account when computing cost of goods sold—Purchases Returns and Allowances and Purchases Discounts.

contra revenue 473 Accounts that are deducted from Sales on the income statement—Sales Returns and Allowances and Sales Discounts.

physical inventory 468 Taking a physical count of the goods on hand.

unearned revenue 470 Cash received in advance.

BUILDING YOUR ACCOUNTING KNOWLEDGE

1. What work sheet amounts are used to compute cost of goods sold?
2. Why are both the debit and credit amounts in the Adjustments columns on the Income Summary line of the work sheet extended to the Adjusted Trial Balance columns?
3. What is an unearned revenue?
4. Give three examples of unearned revenues.
5. List the five steps taken to prepare a work sheet.
6. What does the difference between the Income Statement column totals represent? What does the difference between the Balance Sheet column totals represent?

DEMONSTRATION PROBLEM

Craig Fisher owns and operates Fisher's Bait Shop and Boat Rental. A year-end trial balance is shown on page 484 and adjustment information is provided as follows.

(a–b) Based on a physical count, it was determined that merchandise inventory costing $15,000 is on hand as of December 31, 19--.

(c) Supplies remaining at the end of the year, $200.

(d) Unexpired insurance on December 31, $300.

(e) Depreciation expense on the building for 19-- was $2,000.

(f) Depreciation expense on the store equipment for 19-- was $1,500.

(g) Wages earned but not paid as of December 31, $225.

(h) Unearned boat rental revenue as of December 31, $1,000.

Required
1. Prepare a year-end work sheet.
2. Journalize the adjusting entries.

Fisher's Bait Shop and Boat Rental
Trial Balance
December 31, 19--

ACCOUNT TITLE	ACCOUNT NO.	DEBIT BALANCE	CREDIT BALANCE
Cash		10 000 00	
Accounts Receivable		7 500 00	
Merchandise Inventory		19 000 00	
Supplies		900 00	
Prepaid Insurance		1 200 00	
Land		5 000 00	
Building		45 000 00	
Accum. Deprec.—Building			8 000 00
Store Equipment		25 000 00	
Accum. Deprec.—Store Equip.			7 500 00
Notes Payable			2 500 00
Accounts Payable			5 000 00
Unearned Boat Rental Revenue			11 000 00
Craig Fisher, Capital			77 900 00
Craig Fisher, Drawing		10 000 00	
Sales			100 250 00
Sales Returns & Allowances		600 00	
Purchases		52 500 00	
Purch. Returns & Allowances			400 00
Purchases Discounts			500 00
Freight-In		150 00	
Wages Expense		21 000 00	
Telephone Expense		1 750 00	
Utilities Expense		600 00	
Advertising Expense		3 750 00	
Miscellaneous Expense		3 625 00	
Interest Expense		75 00	
		213 050 00	213 050 00

SOLUTION

2.

	DATE		DESCRIPTION	POST. REF.	DEBIT	CREDIT	
1			Adjusting Entries				1
2	19-- Dec.	31	Income Summary		19 0 0 0 00		2
3			Merchandise Inventory			19 0 0 0 00	3
4							4
5		31	Merchandise Inventory		15 0 0 0 00		5
6			Income Summary			15 0 0 0 00	6
7							7
8		31	Supplies Expense		7 0 0 00		8
9			Supplies			7 0 0 00	9
10							10
11		31	Insurance Expense		9 0 0 00		11
12			Prepaid Insurance			9 0 0 00	12
13							13
14		31	Depreciation Expense—Building		2 0 0 0 00		14
15			Accum. Deprec.—Building			2 0 0 0 00	15
16							16
17		31	Depreciation Expense—Store Equip.		1 5 0 0 00		17
18			Accum. Deprec.—Store Equip.			1 5 0 0 00	18
19							19
20		31	Wages Expense		2 2 5 00		20
21			Wages Payable			2 2 5 00	21
22							22
23		31	Unearned Boat Rental Revenue		10 0 0 0 00		23
24			Boat Rental Revenue			10 0 0 0 00	24
25							25
26							26
27							27
28							28
29							29
30							30
31							31
32							32
33							33
34							34
35							35
36							36
37							37

GENERAL JOURNAL   PAGE 3

1.

Fisher's Bait Shop and Boat Rental
Work Sheet
For the Year Ended December 31, 19--

ACCOUNT TITLE	TRIAL BALANCE DEBIT	TRIAL BALANCE CREDIT	ADJUSTMENTS DEBIT	ADJUSTMENTS CREDIT	ADJUSTED TRIAL BALANCE DEBIT	ADJUSTED TRIAL BALANCE CREDIT	INCOME STATEMENT DEBIT	INCOME STATEMENT CREDIT	BALANCE SHEET DEBIT	BALANCE SHEET CREDIT
Cash	10 000 00				10 000 00				10 000 00	
Accounts Receivable	7 500 00				7 500 00				7 500 00	
Merchandise Inventory	19 000 00		(b)15 000 00	(a)19 000 00	15 000 00				15 000 00	
Supplies	9 000 00			(c) 7 000 00	2 000 00				2 000 00	
Prepaid Insurance	1 200 00			(d) 900 00	300 00				300 00	
Land	5 000 00				5 000 00				5 000 00	
Building	45 000 00				45 000 00				45 000 00	
Accum. Dep.—Building		8 000 00		(e) 2 000 00		10 000 00				10 000 00
Store Equipment	25 000 00				25 000 00				25 000 00	
Accum. Dep.—Store Eq.		7 500 00		(f) 1 500 00		9 000 00				9 000 00
Notes Payable		2 500 00				2 500 00				2 500 00
Accounts Payable		5 000 00				5 000 00				5 000 00
Unearned Boat Rent. Rev.		11 000 00	(h)10 000 00			1 000 00				1 000 00
Craig Fisher, Capital		77 900 00				77 900 00				77 900 00
Craig Fisher, Drawing	10 000 00				10 000 00				10 000 00	
Sales		100 250 00				100 250 00		100 250 00		
Sales Returns & Allow.	600 00				600 00		600 00			

#	Account	Trial Balance Dr.	Trial Balance Cr.	Adjustments Dr.	Adjustments Cr.	Adjusted Trial Balance Dr.	Adjusted Trial Balance Cr.	Income Statement Dr.	Income Statement Cr.	Balance Sheet Dr.	Balance Sheet Cr.
18	Purchases	52 5 0 0 00				52 5 0 0 00		52 5 0 0 00			
19	Purch. Ret. & Allow.		4 0 0 00				4 0 0 00		4 0 0 00		
20	Purchases Discounts		5 0 0 00				5 0 0 00		5 0 0 00		
21	Freight-In	1 5 0 00				1 5 0 00		1 5 0 00			
22	Wages Expense	21 0 0 0 00		(g) 2 2 5 00		21 2 2 5 00		21 2 2 5 00			
23	Telephone Expense	1 7 5 00				1 7 5 00		1 7 5 00			
24	Utilities Expense	6 0 0 00				6 0 0 00		6 0 0 00			
25	Advertising Expense	3 7 5 00				3 7 5 00		3 7 5 00			
26	Miscellaneous Expense	3 6 2 5 00				3 6 2 5 00		3 6 2 5 00			
27	Interest Expense	7 5 00				7 5 00		7 5 00			
28		213 0 5 0 00	213 0 5 0 00								
29	Income Summary			(a)19 0 0 0 00	(b)15 0 0 0 00	19 0 0 0 00	15 0 0 0 00	19 0 0 0 00	15 0 0 0 00		
30	Supplies Expense			(c) 7 0 0 00		7 0 0 00		7 0 0 00			
31	Insurance Expense			(d) 9 0 0 00		9 0 0 00		9 0 0 00			
32	Dep. Exp.—Building			(e) 2 0 0 0 00		2 0 0 0 00		2 0 0 0 00			
33	Dep. Exp.—Store Equip.			(f) 1 5 0 0 00		1 5 0 0 00		1 5 0 0 00			
34	Boat Rental Revenue				(h)10 0 0 0 00		10 0 0 0 00		10 0 0 0 00		
35	Wages Payable				(g) 2 2 5 00		2 2 5 00				2 2 5 00
36				49 3 2 5 00	49 3 2 5 00	231 7 7 5 00	231 7 7 5 00	113 7 7 5 00	126 1 5 0 00	105 6 2 5 00	118 0 0 0 00
37	Net Income							12 3 7 5 00			12 3 7 5 00
38								126 1 5 0 00	126 1 5 0 00	118 0 0 0 00	118 0 0 0 00

EXERCISE 14A1

Adjustment for Merchandising Inventory Using T Accounts

1 Sam Baker owns a business called Sam's Sporting Goods. His beginning inventory as of January 1, 19--, was $47,000 and his ending inventory as of December 31, 19--, was $53,000. Set up T accounts for Merchandise Inventory and Income Summary and perform the year-end adjustment for merchandise inventory.

EXERCISE 14A2

Calculation of Cost of Goods Sold

1 Calculate the Cost of Goods Sold section for Adams Gift Shop. The following account balances are taken from Adams Gift Shop.

Beginning Merchandise Inventory	$26,000
Ending Merchandise Inventory	23,000
Purchases	71,000
Purchases Returns and Allowances	3,500
Purchases Discounts	5,500

EXERCISE 14A3

Adjustment for Unearned Revenues Using T Accounts

2 Set up T accounts for Cash, Unearned Ticket Revenue, and Ticket Revenue. Post the following two transactions to the appropriate accounts indicating each transaction by letter. These two transactions took place for Kennington Theaters.

(a) Sold 1,500 season tickets at $30 each, receiving cash of $45,000.

(b) An end of period adjustment is needed to recognize that $35,000 in ticket revenue has been earned.

EXERCISE 14A4

Work Sheet Extensions for Merchandise Inventory Adjustments

3 The following partial work sheet is taken from Kevin's Gift Shop for the year ended December 31, 19--. The ending merchandise inventory is $50,000.

1. Complete the adjustment columns for the merchandise inventory.
2. Extend the merchandise inventory to the Adjusted Trial Balance, Income Statement columns, and Balance Sheet columns.
3. Extend the remaining accounts to the Adjusted Trial Balance and Income Statement columns.
4. Prepare a Cost of Goods Sold Section from the partial work sheet.

Kevin's Gift Shop
Work Sheet (Partial)
For the Year Ended December 31, 19--

	ACCOUNT TITLE	TRIAL BALANCE DEBIT	TRIAL BALANCE CREDIT	ADJUSTMENTS DEBIT	ADJUSTMENTS CREDIT	
1	Merchandise Inventory	40 000 00				1
2	Income Summary					2
3	Purchases	90 000 00				3
4	Purchases Ret. & Allow.		2 000 00			4
5	Purchases Discounts		3 000 00			5

EXERCISE 14A5

Determining the Beginning and Ending Inventory from a Partial Work Sheet

3 From the following partial work sheet, indicate by dollar amount, the beginning inventory and the ending merchandise inventory.

	ACCOUNT TITLE	ACCT. NO.	TRIAL BALANCE		ADJUSTMENTS		
			DEBIT	CREDIT	DEBIT	CREDIT	
1	Merchandise Inventory				(b) 60 0 0 0 00	(a) 55 0 0 0 00	1
2	Income Summary				(a) 55 0 0 0 00	(b) 60 0 0 0 00	2

	ADJUSTED TRIAL BALANCE		INCOME STATEMENT		BALANCE SHEET		
	DEBIT	CREDIT	DEBIT	CREDIT	DEBIT	CREDIT	
1	60 0 0 0 00				60 0 0 0 00		1
2	55 0 0 0 00	60 0 0 0 00	55 0 0 0 00	60 0 0 0 00			2

EXERCISE 14A6

Journalize Adjusting Entries for a Merchandising Firm

5 The following partial work sheet is taken from the books of Kelly's Kittens, a local pet kennel, for the year ended December 31, 19--. Journalize the adjustments in a two-column general journal.

Kelly's Kittens
Work Sheet (Partial)
For the Year Ended December 31, 19--

	ACCOUNT TITLE	TRIAL BALANCE		ADJUSTMENTS		
		DEBIT	CREDIT	DEBIT	CREDIT	
1	Merchandise Inventory	45 0 0 0 00		(a) 50 0 0 0 00	(b) 45 0 0 0 00	1
2	Supplies	10 0 0 0 00			(d) 7 0 0 0 00	2
3	Building	60 0 0 0 00				3
4	Accum. Deprec.—Bldg.		15 0 0 0 00		(e) 5 0 0 0 00	4
5	Unearned Deposit Fees		3 0 0 0 00	(c) 2 0 0 0 00		5
6	Deposit Fee Revenue		20 0 0 0 00		(c) 2 0 0 0 00	6
7	Wages Expense	37 0 0 0 00		(f) 1 2 0 0 00		7
8	Income Summary			(b) 45 0 0 0 00	(a) 50 0 0 0 00	8
9	Supplies Expense			(d) 7 0 0 0 00		9
10	Depreciation Expense			(e) 5 0 0 0 00		10
11	Wages Payable				(f) 1 2 0 0 00	11
12				110 2 0 0 00	110 2 0 0 00	12

PROBLEMS

PROBLEM 14A1

Completion of a Work Sheet Showing a Net Income

1/2/3/4 The trial balance and additional acccounts for adjustments for Seaside Kite Shop, a business owned by Joyce Kennington, for the year ended December 31, 19--, is shown on page 490.

Seaside Kite Shop
Trial Balance
December 31, 19--

Account Title	Debit	Credit
Cash	20,000	
Accounts Receivable	14,000	
Merchandise Inventory	25,000	
Supplies	8,000	
Prepaid Insurance	5,400	
Land	30,000	
Building	50,000	
Accum. Depr.—Building		20,000
Store Equipment	35,000	
Accum. Depr.—Store Equip.		14,000
Accounts Payable		9,600
Sales Tax Payable		5,900
Mortgage Payable		45,000
Unearned Revenue		8,900
J. Kennington, Capital		65,410
J. Kennington, Drawing	26,000	
Sales		118,000
Sales Returns & Allow.	1,700	
Purchases	27,000	
Purch. Returns & Allow.		1,400
Purchases Discounts		1,800
Freight-In	2,100	
Wages Expense	32,000	
Telephone Expense	1,350	
Utilities Expense	8,000	
Advertising Expense	3,600	
Miscellaneous Expense	860	
	290,010	290,010
Income Summary		
Supplies Expense		
Insurance Expense		
Depr. Exp.—Building		
Depr. Exp.—Store Equip.		
Earned Revenue		
Wages Payable		

Required

1. Complete the adjustments columns, identifying each adjustment with its corresponding letter.
   (a) Merchandise inventory costing $30,000 is on hand as of December 31, 19--.
   (b) Supplies remaining at end of the year, $2,700.
   (c) Unexpired insurance on December 31, $2,900.
   (d) Depreciation expense on the building for 19--, $5,000.
   (e) Depreciation expense on the store equipment for 19--, $3,200.
   (f) Unearned revenue as of December 31, $2,200.
   (g) Wages earned but not paid as of December 31, $900.

2. Complete the work sheet.

3. Enter the adjustments in a two-column general journal.

1/2/3/4 The trial balance and additional accounts for adjustments for Cascade Bicycle Shop, a business owned by David Lamond, for the year ending December 31, 19--, are shown below.

Cascade Bicycle Shop
Trial Balance
December 31, 19--

Account Title	Debit	Credit
Cash	23,000	
Accounts Receivable	15,000	
Merchandise Inventory	31,000	
Supplies	7,200	
Prepaid Insurance	4,600	
Land	28,000	
Building	53,000	
Accum. Depr.—Building		17,000
Store Equipment	27,000	
Accum. Depr.—Store Equip.		9,000
Accounts Payable		3,800
Sales Tax Payable		3,050
Mortgage Payable		42,000
Unearned Revenue		5,600
D. Lamond, Capital		165,760
D. Lamond, Drawing	33,000	
Sales		51,000
Sales Returns & Allow.	2,400	
Purchases	21,000	
Purch. Returns & Allow.		1,300
Purchases Discounts		1,900
Freight-In	1,800	
Wages Expense	35,000	
Telephone Expense	2,200	
Utilities Expense	9,600	
Advertising Expense	5,700	
Miscellaneous Expense	910	
	300,410	300,410
Income Summary		
Supplies Expense		
Insurance Expense		
Depr. Exp.—Building		
Depr. Exp.—Store Equip.		
Earned Revenue		
Wages Payable		

Required

1. Complete the adjustments columns, identifying each adjustment with its corresponding letter.

(a) Merchandise inventory costing $22,000 is on hand as of December 31, 19--.

(b) Supplies remaining at end of the year, $2,400.

(c) Unexpired insurance on December 31, $1,750.

       (d) Depreciation expense on the building for 19--, $4,000.
       (e) Depreciation expense on the store equipment for 19--, $3,600.
       (f) Unearned revenue as of December 31, $1,950.
       (g) Wages earned but not paid as of December 31, $750.
  2. Complete the work sheet.
  3. Enter the adjustments in a two-column general journal.

PROBLEM 14A3

Working Backwards From Adjusted Trial Balance to Determine Adjusting Entries.

1/2/4 The following partial work sheet is taken from the books of Stark Street Computer Repair, a business owned by Logan Cowart, for the year ended December 31, 19--.

Stark Street Computer Repair
Work Sheet (Partial)
For the Year Ended December 31, 19--

Account Title	Trial Balance Debit	Trial Balance Credit	Adjustments Debit	Adjustments Credit	Adjusted Trial Balance Debit	Adjusted Trial Balance Credit
Cash	18,000				18,000	
Accounts Receivable	11,000				11,000	
Merchandise Inventory	25,000				35,000	
Supplies	8,000				2,820	
Prepaid Insurance	5,400				1,225	
Land	27,000				27,000	
Building	48,000				48,000	
Accum. Depr.—Building		20,000				27,000
Store Equipment	33,000				33,000	
Accum. Depr.—Store Equip.		8,700				12,800
Accounts Payable		6,400				6,400
Sales Tax Payable		5,700				5,700
Mortgage Payable		44,000				44,000
Unearned Revenue		8,200				1,800
Logan Cowart, Capital		80,025				80,025
Logan Cowart, Drawing	35,000				35,000	
Sales		122,000				122,000
Sales Returns & Allow.	2,250				2,250	
Purchases	29,750				29,750	
Purch. Returns & Allow.		1,850				1,850
Purchases Discounts		1,425				1,425
Freight-In	3,200				3,200	
Wages Expense	37,000				38,300	
Telephone Expense	1,650				1,650	
Utilities Expense	9,150				9,150	
Advertising Expense	4,125				4,125	
Miscellaneous Expense	775				775	
	298,300	298,300				
Income Summary					25,000	35,000
Supplies Expense					5,180	
Insurance Expense					4,175	
Depr. Expense—Building					7,000	
Depr. Expense—Store Equip.					4,100	
Earned Revenue						6,400
Wages Payable						1,300
					345,700	345,700

Required

1. Determine the adjusting entries by analyzing the difference between the adjusted trial balance and the trial balance.
2. Journalize the adjusting entries in a two-column general journal.

PROBLEM 14A4

Working Backwards from the Income Statement and Balance Sheet Columns of the Work Sheet to Determine Adjusted Trial Balance and Adjusting Entries

1/2/3 The partial work sheet from the books of Lewis Music Store, a business owned by Hugo Lewis, for the year ended December 31, 19--, follows.

Lewis Music Store
Work Sheet (Partial)
For the Year Ended December 31, 19--

Account Title	Trial Balance Debit	Trial Balance Credit	Income Statement Debit	Income Statement Credit	Balance Sheet Debit	Balance Sheet Credit
Cash	27,000				27,000	
Accounts Receivable	13,300				13,300	
Merchandise Inventory	34,000				38,000	
Supplies	5,300				1,500	
Prepaid Insurance	6,100				1,785	
Land	31,000				31,000	
Building	52,000				52,000	
Accum. Depr.—Building		17,000				21,145
Store Equipment	39,000				39,000	
Accum. Depr.—Store Equip.		11,900				14,875
Accounts Payable		6,250				6,250
Sales Tax Payable		6,200				6,200
Mortgage Payable		46,000				46,000
Unearned Revenue		7,400				3,175
Hugo Lewis, Capital		111,620				111,620
Hugo Lewis, Drawing	37,000				37,000	
Sales		136,000		136,000		
Sales Returns & Allow.	3,500		3,500			
Purchases	39,000		39,000			
Purch. Returns & Allow.		2,530		2,530		
Purchases Discounts		1,975		1,975		
Freight-In	2,650		2,650			
Wages Expense	42,000		42,875			
Telephone Expense	1,980		1,980			
Utilities Expense	7,945		7,945			
Advertising Expense	4,175		4,175			
Miscellaneous Expense	925		925			
	346,875	346,875				
Income Summary			34,000	38,000		
Supplies Expense			3,800			
Insurance Expense			4,315			
Depr. Expense—Building			4,145			
Depr. Expense—Store Equip.			2,975			
Earned Revenue				4,225		
Wages Payable						875
			152,285	182,730	240,585	210,140
Net Income			30,445			30,445
			182,730	182,730	240,585	240,585

Required

Analyze the work sheet and determine the adjusted trial balance and the adjusting entries by working backwards from the income statement and balance sheet columns.

SERIES B

EXERCISES

EXERCISE 14B1

Adjustment for Merchandise Inventory Using T Accounts

1 Sandra Owens owns a business called Sandra's Sporting Goods. Her beginning inventory as of January 1, 19--, was $33,000 and her ending inventory as of December 31, 19--, was $36,000. Set up T accounts for Merchandise Inventory and Income Summary and perform the year-end adjustment for merchandise inventory.

EXERCISE 14B2

Calculation of Cost of Goods Sold

1 Calculate the Cost of Goods Sold section for Havens Gift Shop. The following account balances are taken from Havens Gift Shop:

Beginning merchandise inventory	$29,000
Ending merchandise inventory	27,000
Purchases	62,000
Purchases returns and allowances	2,800
Purchases discounts	3,400

EXERCISE 14B3

Adjustment for Unearned Revenues Using T Accounts

2 Set up T accounts for Cash, Unearned Ticket Revenue, and Ticket Revenue. Post the following two transactions to the appropriate accounts indicating each transaction by letter. These two transactions took place for Act II Theaters.

(a) Sold 1,200 season tickets at $20 each, receiving cash of $24,000.

(b) An end of period adjustment is needed to recognize that $19,000 in ticket revenue has been earned.

EXERCISE 14B4

Work Sheet Extensions for Merchandise Inventory Adjustments

3 The partial work sheet on page 495 is taken from Nicole's Gift Shop for the year ended December 31, 19--. The ending merchandise inventory is $37,000.

1. Complete the adjustment columns for the merchandise inventory.
2. Extend the merchandise inventory to the Adjusted Trial Balance, Income Statement columns, and Balance Sheet columns.

3. Extend the remaining accounts to the Adjusted Trial Balance and Income Statement columns.
4. Prepare a Cost of Goods Sold Section from the partial work sheet.

Nicole's Gift Shop
Work Sheet (Partial)
For the Year Ended December 31, 19--

	ACCOUNT TITLE	TRIAL BALANCE DEBIT	TRIAL BALANCE CREDIT	ADJUSTMENTS DEBIT	ADJUSTMENTS CREDIT	
1	Merchandise Inventory	30 0 0 0 00				1
2	Income Summary					2
3	Purchases	85 0 0 0 00				3
4	Purchases Ret. & Allow.		2 2 0 0 00			4
5	Purchases Discounts		2 5 0 0 00			5
6						6
7						7
8						8
9						9
10						10

EXERCISE 14B5

Determining the Beginning and Ending Inventory from a Partial Work Sheet

3 From the following partial work sheet, indicate by dollar amount, the beginning inventory and the ending merchandise inventory.

	ACCOUNT TITLE	ACCT. NO.	TRIAL BALANCE DEBIT	TRIAL BALANCE CREDIT	ADJUSTMENTS DEBIT	ADJUSTMENTS CREDIT	
1	Merchandise Inventory				(b)45 0 0 0 00	(a)49 0 0 0 00	1
2	Income Summary				(a)49 0 0 0 00	(b)45 0 0 0 00	2
3							3

	ADJUSTED TRIAL BALANCE DEBIT	ADJUSTED TRIAL BALANCE CREDIT	INCOME STATEMENT DEBIT	INCOME STATEMENT CREDIT	BALANCE SHEET DEBIT	BALANCE SHEET CREDIT	
1	45 0 0 0 00				45 0 0 0 00		1
2	49 0 0 0 00	45 0 0 0 00	49 0 0 0 00	45 0 0 0 00			2
3							3

5 The following partial work sheet is taken from the books of Carmen's Collies, a local pet kennel, for the year ended December 31, 19--. Journalize the adjustments in a two-column general journal.

Carmen's Collies
Work Sheet (Partial)
For Year Ended December 31, 19--

	ACCOUNT TITLE	TRIAL BALANCE		ADJUSTMENTS		
		DEBIT	CREDIT	DEBIT	CREDIT	
1	Merchandise Inventory	35 000 00		(a) 30 000 00	(b) 35 000 00	1
2	Supplies	4 500 00			(d) 3 100 00	2
3	Building	50 000 00				3
4	Accum. Deprec.—Bldg.		23 000 00		(e) 6 000 00	4
5	Unearned Deposit Fees		7 000 00	(c) 5 500 00		5
6	Deposit Fee Revenue		24 000 00		(c) 5 500 00	6
7	Wages Expense	41 000 00		(f) 1 300 00		7
8	Income Summary			(b) 35 000 00	(a) 30 000 00	8
9	Supplies Expense			(d) 3 100 00		9
10	Depreciation Expense			(e) 6 000 00		10
11	Wages Payable				(f) 1 300 00	11
12				80 900 00	80 900 00	12
13						13
14						14

1/2/3/4 A trial balance and additional accounts for adjustments for Basket Corner, a business owned by Linda Parker, for the year ended December 31, 19--, follows.

Basket Corner
Trial Balance
December 31, 19--

Account Title	Debit	Credit
Cash	25,000	
Accounts Receivable	8,100	
Merchandise Inventory	32,000	
Supplies	7,100	
Prepaid Insurance	3,600	
Land	40,000	
Building	45,000	
Accum. Depr.—Building		16,000
Store Equipment	27,000	

Account Title	Debit	Credit
Accum. Depr.—Store Equip. ..		5,500
Accounts Payable		3,600
Sales Tax Payable		6,200
Mortgage Payable		36,000
Unearned Revenues		6,300
Linda Parker, Capital		112,050
Linda Parker, Drawing	31,000	
Sales		125,000
Sales Returns & Allow.	2,600	
Purchases	38,000	
Purch. Returns & Allow.		2,200
Purchases Discounts		1,700
Freight-In	1,900	
Wages Expense	38,000	
Telephone Expense	1,870	
Utilities Expense	8,400	
Advertising Expense	4,200	
Miscellaneous Expense	780	
	314,550	314,550
Income Summary		
Supplies Expense		
Insurance Expense		
Depr. Exp.—Building		
Depr. Exp.—Store Equip.		
Earned Revenue		
Wages Payable		

Required

1. Complete the adjustments columns, identifying each adjustment with its corresponding letter.
   (a) Merchandise inventory costing $24,000 is on hand as of December 31, 19--.
   (b) Supplies remaining at end of the year, $2,100.
   (c) Unexpired insurance on December 31, $2,600.
   (d) Depreciation expense on the building for 19--, $5,300.
   (e) Depreciation expense on the store equipment for 19--, $3,800.
   (f) Unearned revenue as of December 31, $1,650.
   (g) Wages earned but not paid as of December 31, $750.
2. Complete the work sheet.
3. Enter the adjustments in a two-column general journal.

PROBLEM 14B2

Completion of a Work Sheet Showing a Net Loss

1/2/3/4 The trial balance and additional accounts for adjustments (on page 498) is taken from the books of Oregon Rental Company for the year ended December 31, 19--. The business is owned by Craig Moody.

Oregon Rental Company
Trial Balance
December 31, 19--

Account Title	Debit	Credit
Cash	27,000	
Accounts Receivable	12,000	
Merchandise Inventory	39,000	
Supplies	6,200	
Prepaid Insurance	5,800	
Land	32,000	
Building	58,000	
Accum. Depr.—Building		27,000
Store Equipment	31,000	
Accum. Depr.—Store Equip.		14,000
Accounts Payable		4,900
Sales Tax Payable		2,900
Mortgage Payable		49,000
Unearned Revenues		6,100
C. Moody, Capital		169,500
C. Moody, Drawing	36,000	
Sales		58,000
Sales Returns & Allow.	3,300	
Purchases	19,000	
Purch. Returns & Allow.		900
Purchases Discounts		1,450
Freight-In	800	
Wages Expense	47,000	
Telephone Expense	1,860	
Utilities Expense	8,100	
Advertising Expense	6,200	
Miscellaneous Expense	490	
	333,750	333,750

Income Summary
Supplies Expense
Insurance Expense
Depr. Exp.—Building
Depr. Exp.—Store Equip.
Earned Revenue
Wages Payable

Required

1. Complete the adjustments columns, identifying each adjustment with its corresponding letter.

(a) Merchandise inventory costing $26,000 is on hand as of December 31, 19--.

(b) Supplies remaining at end of the year, $2,500.

(c) Unexpired insurance on December 31, $1,820.

(d) Depreciation expense on the building for 19--, $6,400.

(e) Depreciation expense on the store equipment for 19--, $2,800.

(f) Unearned revenue as of December 31, $2,350.

(g) Wages earned but not paid as of December 31, $1,100.

2. Complete the work sheet.

3. Enter the adjustments in a two-column general journal.

PROBLEM 14B3

Working Backwards from Adjusted Trial Balance to Determine Adjusting Entries

1/2/4 The following partial work sheet is taken from the books of Burnside Auto Parts, a business owned by Barbara Davis, for the year ended December 31, 19--.

Burnside Auto Parts
Work Sheet (Partial)
For the Year Ended December 31, 19--

Account Title	Trial Balance Debit	Trial Balance Credit	Adjustments Debit	Adjustments Credit	Adjusted Trial Balance Debit	Adjusted Trial Balance Credit
Cash	21,000				21,000	
Accounts Receivable	8,300				8,300	
Merchandise Inventory	32,000				36,000	
Supplies	6,150				1,865	
Prepaid Insurance	5,925				1,835	
Land	41,750				41,750	
Building	43,000				43,000	
Accum. Depr.—Building		24,000				27,500
Store Equipment	25,400				25,400	
Accum. Depr.—Store Equip.		12,400				14,750
Accounts Payable		8,100				8,100
Sales Tax Payable		5,200				5,200
Mortgage Payable		26,000				26,000
Unearned Revenues		7,950				2,350
B. Davis, Capital		109,130				109,130
B. Davis, Drawing	40,000				40,000	
Sales		123,500				123,500
Sales Returns & Allow.	2,860				2,860	
Purchases	32,525				32,525	
Purch. Returns & Allow.		2,150				2,150
Purchases Discounts		2,400				2,400
Freight-In	3,175				3,175	
Wages Expense	44,175				45,155	
Telephone Expense	2,200				2,200	
Utilities Expense	8,250				8,250	
Advertising Expense	3,275				3,275	
Miscellaneous Expense	845				845	
	320,830	320,830				
Income Summary					32,000	36,000
Supplies Expense					4,285	
Insurance Expense					4,090	
Depr. Expense—Building					3,500	
Depr. Expense—Store Equip.					2,350	
Earned Revenue						5,600
Wages Payable						980
					363,660	363,660

Required

1. Determine the adjusting entries by analyzing the difference between the adjusted trial balance and the trial balance.
2. Journalize the adjusting entries in a two-column general journal.

PROBLEM 14B4

Working Backwards from the Income Statement and Balance Sheet Columns of the Work Sheet to Determine Adjusted Trial Balance and Adjusting Entries

1/2/3 The following partial work sheet is taken from the books of Diamond Music Store, a business owned by Ned Diamond, for the year ended December 31, 19--.

Diamond Music Store
Work Sheet (Partial)
For the Year Ended December 31, 19--

Account Title	Trial Balance Debit	Trial Balance Credit	Income Statement Debit	Income Statement Credit	Balance Sheet Debit	Balance Sheet Credit
Cash	31,000				31,000	
Accounts Receivable	11,980				11,980	
Merchandise Inventory	33,600				39,100	
Supplies	7,140				1,965	
Prepaid Insurance	5,985				1,235	
Land	36,200				36,200	
Building	51,850				51,850	
Accum. Depr.—Building		13,590				18,875
Store Equipment	32,675				32,675	
Accum. Depr.—Store Equip.		10,290				14,755
Accounts Payable		5,895				5,895
Sales Tax Payable		6,375				6,375
Mortgage Payable		42,400				42,400
Unearned Revenue		8,850				2,930
Ned Diamond, Capital		116,350				116,350
Ned Diamond, Drawing	39,500				39,500	
Sales		148,000		148,000		
Sales Returns & Allow.	2,800		2,800			
Purchases	40,700		40,700			
Purch. Returns & Allow.		2,775		2,775		
Purchases Discounts		2,325		2,325		
Freight-In	1,875		1,875			
Wages Expense	47,000		48,250			
Telephone Expense	2,250		2,250			
Utilities Expense	6,825		6,825			
Advertising Expense	4,695		4,695			
Miscellaneous Expense	775		775			
	356,850	356,850				
Income Summary			33,600	39,100		
Supplies Expense			5,175			
Insurance Expense			4,750			
Depr. Expense—Building			5,285			
Depr. Expense—Store Equip.			4,465			
Earned Revenue				5,920		
Wages Payable						1,250
			161,445	198,120	245,505	208,830
Net Income			36,675			36,675
			198,120	198,120	245,505	245,505

Required
Analyze the work sheet and determine the adjusted trial balance and the adjusting entries by working backwards from the income statement and balance sheet columns.

MASTERY PROBLEM

John Neff owns and operates the Waikiki Surf Shop. A year-end trial balance and adjustment information are provided below.

Required
1. Prepare a year-end work sheet.
2. Journalize the adjusting entries.

Waikiki Surf Shop
Trial Balance
December 31, 19--

Account Title	Debit	Credit
Cash	30,000	
Accounts Receivable	22,500	
Merchandise Inventory	57,000	
Supplies	2,700	
Prepaid Insurance	3,600	
Land	15,000	
Building	135,000	
Accum. Depr.—Building		24,000
Store Equipment	75,000	
Accum. Depr.—Store Equip.		22,500
Notes Payable		7,500
Accounts Payable		15,000
Unearned Rental Revenue		33,000
John Neff, Capital		233,700
John Neff, Drawing	30,000	
Sales		300,750
Sales Returns & Allowances	1,800	
Purchases	157,500	
Purchases Returns & Allowances		1,200
Purchases Discounts		1,500
Freight-In	450	
Wages Expense	63,000	
Telephone Expense	5,250	
Utilities Expense	18,000	
Advertising Expense	11,250	
Miscellaneous Expense	10,875	
Interest Expense	225	
	639,150	639,150

The year-end adjustment data for the Waikiki Surf Shop follows.

(a–b) Based on a physical count, it was determined that merchandise inventory costing $45,000 is on hand as of December 31, 19--.

(c) Supplies remaining at the end of the year, $600.
(d) Unexpired insurance on December 31, $900.
(e) Depreciation expense on the building for 19--, $6,000.
(f) Depreciation expense on the store equipment for 19--, $4,500.
(g) Wages earned but not paid as of December 31, $675,
(h) Unearned boat rental revenue as of December 31, $3,000.

Expense Method of Accounting for Prepaid Expenses

Under the **expense method** of accounting for prepaid expenses, supplies and other prepaid items are entered as expenses when purchased. Under this method, we must adjust the accounts at the end of each accounting period to record the unused portions as assets. To illustrate, let's assume that Office Supplies Expense was debited for a total of $425 during the period. An inventory taken at the end of the period shows that supplies remaining on hand amount to $150. The following adjusting entry is made for supplies on hand:

19		Office Supplies			1 5 0 00			19
20		Office Supplies Expense				1 5 0 00		20
21		Office supplies on hand.						21

As shown in the T accounts below, after this entry is posted, the office supplies expense account has a debit balance of $275. This amount is reported on the income statement as an operating expense. The office supplies account has a debit balance of $150. It is reported on the balance sheet as a current asset.

Office Supplies			Office Supplies Expense		
				425	
Adj.	150		Adj.	150	
			Bal.	275	

To simplify accounting procedures in the following period, reverse this type of adjustment at the start of the new period. The reversing entry for office supplies is shown below.

3			Office Supplies Expense			1	5	0	00									3
4			Office Supplies									1	5	0	00		4
5			Reversing entry for supplies.														5

The asset and expense methods of accounting for prepaid expenses give the same final result. In the **asset method,** the prepaid item is first put into an asset account. At the end of each period, the amount consumed is debited to an expense account. In the **expense method,** the original amount is first debited to an expense account. At the end of each accounting period, the portion not consumed is debited to an asset account.

CHAPTER 15

*F*inancial Statements and Year-End Accounting for a Merchandising Business

The first six chapters of this text illustrated the accounting cycle for a service business. Chapter 7 demonstrated accounting procedures for a professional enterprise. Now we are ready to complete the accounting cycle for a merchandising firm.

In Chapter 14 we prepared the year-end work sheet and adjusting entries for Northern Micro. In this chapter, we will develop the financial statements, prepare closing and reversing entries and take an introductory look at financial statement analysis.

PREPARATION OF THE FINANCIAL STATEMENTS

As you know, a primary purpose of the work sheet is to serve as an aid in the preparation of the financial statements. The completed work sheet for Northern Micro is provided in figure 15-1 on pages 506 and 507. We will use it to prepare financial statements.

THE INCOME STATEMENT

The purpose of an income statement is to summarize the results of operations during an accounting period. The income statement shows the sources of revenue, types of expenses, and the amount of the net income

505

FIGURE 15-1 Work Sheet for Northern Micro

Northern Micro
Work Sheet
For the Year Ended December 31, 19--

	ACCOUNT TITLE	TRIAL BALANCE DEBIT	TRIAL BALANCE CREDIT	ADJUSTMENTS DEBIT	ADJUSTMENTS CREDIT	ADJUSTED TRIAL BALANCE DEBIT	ADJUSTED TRIAL BALANCE CREDIT	INCOME STATEMENT DEBIT	INCOME STATEMENT CREDIT	BALANCE SHEET DEBIT	BALANCE SHEET CREDIT	
1	Cash	20 000 00				20 000 00				20 000 00		1
2	Accounts Receivable	15 000 00				15 000 00				15 000 00		2
3	Merchandise Inventory	26 000 00		(b)18 000 00	(a)26 000 00	18 000 00				18 000 00		3
4	Supplies	1 800 00			(c) 1 400 00	4 000 00				4 000 00		4
5	Prepaid Insurance	2 400 00			(d) 1 800 00	6 000 00				6 000 00		5
6	Land	10 000 00				10 000 00				10 000 00		6
7	Building	90 000 00				90 000 00				90 000 00		7
8	Acc. Dep.—Building		16 000 00		(e) 4 000 00		20 000 00				20 000 00	8
9	Store Equipment	50 000 00				50 000 00				50 000 00		9
10	Acc. Dep.—Store Eq.		15 000 00		(f) 3 000 00		18 000 00				18 000 00	10
11	Notes Payable		5 000 00				5 000 00				5 000 00	11
12	Accounts Payable		10 000 00				10 000 00				10 000 00	12
13	Sales Tax Payable		1 500 00				1 500 00				1 500 00	13
14	Unearned Subscrip. Rev.		12 000 00	(h)10 000 00			2 000 00				2 000 00	14
15	Mortgage Payable		30 000 00				30 000 00				30 000 00	15
16	Gary L. Fishel, Capital		114 400 00				114 400 00				114 400 00	16
17	Gary L. Fishel, Drawing	20 000 00				20 000 00				20 000 00		17

#	Account	Trial Balance Dr	Trial Balance Cr	Adjustments Dr	Adjustments Cr	Adjusted Trial Balance Dr	Adjusted Trial Balance Cr	Income Statement Dr	Income Statement Cr	Balance Sheet Dr	Balance Sheet Cr
18	Sales		200,500.00				200,500.00		200,500.00		
19	Sales Ret. & Allow.	1,200.00				1,200.00		1,200.00			
20	Interest Revenue		900.00				900.00		900.00		
21	Purchases	105,000.00				105,000.00		105,000.00			
22	Purch. Ret. & Allow.		800.00				800.00		800.00		
23	Purchases Discounts		1,000.00				1,000.00		1,000.00		
24	Freight-In	300.00				300.00		300.00			
25	Wages Expense	42,000.00		(g) 450.00		42,450.00		42,450.00			
26	Telephone Expense	350.00				350.00		350.00			
27	Utilities Expense	12,000.00				12,000.00		12,000.00			
28	Advertising Expense	250.00				250.00		250.00			
29	Miscellaneous Expense	225.00				225.00		225.00			
30	Interest Expense	315.00				315.00		315.00			
31		407,100.00	407,100.00								
32	Income Summary			(a) 26,000.00	(b) 18,000.00	26,000.00	18,000.00	26,000.00	18,000.00		
33	Supplies Expense			(c) 1,400.00		1,400.00		1,400.00			
34	Insurance Expense			(d) 1,800.00		1,800.00		1,800.00			
35	Dep. Exp.—Building			(e) 4,000.00		4,000.00		4,000.00			
36	Dep. Exp.—Store Eq.			(f) 3,000.00		3,000.00		3,000.00			
37	Subscriptions Revenue				(h) 10,000.00		10,000.00		10,000.00		
38	Wages Payable				(g) 450.00		450.00				450.00
39				64,650.00	64,650.00	432,550.00	432,550.00	208,550.00	231,200.00	201,350.00	224,000.00
40	Net Income							22,650.00			22,650.00
41								231,200.00	231,200.00	224,000.00	224,000.00

or net loss for the period. Two types of income statement forms commonly used are the single step and the multiple step. The **single-step form** of income statement lists all revenue items and their total first, followed by all expense items and their total. The difference, which is either net income or net loss, is then calculated. A single-step income statement for Northern Micro is illustrated in figure 15-2.

FIGURE 15-2 **Single-Step Income Statement**

Northern Micro Income Statement For the Year Ended December 31, 19--			
Revenues:			
Net sales	$199 3 0 0 00		
Subscriptions revenue	10 0 0 0 00		
Interest revenue	9 0 0 00		
Total revenues			$ 210 2 0 0 00
Expenses:			
Cost of merchandise sold	$111 5 0 0 00		
Wages expense	42 4 5 0 00		
Utilities expense	12 0 0 0 00		
Depreciation expense—building	4 0 0 0 00		
Telephone expense	3 5 0 0 00		
Interest expense	3 1 5 0 00		
Depreciation expense—store equipment	3 0 0 0 00		
Advertising expense	2 5 0 0 00		
Insurance expense	1 8 0 0 00		
Supplies expense	1 4 0 0 00		
Miscellaneous expense	2 2 5 0 00		
Total expenses			187 5 5 0 00
Net income			$ 22 6 5 0 00

The **multiple-step form** of income statement is commonly used for merchandising businesses. The term "multiple-step" is used because the final net income is calculated on a step-by-step basis. Gross sales is shown first, less sales returns and allowances. This difference is called **net sales.** (Many published income statements begin with the amount of net sales.) Cost of goods sold is next subtracted to arrive at **gross profit** (sometimes called **gross margin**). Operating expenses are then listed, and subtracted from the gross profit to compute **operating income.** Finally, other revenues are added and other expenses are subtracted to arrive at net income (or net loss).

A multiple-step income statement for Northern Micro is shown in figure 15-3. Note that the operating expenses are arranged in descending size

FIGURE 15-3 Multiple-Step Income Statement

Northern Micro Income Statement For the Year Ended December 31, 19--				
Revenue from sales:				
Sales			$200 500 00	
Less: Sales returns and allowances			1 200 00	
Net sales				$199 300 00
Cost of merchandise sold				
Merchandise inventory, January 1, 19--			$ 26 000 00	
Purchases		$105 000 00		
Less: Purchases returns and allowances	$ 800 00			
Purchases discounts	1 000 00	1 800 00		
Net purchases		$103 200 00		
Add: Freight-in		300 00	103 500 00	
Total merchandise available for sale			$129 500 00	
Less: Merchandise inv., Dec. 31, 19--			18 000 00	
Cost of merchandise sold				111 500 00
Gross profit				$ 87 800 00
Operating expenses				
Wages expense			$ 42 450 00	
Utilities expense			12 000 00	
Depreciation expense—building			4 000 00	
Telephone expense			3 500 00	
Depreciation expense—store equip.			3 000 00	
Advertising expense			2 500 00	
Insurance expense			1 800 00	
Supplies expense			1 400 00	
Miscellaneous expense			2 250 00	
Total operating expenses				72 900 00
Income from operations				$ 14 900 00
Other revenue				
Subscriptions revenue			$ 10 000 00	
Interest revenue			900 00	
Total other revenue			$ 10 900 00	
Other expenses				
Interest expense			3 150 00	7 750 00
Net income				$ 22 650 00

order (except for Miscellaneous Expense). This order is fairly common, although not required.

<table>
<tr><td>**2**</td><td></td></tr>
</table>

Prepare a statement of owner's equity.

THE STATEMENT OF OWNER'S EQUITY

The statement of owner's equity summarizes all changes in the owner's equity during the period. It includes the net income or loss and any additional investments or withdrawals by the owner. These changes result in the end-of-period balance shown on this statement and the balance sheet.

To prepare the statement of owner's equity for Northern Micro, two sources of information are needed: (1) the work sheet, and (2) Gary Fishel's capital account (no. 311) in the general ledger. The work sheet (figure 15-1) shows net income of $22,650 and withdrawals of $20,000 during the year. Fishel's capital account (figure 15-4) shows a beginning balance of $104,400. An additional $10,000 was invested in the business in February of the current year. The statement of owner's equity for Northern Micro for the year ended December 31, 19--, is shown in figure 15-5.

FIGURE 15-4 Capital Account for Gary L. Fishel

ACCOUNT Gary L. Fishel, Capital								ACCOUNT NO. 311	
DATE	ITEM	POST. REF.	DEBIT	CREDIT	BALANCE				
					DEBIT		CREDIT		
19-- Jan. 1								104 4 0 0 00	
Feb. 12		CR7		10 0 0 0 00				114 4 0 0 00	

FIGURE 15-5 Statement of Owner's Equity

Northern Micro Statement of Owner's Equity For the Year Ended December 31, 19--			
Gary L. Fishel, capital, January 1, 19--			$104 4 0 0 00
Add: Additional investments			10 0 0 0 00
Total investment			$114 4 0 0 00
Net income for the year	$22 6 5 0 00		
Deduct: Withdrawals	(20 0 0 0 00)		
Increase in owner's equity			2 6 5 0 00
Gary L. Fishel, capital, December 31, 19--			$117 0 5 0 00

	THE BALANCE SHEET
3	
Prepare a classified balance sheet.	The report form of classified balance sheet is illustrated in figure 15-6. The balance sheet classifications used by Northern Micro are explained following the balance sheet.

F I G U R E   1 5 - 6   **Balance Sheet**

<table>
<tr><td colspan="5" align="center">Northern Micro
Balance Sheet
December 31, 19--</td></tr>
<tr><td colspan="5" align="center">Assets</td></tr>
<tr><td>Current assets:</td><td></td><td></td><td></td><td></td></tr>
<tr><td>Cash</td><td></td><td></td><td>$20 0 0 0 00</td><td></td></tr>
<tr><td>Accounts receivable</td><td></td><td></td><td>15 0 0 0 00</td><td></td></tr>
<tr><td>Merchandise inventory</td><td></td><td></td><td>18 0 0 0 00</td><td></td></tr>
<tr><td>Supplies</td><td></td><td></td><td>4 0 0 00</td><td></td></tr>
<tr><td>Prepaid insurance</td><td></td><td></td><td>6 0 0 00</td><td></td></tr>
<tr><td>Total current assets</td><td></td><td></td><td></td><td>$ 54 0 0 0 00</td></tr>
<tr><td>Property, plant, and equipment:</td><td></td><td></td><td></td><td></td></tr>
<tr><td>Land</td><td></td><td></td><td>$10 0 0 0 00</td><td></td></tr>
<tr><td>Building</td><td>$90 0 0 0 00</td><td></td><td></td><td></td></tr>
<tr><td>Less accum. depreciation</td><td>20 0 0 0 00</td><td>70 0 0 0 00</td><td></td><td></td></tr>
<tr><td>Store equipment</td><td>$50 0 0 0 00</td><td></td><td></td><td></td></tr>
<tr><td>Less accum. depreciation</td><td>18 0 0 0 00</td><td>32 0 0 0 00</td><td></td><td></td></tr>
<tr><td>Total property, plant, and equip.</td><td></td><td></td><td></td><td>112 0 0 0 00</td></tr>
<tr><td>Total assets</td><td></td><td></td><td></td><td>$166 0 0 0 00</td></tr>
<tr><td colspan="5" align="center">Liabilities</td></tr>
<tr><td>Current liabilities:</td><td></td><td></td><td></td><td></td></tr>
<tr><td>Notes payable</td><td>$ 5 0 0 0 00</td><td></td><td></td><td></td></tr>
<tr><td>Mortgage payable (current portion)</td><td>5 0 0 00</td><td></td><td></td><td></td></tr>
<tr><td>Accounts payable</td><td>10 0 0 0 00</td><td></td><td></td><td></td></tr>
<tr><td>Wages payable</td><td>4 5 0 00</td><td></td><td></td><td></td></tr>
<tr><td>Sales tax payable</td><td>1 5 0 0 00</td><td></td><td></td><td></td></tr>
<tr><td>Unearned subscriptions revenue</td><td>2 0 0 0 00</td><td></td><td></td><td></td></tr>
<tr><td>Total current liabilities</td><td></td><td>$19 4 5 0 00</td><td></td><td></td></tr>
<tr><td>Long-term liabilities:</td><td></td><td></td><td></td><td></td></tr>
<tr><td>Mortgage payable</td><td>$30 0 0 0 00</td><td></td><td></td><td></td></tr>
<tr><td>Less current portion</td><td>5 0 0 00</td><td>29 5 0 0 00</td><td></td><td></td></tr>
<tr><td>Total liabilities</td><td></td><td></td><td></td><td>$ 48 9 5 0 00</td></tr>
<tr><td colspan="5" align="center">Owner's Equity</td></tr>
<tr><td>Gary L. Fishel, capital</td><td></td><td></td><td></td><td>117 0 5 0 00</td></tr>
<tr><td>Total liabil. & owner's equity</td><td></td><td></td><td></td><td>$166 0 0 0 00</td></tr>
</table>

Current Assets. **Current assets** include cash and all other assets expected to be converted into cash or consumed within one year or the normal operating cycle of the business, whichever is longer. The **operating cycle** is the length of time generally required for a firm to buy inventory, sell it, and collect the cash. This time period is generally less than a year. Thus, most firms use one year for classifying current assets. In a merchandising business, the current assets usually include cash, receivables (such as accounts receivable and notes receivable), and merchandise inventory. Since prepaid expenses, such as unused supplies and unexpired insurance, are likely to be consumed within a year, they also are reported as current assets.

Current assets are listed on the balance sheet from the most liquid to least liquid. **Liquidity** refers to the speed with which the asset can be converted to cash. Cash is the most liquid asset and is always listed first. It is often followed by Notes Receivable, Accounts Receivable and Merchandise Inventory.

Property, Plant, and Equipment. Assets that are expected to be used for multiple years in the operation of a business are called **property, plant, and equipment.** Examples include land, buildings, office equipment, store equipment, and delivery equipment. Of these assets, only land is permanent; however, all of these assets have useful lives that are comparatively long. Typically, assets with longer useful lives are listed first.

The balance sheet of Northern Micro shows land, building and store equipment. The accumulated depreciation amounts are shown as deductions from the costs of the building and store equipment. The difference represents the **undepreciated cost,** or **book value** of the assets. This amount less any salvage value will be written off as depreciation expense in future periods.

Current Liabilities. **Current liabilities** include those obligations that are due within one year or the normal operating cycle of the business, whichever is longer, and will require the use of current assets. As of December 31, the current liabilities of Northern Micro consist of notes payable, accounts payable, wages payable, sales tax payable, unearned subscriptions revenue, and the portion of the mortgage payable that is due within the next year.

Long-Term Liabilities. **Long-term liabilities** include those obligations that will extend beyond one year or the normal operating cycle, whichever is longer. A common long-term liability is a mortgage payable.

A **mortgage** is a written agreement specifying that if the borrower does not repay a debt, the lender has the right to take over the property to satisfy the debt. When the debt is paid, the mortgage becomes void. **Mortgage Payable** is an account that is used to reflect an obligation that is secured by a mortgage on certain property.

Owner's Equity. The permanent owner's equity accounts reported on the balance sheet are determined by the type of organization. The accounts for a sole proprietorship, a partnership, or a corporation differ. Northern Micro is a sole proprietorship and reports one owner's equity account, Gary L. Fishel, Capital. The balance of this account is taken from the statement of owner's equity. Partnerships are illustrated in Chapter 20 and corporations are discussed in Chapters 21 and 22.

<table>
<tr><td>**4**</td></tr>
</table>

Compute standard
financial statement ratios.

FINANCIAL STATEMENT ANALYSIS

Both management and creditors are interested in using the financial statements to evaluate the financial condition and profitability of the firm. This can be done by making a few simple calculations.

Balance Sheet Analysis

Recall the following:

1. Current assets include cash, items that will be converted to cash, and items that will be used up within one year.
2. Current liabilities are obligations that will require the use of current assets.

Thus, the difference between current assets and current liabilities represents the amount of capital the firm has available for current operations. This is called **working capital.**

$$\text{Working Capital} = \text{Current Assets} - \text{Current Liabilities}$$

As shown on the balance sheet in figure 15-6, Northern Micro has current assets of $54,000 and current liabilities of $19,450. Thus, the working capital at year end amounts to $34,550 ($54,000 − $19,450). This amount should be more than adequate to satisfy current operating requirements.

Two measures of the firm's ability to pay its current liabilities are the **current ratio** and **quick ratio.** The formulas for their calculations are shown below.

Northern Micro

$$\text{Current Ratio} = \frac{\text{Current Assets}}{\text{Current Liabilities}} = \frac{\$54,000}{\$19,450} = 2.8 \text{ to } 1$$

$$\text{Quick Ratio} = \frac{\text{Quick Assets}}{\text{Current Liabilities}} = \frac{\$35,000}{\$19,450} = 1.8 \text{ to } 1$$

Northern Micro's current ratio of 2.8 to 1 is quite high, which indicates a favorable financial position. The rough "rule of thumb" traditionally has been that a current ratio should be about 2 to 1, but many businesses operate successfully on a minimum current ratio of 1.5 to 1. Although a rule of thumb is helpful, it is better to compare an individual company to industry averages. These figures are available in most public libraries.

Quick assets include cash and all other current assets that can be converted into cash quickly, such as accounts receivable and temporary investments. Temporary investments are discussed in more advanced textbooks. The balance sheet in figure 15-6 shows total quick assets of $35,000 ($20,000 in cash + $15,000 in accounts receivable). This produces a quick ratio of 1.8 to 1. This indicates that quick assets are more than adequate to meet current obligations. The "rule of thumb" traditionally has been that a quick ratio should be about 1 to 1, but many businesses operate successfully on a minimum quick ratio of 0.6 to 1.

Interstatement Analysis

Interstatement analysis provides a comparison of the relationships between certain amounts in the income statement and the balance sheet. A good example of interstatement analysis is the ratio of net income to owner's equity in the business. This ratio is known as **return on owner's equity.**

$$\text{Return on Owner's Equity} = \frac{\text{Net Income}}{\text{Average Owner's Equity}} = \frac{\text{Northern Micro}}{\frac{\$22,650}{(\$104,400 + \$117,050) \div 2}}$$

$$= \frac{\$22,650}{\$110,725}$$

$$= 20.5\%$$

As shown on the statement of owner's equity in figure 15-5, the owner's equity of Northern Micro was $104,400 on January 1 and $117,050 on December 31. The net income for the year of $22,650 is 20.5% of the average owner's equity. A comparison of this ratio with the return on owner's equity in prior years should be of interest to the owner. It may also be of interest to compare the return on owner's equity of Northern Micro with the same ratio for other stores of comparable nature and size.

A second ratio involving both income statement and balance sheet accounts is the rate of **accounts receivable turnover.** This is the number of times the accounts receivable turned over or were collected during the accounting period. This ratio is calculated as follows:

$$\text{Accounts Receivable Turnover} = \frac{\text{Net Credit Sales for the Period}}{\text{Average Accounts Receivable}}$$

The accounts receivable turnover for Northern Micro for the year ended December 31, 19--, is computed as follows:

Net *credit* sales for the year (determined from the accounting records) $110,000
Accounts receivable balance, Jan. 1, 19-- (taken from last year's balance sheet) 10,000
Accounts receivable balance, Dec. 31, 19-- 15,000

$$\text{Average Receivables} = \frac{\text{Beginning Balance} + \text{Ending Balance}}{2} = \frac{\$10,000 + \$15,000}{2}$$

$$= \$12,500$$

$$\text{Rate of Turnover} = \frac{\text{Net Credit Sales for Year}}{\text{Average Accounts Receivable}} = \frac{\$110,000}{\$12,500}$$
$$= 8.8$$

The number of days in the year divided by this rate of turnover shows that Northern Micro's credit customers are taking about 42 days to pay for their purchases.

$$365 \text{ days} \div 8.8 = 41.5 \text{ days}$$

If Northern Micro allows credit terms of n/45, this means that customers generally are paying on a timely basis.

A third ratio involving both income statement and balance sheet accounts is the rate of **inventory turnover.** This is the number of times the merchandise inventory turned over or was sold during the accounting period. This ratio is calculated as follows:

$$\text{Inventory Turnover} = \frac{\text{Cost of Merchandise Sold for the Period}}{\text{Average Inventory}}$$

If inventory is taken only at the end of each accounting period, the average inventory for the period can be calculated by adding the beginning and ending inventories and dividing their sum by two. The turnover of Northern Micro for the year ended December 31, is computed as follows:

Cost of Merchandise sold for the period	$111,500
Beginning inventory	26,000
Ending inventory	18,000

Northern Micro

$$\text{Average Inventory} = \frac{\text{Beginning Inventory} + \text{Ending Inventory}}{2} = \frac{\$26,000 + \$18,000}{2}$$
$$= \$22,000$$

$$\text{Rate of Turnover} = \frac{\text{Cost of Merchandise Sold for the Period}}{\text{Average inventory}} = \frac{\$111,500}{\$22,000}$$
$$= 5.1$$

The number of days in the year divided by this rate of turnover shows that Northern Micro's inventory turned over about once every two months.

$$365 \text{ days} \div 5.1 = 71.6 \text{ days}$$

The higher the rate of turnover, the smaller the margin needs to be on each dollar of sales to produce a satisfactory total dollar amount of gross margin. This is because the increase in numbers of units sold offsets the smaller amount of gross profit earned per unit. Evaluation of Northern Micro's rate of inventory turnover would require comparison with prior years, other companies, or its industry.

5

Prepare closing entries for a merchandising firm.

CLOSING ENTRIES

Closing entries for a service business were illustrated in Chapter 6. The process is essentially the same for a merchandising firm. All revenues and expenses reported on the income statement must be closed to Income Summary. Then, the Income Summary and Drawing accounts are closed to the owner's Capital account. Keep in mind, however, that a few new accounts were needed for a merchandising firm. These include Sales Returns and Allowances, Sales Discounts, Purchases Returns & Allowances and Purchases Discounts. Since these are temporary accounts reported on the income statement, they also must be closed. The easiest way to accomplish this, as illustrated in figure 15-7, is by using the work sheet to prepare the closing entries in four basic steps.

FIGURE 15-7 Income Summary with Closing Entries for a Merch. Firm

Northern Micro
Work Sheet (Partial)
December 31, 19--

	ACCOUNT TITLE	ACCT. NO.	INCOME STATEMENT		BALANCE SHEET		
			DEBIT	CREDIT	DEBIT	CREDIT	
1	Gary L. Fishel, Capital						1
2	Gary L. Fishel, Drawing				20 000 00		2
3	Sales			200 500 00			3
4	Sales Returns & Allow.		1 200 00				4
5	Interest Revenue			900 00			5
6	Purchases		105 000 00				6
7	Purch. Returns & Allow.			800 00			7
8	Purchase Discounts			1 000 00			8
9	Freight-In		300 00				9
10	Wages Expense		42 450 00				10
11	Telephone Expense		350 00				11
12	Utilities Expense		1 200 00				12
13	Advertising Expense		2 500 00				13
14	Miscellaneous Expense		2 250 00				14
15	Interest Expense		3 150 00				15
16							16
17	Income Summary		26 000 00	18 000 00			17
18	Supplies Expense		1 400 00				18
19	Insurance Expense		1 800 00				19
20	Depr. Exp.—Building		4 000 00				20
21	Depr. Exp.—Store Equip.		3 000 00				21
22	Accrued Interest Payable						22
23	Subscriptions Revenue			10 000 00			23
24	Wages Payable						24
25			208 550 00	231 200 00	224 000 00	201 350 00	25
26	Net Income		22 650 00			22 650 00	26
27			231 200 00	231 200 00	224 000 00	224 000 00	27

F I G U R E   1 5 - 7   Income Summary with Closing Entries for a Merch. Firm, cont'd.

	DATE		DESCRIPTION	POST. REF.	DEBIT	CREDIT	
1			Closing Entries				1
2	19--Dec.	31	Sales		200 5 0 0 00		2
3			Interest Revenue		9 0 0 00		3
4			Purchases Returns & Allowances		8 0 0 00		4
5			Purchases Discounts		1 0 0 0 00		5
6			Subscriptions Revenue		10 0 0 0 00		6
7			Income Summary			213 2 0 0 00	7
8							8
9		31	Income Summary		182 5 5 0 00		9
10			Sales Returns & Allowances			1 2 0 0 00	10
11			Purchases			105 0 0 0 00	11
12			Freight-In			3 0 0 00	12
13			Wages Expense			42 4 5 0 00	13
14			Telephone Expense			3 5 0 0 00	14
15			Utilities Expense			12 0 0 0 00	15
16			Advertising Expense			2 5 0 0 00	16
17			Miscellaneous Expense			2 2 5 0 00	17
18			Interest Expense			3 1 5 0 00	18
19			Supplies Expense			1 4 0 0 00	19
20			Insurance Expense			1 8 0 0 00	20
21			Depreciation Expense—Building			4 0 0 0 00	21
22			Depreciation Expense—Store Eq.			3 0 0 0 00	22
23							23
24		31	Income Summary		22 6 5 0 00		24
25			Gary L. Fishel, Capital			22 6 5 0 00	25
26							26
27		31	Gary L. Fishel, Capital		20 0 0 0 00		27
28			Gary L. Fishel, Drawing			20 0 0 0 00	28

The closing process for a merchandising firm follows.

STEP 1   All income statement accounts with credit balances are debited, with an offsetting credit to Income Summary.

STEP 2   All income statement accounts with debit balances are credited, with an offsetting debit to Income Summary.

STEP 3   The resulting balance in Income Summary, which is the net income or loss for the period, is transferred to the owner's Capital account.

STEP 4   The balance in the owner's Drawing account is transferred to the owner's Capital account.

FIGURE 15-7 **Income Summary with Closing Entries for a Merch. Firm, concl.**

ACCOUNT INCOME SUMMARY							ACCOUNT NO. 331	
DATE	ITEM	POST. REF.	DEBIT	CREDIT	BALANCE DEBIT		BALANCE CREDIT	
19-- Dec. 31	Adjusting	J3	26 0 0 0 00		26 0 0 0 00			⬅ Remove Beg. Inv.
31	Adjusting	J3		18 0 0 0 00	8 0 0 0 00			⬅ Enter End. Inv.
31	Closing	J4		213 2 0 0 00			205 2 0 0 00	⬅ Closing STEP 1
31	Closing	J4	182 5 5 0 00				22 6 5 0 00	⬅ Closing STEP 2
31	Closing	J4	22 6 5 0 00		--------		--------	⬅ Closing STEP 3

Note:
Adjustments to:

Post-Closing Trial Balance

A trial balance of the general ledger accounts taken after the temporary owner's equity accounts have been closed is called a **post-closing trial balance.** The purpose of the post-closing trial balance is to prove that the general ledger is in balance at the beginning of a new accounting period before any transactions for the new accounting period are entered. A post-closing trial balance of the general ledger of Northern Micro is shown in figure 15-8.

FIGURE 15-8 **Post-Closing Trial Balance**

Northern Micro Post-Closing Trial Balance December 31, 19--			
ACCOUNT TITLE	ACCOUNT NO.	DEBIT BALANCE	CREDIT BALANCE
Cash	111	20 0 0 0 00	
Accounts Receivable	131	15 0 0 0 00	
Merchandise Inventory	141	18 0 0 0 00	
Supplies	151	4 0 0 00	
Prepaid Insurance	155	6 0 0 00	
Land	161	10 0 0 0 00	
Building	171	90 0 0 0 00	
Accumulated Depreciation—Building	171.1		20 0 0 0 00
Store Equipment	181	50 0 0 0 00	
Accumulated Depreciation—Store Equipment	181.1		18 0 0 0 00
Notes Payable	216		5 0 0 0 00
Accounts Payable	218		10 0 0 0 00
Wages Payable	219		4 5 0 00
Sales Tax Payable	221		1 5 0 0 00
Unearned Subscriptions Revenue	230		2 0 0 00
Mortgage Payable	262		30 0 0 0 00
Gary L. Fishel, Capital	311		117 0 5 0 00
		204 0 0 0 00	204 0 0 0 00

6

Prepare reversing entries.

REVERSING ENTRIES

Numerous adjusting entries are needed at the end of the accounting period to bring the account balances up to date for presentation in the financial statements. Although not required, some of these adjusting entries should be reversed at the beginning of the next accounting period. This is done to simplify the recording of transactions in the new accounting period. As its name implies, a **reversing entry** is the reverse or opposite of the adjusting entry.

	Adjusting Entry			**Reversing Entry** (opposite)	
Dec. 31	Wages Expense	450	Jan. 1	Wages Payable	450
	Wages Payable	450		Wages Expense	450

To see the advantage of using reversing entries, let's consider the effect of reversing Northern Micro's adjusting entry for wages earned, but not paid at the end of the year. As shown in figure 15-9, accrued wages

FIGURE 15-9 **Adjusting, Closing and Reversing Entries for Wages**

	12/29/-1 Monday	12/30/-1 Tuesday	12/31/-1 Wednesday	1/1/-2 Thursday	1/2/-2 Friday
Wages Earned	150	150	150	150	150
Wages Paid	0	0	0	0	750
Total Earned			450		300
Total Paid			0		750
Accrued Wages on 12/31			450		

Date	Without Reversing Entry		With Reversing Entry	
12/31/-1 Adj. Entry	Wages Expense 450		Wages Expense 450	
	Wages Payable	450	Wages Payable	450
12/31/-1 Close. Entry	Income Summary 42,450		Income Summary 42,450	
	Wages Expense	42,450	Wages Expense	42,450
1/1/-2 Rev. Entry	No Entry		Wages Payable 450	
			Wages Expense	450
1/2/-2 Payment of Payroll	Wages Expense 300		Wages Expense 750	
	Wages Payable 450		Cash	750
	Cash	750		

Wages Expense		**Wages Expense**	
Bal. 42,000		Bal. 42,000	
12/31/-1 Adj 450		12/31/-1 Adj 450	
	42,450 12/31/-1 Close		42,450 12/31/-1 Close
1/2/-2 Payroll 300		1/2/-2 Payroll 750	450 1/1/-2 Rev.
		Bal. 300	

Wages Payable		**Wages Payable**	
1/2/-2 Payroll 450	450 12/31/-1 Adj.	1/1/-2 Rev. 450	450 12/31/-1 Adj.

Cash		**Cash**	
	750 1/2/-2 Payroll		750 1/2/-2 Payroll

on December 31 amounted to $450. These wages are for work performed by the employees on the last three days of the accounting period ($150 × 3 = $450). The employees will be paid on Friday, January 2, the normal payday.

Note that the adjusting and closing entries are the same, regardless of whether a reversing entry is made. However, the reversing entry on January 1 has an impact on the entry made when the employees are paid. *Without* a reversing entry, the payment on January 2, 19-2 must be split between reduction of the Wages Payable account for wages earned in 19-1 and Wages Expense for wages earned in 19-2. *With* a reversing entry, the bookkeeper simply debits Wages Expense and credits Cash as done on every other payday. Thus, the likelihood of error is reduced.

Not all adjusting entries should be reversed. To determine which adjusting entries to reverse, follow this rule:

Except for the first year of operation, reverse all adjusting entries that increase an asset or liability account from a zero balance. Except for the first year of operation, merchandise inventory, and contra assets like accumulated depreciation, will have existing balances. Thus, they should never be reversed. The adjusting entries for Northern Micro are shown in figure 15-10. Note that only the adjustment for accrued wages is reversed in figure 15-11.

F I G U R E   1 5 - 1 0 **Which Adjusting Entries to Reverse?**

	DATE		DESCRIPTION	POST. REF.	DEBIT	CREDIT		Should the adjust. be reversed?
1			Adjusting Entries				1	
2	19-1 Dec.	31	Income Summary		26 0 0 0 00		2	Never reverse adjust.
3			Merchandise Inventory			26 0 0 0 00	3	for merch. inventory.
4							4	
5		31	Merchandise Inventory		18 0 0 0 00		5	Never reverse adjust.
6			Income Summary			18 0 0 0 00	6	for merch. inventory.
7							7	
8		31	Supplies Expense		1 4 0 0 00		8	No. No asset or liab. with
9			Supplies			1 4 0 0 00	9	a 0 bal. has been increased.
10							10	
11		31	Insurance Expense		1 8 0 0 00		11	No. No asset or liab. with
12			Prepaid Insurance			1 8 0 0 00	12	a 0 bal. has been increased.
13							13	
14		31	Depreciation Expense—Building		4 0 0 0 00		14	Never reverse adjust. for
15			Accum. Depreciation—Building			4 0 0 0 00	15	depreciation.
16							16	
17		31	Depreciation Expense—Store Equip.		3 0 0 0 00		17	Never reserse adjust. for
18			Accum. Depreciation—Store Equip.			3 0 0 0 00	18	depreciation.
19							19	

GENERAL JOURNAL   PAGE 3

FIGURE 15-10 Which Adjusting Entries to Reverse? (continued)

	DATE	DESCRIPTION	POST. REF.	DEBIT	CREDIT	
20	31	Wages Expense		4 5 0 00		20
21		Wages Payable			4 5 0 00	21
22						22
23	31	Unearned Subscriptions Revenue		10 0 0 0 00		23
24		Subscriptions Revenue			10 0 0 0 00	24

GENERAL JOURNAL — PAGE 3

Yes. A liab. account with a 0 bal. has been increased.

No. No asset or liab. with a 0 bal. has been increased.

FIGURE 15-11 Reversing Entry for Northern Micro

GENERAL JOURNAL — PAGE 4

	DATE	DESCRIPTION	POST. REF.	DEBIT	CREDIT	
1		Reversing Entries				1
2	19-2 Jan. 1	Wages Payable		4 5 0 00		2
3		Wages Expense			4 5 0 00	3
4						4

KEY POINTS

1 The general format for a single-step and multiple-step income statement is shown below.

Single-Step
Income Statement
For the Year Ended December 31, 19--

Revenues:		
All are listed	xxx	
Total revenues		xxx
Expenses:		
Cost of merchandise sold ..	xxx	
All other expenses	xxx	
	xxx	
Total expenses		xxx
Net income		xxx

Multi-Step
Income Statement
For the Year Ended December 31, 19--

Revenue from sales:		
Sales	xxx	
Less: Sales returns and allowances .	xx	
Net sales		xxx
Cost of merchandise sold		xxx
Gross profit		xxx
Operating expenses		
List all operating expenses	xxx	
Total operating expenses		xxx
Income from operations		xxx
Other revenue		
List all other revenue	xxx	
Total other revenue	xxx	
Other expenses		
List all other expenses	xxx	
Total other expenses	xxx	xxx
Net income		xxx

2 A statement of owner's equity has the following format.

Statement of Owner's Equity
For the Year Ended December 31, 19--

Capital, January 1, 19--		xxx
Add: Additional investments		xxx
Total investment		xxx
Net income for the year	xxx	
Deduct: Withdrawals	(xxx)	
Increase in owner's equity		xxx
Capital, December 31, 19--		xxx

3 A classified balance sheet has the following major headings.

Balance Sheet
December 31, 19--
Assets

Current assets:	
Property, plant, and equipment:	
Total assets	xxx
Liabilities	
Current liabilities:	
Long-term liabilities:	
Total liabilities	xxx
Owner's Equity	
Owner's capital	xxx
Total liabilities and owner's equity	xxx

4 The following measures of financial condition may be computed from financial statement information.

Working Capital	= Current Assets − Current Liabilities
Current Ratio	= Current Assets ÷ Current Liabilities
Quick Ratio	= Quick Assets ÷ Current Liabilities
Return on Owner's Equity	= Net Income ÷ Average Owner's Equity

$$\text{Accounts Receivable Turnover} = \frac{\text{Net Credit Sales}}{\text{Average Accounts Receivable for Year}}$$

$$\text{Inventory Turnover} = \frac{\text{Cost of Merchandise Sold}}{\text{Average Merchandise Inventory for Year}}$$

5 There are four steps in the closing process for a merchandising firm.

1. All income statement accounts with credit balances are debited, with an offsetting credit to Income Summary.
2. All income statement accounts with debit balances are credited, with an offsetting debit to Income Summary.

3. The resulting balance in Income Summary, which is the net income or loss for the period, is transferred to the owner's Capital account.
4. The balance in the owner's Drawing account is transferred to the owner's Capital account.

6 Use the following rule to determine which adjusting entries to reverse. Except for the first year in operations, reverse all adjusting entries that increase an asset or liability account from a zero balance.

KEY TERMS

accounts receivable turnover 514 The number of times the accounts receivable turned over or were collected during the accounting period.

book value 512 Undepreciated cost.

current assets 512 Include cash and all other assets expected to be converted into cash or consumed within one year or the normal operating cycle of the business, whichever is longer.

current liabilities 512 Include those obligations that are due within one year or the normal operating cycle of the business, whichever is longer, and will require the use of current assets.

current ratio 513 Current assets divided by current liabilities.

gross margin 508 *See* gross profit.

gross profit 508 Net sales minus cost of goods sold.

income from operations 509 Gross profit less operating expenses on a multiple-step income statement.

interstatement analysis 514 Compares the relationship between certain amounts in the income statement and balance sheet.

inventory turnover 515 The number of times the merchandise inventory turned over or was sold during the accounting period.

liquidity 512 Refers to the speed with which the asset can be converted to cash.

long-term liabilities 512 Include those obligations that will extend beyond one year or the normal operating cycle, whichever is longer.

mortgage 512 A written agreement specifying that if the borrower does not repay a debt, the lender has the right to take over the property to satisfy the debt.

mortgage payable 512   An account that is used to reflect an obligation that is secured by a mortgage on certain property.

multiple-step income statement 508   Commonly used for merchandising businesses, this statement is calculated on a step-by-step basis.

net sales 508   Gross sales less sales returns and allowances.

operating cycle 512   The length of time generally required for a firm to buy inventory, sell it, and collect the cash.

operating income 508   Gross profit minus operating expenses.

post-closing trial balance 518   A trial balance taken after the temporary owner's equity accounts have been closed.

property, plant, and equipment 512   Assets that are expected to be used for multiple years in the operation of a business.

quick assets 513   Include cash and all other current assets that can be converted into cash quickly, such as accounts receivable and temporary investments.

quick ratio 513   Quick assets divided by current liabilities.

return on owner's equity 514   The ratio of net income to average owner's equity.

reversing entry 519   The opposite of the adjusting entry.

single-step income statement 508   Lists all revenue items and their total first, followed by all expense items and their total.

undepreciated cost 512   *See also* book value. Costs less the accumulated depreciation amounts.

working capital 513   The difference between current assets and current liabilities, which represents the amount of capital the firm has available for current operations.

BUILDING YOUR ACCOUNTING KNOWLEDGE

1. Describe the nature of the two forms of income statement.
2. Name and describe the calculation of two measures which provide an indication of a firm's ability to pay current obligations.
3. Describe how to calculate the following ratios:
   a. Return on owner's equity
   b. Accounts receivable turnover
   c. Inventory turnover

4. From where is the information obtained that is needed in journalizing the closing entries?
5. Explain the function of each of the four closing entries made by Northern Micro.
6. What is the purpose of a post-closing trial balance?
7. What is the primary purpose of reversing entries?
8. What is the customary date for reversing entries?
9. What adjusting entries should be reversed?

DEMONSTRATION PROBLEM

Tom McKinney owns and operates McK's Home Electronics. He has a store where he sells and repairs televisions and stereo equipment. A completed work sheet has been prepared as shown on pages 526 and 527.

Required
1. Prepare a multiple-step income statement.
2. Prepare a statement of owner's equity. (McKinney made a $20,000 additional investment during 19--.)
3. Prepare a balance sheet. The current portion of the mortgage payable is $1,000.
4. Calculate the following measures of performance and financial condition for 19--.
   a. Current ratio
   b. Quick ratio
   c. Working capital
   d. Return on owner's equity
   e. Accounts receivable turnover (Net credit sales were $200,000, and accounts receivable on January 1 was $26,000.)
   f. Inventory turnover
5. Prepare adjusting entries.
6. Prepare closing entries in the general journal.
7. Prepare reversing entries for the adjustments where appropriate.

McK's Home Electronics
Work Sheet
For the Year Ended December 31, 19--

	ACCOUNT TITLE	TRIAL BALANCE DEBIT	TRIAL BALANCE CREDIT	ADJUSTMENTS DEBIT	ADJUSTMENTS CREDIT	ADJUSTED TRIAL BALANCE DEBIT	ADJUSTED TRIAL BALANCE CREDIT	INCOME STATEMENT DEBIT	INCOME STATEMENT CREDIT	BALANCE SHEET DEBIT	BALANCE SHEET CREDIT	
1	Cash	10 000 00				10 000 00				10 000 00		1
2	Accounts Receivable	22 500 00				22 500 00				22 500 00		2
3	Merchandise Inventory	39 000 00		(b)45 000 00	(a)39 000 00	45 000 00				45 000 00		3
4	Supplies	2 700 00			(c) 2 100 00	600 00				600 00		4
5	Prepaid Insurance	3 600 00			(d) 2 700 00	900 00				900 00		5
6	Land	15 000 00				15 000 00				15 000 00		6
7	Building	135 000 00				135 000 00				135 000 00		7
8	Acc. Dep.—Building		24 000 00		(e) 6 000 00		30 000 00				30 000 00	8
9	Store Equipment	75 000 00				75 000 00				75 000 00		9
10	Acc. Dep.—Store Eq.		22 500 00		(f) 4 500 00		27 000 00				27 000 00	10
11	Notes Payable		7 500 00				7 500 00				7 500 00	11
12	Accounts Payable		15 000 00				15 000 00				15 000 00	12
13	Sales Tax Payable		2 250 00				2 250 00				2 250 00	13
14	Unearned Repair Fees		18 000 00	(h)15 000 00			3 000 00				3 000 00	14
15	Mortgage Payable		45 000 00				45 000 00				45 000 00	15
16	Tom McKinney, Capital		151 600 00				151 600 00				151 600 00	16
17	Tom McKinney, Drawing	30 000 00				30 000 00				30 000 00		17

#	Account	Trial Balance Debit	Trial Balance Credit	Adjustments Debit	Adjustments Credit	Adjusted Trial Balance Debit	Adjusted Trial Balance Credit	Income Statement Debit	Income Statement Credit	Balance Sheet Debit	Balance Sheet Credit
18	Sales		300 750 00				300 750 00		300 750 00		
19	Sales Ret. & Allow.	1 800 00				1 800 00		1 800 00			
20	Interest Revenue		1 350 00				1 350 00		1 350 00		
21	Purchases	157 500 00				157 500 00		157 500 00			
22	Purch. Ret. & Allow.		1 200 00				1 200 00		1 200 00		
23	Purchases Discounts		1 500 00				1 500 00		1 500 00		
24	Freight-In	450 00				450 00		450 00			
25	Wages Expense	63 000 00		(g) 675 00		63 675 00		63 675 00			
26	Telephone Expense	525 00				525 00		525 00			
27	Utilities Expense	1 800 00				1 800 00		1 800 00			
28	Advertising Expense	375 00				375 00		375 00			
29	Miscellaneous Expense	3 375 00				3 375 00		3 375 00			
30	Interest Expense	4 725 00				4 725 00		4 725 00			
31		590 650 00	590 650 00								
32	Income Summary			(a) 39 000 00	(b) 45 000 00	39 000 00	45 000 00	39 000 00	45 000 00		
33	Supplies Expense			(c) 2 100 00		2 100 00		2 100 00			
34	Insurance Expense			(d) 2 700 00		2 700 00		2 700 00			
35	Dep. Exp.—Building			(e) 6 000 00		6 000 00		6 000 00			
36	Dep. Exp.—Store Eq.			(f) 4 500 00		4 500 00		4 500 00			
37	Repair Fees				(h) 15 000 00		15 000 00		15 000 00		
38	Wages Payable				(g) 675 00		675 00				675 00
39				114 975 00	114 975 00	646 825 00	646 825 00	312 825 00	364 800 00	334 000 00	282 025 00
40	Net Income							51 975 00			51 975 00
41								364 800 00	364 800 00	334 000 00	334 000 00

SOLUTION

1.

McK's Home Electronics Income Statement For the Year Ended December 31, 19--				
Revenue from sales:				
Sales			$300 750 00	
Less: Sales revenues and allowances			1 800 00	
Net sales				$298 950 00
Cost of merchandise sold:				
Merchandise inventory, January 1, 19--			$ 39 000 00	
Purchases		$157 500 00		
Less: Purchases returns and allowances	$ 1 200 00			
Purchases discounts	1 500 00	2 700 00		
Net purchases		$154 800 00		
Add: Freight-in		4 500 00	155 250 00	
Total merchandise available for sale			$194 250 00	
Less: Merchandise inv., Dec. 31, 19--			45 000 00	
Cost of merchandise sold				149 250 00
Gross profit				$149 700 00
Operating expenses:				
Wages expense			$ 63 675 00	
Utilities expense			18 000 00	
Depreciation expense—building			6 000 00	
Telephone expense			5 250 00	
Depreciation expense—store equip.			4 500 00	
Advertising expense			3 750 00	
Insurance expense			2 700 00	
Supplies expense			2 100 00	
Miscellaneous expense			3 375 00	
Total operating expenses				109 350 00
Income from operations				$ 40 350 00
Other revenue:				
Repair fees			$ 15 000 00	
Interest revenue			1 350 00	
Total other revenue			$ 16 350 00	
Other expenses:				
Interest expense			4 725 00	11 625 00
Net income				$ 51 975 00

2.

McK's Home Electronics Statement of Owner's Equity For the Year Ended December 31, 19--			
Tom McKinney, capital, January 1, 19--			$131 600 00
Add: Additional investments			20 000 00
Total investment			$151 600 00
Net income for the year	$51 975 00		
Deduct: Withdrawals	(30 000 00)		
Increase in owner's equity			21 975 00
Tom McKinney, capital, December 31, 19--			$173 575 00

4.

a. Current Ratio = Current Assets ÷ Current Liabilities

$$79,000 ÷ 29,425 = 2.68 \text{ to } 1$$

b. Quick Ratio = Quick Assets ÷ Current Liabilities

$$32,500 ÷ 29,425 = 1.10 \text{ to } 1$$

c. Working Capital = Current Assets − Current Liabilities

$$= \$79,000 − \$29,425$$
$$= \$49,575$$

d. Return on Owner's Equity = Net income ÷ Average owner's equity

$$= \$51,975 ÷ [(\$131,600 + 173,575) ÷ 2]$$
$$= 34\%$$

e.

$$\text{Accounts Receivable Turnover} = \frac{\text{Net Credit Sales for the Year}}{\text{Average Accounts Receivable}}$$

$$= \frac{\$200,000}{(26,000 + 22,500) ÷ 2}$$

$$= 200,000 ÷ 24,250$$

$$= 8.25$$

365 days per year ÷ 8.25 = 44.24 days. Average number of days to collect an account receivable.

f.

$$\text{Inventory Turnover} = \text{Cost of Goods Sold} \div \text{Average Inventory}$$

$$= \frac{\$149{,}250}{(\$39{,}000 + \$45{,}000) \div 2}$$

$$= \$149{,}250 \div \$42{,}000$$

$$= 3.6$$

$365 \div 3.6 = 101.39$ On average, it takes about 101 days to sell inventory.

3.

McK's Home Electronics Balance Sheet December 31, 19--					
Assets					
Current assets:					
Cash			$10 0 0 0 00		
Accounts receivable			22 5 0 0 00		
Merchandise inventory			45 0 0 0 00		
Supplies			6 0 0 00		
Prepaid insurance			9 0 0 00		
Total current assets				$ 79 0 0 0 00	
Property, plant, and equipment:					
Land			$15 0 0 0 00		
Building	$135 0 0 0 00				
Less accum. depreciation	30 0 0 0 00		105 0 0 0 00		
Store equipment	$ 75 0 0 0 00				
Less accum. depreciation	27 0 0 0 00		48 0 0 0 00		
Total property, plant, and equip.				168 0 0 0 00	
Total assets				$247 0 0 0 00	
Liabilities					
Current liabilities:					
Notes payable	$ 7 5 0 0 00				
Mortgage payable (current portion)	1 0 0 0 00				
Accounts payable	15 0 0 0 00				
Wages payable	6 7 5 00				
Sales tax payable	2 2 5 0 00				
Unearned repair fees	3 0 0 0 00				
Total current liabilities			$29 4 2 5 00		
Long-term liabilities:					
Mortgage payable	$45 0 0 0 00				
Less current portion	1 0 0 0 00		44 0 0 0 00		
Total liabilities				$ 73 4 2 5 00	
Owner's Equity					
Tom McKinney, capital				173 5 7 5 00	
Total liabil. & owner's equity				$247 0 0 0 00	

5.

	DATE		DESCRIPTION	POST. REF.	DEBIT	CREDIT	
			GENERAL JOURNAL			PAGE 3	
1			Adjusting Entries				1
2	19-- Dec.	31	Income Summary		39 00 00		2
3			Merchandise Inventory			39 00 00	3
4							4
5		31	Merchandise Inventory		45 00 00		5
6			Income Summary			45 00 00	6
7							7
8		31	Supplies Expense		2 10 00		8
9			Supplies			2 10 00	9
10							10
11		31	Insurance Expense		2 70 00		11
12			Prepaid Insurance			2 70 00	12
13							13
14		31	Depreciation Expense—Building		6 00 00		14
15			Accumulated Dep.—Building			6 00 00	15
16							16
17		31	Depreciation Expense—Store Equip.		4 50 00		17
18			Accumulated Dep.—Store Equip.			4 50 00	18
19							19
20		31	Wages Expense		6 75 00		20
21			Wages Payable			6 75 00	21
22							22
23		31	Unearned Repair Fees		15 00 00		23
24			Repair Fees			15 00 00	24
25							25
26							26
27							27
28							28
29							29
30							30
31							31
31							32
33							33
34							34
35							35
36							36
37							37
38							38
39							39
40							40
41							41

Should adjust. be reversed?

Never reverse adjust. for merch. inventory.

Never reverse adjust. for merch. inventory.

No. No asset or liab. with 0 bal. has been increased.

No. No asset or liab. with a 0 bal. has been increased.

Never reverse adjust. for depreciation.

Never reverse adjust. for depreciation.

Yes. A liab. account with a 0 bal. has been increased.

No. No asset or liab. with a 0 bal. has been increased.

6.

	DATE		DESCRIPTION	POST. REF.	DEBIT	CREDIT	
			GENERAL JOURNAL			PAGE 4	
1			Closing Entries				1
2	19-- Dec.	31	Sales		300 7 5 0 00		2
3			Interest Revenue		1 3 5 0 00		3
4			Purchases Returns & Allowances		1 2 0 0 00		4
5			Purchases Discounts		1 5 0 0 00		5
6			Repair Fees		15 0 0 0 00		6
7			Income Summary			319 8 0 0 00	7
8							8
9		31	Income Summary		273 8 2 5 00		9
10			Sales Returns & Allowances			1 8 0 0 00	10
11			Purchases			157 5 0 0 00	11
12			Freight-In			4 5 0 00	12
13			Wages Expense			63 6 7 5 00	13
14			Telephone Expense			5 2 5 0 00	14
15			Utilities Expense			18 0 0 0 00	15
16			Advertising Expense			3 7 5 0 00	16
17			Miscellaneous Expense			3 3 7 5 00	17
18			Interest Expense			4 7 2 5 00	18
19			Supplies Expense			2 1 0 0 00	19
20			Insurance Expense			2 7 0 0 00	20
21			Depreciation Expense—Building			6 0 0 0 00	21
22			Depr. Expense—Store Equip.			4 5 0 0 00	22
23							23
24		31	Income Summary		51 9 7 5 00		24
25			Tom McKinney, Capital			51 9 7 5 00	25
26							26
27		31	Tom McKinney, Capital		30 0 0 0 00		27
28			Tom McKinney, Drawing			30 0 0 0 00	28

7.

	DATE		DESCRIPTION	POST. REF.	DEBIT	CREDIT	
			GENERAL JOURNAL			PAGE 5	
1			Reversing Entries				1
2	19-- Jan.	1	Wages Payable		6 7 5 00		2
3			Wages Expense			6 7 5 00	3

SERIES A

APPLYING ACCOUNTING CONCEPTS

EXERCISE 15A1

Revenue Section, Multiple-Step Income Statement

1 Based on the information that follows, prepare the revenue section of a multiple-step income statement (see figure 15-3).

Sales	$140,000
Sales Returns and Allowances	3,500
Sales Discounts	2,800

EXERCISE 15A2

Cost of Merchandise Sold Section, Multiple-Step Income Statement

1 Based on the information that follows, prepare the cost of merchandise sold section of a multiple-step income statement (see figure 15-3).

Merchandise Inventory, January 1, 19--	$ 34,000
Purchases	102,000
Purchases Returns and Allowances	4,200
Purchases Discounts	2,040
Freight-In	800
Merchandise Inventory, December 31, 19--	28,000

EXERCISE 15A3

Multiple-Step Income Statement

1 Based on the information that follows, prepare a multiple-step income statement, including the revenue section and the cost of goods sold section (see figure 15-3).

Sales	$148,300
Sales Returns and Allowances	1,380
Sales Discounts	2,166
Merchandise Inventory, January 1, 19--	26,500
Purchases	98,000
Purchases Returns and Allowances	2,180
Purchases Discounts	1,960
Freight-In	750
Merchandise Inventory, December 31, 19--	33,250
Wages Expense	23,800
Utilities Expense	7,000
Depreciation Expense—Equipment	3,100
Telephone Expense	1,100
Insurance Expense	1,000
Supplies Expense	900
Miscellaneous Expense	720
Interest Expense	3,880
Interest Revenue	240

EXERCISE 15A4

Closing Entries

5 From the worksheet on page 534, prepare closing entries for Gimbel's Gifts and Gadgets, a retail merchandising business. Use a general journal to record the entries.

Gimbel's Gifts and Gadgets
Work Sheet
For the Year Ended December 31, 19--

Account Title	Trial Balance Debit	Trial Balance Credit	Adjustments Debit	Adjustments Credit	Adjusted Trial Balance Debit	Adjusted Trial Balance Credit	Income Statement Debit	Income Statement Credit	Balance Sheet Debit	Balance Sheet Credit
Cash	8,214				8,214				8,214	
Accounts Receivable	6,720				6,720				6,720	
Merchandise Inventory	14,210		(b)16,800	(a)14,210	16,800				16,800	
Supplies	680			(c) 380	300				300	
Prepaid Insurance	800			(d) 200	600				600	
Building	80,000				80,000				80,000	
Accum. Depr.—Bldg.		13,600		(e) 4,000		17,600				17,600
Accounts Payable		5,280				5,280				5,280
Sales Taxes Payable		326				326				326
J.M. Gimbel, Capital		111,566				111,566				111,566
J.M. Gimbel, Drawing	31,683				31,683				31,683	
Sales		86,000				86,000		86,000		
Sales Ret. & Allow.	1,840				1,840		1,840			
Purchases	54,200				54,200		54,200			
Purch. Ret. & Allow.		2,813				2,813		2,813		
Purchases Discounts		1,084				1,084		1,084		
Freight-In	800				800		800			
Wages Expense	16,800		(f) 280		17,080		17,080			
Telephone Exp.	2,100				2,100		2,100			
Utilities Exp.	1,310				1,310		1,310			
Advertising Exp.	784				784		784			
Miscellaneous Exp.	386				386		386			
Interest Exp.	142				142		142			
	220,669	220,669								
Income Summary			(a)14,210	(b)16,800	14,210	16,800	14,210	16,800		
Supplies Expense			(c) 380		380		380			
Insurance Expense			(d) 200		200		200			
Depr. Exp.—Building			(e) 4,000		4,000		4,000			
Wages Payable				(f) 280		280				280
			35,870	35,870	241,749	241,749	97,432	106,697	144,317	135,052
Net Income							9,265			9,265
							106,697	106,697	144,317	144,317

EXERCISE 15A5	
Reversing Entries	

6 From the worksheet used for closing entries in Exercise 15A4, prepare the reversing entry.

EXERCISE 15A6	
Adjusting, Closing, Reversing	

4/5 Based on the information that follows, prepare two sets of entries—one that will have a reversing entry and the other without a reversing entry. Post all entries to T accounts for Wages Expense and Wages Payable and show balances.

Wages paid during 19-1 are $20,800.
Wages earned but not paid (accrued) as of December 31, 19-1 are $300.
On January 15, 19-2, payroll of $800 is paid, which includes the $300 of wages earned but not paid in December.

EXERCISE 15A7	
Financial Statement Ratios	

3 Based on the following financial statements (balance sheet, income statement, and statement of owner's equity), prepare the following financial statement ratios: (Note: All sales are credit sales.)

1. Working capital
2. Current ratio
3. Quick ratio
4. Return on owner's equity
5. Accounts receivable turnover
6. Inventory turnover

Jackson Enterprises
Income Statement
For the Year Ended December 31, 19--

Revenue from sales:				
Sales			$184,200	
Less: Sales returns & allow.			2,100	
Net sales				$182,100
Cost of merchandise sold:				
Mdse. Inv., Jan. 1, 19--			$ 31,300	
Purchases		$ 92,800		
Less: Purchases ret. & allow.	$1,800			
Purchases Discounts	1,856	3,656		
Net purchases		$ 89,144		
Add: Freight-in		933	90,077	
Total Merch. avail. for sale			$121,377	
Less: Merch. inv., Dec. 31, 19--			28,177	
Cost of merchandise sold				93,200
Gross profit				$ 88,900
Operating expenses:				
Wages expense			$ 38,000	
Utilities expense			11,000	
Depreciation expense—building			4,000	
Depreciation expense—equipment			3,800	
Telephone expense			2,210	
Advertising expense			1,180	

Operating expenses (*continued*)

Insurance expense	900	
Supplies expense	380	
Miscellaneous expense	530	
Total operating expenses		62,000
Income from operations		$ 26,900
Other revenue: Interest income	$ 1,800	
Other expenses: Interest expense	900	900
Net income		27,800

Jackson Enterprises
Statement of Owner's Equity
For the Year Ended December 31, 19--

J. B. Gray, capital, January 1, 19--		$ 88,000
Net income for year	$ 27,800	
Less: Withdrawals	11,600	
Increase in owner's equity		16,200
J. B. Gray, capital, December 31, 19--		$104,200

Jackson Enterprises
Balance Sheet
December 31, 19--
Assets

Current assets:

Cash		$ 20,800	
Accounts receivable*		18,900	
Merchandise inventory		28,177	
Supplies		1,323	
Prepaid insurance		900	
Total current assets			$ 70,100

Property, plant, and equipment:

Building	$ 90,000		
Less: Accumulated depreciation	28,000	$ 62,000	
Equipment	$ 33,000		
Less: Accumulated depreciation	7,500	25,500	
Total property, plant and equipment			87,500
Total assets			$157,600

Liabilities

Current liabilities:

Accounts payable		$ 12,600	
Mortgage payable (current portion)		800	
Wages payable		500	
Sales tax payable		1,200	
Total current liabilities			$ 15,100

Long-term liabilities:

Mortgage payable		$ 39,100	
Less current portion		800	
Total long-term liabilities			38,300
Total liabilities			$ 53,400

Owner's Equity

J. B. Gray, capital		104,200
Total liab. and owner's equity		$157,600

*Accounts Receivable January 1, 19--, was $21,600.

PROBLEMS

PROBLEM 15A1

Worksheet, Adjusting, Closing, and Reversing Entries

◀**EPS**▶

4/5 Ellis Fabric Store shows the following trial balance as of December 31, 19--:

Cash	$ 28,000	
Accounts Receivable	14,200	
Merchandise Inventory	33,000	
Supplies	1,600	
Prepaid Insurance	900	
Equipment	6,600	
Accum. Depr.—Equipment		$ 1,000
Accounts Payable		16,620
Wages Payable		0
Sales Tax Payable		850
W. P. Ellis, Capital		71,200
W. P. Ellis, Drawing	21,610	
Sales		78,500
Sales Returns & Allowances	1,850	
Interest Revenue		1,200
Purchases	41,500	
Purchases Returns & Allowances		1,800
Purchases Discounts		830
Freight-In	660	
Wages Expense	14,880	
Telephone Expense	1,210	
Utilities Expense	3,240	
Advertising Expense	810	
Miscellaneous Expense	920	
Interest Expense	1,020	
	$172,000	$172,000

At the end of the year, the following adjustments need to be made:

(a) and **(b)** Merchandise Inventory, December 31 balance is $28,900.
(c) Unused supplies on hand, $1350.
(d) Insurance expired, $300.
(e) Depreciation expense for the year, $500.
(f) Wages earned but not paid (wages payable), $480.

Required

1. Prepare a work sheet.
2. Prepare adjusting entries.
3. Prepare closing entries.
4. Prepare reversing entries.
5. Prepare a post-closing trial balance.

PROBLEM 15A2

Income Statement, Statement of Owner's Equity, Balance Sheet

1/2/3 Paulson's Pet Store completed the worksheet on page 538 for the year ended December 31, 19--. Owner's equity as of January 1, 19--, was $48,000.

Paulson's Pet Store
Work Sheet
For Year Ended December 31, 19--

Account Title	Trial Balance Debit	Trial Balance Credit	Adjustments Debit	Adjustments Credit	Adjusted Trial Balance Debit	Adjusted Trial Balance Credit	Income Statement Debit	Income Statement Credit	Balance Sheet Debit	Balance Sheet Credit
Cash	11,860				11,860				11,860	
Accounts Receivable	2,340				2,340				2,340	
Mdse. Inventory	28,100		(b) 26,500	(a) 28,100	26,500				26,500	
Supplies	800			(c) 200	600				600	
Prepaid Insurance	600			(d) 150	450				450	
Equipment	5,000				5,000				5,000	
Accum. Depr.—Equip.		450		(e) 450		900				900
Accounts Payable		1,890				1,890				1,890
Sales Taxes Payable		860				860				860
B. Paulson, Capital		50,000				50,000				50,000
B. Paulson, Drawing	11,200				11,200				11,200	
Sales		61,510				61,510		61,510		
Sales Ret. & Allow.	1,340				1,340		1,340			
Purchases	40,660				40,660		40,660			
Pur. Ret. & Allow.		1,020				1,020		1,020		
Purchases Discounts		800				800		800		
Freight-In	400				400		400			
Wages Expense	12,300		(f) 300		12,600		12,600			
Telephone Expense	684				684		684			
Utilities Expense	716				716		716			
Advertising Expense	300				300		300			
Miscellaneous Expense	150				150		150			
Interest Expense	80				80		80			
	116,530	116,530								
Income Summary			(a) 28,100	(b) 26,500	28,100	26,500	28,100	26,500		
Supplies Expense			(c) 200		200		200			
Insurance Expense			(d) 150		150		150			
Depr. Exp.—Equip.			(e) 450		450		450			
Wages Payable				(f) 300		300				300
			55,700	55,700	143,780	143,780	85,830	89,830	57,950	53,950
Net Income							4,000			4,000
							89,830	89,830	57,950	57,950

Required
1. Prepare a multiple-step income statement.
2. Prepare a statement of owner's equity.
3. Prepare a balance sheet.

PROBLEM 15A3

Financial Statement Ratios

3 Based on the work sheet and financial statements prepared in Problem 15A2, prepare the following financial statement ratios: (Note: All sales are credit sales.)

1. Working capital
2. Current ratio
3. Quick ratio
4. Return on owner's equity
5. Accounts receivable turnover
6. Inventory turnover

Accounts Receivable balance on January 1, 19--, was $3,800.

SERIES B

EXERCISES

EXERCISE 15B1

Revenue Section, Multiple-Step Income Statement

1 Based on the information that follows, prepare the revenue section of a multiple-step income statement (see figure 15-3).

Sales	$86,200
Sales Returns and Allowances	2,280
Sales Discounts	1,724

EXERCISE 15B2

Cost of Merchandise Sold Section, Multiple-Step Income Statement

1 Based on the information that follows, prepare the cost of merchandise sold section of a multiple-step income statement (see figure 15-3).

Merchandise Inventory, January 1, 19--	$13,800
Purchases	71,300
Purchases Returns and Allowances	3,188
Purchases Discounts	1,460
Freight-In	390
Merchandise Inventory, December 31, 19--	21,400

EXERCISE 15B3

Multiple-Step Income Statement

1 Based on the information at the top of page 540, prepare a multiple-step income statement, including the revenue section and the cost of merchandise sold section (see figure 15-3).

Sales	$166,000
Sales Returns and Allowances	1,620
Sales Discounts	3,320
Merchandise Inventory, January 1, 19--	33,200
Purchases	111,300
Purchases Returns and Allowances	3,600
Purchases Discounts	2,226
Freight-In	640
Merchandise Inventory, December 31, 19--	29,600
Wages Expense	22,000
Utilities Expense	9,000
Depreciation Expense—Building	4,600
Depreciation Expense—Equipment	2,800
Telephone Expense	1,100
Insurance Expense	1,000
Supplies Expense	650
Miscellaneous Expense	214
Interest Revenue	3,184
Interest Expense	1,126

EXERCISE 15B4

Closing Entries

5 From the worksheet on page 541, prepare closing entries for Balloons and Baubbles, a retail merchandising company. Use a general journal to record the entries.

EXERCISE 15B5

Reversing Entries

6 From the worksheet used for closing entries in Exercise 15B4, prepare the reversing entry.

EXERCISE 15B6

Adjusting, Closing, and Reversing

5/6 Based on the information that follows, prepare two sets of entries—one which will have a reversing entry and the other without a reversing entry. Post all entries to T accounts for Wages Expense and Wages Payable and show balances.

Wages paid during 19-1 are 20,080.
Wages earned but not paid (accrued) as of December 31, 19-2 are $280.
On January 15, 19-2, payroll of $840 is paid, which includes the $280 of wages earned but not paid in December.

EXERCISE 15B7

Financial Statement Ratios

4 Based on the following financial statements (balance sheet, income statement, and statement of owner's equity), prepare the following financial statement ratios: (Note: All sales are credit sales.)

1. Working capital
2. Current ratio
3. Quick ratio
4. Return on owner's equity
5. Accounts receivable turnover
6. Inventory turnover

Balloons and Baubbles
Work Sheet
For Year Ended December 31, 19--

Account Title	Trial Balance Debit	Trial Balance Credit	Adjustments Debit	Adjustments Credit	Adjusted Trial Balance Debit	Adjusted Trial Balance Credit	Income Statement Debit	Income Statement Credit	Balance Sheet Debit	Balance Sheet Credit
Cash	2,800				2,800				2,800	
Accounts Receivable	4,200				4,200				4,200	
Merchandise Inventory	8,600		(b) 7,500	(a) 8,600	7,500				7,500	
Supplies	780			(c) 280	500				500	
Prepaid Insurance	620			(d) 120	500				500	
Equipment	3,000				3,000				3,000	
Accum. Depr.—Equip.		600		(e) 300		900				900
Accounts Payable		1,800				1,800				1,800
Sales Taxes Payable		80				80				80
L. Marlow, Capital		12,200				12,200				12,200
L. Marlow, Drawing	2,000				2,000				2,000	
Sales		31,000				31,000		31,000		
Sales Ret. & Allow.	800				800		800			
Purchases	22,000				22,000		22,000			
Purchases Ret. & Allow.		1,800				1,800		1,800		
Purchases Discounts		407				407		407		
Freight-In	200				200		200			
Wages Expense	1,200		(f) 200		1,400		1,400			
Telephone Expense	700				700		700			
Utilities Expense	480				480		480			
Advertising Expense	300				300		300			
Miscellaneous Expense	110				110		110			
Interest Expense	97				97		97			
	47,887	47,887								
Income Summary			(a) 8,600	(b) 7,500	8,600	7,500	8,600	7,500		
Supplies Expense			(c) 280		280		280			
Insurance Expense			(d) 120		120		120			
Depr. Exp.—Equipment			(e) 300		300		300			
Wages Payable				(f) 200		200				200
			17,000	17,000	55,887	55,887	35,387	40,707	20,500	15,180
Net Income							5,320			5,320
							40,707	40,707	20,500	20,500

McDonald Carpeting Co.
Income Statement
For the Year Ended December 31, 19--

Revenue from sales:			
Sales		$122,800	
Less: Sales returns & allow.		1,100	
Net sales			$121,700
Cost of merchandise sold:			
Merch. inv., Jan. 1, 19--		$19,300	
Purchases	$62,800		
Less: Purch. ret. & allow.	$2,800		
Purch. discounts	1,944	4,744	
Net purchases		$58,056	
Add: Freight-in		944	59,000
Total merch. avail. for sale			$78,300
Less: Merch. inv., Jan. 31, 19--			16,700
Cost of merchandise sold			$ 61,600
Gross profit			60,100
Operating expenses:			
Wages expense		$ 18,000	
Utilities expense		8,000	
Depreciation expense—building		3,500	
Depreciation expense—equipment		2,500	
Telephone expense		1,200	
Advertising expense		980	
Insurance expense		800	
Supplies expense		320	
Miscellaneous expense		200	
Total operating expenses			35,500
Income from operations			$ 24,600
Other revenue: Interest income		2,800	
Other expenses: Interest expense		2,100	700
Net income			$ 25,300

McDonald Carpeting Co.
Statement of Owner's Equity
For the Year Ended December 31, 19--

C. S. McDonald capital, January 1, 19--		$52,000
Net income for year	$25,300	
Less: Withdrawals	10,400	
Increase in owner's equity		14,900
C. S. McDonald, capital, January 31, 19--		$66,900

McDonald Carpeting Co.
Balance Sheet
December 31, 19--

Assets

Current assets:		
Cash	$10,400	
Accounts receivable*	8,900	
Merchandise inventory	16,700	
Supplies	1,200	
Prepaid insurance	700	
Total current assets		$37,900

Assets

Property, plant, and equipment:
Building	$60,000		
Less: Accumulated depreciation	18,000	$42,000	
Equipment	$22,000		
Less: Accumulated depreciation	6,200	15,800	
Total property, plant and equipment			57,800
Total assets			$95,700

Liabilities

Current liabilities:
Accounts payable	$ 8,400		
Mortgage payable (current portion)	600		
Wages payable	300		
Sales tax payable	1,000		
Total current liabilities		$10,300	
Long-term liabilities:			
Mortgage payable	$19,100		
Less current portion	600		
Total long-term liabilities		18,500	
Total liabilities			$28,800

Owner's Equity

C. D. McDonald, capital	66,900
Total liab. and owner's equity	$95,700

*Accounts Receivable January 1, 19--, was $6,800.

PROBLEMS

PROBLEM 15B1

Worksheet, Adjusting, Closing, and Reversing Entries

5/6 Darby Kite Store shows the following trial balance as of December 31, 19--:

Cash	$ 11,700	
Accounts Receivable	11,200	
Merchandise Inventory	25,000	
Supplies	1,200	
Prepaid Insurance	800	
Equipment	5,400	
Accum. Depr.—Equipment		$ 800
Accounts Payable		7,600
Wages Payable		0
Sales Tax Payable		250
M. D. Akins, Capital		50,000
M. D. Akins, Drawing	10,500	

Sales		$57,990
Sales Returns & Allowances	$1,450	
Purchases	34,500	
Purchases Returns & Allowances .		1,100
Purchases Discounts		630
Freight-In	360	
Wages Expense	10,880	
Telephone Expense	1,100	
Utilities Expense	2,300	
Advertising Expense	740	
Miscellaneous Expense	320	
Interest Expense	920	
	$118,370	$118,370

At the end of the year, the following adjustments need to be made:

(a) and **(b)** Merchandise Inventory, December 31 balance is $23,600.

(c) Unused supplies on hand, $1,000.

(d) Insurance expired, $200.

(e) Depreciation expense for the year, $400.

(f) Wages earned but not paid (wages payable), $360.

Required

1. Prepare a work sheet.
2. Prepare adjusting entries.
3. Prepare closing entries.
4. Prepare reversing entries.
5. Prepare a post-closing trial balance.

PROBLEM 15B2

Income Statement, Statement of Owner's Equity, Balance Sheet

1/2/3 Backlund Farm Supply completed the worksheet on page 545 for the year ended December 31, 19--. Owner's equity as of January 1, 19-- was $52,000.

Required

1. Prepare a multiple-step income statement.
2. Prepare a statement of owner's equity.
3. Prepare a balance sheet.

PROBLEM 15B3

Financial Statement Ratios

4 Based on the work sheet and financial statements prepared in Problem 15B2, prepare the following financial statement ratios found below and at the top of page 546: (Note: All sales are credit sales.)

1. Working capital
2. Current ratio
3. Quick ratio
4. Return on owner's equity

Backlund Farm Supply
Work Sheet
For Year Ended December 31, 19--

Account Title	Trial Balance Debit	Trial Balance Credit	Adjustments Debit	Adjustments Credit	Adjusted Trial Balance Debit	Adjusted Trial Balance Credit	Income Statement Debit	Income Statement Credit	Balance Sheet Debit	Balance Sheet Credit
Cash	18,180				18,180				18,180	
Accounts Receivable	26,420				26,420				26,420	
Merch. Inventory	82,160		(b) 84,300	(a) 82,160	84,300				84,300	
Supplies	4,360			(c) 860	3,500				3,500	
Prepaid Insurance	3,000			(d) 750	2,250				2,250	
Equipment	18,000				18,000				18,000	
Accum. Depr.—Equip.		6,000		(e) 900		6,900				6,900
Accounts Payable		11,200				11,200				11,200
Sales Taxes Payable		800				800				800
J. Backlund, Capital		73,000				73,000				73,000
J. Backlund, Drawing	6,800				6,800				6,800	
Sales		161,800				161,800		161,800		
Sales Ret. & Allow.	1,310				1,310		1,310			
Purchases	71,300				71,300		71,300			
Purch. Ret. & Allow.		2,900				2,900		2,900		
Purchases Discounts		1,510				1,510		1,510		
Freight-In	600				600		600			
Wages Expense	21,300		(f) 420		21,720		21,720			
Telephone Expense	800				800		800			
Utilities Expense	1,300				1,300		1,300			
Advertising Expense	400				400		400			
Miscellaneous Expense	200				200		200			
Interest Expense	1,080				1,080		1,080			
	257,210	257,210								
Income Summary			(a) 82,160	(b) 84,300	82,160	84,300	82,160	84,300		
Supplies Expense			(c) 860		860		860			
Insurance Expense			(d) 750		750		750			
Depr. Exp.—Equipment			(e) 900		900		900			
Wages Payable				(f) 420		420				420
			169,390	169,390	342,830	342,830	183,380	250,510	159,450	92,320
Net Income							67,130			67,130
							250,510	250,510	159,450	159,450

5. Accounts receivable turnover
6. Inventory turnover

Accounts Receivable balance on January 1, 19--, was $38,200.

MASTERY PROBLEM

Dominique Fouque owns and operates Dominique's Doll House. She has a small shop in which she sells new and antique dolls and is particularly well known for her collection of antique Ken and Barbie dolls. In addition, she will refurbish dolls for a fee or for a commission on the sale. A completed work sheet has been prepared and is shown on page 547.

Required
1. Prepare a multiple-step income statement.
2. Prepare a statement of owner's equity.
3. Prepare a balance sheet. The long-term note payable is due in 19-5.
4. Compute the following measures of performance and financial condition for 19-3.
   a. Current ratio
   b. Quick ratio
   c. Working capital
   d. Return on owner's equity
   e. Accounts receivable turnover (Credit sales for 19-3 were $35,300 and receivables on January 1, were $2,500.)
   f. Inventory turnover
5. Prepare adjusting entries in the general journal.
6. Prepare closing entries in the general journal.
7. Prepare reversing entries in the general journal for the adjustments where appropriate.

COMPREHENSIVE PROBLEM

During the month of December, TJ's Specialty Shop engaged in the following transactions below and on page 548.

Dec. 1 Sold merchandise on account to Anne Clark, $2,000 plus tax of $100. Sale no. 637.
      2 Issued check no. 806 to James Owen in payment of December 1 balance of $1,600, less 2% discount.
      3 Issued check no. 807 to Peter Nathen in payment of December 1 balance of $3,000, less 2% discount.

Dominique's Doll House
Work Sheet
For Year Ended December 31, 19-3

Account Title	Trial Balance Debit	Trial Balance Credit	Adjustments Debit	Adjustments Credit	Adjusted Trial Balance Debit	Adjusted Trial Balance Credit	Income Statement Debit	Income Statement Credit	Balance Sheet Debit	Balance Sheet Credit
Cash	5,200				5,200				5,200	
Accounts Receivable	3,200				3,200				3,200	
Merchandise Inventory	22,300		(b) 24,600	(a) 22,300	24,600				24,600	
Office Supplies	800			(c) 600	200				200	
Prepaid Insurance	1,200			(d) 400	800				800	
Store Equipment	85,000				85,000				85,000	
Accum. Depr.—Store Equip.		15,000		(e) 5,000		20,000				20,000
Notes Payable		6,000				6,000				6,000
Accounts Payable		5,500				5,500				5,500
Sales Taxes Payable		850				850				850
Unearned Repair Fees		1,000	(f) 700			300				300
Salaries Payable				(g) 200		200				200
Long-Term Note Payable		10,000				10,000				10,000
D. Fouque, Capital		75,800				75,800				75,800
D. Fouque, Drawing	21,000				21,000				21,000	
Income Summary			(a) 22,300	(b) 24,600	22,300	24,600	22,300	24,600		
Sales		130,500				130,500		130,500		
Sales Returns and Allow.	900				900		900			
Repair Fees		25,000		(f) 700		25,700		25,700		
Purchases	72,000				72,000		72,000			
Purchases Discounts		750				750		750		
Freight-In	1,200				1,200		1,200			
Rent Expense	6,000				6,000		6,000			
Salaries Expense	42,000		(g) 200		42,200		42,200			
Office Supplies Exp.			(c) 600		600		600			
Telephone Expense	1,500				1,500		1,500			
Depreciation Expense			(e) 5,000		5,000		5,000			
Insurance Expense			(d) 400		400		400			
Utility Expense	7,600				7,600		7,600			
Interest Expense	500				500		500			
	270,400	270,400	53,800	53,800	300,200	300,200	160,200	181,550	140,000	118,650
Net Income							21,350			21,350
							181,550	181,550	140,000	140,000

Dec. 4 Purchased merchandise on account from James Owen, $1,550. Invoice no. 763, dated December 4, terms 2/10, n/30.

4 Issued check no. 808 for $180 in payment of telephone expense for the month of November.

6 Purchased merchandise on account from Jerry Evans, $2,350. Invoice no. 764, dated December 6, terms n/30.

8 Sold merchandise for cash, $4,840, plus tax of $242.

9 Received $490 from Heather Waters in full settlement of account.

9 Sold merchandise on account to Lucy Greene, $800, plus tax of $40. Sale no. 638

10 Issued check no. 809 to Harold West in payment of December 1 balance of $1,000.

11 Issued check no. 810 for $400 in payment of advertising expense for the month of December.

12 Sold merchandise on account to Martha Boyle, $1,260, plus tax of $63. Sale no. 639.

12 Received $1,340 on account from Anne Clark.

13 Issued check no. 811 to James Owen in payment of December 4 purchase. Invoice no. 763, less 2% discount.

13 Received merchandise worth $740 for return from Martha Boyle, plus sales tax of $37.

15 Issued check no. 812 for $1,100 in payment of wages (Wages Expense) for the two week period ended December 14.

15 Received $1,960 on account from Lucy Greene.

16 Sold merchandise on account to Kim Fields, $160 plus sales tax of $8. Sale no. 640.

17 Returned merchandise for credit worth $150 to Jerry Evans.

18 Issued check no. 813 to Jerry Evans in payment of December 1 balance of $1,250, less the credit received on December 17.

19 Sold merchandise on account to Lucy Greene, $620, plus tax of $31. Sale no. 641.

22 Received $1,560 from John Dempsey on account.

23 Issued check no. 814 for the purchase of supplies, $120.

24 Purchased merchandise from Harold West, on account $1,200. Invoice no. 765, dated December 24, terms n/30.

26 Purchased merchandise from Peter Nathen on account, $800. Invoice no. 766, dated December 26, terms 2/10, n/30.

27 Issued check no. 815 for $630 in payment of utilities expense for the month of November.

27 Sold merchandise on account to John Dempsey, $2,020, plus tax of $101. Sale no. 642.

29 Received $2,473 on account from Martha Boyle.

29 Issued check no. 816 for $1,100 in payment of wages (Wages Expense) for the two week period ended December 26.

30 Issued check no. 817 for $200 to Len Meyers for a cash purchase of merchandise.

As of December 1, TJ's account balances were as follows:

Account	Account No.	Debit	Credit
Cash	111	$ 11,500	
Accounts Receivable	131	8,600	
Merchandise Inventory	141	21,800	
Supplies	151	1,035	
Prepaid Insurance	155	1,380	
Land	161	8,700	
Building	171	52,000	
Accum. Dep.—Building	171.1		$ 9,200
Store Equipment	181	28,750	
Accum. Dep.—Store Equip.	181.1		9,300
Accounts Payable	218		6,850
Sales Tax Payable	221		970
Mortgage Payable	231		12,525
Tom Jones, Capital	311		90,000
Tom Jones, Drawing	312	8,500	
Sales	411		116,000
Sales Ret. & Allow.	411.1	690	
Purchases	511	60,500	
Purchases Ret. & Allow.	511.1		460
Purchases Discounts	511.2		575
Freight-In	512	175	
Wages Expense	542	25,000	
Telephone Expense	545	2,000	
Utilities Expense	549	6,900	
Advertising Expense	551	4,300	
Miscellaneous Expense	572	2,700	
Interest Expense	581	1,350	
		$245,880	$245,880

Year-end adjustment data, December 31:

(a–b) Merchandise inventory costing $19,700 is on hand as of December 31.
 (c) Supplies remaining at the end of the year, $525.
 (d) Unexpired insurance on December 31, $1,000.
 (e) Depreciation expense on the building for 19--, $800.
  (f) Depreciation expense on store equipment for 19--, $450.
 (g) Wages earned but not paid as of December 31, $330.

Subsidiary Ledger Balances:

Accounts Receivable

Name	Address	Balance
Martha Boyle	12 Jude Lane Hartford, CT 06117	$3,250
Anne Clark	52 Juniper Road Hartford, CT 06118	$1,340

Name	Address	Balance
John Dempsey	700 Hobbes Dr. Avon, CT 06108	$1,560
Kim Fields	5200 Hamilton Ave. Hartford, CT 06117	$ -0-
Lucy Greene	236 Bally Lane Simsbury, CT 06123	$1,960
Heather Waters	447 Drury Lane West Hartford, CT 06107	$ 490

Accounts Payable

Name	Address	Balance
Jerry Evans	34 Harry Ave. East Hartford, CT 06234	$1,250
Peter Nathen	1009 Drake Rd. Farmington, CT 06082	$3,000
James Owen	43 Lucky Lane Bristol, CT 06007	$1,600
Harold West	888 Anders Street Newington, CT 06789	$1,000

Required

1. If you are not using the working papers, open general ledger and accounts receivable and accounts payable ledgers as of December 1. Enter the December 1 balance of each of the accounts in the T accounts, with a check mark to the left of each balance.
2. Enter the transactions in a sales journal, purchases journal, cash receipts journal, cash payments journal, or general journal.
3. Post from the journals to the general ledger accounts and to the accounts receivable and accounts payable subsidiary ledgers. Then update the account balances.
4. Prepare schedules of accounts receivable and accounts payable from the subsidiary ledgers, and verify that the totals agree with the general ledger account balances.
5. Prepare a year-end worksheet, income statement, statement of owner's equity, and balance sheet.
6. Journalize the adjusting journal entries from the worksheet.
7. Prepare closing entries in the general journal.
   Hint: Close all expense and revenue account balances listed in the Income Statement columns of the worksheet. Then close Income Summary and Tom Jones, Drawing to Tom Jones, Capital.
8. Prepare reversing entries for the adjustments where appropriate.

Chapter 15 Demonstration Problem

The following instructions show you how to complete the Chapter 15 demonstration problem. Refer to Appendix A for additional help as you complete this problem and Problems 15A1 and 15B1.

STEP 1 Load the Electronic Problem Solver software and the opening balance file for Demonstration Problem D-15.

STEP 2 Select the Options Menu and the General Information screen. Enter a date of 12/31/-- (current year) and your name. Do not change any buttons (these buttons indicate that this is a sole proprietorship and a merchandising business). Record your data.

STEP 3 Enter the adjusting entries (a) through (h) in the general journal. Enter 12/31/-- (current year) in the Date field. Enter ADJ.ENT. in the Reference field (figure AC15-1).

    a. Enter the account number for Income Summary. (Remember that F1 will display the chart of accounts.) Enter the debit amount.

    b. Enter the account number for Merchandise Inventory. Enter the credit amount.

    c. Enter the remaining adjusting entries for 12/31.

STEP 4 Display the Posting Summary and post the adjusting entries.

STEP 5 Select the Journals option from the Reports menu. Press the space bar to place an X in the General Journal option to display the adjusting entries in the general journal. Enter ADJ.ENT. in the Reference Restriction field of the Selection Options screen.

STEP 6 Display the financial statements including the income statement, balance sheet, and statement of owner's equity.

STEP 7 Manually compute and record on a separate sheet the following measures of performance and financial condition:

    a. Current ratio
    b. Quick ratio
    c. Working capital
    d. Return on owner's equity
    e. Accounts receivable turnover (credit sales were $200,000 and accounts receivable on 1/1 were $26,000)
    f. Inventory turnover

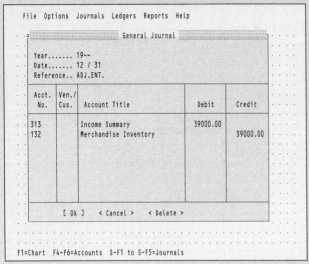

FIGURE AC15-1 **General Journal Data Entry**

```
 File  Options  Journals  Ledgers  Reports  Help
·═══════════════════ General Journal ═══════════════════
· Year....... 19--
· Date....... 12 / 31
· Reference.. ADJ.ENT.

· ┌──────┬──────┬─────────────────────┬─────────┬─────────┐
· │ Acct.│ Ven./│                     │         │         │
· │ No.  │ Cus. │ Account Title       │ Debit   │ Credit  │
· ├──────┼──────┼─────────────────────┼─────────┼─────────┤
· │ 313  │      │ Income Summary      │ 39000.00│         │
· │ 132  │      │ Merchandise Inventory│        │ 39000.00│
· │      │      │                     │         │         │
· │      │      │                     │         │         │
· │      │      │                     │         │         │
· │      │      │                     │         │         │
· │      │      │                     │         │         │
· ├──────┴──────┴─────────────────────┴─────────┴─────────┤
· │        [ Ok ]    < Cancel >    < Delete >             │
· └────────────────────────────────────────────────────────┘

 F1=Chart  F4-F6=Accounts  S-F1 to S-F5=Journals
```

FIGURE AC15-2 **General Journal Display**

```
 File  Options  Journals  Ledgers  Reports  Help
·═══════════════════ General Journal ═══════════════════
· Year....... 19--
· Date....... 01 / 01
· Reference.. REV.ENT.

· ┌──────┬──────┬─────────────────────┬─────────┬─────────┐
· │ Acct.│ Ven./│                     │         │         │
· │ No.  │ Cus. │ Account Title       │ Debit   │ Credit  │
· ├──────┼──────┼─────────────────────┼─────────┼─────────┤
· │ 232  │      │ Wages Payable       │ 675.00  │         │
· │ 611  │      │ Wages Expense       │         │ 675.00  │
· │      │      │                     │         │         │
· │      │      │                     │         │         │
· │      │      │                     │         │         │
· │      │      │                     │         │         │
· │      │      │                     │         │         │
· ├──────┴──────┴─────────────────────┴─────────┴─────────┤
· │        [ Ok ]    < Cancel >    < Delete >             │
· └────────────────────────────────────────────────────────┘

 F1=Chart  F4-F6=Accounts  S-F1 to S-F5=Journals
```

STEP 8 Select the Save As option from the File menu. Save your solution on a data disk under a file such as D-15XXXBC (XXX=your initials). (You should always back up your file before you select the Period-End Closing option.)

STEP 9 Select Options from the menu bar and select Period-End Closing. (The computer will automatically make the closing entries for the period.)

STEP 10 Select Reports and Ledgers. Choose the Trial Balance option, and display a post-closing trial balance.

STEP 11 Select Options and General Information and key a date of 01/01/-- (next year). Record your data.

STEP 12 Enter reversing entries in the general journal for the reversing entries where appropriate. Enter 01/01/-- (next year) in the Date field and REV.ENT. in the Reference field (figure AC15-2).

STEP 13 Select Reports and Journals and display the reversing entries in the general journal. Enter REV.ENT. in the Reference Restriction field of the Selection Options screen.

STEP 14 Select Reports and Ledgers and display a trial balance.

STEP 15 Select the Save As option from the File menu. Save your solution on a data disk under a file such as D-15XXX (XXX=your initials). Select the Quit option to end your session.

552

Accounting and Computers

Computers are used in many accounting applications. Two of the more common types use general ledger software and spreadsheet software. A general ledger program disk and template disk with several opening balances files are available with this textbook. A spreadsheet template disk with opening balances is also available. Your spreadsheet template disk contains instructions. Many books are also available with instructions on using spreadsheet programs.

INTRODUCTION TO THE ELECTRONIC PROBLEM SOLVER

When you use the Electronic Problem Solver general ledger software, you will notice that many accounting steps that are necessary in a manual system are not necessary in a computerized system. For example, a work sheet is not needed with a computerized accounting system. Also, the computer automatically posts all journal entries.

Disk Configuration

The Electronic Problem Solver consists of two 5 1/4″ disks or one 3 1/2″ disk. If you are using the 5 1/4″ disks, you must insert your template disk (Disk 2) in the disk drive after you load the program to load opening balances into computer memory. You should have a formatted data disk available to save your data. (Your DOS manual provides instructions on formatting a data disk.)

Opening Balances on the Template Disk

Your template disk contains the opening balances for several problems in your book. Each opening balance is identified with an EPS icon in the margin.

START-UP INSTRUCTIONS

Use the following steps to start up the Electronic Problem Solver.

STEP 1   Start your computer. At the DOS prompt, place your program disk in the disk drive (Disk 1 if you are using 5 1/4″ disks).

STEP 2   Enter ACCOUNT1 to load the program in the computer memory.

STEP 3   The screen in figure A-1 will appear. Press Enter to display the instructions for this software. (If you are using a mouse, click on the Yes button.)

STEP 4   The screen in figure A-2 will appear. If you are using a monochrome monitor and the display is unclear, choose MonoChrome to improve the image.

STEP 5   The first copyright screen (figure A-3) will appear. The bottom line on the display screen shows the available keys. Use the arrow keys, the PgUp, PgDn, Home, and End keys to scroll through the Help information. Press the F9 key to print the information. Press the Esc key to close this window.

STEP 6   Press the Esc key to close the Help window.

FIGURE A-1 **Opening Screen**   FIGURE A-2 **Select Display Type Screen**

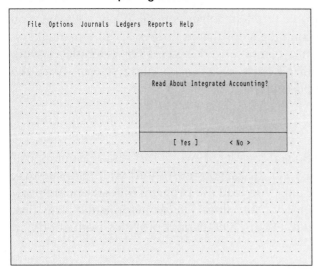

FIGURE A-3 **Select Display Type Screen**

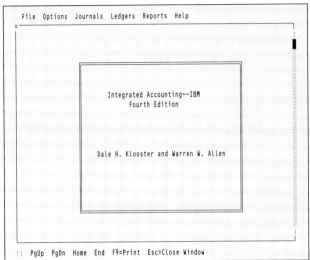

FIGURE A-4 **File Menu**

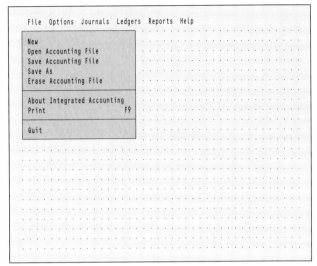

STEP 7   Press the Alt key to activate the menu line. With the reverse bar on the File option, press the Enter key or the Down Arrow key to display the File menu shown in figure A-4. You may also press the F key to pull down the File menu.

THE FILE MENU

The File Menu in figure A-4 is the first menu you will select in order to open an existing file or create a new file. Other file functions in the File menu include saving, printing, erasing files, and exiting from the Electronic Problem Solver.

New Accounting File

The New option on the File menu allows you to erase information from computer memory. The New option is used if you want to create your own problem and enter the opening balances into the computer. If the New option is selected, additional general information is needed to enter data in a new file (using the Options menu).

Open Accounting File

Use the Open Accounting File option to open (load from disk) a file. Enter the disk drive and/or directory name of the file you wish to open in the Path field. Enter the file name of the file you wish to open in the File field. For example, the path and file shown in figure A-5 direct the computer to load File 4A2 from Drive A. File 4A2 contains the opening data for Problem 4A2. The Directory window in figure A-5 shows some of the opening balances that are available. For example, as shown in your text, Problems 11A3, 11B3, 12A4, 12B4, 13A3, 13A4, and several other files are available. File names that begin with the letter "D" are demonstration problems. Use the arrow keys to display additional files in the Directory window.

Follow these steps to display and use the Directory window:

STEP 1   Press the End key to highlight the Directory button. Press the Enter key.

STEP 2   Move the arrow keys to highlight the file name.

STEP 3   Press the Enter key to place that name in the File field.

STEP 4   Press the Ok button to load the selected file.

Select the Cancel button to exit from the Open Accounting File option without opening a file.

Save Accounting File

The Save Accounting File option saves data under the **current** path and file name (as displayed in the upper right corner of the screen), overwriting the previous version of the file. Do not use this option unless you want to overwrite the original data.

Save As

Use the Save As option to save your file under a **different** file name and/or path than the one displayed in the upper right corner of the screen. The Save As option is useful for making a backup copy. Figure A-6 shows File D-4 (Chapter 4 demonstration problem) being saved under a new name of File D-4XXX (XXX = your initials).

Erase Accounting File

Use the Erase Accounting File option to **permanently** remove a file from the directory. Make certain that the correct file name is displayed before selecting the Ok button. Do not erase any files that you need because they cannot be restored.

About Integrated Accounting

The About Integrated Accounting option displays information about menu selection, data entry, alert boxes, scroll boxes, and printing reports. Press F9 to print this information.

FIGURE A-5 **Directory of Files**

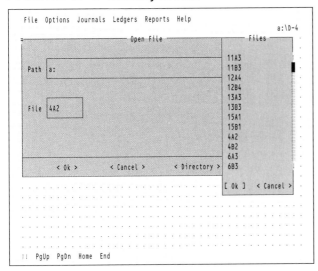

FIGURE A-6 **File Saved Using Initials**

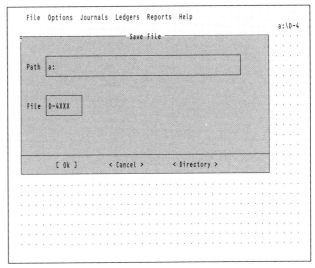

Print

Use the Print option to print a report. The report must be currently displayed. You may also use the F9 hot key to print a displayed report.

Quit

Use the Quit option to end your session and exit the program. If your data have not been saved, an alert window appears (figure A-7). To save the file under the name shown in the right corner of the screen, press the Yes button. To save the file under a different file name, press the Cancel button and choose the Save As option.

FIGURE A-7 **Alert Window**

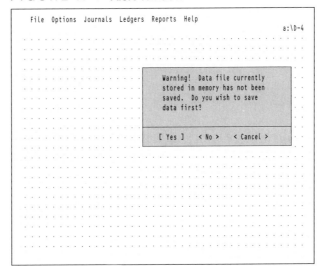

MENU SELECTION

The menu line contains six menu titles, each with its own pull-down menu. Each menu and menu item can be accessed by using either your keyboard or a mouse, unless the menu or menu item is dimmed. The software will not permit access to the dimmed menu or menu items.

Follow these steps to use the keyboard to select pull-down menus:

STEP 1   Press the Alt key to activate the menu line.

STEP 2   Choose the menu you want by moving the arrows keys to highlight the desired menu and pressing Enter, or by pressing the appropriate quick key letter (highlighted letter).

STEP 3   To select a menu item, highlight the item using the arrow keys and press Enter or press the appropriate quick key.

Follow these steps to use the mouse to select pull-down menus:

STEP 1   Click on the menu you would like to pull down.

STEP 2   Click on the menu item you choose.

WINDOWS

Information on the display screen appears within rectangular boxes called **windows**. The Electronic Problem Solver software has five different types of windows: data entry windows, alert windows, list windows, report selection windows, and report windows.

Data Entry Windows

Enter data into data entry windows from left to right and top to bottom. Buttons at the bottom of the windows allow you to accept or cancel the data entered. The hot keys at the bottom of the window allow quick access to the Ledger options (Function keys F4 through F6) and the journals (Shift-F1 to Shift-F5) as shown in figure A-8.

Follow these steps to use the keyboard for data entry:

STEP 1   Move between fields using the Tab key. Press the Shift-Tab keys simultaneously to move backwards through the fields.

STEP 2   Pull-down menus may be displayed during data entry.

STEP 3   Press the Ctrl-Enter keys simultaneously or select the Ok button to save your data. Press the Post button to post a transaction.

STEP 4   Press the Esc key to close the data entry window.

Follow these steps to use the mouse for data entry:

STEP 1   Click on the field where data is to be entered.

STEP 2   Click on the Ok button to accept the data entry window. Click on the Post button to post a transaction.

STEP 3   Click on the Cancel button to erase the data entered.

STEP 4   Click on the = in the upper left corner to close the window.

Alert Windows

Alert windows provide informational and error messages. Figure A-9 shows an alert window.

List Windows

List windows are scroll boxes containing data that can be used in other windows. To scroll through the window, use the keys shown at the bottom of the screen in figure A-10. To scroll through the window using a mouse, click on the arrow icons and the scroll bar on the right side of the window.

FIGURE A-8 **Data Entry Window**   **FIGURE A-9** **Alert Window**

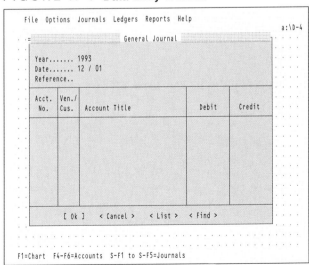

FIGURE A-10 **List Window**

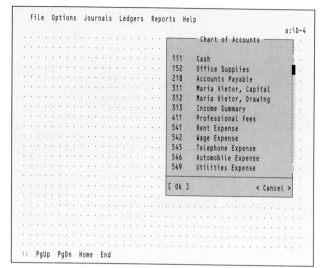

FIGURE A-11 **Report Selection Window**

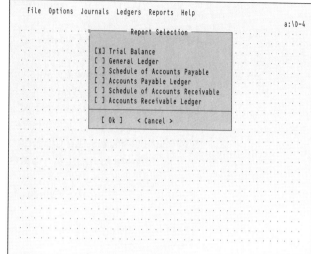

Report Selection Windows

Report selection windows are used to select reports (figure A-11). More than one report may be selected at a time.

Follow these steps to use the keyboard to tag reports to be displayed:

STEP 1   Press the Tab key to position the cursor in the appropriate box.

STEP 2   Press the space bar to place an X inside the box for each report you want to display. (Press the space bar again to remove the X from the box if you decide not to display the report.)

STEP 3   Press the Tab key to move the cursor to the Ok button, then press Enter (or press the Ctrl-Enter keys simultaneously) to accept the Report Selection window.

STEP 4   Press the Esc key or select the Cancel button to close the Report Selection window.

Follow these steps to use the mouse to tag reports to be displayed:

STEP 1   Click on each report you want to display to place an X inside the box. (A second click on the report will remove the X if you decide not to display the report.)

STEP 2   Click on the Ok button to tag a report.

STEP 3   Click on the Cancel button to close the report selection window.

Report Windows

Reports are displayed in report windows. Use the keys shown at the bottom of figure A-12 to scroll through a report. Press the F9 hot key to print a displayed report.

THE OPTIONS MENU

The Options menu in figure A-13 provides access to computer functions for setting up accounting files, as well as computer functions relating to journal entries. You will **not** use the following options unless you enter balances for your own problem: Required Accounts, Account Classification, Extended Classifications, Account Subtotals, Appropriation Accounts, Purge Journal Entries.

General Information

The General Information screen, shown in figure A-14, contains important information for each computerized accounting problem. For each problem, you must enter your name in the Student Name field. You may also need to change the run date. Select the Ok button to save your data. Do not change the Business Organization, Type of Business, Departmentalization, or Accounting System buttons to work the assigned problems.

Period-End Closing

After you select Period-End Closing, an alert window will appear asking if you want to perform the period-end closing. Select the Ok button to perform the period-end closing.

FIGURE A-12 **Report Window**

FIGURE A-13 **Options Menu**

File Options Journals Ledgers Reports Help			
	Vietor/Finan. Plng. Cons.		
	Trial Balance		
	12/31/93		
Acct. Number	Account Title	Debit	Credit
111	Cash	22765.00	
152	Office Supplies	280.00	
218	Accounts Payable		180.00
311	Maria Vietor, Capital		20000.00
312	Maria Vietor, Drawing	1100.00	
411	Professional Fees		6500.00
541	Rent Expense	1000.00	
542	Wage Expense	1200.00	
545	Telephone Expense	100.00	
546	Automobile Expense	60.00	
549	Utilities Expense	75.00	
557	Charitable Contrib. Exp.	100.00	

↑↓ PgUp PgDn Home End F9=Print Esc=Close Window

File Options Journals Ledgers Reports Help   a:\D-4

General Information
Required Accounts
Account Classification
Extended Classifications
Account Subtotals
Appropriation Accounts
Period-End Closing
Purge Journal Entries

Display Type
Set Colors

Before performing the period-end closing, back up your data using the Save As option. As a result of period-end closing: (a) account balances are archived to previous year's balances; (b) temporary account balances are closed; and (c) journal entries are erased.

Display Type and Set Colors

Display Type is used to select the type of monitor that you are using. If the screen image is unclear, choose MonoChrome to improve the image. If you have a color monitor, you may use Set Colors to change the color settings for menus, data entry windows, and report windows.

THE JOURNALS MENU

The Journals Menu in figure A-15 provides access to six journals. If a business uses a voucher system, a New Vouchers Journal would appear in the menu instead of the Purchases Journal.

Opening Balances

Use the opening balances journal to establish a new accounting file. You will not need this journal to complete the assigned problems.

General Journal

Use the general journal shown in figure A-16 to enter adjusting entries, reversing entries, and debit or credit memos. The sum of the debit entries

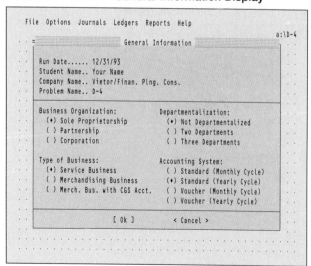

FIGURE A-14 **General Information Display**

```
File Options Journals Ledgers Reports Help
                                                        a:\D-4
 ┌══════════════ General Information ═══════════════┐
 │ Run Date...... 12/31/93                          │
 │ Student Name.. Your Name                          │
 │ Company Name.. Vietor/Finan. Plng. Cons.          │
 │ Problem Name.. D-4                                │
 │                                                   │
 │ Business Organization:    Departmentalization:    │
 │  (•) Sole Proprietorship   (•) Not Departmentalized│
 │  ( ) Partnership           ( ) Two Departments    │
 │  ( ) Corporation           ( ) Three Departments  │
 │                                                   │
 │ Type of Business:         Accounting System:      │
 │  (•) Service Business      ( ) Standard (Monthly Cycle)│
 │  ( ) Merchandising Business (•) Standard (Yearly Cycle)│
 │  ( ) Merch. Bus. with CGS Acct. ( ) Voucher (Monthly Cycle)│
 │                            ( ) Voucher (Yearly Cycle)│
 │                                                   │
 │         [ Ok ]          < Cancel >                │
 └───────────────────────────────────────────────────┘
```

FIGURE A-15 **Journals Menu**

```
File Options Journals Ledgers Reports Help
                                                        a:\D-4
        ┌─────────────────────────┐
        │ Opening Balances         │
        ├─────────────────────────┤
        │ General Journal      S-F1 │
        │ Purchases Journal    S-F2 │
        │ Cash Payments Journal S-F3 │
        │ Sales Journal        S-F4 │
        │ Cash Receipts Journal S-F5 │
        └─────────────────────────┘
```

must equal the sum of the credit entries. The computer displays a "Proof in Balance" message if the debit and credit amounts are equal.

Follow these steps to enter transactions:

STEP 1   Enter the date of the transaction.

STEP 2   Key information in the Reference field to identify the transaction; e.g., check number, invoice number. Key ADJ.ENT. or REV.ENT. if the transaction is an adjusting or reversing entry. The Reference field may be left blank.

STEP 3   To record the debit and credit portions of the transaction, key the account number and debit or credit amounts.

STEP 4   If the account number is Accounts Receivable, you must key a customer number. If the account number is Accounts Payable, you must key a vendor number.

STEP 5   Search windows are available for the Chart of Accounts, Vendors, and Customers by pressing the F1, F2, and F3 keys respectively.

STEP 6   Select the Ok button to obtain a Posting Summary (figure A-17).

STEP 7   Select the Post button if the entry is correct or select the Change button to return and make changes.

FIGURE A-16 **General Journal Data Entry**

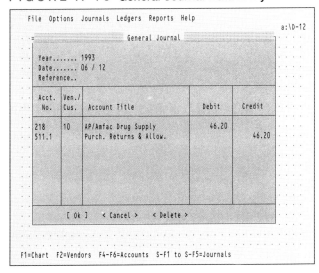

FIGURE A-17 **General Journal Posting Summary**

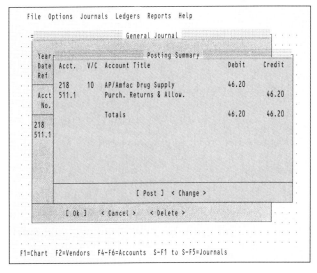

Follow these steps to add a new account, vendor, or customer:

STEP 1   Select either F4, F5, or F6 to display the chart of accounts, vendor list, or customer list.

STEP 2   Select Add New Account (New Vendor or New Customer).

STEP 3   Enter an account number and title of the new account (vendor number and name or customer number and name).
Note: Press Shift-F1 through Shift-F5 for other journals.

Corrections to Journal Entries

To edit a journal entry, select the List button to list the transactions (figure A-18). Highlight the transaction to be edited, then select the Ok button. Change the transaction, and select the Ok button to display a posting summary. Select the Post button.

To search for a journal entry, select the Find button and key into the Find What? field the data you are looking for. If the search is successful, the computer will display the entry in the data entry window for correction or deletion. The computer will not search for the Account Title field.

Purchases Journal

Use the purchases journal to enter purchases on account. Key data in the top part of the entry window. Enter the debit(s) to complete the transaction. The computer automatically credits Accounts Payable.

Cash Payments Journal

Use the cash payments journal to enter cash payments. Key data into the fields in the top part of the data entry window. Enter the debit(s) to complete the transaction. If the transaction involves a purchases discount, record the credit(s) to Purchases Discounts as a negative number in the Debit column (place a minus (−) sign before the number). The computer automatically credits Cash.

Sales Journal

Use the sales journal to enter sales on account. Key data into the fields in the top part of the data entry window. Enter the credit(s) to complete the transaction. The computer automatically debits Accounts Receivable.

Cash Receipts Journal

Use the cash receipts journal to enter all cash receipts. Key data into fields in the top part of the data entry window. Enter the credit(s) to complete the transaction. If the transaction involves a cash discount, record the debit to Sales Discounts as a negative number in the Credit column. The computer automatically debits Cash.

THE LEDGERS MENU

The Ledgers menu in figure A-19 provides access to the chart of accounts, vendors list, and customers list. Use the Maintain screens to add, edit, or delete data in these ledgers.

Chart of Accounts, Vendor List, Customer List

The Chart of Accounts, Vendor List, and Customer List options list the chart of accounts, vendors, and customers. A specific account, vendor, or customer may be selected from the respective list window for entry into a data entry window.

Maintain Accounts, Maintain Vendors, Maintain Customers

Use the Maintain Accounts option to add, edit or delete an account. To add an account, select ——Add New Account—— from the Chart of

FIGURE A-18 **Corrections to Journal Entries**

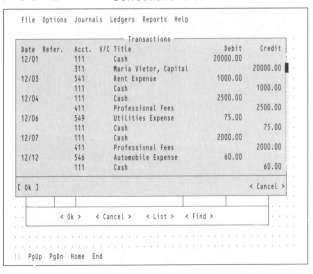

FIGURE A-19 **Ledgers Menu**

Accounts window. Key the acct. no. and title. Select the Ok button. To edit an account, highlight the account to edit, select the Ok button, and make the changes.

THE REPORTS MENU

The Reports menu in figure A-20 provides access to the available reports. The reports may be displayed and printed.

Accounts

Select Accounts from the Reports menu to display a report selection window for the chart of accounts, vendor list, and customer list. Press the space bar to place an X in the box next to the account(s) you want to display. Select the Ok button. Press the F9 key to print the report.

Journals

Select Journals from the Reports menu to display a report selection window for the six journal reports (figure A-21). Follow the same steps that you followed with the Accounts option to display and print these reports.

Enter the date range of the transactions you want to include in the report and add a reference restriction, if appropriate. For example, ADJ.ENT. would be entered in the Reference restriction area if the report is for adjusting entries only (figure A-22).

FIGURE A-20   **Reports Menu**

```
 File  Options  Journals  Ledgers  Reports  Help
                                                          a:\D-4
 . . . . . . . . . . . . . . . . .  ┌──────────────────┐ . . . . . . . . . .
 . . . . . . . . . . . . . . . . .  │ Accounts          │ . . . . . . . . . .
 . . . . . . . . . . . . . . . . .  │ Journals          │ . . . . . . . . . .
 . . . . . . . . . . . . . . . . .  │ Ledgers           │ . . . . . . . . . .
 . . . . . . . . . . . . . . . . .  │ Financial Statements│ . . . . . . . . .
 . . . . . . . . . . . . . . . . .  │ Financial Analysis  │ . . . . . . . . .
 . . . . . . . . . . . . . . . . .  │ Special           │ . . . . . . . . . .
                                     └──────────────────┘
```

FIGURE A-21 **Journals Report Selection**   FIGURE A-22 **Selection Options**

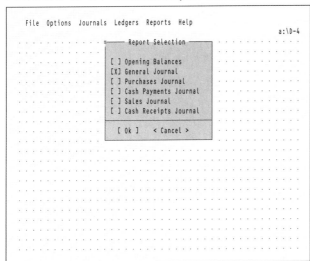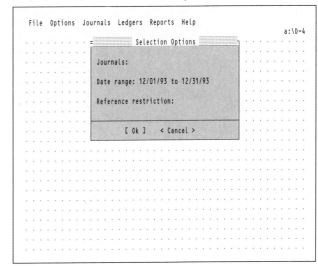

Ledgers

Select Ledgers from the Reports menu to display a report selection window for the six ledger reports: the trial balance, general ledger, schedule of accounts payable, accounts payable ledger, schedule of accounts receivable, and accounts receivable ledger.

Financial Statements, Financial Analysis, and Special

Select Financial Statements from the Reports menu to display a report selection window for the income statement, balance sheet and/or statement of owner's equity. Financial Analysis contains six financial analysis reports, which you will not need for the assigned problems. The Special option, available for a voucher system, contains a selection window for checks and statements.

APPENDIX B

*F*ICA Taxes for 1993 and 1992

FICA TAXES FOR 1993

As discussed in Chapters 9 and 10, the Federal Insurance Contributions Act (FICA) taxes include amounts for both OASDI (old-age, survivors and disability insurance) and HI (hospital insurance). OASDI taxes may also be referred to as social security taxes, and HI taxes may be referred to as Medicare taxes.

The actual FICA rates and limits for 1993 were announced in late October, 1992. For 1993, the OASDI (social security) rate is 6.2% on maximum earnings of $57,600. The HI (Medicare) rate is 1.45% on maximum earnings of $135,000.

FICA TAXES FOR 1992

The 1992 rates were discussed in Chapters 9 and 10. For 1992, the OASDI (social security) rate was 6.2% on maximum earnings of $55,500. The HI (Medicare) rate was 1.45% on maximum earnings of $130,200.

On Page 283, Sara Cadrain's FICA tax is shown. Since Sara Cadrain did not make $57,600, the following presentation uses the 1992 limit for the OASDI tax. Compare the presentation on Page 283 with the following calculation of the FICA tax for Sarah Cadrain:

Pay Period	Earnings	
	Week	Year-to-Date
Nov. 8–14	$1,100	$48,400
......	.	.
......	.	.
......	.	.
Dec. 13–19	$1,260	$55,800

B-1

For the week of November 8–14, FICA taxes on Caldrain's earnings would be:

	Taxable Earnings	×	Tax Rates	=	Tax
OASDI	$1,100		6.20%	=	$68.20
HI	$1,100		1.45%	=	15.95
Total FICA tax					$84.15

During the week of December 13–19, Cadrain's earnings for the calendar year went over the $55,500 OASDI (social security) maximum by $300 (55,800–55,500). Therefore, $300 of her $1,260 earnings for the week would not be subject to the OASDI tax.

Year-to-date earnings	$55,800
OASDI maximum	55,500
Amount not subject to OASDI tax ...	$ 300

The OASDI tax on Cadrain's December 13–19 earnings would be:

Gross pay	$1,260.00
Amount not subject to OASDI tax ...	300.00
Amount subject to OASDI tax	$ 960.00
Tax rate	6.2%
OASDI tax	$ 59.52

Since the HI maximum is $130,200, all of Cadrain's earnings would be subject to the HI tax. The HI tax on Cadrain's December 13–19 earnings would be:

Gross pay	$1,260.00
Amount not subject to HI tax	0.00
Amount subject to HI tax	$1,260.00
Tax rate	1.45%
HI tax	$ 18.27

The total FICA tax would be:

OASDI tax	$59.52
HI tax	18.27
Total FICA tax	$77.79

For the rest of the calendar year through December 31, Cadrain's earnings would be subject only to HI taxes.

COMPUTING NET PAY

Page 284 shows how to calculate Ken Istone's net pay. Compare the illustration on Page 284 to the following illustration, which uses the exact rates for both OASDI and HI. (Ken Istone's cumulative earnings are $22,025.00.) Ken Istone's net pay for the week ended December 19 would be calculated as follows.

Gross pay	$425.00
Deductions:	
Federal income tax withholding $16.00	
OASDI withholding 26.35	
HI withholding 6.16	
Health insurance premiums 10.00	
Total deductions	58.51
Net pay	$366.49

PAYROLL RECORDS

The payroll register for Figure 9-5 on Page 285 appears as follows when the OASDI and the HI taxes are split into the two amounts and two limits for 1992.

PAYROLL

	NAME	ALLOW-ANCES	MARITAL STATUS	EARNINGS				TAXABLE EARNINGS			
				REGULAR	OVER-TIME	TOTAL	CUMULATIVE TOTAL	UNEMPLOY. COMP.	OASDI	HI	
1	Cadrain, Sarah	4	M	1 100 00	160 00	1 260 00	55 800 00		960 00	1 260 00	1
2	Gunther, James	1	S	860 00	40 00	900 00	43 400 00		900 00	900 00	2
3	Istone, Ken	6	M	425 00		425 00	22 025 00		425 00	425 00	3
4	Kuzmik, Helen	2	M	480 00	294 00	774 00	31 000 00		774 00	774 00	4
5	Raines, Russell	3	M	440 00		440 00	22 340 00		440 00	440 00	5
6	Swaney, Linda	2	S	528 00	198 00	726 00	27 500 00		726 00	726 00	6
7	Tamin, Paul	5	M	490 00		490 00	25 650 00		490 00	490 00	7
8	Wiles, Harry	1	S	300 00		300 00	6 300 00	300 00	300 00	300 00	8
9				4 623 00	692 00	5 315 00	234 015 00	300 00	5 015 00	5 315 00	9

REGISTER— WEEK ENDED 12/19/--

	DEDUCTIONS							NET PAY	CK. NO.	
	FEDERAL INC. TAX	OASDI	HI	HEALTH INS.	UNITED WAY	OTHER	TOTAL			
1	204 00	59 52	18 27				281 79	978 21	409	1
2	138 00	55 80	13 05		20 00		226 85	673 15	410	2
3	16 00	26 35	6 16	10 00			58 51	366 49	411	3
4	97 00	47 99	11 22	13 00	20 00		189 21	584 79	412	4
5	38 00	27 28	6 38	13 00			84 66	355 34	413	5
6	122 00	45 01	10 52				177 53	548 47	414	6
7	33 00	30 38	7 11	10 00			80 49	409 51	415	7
8	36 00	18 60	4 35				58 95	241 05	416	8
9	684 00	310 93	77 06	46 00	40 00		1 157 99	4 157 01		9

EMPLOYER'S FICA TAX

The employer FICA tax is levied on employers at the same rate and on the same earnings base as the employee FICA tax. The employer withholds this tax from the employee and then pays both employer and employee OASDI and HI using Form 941. The actual Form 941 for 1992 is illustrated on Page 320. Notice that the rates are 12.4% (6.2% $\times$ 2) and 2.9% (1.45% $\times$ 2).

WORKING PAPERS

Working papers with an additional column for the second FICA amount are available so that you can solve the problems in Chapters 9 and 10 using up-to-date FICA rates and up-to-date maximum amounts.

*I*ndex